$1.50

THE LITTLE RED BOOK OF BASEBALL 1966

41st ANNUAL EDITION

BASEBALL'S BOOK OF OFFICIAL RECORDS

Endorsed by American and National Leagues. The authentic publication of all official Major League baseball records, including World Series and All Star games.

PLAY TO <u>WIN</u> WITH THE

Wilson A2000®

First choice of these major league "glove men":

- Luis Aparicio
- Al Kaline
- Ron Santo
- Harmon Killebrew
- Jerry Adair
- Bob Allison

Members of the Wilson Advisory Staff

PLAY TO <u>WIN</u> WITH

Wilson

Wilson Sporting Goods Co., Chicago
(A subsidiary of Wilson & Co., Inc.)

Wilson baseball shoes, genuine kangaroo leather

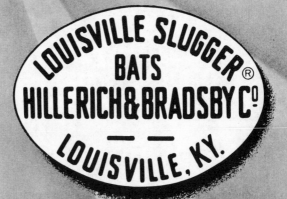

CURRENT PLAYERS—1,000 OR MORE GAMES—AMERICAN LEAGUE

Player	Yrs.	G	AB	R	H	TB	1B	2B	3B	HR	RBI	SB	BB	HP	SO	BA	SLG
Adcock, Joseph	16	1876	6375	790	1769	3072	1134	285	32	318	1074	18	563	17	1011	.277	.482
Allison, W. Robert	8	1045	3638	608	942	1753	553	160	36	193	616	60	596	25	728	.259	.482
Aparicio, Luis	10	1490	5826	806	1502	1988	1183	204	63	52	456	392	417	16	446	.258	.341
Blasingame, Donald	11	1364	5077	712	1320	1673	1069	169	62	20	296	103	532	15	438	.260	.330
Boyer, Cletis	10	1048	3366	393	809	1221	583	122	22	82	346	22	265	14	601	.240	.363
Brandt, John	9	1082	3623	516	956	1520	647	164	35	110	454	45	326	12	523	.264	.420
Bressoud, Edward	10	1001	3200	387	825	1310	540	168	34	83	315	7	303	11	598	.258	.409
Burgess, Forrest	16	1535	4344	483	1289	1951	908	224	33	124	647	13	452	11	254	.297	.449
Colavito, Rocco	11	1488	5385	852	1472	2744	874	252	18	328	1013	14	797	24	723	.273	.510
Cunningham, Joseph	11	1138	3354	525	979	1400	712	177	26	64	436	16	599	49	367	.292	.417
Freese, Gene	11	1046	3307	420	852	1403	553	159	28	112	422	48	230	19	504	.258	.424
Held, Woodson	10	1121	3593	481	886	1575	558	137	21	170	521	14	450	48	813	.247	.438
Howard, Elston	11	1300	4435	537	1261	1999	875	186	48	152	681	8	293	21	616	.284	.451
Kaline, Albert	13	1720	6378	1030	1949	3136	1323	315	61	250	1029	104	723	31	565	.306	.492
Killebrew, Harmon	12	1108	3828	651	998	2046	557	131	13	297	745	6	634	31	875	.261	.534
Kirkland, Willie	8	1025	3331	422	806	1420	504	132	28	142	492	50	307	15	598	.242	.426
Kubek, Anthony	9	1092	4167	522	1109	1518	844	178	30	57	373	29	217	13	441	.266	.364
Landis, James	9	1181	3932	578	979	1486	692	153	48	86	434	135	540	56	692	.249	.378
Lopez, Hector	11	1396	4527	609	1226	1883	869	189	36	132	575	16	410	22	676	.271	.416
Lumpe, Jerry	10	1177	4350	571	1184	1580	921	172	49	42	411	20	388	8	349	.272	.363
Malzone, Frank	11	1359	5273	641	1454	2123	1068	234	21	131	716	14	327	25	420	.276	.403
Mantle, Mickey	15	2005	6894	1517	2108	3968	1264	301	70	473	1344	145	1464	11	1424	.306	.576
Maris, Roger	9	1119	4033	700	1058	2014	629	150	31	248	708	21	540	36	574	.262	.499
Piersall, James	15	1654	5764	797	1578	2245	1171	251	52	104	577	114	510	25	562	.274	.389
Power, Victor	12	1627	6046	765	1716	2482	1251	290	49	126	658	45	279	15	247	.284	.411
Richardson, Robert	11	1263	4776	572	1279	1603	1043	175	34	27	348	67	237	6	215	.268	.336
Robinson, Brooks	11	1249	4616	548	1306	1940	934	221	40	111	572	16	324	20	484	.283	.420
Siebern, Norman	9	1175	4013	625	1114	1754	762	191	34	127	584	18	625	25	661	.278	.437
Sievers, Roy	17	1887	6387	945	1703	3033	1051	292	42	318	1147	14	841	51	920	.267	.475
Skowron, William	12	1468	5079	646	1455	2393	975	226	50	204	848	15	353	47	796	.286	.471
Zimmer, Donald	12	1095	3283	353	773	1220	530	130	22	91	352	45	246	13	678	.235	.372

CURRENT PLAYERS—1,000 OR MORE GAMES—NATIONAL LEAGUE

Player	Yrs.	G	AB	R	H	TB	1B	2B	3B	HR	RBI	SB	BB	HP	SO	BA	SLG
Aaron, Henry	12	1806	7080	1289	2266	4011	1397	391	80	398	1305	149	663	21	736	.320	.567
Bailey, L. Edgar	13	1207	3578	432	915	1538	617	128	15	155	540	17	544	25	576	.256	.430
Banks, Ernest	13	1820	6915	1025	1935	3601	1152	304	75	404	1227	46	612	49	869	.280	.521
Berra, Lawrence	19	2120	7555	1175	2150	3643	1422	321	49	358	1430	30	704	49	414	.285	.482
Bolling, Frank	11	1465	5335	676	1367	1976	1008	214	40	105	538	39	452	29	544	.256	.370
Boyer, Kenton	11	1667	6334	988	1855	3011	1270	269	61	255	1001	97	631	19	859	.293	.475
Cepeda, Orlando	8	1095	4129	647	1272	2209	803	224	22	223	752	92	255	49	625	.308	.535
Clemente, Roberto	11	1520	5910	832	1827	2636	1342	275	96	114	722	57	334	26	688	.309	.446
Covington, J. Wesley	10	1029	2934	354	827	1377	553	128	16	130	493	7	240	22	407	.282	.469
Crandall, Delmar	15	1523	4918	575	1251	1989	881	177	18	175	649	26	410	21	468	.254	.404
Davenport, James	8	1019	3215	418	842	1231	603	149	30	60	333	14	259	18	508	.262	.383
Flood, Curtis	10	1149	3958	564	1156	1579	886	178	31	61	389	52	295	34	396	.292	.399
Fox, J. Nelson	19	2367	9232	1279	2663	3347	2161	355	112	35	790	76	719	142	216	.288	.363
Francona, John	10	1238	4021	546	1107	1679	779	191	30	107	512	41	422	29	536	.275	.418
Gilliam, James	13	1868	6884	1133	1838	2467	1408	295	71	64	542	201	1002	33	399	.267	.358
Groat, Richard	12	1730	6804	764	1971	2536	1542	330	62	37	649	12	440	26	463	.290	.373
Kasko, Edward	9	1019	3410	400	906	1134	733	139	13	21	249	30	250	20	334	.266	.333
Kuenn, Harvey	14	1744	6752	936	2044	2764	1554	347	56	87	656	68	584	15	385	.303	.409
Lynch, Gerald	12	1120	2823	359	786	1318	516	122	34	114	464	12	220	9	406	.278	.467
Mathews, Edwin	14	2089	7597	1380	2088	3968	1228	317	66	477	1355	65	1313	23	1305	.275	.522
Mays, Willie	14	2005	7594	1497	2381	4507	1383	375	118	505	1402	276	949	27	893	.314	.593
Mazeroski, William	10	1412	5138	553	1362	1956	1014	201	48	99	569	16	281	13	482	.265	.381
McMillan, Roy	15	2017	6532	715	1592	2105	1247	244	34	67	582	40	645	55	686	.244	.322
Moon, Wallace	12	1457	4843	737	1399	2157	985	212	60	142	661	89	644	13	591	.289	.445
Pinson, Vada	8	1121	4568	758	1381	2214	913	250	71	147	624	160	318	25	603	.302	.485
Robinson, Frank	10	1502	5527	1043	1673	3063	981	318	50	324	1009	161	698	118	789	.303	.554
Roseboro, John	9	1031	3241	357	795	1233	555	121	40	79	394	54	362	29	482	.245	.380
Skinner, Robert	11	1332	4273	640	1191	1809	835	196	58	102	526	67	483	16	629	.279	.423
Stuart, Richard	8	1021	3768	492	1004	1878	600	154	30	220	717	2	278	20	893	.266	.498
Taylor, Antonio	8	1111	4260	578	1116	1481	876	155	45	40	300	142	333	55	649	.262	.348
Thomas, Frank	15	1761	6280	792	1671	2853	1092	262	31	286	962	15	484	51	913	.266	.454
Triandos, Gus	13	1206	3907	389	954	1614	634	147	6	167	608	1	440	21	636	.244	.413
Virdon, William	11	1577	5977	734	1595	2264	1187	237	81	90	500	47	442	8	645	.267	.379
White, William	9	1228	4645	688	1366	2197	916	232	55	163	690	80	426	20	663	.294	.473

CURRENT PITCHERS—100 OR MORE WINS—LIFETIME

Player	Yrs.	Won	Lost	Pct.	ERA	G	GS	CG	SHO	IP	H	HR	R	ER	BB	HB	SO	°BA
Buhl, Robert	13	160	124	.563	3.46	421	350	110	20	2450	2280	225	1080	941	1063	33	1207	.248
Bunning, James	11	156	104	.600	3.25	384	329	106	28	2442	2193	269	987	882	672	99	1893	.238
Burdette, S. Lewis	16	195	142	.579	3.65	553	373	158	33	2970	3090	281	1358	1206	616	54	1039	.268
Donovan, Richard	15	122	99	.552	3.66	345	273	101	25	2020	1988	199	909	822	495	45	880	.258
Drysdale, Donald	10	164	118	.582	2.96	397	344	134	34	2574	2264	220	975	846	681	115	1934	.234
Ford, Edward	14	232	97	.705	2.77	469	422	153	34	3054	2647	218	1063	939	1053	28	1892	.234
Friend, Robert	15	191	218	.467	3.55	568	477	161	35	3481	3610	273	1575	1372	869	45	1682	.268
Haddix, Harvey	14	136	113	.546	3.63	453	285	99	20	2235	2154	240	1012	901	601	43	1575	.252
Herbert, Raymond	13	102	102	.500	4.00	384	234	68	13	1833	1945	160	901	815	549	23	849	.275
Jackson, Lawrence	11	153	136	.529	3.50	446	323	114	26	2501	2478	208	1102	974	648	53	1331	.258
Klippstein, John	16	100	117	.461	4.25	680	162	37	6	1923	1874	200	1040	908	957	68	1128	.258
Koufax, Sanford	11	138	78	.639	2.93	356	273	110	35	2002	1513	185	732	651	740	18	2079	.205
Lary, Frank	12	128	116	.525	3.49	350	292	126	21	2162	2123	197	960	838	616	97	1099	.257
Law, Vernon	14	148	133	.527	3.73	427	326	110	24	2398	2508	246	1132	993	555	35	961	.269
Marichal, Juan	6	105	52	.669	2.75	190	184	97	26	1414	1199	135	498	432	325	12	1029	.226
Mossi, Donald	12	101	80	.558	3.43	460	165	55	8	1548	1493	156	672	590	385	19	932	.252
Nuxhall, Joseph	15	129	109	.542	3.86	491	271	81	19	2174	2174	195	1022	933	734	61	1301	.262
Pappas, Milton	9	110	74	.598	3.24	264	232	82	26	1632	1437	142	653	587	531	36	944	.237
Pascual, Camilo	12	137	135	.504	3.60	411	312	117	31	2362	2170	205	1064	946	879	45	1829	.243
Podres, John	12	136	104	.567	3.67	365	310	74	23	2028	2007	211	915	826	669	25	1330	.259
Purkey, Robert	12	129	114	.531	3.81	376	276	92	13	2095	2154	195	995	888	506	71	788	.266
Ramos, Pedro	11	110	147	.428	4.03	477	267	73	13	2177	2161	292	1107	975	670	60	1192	.258
Roberts, Robin	18	281	237	.542	3.37	652	588	303	44	4577	4441	487	1896	1714	881	53	2303	.253
Sanford, John	10	120	90	.571	3.63	316	277	76	14	1869	1722	156	857	754	689	40	1094	.244
Simmons, Curtis	18	183	167	.523	3.49	509	428	155	34	3121	3055	234	1430	1211	996	48	1615	.257
Spahn, Warren	21	363	245	.597	3.08	750	665	382	63	5246	4830	434	2016	1798	1434	42	2583	.244
Terry, Ralph	10	106	93	.533	3.60	310	246	75	20	1758	1655	208	795	704	420	23	948	.248
Wilhelm, J. Hoyt	14	113	99	.533	2.61	770	52	20	5	1784	1425	123	633	517	619	50	1241	.221

° Opponents' batting average against pitcher.

ELECTED TO HALL OF FAME

THEODORE "TED" WILLIAMS

ZOILO VERSALLES
Minnesota Twins
1965 American League M.V.P.

WILLIE MAYS
San Francisco Giants
1965 National League M.V.P.

SANDY KOUFAX
Los Angeles Dodgers
Cy Young Award Winner, 1965

TONY OLIVA
Minnesota Twins
A.L. Batting Champ .321

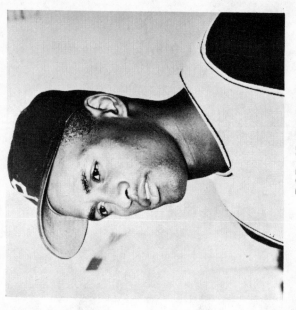

BOB CLEMENTE
Pittsburgh Pirates
N.L. Batting Champ .329

1966—FORTY-FIRST ANNUAL EDITION—1966

THE
LITTLE RED BOOK
OF
MAJOR LEAGUE BASEBALL

A Complete record book of all important records made in
major league baseball from 1876 to and including 1965.
World Series records from 1903 to 1965 inclusive.
All Star Game records

Editor: SEYMOUR SIWOFF
Asst. Editor: Jay Chesler

PUBLISHED BY

ELIAS SPORTS BUREAU, INC.

SEYMOUR SIWOFF, Pres.
11 West 42nd St., New York, N. Y. 10036

PROFESSIONAL BASE BALL GOVERNMENT
Commissioner: WILLIAM D. ECKERT
Administrator: Leland S. MacPhail, Jr.
Secretary-Treasurer: Charles M. Segar
Director, Public Relations: Joseph Reichler

COMMISSIONERS

Kenesaw M. Landis (Nov. 12, 1920—Nov. 25, 1944). Died in office.
Albert B. Chandler (Apr. 24, 1945—July 15, 1951). Resigned
Ford C. Frick (Oct. 8, 1951—November 17, 1965).
William D. Eckert (November 17, 1965 to date).

NATIONAL ASSOCIATION
President: PHILIP PITON

NATIONAL LEAGUE
President: WARREN C. GILES
Secretary: Fred G. Fleig
Director, Public Relations: David J. Grote

PRESIDENTS

1876 (one year)—Hon. Morgan G. Bulkeley, Hartford, Conn. (died November 6, 1922).
1877-1882 (six years)—Mr. William A. Hulbert, Chicago (died April 10, 1882).
1883-1884 (two years)—Col. A. G. Mills, New York (died August 26, 1929).
1885-1902 (eighteen years)—Mr. Nicholas E. Young, Washington, D. C. (died October 31, 1916).
1903-1909 (seven years)—Mr. Harry C. Pulliam, New York (died July 29, 1909).
1909 (part 1909)—Mr. John A. Heydler, New York.
1910-1913 (four years)—Mr. Thomas J. Lynch, New Britain, Conn. (died February 27, 1924).
1913-1918 (six years)—Hon. John K. Tener, ex-Gov. of Pennsylvania. Resigned August 6, 1918.
1918-1934 (seventeen years)—Mr. John A. Heydler, New York. (December 13, 1932, re-elected for four years 1933, 1934, 1935, 1936) resigned to take effect December 14, 1934.
1934-1951 (eighteen years)—Mr. Ford C. Frick (assumed office December 11) re-elected for two years, December 10, 1935; re-elected for three years, December 6, 1937; re-elected for four years, December 10, 1940; re-elected for four years, December 11, 1944; re-elected for four years, July 7, 1947, to take effect December 9, 1947; re-elected for 4 years, December 11, 1950. Elected Commissioner September 20, 1951, to take effect October 16, 1951.
1951—Mr. Warren C. Giles, elected September, 1951. Re-elected December, 1954. Re-elected December, 1958. Re-elected December, 1962. Re-elected November, 1965.

VICE-PRESIDENTS

Mr. Barney Dreyfuss, elected February 5, 1929 (office created); re-elected 1930 and 1931 (died February 5, 1932).
Mr. Charles A. Stoneham, elected December 12, 1933, re-elected 1934, re-elected 1935 (died January 6, 1936).
Mr. Samuel Breadon, elected February 4, 1936, re-elected December 6, 1937. Re-elected 1938, 1939, 1940, 1941, 1942, 1943, 1944, 1945, 1946 (elected honorary vice-president for life, January 30, 1948) (died May 10, 1949).
Mr. Philip K. Wrigley, elected December 9, 1947, re-elected annually to date.

SECRETARIES

1876-1902 (twenty-seven years)—Mr. Nicholas E. Young served as Secretary and Treasurer of the National League from its organization in 1876 to 1902, inclusive. Mr. Young also served as Secretary of the original National Association of Professional Base Ball Players from 1871 to 1875, inclusive—five years—covering a continuous period of thirty-two years.
1903-1907 (four years)—Mr. Harry C. Pulliam was elected Secretary and Treasurer in 1903.
1907-1934 (twenty-eight years)—Mr. John A. Heydler, New York, resigned November 2, 1934 to take effect December 14, 1934.
1934-1951—Mr. Harvey Traband (elected Secretary-Treasurer November 8, 1934 to take office December 11). Re-elected for one year, December 10, 1935. Re-elected 1936, re-elected annually.
1951—Mr. Fred G. Fleig, appointed Asst. Secretary-Treasurer, November 1, 1951 to December 5, 1960. Elected Secretary December 5, 1960.

Honorary Members—Date of Election

A. G. Mills, New York......Nov. 20, 1884	John I. Rogers, Phila......March 6, 1903
Albert G. Spalding, Chicago..Nov. 12, 1891	James A. Hart, Chicago.....Dec. 12, 1905
George W. Howe, Cleveland..Nov. 7, 1892	Arthur H. Soden, Boston....Dec. 12, 1906
Henry Chadwick, Brooklyn..Nov. 5, 1894	William H. Conant, Boston..Dec. 11, 1906
Nicholas E. Young, Wash....Dec. 12, 1902	James C. Jones, St. Louis...June 9, 1922
Alfred J. Reach, Phila.....March 4, 1903	August Herrmann, Cincinnati. Dec. 13, 1927

2

No. 1. Chicago Club°
William A. Hulbert...........1876-1881
Albert G. Spalding...........1882-1891
James A. Hart................1892-1905
Charles W. Murphy...........1906-1913
Charles H. Thomas...........1914-1915
Charles H. Weeghman........1916-1918
Fred F. Mitchell.............(part) 1919
William L. Veeck.............1919-1933
William M. Walker............1934
Philip K. Wrigley ....1934 to date

No. 2. Boston Club°
N. T. Appolonio..................1876
Arthur H. Soden..............1877-1906
George B. Dovey.............1907-1909
John S. C. Dovey............1909-1910
W. Hepburn Russell...............1911
John M. Ward...............(part) 1912
James E. Gaffney............1912-1915
Percy D. Haughton...........1916-1918
George W. Grant.............1919-1922
Christopher Mathewson.......1923-1925
Emil Fuchs.............1925-(part) 1935
J. A. (Robert) Quinn........1936-1945
Louis R. Perini 1945-1952

No. 3. Mutual Club (N. Y.)° (expelled)
William H. Cammeyer...............1876

No. 4. Athletic Club of Phila.° (expelled)
Thomas J. Smith..................1876

No. 5. Hartford Club° (resigned 1877)
Morgan G. Bulkeley...........1876-1877

No. 6. St. Louis Club° (resigned 1877)
J. R. C. Lucas (see No. 20 and 28) 1876-1877

No. 7. Cincinnati Club° (expelled 1880)
J. L. Keck, J. M. W. Neff......1876-1879
Justus Thorner (see 27)..........1880

No. 8. Louisville Club° (resigned 1878)
W. W. Haldeman (see No. 30)...1876-1877

No. 9. Indianapolis Club (resigned 1878)
W. B. Pettit (see No. 24)..........1878

No. 10. Milwaukee Club (resigned 1878)
J. R. Kaine......................1878

No. 11. Providence Club (resigned 1885)
John D. Thurston.................1878
Henry J. Root.......1879-81 also 1884-85
Henry B. Winship............1882-1883

No. 12. Buffalo Club (resigned 1885)
E. B. Smith, John B. Sage......1879-1880
Josiah Jewett...............1881-1885

No. 13. Cleveland Club (resigned 1884)
J. Ford Evans...............1879-1881
C. H. Bulkley...............1882-1884

No. 14. Syracuse Club (forfeited 1879)
Hamilton S. White...............1879

No. 15. Troy Club (resigned 1882)
Gardner Earl................1879-1880
A. L. Hotchkin, Francis N. Mann.1881-1882

No. 16. Worcester Club (resigned 1882)
C. B. Pratt.................1880-1882

No. 17. Detroit Club (resigned 1888)
W. G. Thompson.............1881-1884
Joseph H. Marsh.............1885-1886
Fred K. Stearns, Charles W. Smith 1887-1888

No. 18. New York Club
John B. Day.................1883-1892
C. C. VanCott..............1893-1894
Andrew Freedman 1895-1902
John T. Brush 1903-1912
Harry N. Hempstead..........1912-1918
Charles A. Stoneham 1919-1935
Horace C. Stoneham 1936-1957

No. 19. Philadelphia Club
Alfred J. Reach.............1883-1902
James Potter................1903-1904
William J. Shettsline.......1905-1908
Israel W. Durham...........(part) 1909
Horace S. Fogel.............1909-1912
William H. Locke...........(part) 1913

William F. Baker............1913-1930
L. Charles Ruch.............1931-1932
Gerald P. Nugent............1933-1942
William D. Cox...............1943
Robert R. M. Carpenter, Jr. ..1943 to date

No. 20. St. Louis (resigned 1886)
Henry V. Lucas (see 6 and 28)...1885-1886

No. 21. Washington Club (resigned 1889)
Robert C. Hewett............1886-1888
Walter F. Hewett..............1889

No. 22. Kansas City Club (resigned 1886)
Joseph J. Heim..................1886

No. 23. Pittsburgh Club
W. A. Nimick................1887-1890
J. Palmer O'Neill, Wm. C. Temple.1891-92
A. C. Buckenberger, W. H. Watkins.1893-98
W. W. Kerr.................1894-1899
Barney Dreyfuss.............1900-1931
William E. Benswanger.......1932-1946
Frank E. McKinney .....1946-1950 (Part)
John W. Galbreath ...1950 (Part) to date

No. 24. Indianapolis Club (resigned 1889)
John T. Brush (see No. 9)...1887-1888-1889

No. 25. Cleveland Club (resigned 1900)
Frank DeHaas Robison........1889-1898
M. Stanley Robison............1899

No. 26. Brooklyn Club
Charles H. Byrne............1890-1897
Charles H. Ebbets...........1898-1925
Wilbert Robinson...........1925-1929
Frank B. York...............1930-1932
Stephen W. McKeever........1933-1937
L. S. MacPhail, Exec. V-P ...1938-1939
L. S. MacPhail.............1939-1942
Branch Rickey ....1943-1950 (Part)
Walter F. O'Malley ..1950 (Part)—1957

No. 27. Cincinnati Club (No. 7)
A. S. Stern, John T. Brush..1890-1891-1902
August Herrmann.............1903-1927
C. J. McDiarmid.............1928-1929
Sidney Weil.................1930-1933
Powell Crosley, Jr..........1934-1946
Warren C. Giles.........1946-1951 (Part)
Powell Crosley, Jr. 1951 (Part) 1961 (Part)
William O. DeWitt ..1961 (Part) to date

No. 28. St. Louis Club
Chris Von der Ahe...........1892-1897
B. S. Muckenfuss.............1898
Frank De Haas Robison.......1899-1906
M. Stanley Robison..........1907-1910
E. A. Steininger, James C. Jones.1911-1912
Schuyler P. Britton.........1913-1916
Mrs. Schuyler P. Britton....1916
Branch Rickey...............1917-1919
Samuel Breadon.............1920-1947
Robert E. Hannegan.....1947-(part) 1949
Fred M. Saigh, Jr. 1949-1952
August A. Busch, Jr. ....1953 to date

No. 29. Baltimore Club (retired 1900)
H. B. Von der Horst............1892
Edward H. Hanlon............1893-1900

No. 30. Louisville Club (see No. 8 retired 1900)
T. Hunt Stucky.................1892
Fred Drexler................1893-1896
Harry C. Pulliam............1897-1898
Barney Dreyfuss, H. C. Pulliam..1899-1900

No. 31. Washington Club (retired 1900)
George W. Wagner...........1892-1900

No. 32. Milwaukee Club
Louis R. Perini 1953-1956
Joseph F. Cairnes ....1957 to 1961 (Part)
John J. McHale ....1961 to 1965

No. 33. San Francisco Club
Horace C. Stoneham ......1958 to date

No. 34. Los Angeles Club
Walter F. O'Malley ....1958 to date

No. 35. Houston Club
Craig Cullinan, Jr. 1962
Roy Hofheinz ....1963 to date

No. 36. New York Club
George M. Weiss .....1962 to date

°Charter Members.

3

AMERICAN LEAGUE

Chairman of Board: WILLIAM HARRIDGE

President-Secretary-Treasurer: JOSEPH E. CRONIN

Director, Public Relations: Joseph McKenney
Asst. to the President: William S. Cutler

PRESIDENTS

1901-1927 (26 years)—Byron Bancroft Johnson, originally elected for 10 years, re-elected for a term of 20 years. Retired on account of ill health October 18, 1927.

1927-1931 (4 years)—Ernest S. Barnard, elected for 3 years, re-elected for 5 years but died in office March 27, 1931.

1931-1959 (28 years)—William Harridge, elected for 3 years, re-elected in 1933 for 5 years, re-elected in 1938 for 10 years, re-elected in 1947 for 10 years, re-elected in 1956 for 10 years. Resigned effective February 1, 1959 and elected Chairman of Board.

1959—Joseph Edward Cronin, elected for 7 years February 1, 1959, re-elected for 7 years November 17, 1965.

VICE PRESIDENTS

Vice-Presidents—Charles W. Somers, 1901-1916; Charles A. Comiskey, Chicago, 1917-1919; Frank J. Navin, Detroit, 1921-1935; Col. Jacob Ruppert, New York, 1935-1938; Clark C. Griffith, Washington, 1939-1955; Thomas A. Yawkey, Boston, 1955 to date.

SECRETARIES

Secretaries—William Harridge, 1927-1959; Earl J. Hilligan, 1959; Joseph E. Cronin, 1960 to date.

PRESIDENTS OF LEAGUE CLUBS

No. 1. Chicago Club.
Charles A. Comiskey, 1901-1931; J. Louis Comiskey, part of 1931-1938. Harry Grabiner, V.P., 1931-46; Mrs. Grace R. Comiskey, 1941-1956; William L. Veeck, Jr., 1959-1961 (part); Arthur C. Allyn, Jr., 1961 (part) to date.

No. 2. Milwaukee Club.
Matthew Killilea, 1901.

No. 3. Cleveland Club.
John F. Kilfoyl, 1901-1909; Charles W. Somers, 1910-1915; James C. Dunn, 1916-1922; Ernest S. Barnard, 1922-1927; Alva Bradley, 1928-1946 (part); William L. Veeck, Jr., (part) 1946-(part 1949); Ellis W. Ryan (part) 1949-1952 (part); Myron H. Wilson, Jr. 1952 (part) to 1962. Gabriel H. Paul 1963 to date.

No. 4. Detroit Club.
James D. Burns, 1901; Samuel F. Angus, 1902-1903; W. H. Yawkey, 1904-1907; Frank J. Navin, 1908-1935 (part); Walter O. Briggs, Sr., (part) 1935-1951 (part); Walter O. Briggs, Jr. 1951-1956 (part); Frederick A. Knorr, 1956 (part)-1957 (part); Harvey R. Hansen, 1957 (part)-1959; William O. DeWitt, 1960; John E. Fetzer, 1961 to date.

No. 5. Washington Club.
Fred Postal, 1901-1903; Thomas J. Loftus, 1904; Thomas C. Noyes, 1905-1912; Benjamin S. Minor, 1912-1919; Clark C. Griffith, 1920 to 1955 (part); Calvin Griffith 1955 (part)-1961.

No. 6. Boston Club.
Charles W. Somers, 1901-1902; Henry J. Killilea, 1903; John I. Taylor. 1904-1911; James R. McAleer, 1912-1913; Joseph J. Lannin, 1913-1916; H. H. Frazee, 1917-1923; J. A. (Robert) Quinn, part of 1923-1932; Thomas A. Yawkey, 1933 to date.

No. 7. Baltimore Club.
Sidney W. Frank, 1901; John J. Mahon, 1902.

No. 8. Philadelphia Club.
Benjamin F. Shibe, 1901-1921; Thomas S. Shibe, 1922-part 1936; John D. Shibe, (part 1936; Connie Mack, 1937-1953.

No. 9. St. Louis Club.
Ralph Orthwein, 1902; Robert L. Hedges, 1903-1915; Philip D. C. Ball, 1916-1933; Louis B. Von Weise, 1934-1936; Donald L. Barnes, (part) 1936-(part) 1945; Richard C. Muckerman, 1945-(part) 1949; William O. DeWitt, 1949-51 (part); William L. Veeck, Jr., 1951 (part)-1952.

No. 10. New York Club.
Joseph W. Gordon, 1903-1906; Frank J. Farrell, 1907-1914; Col. Jacob Ruppert, 1915-1938; Edward G. Barrow, 1939-1949 (part); Col. Leland S. McPhail, 1945-1947 (part); Daniel R. Topping, 1947 to date.

No. 11 Baltimore Club.
Clarence W. Miles, 1953-1955 (part); James Keelty, 1955 (part)-1959; Leland S. MacPhail, Jr., 1960-1965.

No. 12 Kansas City Club.
Arnold Johnson, 1954-1959; Parke Carroll, V.P., 1960; Charles O. Finley, 1961 to date.

No. 13. Minnesota Club.
Calvin Griffith, 1961 to date.

No. 14. Washington Club.
Elwood Quesada, 1961-1962; James M. Johnston (Bd. Ch.), 1963 to date.

No. 15. Los Angeles Club.
Robert Reynolds, 1961 to date.

NATIONAL LEAGUE CHAMPIONS

Year	Club	Manager	Won	Lost	PC
1876	Chicago	Albert G. Spalding	52	14	.788
1877	Boston	Harry Wright	42	18	.700
1878	Boston	Harry Wright	41	19	.683
1879	Providence	George Wright	55	23	.705
1880	Chicago	Adrian C. Anson	67	17	.798
1881	Chicago	Adrian C. Anson	56	28	.667
1882	Chicago	Adrian C. Anson	55	29	.655
1883	Boston	John F. Morrill	63	35	.643
1884	Providence	Frank C. Bancroft	84	28	.750
1885	Chicago	Adrian C. Anson	87	25	.777
1886	Chicago	Adrian C. Anson	90	34	.726
1887	Detroit	W. H. Watkins	79	45	.637
1888	New York	James J. Mutrie	84	47	.641
1889	New York	James J. Mutrie	83	43	.659
1890	Brooklyn	William H. McGunnigle	86	43	.667
1891	Boston	Frank G. Selee	87	51	.630
1892	Boston	Frank C. Selee	102	48	.680
1893	Boston	Frank C. Selee	86	44	.662
1894	Baltimore	Edward H. Hanlon	89	39	.695
1895	Baltimore	Edward H. Hanlon	87	43	.669
1896	Baltimore	Edward H. Hanlon	90	39	.698
1897	Boston	Frank G. Selee	93	39	.705
1898	Boston	Frank G. Selee	102	47	.685
1899	Brooklyn	Edward H. Hanlon	88	42	.677
1900	Brooklyn	Edward H. Hanlon	82	54	.603
1901	Pittsburgh	Fred C. Clarke	90	49	.647
1902	Pittsburgh	Fred C. Clarke	103	36	.741
1903	Pittsburgh	Fred C. Clarke	91	49	.650
1904	New York	John J. McGraw	106	47	.693
1905†	New York	John J. McGraw	105	48	.686
1906	Chicago	Frank L. Chance	116	36	.763
1907†	Chicago	Frank L. Chance	107	45	.704
1908†	Chicago	Frank L. Chance	99	55	.643
1909†	Pittsburgh	Fred C. Clarke	110	42	.724
1910	Chicago	Frank L. Chance	104	50	.675
1911	New York	John J. McGraw	99	54	.647
1912	New York	John J. McGraw	103	48	.682
1913	New York	John J. McGraw	101	51	.664
1914†	Boston	George T. Stallings	94	59	.614
1915	Philadelphia	Patrick J. Moran	90	62	.592
1916	Brooklyn	Wilbert Robinson	94	60	.610
1917	New York	John J. McGraw	98	56	.636
1918	Chicago	Fred L. Mitchell	84	45	.651
1919†	Cincinnati	Patrick J. Moran	96	44	.686
1920	Brooklyn	Wilbert Robinson	93	61	.604
1921†	New York	John J. McGraw	94	59	.614
1922†	New York	John J. McGraw	93	61	.604
1923	New York	John J. McGraw	95	58	.621
1924	New York	John J. McGraw	93	60	.608
1925†	Pittsburgh	William B. McKechnie	95	58	.621
1926†	St. Louis	Rogers Hornsby	89	65	.578
1927	Pittsburgh	Owen J. Bush	94	60	.610
1928	St. Louis	William B. McKechnie	95	59	.617
1929	Chicago	Joseph V. McCarthy	98	54	.645
1930	St. Louis	Charles E. Street	92	62	.597
1931†	St. Louis	Charles E. Street	101	53	.656
1932	Chicago	Charles J. Grimm	90	64	.584
1933†	New York	William H. Terry	91	61	.599
1934†	St. Louis	Frank F. Frisch	95	58	.621
1935	Chicago	Charles J. Grimm	100	54	.649
1936	New York	William H. Terry	92	62	.597
1937	New York	William H. Terry	95	57	.625
1938	Chicago	Charles L. Hartnett	89	63	.586
1939	Cincinnati	William B. McKechnie	97	57	.630
1940†	Cincinnati	William B. McKechnie	100	53	.654
1941	Brooklyn	Leo E. Durocher	100	54	.649
1942†	St. Louis	William H. Southworth	106	48	.688
1943	St. Louis	William H. Southworth	105	49	.682
1944†	St. Louis	William H. Southworth	105	49	.682
1945	Chicago	Charles J. Grimm	98	56	.636
1946†	St. Louis	Edwin H. Dyer	98	58	.628
1947	Brooklyn	Burton E. Shotton	94	60	.610
1948	Boston	William H. Southworth	91	62	.595
1949	Brooklyn	Burton E. Shotton	97	57	.630
1950	Philadelphia	Edwin M. Sawyer	91	63	.591
1951	New York	Leo E. Durocher	98	59	.624
1952	Brooklyn	Charles W. Dressen	96	57	.627
1953	Brooklyn	Charles W. Dressen	105	49	.682
1954†	New York	Leo E. Durocher	97	57	.630
1955†	Brooklyn	Walter E. Alston	98	55	.641

5

NATIONAL LEAGUE CHAMPIONS (Cont'd)

			Won	Lost	PC
1956	Brooklyn	Walter E. Alston	93	61	.604
1957‡	Milwaukee	Fred G. Haney	95	59	.617
1958	Milwaukee	Fred G. Haney	92	62	.597
1959‡	Los Angeles	Walter E. Alston	88	68	.564
1960‡	Pittsburgh	Daniel E. Murtaugh	95	59	.617
1961	Cincinnati	Frederick C. Hutchinson	93	61	.604
1962	San Francisco	Alvin R. Dark	103	62	.624
1963‡	Los Angeles	Walter E. Alston	99	63	.611
1964‡	St. Louis	John J. Keane	93	69	.574
1965†	Los Angeles	Walter E. Alston	97	65	.599

‡World Series Winner.

AMERICAN LEAGUE CHAMPIONS

Year	Club	Manager	Won	Lost	PC
1901	Chicago	Clark C. Griffith	83	53	.610
1902	Philadelphia	Connie Mack	83	53	.610
1903‡	Boston	James J. Collins	91	47	.659
1904	Boston	James J. Collins	95	59	.617
1905	Philadelphia	Connie Mack	92	56	.622
1906‡	Chicago	Fielder A. Jones	93	58	.616
1907	Detroit	Hugh A. Jennings	92	58	.613
1908	Detroit	Hugh A. Jennings	90	63	.588
1909	Detroit	Hugh A. Jennings	98	54	.645
1910‡	Philadelphia	Connie Mack	102	48	.680
1911‡	Philadelphia	Connie Mack	101	50	.669
1912‡	Boston	J. Garland Stahl	105	47	.691
1913‡	Philadelphia	Connie Mack	96	57	.627
1914	Philadelphia	Connie Mack	99	53	.651
1915‡	Boston	William F. Carrigan	101	50	.669
1916‡	Boston	William F. Carrigan	91	63	.591
1917‡	Chicago	Clarence H. Rowland	100	54	.649
1918‡	Boston	Edward G. Barrow	75	51	.595
1919	Chicago	William Gleason	88	52	.629
1920‡	Cleveland	Tris E. Speaker	98	56	.636
1921	New York	Miller J. Huggins	98	55	.641
1922	New York	Miller J. Huggins	94	60	.610
1923‡	New York	Miller J. Huggins	98	54	.645
1924‡	Washington	Stanley R. Harris	92	62	.597
1925	Washington	Stanley R. Harris	96	55	.636
1926	New York	Miller J. Huggins	91	63	.591
1927‡	New York	Miller J. Huggins	110	44	.714
1928‡	New York	Miller J. Huggins	101	53	.656
1929‡	Philadelphia	Connie Mack	104	46	.693
1930‡	Philadelphia	Connie Mack	102	52	.662
1931	Philadelphia	Connie Mack	107	45	.704
1932‡	New York	Joseph V. McCarthy	107	47	.695
1933	Washington	Joseph E. Cronin	99	53	.651
1934	Detroit	Gordon S. Cochrane	101	53	.656
1935‡	Detroit	Gordon S. Cochrane	93	58	.616
1936‡	New York	Joseph V. McCarthy	102	51	.667
1937‡	New York	Joseph V. McCarthy	102	52	.662
1938‡	New York	Joseph V. McCarthy	99	53	.651
1939‡	New York	Joseph V. McCarthy	106	45	.702
1940	Detroit	Delmar D. Baker	90	64	.584
1941‡	New York	Joseph V. McCarthy	101	53	.656
1942	New York	Joseph V. McCarthy	103	51	.669
1943‡	New York	Joseph V. McCarthy	98	56	.636
1944	St. Louis	James L. Sewell	89	65	.578
1945‡	Detroit	Stephen F. O'Neill	88	65	.575
1946	Boston	Joseph E. Cronin	104	50	.675
1947‡	New York	Stanley R. Harris	97	57	.630
1948‡	Cleveland	Louis Boudreau	97	58	.626
1949‡	New York	Charles D. Stengel	97	57	.630
1950‡	New York	Charles D. Stengel	98	56	.636
1951‡	New York	Charles D. Stengel	98	56	.636
1952‡	New York	Charles D. Stengel	95	59	.617
1953‡	New York	Charles D. Stengel	99	52	.656
1954	Cleveland	Alfonso R. Lopez	111	43	.721
1955	New York	Charles D. Stengel	96	58	.623
1956‡	New York	Charles D. Stengel	97	57	.630
1957	New York	Charles D. Stengel	98	56	.636
1958‡	New York	Charles D. Stengel	92	62	.597
1959	Chicago	Alfonso R. Lopez	94	60	.610
1960	New York	Charles D. Stengel	97	57	.630
1961‡	New York	Ralph G. Houk	109	53	.673
1962‡	New York	Ralph G. Houk	96	66	.593
1963	New York	Ralph G. Houk	104	57	.646
1964	New York	Lawrence P. Berra	99	63	.611
1965	Minnesota	Sabath A. Mele	102	60	.630

‡World Series Winner.

Position of Major League Clubs
*Indicates ties.

NATIONAL LEAGUE

	Bos.-Mil.	Brooklyn	Chicago	Cincinnati	New York	Philadelphia	Pittsburgh	St. Louis
1901	5	3	6	8	7	2	1	4
1902	3	2	5	4	8	7	1	6
1903	6	5	3	4	2	7	1	8
1904	7	6	2	3	1	8	4	5
1905	7	8	3	5	1	4	2	6
1906	8	5	1	6	2	4	3	7
1907	7	5	1	6	4	3	2	8
1908	6	7	1	5	2°	4	2°	8
1909	8	6	2	4	3	5	1	7
1910	8	6	1	5	2	4	3	7
1911	8	7	2	6	1	4	3	5
1912	8	7	3	4	1	5	2	6
1913	5	6	3	7	1	2	4	8
1914	1	5	4	8	2	6	7	3
1915	2	3	4	7	8	1	5	6
1916	3	1	5	7°	4	2	6	7°
1917	6	7	5	4	1	2	8	3
1918	7	5	1	3	2	6	4	8.
1919	6	5	3	1	2	8	4	7
1920	7	1	5°	3	2	8	4	5°
1921	4	5	7	6	1	8	2	3
1922	8	6	5	2	1	7	3°	3°
1923	7	6	4	2	1	8	3	5
1924	8	2	5	4	1	7	3	6
1925	5	6°	8	3	2	6°	1	4
1926	7	6	4	2	5	8	3	1
1927	7	6	4	5	3	8	1	2
1928	7	6	3	5	2	8	4	1
1929	8	6	1	7	3	5	2	4
1930	6	4	2	7	3	8	5	1
1931	7	4	3	8	2	6	5	1
1932	5	3	1	8	6°	4	2	6°
1933	4	6	3	8	1	7	2	5
1934	4	6	3	8	2	7	5	1
1935	8	5	1	6	3	7	4	2
1936	6	7	2°	5	1	8	4	2°
1937	5	6	2	8	1	7	3	4
1938	5	7	1	4	3	8	2	6
1939	7	3	4	1	5	8	6	2
1940	7	2	5	1	6	8	4	3
1941	7	1	6	3	5	8	4	2
1942	7	2	6	4	3	8	5	1
1943	6	3	5	2	8	7	4	1
1944	6	7	4	3	5	8	2	1
1945	6	3	1	7	5	8	4	2
1946	4	2	3	6	8	5	7	1
1947	3	1	6	5	4	7°	7°	2
1948	1	3	8	7	5	6	4	2
1949	4	1	8	7	5	3	6	2
1950	4	2	7	6	3	1	8	5
1951	4	2	8	6	1	5	7	3
1952	7	1	5	6	2	4	8	3
1953	2	1	7	6	5	3°	8	3°
1954	3	2	7	5	1	4	8	6
1955	2	1	6	5	3	4	8	7
1956	2	1	8	3	6	5	7	4
1957	1	3	7°	4	6	5	7°	2

Boston transferred to Milwaukee 1953.

AMERICAN LEAGUE

	Boston	Chicago	Cleveland	Detroit	Balt.-N.Y.	Phil.-K.C.	St.L.-Balt.	Washington
1901	2	1	7	3	5	4	8	6
1902	3	4	5	7	8	1	2	6
1903	1	7	3	5	4	2	6	8
1904	1	3	4	7	2	5	6	8
1905	4	2	5	3	6	1	7	8
1906	8	1	3	6	2	4	5	7
1907	7	3	4	1	5	2	6	8
1908	5	3	2	1	8	6	4	7
1909	3	4	6	1	5	2	7	8
1910	4	6	5	3	2	1	8	7
1911	5	4	3	2	6	1	8	7
1912	1	4	5	6	8	3	7	2
1913	4	5	3	6	7	1	8	2
1914	2	6°	8	4	6°	1	5	3
1915	1	3	6	2	5	8	7	4
1916	1	2	6	3	4	8	5	7
1917	2	1	3	4	6	8	7	5
1918	1	6	2	7	4	8	5	3
1919	6	1	2	4	3	8	5	7
1920	5	2	1	7	3	8	4	6
1921	5	7	2	6	1	8	3	4
1922	8	5	4	3	1	7	2	6
1923	8	6	3	2	1	7	5	4
1924	7	8	6	3	2	5	4	1
1925	8	5	6	4	7	2	3	1
1926	8	5	2	6	1	3	7	4
1927	8	5	6	4	1	2	7	3
1928	8	5	7	6	1	2	3	4
1929	8	7	3	6	2	1	4	5
1930	8	7	4	5	3	1	6	2
1931	6	8	4	7	2	1	5	3
1932	8	7	4	5	1	2	6	3
1933	7	6	4	5	2	3	8	1
1934	4	8	3	1	2	5	6	7
1935	4	5	3	1	2	8	7	6
1936	6	3	5	2	1	8	7	4
1937	5	3	4	2	1	7	8	6
1938	2	6	3	4	1	8	7	5
1939	2	4	3	5	1	7	8	6
1940	4°	4°	2	1	3	8	6°	6°
1941	2	3	4°	4°	1	8	6°	6°
1942	2	6	4	5	1	8	3	7
1943	7	4	3	5	1	8	6	2
1944	4	7	5°	2	3	5°	1	8
1945	7	6	5	1	4	8	3	2
1946	1	5	6	2	3	8	7	4
1947	3	6	4	2	1	5	8	7
1948	2	8	1	5	3	4	6	7
1949	2	6	3	4	1	5	7	8
1950	3	6	4	2	1	8	7	5
1951	3	4	2	5	1	6	8	7
1952	6	3	2	8	1	4	7	5
1953	4	3	2	6	1	7	8	5
1954	4	3	1	5	2	8	7	6
1955	4	3	2	5	1	6	7	8
1956	4	3	2	5	1	8	6	7
1957	3	2	6	4	1	7	5	8

Baltimore transferred to New York 1903.
St. Louis transferred to Baltimore 1954.
Philadelphia transferred to K.C. 1955.

Position of Major League Clubs—Continued

°Indicates ties.

NATIONAL LEAGUE

	Chicago	Cincinnati	Houston	Los Angeles	Milwaukee	New York	Philadelphia	Pittsburgh	St. Louis	San Francisco
1958	5°	4	—	7	1	—	8	2	5°	3
1959	5°	5°	—	1	2	—	8	4	7	3
1960	7	6	—	4	2	—	8	1	3	5
1961	7	1	—	2	4	—	8	6	5	3
1962	9	3	8	2	5	10	7	4	6	1
1963	7	5	9	1	6	10	4	8	2	3
1964	8	2°	9	6°	5	10	2°	6°	1	4
1965	8	4	9	1	5	10	6	3	7	2

AMERICAN LEAGUE

	Baltimore	Boston	Chicago	Cleveland	Detroit	Kansas City	L.A.-Cal.	Minnesota	New York	Washington
1958	6	3	2	4	5	7	—	—	1	8
1959	6	5	1	2	4	7	—	—	3	8
1960	2	7	3	4	6	8	—	—	1	5
1961	3	6	4	5	2	9°	8	7	1	9°
1962	7	8	5	6	4	9	3	2	1	10
1963	4	7	2	5°	5°	8	9	3	1	10
1964	3	8	2	6°	4	10	5	6°	1	9
1965	3	9	2	5	4	10	7	1	6	8

BASEBALL HALL OF FAME

†Special Committee Nominee

SELECTED FOR MERITORIOUS SERVICE TO BASEBALL

EDWARD BARROW Manager-Executive
MORGAN G. BULKELEY Executive
ALEXANDER J. CARTWRIGHT Executive
HENRY CHADWICK Writer-Statistician
THOMAS CONNOLLY AL Umpire
WILLIAM A. CUMMINGS Early Pitcher
MILLER J. HUGGINS Manager
B. BANCROFT JOHNSON Executive

WILLIAM KLEM NL Umpire
KENESAW M. LANDIS Commissioner
CONNIE MACK Manager-Executive
JOSEPH McCARTHY Manager
WILLIAM B. McKECHNIE Manager
ALBERT G. SPALDING Early Player
GEORGE WRIGHT Early Player
HARRY WRIGHT Manager

PITCHERS

	Selected	Years	G	IP	W	L	PCT.
Alexander, Grover	(1938)	1911-1930	696	5189	373	208	.642
†Bender, Charles	(1953)	1903-1925	452	3026	212	128	.624
†Brown, Mordecai	(1949)	1903-1916	480	3168	239	130	.648
†Chesbro, John	(1946)	1899-1909	384	2859	199	128	.609
†Clarkson, John	(1963)	1882-1894	529	4514	328	175	.652
Dean, Jerome	(1953)	1930-1947	317	1966	150	83	.644
†Faber, Urban	(1964)	1914-1933	669	4087	253	211	.545
Feller, Robert	(1962)	1936-1956	570	3828	266	162	.621
†Galvin, James	(1965)	1876-1892	680	5959	365	309	.542
†Griffith, Clark	(1946)	1891-1914	428	3370	237	140	.629
†Grimes, Burleigh	(1964)	1916-1934	615	4178	270	212	.560
Grove, Robert	(1947)	1925-1941	616	3940	300	141	.680
Hubbell, Carl	(1947)	1928-1943	535	3591	253	154	.622
Johnson, Walter	(1936)	1907-1927	802	5924	416	279	.599
†Keefe, Timothy	(1964)	1880-1893	577	5039	346	225	.606
Lyons, Theodore	(1955)	1923-1946	594	4162	260	230	.531
Mathewson, Christy	(1936)	1900-1916	634	4789	373	188	.665
†McGinnity, Joseph	(1946)	1899-1908	467	3455	247	142	.633
†Nichols, Charles	(1949)	1890-1906	582	5015	360	202	.641
Pennock, Herbert	(1948)	1912-1934	617	3559	241	163	.597
†Plank, Edward	(1946)	1901-1917	620	4503	325	190	.631
†Radbourne, Charles	(1939)	1880-1891	517	4543	308	191	.617
†Rixey, Eppa	(1963)	1912-1933	692	4494	266	251	.515
Ruth, George	(1936)	1914-1933	163	1220	92	44	.676
Vance, Arthur	(1955)	1915-1935	442	2967	197	140	.585
†Waddell, George	(1946)	1897-1910	407	2958	193	140	.580
†Walsh, Edward	(1946)	1904-1917	431	2968	195	126	.607
Young, Denton	(1937)	1890-1911	906	7377	511	315	.619

BATTERS

	Selected	Years	G	AB	R	H	PCT
†Anson, Adrian	(1939)	1876-1897	2253	9084	1712	3081	.339
Appling, Lucius B.	(1964)	1930-1950	2422	8857	1319	2749	.310
†Baker, J. Frank	(1955)	1908-1922	1575	5985	887	1838	.307
†Bresnahan, Roger	(1945)	1897-1915	1410	4480	684	1251	.279
Brouthers, Dennis	(1945)	1879-1896	1655	6737	1507	2347	.348
†Burkett, Jesse	(1946)	1890-1905	2063	8389	1708	2872	.342
†Carey, Max	(1961)	1910-1929	2469	9363	1545	2665	.285
†Chance, Frank	(1946)	1898-1914	1232	4279	796	1273	.297
†Clarke, Fred	(1945)	1894-1915	2204	8584	1620	2703	.315
Cobb, Tyrus	(1936)	1905-1928	3033	11429	2244	4191	.367
†Cochrane, Gordon	(1947)	1925-1937	1482	5169	1041	1652	.320
Collins, Edward	(1939)	1906-1930	2826	9952	1818	3313	.333
†Collins, James	(1945)	1895-1908	1718	6792	1057	1999	.294
†Comiskey, Charles	(1939)	1882-1894	1383	5813	984	1564	.269
†Crawford, Samuel	(1957)	1899-1917	2505	9579	1392	2964	.309
Cronin, Joseph	(1956)	1926-1945	2124	7577	1233	2285	.302
†Delahanty, Edward	(1945)	1888-1903	1825	7493	1596	2593	.346
Dickey, William	(1954)	1928-1946	1789	6300	930	1969	.313
DiMaggio, Joseph	(1955)	1936-1951	1736	6821	1390	2214	.325
†Duffy, Hugh	(1945)	1888-1906	1722	6999	1545	2307	.330
†Evers, John	(1946)	1902-1919	1776	6136	919	1569	.270
†Ewing, William	(1946)	1880-1897	1280	5348	1119	1663	.311
†Flick, Elmer	(1963)	1898-1910	1480	5597	948	1764	.315
Foxx, James	(1951)	1925-1945	2317	8134	1751	2646	.325
Frisch, Frank	(1947)	1919-1937	2311	9112	1532	2880	.316
Gehrig, H. Louis	(1939)	1923-1939	2164	8001	1888	2721	.340
Gehringer, Charles	(1949)	1924-1942	2323	8858	1773	2839	.321
Greenberg, Henry	(1956)	1933-1947	1394	5193	1051	1628	.313
†Hamilton, William	(1961)	1909-1901	1578	6262	1691	2157	.344
Hartnett, Charles	(1955)	1922-1941	1990	6432	867	1912	.297
Heilmann, Harry	(1952)	1914-1932	2146	7787	1291	2660	.342
Hornsby, Rogers	(1942)	1915-1937	2259	8173	1579	2930	.358
†Jennings, Hugh	(1945)	1891-1918	1264	4840	969	1520	.314
Keeler, William	(1939)	1892-1910	2124	8564	1720	2955	.345
†Kelly, Michael	(1945)	1878-1893	1493	6178	1434	1944	.315
Lajoie, Napoleon	(1937)	1896-1916	2475	9589	1503	3251	.339
†Manush, Henry	(1964)	1923-1939	2009	7653	1287	2524	.330
Maranville, Walter	(1954)	1912-1935	2670	10078	1255	2605	.258
†McCarthy, Thomas	(1946)	1884-1896	1268	5098	1062	1498	.294
†McGraw, John	(1937)	1891-1906	1082	3919	1019	1307	.334
†O'Rourke, James	(1945)	1876-1894	1750	7335	1425	2314	.315
Ott, Melvin	(1951)	1926-1947	2730	9456	1859	2876	.304
†Rice, Edgar	(1963)	1915-1934	2404	9269	1515	2987	.322
†Robinson, Jack	(1962)	1947-1956	1382	4877	947	1518	.311
†Robinson, Wilbert	(1945)	1886-1902	1316	4942	629	1386	.280
Roush, Ed	(1962)	1913-1931	1967	7361	1097	2377	.323
Ruth, George	(1936)	1914-1935	2503	8399	2174	2873	.342
†Schalk, Raymond	(1955)	1912-1929	1760	5306	579	1345	.253
Simmons, Al	(1953)	1924-1944	2215	8761	1507	2927	.334
Sisler, George	(1939)	1915-1930	2055	8267	1284	2812	.340
Speaker, Tris	(1937)	1907-1928	2789	10208	1881	3515	.344
Terry, William	(1954)	1923-1936	1721	6428	1120	2193	.341
†Tinker, Joseph	(1946)	1902-1916	1641	5937	710	1565	.264
Traynor, Harold	(1948)	1920-1937	1941	7559	1183	2416	.320
†Wallace, Roderick	(1953)	1894-1918	2369	8629	1056	2308	.267
Waner, Paul	(1952)	1926-1945	2549	9459	1626	3152	.333
†Ward, John	(1964)	1878-1894	1810	7598	1402	2151	.283
†Wheat, Zach	(1959)	1909-1927	2406	9106	1289	2884	.317
Williams, Theodore	(1966)	1939-1960	2292	7706	1798	2654	.344

MAJOR LEAGUE ATTENDANCE RECORDS

LEAGUE RECORDS FOR SEASON

AMERICAN LEAGUE......11,150,099—1948   NATIONAL LEAGUE .....12,045,190—1964

Largest paid attendance by clubs, at home, season

AMERICAN LEAGUE		NATIONAL LEAGUE	
Cleveland	2,620,627—1948	Los Angeles	2,755,184—1962
New York	2,373,901—1948	Milwaukee	2,215,404—1957
Detroit	1,951,474—1950	Houston	2,151,470—1965
Chicago	1,644,460—1960	San Francisco	1,795,356—1960
Boston	1,596,650—1949	New York	1,768,389—1965
Minnesota	1,463,258—1965	Pittsburgh	1,705,828—1960
Kansas City	1,393,054—1955	Chicago	1,485,166—1929
Baltimore	1,187,849—1960	St. Louis	1,430,676—1949
Los Angeles	1,144,063—1962	Philadelphia	1,425,891—1964
Washington	729,775—1962	Cincinnati	1,125,928—1956

Largest paid attendance, clubs, day

AMERICAN LEAGUE	NATIONAL LEAGUE
Cleveland (vs. N.Y.) . .84,587—Sept. 12, 1954°	New York (vs. L.A.) . .57,175—June 13, 1965°
New York (vs. Boston) .81,841—May 30, 1938°	Los Angeles (vs. S.F.) 54,418—Sept. 3, 1962
Detroit (vs. N. Y.)....58,369—July 20, 1947°	Houston (vs. L.A.) . . .49,442—Sept. 5, 1965
Chicago (vs. N.Y.) ....54,215—July 19, 1953°	Milwaukee (vs. Phil.)..48,642—Sept. 27, 1959
Balt. (vs. N.Y.) ......46,796—May 16, 1954°	Chicago (vs. Pitts.)...46,965—May 31, 1948°
Los Angeles (vs. N.Y.) .44,912—June 3, 1962	St. Louis (vs. Chi.)....45,770—July 12, 1931°
Washington (vs. Bos.) .43,554—Apr. 12, 1965	Pitts. (vs. Brk.) ......44,932—Sept. 23, 1956
Boston (vs. N. Y.)....41,766—Aug. 12, 1934°	San Francisco (vs. Mil.) 42,894—Apr. 14, 1964
Minnesota (vs. Balt.) . .41,021—Aug. 1, 1965	Phila. (vs. Bklyn.) .....40,720—May 11, 1947°
Kansas City (vs. N.Y.) .34,065—Aug. 27, 1961	Cincinnati (vs. Pitts.)..36,961—Apr. 27, 1947°

Largest paid attendance by clubs on road

AMERICAN LEAGUE		NATIONAL LEAGUE	
New York	2,216,159—1962	Los Angeles	1,918,669—1965
Boston	1,779,936—1946	San Francisco	1,810,414—1965
Cleveland	1,762,564—1948	Milwaukee	1,633,569—1959
Detroit	1,414,126—1950	Pittsburgh	1,581,129—1960
Chicago	1,280,554—1955	St. Louis	1,518,545—1946
Minnesota	1,178,475—1965	Cincinnati	1,451,838—1965
Baltimore	1,151,055—1960	Philadelphia	1,391,812—1964
Los Angeles	861,699—1962	Chicago	1,245,920—1960
Kansas City	778,870—1960	New York	1,075,431—1965
Washington	627,761—1965	Houston	952,749—1965

Largest opening day attendance

AMERICAN LEAGUE		NATIONAL LEAGUE	
Cleveland	73,163—1948	Los Angeles	52,564—1962
New York	54,404—1946	New York	48,736—1964
Detroit	53,563—1960	Chicago	43,824—1929
Baltimore	46,354—1954	Milwaukee	43,640—1955
Washington	43,554—1965	San Francisco	42,894—1964
Chicago	41,660—1960	Houston	42,652—1965†
Boston	35,223—1958	Pittsburgh	38,546—1948
Kansas City	31,895—1955	Philadelphia	37,667—1957
Minnesota	24,606—1961	Cincinnati	35,747—1924
Los Angeles	21,864—1963	St. Louis	26,246—1958†

Largest night game attendance

AMERICAN LEAGUE	NATIONAL LEAGUE
Cleveland (vs Chic.) . .78,382—Aug. 20, 1948	New York (vs S.F.) ...56,167—Aug. 27, 1965
New York (vs Bost.) ..74,747—May 26, 1947	Los Angeles (vs. S.F.) .54,395—Sept. 5, 1962
Detroit (vs Cleve.) ....56,586—Aug. 9, 1948	Houston (vs L.A.) ....50,136—July 3, 1965
Chicago (vs N.Y.) ....53,940—June 8, 1951	Milwaukee (vs N.Y.) ..46,944—Aug. 27, 1954
Los Angeles (vs. N.Y.) 53,591—July 13, 1962	Pittsburgh (vs Cinn.) . .42,254—Aug. 12, 1940
Washington (vs N.Y.) .48,147—Aug. 1, 1962°	San Francisco (vs Mil.) 41,943—May 2, 1960
Baltimore (vs. N.Y.) . .47,987—Aug. 15, 1964	Philadelphia (vs Cinn.) 40,007—Sept. 19, 1946
Minnesota (vs N.Y.) . . .42,034—July 17, 1963	St. Louis (vs Bklyn.) . .33,323—Aug. 25, 1942
Boston (vs N.Y.) ......36,228—June 28, 1949	Cincinnati (vs Chic.) . .32,916—June 29, 1936
Kansas City (vs. N.Y.) 35,147—Aug. 18, 1962°	

° Doubleheader.
† Night game.

CHAMPION BATTERS IN MAJOR LEAGUES

Year	League	P.C.	League	P.C.	League	P.C.
	National League					
1876	R. Barnes, Chi.	403				
1877	J. L. White, Bos.	385				
1878	A. Dalrymple, Mil.	356				
1879	A. C. Anson, Chi.	407	**American Association**			
1880	G. F. Gore, Chi.	365			**Union Association**	
1881	A. C. Anson, Chi.	399	L. Browning, Lou.	382		
1882	D. Brouthers, Buf.	367	C. E. Swartwood, Alle.	368		
1883	D. Brouthers, Buf.	371	T. Esterbrook, Met.	408	F. Dunlap, St. L.	420
1884	J. O'Rourke, Buf.	350	L. Browning, Lou.	367		
1885	R. Connor, N.Y.	371	David Orr, Met.	346		
1886	M. J. Kelly, Chi.	388	J. F. O'Neill, St. L.	492	**Players League**	
1887	A. C. Anson, Chi.	421	J. F. O'Neill, St. L.	332		
1888	A. C. Anson, Chi.	343	T. Tucker, Balt.	375	L. Browning, Cleve.	391
1889	D. Brouthers, Bos.	373	W. V. Wolf, Lou.	366		
1890	J. Glasscock, N.Y.	336	D. Brouthers, Bost.	349		
1891	W. Hamilton, Phil.	338				
1892	C. Childs, Cleve.	335				
1893	Hugh Duffy, Bos.	378				
1894	Hugh Duffy, Bos.	438				
1895	J. Burkett, Cleve.	423				
1896	J. Burkett, Cleve.	410				
1897	W. Keeler, Balt.	432				
1898	W. Keeler, Balt.	379	**American League**			
1899	E. J. Delahanty, Phil.	408				
1900	J. P. Wagner, Pitts.	381				
1901	J. Burkett, St. L.	382	N. Lajoie, Phil.	422		
1902	C. H. Beaumont, Pitts.	357	E. J. Delahanty, Wash.	376		
1903	J. P. Wagner, Pitts.	355	N. Lajoie, Cleve.	355		
1904	J. P. Wagner, Pitts.	349	N. Lajoie, Cleve.	381		
1905	J. B. Seymour, Cin.	377	Elmer Flick, Cleve.	306		
1906	J. P. Wagner, Pitts.	339	G. Stone, St. L.	358		
1907	J. P. Wagner, Pitts.	350	T. R. Cobb, Det.	350		
1908	J. P. Wagner, Pitts.	354	T. R. Cobb, Det.	324		
1909	J. P. Wagner, Pitts.	339	T. R. Cobb, Det.	377		
1910	S. N. Magee, Phil.	331	T. R. Cobb, Det.	385		
1911	J. P. Wagner, Pitts.	334	T. R. Cobb, Det.	420		
1912	H. Zimmerman, Chi.	372	T. R. Cobb, Det.	410		
1913	J. Daubert, Brklyn.	350	T. R. Cobb, Det.	390		
1914	J. Daubert, Brklyn.	329	T. R. Cobb, Det.	368	**Federal League** B. Kauff, Ind.	366
1915	L. Doyle, N.Y.	320	T. R. Cobb, Det.	369	B. Kauff, Brklyn.	344
1916	H. Chase, Cin.	339	T. Speaker, Cleve.	386		
1917	E. J. Roush, Cin.	341	T. R. Cobb, Det.	383		
1918	Z. D. Wheat, Brklyn.	335	T. R. Cobb, Det.	382		
1919	E. J. Roush, Cin.	321	T. R. Cobb, Det.	384		
1920	Rogers Hornsby, St. L.	370	G. H. Sisler, St. L.	407		
1921	Rogers Hornsby, St. L.	397	H. E. Heilmann, Det.	394		
1922	Rogers Hornsby, St. L.	401	G. H. Sisler, St. L.	420		
1923	Rogers Hornsby, St. L.	384	H. E. Heilmann, Det.	403		
1924	Rogers Hornsby, St. L.	424	G. H. Ruth, N.Y.	378		
1925	Rogers Hornsby, St. L.	403	H. E. Heilmann, Det.	393		
1926	Eugene Hargrave, Cin.	353	H. E. Manush, Det.	378		
1927	Paul G. Waner, Pitts.	380	H. E. Heilmann, Det.	398		
1928	Rogers Hornsby, Bos.	387	L. A. Goslin, Wash.	379		
1929	Frank J. O'Doul, Phil.	398	L. A. Fonseca, Cleve.	369		
1930	Wm. H. Terry, N.Y.	401	A. H. Simmons, Phil.	381		
1931°	C. J. Hafey, St. L.	349	A. H. Simmons, Phil.	390		
1932	F. J. O'Doul, Brklyn.	368	D. Alexander, Det.-Bos.	367		
1933	C. H. Klein, Phil.	368	J. E. Foxx, Phil.	356		
1934	P. G. Waner, Pitts.	362	H. L. Gehrig, N.Y.	363		
1935	F. Vaughan, Pitts.	385	C. S. Myer, Wash.	349		
1936	P. G. Waner, Pitts.	373	L. B. Appling, Chi.	388		
1937	J. M. Medwick, St. L.	374	C. L. Gehringer, Det.	371		
1938	E. N. Lombardi, Cin.	342	J. E. Foxx, Bos.	349		
1939	J. R. Mize, St. L.	349	J. P. DiMaggio, N.Y.	381		
1940	D. Garms, Pitts.	355	J. P. DiMaggio, N.Y.	352		
1941	P. H. Reiser, Brklyn.	343	T. S. Williams, Bos.	406		
1942	E. N. Lombardi, Bos.	330	T. S. Williams, Bos.	356		
1943	S. F. Musial, St. L.	357	L. B. Appling, Chi.	328		
1944	F. Walker, Brklyn.	357	L. Boudreau, Cleve.	327		
1945	P. J. Cavarretta, Chi.	355	G. H. Stirnweiss, N.Y.	309		

°In 1931 Hafey led, with percentage .3489; Terry, N. Y., second, .3486; Bottomley, St. L., third, .3482.

CHAMPION BATTERS IN MAJOR LEAGUES—Continued

1946—S. F. Musial, St. L......**365** J. B. Vernon, Wash.....353
1947—H. Walker, St. L.-Phil. .363 T. S. Williams, Bos.....343
1948—S. F. Musial, St. L.....**376** T. S. Williams, Bos.....369
1949—J. R. Robinson, Brklyn..342 °G. C. Kell, Det.......343 °In 1949 Kell led with
1950—S. F. Musial, St. L.....**346** W. D. Goodman, Bos. ...354 percentage, .3429, Wil-
1951—S. F. Musial, St. L.....**355** F. R. Fain, Phil........344 liams second, .3427.
1952—S. F. Musial, St. L.....**336** F. R. Fain, Phil........327
1953—C. A. Furillo, Bklyn.....**344** J. B. Vernon, Wash.....337
1954—W. H. Mays, N. Y......**345** R. F. Avila, Cleve.....341
1955—R. Ashburn, Phila......**338** A. W. Kaline, Det.....340
1956—H. Aaron, Milw.......**328** M. C. Mantle, N.Y. 353
1957—S. F. Musial, St. L.....**351** T. S. Williams, Bos.....388
1958—R. Ashburn, Phila......**350** T. S. Williams, Bos. ...328
1959—H. Aaron, Milw. .....**355** H. Kuenn, Det. 353
1960—R. M. Groat, Pitt......**325** J. E. Runnels, Bos.....320
1961—R. W. Clemente, Pitt. ..**351** N. D. Cash, Det. 361
1962—H. T. Davis, L.A. .....**346** J. E. Runnels, Bos. 326
1963—H. T. Davis, L.A......**326** C. Yastrzemski, Bos....321
1964—R. W. Clemente, Pitt .339 P. Oliva, Minn 323
1965—R. W. Clemente, Pitt....**329** P. Oliva, Minn........321

RUNS BATTED IN LEADERS
(official tabulation adopted in 1920)

NATIONAL LEAGUE	AMERICAN LEAGUE
1920—Kelly, George L., New York.......... 94	Ruth, George H., New York......137
Hornsby, Rogers, St. Louis.......... 94	
1921—Hornsby, Rogers, St. Louis..........126	Ruth, George H., New York......170
1922—Hornsby, Rogers, St. Louis..........152	Williams, Kenneth R., St. Louis....155
1923—Meusel, Emil F., New York.........125	{ Speaker, Tris, Cleveland..........130
	{ Ruth, George H., New York.......130
1924—Kelly, George L., New York.........**136**	Goslin, Leon A., Washington......129
1925—Hornsby, Rogers, St. Louis.........143	Meusel, Robert W., New York......138
1926—Bottomley, James L., St. Louis......120	Ruth, George H., New York......155
1927—Waner, Paul G., Pittsburgh..........131	Gehrig, Henry L., New York.....175
1928—Bottomley, James L., St. Louis.......**136**	{ Ruth, George H., New York.....142
	{ Gehrig, Henry L., New York.....142
1929—Wilson, Lewis R., Chicago..........159	Simmons, Al H., Philadelphia......157
1930—Wilson, Lewis R., Chicago..........190	Gehrig, Henry L., New York......174
1931—Klein, Charles H. Philadelphia.......121	Gehrig, Henry L., New York.....184
1932—Hurst, Frank O., Philadelphia......143	Foxx, James E., Philadelphia.....169
1933—Klein, Charles H., Philadelphia......120	Foxx, James E., Philadelphia......163
1934—Ott, Melvin T., New York.........135	Gehrig, Henry L., New York.....165
1935—Berger, Walter A., Boston..........130	Greenberg, Henry, Detroit.......170
1936—Medwick, Joseph M., St. Louis.........138	Trosky, Harold, Cleveland........162
1937—Medwick, Joseph M., St. Louis.......154	Greenberg, Henry, Detroit.......183
1938—Medwick, Joseph M., St. Louis.......122	Foxx, James E., Boston.........175
1939—McCormick, Frank A., Cincinnati ...128	Williams, Theodore S., Boston......145
1940—Mize, John R., St. Louis...........137	Greenberg, Henry, Detroit.......150
1941—Camilli, Adolph, Brooklyn..........120	DiMaggio, Jos. P., New York......125
1942—Mize, John R., New York..........110	Williams, Theodore S., Boston.. ...137
1943—Nicholson, William B., Chicago......128	York, P. Rudolph, Detroit.........118
1944—Nicholson, William B., Chicago......122	Stephens, Vernon D., St. Louis.....109
1945—Walker, Frederick, Brooklyn.......124	Etten, Nicholas R., New York......111
1946—Slaughter, Enos B., St. Louis.......130	Greenberg, Henry B., Detroit......127
1947—Mize, John R., New York.........138	Williams, Theodore S., Boston......114
1948—Musial, Stanley F., St. Louis........131	DiMaggio, Joseph P., New York....155
1949—Kiner, Ralph M., Pittsburgh.........127	{ Williams, Theodore S., Boston......159
	{ Stephens, Vernon D., Boston......159
1950—Ennis, Delmer, Philadelphia 126	{ Stephens, Vernon D., Boston......144
	{ Dropo, Walter O., Boston........144
1951—Irvin, Monford, New York 121	Zernial, Gus E., Chic.-Phila......129
1952—Sauer, Henry J., Chicago 121	Rosen, Albert L., Cleveland 105
1953—Campanella, Roy, Brooklyn.........142	Rosen, Albert L., Cleveland 145
1954—Kluszewski, Theo. B., Cincinnati......141	Doby, Lawrence E., Cleveland 126
1955—Snider, Edwin D., Brooklyn..........136	{ Boone, Raymond O., Detroit.......116
	{ Jensen, Jack E., Boston............116
1956—Musial, Stanley F., St. Louis 109	Mantle, Mickey C., New York 130
1957—Aaron, Henry, Milwaukee 132	Sievers, Roy, Washington 114
1958—Banks, Ernest, Chicago 129	Jensen, Jack E., Boston 122
1959—Banks, Ernest, Chicago 143	Jensen, Jack E., Boston 112
1960—Aaron, Henry, Milwaukee 126	Maris, Roger E., New York 112
1961—Cepeda, Orlando, San Francisco 142	Maris, Roger E., New York 142
1962—Davis, H. Thomas, Los Angeles 153	Killebrew, Harmon C., Minnesota ..126
1963—Aaron, Henry, Milwaukee 130	Stuart, Richard L., Boston 118
1964—Boyer, Kenton L., St. Louis 119	Robinson, Brooks C., Baltimore 118
1965—Johnson, Deron R., Cincinnati 130	Colavito, Rocco D., Cleveland 108

MAJOR LEAGUE RECORDS

INDIVIDUAL BATTING RECORDS

A—Highest percentage (100 or more games), season—
.438—Hugh Duffy, Boston NL, 124 games, 539-ab, 236 hits, 1894.
.432—William H. Keeler, Baltimore NL, 128 games, 562-ab, 243 hits, 1897.
.424—Rogers Hornsby, St. Louis NL, 143 games, 536-ab, 227 hits, 1924.
.422—Napoleon Lajoie, Philadelphia AL, 131 games, 543-ab, 229 hits, 1901.
.420—George H. Sisler, St. Louis AL (.41979), 142 games, 586-ab, 246 hits, 1922.
    Tyrus R. Cobb, Detroit AL (.41962), 146 games, 591-ab, 248 hits, 1911.
    (In 1887, when a base on balls was scored as a base hit, J. F. O'Neill, St. Louis A.A, had a percentage of .492.)

B—Highest percentage (10 or more years), lifetime—
.367—Tyrus R. Cobb, Detroit AL, 1905-26; Phila. AL, 1927-28; 24 years; 11,429 ab, 4,191 hits.
.358—Rogers Hornsby, St. Louis NL, 1915-1926; New York NL, 1927; Boston NL, 1928; Chicago NL, 1929-1932 (part); St. Louis AL, 1933 (part) 1937, 23 years, 8,173 ab, 2,930 hits.

C—Lowest percentage, leading batsman, 100 or more games, season—
.306—Elmer H. Flick, Cleveland AL, 131 games, 496-ab, 152 hits, 1905.
.320—Lawrence J. Doyle, New York NL, 150 games, 591-ab, 189 hits, 1915.

D—Most years leading league (percentage)—
12—Tyrus R. Cobb, Detroit AL, 1907-8-9-10-11-12-13-14-15-17-18-19.
8—John P. Wagner, Pittsburgh NL, 1900-03-04-06-07-08-09-11.

E—Most consecutive years leading (percentage)—
9—Tyrus R. Cobb, Detroit, AL, 1907-15, inclusive.
6—Rogers Hornsby, St. Louis NL, 1920-25.

F—Leading both leagues in batting
.408—Edward J. Delahanty, Philadelphia, 1899, National.
.376—Edward J. Delahanty, Washington 1902, American.

G—Most years batting .400 or better—
3—Jesse C. Burkett, Cleveland NL, .423—1895; .410—1896; St. Louis NL, .402—1899.
    Tyrus R. Cobb, Detroit AL, .420—1911; .410—1912; .401—1922.
    Rogers Hornsby, St. L., NL., .401—1922; .424—1924; .403—1925.
    (For .400 hitters see table page 19)

H—Most consecutive years batting .400 or better—

2—Jesse C. Burkett, Cleveland NL..........................423—1895	.410—1896
Tyrus R. Cobb, Detroit AL..........................420—1911	.410—1912
Rogers Hornsby, St. Louis NL..........................424—1924	.403—1925

I—Most years batting .300 or better—
23—Tyrus R. Cobb, Detroit AL, 1906-26; Phila. AL, 1927-28.
20—Adrian C. Anson, Chicago NL, 1876-97 (except 1891, 1892).
17—John P. Wagner, Louisville NL, 1897-98-99; Pitts. NL 1900-13.
    Stanley F. Musial, St. Louis NL, 1942-44, 46-58, 62.

J—Most consecutive years batting .300 or better—
23—Tyrus R. Cobb, Detroit AL, 1906-26; Philadelphia AL, 1927-28.
17—John P. Wagner, Louisville NL, 1897-98-99; Pittsburgh NL 1900-13.

GAMES PLAYED

K—Most games played, season—(154 game schedule)—
162—James E. Barrett, Detroit AL, 1904.
160—Thomas H. Griffith, Cincinnati NL, 1915.
    Henry K. Groh, Cincinnati NL, 1915.

L—Most games played, season (162 game schedule)—
165—Maurice M. Wills, Los Angeles NL, 1962.
163—Rocco D. Colavito, Detroit AL, 1961.
    Brooks C. Robinson, Baltimore AL, 1961, 64.
    Leon L. Wagner, Cleveland AL, 1964.

M—Most years playing 150 or more games, league—
12—Henry L. Gehrig, New York AL, 1926-32, 34-38.
    Willie H. Mays, N.Y. NL, 1954-57; S.F. NL, 1958-65.

N—Most consecutive years playing 150 or more games, league—
12—Willie H. Mays, N.Y. NL, 1954-57; S.F. NL, 1958-65.
11—J. Nelson Fox, Chi. AL, 1952-62.

A—Most years playing 100 or more games, league or lifetime—
21—Stanley F. Musial, St. L. NL, 1942-44, 46-63 (Mil. Service 1945).
19—Tyrus R. Cobb, Det. AL, 1907-13, 15-25; Phil. AL, 1927.
Tris E. Speaker, Bos. AL, 1909-15; Clev. AL, 1916-26; Wash. AL, 1927.

B—Most consecutive years, playing 100 or more games, league—
21—Stanley F. Musial, St. L. NL, 1942-44, 46-63 (Mil. Service 1945).
19—Tris E. Speaker, Bos. AL, 1909-15; Clev. AL, 1916-26; Wash. AL, 1927.

C—Most games played, league—
3,033—Tyrus R. Cobb, Detroit (2804) AL, 1905-26; Philadelphia (229) AL, 1927-28. (24 years).
3,026—Stanley F. Musial, St. Louis NL, 1941-44, 46-63. (21 years.)

D—Most years leading league in games played, season—
7—Henry L. Gehrig, New York AL, 1927-1930-1932-1934-1936-1937-1938.
6—Ernest Banks, Chicago NL, 1954, 55, 57, 58, 59, 60 (tied in 1954-55-57-59-60).

E—Most consecutive games played, league—
2,130—Henry L. Gehrig, N.Y. AL, June 1, 1925 thru Apr. 30, 1939.
895—Stanley F. Musial, St. L. NL, Apr. 15, 1952 thru Aug. 22, 1957.

F—Most consecutive games played, start of major league career—
424—Ernest Banks, Chicago NL, 1953 (10), 1954 (154), 1955 (154), 1956 (106).
394—Aloysius H. Simmons, Phila. AL, 1924 (152), 1925 (153), 1926 (89).

SERVICE YEARS

G—Most years, lifetime—
26—James T. McGuire (AA) Tol.1884;Clev.88;Roch.90;Wash.91 (NL) Det.85,88;Phil.86-88; Wash.92-99;Brk.99-01 (AL) Det.02-03,12;N.Y.04-07;Bos.07-08;Clev.08,10.

Most years, league
25—Edward T. Collins (AL) Philadelphia 1906-14, 27-30; Chicago 1915-26.
23—Walter J. Maranville (NL) Boston 1912-20, 29-33, 35; Pittsburgh 1921-24; Chicago 1925; Brooklyn 1926; St. Louis 1927-28.

Most years, one club—
22—Adrian C. Anson, Chicago NL, 1876-1897.
Tyrus R. Cobb, Detroit AL, 1905-1926.
Melvin T. Ott, New York NL, 1926-1947.
Stanley F. Musial, St. Louis NL, 1941-44, 46-63.

H—Playing on most clubs, lifetime—
12—James T. McGuire, Toledo, Clev., Roch., Wash. AA; Det., Phil., Wash., Brk. NL; Det., N.Y., Bos., Clev. AL, 1884-1912.

Playing on most clubs (since 1900)—
10—Richard B. Littlefield, Bos., Chi., Det., St.L., Balt. AL; Pitt., St.L., N.Y., Chi., Mil. NL, 1950-58.

Playing on most clubs, league—
9—Dennis L. Brouthers (NL) Troy 1879-80;Buff.81-85;Det.86-88;Bos.89;Brk.92-93;Balt.94-95; Lou.95;Phil.96;N.Y.1904.
8—W. Edward Robinson (AL) Clev.1942,46-48,57;Wash.49-50;Chi.50-52;Phil.53;N.Y.54-56;K.C. 56; Det.57;Balt.57.
7—John C. Barry (NL) Wash.1899;Bos.1900-01;Phil.01-04;Chi.04-05;Cin.05-06;St.L.06-08;N.Y.08.
Joseph C. Schultz (NL) Bos.1912-13;Brk.15;Chi.15;Pitt.16;St.L.19-24;Phil.24-25;Cin.25.
W. Walker Cooper (NL) St.L.1940-45,56-57;N.Y.46-49;Cin.49-50;Bos.50-52;Mil.53;Pitt.54; Chi.54-55.
Frank J. Thomas (NL) Pitt.1951-58;Cin.59;Chi.60-61;Mil.61,65;N.Y.62-64;Phil.64-65;Hou.65.

TIMES AT BAT—INDIVIDUAL

I—Most times at bat, lifetime—
11,429—Tyrus R. Cobb, Detroit AL, 1905-1926; Philadelphia AL, 1927-28; 24 years.
10,972—Stanley F. Musial, St. Louis NL, 1941-44, 46-63; 22 years.

J—Most years 600 or more times at bat, league—
12—J. Nelson Fox, Chicago AL, 1951-62.
7—George J. Burns, N.Y.NL,1913,15-16,20-21;Cin.NL,22-23.
Albert F. Schoendienst,St.L.NL,1946-47,49-50,52,54;N.Y.-Mil.NL,1957.
Richie Ashburn, Philadelphia NL, 1949, 51-53, 56-58.
Henry Aaron, Milwaukee NL, 1955-59, 61, 63.
Vada E. Pinson, Cin. NL, 1959-65.

K—Most consecutive years leading league, times at bat—
3—Earl J. Adams, Chi. NL, 1925-27.
Roger M. Cramer, Phil. AL, 1933-35; Bos. AL, 1940, Wash. AL, 1941, Det. AL, 1942.
Robert C. Richardson, N.Y. AL, 1962-64.

L—Most years leading league, times at bat—
7—Roger M. Cramer, Phil., Bos., Wash., Det., AL, 1933-34-35-38-40-41-42.
4—Abner F. Dalrymple, Chicago NL, 1880-82-84-85.
3—Earl J. Adams, Chicago NL, 1925-26-27
Lloyd J. Waner, Pittsburgh NL, 1928-29-31.

INDIVIDUAL BATTING RECORDS—Continued

A—Most times at bat, season—
696—Forrest Jensen, Pittsburgh NL, 153 games, 1936.
692—Robert C. Richardson, New York AL, 161 games, 1962.

B—Most times facing pitcher as a batsman, 9 inning game—
8—By many players.
Last performed by: Clyde F. Vollmer, Boston AL, June 8, 1950.

C—Most times facing pitcher as batsman, inning—
3—E. Williamson, T. E. Burns, F. Pfeffer, F. Goldsmith, W. A. Sunday, Chi. NL, 7th inning, Sept. 6, 1883.
Robert L. Lowe, H. A. Long, H. Duffy and T. F. McCarthy, Bos. NL, 1st inning, A.M. game, June 18, 1894.
Martin Callaghan, Chicago NL, 4th inning, Aug. 25, 1922.
Theodore S. Williams, Boston AL, 7th inning, July 8, 1948.
Harold Reese, William Cox, Edwin Snider, Brooklyn NL, 1st inning, May 21, 1952.
Samuel White, Eugene Stephens, George Kell, Thomas Umphlett, John J. Lipon, Boston AL, 7th inning, June 18, 1953.
Gilbert R. Hodges, Brooklyn NL, 8th inning, Aug. 8, 1954.

CC—Most times faced pitcher, game, no official at bats—
6—Charles M. Smith, Boston NL, 5 BB, 1 HP, April 17, 1890.
Walter Wilmot, Chicago NL, 6 BB, Aug. 22, 1891.
Miller J. Huggins, St. Louis NL, 4 BB, 2 SH, June 1, 1910.
William J. Urbanski, Boston NL, 4 BB, 2 SH, June 13, 1934.
James E. Foxx, Boston AL, 6 BB, June 16, 1938.

RUNS—INDIVIDUAL

D—Most runs, league or lifetime—
2,244—Tyrus R. Cobb, Detroit AL, 1905-1926; Phila. AL, 1927-28; 24 years.
1,949—Stanley F. Musial, St. Louis NL, 1941-44, 46-63, 22 years.

E—Most runs, season—
196—William R. Hamilton, Philadelphia NL, 131 games, 1894.
177—George H. Ruth, New York AL, 152 games, 1921.
158—Charles H. Klein, Philadelphia NL, 156 games, 1930.

F—Most runs, game—
7—Guy Hecker, Louisville AA, 2nd game, Aug. 15, 1886.
6—By many players prior to 1900.
Melvin T. Ott, New York NL, Aug. 4, 1934; April 30, 1944.
John M. Pesky, Boston AL, May 8, 1946.
Frank J. Torre, Milwaukee NL, 1st game, Sept. 2, 1957.

G—Most runs, inning—
3—Thomas E. Burns, Edward Williamson, Chicago NL, 7th inning, Sept. 6, 1883.
Samuel White, Boston AL, 7th inning, June 18, 1953.

H—Most consecutive games, scoring runs—
24—William R. Hamilton, Philadelphia NL, July 6 to August 2, 1894; (35 runs).
18—Robert A. Rolfe, New York AL, Aug. 9-25, 1939 (30 runs)
17—Theodore B. Kluszewski, Cincinnati NL, Aug. 27 to Sept. 13, 1954; (24 runs).

I—Most years leading league, in runs—
8—George H. Ruth, Boston AL, 1919; New York AL, 1920-21-23-24-26-27-28.
5—George J. Burns, New York NL, 1914-16-17-19-20.
Rogers Hornsby, St. Louis NL, 1921-22-24; New York NL, 1927; Chicago NL, 1929.
Stanley F. Musial, St. Louis NL, 1946-48,51-52-54.

J—Most consecutive years leading league in runs—
5—Theodore S. Williams, Boston AL; 134—1940, 135—1941, 141—1942, 142—1946, 125—1947. (In Service, 1943-1945.)
3—Michael J. Kelly, Chicago NL, 120—1884, 124—1885, 155—1886.
Charles H. Klein, Philadelphia NL, 158—1930, 121—1931, 152—1932.
Edwin D. Snider, Brooklyn NL, 132—1953, 120—1954, 126—1955.

K—Most years 100 runs or more, league or lifetime—
13—Henry L. Gehrig, N.Y. AL, 1926-38.
12—Willie H. Mays, N.Y. NL, 1954-57; S.F. NL, 1958-65.

L—Most consecutive years 100 or more runs—
13—Henry L. Gehrig, N.Y. AL, 1926-38.
12—Willie H. Mays, N.Y. NL, 1954-57; S.F. NL, 1958-65.

13

INDIVIDUAL BATTING RECORDS—Continued
RUNS BATTED IN

A—Most runs batted in, league or lifetime (unofficial tabulation inaugurated 1907; official tabulation adopted 1920)—
2,209—George H. Ruth, Bos. AL, NL; New York AL, 1914-1935 (22 years).
1,951—Stanley F. Musial, St. Louis NL, 1941-44, 46-63 (22 years).

B—Most years, leading league, runs batted in—
6—George H. Ruth, New York AL, 1919-20-21-23-26-28.
4—Rogers Hornsby, St. Louis NL, 1920-21-22-25.

BB—Most consecutive years leading league, runs batted in—
3—George H. Ruth, Boston-New York AL, 1919, 1920, 1921.
Rogers Hornsby, St. Louis NL, 1920 (tied), 1921, 1922.
Joseph M. Medwick, St. Louis NL, 1936, 1937, 1938.

C—Most years 100 or more runs batted in, league—
13—George H. Ruth, Boston AL, 1919; New York AL, 1920-21-23-24-26-27-28-29-30-31-32-33
Henry L. Gehrig, New York AL, 1926-27-28-29-30-31-32-33-34-35-36-37-38.
James E. Foxx, Phila. AL, 1929-30-31-32-33-34-35; Bos. AL, 1936-37-38-39-40-41.
10—Stanley F. Musial, St. Louis NL, 1946-48-49-50-51-53-54-55-56-57.

D—Most years 150 or more runs batted in, league—
7—Henry L. Gehrig, New York AL, 1927-30-31-32-34-36-37.
2—Lewis R. Wilson, Chicago NL, 1929-1930.

E—Most consecutive years, 100 or more runs batted in—
13—H. L. Gehrig, New York AL, 1926—107, 27—175, 28—142, 29—126, 30—174, 31—184, 32—151,
33—139, 34—165, 35—119, 36—152, 37—159, 38—114.
James E. Foxx, Phila.-Bos. AL, 1929—117, 30—156, 31—120, 32—169, 33—163, 34—130,
35—115, 36—143, 37—127, 38—175, 39—105, 40—119, 41—105.
8—M. T. Ott, New York NL, 1929—151, 30—119, 31—115, 32—123, 33—103, 34—135, 35—114,
36—135.

F—Most runs batted in, season—
190—Lewis R. Wilson, Chicago NL, 155 games, 1930.
184—Henry L. Gehrig, New York AL, 155 games, 1931.

G—Most runs batted in, season, by a catcher—
142—Roy Campanella, Brooklyn, NL, 1953 (only catcher to lead league)
133—William Dickey, New York, AL, 1937

H—Most runs batted in, game—
12—James L. Bottomley, St. Louis NL, Sept. 16, 1924.
11—Anthony M. Lazzeri, New York AL, May 24, 1936.

HH—Most consecutive games, runs batted in—
11—Melvin T. Ott, New York NL, June 11-20, 1929 (27 RBIs).
10—Henry L. Gehrig, New York AL, Aug. 23-Sept. 1, 1931 (27 RBIs).

I—Most runs batted in, game, by pitcher—
7—Victor Raschi, New York, AL, August 4, 1953.

J—Most runs batted in, inning—
7—Edward Cartwright, St. Louis AA, Sept. 23, 1890.
6—Fred C. Merkle, New York NL, 1st inning, May 13, 1911.
Robert L. Johnson, Philadelphia AL, 1st inning, Aug. 29, 1937, first game.
Thomas R. McBride, Boston AL, 4th inning, Aug. 4, 1945, second game.
Joseph H. Astroth, Philadelphia AL, 6th inning, Sept. 22, 1950.
Gilbert J. McDougald, New York AL, 9th inning, May 3, 1951.
Sabath A. Mele, Chicago AL, 4th inning, June 10, 1952.
James R. Lemon, Washington AL, 3rd inning, Sept. 5, 1959.

JJ—Most runs batted in, two consecutive innings—
8—James E. Gentile, Baltimore AL (4—1st, 4—2nd), May 9, 1961.
7—By many—last:
Ralph M. Kiner, Pittsburgh NL (4—3rd, 3—4th) 2nd g, July 4, 1951.

BASE HITS—INDIVIDUAL

K—Most base hits, league—
4,191—Tyrus R. Cobb, Detroit AL, 1905-26; Phila. AL. 1927-28; 24 years.
3,630—Stanley F. Musial, St. Louis NL, 1941-44, 46-63; 22 years.

L—Most years leading league in base hits—
8—Tyrus R. Cobb, Detroit AL, 1907-08-09-11-12-15-17-19.
6—Stanley F. Musial, St. Louis NL, 1943-44-46-48-49-52.

M—Three thousand (3000) or more hits—

Player	Hits	Player	Hits
Tyrus R. Cobb	4191	Edward T. Collins	3313
Stanley F. Musial	3630	Napoleon Lajoie	3251
Tris E. Speaker	3515	Paul G. Waner	3152
John P. Wagner	3430	Adrian C. Anson	3081

INDIVIDUAL BATTING RECORDS—BASE HITS

A—Most base hits, 2 consecutive seasons—
485—Rogers Hornsby, St. Louis NL, 235—1921, 250—1922.
475—Tyrus R. Cobb, Detroit AL, 248—1911, 227—1912.

B—Most base hits, season—
257—George H. Sisler, St. Louis AL, 154 games, 1920.
254—Frank J. O'Doul, Philadelphia NL, 154 games, 1929.
William H. Terry, New York NL, 154 games, 1930.

C—Most base hits, consecutive, game—
7—Wilbert Robinson, Baltimore NL, June 10, 1892, 1st game, 7-ab, 6-1b, 1-2b.
6—By many players. (For 6 base hits in 6 times at bat, see table.)

D—Most base hits, first major league game—
5—Fred E. Clarke, Louisville NL, June 30, 1894.
Cecil H. Travis, Washington AL, May 16, 1933 (12 inn.).
4—Since 1900—By many players.
Last: Mack Jones, Milwaukee NL, July 13, 1961.

E—Most base hits in an extra inning game—
9—John Burnett, Cleveland AL, 18 inn., 11-ab, 9 hits (2-2b) July 10, 1932.

F—Most base hits, inning—
3—T. E. Burns, E. Williamson, F. Pfeffer, Chicago NL, 7th inn. Sept. 6, 1883.
Eugene Stephens, Boston, AL, 7th inning, June 18th, 1953.

G—Most times 2 hits, one inning, one game—
2—Max Carey, Pittsburgh NL, 2 in 1st inn., 2 in 8th inn., June 22, 1925.
Urban J. Hodapp, Cleveland AL, 2 in 2d inn., 2 in 6th inn., July 29, 1928.
Sherman Lollar, Chicago AL, 2 in 2nd inn., 2 in 6th inn., April 23, 1955.

H—Most years 200 or more hits—
9—Tyrus R. Cobb, Detroit AL, 1907, 09, 11, 12, 15, 16, 17, 22, 1924.
8—William H. Keeler, Baltimore-Bklyn. NL, 1894, 95, 96, 97, 98, 99, 1900, 01.
Paul G. Waner, Pittsburgh NL, 1927, 28, 29, 30, 32, 34, 36, 1937.

H-H—Batter reaching base most times in inning (since 1900)—
3—Harold Reese, Brooklyn, 1st inning, May 21, 1952.
Samuel White, Eugene Stephens, Thomas Umphlett, Boston, AL, 7th inning, June 18, 1953.

I—Making 200 or more hits in their first full season—
William H. Keeler, Baltimore NL (218 hits in 128 games), 1894.
James T. Williams, Pittsburgh NL, (219 hits in 153 games), 1899.
Joseph J. Jackson, Cleveland AL (233 hits in 147 games), 1911.
Earle B. Combs, New York AL (203 hits in 150 games), 1925.
Lloyd J. Waner, Pittsburgh NL (223 hits in 150 games), 1927.
Dale Alexander, Detroit AL (215 hits in 155 games, 1929.
John H. Frederick, Brooklyn NL (206 hits in 148 games), 1929.
Roy C. Johnson, Detroit AL (201 hits in 148 games), 1929.
Charles H. Klein, Philadelphia NL (219 hits in 150 games), 1929.
William J. Herman, Chicago NL (206 hits in 154 games), 1932.
Harold A. Trosky, Cleveland AL (206 hits in 154 games), 1934.
Roy C. Bell, St. Louis AL (212 hits in 155 games), 1936.
Joseph P. DiMaggio, New York AL (206 hits in 138 games), 1936.
Frank A. McCormick, Cincinnati NL (209 hits in 151 games), 1938.
John Pesky, Boston AL (205 hits in 147 games), 1942.
Richard Wakefield, Detroit AL (200 hits in 155 games), 1943.
Harvey E. Kuenn, Detroit, AL (209 hits in 155 games), 1953.
Vada Pinson, Cincinnati NL (205 in 154 games), 1959.
Richard A. Allen, Philadelphia NL (201 hits in 162 games), 1964.
Pedro, (Tony) Oliva, Minnesota AL (217 hits in 161 games), 1964.

J—Most times 5 hits in one game, season—
4—William H. Keeler, Baltimore NL, July 17, Aug. 14, Sept. 3, Sept. 6, 1st game, 1897.
Tyrus R. Cobb, Detroit AL, May 7, July 7, 2d game; July 12, 1922.
Stanley F. Musial, St. Louis NL, April 30, May 19, June 22, Sept. 22, 1948.

K—Most times 5 or more hits in one game, league—
14—Tyrus R. Cobb, Detroit AL, 1908, 11, 12, 17 (twice), 18, 20, 22 (four), 24, 25, 27.
9—Max Carey, Pittsburgh (8), Brooklyn (1), NL, 1914, 15 (twice), 18, 21, 22, 23, 25, 27.

L—Most hits in succession—
12—Higgins, M. Frank, Boston AL, June 19, 2 games, 21, 2 games.............1938
Dropo, Walter, Detroit AL, July 14, July 15, 2 games 1952
10—Delahanty, Edward J., Philadelphia NL, July 13, 2 games, 14.............1897
Gettman, Jacob, Washington NL, Sept. 10, 11, 11........................1897
Konetchy, Edward J., Brooklyn NL, June 28, 29, July 1....................1919
Cuyler, Hazen S., Pittsburgh NL, Sept. 18, 19, 21......................1925
Hafey, Charles J., St. Louis NL, July 6, 7, 8, 9 1929
Medwick, Joseph M., St. Louis NL, July 19, 2 games, July 21.............1936
Hassett, John A., Boston NL, 2d game, June 9, 10, 14....................1940
Williams, Woodrow, Cincinnati NL, Sept. 5, 6, 6.......................1943

M—Most consecutive games batted safely season—
56—Jos. P. DiMaggio, New York AL (91 hits—16-2b, 4-3b, 15 hr), May 15 to July 16, 1941.
44—William H. Keeler, Baltimore NL (82 hits—11-2b, 10-3b), April 22 to June 18, 1897.
37—Thomas F. Holmes, Boston NL (66 hits—11-2b, 3-3b, 9 hr), June 6 to July 8, 1945.

Lifetime record, players who have made two thousand (2,000) or more base hits, 1876 to date

Name and Club	Years	G	AB	R	H	PC.
Aaron, Henry L., Milwaukee NL	12, 1954-1965	1806	7080	1289	2266	.320
Anson, Adrian C., Chicago NL	22, 1876-1897	2253	9084	1712	3081	.339
Appling, Lucius B., Chicago AL	20, 1930-1950	2422	8857	1319	2749	.310
Ashburn, Richie, Phil.-Chi.-N.Y. NL	15, 1948-1962	2189	8365	1322	2574	.308
Averill, H. Earl, Clev.-Det. AL; Bos. NL	13, 1929-1941	1669	6359	1224	2020	.318
Bancroft, David J., Three Clubs NL	16, 1915-1930	1913	7182	1048	2004	.279
Bartell, Rich., Pts.-Phil.-N.Y.-Chi. NL, Det. AL	18, 1927-1946	2016	7629	1130	2165	.284
Beckley, Jacob, Four Clubs NL, One Club PL	20, 1888-1907	2373	9476	1601	2930	.309
Berra, Lawrence P., N.Y. AL; N.Y. NL	19, 1946-1965	2120	7555	1175	2150	.285
Bottomley, Jas. L., St. L. NL-AL; Cinn. NL	16, 1922-1937	1991	7471	1177	2313	.310
Brouthers, Dennis, Eleven Clubs NL-PL-AA	19, 1879-1904	1655	6737	1507	2347	.348
Burkett, Jesse C., Five Clubs NL-AL	16, 1890-1905	2063	8389	1708	2872	.342
Burns, George H., Four Clubs AL	16, 1914-1929	1866	6573	901	2018	.307
Burns, George J., N.Y.-Cinn.-Phil, NL	15, 1911-1925	1853	7241	1188	2077	.273
Carey, Max G., Pitts.-Brook. NL	20, 1910-1929	2469	9363	1545	2665	.285
Chase, Harold H., Five Clubs AL-NL-FL	15, 1905-1919	1917	7416	981	2156	.291
Clarke, Fred C., Louisville-Pitts. NL	21, 1894-1915	2204	8584	1620	2703	.315
Cobb, Tyrus R., Det.-Phila. AL	24, 1905-1928	3033	11429	2244	4191	.367
Collins, Edward T., Phila.-Chi. AL	25, 1906-1930	2826	9952	1818	3313	.333
Connor, Roger, Five Clubs NL-PL	18, 1880-1897	1981	7788	1608	2523	.324
Corcoran, Thos. W., Five Clubs AA, NL, PL	18, 1890-1907	2148	8772	1189	2232	.254
Cramer, Roger M., Phil.-Bos.-Wash.-Det. AL	20, 1929-1948	2239	9140	1357	2705	.296
Crawford, Samuel E., Cinn. NL; Det. AL	19, 1899-1917	2505	9579	1392	2964	.309
Cronin, Joseph E., Pitts. NL; Wash.-Bos. AL	20, 1926-1945	2124	7577	1233	2285	.302
Cross, Lafayette N., Five Clubs NL-AL	21, 1887-1907	2257	9052	1343	2595	.287
Cuyler, Hazen S., Four Clubs NL	18, 1921-1938	1879	7161	1305	2299	.321
Dahlen, William F., Four Clubs NL	21, 1891-1911	2430	9019	1594	2478	.275
Dark, Alvin R., Five Clubs NL	14, 1946-1960	1828	7219	1064	2089	.289
Daubert, Jacob E., Brook.-Cinn. NL	15, 1910-1924	2014	7673	1117	2326	.303
Davis, George S., Cleve.-N.Y. NL, Chic. AL	20, 1890-1909	2370	8996	1556	2674	.297
Delahanty, Edw. J., Three Clubs NL-AL	16, 1888-1903	1825	7493	1596	2593	.346
DiMaggio, Joseph P., New York AL	13, 1936-1951	1736	6821	1390	2214	.325
Doerr, Robert P., Boston AL	14, 1937-1951	1865	7093	1094	2042	.288
Donovan, Patrick J., Six Clubs NL-AL	15, 1890-1904	1808	7518	1320	2261	.301
Duffy, Hugh, Six Clubs NL-AL	17, 1888-1906	1722	6999	1545	2307	.330
Dykes, James J., Phila.-Chi. AL	22, 1918-1939	2282	8046	1108	2256	.280
Elliott, Robert I., 3 NL clubs, 2 AL clubs	15, 1939-1953	1978	7141	1064	2061	.289
Ennis, Delmer, Phil.-St.L.-Cin. NL; Chi. AL	14, 1946-1959	1903	7254	985	2063	.284
Fox, J. Nelson, Phil.-Chi. AL; Hou. NL	19, 1947-1965	2367	9232	1279	2663	.288
Foxx, James E., Phila.-Bos. AL; Chi.-Phila. NL	20, 1925-1945	2317	8134	1751	2646	.325
Frisch, Frank F., N. Y.,-St. Louis NL	19, 1919-1937	2311	9112	1532	2880	.316
Gehrig, Henry L., New York AL	17, 1923-1939	2164	8001	1888	2721	.340
Gehringer, Charles L., Detroit AL	19, 1924-1942	2323	8858	1773	2839	.321
Glasscock, John W., 6 NL Clubs, 1 UA	17, 1879-1895	1724	6996	1065	2079	.297
Goslin, Leon A., Three Clubs AL	18, 1921-1938	2287	8654	1483	2735	.316
Grimm, Charles J., One AL; Three Clubs NL	20, 1916-1936	2166	7917	908	2299	.290
Hack, Stanley C., Chicago NL	16, 1932-1947	1938	7278	1239	2193	.301
Hamilton, William R., Three Clubs AA-NL	14, 1888-1901	1578	6262	1694	2157	.344
Heilmann, Harry E., Det. AL; Cin. NL	17, 1914-1932	2146	7787	1291	2660	.342
Herman, William J., Chi.-Bkn.-Bos.-Pitts. NL	15, 1931-1947	1922	7707	1163	2345	.304
Hooper, Harry B., Bos.-Chicago AL	17, 1909-1925	2308	8784	1429	2466	.281
Hornsby, Rogers, Four Clubs NL-1 AL	23, 1915-1937	2259	8173	1579	2930	.358
Hoy, William E., Six Clubs NL-PL-AL	15, 1888-1902	1920	7600	1534	2198	.289

Name and Club	Years	G	AB	R	H	PC.
Johnson, Robert L., Phila.-Wash.-Bos. AL........13, 1933-1945		1863	6920	1239	2051	.296
Judge, Joseph I., Three Clubs AL-NL...........20, 1915-1934		2170	7901	1184	2350	.297
Keeler, William H., Four Clubs...............19, 1892-1910		2124	8564	1720	2955	.345
Kell, George C., Five Clubs AL................15, 1943-1957		1795	6702	881	2054	.306
Kelley, Joseph J., Six Clubs NL-AL 17, 1891-1908		1829	6989	1425	2245	.321
Klein, Chas. H., Phil.-Chic.-Pitts. NL 17, 1928-1944		1753	6486	1168	2076	.320
Konetchy, Edward J., 5-NL 1-FL............15, 1907-1921		2085	7651	972	2148	.281
Kuenn, Harvey E., Det.-Clev. AL; S.F.-Chi. NL 14, 1952-1965		1744	6752	936	2044	.303
Kuhel, Joseph A., Wash.-Chic. AL............18, 1930-1947		2105	7985	1236	2212	.277
Lajoie, Napoleon, Three Clubs NL-AL...........21, 1896-1916		2475	9589	1503	3251	.339
Leach, Thomas W., Four Clubs NL............19, 1898-1918		2130	7956	1352	2144	.269
Long, Herman, Four Clubs NL-AL-AA..........16, 1889-1904		1869	7653	1459	2148	.279
McInnis, John P., Six Clubs AL-NL............19, 1909-1927		2128	7823	872	2406	.308
McKean, Edwin, Three Clubs NL-AA...........13, 1887-1899		1655	6797	1207	2147	.316
McPhee, John A., Cinn. AA-NL..............18, 1882-1899		2127	8348	1660	2342	.281
Magee, Sherwood R., Three Clubs NL............16, 1904-1919		2084	7441	1112	2169	.291
Mantle, Mickey C., New York AL 15, 1951-1965		2005	6894	1517	2108	.306
Manush, Henry E., Four Clubs AL-2 NL.........17, 1923-1939		2009	7653	1287	2524	.330
Maranville, W. J., Five Clubs NL..............23, 1912-1935		2670	10078	1255	2605	.258
Mathews, Edwin L., Bos.-Mil. NL 14, 1952-1965		2089	7597	1380	2088	.275
Mays, Willie H., N.Y.-S.F. NL 14, 1951-1965		2005	7594	1497	2381	.314
Medwick, J. M., St. L.-Bklyn-N. Y.-Bos. NL......17, 1932-1948		1984	7635	1198	2471	.324
Milan, J. Clyde, Washington AL...............16, 1907-1922		1981	7338	1001	2099	.285
Mize, John R., St. Louis-N.Y. NL, N.Y. AL 16, 1936-1953		1884	6443	1118	2011	.312
Moses, Wallace, Phil.-Chic.-Bos. AL............17, 1935-1951		2012	7356	1124	2138	.291
Musial, Stanley F., St. Louis NL 22, 1941-1963		3026	10972	1949	3630	.331
Myer, Charles S., Wash.-Bos. AL...............17, 1925-1941		1923	7038	1174	2131	.303
O'Rourke, James H., Six Clubs NL-PL..........18, 1876-1893		1750	7335	1425	2314	.315
Ott, Melvin T., New York NL................22, 1926-1947		2730	9456	1859	2876	.304
Reese, Harold H., Brooklyn-Los Angeles NL 16, 1940-1958		2166	8058	1338	2170	.269
Rice, Edgar C., Wash.-Cleve. AL.............20, 1915-1934		2404	9269	1515	2987	.322
Roush, Edd J., 1 Club AL, 2 FL, 2 NL.........18, 1913-1931		1967	7361	1097	2377	.323
Ruth, George H., Two Clubs AL-1 NL..........22, 1914-1935		2503	8399	2174	2873	.342
Ryan, James, Four Clubs NL-PL-AL............18, 1885-1903		2005	8169	1653	2559	.313
Schoendienst, Albert F., St.L.-N.Y.-Mil. NL........19, 1945-1963		2216	8479	1223	2449	.289
Sewell, Joseph W., Cleve.-N.Y. AL............14, 1920-1933		1903	7132	1141	2226	.312
Sheckard, James T., Five Clubs NL-1 AL.........17, 1897-1913		2107	7601	1296	2097	.276
Simmons, Al H., Five Clubs AL-2 NL...........20, 1924-1944		2215	8761	1507	2927	.334
Sisler, George H., Three Clubs AL-NL..........16, 1915-1930		2055	8267	1284	2812	.340
Slaughter, Enos B., St.L.-Mil. NL; K.C.-N.Y. AL ..19, 1938-1959		2380	7946	1247	2383	.300
Snider, Edwin D., Brk.-L.A.-N.Y.-S.F. NL 18, 1947-1964		2143	7161	1259	2116	.295
Speaker, Tris E., Four Clubs AL 22, 1907-1928		2789	10208	1881	3515	.344
Tenney, Fred C., Boston-N. Y. NL.............17, 1894-1911		1969	7587	1271	2239	.295
Terry, William H., New York NL..............14, 1923-1936		1721	6428	1120	2193	.341
Thompson, Samuel, Det.-Phil. NL-Det. AL........15, 1885-1906		1405	6005	1255	2016	.336
Traynor, Harold J., Pittsburgh NL..............17, 1920-1937		1941	7559	1183	2416	.320
Van Haltren, Geo. S., Five Clubs NL-PL-AA......17, 1887-1903		1936	7853	1610	2527	.322
Vaughan, Floyd E., Pitts-Bklyn NL.............14, 1932-1948		1817	6622	1173	2103	.318
Veach, Robert H., Four Clubs AL..............14, 1912-1925		1822	6659	954	2064	.310
Vernon, James B., 3 AL, 2 NL clubs 20, 1939-1960		2409	8731	1196	2495	.286
Wagner, John P., Louisville-Pitts. NL...........21, 1897-1917		2785	10427	1740	3430	.329
Walker, Fred, N. Y.-Chi.-Det. AL-Bkn.-Pts. NL....19, 1931-1949		1905	6740	1037	2064	.306
Wallace, Rhoderick J., Cleve.-St. L. NL-AL......25, 1894-1918		2369	8629	1056	2308	.267
Waner, Lloyd J., Pitts.-Bos.-Cinn.-Phil. NL........18, 1927-1945		1993	7772	1201	2459	.316
Waner, Paul G., Pts.-Bkn.-Bos. NL; N. Y. AL.....20, 1926-1945		2549	9459	1626	3152	.333
Ward, John M., Brooklyn PL, Providence, N.Y. NL..17, 1878-1894		1810	7597	1403	2151	.283
Wheat, Zachary D., Brook-Phil. NL-AL..........19, 1909-1927		2406	9106	1289	2884	.317
Williams, Theodore S., Boston AL 19, 1939-1960		2292	7706	1798	2654	.344

Six Base Hits in Six Consecutive Times at Bat, 1901 to date
9 innings only

Alou, Jesus R., San Francisco NL (1-hr) .... July 10, 1964
Bancroft, David J., New York NL.................................... June 28, 1920
Bottomley, James L., St. Louis NL (1-2b, 2-hr)....................... Sept. 16, 1924
Bottomley, James L., St. Louis NL, 2d game (1-2b)................... Aug. 5, 1931
Brower, Frank W., Cleveland AL (1-2b)............................. Aug. 7, 1923
Burns, George H., Cleveland AL, 1st game, 3-2b, 1-3b)............. June 19, 1924
Campbell, Bruce D., Cleveland AL, 1st game (1-2b) . . .. July 2, 1936
Cobb, Tyrus R., Detroit AL (1-2b, 3-hr)............................ May 5, 1925
Cooper, W. Walker, Cincinnati NL, (3-hr).......................... July 6, 1949
Cramer, Roger M., Philadelphia AL................................. June 20, 1932
Cramer, Roger M., Philadelphia AL, 1st game (1-2b)................ July 13, 1935
Cuccinello, Anthony F., Cincinnati NL 1st game (1-2b, 1-3b)........ Aug. 13, 1931
Cutshaw, George W., Brooklyn NL................................... Aug. 9, 1915
Cuyler, Hazen S., Pittsburgh NL, 1st game (3-2b, 1-3b)............. Aug. 9, 1924
Donlin, Michael J., Baltimore AL (2-2b, 2-3b)...................... June 24, 1901
Fournier, Jacques F., Brooklyn NL (2-2b, 1-hr).................... June 29, 1923
Fridley, James R., Cleveland AL .... Apr. 29, 1952
Frisch, Frank F., New York NL, 1st game (7-ab, 6 h in succession, 1-hr)...... Sept. 10, 1924
Groat, Richard M., Pittsburgh NL (3-2b) .... May 13, 1960
Harvey, Erwin K., Cleveland AL.................................... Apr. 25, 1902
Hoag, Myril O., New York AL, 1st game............................ June 6, 1934
Hopp, John L., Pittsburgh NL, 2d game (2-hr) .... May 14, 1950
Johnson, Robert, Philadelphia AL, 2nd game (1-2b, 2-hr).......... June 16, 1934
Lavagetto, Harry A., Brooklyn NL, 1st game (1-2b, 1-3b)........... Sept. 23, 1939
Lombardi, Ernest N., Cincinnati NL (1-2b)......................... May 9, 1937
Moore, Terry B., St. Louis NL (1-2b)............................... Sept. 5, 1935
Murphy, Daniel F., Philadelphia AL (1-hr)......................... July 8, 1902
Myatt, George E., Washington AL (1-2b)........................... May 1, 1944
Nance, William G., Detroit AL (1-2b).............................. July 13, 1901
Piersall, James A., Boston AL (1-2b)............................... June 10, 1953
Robinson, Floyd A., Chicago AL .... July 22, 1962
Ryan, Cornelius J., Philadelphia NL (2-2b)......................... **April 16, 1953**
Spence, Stanley O., Washington AL (1-hr).......................... June 1, 1944
Steinbacher, Henry, Chicago AL (1-2b)............................. June 22, 1938
Waner, Paul G., Pittsburgh NL (2-2b, 1-3b)........................ Aug. 26, 1926
Williams, James T., Baltimore AL (1-2b, 1-3b)..................... Aug. 25, 1902

INDIVIDUAL BATTING RECORDS
LONG HITS (Doubles, Triples, Homers)

A—Most years leading league in long hits, lifetime—
   7—George H. Ruth, Boston AL, 1918-19; New York AL, 1920-21-23-24-28.
   John P. Wagner, Pittsburgh NL, 1900-02-03-04-07-08-09.
   Stanley F. Musial, St. Louis NL, 1943-44, 1946, 1948-50, 1953.

B—Most long hits, lifetime—
   1,377—Stanley F. Musial, St.L NL, (725-2b, 177-3b, 475-hr).
   1,356—G. H. Ruth, Bos.-N.Y. AL, Bos. NL, (506-2b, 136-3b, 714-hr).

C—Most long hits, season—
   119—George H. Ruth, New York AL (44-2b, 16-3b, 59-hr), 152 games, 1921.
   107—Charles H. Klein, Philadelphia NL (59-2b, 8-3b, 40-hr), 156 games, 1930.

D—Most times, season, four (4) long hits a game—
   2—George H. Burns, Cleveland AL, 1st game, June 19, (3-2b, 1-3b), July 23, 1924 (2-2b, 2-hr).
   James E. Foxx, Philadelphia AL, April 24, (3-2b, 1-hr), July 2, 1933 (1-2b, 1-3b, 2-hr).
   Joseph M. Medwick, St. Louis NL, May 12 (2-2b, 2-hr), August 4 (4-2b), 1937.

E—Hitting 20 or more doubles, triples and home runs, season—
   John B. Freeman, Washington NL, 1899 (20-2b, 26-3b, 25 hr).
   Frank M. Schulte, Chicago NL, 1911 (30-2b, 21-3b, 21 hr).
   James L. Bottomley, St. Louis NL, 1928 (42-2b, 20-3b, 31-hr).
   J. Geoffrey Heath, Cleveland AL, 1941 (32-2b, 20-3b, 24-hr).
   Willie H. Mays, New York NL, 1957 (26-2b, 20-3b, 35 hr).

LONG HITS (Doubles, Triples, Homers)

A—Most long hits, game—

			2B	3B	HR
5—George A. Strief, Philadelphia AA, June 25, 1885			1	4	..
George F. Gore, Chicago NL, July 9, 1885			3	2	..
Lawrence Twitchell, Cleveland NL, Aug. 15, 1889			1	3	1
Louis Boudreau, Cleveland AL, first game, July 14, 1946			4	..	1
Joseph W. Adcock, Milwaukee NL, July 31, 1954			1	..	4

AA—Most long hits, two consecutive games—
7—Edward J. Delahanty, Phil. NL, July 13, 14, 1896 (2-2b, 1-3b, 4-hr).
  Albert F. Schoendienst, St. Louis NL, June 5, 6, 1948 (6-2b, 1-hr).
  Joseph W. Adcock, Milwaukee NL, July 30, 31, 1954 (2-2b, 5-hr).
6—By many players.

B—Most times, four (4) long hits, game (lifetime)—
5—Henry L. Gehrig, New York AL, 1926, 1928, 1930, 1932, 1934.
  Joseph P. DiMaggio, New York AL, 1936, 1937, 1941, 1948, 1950.
3—Lester R. Bell, St. Louis, Boston NL, 1925, 1926, 1928.
  Jos. M. Medwick, St. Louis NL, 1935, 1937 (2).

C—Most long hits, inning—
3—Thomas E. Burns, Chicago NL (2-2b, 1-hr), 7th inn. Sept. 6, 1883.
2—By many players.
  Last: Joseph R. Cunningham, Chi. A.L. (1-2b, 1-3b), 4th inn., Aug. 11, 1962.

EXTRA BASES ON LONG HITS (Doubles, Triples, Homers)

D—Most years leading league in extra bases on long hits—
9—George H. Ruth, Boston AL, 1918-19; New York AL, 1920-21-23-24-26-28-29.
6—John P. Wagner, Pittsburgh NL, 1900-02-03-07-08-09.

E—Most years 100 or more extra bases on long hits, league—
16—Theodore S. Williams, Boston AL, 1939-42. 46-51; 54-58; 60.
14—George H. Ruth, Boston AL, 1919; New York AL, 1920-24; 26-33.
  Henry L. Gehrig, New York AL, 1925-38.
  Melvin T. Ott, New York NL, 1929-39; 41-42; 44.
  Stanley F. Musial, St. Louis NL, 1943-44; 46-57.

F—Most years 200 or more extra bases on long hits, league—
4—George H. Ruth, New York AL, 216—1920, 253—1921, 225—1927, 207—1928.
1—Rogers Hornsby, St. Louis NL, 200—1922.
  Lewis R. Wilson, Chicago NL, 215—1930.

G—Most extra bases on long hits, lifetime—
2,920—George H. Ruth, Bos.-N.Y. AL; Bos. NL (506-2b, 272-3b, 2142-hr).
2,504—Stanley F. Musial, St. L. NL (725-2b, 354-3b, 1425-hr).

H—Most extra bases on long hits, season—
253—George H. Ruth, New York AL (44 on 2b, 32 on 3b, 177 on hr), 152 games, 1921.
215—Lewis R. Wilson, Chicago NL (35 on 2b, 12 on 3b, 168 on hr), 155 games, 1930.

I—Most extra bases on long hits, game—
13—Joseph W. Adcock, Milwaukee NL (on 1-2b, 4-hr), July 31, 1954.
12—By 8 players. (See table page 23B: 4 HRs in game).

J—Most extra bases on long hits, inning—
    (All on two home runs.)
6—Charles Jones, Boston NL, 8th inning, June 10, 1880.
  Louis Bierbauer, Brooklyn PL, 3d inning, July 12, 1890.
  Edward Cartwright, St. Louis AA, 3d inning, Sept. 23, 1890.
  Robert L. Lowe, Boston NL, 3d inning, P.M. game, May 30, 1894.
  Jacob C. Stenzel, Pittsburgh NL, 3d inning, June 6, 1894.
  Kenneth R. Williams, St. Louis AL, 6th inning, Aug. 7, 1922.
  Lewis R. Wilson, New York NL, 3d inning, 2d game, July 1, 1925.
  William Regan, Boston AL, 4th inning, June 16, 1928.
  Henry Leiber, New York NL, 2d inning, Aug. 24, 1935.
  Joseph P. DiMaggio, New York AL, 5th inning, June 24, 1936.
  Andrew W. Seminick, Philadelphia NL, 8th inning, June 2, 1949.
  Sidney Gordon, New York NL, 2d inning, 2d game, July 31, 1949.
  Albert W. Kaline, Detroit AL, 6th inning, April 17, 1955.
  James R. Lemon, Washington AL, 3rd inning, Sept. 5, 1959.
  Joseph A. Pepitone, New York AL, 8th inning, May 23, 1962.

TOTAL BASES—INDIVIDUAL

A—Most total bases, lifetime—

    6,134—Stanley F. Musial, St.L. NL, 1941-44, 46-63.
    5,863—Tyrus R. Cobb, Det.(5475)-Phil.(388) AL, 1905-28.

B—Most consecutive years leading league in total bases—

    4—John P. Wagner, Pittsburgh NL, 237—1906, 264—1907, 308—1908, 242—1909.
        Charles H. Klein, Philadelphia NL, 445—1930, 347—1931, 420—1932, 365—1933.
    3—Tyrus R. Cobb, Detroit AL, 286—1907, 276—1908, 329—1909.
        Theodore S. Williams, Boston AL, 338—1942, 343—1946, 335—1947 (In Service 1943-45).

C—Most total bases, season—

    457—G. H. Ruth, N. Y. AL, 152 g. (85 on 1b, 88 on 2b, 48 on 3b, 236 on hr), 1921.
    450—R. Hornsby, St. L. NL, 154 g. (148 on 1b, 92 on 2b, 42 on 3b, 168 on hr), 1922.

D—Most total bases, game—

    18—Joseph W. Adcock, Milwaukee NL (1-2b, 4-hr), July 31, 1954.
    17—Robert L. Lowe, Bos. NL (4-hr, 1-1b) 2d game, May 30, 1894.
        Edward J. Delahanty, Philadelphia NL (4-hr, 1-1b), July 13, 1896.
        Gilbert R. Hodges, Brooklyn NL (4-hr, 1-1b), Aug. 31, 1950.
    16—Tyrus R. Cobb, Detroit AL (2-1b, 1-2b, 3-hr), May 5, 1925.
        Henry L. Gehrig. New York AL (4-hr) June 3, 1932.
        James E. Foxx, Phil. AL (2-1b, 1-2b, 3-hr) July 10, 1932 (18 inn.).
        James P. Seerey, Chicago AL, (4-hr), 1st game, July 18, 1948 (11 inn.).
        Rocco D. Colavito, Cleveland AL, (4-hr), June 10, 1959.
        Willie H. Mays, San Francisco NL (4-hr), April 30, 1961.

E—Most total bases, inning—

    8—Thomas E. Burns, Chi. NL, 7th inn., Sept. 6, 1883 (2-2b, 1-hr).
        Also by 15 other players who hit 2 hrs. See Item "A", page 24.

F—Most years leading league in total bases—

    7—Rogers Hornsby, St. Louis NL, 1917-20-21-22-24-25; Chicago NL, 1929.
    6—Tyrus R. Cobb, Detroit AL, 1907-08-09-11-15-17.
        George H. Ruth, Boston AL, 1919; New York AL, 1921-23-24-26-28.
        Theodore S. Williams, Bost AL, 1939-42-46-47-49-51.

G—Most years 400 or more total bases, league—

    5—Henry L. Gehrig, New York AL, 447—1927, 419—1930, 410—1931, 409—1934, 403—1936.
    3—Charles H. Klein, Phila. NL, 405—1929, 445—1930, 420—1932.

H—Most years 300 or more total bases, league—

    13—Henry L. Gehrig, New York AL, 313—1926, 447—27, 364—28, 322—29, 419—30, 410—31,
        370—32, 359—33, 409—34, 312—35, 403—36, 366—37, 301—38.
    13—Stanley F. Musial, St. Louis NL, 347—1943, 312—1944, 366—1946, 429—1948, 382—1949,
        331—1950, 355—1951, 311—1952, 361—1953, 359—1954, 318—1955, 310—1956, 307—1957.

I—Most consecutive years 300-or-more Total Bases, league—

    13—Henry L. Gehrig, N.Y. AL, 1926-38.
    12—Willie H. Mays, N.Y. NL, 1954-57; S.F. NL, 1958-65.

J—Most total bases, fewest consecutive official times at bat—

    30—Ralph M. Kiner, Pitts. NL, Aug. 13 (last at bat), 14, 15, 16, 1947, 11-ab, 2-1b, 7-hr
        (a percent. of 2.73 TB to AB).
    25—Joseph W. Adcock, Milwaukee NL, July 30, 31, 1954, 10-ab, 1-1b, 2-2b, 5-hr (a percent
        of 2.50 TB to AB).
    24—Edward J. Delahanty, Phila. NL, July 13 and 14, 1896, 10-ab, 1-1b, 2-2b, 1-3b, 4-hr
        (a percent. of 2.40 TB to AB).
    22—E. J. Smith, Cleve. AL, Sept. 4 and 5, 1921, 7-ab, 3-2b, 4-hr (a percent. of 3.14 TB
        to AB).
    22—Theodore S. Williams, Boston AL, Sept. 17, 20, 21, 22, 23, 24 (first two at bat), 1957
        8-ab, 1-2b, 5-hr (a percent of 2.75 TB to AB).
    21—William B. Nicholson, Chicago NL, July 22 (last at bat), 23, and 23, 1944, 7-ab, 1-1b,
        5-hr (a percent. of 3.00 TB to AB).
    21—Stanley F. Musial, St. Louis NL, May 2 (doubleheader) 1954, 8-ab, 1-1b, 5-hr (a
        percent of 2.63 TB to AB).

SLUGGERS' PERCENTAGE

The percentage is obtained by dividing the "times at bat" into total bases.

A—Highest slugging percentage, league, lifetime (10 yrs or more)—

.692—George H. Ruth, Bos.-N.Y. AL, (8324-ab, 5762-tb), 21 yrs.
.593—Willie H. Mays, N.Y.-S.F. NL (7594-ab, 4507-tb), 14 yrs.

B—Most years leading league in slugging percentage—

13—George H. Ruth, Bos. AL, 1918-19; N.Y. AL, 1920-24, 26-31.
9—Rogers Hornsby, St.L. NL, 1917, 20-25; Bos. NL, 1928; Chi. NL, 1929.

C—Most conecutive years leading league in slugging percentage—
7—George H. Ruth, Bos. AL, 1918-19; N.Y. AL, 1920-24.
6—Rogers Hornsby, St.L. NL, 1920-25.

D—Highest slugging percentage, one season—

.847—G. H. Ruth, N. Y. AL, 142 games, 458 at bat, total bases, 388, 1920 (had .846 in 1921).
.756—Rogers Hornsby, St. Louis NL, 138 games, 504 at bat, 381 total bases, 1925.

LEADING IN MOST BATTING CATEGORIES, SEASON

12—Tyrus R. Cobb, Detroit AL, 1911 (Batting Avg., Slugging Avg., Runs, Hits, Total Bases, Singles, Doubles, Triples, Runs Batted In, Long Hits, Extra Bases, Stolen Bases).
Joseph M. Medwick, St. Louis NL, 1937 (Batting Avg., Slugging Avg., Games, At Bats, Runs, Hits, Total Bases, Doubles, Home Runs, Runs Batted In, Long Hits, Extra Bases).
Stanley F. Musial, St. Louis NL, 1946 (Batting Avg., Slugging Avg., Games, At Bats, Runs, Hits, Total Bases, Singles, Doubles, Triples, Long Hits, Extra Bases).

LEADING LEAGUE, DOUBLES—TRIPLES—HOME RUNS, SEASON
James F. O'Neill, St. Louis AA, 1887 (46-2b, 24-3b, 13-hr, also batting pct.—.492).

TRIPLE CROWN WINNERS

(Players leading league in batting, runs batted in and home runs.)
2—Hornsby, Rogers, St. Louis NL, 1922, 1925.
Williams, Theodore S., Boston AL, 1942, 1947.
1—Cobb, Tyrus R., Detroit AL, 1909.
Zimmerman, Henry, Chicago NL, 1912.
Foxx, James E., Philadelphia AL, 1933.
Klein, Charles H., Philadelphia NL, 1933.
Gehrig, Henry L., New York AL, 1934.
Medwick, Joseph M., St. Louis NL, 1937.
Mantle, Mickey C., New York AL, 1956.

MAJOR LEAGUE PLAYERS WHO HAVE BATTED .400 OR BETTER

Player	Year	Avg.	Player	Year	Avg.
Anson, A. C., Chi.	1879	.407	Hornsby, R., St. L.	1922	.401
	1887	.421		1924	.424
Barnes, R., Chicago	1876	.403		1925	.403
Brouthers, D., Det.	1887	.419	Jackson, J., Cleve.	1911	.408°
Browning, L., Louisville	1887	.471†	Keeler, W., Balto.	1897	.432
	1895	.423	Lajoie, N., Phila.	1901	.422°
Burkett, J., Cle., St. L.	1896	.410	Lyons, D., Athletics	1887	.469‡
	1899	.402	Mack, Joseph, Louisville	1887	.410†
Burns, T. P., Balto.	1887	.401†	O'Neill, J. F., St. L.	1887	.492†
Clarke, F., Louisville	1897	.406	Orr, D., N. Y., Mets	1887	.403†
	1911	.420°	Radford, P., N. Y. Mets	1887	.404†
Cobb, T. R., Det.	1912	.410°	Robinson, W. H., St. L.	1887	.426†
	1922	.401°	Sisler, G. H., St. L.	1920	.407°
Delahanty, E., Phila.	1894	.400		1922	.420°
	1899	.408	Stovey, H., Athletics	1884	.404†
Duffy, Hugh, Boston	1894	.438		1887	.402†
Dunlap, F., St. L.	1884	.420‡	Terry, W. H., N. Y.	1930	.401
Esterbrook, T. J., N. Y. Mets.	1884	.408†	Thompson, S., Det.-Phil.	1887	.406
Heilmann, H. E., Det.	1923	.403°		1894	.403
			Turner, G. A., Phila.	1894	.423
			Williams, T. S., Boston	1941	.406

°American League. †American Association. ‡Union Association.

19

ONE-BASE HITS (singles)

A—Most one-base hits (singles), league—
  3,052—Tyrus R. Cobb, Detroit AL, 1905-26; Philadelphia AL, 1927-28.
  2,426—John P. Wagner, Louisville NL, 1897-98-99; Pittsburgh NL, 1900-17.

B—Most years leading league, one base hits (singles)—
  8—J. Nelson Fox, Chicago AL, 1952-54-55-56-57-58-59-60.
  4—Clarence H. Beaumont, Pitts.-Boston NL, 1902-03-04-07.
     Lloyd J. Waner, Pittsburgh NL, 1927-28-29 (tied)-31.
     Richie Ashburn, Philadelphia NL, 1951-53-57-58.

BB—Most consecutive years, leading league, one-base hits (singles)—
  7—J. Nelson Fox, Chicago AL, 1954-1960.
  3—Clarence H. Beaumont, Pittsburgh NL, 1902, 1903, 1904.
     Lloyd J. Waner, Pittsburgh NL, 1927, 1928, 1929.

C—Most one-base hits (singles), season—
  199—William H. Keeler, Baltimore NL, 128 games, 1897.
  198—Lloyd J. Waner, Pittsburgh NL, 150 games, 1927.
  182—Edgar C. Rice, Washington AL, 152 games, 1925.

TWO-BASE HITS (doubles)

D—Most two-base hits, league—
  793—Tris E. Speaker, Bos.(241)-Clev.(486)-Wash.(43)-Phil.(23) AL, 1907-28.
  725—Stanley F. Musial, St.L. NL, 1941-63.

E—Most years leading league in two-base hits—
  8—John P. Wagner, Pittsburgh NL, 1900-01-02-04-06-07-08-09.
     Tris E. Speaker, Boston AL, 1912-14; Cleveland AL, 1916-18-20-21-22-23.
     Stanley F. Musial, St. Louis NL, 1943-44-46-48-49-52-53-54.

F—Most consecutive years, leading league, two-base hits—
  4—John P. Wagner, Pittsburgh NL, 1906, 1907, 1908, 1909.
     Tris E. Speaker, Cleveland AL, 1920, 1921, 1922, 1923.

G—Most years, 50 or more two-base hits, league—
  5—Tris E. Speaker, Bos. AL, 53—1912; Cleve. AL, 50—1920, 52—1921, 59—1923, 52—1926.
  3—Paul G. Waner, Pittsburgh NL, 50—1928, 62—1932, 53—1936.
     Stanley F. Musial, St. Louis, NL, 51—1944, 50—1946, 53—1953.

H—Most two-base hits, season—
  67—Earl W. Webb, Boston AL, 151 games, 1931.
  64—Joseph M. Medwick, St. Louis NL, 155 games, 1936.

I—Most two-base hits, game—
  4—By many players. Last:
     William H. Bruton, Det. AL, May 19, 1963.

J—Most two-base hits, inning—
  2—By many players.

K—Most two-base hits—by a pitcher, inning—
  2—Frederick Goldsmith, Chicago NL, Sept. 6, 1883.
     Theodore A. Lyons, Chicago AL, July 28, 1935.
     Henry Borowy, Chicago NL, May 5, 1946

THREE-BASE HITS (triples)

L—Most three-base hits, lifetime—
  312—Samuel Crawford, Cinn. NL, 4 years, 1899-1902 (62); Det. AL, 15 years, 1903-17 (250)
  297—Tyrus R. Cobb, Detroit, Philadelphia AL, 1905-1928.
  252—John P. Wagner, Louisville NL, 1897-98-99; Pitts. NL, 1900-17, 21 years.

M—Most consecutive years leading in three-base hits—
  3—Elmer Flick, Cleveland AL, 19—1905, 22—1906, 18—1907.
     Samuel Crawford, Detroit AL, 23—1913, 26—1914, 19—1915.
     Zoilo Versalles, Minnesota AL, 13—1963, 10—1964, 12—1965.
  2—Michael F. Mitchell, Cincinnati NL, 17—1909, 18—1910.
     Henry H. Myers, Brooklyn NL, 14—1919, 22—1920.
     Paul G. Waner, Pittsburgh NL, 22—1926, 17—1927.
     Ival R. Goodman, Cincinnati NL, 18—1935, 14—1936.
     Stanley F. Musial, St. Louis NL, 18—1948, 13 (tied)—1949.
     Willie H. Mays, New York NL, 13—1954, 13 (tied)—1955.

N—Most three-base hits, league—
  297—Tyrus R. Cobb, Detroit AL, 1905-1926; Phila. AL, 1927-28.
  252—John P. Wagner, Louisville NL, 1897-98-99; Pittsburgh NL, 1900-17.

A—Most years leading league in three-base hits, lifetime—
6—Samuel Crawford, Cincinnati NL, 1902; Detroit AL, 1903-10-13-14-15.
5—Stanley F. Musial, St. Louis NL, 1943-46-48-49 (tied), 51 (tied).

B—Most years making 20 or more three-base hits—
5—Samuel Crawford, Cinn. NL, 23—1902; Det. AL, 25—1903, 21—1912, 23—1913, 26—1914.
4—Tyrus R. Cobb, Detroit AL, 20—1908, 24—1911, 23—1912, 23—1917.

C—Most three-base hits, season—
36—J. Owen Wilson, Pittsburgh NL, 152 games, 1912.
26—Joseph J. Jackson, Cleveland AL, 152 games, 1912.
Samuel Crawford, Detroit AL, 157 games, 1914.

D—Most three-base hits in game—
4—George A. Strief, Philadelphia AA, June 25, 1885.
William Joyce, New York NL, May 18, 1897.
3—By 34 players.
Last player: Roberto Clemente, Pittsburgh NL, Sept. 8, 1958.

DD—Most three-base hits in game, bases filled—
2—Elmer W. Valo, Philadelphia AL, May 1, 1949.
William H. Bruton, Milwaukee NL, Aug. 2, 1959.

E—Most three-base hits, inning—
2—Joseph Hornung, Boston NL, 8th inning, May 6, 1882
Harry Wheeler, Cincinnati AA, 11th inning, June 28, 1882.
Harry D. Stovey, Philadelphia AA, 8th inning, Aug. 18, 1884.
Henry Peitz, St. Louis NL, 1st inning, July 2, 1895.
John B. Freeman, Boston NL, 1st inning, July 25, 1900.
William F. Dahlen, Brooklyn NL, 8th inning, Aug. 30, 1900.
W. Curtis Walker, Cincinnati NL, 2d inning, July 22, 1926.
Allen L. Zarilla, St. Louis AL, 4th inning, July 13, 1946.
Gilbert F. Coan, Washington AL, 6th inning, April 21, 1951.

HOME RUNS—INDIVIDUAL

F—Hitting Home Run First Time at Bat—

W. J. Duggleby, Phil. NL, Apr. 21, 1898.
J. W. Bates, Bos. NL, Apr. 12, 1906
H. E. Averill, Clev. AL, Apr. 16, 1929
C. E. Dudley, Brk. NL, Apr. 27, 1929
G. L. Slade, Brk. NL, May 24, 1930
J. C. Ryan, Chi. AL, July 15, 1930
E. Morgan, St.L. NL, Apr. 14, 1936*.
C. M. Parker, Phil. AL, Apr. 30, 1937*
E. Koy, Brk. NL, Apr. 19, 1938.
E. J. Mueller, Phil. NL, Apr. 19, 1938
W. H. LeFebvre, Bos. AL, June 10, 1938.
C. F. Vollmer, Cin. NL, May 31, 1942.
J. J. Kerr, N.Y. NL, Sept. 8, 1943.
J. E. Miller, Det. AL, Apr. 23, 1944.
C. W. Lockman, N.Y. NL, July 5, 1945
E. C. Pellagrini, Bos. AL, Apr. 22, 1946.
D. P. Bankhead, Brk. NL, Aug. 26, 1947.
G. S. Vico, Det. AL, Apr. 20, 1948

L. L. Layton, N.Y. NL, May 21, 1948*.
E. R. Sanicki, Phil. NL, Sept. 14, 1949.
T. N. Tappe, Cin. NL, Sept. 14, 1950*.
R. C. Nieman, St.L. AL, Sept. 14, 1951.
H. J. Wilhelm, N.Y. NL, Apr. 23, 1952.
W. W. Moon, St.L. NL, Apr. 13, 1954.
C. W. Tanner, Mil. NL, Apr. 12, 1955*.
W. D. White, N.Y. NL, May 7, 1956.
F. J. Ernaga, Chi. NL, May 24, 1957.
D. G. Leppert, Pitt. NL, June 18, 1961.
F. A. Barragan, Chi. NL, Sept. 1, 1961.
J. E. Kennedy, Wash. AL, Sept. 5, 1962*.
L. F. Narum, Bal. AL, May 3, 1963
W. G. Brown, Det. AL, June 19, 1963*
D. B. Campaneris, K.C. AL, July 23, 1964
W. A. Roman, Det. AL, Sept. 30, 1964*
B. R. Alyea, Wash. AL, Sept. 12, 1965*

*Pinch-hitter.

G—Most times switch-hitting 2 home runs, game—
10—Mickey C. Mantle, New York AL vs. Detroit (Gromek-R. Miller), May 13, 1955; vs. Baltimore (Schallock-Moore), Aug. 15, 1955; vs. Chicago (Pierce-Howell), May 18, 1956; vs. Washington (Stone-Byerly), July 1, 1956; vs. Chicago (Harshman-Keegan), June 12, 1957; vs. Kansas City (Tomanek-Herbert), July 28, 1958, vs. Chicago (Pierce-Shaw), Sept. 15, 1959; vs. Detroit (Donohue-Aguirre), April 26, 1961, vs. Washington (Burnside-Hannan), May 6, 1962; vs. Chicago (Herbert-Baumann), Aug. 12, 1964.
2—James W. Russell, Boston NL vs. Chicago (McCall-Hamner), June 7, 1948; Brooklyn NL vs. St. Louis (Brecheen-Munger) July 26, 1950.
Ellis N. Burton, Chicago NL vs. Milwaukee (Lemaster-Piche), Aug. 1, 1963; vs. Milwaukee (Fischer-Blasingame), Sept. 7, 1964, 1st g.

H—Most home runs, lifetime—
714—George H. Ruth, 22 years, Boston AL, 0—1914, 4—1915, 3—1916, 2—1917, 11—1918, 29—1919; New York AL, 54—1920, 59—1921, 35—1922, 41—1923, 46—1924, 25—1925, 47—1926, 60—1927, 54—1928, 46—1929, 49—1930, 46—1931, 41—1932, 34—1933, 22—1934; Boston NL, 6—1935.
511—Melvin T. Ott, 22 years, New York NL, 0—1926, 1—1927, 18—1928, 42—1929, 25—1930, 29—1931, 38—1932, 23—1933, 35—1934, 31—1935, 33—1936, 31—1937, 36—1938, 27—1939, 19—1940, 27—1941, 30—1942, 18—1943, 26—1944, 21—1945, 1—1946, 0—1947.

HOME RUNS—INDIVIDUAL

A—Most home runs, season (154 game schedule)—
60—George H. Ruth, N.Y. AL (28 home, 32 away), 151 gs, 1927.
56—Lewis R. Wilson, Chi. NL (33 home, 23 away), 155 gs, 1930.

B—Most home runs, season (162 game schedule)—
61—Roger E. Maris, N.Y. AL (30 home, 31 away), 161 gs, 1961.

C—Most home runs, rookie season—
38—Walter A. Berger, Boston NL, 1930.
  Frank Robinson, Cincinnati NL, 1956.
37—Albert L. Rosen, Cleveland AL, 1950.

D—Most home runs in one season, at home—
39—Henry Greenberg, Detroit AL, 1938.
34—Theodore B. Kluszewski, Cincinnati NL, 1954.

E—Most home runs in one season, on road—
34—George H. Ruth, New York AL, 1921.
30—Edwin L. Mathews, Milwaukee NL, 1953.

F—Most home runs against one club, season—
14—Henry L. Gehrig, New York AL vs. Cleveland, 1936.
13—Henry J. Sauer, Chicago NL vs Pittsburgh, 1954.
  Joseph W. Adcock, Milwaukee NL vs Brooklyn, 1956.

G—Leading league in home runs, first season in majors, (1901 to date)—
Harry G. Lumley, Brooklyn NL, 1904 (9).
Ralph M. Kiner, Pittsburgh NL, 1946 (23).

H—Most home runs, 2 consecutive seasons—
114—George H. Ruth, New York AL, 60—1927; 54—1928.
101—Ralph M. Kiner, Pittsburgh NL, 54—1949; 47—1950.

I—Most years leading league, home runs—
12—George H. Ruth, Bos. AL 1918-19; N.Y. AL 1920-21, 23-24, 26-31.
7—Ralph M. Kiner, Pitt. NL 1946-52.

J—Most years, 50 or more home runs—
4—George H. Ruth, N.Y. AL 1920-21, 27-28.
2—Ralph M. Kiner, Pitt. NL 1947, 49.
  Willie H. Mays, N.Y. NL, 1955; S.F. NL, 1965.

K—Most years, 40 or more home runs—
11—George H. Ruth, N.Y. AL 1920-21, 23-24, 26-32.
6—Willie H. Mays, N.Y. NL, 1954-55; S.F. NL, 1961-62, 64-65.

L—Most years, 30 or more home runs—
13—George H. Ruth, N.Y. AL 1920-24, 26-33.
12—James E. Foxx, Phil. AL 1929-35, Bos. AL 36-40.
10—Edwin L. Mathews, Mil. NL, 1953-61, 65.
  Willie H. Mays, N.Y. NL, 1954-57; S.F. NL, 1959, 61-65.

M—Most home runs, one month—
18—P. Rudolph York, Det. AL Aug. 1937.
17—Willie H. Mays, S.F. NL Aug. 1965.

N—Most Home runs, first game—
2—Charles T. Reilly, Col. AA, Oct. 9, 1889.
  Robert C. Nieman, St.L. AL, Sept. 14, 1951 (first 2 at bats).
  Dagoberto B. Campaneris, K.C. AL, July 23, 1964.

O—MOST HOME RUNS, LEAGUE, SEASON, BY POSITION

National League			American League
Mize, N.Y. 1947 (154 gs) 51	1B	58..........Greenberg, Det. 1938 (154 gs)
Hornsby, St.L. 1922 (154 gs) 42	2B	32..........Gordon, Clev. 1948 (144 gs)
Mathews, Mil. 1953 (157 gs) 47	3B	43..........Rosen, Clev. 1953 (154 gs)
Banks, Chi. 1958 (154 gs) 47	SS	39..........Stephens, Bos. 1949 (155 gs)
Wilson, L., Chi. 1930 (155 gs) 56	OF	61..........Maris, N.Y. 1961 (161 gs)
Campanella, Brk. 1953 (140 gs) 41	C	30..........Berra, N.Y. 1956 (135 gs)
		30..........Triandos, Balt. 1958 (132 gs)
Newcombe, Brk. 1955 (57 gs) 7	P	9..........Ferrell, W. Clev. 1931 (48 gs)
Drysdale, L.A. 1958 (47 gs); 1965 (58 gs) 7		

HOME RUN LEADERS

NATIONAL LEAGUE	No.	AMERICAN LEAGUE	No.
1901—Crawford, Samuel, Cincinnati	16	Lajoie, Napoleon, Philadelphia	13
1902—Leach, Thomas W., Pittsburgh	6	Seybold, Ralph O., Philadelphia	16
1903—Sheckard, James, T., Brooklyn	9	Freeman, John B., Boston	13
1904—Lumley, Harry G., Brooklyn	9	Davis, Harry H., Philadelphia	10
1905—Odwell, Fred, Cincinnati	9	Davis, Harry H., Philadelphia	8
1906—Jordan, Timothy J., Brooklyn	12	Davis, Harry H., Philadelphia	12
1907—Brain, David L., Boston	10	Davis, Harry H., Philadelphia	8
1908—Jordan, Timothy J., Brooklyn	12	Crawford, Samuel, Detroit	7
1909—Murray, John J., New York	7	Cobb, Tyrus R., Detroit	9
1910—Beck, Boston, Schulte, Chicago	10	Stahl, J. Garland, Boston	10
1911—Schulte, Frank, Chicago	21	Baker, J. Franklin, Philadelphia	9
1912—Zimmerman, Henry, Chicago	14	Baker, J. Franklin, Philadelphia	10
1913—Cravath, Clifford C., Philadelphia	19	Baker, J. Franklin, Philadelphia	12
1914—Cravath, Clifford C., Philadelphia	19	Baker, Phila.; Crawford, Detroit	8
1915—Cravath, Clifford C., Philadelphia	24	Roth, Robert F., Chicago-Cleveland	7
1916—Robertson, N. Y., Williams, Chicago	12	Pipp, Walter C., New York	12
1917—Robertson, N. Y., Cravath, Phila.	12	Pipp, Walter C., New York	9
1918—Cravath, Clifford C., Philadelphia	8	Walker, Phila.; Ruth, Boston	11
1919—Cravath, Clifford C., Philadelphia	12	Ruth, George H., Boston	29
1920—Williams, Fred C., Philadelphia	15	Ruth, George H., New York	54
1921—Kelly, George L., New York	23	Ruth, George H., New York	59
1922—Hornsby, Rogers, St. Louis	42	Williams, Kenneth R., St. Louis	39
1923—Williams, Fred C., Philadelphia	41	Ruth, George H., New York	41
1924—Fournier, Jacques F., Brooklyn	27	Ruth, George H., New York	46
1925—Hornsby, Rogers, St. Louis	39	Meusel, Robert W., New York	33
1926—Wilson, Lewis R., Chicago	21	Ruth, George H., New York	47
1927—Wilson, Chi., Williams, Philadelphia	30	Ruth, George H., New York	60
1928—Bottomley, St. Louis; Wilson, Chi.	31	Ruth, George H., New York	54
1929—Klein, Charles H., Philadelphia	43	Ruth, George H., New York	46
1930—Wilson, Lewis R., Chicago	56	Ruth, George H., New York	49
1931—Klein, Charles H., Philadelphia	31	Ruth, New York; Gehrig, New York	46
1932—Klein, Phila., Ott, New York	38	Foxx, James E., Philadelphia	58
1933—Klein, Charles H., Philadelphia	28	Foxx, James E., Philadelphia	48
1934—Collins, St. Louis; Ott, New York	35	Gehrig, Henry L., New York	49
1935—Berger, Walter A., Boston	34	Foxx, Phila.; Greenberg, Detroit	36
1936—Ott, Melvin T., New York	33	Gehrig, Henry L., New York	49
1937—Ott, New York; Medwick, St. Louis	31	DiMaggio, Joseph P., New York	46
1938—Ott, Melvin T., New York	36	Greenberg, Henry, Detroit	58
1939—Mize, John R., St. Louis	28	Foxx, James E., Boston	35
1940—Mize, John R., St. Louis	43	Greenberg, Henry, Detroit	41
1941—Camilli, Adolph, Brooklyn	34	Williams, Theodore S., Boston	37
1942—Ott, Melvin T., New York	30	Williams, Theodore S., Boston	36
1943—Nicholson, William B., Chicago	29	York, P. Rudolph, Detroit	34
1944—Nicholson, William B., Chicago	33	Etten, Nicholas R., New York	22
1945—Holmes, Thomas F., Boston	28	Stephens, Vernon D., St. Louis	24
1946—Kiner, Ralph M., Pittsburgh	23	Greenberg, Henry B., Detroit	44
1947—Kiner, Pitts.; Mize, New York	51	Williams, Theodore S., Boston	32
1948—Kiner, Pitts.; Mize, New York	40	DiMaggio, Joseph P., New York	39
1949—Kiner, Ralph M., Pittsburgh	54	Williams, Theodore S., Boston	43
1950—Kiner, Ralph M., Pittsburgh	47	Rosen, Albert L., Cleveland	37
1951—Kiner, Ralph M., Pittsburgh	42	Zernial, Gus E., Chic.-Phila.	33
1952—Kiner, Pitts., Sauer, Chicago	37	Doby, Lawrence E., Cleveland	32
1953—Mathews, Edwin L., Milwaukee	47	Rosen, Albert L., Cleveland	43
1954—Kluszewski, Theo. B., Cincinnati	49	Doby, Lawrence E., Cleveland	32
1955—Mays, Willie H., New York	51	Mantle, Mickey C., New York	37
1956—Snider, Edwin D., Brooklyn	43	Mantle, Mickey C., New York	52
1957—Aaron, Henry, Milwaukee	44	Sievers, Roy, Washington	42
1958—Banks, Ernest, Chicago	47	Mantle, Mickey C., New York	42
1959—Mathews, Edwin L., Milwaukee	46	Colavito, Clev.; Killebrew, Wash.	42
1960—Banks, Ernest, Chicago	41	Mantle, Mickey C., New York	40
1961—Cepeda, Orlando, San Francisco	46	Maris, Roger E., New York	61
1962—Mays, Willie H., San Francisco	49	Killebrew, Harmon C., Minnesota	48
1963—Aaron, Mil.; McCovey, S.F.	44	Killebrew, Harmon C., Minnesota	45
1964—Mays, Willie H., San Francisco	47	Killebrew, Harmon C., Minnesota	49
1965—Mays, Willie H., San Francisco	52	Conigliaro, Anthony R., Boston	32

PLAYERS WITH 200 OR MORE HOME RUNS

INACTIVE

George H. Ruth	714	Robert B. Thomson	264
James E. Foxx	534	Joseph L. Gordon	253
Theodore S. Williams	521	Lawrence E. Doby	253
Melvin T. Ott	511	Fred Williams	251
H. Louis Gehrig	493	Leon A. Goslin	248
Stanley F. Musial	475	Vernon D. Stephens	247
Edwin D. Snider	407	Lewis R. Wilson	244
Gilbert R. Hodges	370	Walter A. Berger	242
Ralph M. Kiner	369	Roy Campanella	242
Joseph P. DiMaggio	361	Adolph Camilli	239
John R. Mize	359	H. Earl Averill	238
Lawrence P. Berra	358	Gus E. Zernial	237
Henry B. Greenberg	331	Charles L. Hartnett	236
Roy E. Sievers	318	William B. Nicholson	235
Al H. Simmons	307	Harold A. Trosky	228
Rogers Hornsby	302	Robert P. Doerr	223
Charles H. Klein	300	James L. Bottomley	219
Delmer Ennis	288	Andrew Pafko	213
Robert L. Johnson	288	Walter C. Post	210
Henry J. Sauer	288	David R. Bell	206
Theodore B. Kluszewski	279	Joseph M. Medwick	205
Rudolph P. York	277	Sidney Gordon	202
Victor W. Wertz	266	William M. Dickey	202

ACTIVE

Willie H. Mays	505	Harmon C. Killebrew	297
Edwin L. Mathews	477	Frank J. Thomas	286
Mickey C. Mantle	473	Kenton L. Boyer	255
Ernest Banks	404	Albert W. Kaline	250
Henry L. Aaron	398	Roger E. Maris	248
Rocco D. Colavito	328	Orlando Cepeda	223
Frank Robinson	324	Richard L. Stuart	220
Joseph W. Adcock	318	William J. Skowron	204

MOST HOME RUNS, LEAGUE, LIFETIME, BY POSITION

National League		Pos.	American League	
Gilbert R. Hodges, Brk.-L.A.-N.Y.	355	1B	H. Louis Gehrig, N.Y.	493
Rogers Hornsby, St.-L.-N.Y.-Bos.-Chi.	299	2B	Joseph L. Gordon, N.Y.-Clev.	253
Edwin L. Mathews, Bos.-Mil.	464	3B	Albert L. Rosen, Clev.	192
Ernest Banks, Chi.	293	SS	Vernon D. Stephens, 4 clubs	247
Melvin T. Ott, N.Y.	511	OF	George H. Ruth, Bos.-N.Y.	699
Roy Campanella, Brk.	242	C	Lawrence P. Berra, N.Y.	313
Warren E. Spahn, Bos.-Mil.	35	P	Wesley C. Ferrell, 4 clubs	37

CLUB HOME RUN LEADERS

AMERICAN LEAGUE		NATIONAL LEAGUE	
New York—Roger Maris, 1961	61	Chicago—Lewis Wilson, 1930	56
Detroit—Henry Greenberg, 1938	58	Pittsburgh—Ralph Kiner, 1949	54
Boston—James Foxx, 1938	50	San Francisco—Willie Mays, 1965	52
Minnesota-Harmon Killebrew, 1964	49	Cincinnati—Theo. Kluszewski, 1954	49
Baltimore—James Gentile, 1961	46	Milwaukee—Edward Mathews, 1953	47
Cleveland—Albert Rosen, 1953	43	Philadelphia—Charles Klein, 1929	43
Kansas City—Robert Cerv, 1958	38	St. Louis—John Mize, 1940	43
Los Angeles—Leon Wagner, 1962	37	New York—Frank Thomas, 1962	34
Chicago—Zernial, '50, Robinson, '51	29	Los Angeles—Frank Howard, 1962	31
Washington-Don Lock, 1964	28	Houston—Roman Mejias, 1962	24

FOUR HOME RUNS, ONE GAME

Robert L. Lowe, Boston NL, consecutive (3d (2) 5th, 6th inn.), May 30, 1894.
Edward J. Delahanty, Philadelphia NL, 1st, 5th, 7th, 9th inn., July 13, 1896.
Henry L. Gehrig, N. Y. AL (all consecutive), 1st, 4th, 5th and 7th inn., June 3, 1932.
Charles H. Klein, Philadelphia NL, 1st, 5th, 7th, 10th inn., July 10, 1936.
James P. Seerey, Chicago AL, 4th, 5th, 6th, 11th inn., 1st game, July 18, 1948.
Gilbert R. Hodges, Brooklyn NL. 2d, 3d, 6th, 8th inn. Aug. 31, 1950.
Joseph W. Adcock, Milwaukee NL, 2d, 5th, 7th, 9th inn. July 31, 1954.
Rocco D. Colavito, Cleveland AL (consecutive), 3d, 5th, 6th, 9th inn. June 10, 1959.
Willie H. Mays, San Francisco NL, 1st, 3d, 6th, 8th inn. April 30, 1961.

THREE HOME RUNS, ONE GAME

Aaron, Henry L., Milwaukee NL..June 21, 1959
Allison, W. Robert, Minn. AL.....May 17, 1963
Anson, Adrian C., Chicago NL.....Aug. 6, 1884*
Averill, H. E., Cleve. AL (1st g.)..Sept. 17, 1930*
Avila, Roberto, Cleveland AL.....June 20, 1951
Bailey, Edgar, Cincinnati NL.....June 24, 1956
Banks, Ernest, Chicago NL........Aug. 4, 1955
Banks, Ernest, Chicago NL........Sept. 14, 1957*
Banks, Ernest, Chicago NL........May 29, 1962*
Banks, Ernest, Chicago NL........June 9, 1963
Beckley, J. C., Cinn. NL (1st g.)..Sept. 26, 1897
Bell, Lester R., Boston NL........June 2, 1928
Bell, David R., Cincinnati NL.....July 21, 1955*
Bell, David R., Cincinnati NL.....May 29, 1956*
Boros, Stephen, Detroit AL........Aug. 6, 1962
Brouthers, Dennis L., Detroit NL.Sept. 10, 1886
Brown, Thomas M., Brooklyn NL.Sept. 18, 1950*
Burgess, Forrest H., Cinn. NL....July 29, 1955
Callison, John W., Phil. NL.......Sept. 27, 1964
Callison, John W., Phil. NL (2d g.)..June 6, 1965
Campanella, Roy, Brooklyn NL...Aug. 26, 1950*
Cerv, Robert H., K. C. AL........Aug. 20, 1959
Chapman, Samuel B., Phila. AL...Aug. 15, 1946
Chapman, W. B., N. Y. AL (2d g.)July 9, 1932
Cobb, Tyrus R., Detroit AL.......May 5, 1925
Cochrane, Gordon S., Phila. AL...May 21, 1925
Colavito, Rocco, Det. AL (2d g.)..Aug. 27, 1961
Colavito, Rocco, Detroit AL.......July 5, 1962*
Coleman, P. E., Phila. AL (1st g.).Aug. 17, 1934*
Connor, Roger, New York NL.....May 10, 1888
Connors, Mervyn, Chicago AL....Sept. 17, 1938*
Cooper, W. W., Cincinnati NL....July 6, 1949
Demeter, Donald L., L.A., NL....Apr. 21, 1959
Demeter, Donald L., Phil. NL.....Sept. 12, 1961
Dickey, Wm. M., N. Y. AL.......July 26, 1939
DiMaggio, J. P., N. Y. AL (2d g.).June 13, 1937
DiMaggio, J. P., N. Y. AL (1st g.).May 23, 1948*
DiMaggio, J. P., New York AL....Sept. 10, 1950
Doby, Lawrence E., Cleveland AL..Aug. 2, 1950*
Doerr, Robert P., Boston AL......June 8, 1950*
Elliott, Robert I., Boston NL......Sept. 24, 1949
Ennis, Delmer, Philadelphia NL...July 23, 1955
Fournier, Jacques F., Bklyn NL...July 13, 1926*
Foxx, James E., Philadelphia AL..June 8, 1933*
Foxx, Jas. E., Phila. AL (18 inn.).July 10, 1932
Gehrig, Henry L., New York AL...June 23, 1927
Gehrig, Henry L., New York AL...May 4, 1929*
Gehrig, H. L., N. Y. AL (2d g.)...May 22, 1930
Glynn, William V., Cleve. AL(1st g.)July 5, 1954*
Goslin, Leon A., Washington AL...June 19, 1925
Goslin, L. A., St. L. AL (1st g.)...Aug. 19, 1930*
Goslin, L. A., St. Louis AL.......June 23, 1932
Harper, G. W., St. L. NL (1st g.)..Sept.'20, 1928
Hauser, Joseph J., Phila. AL......Aug. 2, 1924
Hecker, Guy, Louis'e A.A. (2d g.)..Aug. 15, 1886*
Henline, Walter J., Phila. NL.....Sept. 15, 1922
Herman, Floyd C., Chicago NL...July 20, 1933
Hermanski, Eugene V., Bklyn NL..Aug. 5, 1948*
Hickman, James L., N.Y. NL.....Sept. 3, 1965*
Higgins, M. F., Phila. AL.........June 27, 1935
Higgins, M. F., Detroit AL.......May 20, 1940*
Hornsby, Rogers, Chicago NL....April 24, 1931*
Jimenez, Manuel E., K. C. AL....July 4, 1964*
Joyce, William, Washington NL...Aug. 20, 1894*
Kaline, Albert W., Detroit AL....April 17, 1955
Kampouris, Alexis, Cinn. NL.....May 9, 1937
Keller, C. E., N. Y. AL (1st g.)...July 28, 1940
Kelly, George L., New York NL...Sept. 17, 1923*
Kelly, George L., New York NL...June 14, 1924
Keltner, Kenneth F., Cleve. AL...May 25, 1939*
Killebrew, H. C., Minn. AL (1st g.).Sept. 21, 1963
Kiner, Ralph M., Pitts. NL.......Aug. 16, 1947*
Kiner, R. M., Pitts. NL (2d g.)...Sept. 11, 1947
Kiner, R. M., Pitts. NL (1st g.)...July 5, 1948
Kiner, Ralph M., Pitts. NL.......July 18, 1951
King, James H., Wash. AL.......June 8, 1964
Kirkland, Willie C., Clev. AL (2d g.).July 9, 1961*
Kluszewski, Theo., Cinn. NL(1st g.)July 1, 1956
Lazzeri, Anthony M., New York AL.June 8, 1927
Lazzeri, Anthony M., New York AL.May 24, 1936

Lee, Harold B., Boston NL........July 6, 1934
Leiber, Henry, Chicago NL (1st g.).July 4, 1939
Lemon, James R., Washington AL.Aug. 31, 1958
Leppert, Donald G., Wash. AL....April 11, 1963
Lopez, Hector H., K.C. AL (12 inn.).June 26, 1956
Manning, John, Phila. NL........Oct. 9, 1884
Mantle, Mickey C., New York AL.May 13, 1955
Marshall, Willard W., N. Y. NL...July 18, 1947*
Mathews, Edwin, Boston NL.....Sept. 27, 1952*
Maxwell, Chas. R., Det. AL (2d g.).May 3, 1959*
Mays, Willie H., S. F. NL (10 inn.).June 29, 1961
Mays, Willie H., S. F. NL........June 2, 1963
McCovey, Willie L., S. F. NL.....Sept. 22, 1963*
McCovey, Willie L., S. F. NL.....April 22, 1964*
McCreery, Thos. L., Louisville NL.July 12, 1897*
McCullough, C. E., Chi. NL (1st g.).July 26, 1942*
Mejias, Roman G., Pitts. NL.....May 4, 1958
Mize, John R., St. Louis NL......July 13, 1938*
Mize, J. R., St. L. NL (2d g.).....July 20, 1938
Mize, J. R., St. L. NL (14 inn.)....May 13, 1940
Mize, J. R., St. L. NL (1st g.)....Sept. 8, 1940*
Mize, John R., New York NL.....April 24, 1947*
Mize, John R., New York AL.....Sept. 15, 1950*
Moore, John F., Phila. NL........July 22, 1936*
Moryn, Walter J., Chi. NL (2d g.).May 30, 1958
Mueller, Donald F., New York NL.Sept. 1, 1951
Mullin, Patrick J., Detroit AL (2d g.)June 26, 1949
Musial, Stanley F., St. L. NL (1st g.).May 2, 1954
Musial, Stanley F., St. L. NL.....July 8, 1962*
Nicholson, Wm. B., Chic. NL(1st g.)July 23, 1944*
Ott, M. T., N. Y. NL (2d g.).....Aug. 31, 1930
Pafko, Andrew, Chicago NL......Aug. 2, 1950
Pendleton, Jas. E., Mil. NL (1st g.).Aug. 30, 1953*
Powell, John W., Baltimore AL...Aug. 10, 1963*
Powell, John W., Balt. AL........June 27, 1964
Reynolds, C. N., Chi. AL (2d g.)..July 2, 1930*
Rhodes, James L., New York NL..Aug. 26, 1953
Rhodes, James L., New York NL..July 28, 1954*
Robinson, Frank, Cincinnati NL..Aug. 22, 1959
Rosen, Albert L., Cleveland AL...April 29, 1952
Ruth, G. H., N. Y. AL (1st g.)....May 21, 1930
Ruth, George H., Boston NL......May 25, 1935
Sauer, Henry J., Chicago NL.....Aug. 28, 1950
Sauer, Henry J., Chicago NL.....June 11, 1952
Seerey, James P., Cleveland AL...July 13, 1945
Seminick, Andrew W., Phila. NL..June 2, 1949*
Shugart, William F., St. Louis NL..May 10, 1894*
Simmons, Al H., Phila. AL.......July 15, 1932
Snider, E. D., Brklyn NL (2d g.)..May 30, 1950*
Snider, Edwin D., Brooklyn NL...June 1, 1955
Solters, J. J., St. Louis AL.......July 7, 1935*
Stargell, Wilver D., Pitt. NL.....June 24, 1965
Stuart, Richard L., Pitt. NL (2d g.).June 30, 1960*
Tabor, James R., Boston AL (2d g.).July 4, 1939
Terry, William H., N. Y. NL.....Aug. 13, 1932*
Thomas, Frank J., Pittsburgh NL..Aug. 16, 1958
Thomas J. Leroy, L.A. AL (2d g.)..Sept. 5, 1961
Thompson, Henry J., N. Y. NL...June 3, 1954*
Thurman, Robert B., Cinn. NL...Aug. 18, 1956*
Tobin, James P., Boston NL......May 13, 1942*
Tresh, Thomas M., N. Y. AL (2d g.).June 6, 1965*
Trosky, H. A., Cleve. AL (2d g.)..May 30, 1934
Trosky, H. A., Cleve. AL (1st g.)..July 5, 1937
Vollmer, Clyde F., Boston AL....July 26, 1951
Walls, R. Lee, Chicago NL.......April 24, 1958
Ward, Preston M., Kansas City AL.Sept. 9, 1958*
Watkins, G., St. Louis NL (2d g.)..June 24, 1931*
Westrum, Wesley W., N. Y. NL...June 24, 1950
Wilte, William D., St. L..........July 5, 1961*
Wilber, Delbert Q., Phila. NL....Aug. 27, 1951*
Williams, Fred C., Phila. NL.....May 11, 1923
Williams, Kenneth R., St. L. AL...April 22, 1922
Williams, Theo. S., Bos. AL (1st g.).July 14, 1946
Williams, Theo. S., Boston AL....May 8, 1957
Williams, Theo. S., Boston AL....June 13, 1957
Williamson, Edw., Chi. NL (2d g.).May 30, 1884
Wilson, Lewis R., Chicago NL....July 26, 1930
York, R. P., Detroit AL (1st g.)...Sept. 1, 1941
Zauchin, Norbert H., Boston AL...May 27, 1955
Zernial, Gus. E., Chigo. AL (2d g.)..Oct. 1, 1950

* Successive

A—Most home runs, inning—

2—Charles Jones, Boston NL, 8th inning, June 10, 1880.
Louis Bierbauer, Brooklyn PL, 3d inning, July 12, 1890.
Edward Cartwright, St. Louis AA, 3d inning, Sept. 23, 1890.
Robert L. Lowe, Boston NL, 3d inning, afternoon game, May 30, 1894.
Jacob C. Stenzel, Pittsburg NL, 3d inning, June 6, 1894.
Kenneth R. Williams, St. Louis AL, 6th inning, Aug. 7, 1922.
Lewis R. Wilson, New York NL, 3d inning, 2d game, July 1, 1925.
William Regan, Boston AL, 4th inning, June 16, 1928.
Henry Leiber, New York NL, 2d inning, Aug. 24, 1935.
Joseph P. DiMaggio, Jr., New York AL, 5th inning, June 24, 1936.
Sidney Gordon, New York NL, 2d inning, (2d game), July 31, 1949.
Andrew W. Seminick, Philadelphia NL, 8th inning, June 2, 1949.
Albert W. Kaline, Detroit AL, 6th inning, April 17, 1955.
James E. Lemon, Washington AL, 3rd inn., Sept. 5, 1959.
Joseph A. Pepitone, New York AL, 8th inn., May 23, 1962.

B—Most home runs, 2 consecutive games—

5—Adrian C. Anson, Chicago NL, Aug. 5 (2), 6 (3 in succession), 1884.
Tyrus R. Cobb, Detroit AL, May 5 (3), May 6 (2), 1925.
Anthony M. Lazzeri, New York AL, May 23. 2d g. (2), May 24 (3), 1936.
Ralph M. Kiner, Pitt. NL, Aug. 15 (2), 16 (3); Sept. 11 (3), 12 (2), 1947.
Donald F. Mueller, New York NL, Sept. 1, (3), Sept. 2 (2), 1951.
Stanley F. Musial, St. Louis NL, 1st game (3), 2nd game (2), May 2, 1954.
Joseph W. Adcock, Milwaukee NL, July 30 (1), July 31 (4), 1954.

C—Most home runs, 3 consecutive games—

6—Anthony M. Lazzeri, New York AL, May 23, 1st g. (1), 2d g. (2), May 24 (3), 1936.
Gus E. Zernial, Philadelphia AL, May 13, 2nd g. (2), May 15 (2), May 16 (2), 1951
Ralph M. Kiner, Pittsburgh NL, (thrice), Aug. 14, 15 (2). 16 (3); Sept. 10 (2), 11, 1st g., (1), 2d g. (3), or 11, 1st g. (1), 2d g. (3), 12 (2), 1947.
Frank J. Thomas, New York NL, Aug. 1 (2), Aug. 2 (2), Aug. 3 (2), 1962.

D—Most home runs, 4 consecutive games—

8—Ralph M. Kiner, Pittsburgh NL, Sept. 10 (2), 11, 1st g., 11 2d g. (3), 12 (2), 1947.
7—Anthony M. Lazzeri, New York AL, May 21, (1) 23, 1st g. (1), 2d g. (2), 24 (3), 1936.
Gus E. Zernial, Philadelphia AL, May 13, 2nd g. (2), May 15 (2), May 16 (2), May 17 (1), 1951.

E—Most home runs, 5 consecutive games—

7—George H. Ruth, New York AL, June 10, 11, 12, 13 (2), 14 (2), 1921.
Victor W. Wertz, Detroit AL, July 27, 28 (2), 29, 30, Aug. 1 (2), 1950.
James L. Bottomley, St. Louis NL, July 5, 6, 1st g. (2), 2d g. (1), 8, 9 (2), 1929.

F—Most home runs, 6 consecutive games—

7—George L. Kelly, New York NL, July 11, 12 (2), 13, 14, 15, 16, 1924.
W. Walker Cooper, New York NL, June 22 (2), 23, 24, 25. 27, 28. 1947.
Willie H. Mays, New York NL, Sept. 14 (2), 16, 17, 18, 20 (2), 1955.
Roger E. Maris, New York AL, Aug. 11, 12, 13, 13, 15, 16 (2), 1961.

G—Most home runs, 8 consecutive games—

8—R. Dale Long, Pittsburgh NL, May 19, 20, 20, 22, 23, 25, 26, 28, 1956.

H—Most home runs, one double header—

5—Stanley F. Musial, St. Louis NL, 1st game (3), 2d game (2), May 2, 1954.
4—H. Earl Averill, Cleveland AL, 1st game (3), 2d game (1), Sept. 17, 1930.
James E. Foxx, Philadelphia AL, 1st game (2), 2d game (2), July 2, 1933.
James R. Tabor, Boston AL, 1st game (1), 2d game (3), July 4, 1939.
Gus E. Zernial, Chicago AL, 1st game (1), 2d game (3), Oct. 1, 1950.
Charles R. Maxwell, Detroit AL, 1st game (1), 2d game (3), May 3, 1959.
Roger E. Maris, New York AL, 1st game (2), 2d game (2), July 25, 1961.
Rocco D. Colavito, Detroit AL, 1st game (1), 2d game (3), Aug. 27, 1961.
Harmon C. Killebrew, Minn. AL, 1st game (3), 2d game (1), Sept. 21, 1963.

I—Most home runs, consecutive times at bat—

4—Robert L. Lowe, Boston NL, consecutive (3d (2), 5th, 6th inn.), May 30, 1894.
Henry L. Gehrig, New York AL, 1st, 4th, 5th, 7th innings, June 3, 1932.
James E. Foxx, Phila. AL, June 7 (last time up), June 8, 2d, 4th, 5th innings. 1933.
Henry Greenberg, Detroit AL, July 26 (last 2 times) July 27 (first 2 times) 1938.
William B. Nicholson, Chicago NL, July 22 (last time up), July 23, (1st g.) 2d—b.b., 4th, 6th, 8th innings—hr., 1944.
Ralph M. Kiner, Pittsburgh NL, Aug. 15 (last time up), 16—2 bb.b., 3 hr., 1947.
Ralph M. Kiner, Pittsburgh NL, Sept. 11 (last 2 times), Sept. 13 (first 2 times), 1949.
Theodore S. Williams, Boston AL, Sept. 17, 8th inn.; 18, bb; 20, 9th inn.; 21, 2nd inn., 3 bb.; 22, bb., 2nd inn., 1957.
Charles R. Maxwell, Detroit AL, May 3 (1st game, last time up), May 3 (2nd game, first 3 times) 1959.
Rocco D. Colavito, Cleveland AL, June 10, 3rd, 5th, 6th, 9th inn., 1959.
Willie C. Kirkland, Cleveland AL, July 9, 2d game (3-hr, bb, sh), July 13 (bb, hr), 1961.
John E. Blanchard, New York AL, July 21, 9th inn.; 22, 9th inn.; 26, 1st, 4th inns., 1961.
Mickey C. Mantle, New York AL, July 4 (2d g) 5th, 6th inns.; July 6, 1st, 3rd inns., 1962.
Stanley F. Musial, St. Louis NL, July 7, (2d g) 8th inn.; July 8, 1st, 4th, 7th inns., 1962.

A—Most times two or more home runs, game, season—
11—H. Greenberg, Detroit AL, 1938; May 25, June 24, July 9, 26, 27, 29, Aug. 19, Sept. 11, 17, 23, 27.
10—Ralph M. Kiner, Pittsburgh NL, 1947; May 15, June 1 (2d g.), June 15 (1st g.), June 28 (2d g.), July 23, Aug. 15, 16 (3), Sept. 10, 11 (2d g.–3), 12.

B—Most times two or more home runs, game, lifetime—
72—George H. Ruth, Bos. AL 1919; N.Y. AL 1920-34; Bos. N.L. 1935.
54—Willie H. Mays, N.Y. NL, 1951, 54-57; S.F. NL, 1958-65.

C—Most times, three or more home runs, game, lifetime—
6—John R. Mize, St. Louis NL, July 13, 20 (2d g.), 1938, May 13, Sept. 8 (1st g.), 1940; New York NL, Apr. 24, 1947; New York AL, Sept. 15, 1950.
4—Henry L. Gehrig, New York AL, June 23, 1927, May 4, 1929, May 22 (2d g.), 1930, June 3, 1932 (4 home runs).

CC—Most times three or more home runs, game, season—
2—John R. Mize, St. Louis NL (twice) 1938, 1940.
Ralph M. Kiner, Pittsburgh NL, 1947.
Theodore S. Williams, Boston AL, 1957.
Willie H. Mays, San Francisco NL, 1961.

D—Most home runs with bases filled, lifetime—
23—Henry L. Gehrig, New York AL, 1927-1938.
14—Gilbert R. Hodges, Bklyn. NL, 1943-57; L.A. NL, 1958.

E—Most home runs with bases filled, season—
5—Ernest Banks, Chicago NL, May 11, 19, July 17 (1st game). Aug. 2, Sept. 19, 1955
James E. Gentile, Baltimore AL, May 9 (2), July 2, 7, Sept. 22, 1961.

F—Most home runs, with bases filled, same game—
2—Anthony M. Lazzeri, New York AL, May 24, 1936.
James R. Tabor, Boston AL (2d game), July 4, 1939.
Rudolph P. York, Boston AL. July 27, 1946.
James E. Gentile, Baltimore AL, May 9, 1961.

G—Most home runs, bases filled, two consecutive games—
2—George H. Ruth, N.Y. AL, Sept. 27-29, 1927; Aug. 6-7, 1929.
1—James T. Sheckard, Brk. NL, Sept. 23-24, 1901.
William M. Dickey, N.Y. AL, Aug. 3-4, 1937.
James E. Foxx, Bos. AL, May 20-21, 1940.
James F. Busby, Clev. AL, July 5-6, 1956.
Brooks C. Robinson, Balt. AL, May 6-9, 1962.

H—Hitting Home Run in all Major League Parks, Career—
Harry E. Heilmann, Detroit AL, Cincinnati NL, 1914-1932.
J. Geoffrey Heath, Cleveland, Wash., St. Louis AL, Boston NL, 1936-1949
John R. Mize, St. Louis, New York NL, New York AL, 1936-1953.

I—Most home runs by pitcher, game—
3—Guy J. Hecker, Louisville AA, August 15, 1886 (2d game).
James A. Tobin, Boston NL, May 13, 1942. (Consecutive.)

SACRIFICE HITS

J—Most sacrifice hits, league—
509—Edward T. Collins, Philadelphia-Chicago-Philadelphia AL, 25 years, 1906-1930.
392—Jacob E. Daubert, 15 years, Bklyn. NL, 1910-18; Cincinnati NL, 1919-20-21-22-23-24.

K—Most years leading league in sacrifice hits—
6—George W. Haas, Philadelphia AL, 1930-31-32; Chicago AL, 1933-34-36.
4—F. Otto Knabe, Philadelphia NL, 1907-08-10-13.

L—Pitcher leading league in sacrifice hits, season—
John F. Sain, Boston NL, 16, 1948.
Robert A. Harris, St. Louis AL, 14 (tied), 1941.

M—Most sacrifice hits, season—
67—Ray J. Chapman, Cleveland AL, 156 games, 1917.
46—James T. Sheckard, Chicago NL, 148 games, 1909.

N—Most sacrifice hits, game—
4—Jacob E. Daubert, Brooklyn NL, 2d game, Aug. 15, 1914.
Wade Killefer, Washington AL, vs. Detroit, 1st game, Aug. 27, 1910.
John J. Barry, Boston AL, Aug. 21, 1916.
Ray J. Chapman, Cleveland AL, Aug. 31, 1919.

O—Most sacrifice flies, season—
19—Gilbert R. Hodges, Brooklyn NL, 1954.
16—Samuel Crawford, Detroit AL, 1914.
Charles A. Gandil, Washington AL, 1914.

P—Most sacrifice flies, game—
3—Harry M. Steinfeldt, Chicago NL, May 5, 1909.
Robert W. Meusel, New York AL, Sept. 15, 1926.
Ernest Banks, Chicago NL, June 2, 1961.
Russell E. Nixon, Bos. AL, Aug. 30, 1965.

INDIVIDUAL BATTING RECORDS—Continued
BASES ON BALLS

A—Most bases on balls, lifetime—
  2056—George H. Ruth, Boston-New York AL, 1914-1934 (2036), Boston NL, 1935 (20).
  1708—Melvin T. Ott, New York NL, 1926-1947.

B—Most years leading league, bases on balls—
  11—George H. Ruth, New York AL, 1920-21-23-24-26-27-28-30-31-32-33.
  6—Melvin T. Ott, New York NL, 1929-31-32-33-37-42.

C—Most consecutive years leading in bases on balls—
  6—Theodore S. Williams, Boston AL, 145—1941, 145—1942, 156—1946, 162—1947, 126—**1948.**
    162—1949. (In Service 1943-45.)
  4—George H. Ruth, New York AL, 136—1930, 128—1931, 130—1932, 114—1933.
  3—George J. Burns, New York NL, 82—1919, 76—1920, 80—1921.
    Melvin T. Ott, New York NL, 80—1931, 100—1932, 75—1933.
    Floyd E. Vaughan, Pittsburgh NL, 94—1934, 97—1935, 118—1936.
    Edwin L. Mathews, Milwaukee NL, 93-1961, 101-1962, 124-1963.

D—Most years 100 or more bases on balls—
  13—George H. Ruth, Boston and New York AL, 1919 to 1934.
  10—Melvin T. Ott, New York NL, 1929 to 1942.

E—Most consecutive years 100 or more bases on balls, league—
  7—Melvin T. Ott, New York NL, 1936-42.
  6—Theodore S. Williams, Boston AL, 1941-42; 1946-49. (In Service 1943-**45.)**
    Edwin D. Joost, Philadelphia AL, 1947-1952.

F—Most bases on balls, season—
  170—George H. Ruth, New York AL, 152 games, 1923.
  148—Edward R. Stanky, Brooklyn NL, 153 games, 1945.

G—Fewest bases on balls, 150 or more games, season—
  13—Henry H. Myers, Brooklyn NL, 153 games, 1922.
  18—George D. Weaver, Chicago AL, 151 games, 1913.

H—Most intentional bases on balls, game (since 1955)—
  4—Roger E. Maris, New York AL, May 22, 1962 (12 inns.).
  3—Robert B. Thomson, Chicago NL, June 4, 1958.
    Daniel J. Dobbek, Washington AL, Apr. 22, 1960.
    Billy R. Bryan, Kansas City AL, Apr. 27, 1963.
    Roberto W. Clemente, Pittsburgh NL Apr. 21, 1964.
    Denis J. Menke, Milwaukee NL, May 23, 1964.
    Clayton E. Dalrymple, Philadelphia NL, June 11, 1965.
    William D. White, St. Louis NL, July 23, 1965.

HH—Most intentional bases on balls, season (since 1955)—
  33—Theodore S. Williams, Boston AL, 1957.
  28—Ernest Banks, Chicago NL, 1960.

I—Most bases on balls, game—
  6—Walter Wilmot, Chicago NL, Aug. 22, 1891.
    James E. Foxx, Boston AL, June 16, 1938.
  5—(NL since 1900) By 12 players.

J—Most consecutive games, one or more base on balls—
  19—Theodore S. Williams, Boston AL, Aug. 24 to Sept. 14, 1941.
  10—Edwin L. Mathews, Milwaukee NL, August 2 to August 13, 1954.

K—Most consecutive bases on balls, season—
  7—William G. Rogell, Detroit AL, Aug. 17, 18, 19, 1938.
    Melvin T. Ott, New York NL, June 16, 17, 18, 1943.
    Edward R. Stanky, New York NL, Aug. 29, 30, 1950.

L—Most bases on balls, inning—
  2—By many players:

BATSMEN HIT BY PITCHER

M—Most hit by pitcher, season—
  49—Hugh Jennings, Baltimore NL, 129 games, 1896.
  31—Louis R. Evans, St. Louis NL, 151 games, 1910.
  23—Orestes Minoso, Chicago AL, 1956.

N—Most hit by pitcher, game—
  3—By many players.
    Last player: Sherman Lollar, Chicago AL, June 8, 1956.

O—Most hit by pitcher, inning—
  2—Willard R. Schmidt, Cincinnati NL, April 26 (3rd inn.), 1959.
    Frank J. Thomas, New York NL, April 29, 1st g (4th inn.), 1962.

P—Most years leading league, hit by pitcher—
  10—S. Orestes Minoso, Chi.-Clev. AL, 1951-54, 56-61.
  6—Frank Robinson, Cin. NL, 1956, 59-60, 62-63, 65.

26

STRIKEOUTS

A—Most strikeouts, lifetime—
1424—Mickey C. Mantle, N.Y. AL, 1951-65.

B—Most strikeouts, league, lifetime—
1424—Mickey C. Mantle, N.Y. AL, 1951-65.
1305—Edwin L. Mathews, Bos. (115)-Mil. (1190) NL, 1952-65.

C—Most strikeouts, season (154 game schedule)—
138—James R. Lemon, Washington AL, 1956.
136—J. Francisco Herrera, Philadelphia NL, 1960.

D—Most strikeouts, season (162 game schedule)—
175—David L. Nicholson, Chi. AL, 1963.
150—Richard A. Allen, Phil. NL, 1965.

E—Most years leading league, strikeouts—
7—James E. Foxx, Philadelphia AL, 1929, 30 (tie), 31, 33, 35, 36, 41.
6—Vincent P. DiMaggio, Boston NL, 1937-38; Pittsburgh, 1942-43-44; Philadelphia, 1945.

F—Most consecutive years leading in strikeouts—
4—Lewis R. Wilson, Chicago NL, 1927-30.
  Vincent P. DiMaggio, Pitt.-Phil. NL, 1942-44; 45.
3—James E. Foxx, Philadelphia AL, 1929-31.
  James P. Seerey, Cleveland AL, 1944-46.
  James R. Lemon, Washington AL, 1956-58.
  Mickey C. Mantle, New York AL, 1958-60.

G—Most strikeouts, 9 inning game—
5—By many players.

H—Most strikeouts, extra inning game—
6—Carl Weilman, St. Louis AL, July 25, 1913 (15 inn.)
  Donald A. Hoak, Chicago NL, May 2, 1956 (17 inn.)

I—Most strikeouts, player, 2 consecutive games—
8—Pedro Ramos, Cleveland AL, Aug. 19-23, 1963.
7—J. Patrick Seerey, Chicago AL, July 24-24, 1948.
  Gerald D. Kindall, Chicago NL, Aug. 14-16, 1960.
  David L. Nicholson, Chicago AL, June 12-12, 1963.
  Wilver D. Stargell, Pittsburgh NL, Sept. 24-25, 1964.
  Sanford Koufax, Los Angeles NL, May 5-9, 1965.
  Frank O. Howard, Washington AL, July 9-9, 1965.
  Joseph O. Christopher, New York NL, Oct. 2-3, 1965.

J—Most strikeouts, inning—
2—By many players

K—Fewest strikeouts, lifetime (7000 or more at bats)—
114—Joseph W. Sewell, Cleveland, New York AL, 1920-1933.
173—Lloyd J. Waner, Pitts., Bost., Cinn., Phil., Bkn., NL 1927-1945.

L—Fewest strikeouts, season (150 or more games)—
4—Joseph W. Sewell, Cleveland AL, 155 games, 1925; also 152 games, 1929.
5—Charles J. Hollocher, Chicago NL, 152 games, 1922.

M—Most years leading league, fewest strikeouts, season—
13—J. Nelson Fox, Chi. AL, 1952-63; Hou. NL, 1964.
4—Stanley F. Musial, St. Louis NL, 1943, 48, 52, 56.

N—Most consecutive game, no strikeouts—
98—J. Nelson Fox, Chicago AL, May 17 to Aug. 22, 1958.
77—Lloyd J. Waner, Pitts. Bos. Cinn. NL, April 24 to Sept. 16, 1941.

GROUNDED INTO DOUBLE PLAYS

O—Most times, season—
32—Jack E. Jensen, Boston AL, 1954.
30—Ernest N. Lombardi, Cincinnati NL, 1938.

P—Most Years Leading League—
4—Ernest N. Lombardi, Cinn. New York NL, 1933, 1934, 1938, 1944.
3—Jack E. Jensen, Boston AL, 1954, 1956, 1957.

Q—Most times, game—
4—Leon A. Goslin, Detroit AL (consecutive) vs. Cleveland, April 28, 1934.
  Michael A. Kreevich, Chicago AL (consecutive) vs. Washington, Aug. 4, 1939.
3—By Many Players:
  Last Player: Richie Ashburn, Philadelphia NL, June 28, 1959.

R—Fewest times, season (500 or more at bats)—
0—August J. Galan Chi. NL, 1935 (154 gs, 646 at-bat)
1—Donald L. Blasingame, Wash. AL, 1964 (143 gs, 506 at-bat)

27

LEADER IN BASES ON BALLS AND STRIKE OUTS, 1913 TO DATE

	BASE ON BALLS		STRIKE OUTS	
	NATIONAL	AMERICAN	NATIONAL	AMERICAN
1913	Bescher, Cinn.... 94	Shotton, St. L...102	Burns, N. Y. ... 74	Moeller, Wash...106
1914	Huggins, St. L...105	Bush, Det......112	Merkle, N. Y.... 80	Williams, St. L..120
1915	Cravath, Phila... 86	Collins, Chi.....119	Baird, Pitts..... 88	Lavan, St. L.... 83
1916	Groh, Cinn. 84	Shotton, St. L...111	Cravath, Phila... 89	Pipp, N. Y...... 82
1917	Burns, N. Y......75	Graney, Cleve... 94	Williams, Chi... 78	Roth, Cleve..... 73
1918	Carey, Pitts......62	Chapman, Cleve. 84	{Youngs, N. Y. .. 49 / Paskert, Chi.... 49}	Ruth, Bos....... 58
1919	Burns, N. Y......82	Graney, Cleve. ..105	Powell, Bos..... 79	Shannon, Bos.... 70
1920	Burns, N. Y......76	Ruth, N. Y.....148	Kelly, N. Y..... 92	Ward, N. Y..... 84
1921	Burns, N. Y......80	Ruth, N. Y.....144	Powell, Bos..... 85	Meusel, N. Y.... 88
1922	Carey, Pitts 80	Witt, N. Y..... 89	Parkinson, Phila. 93	Dykes, Phila.... 98
1923	Burns, Cinn.....101	Ruth, N. Y.....170	Grantham, Chi.. 92	Ruth, N. Y..... 93
1924	Hornsby, St. L... 89	Ruth, N. Y.....142	Grantham, Chi.. 63	Ruth, N. Y..... 81
1925	Fournier, Bklyn... 86	{Kamm, Chi. ... 90 / Mostil, Chi.... 90}	Hartnett, Chi.... 77	McManus, St. L.. 69
1926	Wilson, Chi...... 69	Ruth, N. Y.....144	Friberg, Phila... 77	Lazzeri, N. Y.... 96
1927	Hornsby, N. Y... 86	Ruth, N. Y.....138	Wilson, Chi..... 70	Ruth, N. Y..... 89
1928	Hornsby, Bos....107	Ruth, N. Y.....135	Wilson, Chi..... 94	Ruth, N. Y..... 87
1929	Ott, N. Y.......113	Bishop, Phila....128	Wilson, Chi..... 83	Foxx, Phila.... 70
1930	Wilson, Chi. 105	Ruth, N. Y.....136	Wilson, Chi..... 84	{Foxx, Phila.... 66 / Morgan, Cleve.. 66}
1931	Ott, N. Y........ 80	Ruth, N. Y.....128	Cullop, Cinn.... 86	Foxx, Phila.... 84
1932	Ott, N. Y........100	Ruth, N. Y.....130	Wilson, Bklyn... 85	Campbell, St. L..104
1933	Ott, N. Y........ 75	Ruth, N. Y.....114	Berger, Bos..... 77	Foxx, Phila.... 93
1934	Vaughan, Pitts... 94	Foxx, Phila.....111	Camilli, Chi..... 94	Clift, St. L.....100
1935	Vaughan. Pitts... 97	Gehrig, N. Y...132	Camilli, Phila....113	Foxx, Phila..... 99
1936	Vaughan. Pitts ..118	Gehrig, N. Y...130	Brubaker, Pitts.. 96	Foxx, Bos......119
1937	Ott, N. Y........102	Gehrig, N. Y...127	DiMaggio, Bos...111	Crosetti, N. Y...105
1938	Camilli, Bklyn...119	{Foxx, Bos.....119 / Greenberg, Det.119}	DiMaggio, Bos...134	Crosetti, N. Y... 97
1939	Camilli, Bklyn....110	Clift, St. L.....111	Camilli, Bklyn...107	Greenberg, Det.. 95
1940	Fletcher, Pitts....118	Keller, N. Y. ...106	Ross, Bos......127	S. Chapman, Phil.96
1941	Fletcher, Pitts...118	Williams, Bos...145	Camilli, Bklyn...115	Foxx, Bos......103
1942	Ott, N. Y.......109	Williams, Bos...145	DiMaggio, Pitts.. 87	Gordon, N. Y... 95
1943	Galan, Bklyn...103	Keller, N. Y. ...106	DiMaggio, Pitts.126	Laabs, St. L.....105
1944	Galan, Bklyn....101	Etten, N. Y. 97	DiMaggio, Pitts.. 83	Seerey, Cleve.... 99
1945	Stanky, Bklyn....148	Cullenbine, Cl-Dt.112	DiMaggio, Phila. 91	Seerey, Cleve.... 97
1946	Stanky, Bklyn....137	Williams, Bos...156		{Seerey, Cleve..101 / Keller, N. Y....101}
1947	{Greenberg, Pitts. 104 / Reese, Bklyn....104}	Williams, Bos...162	Kiner, Pitts.....109	Joost, Phila.....110
1948	Elliott, Boston ...131	Williams, Bos...126	Nicholson, Chi... 83	Seerey, Cle.-Chi. 102
1949	Kiner, Pitts......117	Williams, Bos...162	Sauer, Cinn..... 85	Kokos, St. L. ... 91
1950	Stanky, N.Y......144	Yost, Wash......141	Snider, Bklyn... 92	Zernial, Chi.....110
1951	Kiner, Pitts. 137	Williams, Bos...143	Smalley, Chi. ...114	Zernial, Chi.-Phil.101
1952	Kiner, Pitts......110	Yost, Wash. 129	Mathews, Bos. ...115	{Doby, Clev. ...111 / Mantle, N.Y. ...111}
1953	Musial, St. Louis.105	Yost, Wash......123	Bilko, St. Louis ..125	Doby, Cleveland.121
1954	Ashburn, Phila. ..125	Williams, Bos. ..136	Snider, Bkn. ... 96	Mantle, N. Y. ...107
1955	Mathews, Milw. ..109	Mantle, N. Y....113	Post, Cinn. 102	Zauchin, Bos. ...105
1956	Snider, Bklyn .. 99	Yost, Wash......151	Post, Cinn......124	Lemon, Wash...138
1957	{Ashburn, Phila.. 94 / Temple, Cinn.. 94}	Mantle, N.Y. ...146	Snider, Bkn. ...104	Lemon, Wash .. 94
1958	Ashburn, Phil. .. 97	Mantle, N.Y. ...129	H. Anderson, Phil 95	{Lemon, Wash. 120 / Mantle, N.Y. ...120}
1959	Gilliam, L.A. ... 96	Yost, Det. 135	Post, Phil. 101	Mantle, N.Y. ...126
1960	Ashburn, Chi. ...116	Yost, Det. 125	Herrera, Phil. ..136	Mantle, N.Y. ...125
1961	Mathews, Mil. .. 93	Mantle, N.Y. ...126	Stuart, Pitt. ...121	Wood, Det. 141
1962	Mathews, Mil. ..101	Mantle, N.Y. ...122	Hubbs, Chi. 129	Killebrew, Minn. 142
1963	Mathews, Mil. ..124	Yastrzemski, Bos. 95	Clendenon, Pitt. 136	Nicholson, Chi. ..175
1964	Santo, Chi. 86	Siebern, Balt. ...106	Allen, Phil. 138	Mathews, K.C. ..143
1965	Morgan, Hou. ... 97	Colavito, Clev. . 93	Allen, Phil. 150	Versalles, Minn. 122

INDIVIDUAL PINCH HITTING RECORDS

A—Most games in a season—
81—Elmer W. Valo, N.Y. (5)—Wash. (76), AL, 1960.
80—Albe t F. Schoendienst, St.L. NL, 1962.

B—Most times at bat, season—
72—Samuel A. Leslie, New York NL, 1932.
Albert F. Schoendienst, St. Louis NL, 1962.
David E. Philley, Baltimore AL, 1961.

C—Most times reaching base, season—
33—Elmer W. Valo, N.Y.-Wash. AL, 1960.

D—Most consecutive hits, lifetime—
9—David E. Philley, Phil. NL, Sept. 9, 11, 12, 13, 19, 20, 27, 28, 1958; Apr. 16, 1959.

E—Most consecutive hits, season—
8—David E. Philley, Phil. NL, Sept. 9, 11, 12, 13, 19, 20, 27, 28, 1958
6—Robert W. Johnson, Balt. AL, June 26, 30, July 2, 9, 13, 14, 1964.

F—Most hits season—
24—David E. Philley, Baltimore AL, 1961.
22—Samuel A. Leslie, New York NL, 1932.
Albert F. Schoendienst, St. Louis NL, 1962.

G—Most hits lifetime—
115—Forrest H. Burgess, Chi.-Phil.-Cin.-Pitt. NL; Chi. AL (389 games).
107—Charles F. Lucas, Bos.-Cin.-Pitts. NL (440 games).
76—Robert R. Fothergill, Det.-Chic.-Bos. AL (257 games).

H—Most home runs, season—
6—John F. Frederick, Bkn. NL, 1932.
5—Joseph E. Cronin, Bos. AL, 1943.

I—Most home runs, lifetime—
17—Gerald T. Lynch, Pitt.-Cin. NL, 1957 (3), 58, 59, 61 (5), 62, 63 (4), 64, 65.
12—Robert H. Cerv, N.Y.-K.C. AL, 1954, 55(2), 57(3), 58, 60(2), 61(3).

J—Most home runs, double-header—
2—Joseph E. Cronin, Bos. AL, June 17, 1943.

K—Most home runs, consecutive appearances—
2—Raymond B. Caldwell, New York AL, June 10, 11, 1915.
Fred Williams, Philadelphia NL, June 2, 6, 1928.
Joseph E. Cronin, Boston AL, June 17 (doubleheader), 1943.
Charles E. Keller, New York AL, Sept. 12, 14, 1948.
Delbert Q. Wilber, Boston AL, May 6, 10, 1953.
Eldon J. Repulski, Philadelphia NL, Aug. 22, 24, 1958.
Gene L. Freese, Philadelphia NL, April 18, 23, 1959.
R. Dale Long, Chicago NL, August 13, 14, 1959.
Gerald T. Lynch, Cincinnati NL, Apr. 23, 26, 1961.
John E. Blanchard, New York AL, July 21, 22, 1961.
Charles T. Schilling, Boston AL, Apr. 30, May 1, 1965.
Raymond H. Barker, New York AL, June 20, 22, 1965.

L—Most home runs with bases filled, season—
1—By many players.

M—Most home runs with bases filled, lifetime—
3—Ronald J. Northey, St. Louis NL, Sept. 3, 1947; May 30, 1948; Chicago NL, Sept. 18, 1950.
2—William J. Skowron, New York AL, Aug. 17, 1954; July 14, 1957 (2nd game).
Victor W. Wertz, Boston AL, Aug. 14, 1959; Aug. 25, 1960.

N—Most bases on balls, lifetime—
91—Elmer W. Valo, 5 AL-3 NL clubs, 1940-61.

O—Most bases on balls, season—
18—Elmer W. Valo, N.Y. (0)-Wash. (18) AL, 1960.

Individual Base Running Records

A—Most stolen bases, league—

892—Tyrus R. Cobb, Det. AL, 1905-26; Phila. AL, 1927-28.
797—Wm. R. Hamilton, Phila. NL, 1890-95; Boston NL 1896-1901.
744—Edward T. Collins, Phil. AL, 1906-14; 1927-30; Chic. AL 1915-26.
738—Max G. Carey, Pitts. NL, 1911-26; Bklyn NL, 1926-28.

B—Most years leading league, stolen bases—

10—Max G. Carey, Pitt. NL, 1913, 15-18, 20, 22-25.
9—Luis E. Aparicio, Chi. AL, 1956-62; Balt. AL, 1963-64.

C—Most consecutive years, leading league—

9—Luis E. Aparicio, Chi. AL, 1956-62; Balt. AL, 1963-64.
6—Maurice M. Wills, L.A. NL, 1960-65.

D—Most stolen bases, season (154 game schedule)—

156—Harry Stovey, Phila. AA, 130 games, 1888.
115 William R. Hamilton, Philadelphia NL, 133 games, 1891.
96—Tyrus R. Cobb, Detroit AL, 156 games, 1915.
80—Robert H. Bescher, Cincinnati NL, 153 games, 1911.

Most stolen bases, season (162 game schedule)—

104—Maurice M. Wills, Los Angeles NL, 165 games, 1962.

E—Fewest stolen bases, 150 or more games, season—

0—By many players.

F—Most stolen bases, game—

7—George F. Gore, Chicago NL, June 25, 1881.
   Wm. R. Hamilton, Phila NL, 2d game, 8 inn., Aug. 31, 1894.
6—E. T. Collins, Phila. AL, Sept. 11, 1912, 1st g., Sept. 22, 1912.
5—Dennis L. McGann, New York NL, May 27, 1904.

G—Most stolen bases, inning—

3—By many players. Last:
   Robert W. Meusel, New York AL, (3rd inn.), May 16, 1927.

H—Most times stealing home, game—

2—Joseph B. Tinker, Chicago NL, June 28, 1910.
   Lawrence J. Doyle, New York NL, Sept. 18, 1911.
   Victor P. Power, Cleveland AL, Aug. 14, 1958.

I—Most times stealing home, season—

7—Harold P. Reiser, Brooklyn NL, 1946.
6—Robert F. Roth, Cleveland AL, 1917.

J—Most times stealing home, lifetime—

13—Tyrus R. Cobb, Det.-Phil. AL, 1905-28.
9—Harold P. Reiser, Brk.-Bos.-Pitt. NL, 1940-42, 46-51; Clev. AL, 1952.

K—Fewest caught stealing, season (50 attempts)—

2—Max G. Carey, Pittsburgh NL, in 53 times, 1922.
8—Luis E. Aparicio, Chicago AL, in 59 times, 1960.

L—Most caught stealing, season—

38—Tyrus R. Cobb, Detroit AL, 156 games, 1915.
36—Miller J. Huggins, St. Louis NL, 148 games, 1914.

M—Most caught stealing, game—

3—By many players.

MAJOR LEAGUE FIELDING RECORDS
First Basemen's Fielding

A—Most games played, lifetime—
2368—Jacob C. Beckley, Pitts.-New York-Cinn.-St. L. NL, 19 yrs., 1888-89; 1891-1907 (2247) games; Pitts. PL, 1 yr., 1890 (121 games).
2237—James B. Vernon, 4 clubs AL-NL, 19 yrs., 1939-1959.
2132—Charles J. Grimm, St. L.-Pitts.-Chi. NL, 19 years, 1918-36.

B—Most games played, season—
162—Norman L. Siebern, Kansas City AL, 1962. (162 game schedule).
William D. White, St. Louis NL, 1963. (162 game schedule.)
Ernest Banks, Chicago NL, 1965. (162 game schedule).

C—Highest fielding percentage, season—
.9993—John P. McInnis, Boston AL, 152 games), 1921.
.9992—Frank A. McCormick, Philadelphia NL, (134 games), 1946.
.9974—Walter L. Holke, Boston NL, (150 games), 1921.

D—Consecutive years leading league in percentage—
5—Theodore B. Kluszewski, Cincinnati NL, 1951-52-53-54-55.
4—Charles A. Gandil, Cleve.-Chicago AL, 1916-17-18-19.

E—Most years leading league, 100 or more games—
9—Charles J. Grimm, Pitt.-Chi. NL, 1920, 22-24; 28, 30-33.
6—Joseph I. Judge, Wash. AL, 1923-25, 27, 29-30.

CHANCES ACCEPTED—FIRST BASEMEN

EE—Most chances accepted, lifetime—
23,687—Jacob P. Beckley, 4 clubs NL-PL, 20 yrs., 1888-89; 1891-1907.
21,914—Charles J. Grimm, 3 clubs NL, 19 yrs., 1918-1936.
21,256—James B. Vernon, 4 clubs, AL-NL, 19 years, 1939-1959.

F—Most chances accepted, season—
1986—John A. Donohue, Chicago AL, 157 games, 1907.
1862—George L. Kelly, New York NL, 155 games, 1920.

G—Most chances accepted, 9-inning game—
22—By many. Last:
Ernest Banks, Chicago NL, May 9, 1963 (22-po).

H—Fewest chances offered, games, 9 innings—
0—Guy Hecker, Louisville AA, October 9, 1887.
A. B. McCauley, Washington AA, Aug. 6, 1891.
John W. Clancy, Chicago AL, April 27, 1930.
James A. Collins, Chicago AL, June 29, 1937.
Norman D. Cash, Detroit AL, June 27, 1963.

I—Most consecutive chances accepted, no errors—
1625—John P. McInnis, Bos-Cleve. AL, May 31, 1921—June 2, 1922.
1337—Frank A. McCormick, Cinn.-Phila. NL, Sept. 23, 1945-Sept. 25, 1946.

PUTOUTS—FIRST BASEMEN

J—Most putouts, season—
1846—John A. Donohue, Chicago AL, 157 games, 1907.
1759—George L. Kelly, New York NL, 155 games, 1920.

JJ—Most putouts, league, lifetime—
22,438—Jacob P. Beckley, 4 clubs NL, 1888-89; 1891-1907.
20,700—Charles J. Grimm, 3 clubs NL, 1918-1936.
19,753—James B. Vernon, 3 clubs AL, 1939-1958.

K—Most putouts, 9-inning game—
22—Tom Jones, St. Louis AL, May 11, 1906.
Hal Chase, New York AL, 1st game, Sept. 21, 1906.
Ernest Banks, Chicago NL, May 9, 1963.

L—Fewest putouts, game—
0—Guy Hecker, Louisville AA, Oct. 9, 1887.
A. B. McCauley, Washington AA, August 6, 1891.
A. F. Hofman, Chicago NL, June 24, 1910.
John W. Clancy, Chicago AL, April 27, 1930.
James A. Collins, St. Louis NL, August 21, 1935.
James A. Collins, Chicago NL, June 29, 1937.
Adolph Camilli, Philadelphia NL, July 30, 1937.
Rudolph P. York, Detroit AL, June 18, 1943.
C. Earl Torgeson, Boston NL, 1st game, May 30, 1947.
Norman D. Cash, Detroit AL, June 27, 1963.

FIRST BASEMEN'S FIELDING RECORDS—Continued
ASSISTS—FIRST BASEMEN

A—Most assists, league, lifetime—
1446—James B. Vernon, 3 clubs AL, 18 yrs., 1939-1958.
1365—Fred C. Tenney, Bost.-N.Y. NL, 14 yrs., 1897-1909; 1911.
AA—Most assists, season—
155—James B. Vernon, Cleveland AL, 153 games, 1949.
152—Fred C. Tenney, Boston NL, 148 games, 1905.
B—Most years leading league in assists—
8—Frederick Tenney, Bos. NL, 1899, 1901-07.
6—George H. Sisler, St. L. AL, 1919-20, 22, 24-25, 27.
Victor P. Power, K.C. 1955, 57, Clev. 59-61, Minn., AL, 62.
C—Most assists, game—
7—Wm. E. Bransfield, Pittsburgh NL, May 3, 1904.
Fred W. Luderus, Philadelphia NL, August 22, 1918.
G. T. Stovall, St. Louis AL, August 7, 1912.

ERRORS—FIRST BASEMEN

D—Most errors, season—
58—Adrian C. Anson, Chicago NL, 108 games, 1884.
43—John J. Doyle, New York NL, 130 games, 1900.
41—Jerry B. Freeman, Washington AL, 154 games, 1908.
E—Fewest errors, season (100 or more games)—
1—John P. McInnis, Boston AL, (152 games), 1921.
Frank A. McCormick, Philadelphia NL (134 games), 1946.
F—Most consecutive games, no errors—
163—John P. McInnis, Bos.-Cleve. AL (119) May 31, 1921, (44) June 2, 1922.
138—Frank A. McCormick, Cinn. (7)—Phila. (131), 1st game, Sept. 26, 1945-Sept. 23, 1946.
G—Most errors, game—
5—J. C. Carbine, Louisville NL, April 29, 1876.
Also by eight (8) players, 1876-1901.
4—By 7 players.
Last player: James C. Wasdell, Washington AL, May 3, 1939.
H—Most errors in an inning—
3—Adolph Camilli, Philadelphia NL, 1st inning, Aug. 2, 1935.
George M. Metkovich, Boston AL, 7th inning, April 17, 1945.

DOUBLE PLAYS—FIRST BASEMEN

I—Participating in most double plays, season—
194—Ferris R. Fain, Philadelphia AL, 150 games, 1949.
171—Gilbert R. Hodges, Brooklyn NL, 158 games, 1951.
J—Most double plays, unassisted, season—
8—James L. Bottomley, St. Louis AL, Apr. 23; May 26; June 28; July 2, 5, 11; Aug. 4; Sept. 13, 1936.
William D. White, St. Louis NL, May 13; July 16, 20, 22, 23, 25; Aug. 23; Sept. 26, 1961.
K—Participating in most double plays, game—
6—By 6 players.
Last: J. Leroy Thomas, Los Angeles AL, Aug. 23, 1963.
L—Most double plays, unassisted, game—
2—By many players.
M—Most years leading league, Double plays—
4—Frank A. McCormick, Cincinnati NL, 1939-40-41-42.
Theodore B. Kluszewski, Cincinnati NL, 1953-54-55-56.
Gilbert R. Hodges, Bklyn.-L.A. NL, 1949-50-51-58.
3—Irving J. Burns, St. Louis AL, 1931-32-33.
James B. Vernon, Wash. AL, 1941, 53-54.
Victor P. Power, K.C.-Clev. AL, 1955; 59-60.

Second Basemen's Fielding Records

N—Most games played, lifetime—
2651—Edward T. Collins, Phil. (995), Chi. (1656), AL, 1906-28.
1834—Albert F. Schoendienst, St.L. (1429), N.Y. (142), Mil. (263), NL, 1945-62.
O—Most years leading league, games played—
8—J. Nelson Fox, Chi. AL, 1952-59.
7—William J. Herman, Chi. NL, 1932-33, 35-36, 38-39; Brk. NL, 1942.
P—Most games played, season—
162—Jacob Wood, Detroit AL, 1961 (162 game schedule).
William S. Mazeroski, Pittsburgh NL, 1964 (162 game schedule).
Peter E. Rose, Cincinnati NL, 1965 (162 game schedule).
Q—Most consecutive games played—
798—J. Nelson Fox, Chicago AL, Aug. 7, 1955, thru Sept. 3, 1960.

SECOND BASEMEN'S FIELDING RECORDS—Continued

A—Highest fielding percentage (100 or more games), season—
.9939—Kenneth J. Adair, Baltimore AL, 153 games, 1964.
.9934—Albert F. Schoendienst, St.L.-N.Y. NL, 121 games, 1956.
B—Most years leading league in percentage—
9—E. T. Collins, Phila. AL, 1909-10-14, Chi. 1915-16-20-21-22-24.
7—Albert F. Schoendienst, St. L.-N.Y.-Milw. NL, 1946-49-53-55-56-57 (tied)-58.

CHANCES ACCEPTED—SECOND BASEMEN

C—Most chances accepted, season—
1037—Frank F. Frisch, St. Louis NL, 153 games, 1927.
988—Napoleon Lajoie, Cleveland AL, 156 games, 1908.
CC—Most years leading league, chances accepted—
9—J. Nelson Fox, Chicago AL, 1952-60.
6—Fred N. Pfeffer, Chicago NL, 1884-85; 87-89; 91.
William S. Mazeroski, Pittsburgh NL, 1958, 60-64.
D—Most consecutive chances accepted, no errors—
458—Kenneth J. Adair, Baltimore AL, July 22, 1964-May 8, 1965.
418—Kenneth D. Hubbs, Chicago NL, June 13-Sept. 5 (1st g.), 1962.
E—Most chances accepted, game—
18—C. L. Childs, Syracuse AA, (9-po, 9-a), June 1, 1890.
17—Fred C. Dunlap, Cleve. NL, (6-po, 11-a, 1-e), July 24, 1882.
James J. Dykes, Phila AL (9-po, 8-a), Aug. 28, 1921.
Nelson Fox, Chicago, AL (10-po, 7-a), June 12, 1952.
16—M. J. Huggins, St. L. NL, (8-po, 8-a, 1-e), July 13, 1911.
James B. Partridge, Brklyn NL, (8-po, 8-a), April 21, 1927.
F. F. Frisch, St. L. NL, (6-po, 10-a), July 5, 1930.
F—Fewest chances offered game, 10 or more innings—
0—S. D. Yerkes, Bos. AL, June 11, 1913 (15 innings).
Raymond Charles, St. L. NL, June 26, 1909 (11 innings).
Casimer E. Michaels, Washington AL, May 1, 1951 (13 innings).

PUTOUTS—SECOND BASEMEN

G—Most putouts, season—
479—Stanley R. Harris, Wash. AL, 154 games, 1922.
466—William Herman, Chicago NL, 153 games, 1933.
GG—Most years leading league, putouts—
10—J. Nelson Fox, Chicago AL, 1952-61.
7—Fred N. Pfeffer, Chicago NL, 1884-89; 91.
William J. Herman, Chic.-Bklyn. NL, 1933; 35-36; 38-39; 40 (tied); 42.

H—Most putouts, game—
12—Louis Bierbauer, Philadelphia AA, June 22, 1888.
11—Held by many.
Last: M. Julian Javier, St. L. NL, June 27, 1964.

ASSISTS—SECOND BASEMEN

I—Most assists, season—
641—Frank F. Frisch, St. Louis NL, 153 games, 1927.
572—Oscar D. Melillo, St. Louis AL, 148 games, 1930.
J—Most assists, game—
12—John M. Ward, Bklyn. NL, 1st g., June 10, 1892.
James Gilliam, Brooklyn NL, July 21, 1956.
11—By many AL players.

ERRORS—SECOND BASEMEN

K—Most errors, season—
92—William H. Robinson, St. Louis AA, 129 games, 1886.
88—Charles M. Smith, Cincinnati NL, 80 games, 1880.
Robert V. Ferguson, Philadelphia NL, 85 games, 1883.
61—Hobe Ferris, Boston AL, 138 games, 1901.
William Gleason, Detroit AL, 136 games, 1901.
55—George F. Grantham, Chicago NL, 150 games, 1923.
L—Most errors, game—
9—Andrew Leonard, Boston NL, June 14, 1876.
5—Charles Hickman, Washington AL, Sept. 29, 1905.
Napoleon Lajoie, Philadelphia AL, April 22, 1915.
4—By many. Last performed by Kendall C. Wise, Chicago NL, May 3, 1957
M—Most consecutive games, no errors—
89—Kenneth J. Adair, Baltimore AL, July 22, 1964-May 6, 1965.
78—Kenneth D. Hubbs, Chicago NL, June 14-Sept. 5 (1st g.), 1962.
N—Fewest errors, season (150 or more games)—
5—Kenneth J. Adair, Baltimore AL, 1964 (153 games).
7—Jack R. Robinson, Brooklyn NL, 1951 (150 games).

DOUBLE PLAYS—SECOND BASEMEN

O—Participating in most double plays, season—
150—Gerald E. Priddy, Detroit AL, 157 games, 1950
144—William S. Mazeroski, Pittsburgh NL, 152 games, 1961.

SECOND BASEMEN'S FIELDING RECORDS—Continued

A—Participating in most double plays, game—
  5—By many players. Last:
    M. Julian Javier, St. Louis NL, Sept. 24, 1961.
    Donald A. Buford Chicago AL, Sept. 26, 1964.
AA—Most years leading league, double plays—
  6—William S. Mazeroski, Pitt. NL, 1960-65.
  5—Robert P. Doerr, Bos. AL, 1938, 40, 43, 46-47.
    J. Nelson Fox, Chi. AL, 1954, 56-58, 60.

Third Basemen's Fielding Records

B—Most games played, lifetime—
  2008—Edward F. Yost, Wash. (1625), Det. (288), L.A. (95), AL, 17 years, 1946-62.
  2003—Edwin L. Mathews, Bos. (142), Mil. (1861), NL, 14 years, 1952-65.
C—Most games played, season—
  164—Ronald E. Santo, Chi. NL, 1965 (162 game schedule).
  163—Brooks C. Robinson, Balt. AL, 1961, 64 (162 game schedule)
D—Highest fielding percentage (100 or more games), season—
  .988—Henry Majeski, Philadelphia AL, 134 games, 1947.
  .983—Henry K. Groh, New York NL, 145 games, 1924.
E—Most years leading league in percentage—
  8—Wm. E. Kamm, Chi. AL, 1924-25-26-27-28-29, Cleve. AL, 1933-34.
  6—Henry K. Groh, Cinn. NL, 1915-17-18, N. Y. NL, 1922-23-24.
          CHANCES ACCEPTED—THIRD BASEMEN
G—Most chances accepted, season—
  603—Harlond B. Clift, St. Louis AL, 155 games, 1937.
  601—James J. Collins, Boston NL, 151 games, 1899.
  583—Thomas W. Leach, Pittsburgh NL, 146 games, 1904.
GG—Most consecutive chances accepted, no errors—
  242—William E. Kamm, Chi. AL, June 26-Sept. 11, 1928 (75 gms).
  155—Stanley C. Hack, Chi. NL, Apr. 30-July 4, 1942 (54 gms).
H—Most chances accepted, game—
  13—By 8 players. (9 inn. game).
    Last: Roy J. Hughes, Chi. NL, Aug. 29, 1944 (2d gm).
I—Fewest chances offered, game, 15 or more innings—
  0—Harry Steinfeldt, Chi. NL, (15 inn.), Aug. 22, 1908.
    Henry K. Groh, Cinn. NL, 2d g. (15 inn.), Aug. 26, 1919.
    Norman D. Boeckel, Bos. NL, June 16, 1921 (15 inn.), also 1st game (15 inn.), Sept. 12, 1921.
          PUTOUTS—THIRD BASEMEN
J—Most putouts, season—
  252—James J. Collins, Boston NL, 142 games, 1900.
  243—William E. Kamm, Chicago AL, 155 games, 1928.
K—Most putouts, game—
  10—William Kuehne, Pittsburgh NL, May 24, 1889.
  9—Patrick Dillard, St. Louis NL, June 18, 1900.
  7—W. J. Bradley, Cleve. AL, 1st g., Sept. 21, 1901; also May 13, 1909.
    Harry P. Riconda, Philadelphia AL, 2d g., July 5, 1924.
    Oswald L. Bluege, Washington AL, June 18, 1927.
    Raymond O. Boone, Detroit AL, Apr. 24, 1954.
KK—Most years leading, putouts—
  8—Edward F. Yost, Wash.-Det. 1948; 1950-51-52-53-54; 1956; 1959.
  7—Harold J. Traynor, Pittsburgh NL, 1923; 1925-26-27; 1931; 1933-34.
    Willie E. Jones, Philadelphia NL, 1949; 1950; 1952-53-54-55-56.
          ASSISTS—THIRD BASEMEN
L—Most assists, season—
  405—Harlond B. Clift, St. Louis AL, 155 games, 1937.
  384—William Shindle, Baltimore NL, 134 games, 1892.
  374—Ronald E. Santo, Chicago NL, 162 games, 1963.
M—Most assists, game—
  11—James L. White, Buffalo NL, May 16, 1884.
    Jerry Denny, New York NL, May 29, 1890.
    Damon R. Phillips, Boston NL, Aug. 29, 1944.
  10—Lucius B. Appling, Chicago AL, 1st game, June 20, 1948.
    Vernon D. Stephens, Boston AL, May 23, 1951.
    Henry Majeski, Phila. AL, April 19, 1952.
    Frank J. Malzone, Boston AL, Sept. 24, 1957.
          ERRORS—THIRD BASEMEN
N—Most errors, season—
  91—Charles Hickman, New York NL, 118 games, 1900.
  64—Samuel Strang (Nicklin), Chicago AL, 137 games, 1902.
O—Most consecutive games, no errors—
  75—William E. Kamm, Chicago AL, June 26 to Sept. 11, 1928.
    (246 chances.)
  57—Robert T. Aspromonte, Houston NL, July 15 (2d g.) to Sept. 20 (1st g.). 1962. (150 chances.)
P—Fewest errors, season—
  9—George Kell, Detroit AL, 157 games, 1950.
  11—Robert T. Aspromonte, Houston NL, 155 games, 1964.

A—Most errors, game—
    6—Joseph H. Mulvey, Philadelphia NL, July 30, 1884.
      and 4 other players prior to 1900.
    5—David L. Brain, Boston NL, June 11, 1906.
    4—By many players. Last:
      Stephen Boros, Detroit AL, Aug. 23, 1962.

B—Most errors, inning—
    4—James T. Burke, Milwaukee AL, 4th inn., May 27, 1901.
      Lew Whistler, N. Y. NL, 4th inn., June 19, 1891.
    3—By many players. Last:
      Ronald E. Santo, Chi. NL (2d inn), Sept. 3, 1963.

DOUBLE PLAYS—THIRD BASEMEN

C—Participating in most double plays, season—
    50—Harlond B. Clift, St. Louis AL, 155 games, 1937.
    43—Henry Thompson, New York NL, 138 games, 1950.

D—Participating in most double plays, game—
    4—By many players.

E—Most unassisted double plays, season—
    4—Joseph A. Dugan, N. Y. AL, April 17, 24; May 7; Sept. 15, 1924.

F—Most Years Leading League, Double Plays—
    5—Kenneth F. Keltner, Clev. AL, 1939, 41, 42, 44, 47.
      Frank J. Malzone, Bos. AL, 1957-58-59-60-61.
      Kenton L. Boyer, St.L. NL, 1956, 58, 59, 60, 62.

Shortstops' Fielding Records

G—Most games played, lifetime—
    2218—Lucius B. Appling, Chicago AL, 20 years, 1930-1950. (In Service 1944.)
    2153—Walter J. Maranville, Bos.-Pitts.-Chi.-Bklyn.-St. L. NL, 19 years, 1912-23; 1925-31.

H—Most games played, season—
    165—Maurice M. Wills, Los Angeles NL, 1962 (162 game schedule).
    162—Richard D. Howser, Cleveland AL, 1964 (162 game schedule).

I—Highest fielding percentage (100 or more games), season—
    .985—Ernest Banks, Chicago NL (154 games), 1959.
    .983—Luis E. Aparicio, Baltimore AL (145 games), 1963.

J—Most years leading league in percentage—
    8—L. Everett Scott, Boston AL, 1916-17-18-19-20-21; New York AL, 1922-23
      (8 years in succession).
      Louis Boudreau, Cleveland AL, 1940-41-42-43-44-46-47-48.
    5—Hugh A. Jennings, Baltimore NL, 1894-5-6-7-8 (consecutive).
      Jos. B. Tinker, Chi. NL, 1906-08-09-11; Cinn. 1913.
      Edward R. Miller, Boston NL, 1940-41-42; Cincinnati 1943, 45.

K—Shortstops, who were LEFT HAND throwers—
    Wm. F. Greenwood, A's NL, 1882-83; Wm. Hulen, Phil. NL, 1896; Wm. McClellan, Chi. NL, 1878; Irving Ray, Bos. NL, 1888-89; Geo. Van Haltren, Balt. AA, 1891.

CHANCES ACCEPTED—SHORTSTOPS

L—Most chances accepted, season—
    984—David J. Bancroft, New York NL, 156 games, 1922.
    969—Owen J. Bush, Detroit AL, 157 games, 1914.

M—Most chances accepted, game—
    19—D. Richardson, Washington NL, (6-po, 13-a, 1-e), 1st g., June 20, 1892.
      Edwin Joost, Cincinnati NL, (9-po, 10-a, 1-e), May 7, 1941.
    17—R. J. Wallace, St. Louis AL, (6-po, 11-a, 2-e), June 10, 1902.

N—Most consecutive chances accepted, no errors—
    383—John J. Kerr, New York NL, (1st g.) July 28, 1946-May 25, 1947.
    297—Alfonso Carrasquel, Chicago AL, May 27 (2d g.)—July 18, 1951.

O—Fewest chances offered game, 12 or more innings—
    0—Irving Ray, Boston NL, August 15, 1888 (12 innings).
      John P. Gochnauer, Cleveland AL, July 14, 1903 (12 innings).
      William Rogell, Detroit AL, June 16, 1937 (12 innings).
      Edward Feinberg, Philadelphia NL, May 19, 1939 (12 innings).
      William F. Jurges, New York NL, Sept. 22, 1942 (12 innings).

PUTOUTS—SHORTSTOPS

A—Most putouts, season—
433—Robert G. Allen, Philadelphia NL, 148 games, 1892.
425—Owen J. Bush, Detroit AL, 157 games, 1914.
407—Walter J. Maranville, Boston NL, 156 games, 1914.

B—Most putouts, game—
11—William Fuller, New York NL, Aug. 20, 1895.
Horace H. Ford, Cincinnati NL, Sept. 18, 1929.
10—Napoleon Lajoie, Philadelphia AL, Sept. 24, 1901.
Lamar Newsome, Philadelphia AL, May 15, 1939.

ASSISTS—SHORTSTOPS

C—Most assists, season—
601—F. Glenn Wright, Pittsburgh NL, 153 games, 1924.
570—Terry L. Turner, Cleveland AL, 147 games, 1906.

D—Most assists, game—
14—Thos. W. Corcoran, Cincinnati NL, Aug. 7, 1903.
13—Robert E. Reeves, Washington AL, Aug. 7, 1927.

ERRORS—SHORTSTOPS

E—Most errors, season—
115—Wm. Shindle, Philadelphia PL, 132 games, 1890.
106—Joseph Sullivan, Washington NL, 127 games, 1893.
81—Rudolph E. Hulswitt, Philadelphia NL, 138 games, 1903.
95—John P. Gochnauer, Cleveland AL, 128 games, 1903.

EE—Fewest errors, season—
12—Ernest Banks, Chicago NL, 154 games, 1959.
14—Philip F. Rizzuto, New York AL, 155 games, 1950

F—Most errors, game—
7—George Smith, Brooklyn AA, June 17, 1885.
J. Hallinan, Mutuals NL (New York) July 29, 1876.
5—Charles Babb, New York NL, Aug. 24, 1903; Brooklyn NL, June 20, 1904.
Philip Lewis, Brooklyn NL, July 20, 1905.
Owen J. Bush, Detroit AL, 1st game, Aug. 25, 1911.

G—Most errors, inning—
4—William Fuller, Washington NL, 2nd inn., Aug. 17, 1888.
Raymond J. Chapman, Cleveland AL, 5th inn., June 20, 1914.
Leonard R. Merullo, Chicago NL, 2nd inn., Sept. 13, 1942.

H—Most consecutive games, no errors—
68—John J. Kerr, New York NL, (2d g.) July 28, 1946-May 24, 1947.
58—Philip F. Rizzuto, New York AL, Sept. 18, 1949-June 7, 1950.

DOUBLE PLAYS—SHORTSTOPS

I—Participating in most double plays, season—
134—Louis Boudreau, Cleveland AL, 149 games, 1944.
129—Roy D. McMillan, Cincinnati NL, 154 games, 1954.

J—Participating in most double plays, game—
5—By many players.
Last: K. Andre Rodgers, Chicago NL, June 29, 1962.

JJ—Most years leading in double plays—
5—Louis Boudreau, Clev. AL, 1940, 43-44, 47-48.
Richard M. Groat, Pitt. NL, 1958-59, 61-62; St. L. NL, 1964

Outfielders' Fielding Records

K—Most games played, lifetime—
2938—Tyrus R. Cobb, Detroit-Philadelphia AL, 24 years, 1905-28.
2421—Max G. Carey, Pittsburgh-Brooklyn NL, 20 years, 1910-29.

L—Most games played, season (162 game schedule)
164—Billy L. Williams, Chicago NL, 1965.
163—Leon L. Wagner, Cleveland AL, 1964.

M—Highest fielding pct. (150 or more games), season—
1.000—Daniel W. Litwhiler, Phil. NL, 1942 (151 gms, 317 chances).
Rocco D. Colavito, Clev. AL, 1965 (162 gms, 274 chances).

N—Most years leading league in percentage, (100 or more games)—
5—Amos Strunk, Phila. 1912-14-17; Bos. 1918: Phila.-Chi. AL, 1920.
3—Stanley F. Musial, St. Louis NL, 1949, 54, 61.

CHANCES ACCEPTED—OUTFIELDERS

O—Most chances accepted, season—
557—Taylor L. Douthit, St. Louis NL, 154 games, 1928.
516—Dominic P. DiMaggio, Boston AL, 155 games, 1948.

P—Most chances accepted, game—
13—Earl B. Clark, Boston NL, (12-po, 1-a), May 10, 1929.
12—Oscar C. Felsch, Chicago AL, (11-po, 1-a), June 23, 1919.
John B. Mostil, Chicago AL, (11-po, 1-a), May 22, 1928.

Q—Fewest chances accepted, extra inning game—
0—William H. Bruton, Det. AL, June 24, 1962 (22 inns.).

OUTFIELDERS' FIELDING RECORDS—Continued
PUTOUTS—OUTFIELDERS
A—Most putouts, season—
547—Taylor L. Douthit, St. Louis NL, 154 games, 1928.
503—Dominic P. DiMaggio, Boston AL, 155 games, 1948.
B—Most years, 400 or more putouts, league—
9—Richie Ashburn, Philadelphia NL, 1949-50-51-52-53-54-56-57-58.
4—Samuel West, Washington AL, 1931, 1932; St. Louis AL, 1935, 1936.
Dominic P. DiMaggio, Boston AL, 1942, 1947, 1948, 1949.
Samuel B. Chapman, Philadelphia AL, 1942, 1947, 1949, 1950.
C—Most years leading league, putouts—
9—Max Carey, Pitt. NL, 1912-13, 16-18, 21-24.
Richie Ashburn, Phil. NL, 1949-54, 56-58.
7—Tristram E. Speaker, Bos. AL, 1909-10, 13-15; Clev. AL, 1918-19.
D—Most putouts, game—
12—Earl B. Clark, Boston NL, May 10, 1929.
11—Oscar C. Felsch, Chicago AL, June 23, 1919.
John A. Mostil, Chicago AL, May 22, 1928.
Harry F. Rice, New York AL, June 12, 1930.
Paul E. Lehner, Philadelphia AL, 2d game, June 25, 1950.
Irving A. Noren, Washington AL, September 22, 1951.

ASSISTS—OUTFIELDERS
E—Most assists, season (1900 to date)—
44—Charles H. Klein, Philadelphia NL, 156 games, 1930.
35—Samuel Mertes, Chicago AL, 123 games, 1902.
Tris E. Speaker, Boston AL, 142 games, 1909; 153 games, 1912.
F—Most assists, game—
4—William Holmes, Chicago AL, Aug. 21, 1903.
Fred C. Clarke, Pittsburgh NL, Aug. 23, 1910.
Also by many players.
FF—Most assists, inning—
2—By many players. Last:
David R. Bell, N.Y. NL, April 11, 1962 (3rd inn.).

ERRORS—OUTFIELDERS
G—Most errors, season (1900 to date)—
36—·J. Bentley (Cy) Seymour, Cincinnati NL, 135 games, 1903
31—Roy C. Johnson, Detroit AL, 146 games, 1929.
H—Fewest errors (150 or more games), season—
0—Daniel W. Litwhiler, Phil. NL, 1942 (151 gms, 317 chances).
Rocco D. Colavito, Clev. AL, 1965 (162 gms, 274 chances).
I—Most errors, game—
5—By 9 players prior to 1900—
Albert C. Selbach, Baltimore AL, Aug. 19, 1902.
4—Fred Nicholson, Boston NL, June 16, 1922.
II—Most consecutive games, no errors—
266—Donald L. Demeter, Phil. (140) NL, 1962-63; Det. (126) AL, 1964-65.
205—A. Antonio Gonzalez, Philadelphia NL, 1961-63.
194—Charles R. Maxwell, Detroit AL, 1957-58.

DOUBLE PLAYS—OUTFIELDERS
J—Participating in most double plays, season—
15—Oscar C. Felsch, Chicago AL, 135 games, 1919.
12—Melvin T. Ott, New York NL, 149 games, 1929.
K—Most double plays, unassisted, season—
2—Ralph O. Seybold, Philadelphia AL, Aug. 15 and Sept. 10, 1907.
Tris E. Speaker, Cleveland AL, April 18 and 29, 1918.
Adam Comorosky, Pittsburgh NL, May 31, and June 13, 1931.

Catchers' Fielding Records
L—Most games caught, lifetime—
1918—Alfonso R. Lopez, Bklyn.-Bos.-Pitts. NL, 18 years, 1928-46 (1861 games);
Cleveland AL, 1 years, 1947 (57 games).
1806—Richard B. Ferrell, St. L.-Bos.-Wash. AL, 18 years, 1929-45; 1947.
M—Most games caught, season—
155—Ray C. Mueller, Cincinnati NL, 1944.
Frank W. Hayes, Philadelphia AL, 1944.
N—Highest fielding percentage (100 or more games), season—
1.000—Warren V. Rosar, Philadelphia AL, 117 games, 1946.
.999—Wesley W. Westrum, New York NL, 139 games, 1950.
O—Most years leading league, percentage (100 or more games)—
8—Ray W. Schalk, Chicago AL, 1913-14-15-16-17-20-21-22.
7—Charles L. Hartnett, Chicago NL, 1925-28-30-34-35-36-37.
P—Most consecutive games caught, league—
312—Frank W. Hayes, St. Louis AL, 1943 (2); Philadelphia AL, 1944 (155);
Philadelphia AL (32)-Cleveland AL (119), 1945 (151); Cleveland AL,
1946 (4); Oct. 2, 1943 (2d game)-April 21, 1946.
233—Ray. C. Mueller, Cincinnati NL, 1943 (62); 1944 (155); 1946 (16); July 31,
1943-May 5, 1946. (In service during 1945.)

CATCHERS' FIELDING RECORDS—Continued

A—Most years catching 100 or more games—
  13—William M. Dickey, New York AL, 1929-1941.
  12—Charles L. Hartnett, Chicago NL, 1924-1925; 1927-1928; 1930-1937.
    Alfonso R. Lopez, Brooklyn NL, 1930-1935; Boston NL, 1936-1937, 1939,
      Pittsburgh NL, 1941, 1943-1944.
AA—Most consecutive games caught, season—
  155—Ray C. Mueller, Cincinnati NL, 1944.
    Frank W. Hayes, Philadelphia AL, 1944.
B—Most consecutive years, catching 100 or more games—
  13—William M. Dickey, New York AL, 1929-1941.
  9—Roy Campanella, Brooklyn NL, 1949-1957.
C—Most years catching, league—
  21—Robert A. O'Farrell, Chicago, St. L., N.Y., Cinn. NL, 1915-1935.
  20—J. Luther Sewell, Cleve., Wash., Chic., St. L., AL, 1921-1942, except 1940-41.

CHANCES ACCEPTED—CATCHERS

D—Most consecutive chances, no errors, league—
  950—Lawrence P. Berra, New York AL, July 28, 1957 to May 10, 1959.
  511—Arnold M. Owen, St. Louis-Brooklyn NL, Sept. 22, 1940 to Aug. 29, 1941.
E—Most consecutive chances, no errors, season—
  605—Warren V. Rosar, Philadelphia AL, 1946.
  479—Arnold M. Owen, Brooklyn NL, 1941.
F—Most chances accepted, season—
  1095—John A. Edwards, Cincinnati NL, 148 games, 1963.
  1006—Elston G. Howard, New York AL, 146 games, 1964.
FF—Most years leading league, chances accepted—
  8—Raymond W. Schalk, Chicago AL, 1913-14-15-16-17-19-20-22.
    Lawrence P. Berra, New York AL, 1950, 51, 52, 54, 55, 56, 57, 59.
  6—Roy Campanella, Brooklyn NL, 1949-50-51-53-55-56.
G—Most chances accepted, game—
  25—Maurice R. Powers, Phil. AL, (18-po, 7-a), Sept. 1, 1906 (24 inn.).
  23—G. Bignall, Milwaukee U. Asso. (17-po, 6-a, 2-e), Oct. 3, 1884.
  22—Vincent Nava, Providence NL, (19-po, 3-a), June 7, 1884.
    Robert B. Schmidt, S.F. NL, (22-po), 1st g, June 22, 1958 (14 inn.).
  19—William Bergen, Brooklyn NL, (16-po, 3-a), 2d g., July 24, 1909.
    John Roseboro, Los Angeles NL, (19-po), Aug. 31, 1959.
    William A. Freehan, Detroit AL, (19-po), June 15, 1965.
H—Fewest chances, offered, extra inning game—
  0—Eugene Desautels, Cleveland AL, 14 innings, Aug. 11, 1942.
    James Wilson, Philadelphia NL, 13 innings, 1st g., Aug. 31, 1927.

PUTOUTS—CATCHERS

I—Most putouts, season—
  1008—John A. Edwards, Cincinnati NL, 148 games, 1963.
  939—Elston G. Howard, New York AL, 146 games, 1964.
J—Most putouts. game—
  22—Robert B. Schmidt, San Francisco NL, 1st game, June 22. 1958 (14 inn.).
  20—Kenneth L. Retzer, Washington AL, Sept. 12, 1962 (15 inns.).
  19—Vincent Nava, Providence NL. June 7, 1884.
  19—John Roseboro, Los Angeles NL, Aug. 31, 1959.
    N. Michael Grasso, Washington AL, May 1, 1951 (13 inn.).
    William A. Freehan, Detroit AL, June 15, 1965.
K—Most consecutive putouts—
  9—Arthur Wilson, New York NL, vs. Brooklyn (put out the first 9 men),
      morning game, May 30, 1911.
KK—Most years leading league, put outs—
  9—Raymond W. Schalk, Chicago AL, 1913-14-15-16-17-18-19-20-22.
  6—John G. Kling, Chicago NL, 1902-03-04-05-06-07 (tied).
    Roy Campanella, Brooklyn NL, 1949-50-51-53-55-56.

ASSISTS—CATCHERS

L—Most assists, season—
  236—William Rariden, Newark FL, 142 games, 1915.
  214—Patrick J. Moran, Boston NL. 107 games, 1903.
  212—Oscar Stanage, Detroit AL, 141 games, 1911.
M—Most assists, game—
  9—Michael P. Hines, Boston NL, May 1, 1883.
  8—Walter H. Schang, Boston AL, May 12, 1920.
  7—Wm. Bergen. Brooklyn NL. 2d game, Aug. 23, 1909.
    James P. Archer, Pittsburgh NL, May 24, 1918.
    John B. Adams, Philadelphia NL, Aug. 21, 1919.
N—Most assists, inning—
  3—Leslie Nunamaker, New York AL, 2d inn., Aug. 3, 1914.
    Ray W. Schalk, Chicago AL, 8th inn. (consecutive), Sept. 30, 1921.
    William M. Dickey, New York AL, 6th inn., May 13, 1929.
    C. Bruce Edwards. Brooklyn NL, 4th inn. (consecutive), Aug. 15, 1946.
    James R. Campbell, Houston NL, 3rd inn., 2d gm, June 16, 1963.

A—Most errors, season—
  41—Oscar Stanage, Detroit AL, 141 games, 1911.
  40—Charles Dooin, Philadelphia NL, 140 games, 1909.

B—Most errors, game—
  4—Charles E. Street, Boston NL, June 7, 1905.
  John Peters, Cleveland AL, May 16, 1918.
  William G. Styles, Philadelphia AL, July 29, 1921.
  Wm. H. Moore, Boston AL, 2d game, Sept. 26, 1927.

C—Most errors in inning (since 1900)—
  3—Edward Sweeney, New York AL, 1st inn. July 10, 1912.
  John Peters, Cleveland AL, 1st inn., May 16, 1918.
  2—Held by many players.
  Last player: Andrew Seminick, Cinn. NL, July 16, 1952.

D—Fewest errors, season (100 or more games)—
  0—Warren V. Rosar, Philadelphia AL, 117 games, 1946.
  1—Earl Grace, Pittsburgh NL, 114 games, 1932.
  Wesley W. Westrum, New York NL, 139 games, 1950.

E—Most consecutive games, no error—
  148—Lawrence P. Berra, New York AL, July 28, 1957 to May 10, 1959.
  121—J. Frank Hogan, Boston NL, May 17, 1933 to August 2, 1934.

F—Most passed balls, season (1900 to date)—
  33—Joseph C. Martin, Chi. AL, 1965 (112 games).
  29—Frank Bowerman, N.Y. NL, 1900 (73 games).

G—Most passed balls, game (1900 to date)—
  6—Harry Vickers, Cincinnati NL, October 4, 1902.
  4—By many AL catchers. Last:
  Charles R. Lau, Baltimore AL, June 14, 1962.

H—Most passed balls, inning—
  4—Raymond Katt, New York NL, 8th inn., September 10, 1954.
  3—Gus Triandos, Balt. AL, 6th inn., May 4, 1960.
  Myron N. Ginsberg, Balt. AL, 2d inn., May 10, 1960.
  Charles R. Lau, Balt. AL, 8th inn., June 14, 1962.

I—Fewest passed balls, 100 or more games, season—
  0—William M. Dickey, New York AL, 125 games, 1931.
  Alfred C. Todd, Pittsburgh NL, 128 games, 1937.
  Alfonso R. Lopez, Pittsburgh NL, 114 games, 1941.

J—Most runners thrown out in attempts to steal base, game—
  8—Charles A. Farrell, Washington NL, May 11, 1897.
  7—William Bergen, Brooklyn NL, 2d game, Aug. 23, 1909.
  6—Walter H. Schang, Philadelphia AL, May 12, 1915.

K—Most runners thrown out in attempts to steal base, inning—
  3—John Milligan, Philadelphia A.A. vs. Cinn., 3d inn., July 26, 1887.
  Leslie G. Nunamaker, New York AL, 2nd inn., Aug. 3, 1914.
  2—Held by many catchers.

L—Participating in double plays, season—
  29—Frank W. Hayes, Philadelphia-Cleveland AL, 151 games, 1945.
  22—Robert A. O'Farrell, Chicago NL, 125 games, 1922.

M—Most unassisted double plays, lifetime—
  2—Charles Schmidt, Det. AL, 1906-07.
  Frank P. Crossin, St. L. AL, 1914 (2).
  Miguel A. Gonzales, St. L. NL, 1915, 18.
  Clinton D. Courtney, Balt. AL, 1954, 60.
  Lawrence P. Berra, N.Y. AL, 1947, 62.
  L. Edgar Bailey, S.F. NL, 1963; Chi. NL, 1965.
  Christopher J. Cannizzaro, N.Y. NL, 1964-65.

Pitchers' Fielding Records

N—Most games played, lifetime—
  906—Denton T. Young, Cleve.-St. L.-Bos. NL, 1890-1900; 1911; Bos.-Cleve.
  AL, 1901-11, 22 years.
  802—Walter P. Johnson, Wash. AL, 1907-27, 21 years.
  750—Warren E. Spahn, Bos.-Mil.-N.Y.-S.F. NL, 1942, 46-65, 21 years.

O—Most games played, season—
  84—Ted W. Abernathy, Chi. NL, 1965 (all relief).
  82—Eddie G. Fisher, Chi. AL, 1965 (all relief).

P—Highest percentage (with most chances accepted), season—
  1.000—Lawrence C. Jackson, Chi. NL, 1964 (109: 24-po, 85-a) 40 gs.
  Walter P. Johnson, Wash. AL, 1913 (103: 21-po, 82-a) 51 gs.

CHANCES ACCEPTED—PITCHERS

Q—Most chances accepted, season (1900 to date)—
  262—Edward A. Walsh, Chicago AL, 56 games, 1907.
  168—Christopher Mathewson, New York NL, 56 games, 1908.

A—Most chances accepted, game—
    13—Nick Altrock, Chicago AL (3-po, 10-a), Aug. 6, 1904.
        Edward A. Walsh, Chicago AL (2-po, 11-a), April 19, 1907.
    12—Truett B. Sewell, Pittsburgh NL (1-po,11-a), June 6, 1941

B—Fewest chances accepted, extra inning game—
    0—Milton Watson, Philadelphia NL, July 17, 1918, 21 innings.
        Charles H. Ruffing, N.Y. AL. vs. Bos. July 23, 1932, 15 ins.

C—Most consecutive chances accepted, without error—
    273—Claude W. Passeau, Chicago NL. Started Sept. 21, 1941, ended May
        28, 1946 (145 games).
    159—Theodore A. Lyons, Chicago AL, Aug. 11, 1934 to June 12, 1938 (88
        games).

PUTOUTS—PITCHER

D—Most putouts, season—
    49—Nick Altrock, Chicago AL, 38 games, 1904.
    47—Larry Corcoran, Chicago NL, 59 games, 1884.
    39—Victor G. Willis, Boston NL, 43 games, 1904.

E—Most putouts, game—
    5—By many pitchers.

ASSISTS—PITCHER

F—Most assists, season—
    227—Edward A. Walsh, Chicago AL, 56 games, 1907.
    141—Christopher Mathewson, N. Y., NL, 56 games, 1908.

G—Most assists, game—
    11—Albert C. Orth, New York AL, Aug. 12, 1906.
        Edward A. Walsh, Chi. AL, April 19, and Aug. 12, 1907. (2).
        George McConnell, N. Y. AL, 2d game, Sept. 2, 1912.
        Meldon G. Wolfgang, Chicago AL, Aug. 29, 1914.
        Truett B. Sewell, Pittsburgh, NL, June 6, 1941.

ERRORS—PITCHERS

H—Most errors, season (1900 to date)—
    17—Eustace J. Newton, Cinn. Brooklyn NL, 33 games, 1901.
    15—John D. Chesbro, New York AL, 55 games, 1904.
        George E. Waddell, Philadelphia AL, 46 games, 1905.
        Edward A. Walsh, Chicago AL, 62 games, 1912.

I—Most errors (1900 to date), game—
    4—Eustace J. Newton, Cincinnati NL, 1st game, Sept. 13, 1900.
        Lafayette S. Winham, Pittsburgh NL, 1st game, Sept. 21, 1903.
        Chester Ross, Boston AL, May 17, 1925.

I-I—Most consecutive games, no errors—
    219—Marvin E. Grissom, N.Y.-S.F.-St.L. NL, Aug. 28, 1954 thru June 11, 1959.
        (75 chances).
    183—J. Hoyt Wilhelm, Chi. AL, May 16, 1963 thru Oct. 3, 1965. (69 chances).

DOUBLE PLAYS—PITCHER

J—Participating in most double plays, season—
    15—Robert G. Lemon, Cleveland AL, 41 games, 1953.
    12—Arthur N. Nehf, New York NL, 40 games, 1920.
        Edwin A. Rommel, Philadelphia AL, 43 games, 1924.
        Curtis B. Davis, Phila. NL, 51 games, 1934.

K—Most double plays started, game—
    4—Milton Gaston, Chicago AL, May 17, 1932.
        Harold Newhouser, Detroit AL, May 19, 1948.
    3—By 5 NL players. Last:
        Eugene Conley, Milwaukee NL, July 19, 1957.

L—Unassisted double plays, game—
    1—William L. Doak, St. Louis NL vs. Phila., July 16, 1914.
        W. C. Noyes, Philadelphia AL vs. Detroit, July 26, 1917.
        Also by many pitchers.

AMERICAN LEAGUE MANAGERS, 1901-to-Date

Armour, William R., Cleveland, Detroit (5)....1902, 03, 04; 1905-06
Austin, James P., St. Louis (1)......................1923
Baker, Delmar, Detroit (5).........................1938-42
Barrow, Edward G., Detroit, Boston (5)....1903, 04; 18, 19, 20
Barry, John J., Boston (1)..........................1917
Bauer, Henry A., Kansas City, Baltimore (4)....1961-62; 64-65
Berra, Lawrence P., New York (1)..................1964
Birmingham, Joseph L., Cleveland (4)....1912, 13, 14, 15
Blackburne, Russell A., Chicago (2)....1928, 29
Bluege, Oswald L., Washington (5)....1943-1947
Bottomley, James L., St. Louis (1)....1937
Boudreau, Louis, Cleveland, Boston, K.C. (15) 1942-50; 52-54; 55-57
Bragan, Robert R., (1), Cleveland.................1958
Burke, James T., St. Louis (3)....1918, 19, 20
Bush, Owen J., Wash., Chicago (3)....1923; 1930, 31
Callahan, James J., Chicago (5)....1903, 04, 12, 13, 14
Cantillon, Joseph, Washington (3)....1907, 08, 09
Carrigan, William F., Boston (7)....1913, 14, 15, 16; 27, 28, 29
Chance, Frank L., New York, Boston (3)....1913, 14; 1923
Chase, Harold H., New York (2)....1910, 11
Cobb, Tyrus R., Detroit (6)....1921, 22, 23, 24, 25, 26
Cochrane, Gordon S., Detroit (5)....1934-38
Collins, Edward T., Chicago (2)....1925, 26
Collins, James J., Boston (6)....1901, 02, 03, 04, 05, 06
Collins, John F., Boston (2)....1931, 32
Corriden, John M., Chicago (1)....1950
Craft, Harry F., Kansas City (3)....1957-59
Cronin, Joseph E., Washington, Boston (15)....1933-34; 35-47
Davis, Harry H., Cleveland (1)....1912
Dickey, William M., New York (1)....1946
Donovan, Patrick J., Washington, Boston (3)....1904, 10, 11
Donovan, William E., New York (3)....1915, 16, 17

Dressen, Charles W., Washington, Detroit (6)....1955-57, 63-65
Duffy, Hugh, Milwaukee, Chicago, Boston (5)....1901; 10, 11, 21, 22
Dwyer, Frank J., Detroit (1)....1902
Dykes, James J., Chi., Phil., Balt., Det., Clev. (20)....1934-46; 51-53; 54; 59-60; 60-61
Elberfeld, Norman, New York (1)....1908
Elliott, Robert I., Kansas City (1)....1960
Evers, John J., Chicago (1)....1924
Farrell, M. Kerby, Cleveland (1)....1957
Fohl, Lee A. Cleve., St. L., Bos. (11)....1915-19; 1921-23; 1924, 25, 26
Fonseca, Lewis A., Chicago (3)....1932, 33, 34
Gleason, William, Chicago (5)....1919, 20, 21, 22, 23
Gordon, Joseph L., Clev., Det., K.C. (4)....1958-60; 60; 61
Griffith, Clark C., Chi., N. Y., Wash. (17)....1901-02; 1903-08; 1912-20
Haney, Fred, St. Louis (3)....1939-41
Harris, C. Luman, Baltimore (1)....1961
Harris, Stanley R., Wash., Det. Bos., New York, Wash., Det. (28)....1924-28; 29-33; 34; 35-42; 47-48; 50-54; 55-56
Herman, William J., Boston (1)....1965
Higgins, Michael F., Boston (8)....1955-62
Hitchcock, William C., Baltimore (2)....1962-63
Hodges, Gilbert R., Washington (3)....1963-65
Hornsby, Rogers, St. Louis (6)....1933, 34, 35, 36, 37, 52
Houk, Ralph G., New York (3)....1961-63
Howley, Daniel P., St. Louis (3)....1927, 28, 29
Huggins, Miller J., New York (12)....1918-29
Huff, George, Boston (1)....1907
Hutchinson, Frederick C., Detroit (3)....1952-54
Jennings, Hugh A., Detroit (14)....1907-20
Johnson, Walter A., Washington-Cleveland (7)....1929-32; 1933-35
Jones, Fielder A., Chicago-St. Louis (8)....1904-08; 16, 17, 18
Joost, Edwin D., Philadelphia (1)....1954
Jurges, William F., Boston (2)....1959-60
Keane, John J., New York (1)....1965
Killefer, William, St. Louis (4)....1930, 31, 32, 33

Kittridge, M. J., Washington (1)............1904	Pesky, John M., Boston (2)................1963-64
Kuhel, Joseph A., Washington (2)........1948-49	Richards, Paul R., Chicago, Baltimore (11)....1951-54; 55-61
Lajoie, Napoleon, Cleveland (5)...........1905-09	Rickey, Branch, St. Louis (3).............1913, 14, 15
Lake, Fred, Boston (2)....................1908, 09	Rigney, William J., Los Angeles (5).......1961-65
Lavagetto, Harry A., Washington, Minnesota (5)....1957-60; 61	Robinson, Wilbert, Baltimore (1)..........1902
Loftus, Thomas J., Washington (2)..........1902, 03	Rolfe, Robert A., Detroit (4).............1949-52
Lopat, Edmund W., Kansas City (2)..........1963-64	Rowland, Clarence H., Chicago (4).........1915, 16, 17, 18
Lopez, Alfonso R., Cleveland, Chicago (15)...1951-56, 57-65	Ruel, Herold D., St. Louis (1)............1947
Lowe, Robert L., Detroit (1)...............1904	Schalk, Ray W., Chicago (2)...............1927, 28
Lyons, Theodore A., Chicago (3)............1946-48	Scheffing, Robert B., Detroit (3).........1961-63
Mack, Connie, Philadelphia (50)...........1901-50	Sewell, J. Luther, St. Louis (6)..........1941-46
Manning, James H., Washington (1).........1901	Shawkey, J. Robert, New York (1)..........1930
Marion, Martin, St. Louis, Chicago (4)....1952-53; 1955-56	Sisler, George H., St. Louis (3)..........1924, 25, 26
McAleer, James R., Cleve., St. L., Wash. (11)...1901; 1902-09; 1910-11	Speaker, Tris E., Cleveland (8)...........1919-1926
McBride, George F., Washington (1)........1921	Stahl, J. Garland, Washington, Boston (4)...1905, 06; 1912, 13
McCallister, John, Cleveland (1)..........1927	Stahl, Charles S., Boston (1).............1906
McCarthy, Joseph V., New York-Boston (19)...1931-46; 48-50	Stallings, George T., Detroit, New York (3)...1901; 1909, 10
McGaha, F. Melvin, Cleveland, Kansas City (3)...1962, 64-65	Stengel, Charles D., New York (12)........1949-60
McGraw, John J., Baltimore (2)............1901, 02	Stovall, George T., Cleveland, St. Louis (3)...1911, 12, 13
McGuire, James T., Boston, Cleveland (5)...1907, 08; 1909, 10, 11	Street, Charles E., St. Louis (1).........1938
McManus, Martin J., Boston (2)............1932, 33	Sullivan, Haywood C., Kansas City (1).....1965
Mele, Sabath A., Minnesota (5)............1961-65	Sullivan, William D., Chicago (1).........1909
Melillo, Oscar D., St. Louis (1)..........1938	Taylor, James W., St. Louis (4)...........1948-51
Milan, J. Clyde, Washington (1)...........1922	Tebbetts, George R., Cleveland (3)........1963-65
Moriarty, George J., Detroit (2)..........1927, 28	Tighe, John T., Detroit (2)...............1957-58
Neun, John H., New York (1)...............1946	Unglaub, Robert A., Boston (1)............1907
Norman, Willis P., Detroit (2)............1958-59	Vernon, James B., Washington (3)..........1961-63
O'Connor, John, St. Louis (1).............1910	Vitt, Oscar J., Cleveland (3).............1938-40
O'Neill, Stephen F., Clev., Det., Bos. (11)...1935-37; 43-48; 50-51	Wagner, Charles H., Boston (1)............1930
Onslow, John J., Chicago (2)..............1949-50	Wallace, Rhoderick J., St. Louis (2)......1911, 12
Peckinpaugh, Roger, New York, Cleveland (8)...1914; 1928-33; 1941	Wolverton, Harry S., New York (1).........1912

NATIONAL LEAGUE MANAGERS, 1901-to-Date

Alston, Walter E., Brooklyn, Los Angeles (12)	1954-57, 58-65
Bancroft, Frank C., Cincinnati (1)	1902
Bancroft, David J., Boston (4)	1924, 25, 26, 27
Bezdek, Hugo, Pittsburgh (3)	1917, 18, 19
Bissonette, Adelphia L., Boston (1)	1945
Blades, Raymond F., St. Louis (2)	1939-40
Bowerman, Frank, Boston (1)	1909
Boudreau, Louis, Chicago (1)	1960
Bragan, Robert R., Pittsburgh, Milwaukee (5)	1956-57, 63-65
Bresnahan, Roger P., St. L., Chi. (5)	1909, 10, 11, 12; 1915
Buckenberger, Al. C., Boston (3)	1902, 03, 04
Burke, James T., St. Louis (1)	1905
Bush, Owen J., Pittsburgh, Cincinnati (4)	1927, 28, 29; 1933
Callahan, James J., Pittsburgh (2)	1916, 17
Carey, Max G., Brooklyn (2)	1932, 33
Cavaretta, Philip J. Chicago (3)	1951-53
Chance, Frank L., Chicago (7)	1906-1912
Chapman, W. Benjamin, Philadelphia (4)	1945-48
Clarke, Fred C., Pittsburgh (15)	1901-15
Coleman, Robert H., Boston (2)	1944-45
Coombs, John W., Philadelphia (1)	1919
Craft, Harry, Houston (3)	1962-64
Cravath, Clifford C., Philadelphia (2)	1919-20
Dahlen, William F., Brooklyn (4)	1910, 11, 12, 13
Dark, Alvin R., San Francisco (4)	1961-64
Davis, George S., New York (1)	1901
Donovan, Patrick J., St. Louis, Bklyn (6)	1901, 02, 03; 06, 07, 08
Donovan, William E., Philadelphia (1)	1921
Dooin, Charles S., Philadelphia (5)	1910, 11, 12, 13, 14
Dressen, Charles W., Cin., Brk., Mil (9)	1934-37; 51-53; 60-61
Duffy, Hugh, Philadelphia (3)	1904, 05, 06
Durocher, Leo E., Brooklyn, New York (16)	1939-46, 48; 48-55
Dyer, Edwin H., St. Louis (5)	1946-50
Dykes, James J., Cincinnati (1)	1958
Ens, Jewel, Pittsburgh (2)	1930, 31
Evers, John J., Chicago (2)	1913, 1921
Fitzsimmons, Fred L., Philadelphia (3)	1943-45
Fletcher, Arthur, Philadelphia (4)	1923, 24, 25, 26
Fogel, Horace S., New York (1)	1902
Franks, Herman L., San Francisco (1)	1965
Frisch, Frank E., St. L., Pitts, Chi. (16)	1933-38; 1940-46; 1949-51
Fuchs, Emil E., Boston (1)	1929
Ganzel, John, Cincinnati (1)	1908
Gibson, Geo., Pitts., Chi., Pitt. (7)	1920, 21, 22; 1925; 1932, 33, 34
Gonzales, Miguel A., St. Louis (1)	1938
Griffith, Clark C., Cincinnati (3)	1909, 10, 11
Grimm, Chas., L., Chi.; Bos.; Mil. (19)	1932-38; 44-49; 52-56; 60
Hack, Stanley C., Chicago (3)	1954-56
Haney, Fred, Pitts., Milwaukee (7)	1953-55; 56-59
Hanlon, Edward H., Brooklyn, Cincinnati (7)	1901-06; 1906-07
Harris, C. Luman, Houston (2)	1964-65
Harris, Stanley R., Philadelphia (1)	1943
Hartnett, Charles L., Chicago (3)	1938-40
Hemus, Solomon J., St. Louis (3)	1959-61
Hendricks, John C., St. Louis, Cincinnati (7)	1918; 1924-29
Herman, William J., Pittsburgh (1)	1947
Herzog, Charles L., Cincinnati (3)	1914, 15, 16
Holmes, Thomas F., Boston (2)	1951-52
Hornsby, Rogers, St.L., Bos., Chi., Cin. (8)	1925-26; 28; 30-32; 52-53
Howley, Daniel P., Cincinnati (3)	1930, 31, 32
Huggins, Miller J., St. Louis (5)	1913, 14, 15, 16, 17
Hutchinson, Frederick C., St. Louis, Cincinnati (9)	1956-58; 59-64
Keane, John J., St. Louis (4)	1961-64
Kelley, Joseph J., Cincinnati, Boston (5)	1902-05, 08
Killefer, William J., Chicago (5)	1921, 22, 23, 24, 25
Kling, John G., Boston (1)	1912
Lake, Fred, Boston (1)	1910
Lobert, John B., Philadelphia (1)	1942

NATIONAL LEAGUE MANAGERS, 1901-to-Date—Continued

Loftus, Thomas J., Chicago (1)..........1901
Lumley, Harry G., Brooklyn (1)..........1909
Maranville, Walter J., Chicago, Boston (2)....1925; 1929
Marion, Martin W., St. Louis (1) 1951
Mathewson, Christopher, Cincinnati (3)....1916, 17, 18
Mauch, Gene W., Philadelphia (6)....1960-65
McCarthy, Joseph V., Chicago (5)....1926, 27, 28, 29, 30
McCloskey, John J., St. Louis (3)....1906, 07, 08
McGraw, John J., New York (31)....1902-32
McInnis, John P., Philadelphia (1)....1927
McKechnie, William B., Pitts., St. L., Bos., Cinn. (24)
....1922-26; 28-29; 30-37; 38-46
McPhee, John A., Cincinnati (2)....1901, 02
Meyer, William A., Pittsburgh (5)....1948-52
Mitchell, Fred L., Chicago, Boston (7)....1917-20; 1921-23
Moore, Terry B., Philadelphia (1)....1954
Moran, Patrick J., Phila., Cincinnati (9)....1915-18; 1919-23
Murray, William J., Philadelphia (3)....1907, 08, 09
Murtaugh, Daniel E., Pittsburgh (8)....1957-64
Nichols, Charles A., St. Louis (2)....1904, 05
Neun, John H., Cincinnati (2)....1947-48
O'Day, Henry, Cincinnati, Chicago (2)....1912; 1914
O'Farrell, Robert F., St. Louis, Cincinnati (2)....1927; 1934
O'Neill, Stephen F., Philadelphia (3)....1952-54
Ott, Melvin T., New York (7)....1942-48
Prothro, James T., Philadelphia (3)....1939-41
Rickey, Branch, St. Louis (7)....1919-25
Rigney, William J., New York, San Francisco (5)....1956-57; 58-60
Robinson, Wilbert, Brooklyn (18)....1914-31

Sawyer, Edwin M., Philadelphia (8) 1948-52; 58-60
Scheffing, Robert B., Chicago (3)....1957-59
Schoendienst, Albert F., St. Louis (1)....1965
Selee, Frank G., Boston, Chicago (5)....1901; 1902, 03, 04, 05
Sewell, J. Luther, Cincinnati (3)....1950-52
Sheehan, Thomas, San Francisco (1)....1960
Shettsline, William, Philadelphia (2)....1901, 02
Shotton, Burton E., Philadelphia, Brooklyn (10)....1928-33; 1947-50
Sisler, Richard A., Cincinnati (1)....1965
Slattery, Jack, Boston (1)....1928
Smith, George H., New York (1)....1902
Smith, Harry, Boston (1)....1909
Smith, E. Mayo, Philadelphia, Cincinnati (5)....1955-58; 59
Southworth, William H., St. L., Boston (13)....1929; 1940-45; 1946-51
Stallings, George T., Boston (8)....1913-20
Stanky, Edward R., St. Louis (4)....1952-55
Stengel, Charles D., Brk., Bos., N.Y. (13)....1934-36, 38-43, 62-65
Street, Charles, St. Louis (4)....1930, 31, 32, 33
Tebbetts, George R., Cincinnati, Milwaukee (7)....1954-58; 61-62
Tenney, Fred, Boston (4)....1905, 06, 07, 11
Terry, William H., New York (10)....1932-41
Tinker, Joseph B., Cincinnati, Chicago (2)....1913; 1916
Traynor, Harold J., Pittsburgh (6)....1934-39
Wagner, John P., Pittsburgh (1)....1917
Walker, Harry W., St. Louis, Pittsburgh (2)....1955, 65
Wallace, Rhoderick J., Cincinnati (1)....1937
Walters, William H., Cincinnati (2)....1948-49
Wilhelm, Irvin K., Philadelphia (2)....1921, 22
Wilson, James, Philadelphia, Chicago (9)....1934-38; 1941-44
Zimmer, Charles, Philadelphia (1)....1903

MAJOR LEAGUE PITCHING RECORDS

SERVICE

A—Most years pitched, lifetime—
    23—John P. Quinn, AL: N.Y. 1909-12, 19-21; Bos. 1913; 22-25; Chi. 1918; Phil. 1925-30; FL: Bal. 1914-15; NL: Brk. 1931-32; Cin. 1933.
    Early Wynn, AL: Wash. 1939, 41-44, 46-48; Clev. 1949-57, 63; Chi. 1958-62.
B—Most years pitched, league—
    23—Early Wynn, Wash. AL, 1939, 41-44, 46-48; Clev. AL, 1949-57, 63; Chi. AL, 1958-62.
    21—Eppa J. Rixey, Phil. NL, 1912-17, 19-20; Cin. NL, 1921-33.
    Warren E. Spahn, Bos. 1942, 46-52; Mil. 1953-64; N.Y.-S.F., NL, 1965.
C—Most years pitched, one club—
    21—Walter P. Johnson, Wash. AL, 1907-27.
    Theodore A. Lyons, Chi. AL, 1923-42, 46.
    20—Warren E. Spahn, Bos.-Mil. NL, 1942, 46-64.

GAMES

D—Most games, lifetime—
    906—Denton T. Young, Clev. NL, 1890-98; St.L. NL, 1899-00; Bos. AL, 1901-08; Clev. AL, 1909-11; Bos. NL 1911. (NL—516, AL—390.)
E—Most games, league—
    802—Walter J. Johnson, Wash. AL, 1907-27.
    750—Warren E. Spahn, Bos. (262); Mil. (452); N.Y. (20); S.F. (16), NL, 1942, 46-65.
F—Most games, relief pitcher, lifetime—
    718—J. Hoyt Wilhelm, N.Y. (319)-St. L. (40) NL (359), 1952-57; Clev. (26)—Balt. (142)—Chi. (191) AL (359), 1957-65.
    617—El Roy Face, Pitt. NL, 1953, 55-65.
    382—Tom S. Morgan, N.Y. (110)-K.C. (33)-Det. (105)-Wash. (14)-L.A. (120) AL, 1951-63.
G—Most games season—
    84—Ted W. Abernathy, Chi. NL, 1965 (all relief).
    82—Eddie G. Fisher, Chi. AL, 1965 (all relief).
H—Most consecutive games, relief pitcher—
    9—El Roy Face, Pitt. NL, Aug. 3-13, 1956.
    George W. Schultz, Chi. NL, May 4-13, 1962.
    8—Bennett Flowers, Bos. AL, July 25-Aug. 1, 1953.

GAMES STARTED

I—Most games started, lifetime—
    818—Denton T. Young, Clev.-St.L.-Bos. NL; Bos.-Clev. AL, 1890-1911.
J—Most games started, league—
    666—Walter P Johnson, Wash. AL, 1907-27.
    665—Warren E. Spahn, Bos. (236) 1942, 46-52; Mil. (399) 1953-64; N.Y. (19) 1965; S.F. (11) NL, 1965.
K—Most games started, season—
    74—William H. White, Cin. NL, 1879.
    51—John D. Chesbro, N.Y. AL, 1904.
    48—Joseph J. McGinnity, N.Y. NL, 1903.

COMPLETE GAMES

L—Most complete games, lifetime—
    751—Denton T. Young, Clev.-St.L.-Bos. NL (428); Bos.-Clev. AL (323). 1890-1911.
    560—James F. Galvin, Buff.-Pitt.-St. L. NL, 1879-92.
    531—Walter P. Johnson, Wash. AL, 1907-27.
    440—Grover C. Alexander, Phil. NL (221) 1911-17, 30; Chi. NL (159) 1918-26; St. L. NL (60) 1926-29.
M—Most years leading, complete games—
    9—Warren E. Spahn, Bos. NL, 1949, 51; Mil. NL, 1957-63.
    6—Walter P. Johnson, Wash. AL, 1910-11, 13-16.
N—Most complete games, season—
    74—William H. White, Cin. NL, 1879.
    48—John D. Chesbro, N.Y. AL, 1904.
    45—Victor G. Willis, Bos. NL, 1902.
O—Most consecutive complete games—
    37—William H. Dinneen, Bos. AL, Apr. 16-Oct. 10, 1904.
    23—John W. Taylor, St.L. NL, Apr 15-July 30, 1904.

GAMES FINISHED

P—Most games finished, lifetime—
    455—J. Hoyt Wilhelm, N.Y. (153)-St. L. (30) NL (183), 1952-57; Clev. (18)-Balt. (114)-Chi. (140) AL (272), 1957-65.
    427—El Roy Face, Pitt. NL, 1953, 55-65.
    293—John J. Murphy, N.Y.-Bos. AL, 1932, 34-43, 46-47.
Q—Most games finished, season—
    67—Richard R. Radatz, Bos. AL, 1964.
    62—C. James Konstanty, Phil. NL, 1950.
    Ted W. Abernathy, Chi. NL, 1965.

PITCHERS' RECORDS—Continued

INNINGS PITCHED

A—Most innings pitched, lifetime—
7377—Denton T. Young, Clev.-St.L.-Bos. (4143) NL; Bos.-Clev. (3234) AL, 1890-1911.
5959—James F. Galvin, Buff.-Pitt.-St.L. (5211) NL; Alghy (532) AA; Pitt. (216) PL, 1879-92.
5924—Walter P. Johnson, Wash. AL, 1907-27.
5246—Warren E. Spahn, Bos. (1885)—Mil. (3163)—N.Y. (126)—S.F. (72) NL, 1942, 46-65.

B—Most innings pitched, season—
683—William H. White, Cin. NL, 1879.
464—Edward A. Walsh, Chi. AL, 1908.
434—Joseph J. McGinnity, N.Y. NL, 1903.

C—Most years leading league, innings pitched—
7—Grover C. Alexander, Phil. NL, 1911-12, 14-17; Chi. NL, 1920.
5—Walter P. Johnson, Wash. AL, 1910, 13-16.
  Robert A. Feller, Clev. AL, 1939-41, 46-47.

D—Most innings pitched, game—
26—Leon J. Cadore, Brk. NL, May 1, 1920.
  Joseph Oeschger, Bos. NL, May 1, 1920.
24—John W. Coombs, Phil. AL, Sept. 1, 1906.
  Joseph W. Harris, Bos. AL, Sept. 1, 1906.

Most innings pitched, relief, game—
18⅓—George W. Zabel, Chi. NL, June 17, 1915. (won)
17 —Edwin A. Rommel, Phil. AL, July 10, 1932. (won)

RUNS ALLOWED

E—Most runs off pitcher, season—
544—John Coleman, Philadelphia NL, 1883.
211—Joseph J. McGinnity, Baltimore AL, 1901.
196—Charles Pittinger, Boston NL, 1903.

F—Most runs off pitcher, game—
35—David E. Rowe, Cleveland NL, July 24, 1882.
24—J. Travers, Detroit AL vs. Philadelphia, May 18, 1912.
21—Harley Parker, Cincinnati NL vs Brooklyn, June 21, 1901.

G—Most runs off pitcher, inning—
16—Anthony J. Mullane, Baltimore, NL, 1st inn., 1st game, June 18, 1894.
13—Frank J. O'Doul, Boston AL, 6th inn., July 7, 1923.
12—Harold Kelleher, Philadelphia NL, 8th inn., May 5, 1938.

H—Fewest runs, double-header—
0—Edward M. Reulbach, Chicago NL, vs. Brooklyn (5-0, 3-0), Sept. 26, 1908.
1—Edward A. Walsh, Chicago AL, vs. Boston (5-1, 2-0), Sept. 29, 1908.
  Carl W. Mays, Boston AL, vs. Philadelphia (12-0, 4-1), Aug. 30, 1918.

I—Most runs earned off pitcher, season (1912 to date)—
186—Louis N. Newsom, St. Louis AL, 330 innings, 1938.
155—Guy T. Bush, Chicago NL, 225 innings, 1930.

EARNED RUN AVERAGE

J—Lowest earned run average (1912 to date)—
0.90—Ferd. M. Schupp, New York NL, 30 games, 140 innings, 1916.
    (Nominal leader for 1916.)
1.01—Hubert B. Leonard, Boston AL, 35 games, 222 innings, 1914.
1.22—Grover C. Alexander, Philadelphia NL, 49 games, 376 innings, 1915.

K—Most years leading league, earned run average—
9—Robert M. Grove, Phil. AL, 1926, 29-32; Bos. AL, 1935-36, 38-39.
5—Grover C. Alexander, Phil. NL, 1915-17; Chi. NL, 1919-20.

L—Most consecutive years leading league, earned run average—
4—Robert M. Grove, Phil. AL, 1929-32.
  Sanford Koufax, L.A. NL, 1962-65.

M—Leading league, first season, earned run average—
2.28—W. Wilcy Moore, New York AL, 1927.
2.59—Darrell E. Blanton, Pittsburgh NL, 1935.
2.38—James R. Turner, Boston NL, 1937.
2.43—H. Eugene Bearden, Cleveland AL, 1948.
2.88—Chester Nichols, Boston NL, 1951.
2.43—J. Hoyt Wilhelm, New York NL, 1952.

N—Leading N.L. & A.L., earned run average, season—
J. Hoyt Wilhelm, N.Y. NL, 1952 (2.43); Balt. AL, 1959 (2.19).

BASE HITS—OFF PITCHER

A—Most hits off one pitcher, season (1900 to date)—
    401—Joseph J. McGinnity, Baltimore AL, 1901.
    394—Charles Pittinger, Boston NL, 1903.

B—Most hits off one pitcher, one game—
    36—John Wadsworth, Louisville NL, vs. Philadelphia, Aug. 17, 1894.
    26—Harley Parker, Cincinnati NL, vs. Brooklyn, June 21, 1901.
    Horace Lisenbee, Philadelphia AL, vs. Chicago, Sept. 11, 1936.

C—Most hits off one pitcher, inning—
    13—George E. Weidman, Detroit NL, 7th inn., Sept. 6, 1883.
    12—Merle T. Adkins, Boston AL, 6th inn., July 8th, 1902.
    11—Reginald Grabowski, Philadelphia NL, 9th inn., Aug. 4, 1934.

D—Fewest hits allowed, two consecutive games—
    0—John Vander Meer, Cincinnati NL, June 11 (0), June 15 (0), 1938.
    1—Howard J. Ehmke, Boston AL, Sept. 7 (0), Sept. 11 (1), 1923.

E—Most consecutive hitless innings, season—
    23—Denton T. Young, Boston AL, April 25th (2), 30th (6), May 5th (9), 11th (6), 1904.
    21 2-3—John Vander Meer, Cin. NL, June 5th (1-3), 11th (9), 15th (9), 19th (3 1-3), 1938.

F—Most consecutive hitless innings, game—
    12—Harvey Haddix, Pitts. NL (vs. Milw.), May 26, 1959. (Allowed one hit in 13th inn. and lost 1-0.)

G—Most one-hit games, lifetime—
    12—Robert A. Feller, Cleveland AL.
    7—Charles G. Radbourne, Prov.-Boston NL.
    5—Mordecai P. Brown, Chicago NL.
    Grover C. Alexander, Philadelphia NL.

H—Most consecutive one-hit games (since 1900)—
    2—Lonnie Warneke, Chi. NL, Apr. 17-22, 1934.
    Morton C. Cooper, St. L. NL, May 31-June 4, 1943.
    Edward C. Ford, N.Y. AL, Sept. 2-7, 1955.

I—Most one-hit games, season—
    4—Grover C. Alexander, Philadelphia NL, June 5, 26, July 5, Sept. 29, 1915.
    3—Adrian C. Joss, Cleveland AL; April 20, Sept. 5, 25, 1907.

J—Most home runs allowed, lifetime—
    487—Robin E. Roberts, Phil.-Hou. (400) NL; Balt. (87) AL, 1948-65.
    434—Warren E. Spahn, Bos.—Mil.—N.Y.—S.F. NL, 1942, 46-65.
    335—Early Wynn, Wash.-Clev.-Chi. AL, 1939, 41-44, 46-63.

K—Most home runs allowed, season—
    46—Robin E. Roberts, Philadelphia NL, 1956.
    43—Pedro Ramos, Washington AL, 1957.

L—Most home runs allowed, game—
    6—Lawrence J. Benton, New York NL, May 12, 1930.
    Hollis J. Thurston, Brooklyn NL, August 13, 1932.
    Alphonse T. Thomas, St. Louis AL, June 27, 1936.
    Wayman W. Kerksieck, Phila. NL, August 13, 1939.
    George J. Caster, Phila. AL, September 24, 1940.

M—Most home runs allowed, inning—
    4—William Lampe, Boston NL, 3rd inn., June 6, 1894.
    Lawrence J. Benton, New York NL, 7th inn., May 12, 1930.
    Wayman W. Kerksieck, Phila. NL, 4th inn., Aug. 13, 1939.
    George J. Caster, Phila. AL, 6th inn., Sept. 24, 1940.
    Charles Bicknell, Phila. NL, 6th inn., June 6, 1948.
    Benjamin Wade, Brooklyn NL, 8th inn., May 28, 1954.
    Calvin C. McLish, Cleveland AL, 6th inn., May 22, 1957.
    Paul E. Foytack, Los Angeles AL, 6th inn., July 31, 1963.

N—Most home runs, bases full, lifetime—
    8—Robert A. Feller, Clev. AL, 1937, 39, 41, 46, 47, 48 (2), 51.
    7—Lawrence H. French, Pitt. NL, 1929, 30, 33; Chi. NL, 1935, 37, 38 (2).
    James T. Hearn, N.Y. NL, 1952 (3), 56 (3); Phil. NL, 1959.
    John S. Sanford, Phil. NL, 1957, 58; S.F. NL, 1959, 60 (2), 62, 65.

O—Most home runs allowed, bases full, season—
    4—Raymond E. Narleski, Detroit AL, 1959.
    3—By many pitchers. Last:
    Lyndall D. McDaniel, Chicago NL, 1963.

PERCENTAGE

P—Highest percentage, games won, season (since 1900)—
    .947—El Roy Face, Pittsburgh NL, (won 18, lost 1), 1959.
    .938—John T. Allen, Cleveland AL (won 15, lost 1), 1937.

Q—Most years leading league, W&L pct.—
    5—Robert M. Grove, Phila.-Boston AL, 1929, 30, 31, 33, 38.
    3—Samuel L. Leever, Pittsburgh NL, 1901, 03, 05.
    Edward M. Reulbach, Chicago NL, 1906, 07, 08.
    Sanford Koufax, Los Angeles NL, 1963, 64, 65.

R—Leading league W&L pct. and ERA, first year—
    J. Hoyt Wilhelm, New York NL, 1952

S—Leading N.L. and A.L. in percentage, games won—
    John D. Chesbro, Pitt. NL, 1902; N.Y. AL, 1904.

GAMES WON

A—Most games won, lifetime—
511—Denton T. Young, Clev. NL (239) 1890-98; St.L. NL (46) 1899-00; Bos. AL (193) 1901-08; Clev. AL (29) 1909-11; Bos. NL (4) 1911.

B—Most games won, relief pitcher, lifetime—
94—J. Hoyt Wilhelm, N.Y. (42) NL, 1952-56; St. L. (1) NL, 1957; Clev. (3) AL, 1957-58; Balt. (24) AL, 1958-62; Chi. (24) AL, 1963-65.
77—El Roy Face, Pitt. NL, 1953, 55-65.
73—John J. Murphy, N.Y. AL, 1934-46.

C—Most games won, league, righthanded pitcher—
416—Walter P. Johnson, Wash. AL, 21 years, 1907-27.
373—G. C. Alexander, Phila.-Chi-St. L. NL, 20 years, 1911-1930.
    Christy Mathewson, N. Y.-Cin. NL, 17 years, 1900-1916.

D—Most games won, league, lefthanded pitcher—
363—Warren E. Spahn, Bos.—N.Y.—S.F. NL, 1946-65.
305—Edward S. Plank, Phil.-St. L. AL, 1901-14, 16-17.

E—Most games won, righthanded pitcher, season—
60—Charles Radbourne, Providence NL, 1884.
41—John D. Chesbro, New York AL, 1904.
37—Christopher Mathewson, New York NL, 1908.
Most games won, lefthanded pitcher, season—
42—Charles B. Baldwin, Det. NL, 1886.
31—Robert M. Grove, Phil. AL, 1931.
26—Richard M. Marquard, N.Y. NL, 1912.
    Carl O. Hubbell, N.Y. NL, 1936.
    Sanford Koufax, L.A. NL, 1965.

F—Most years leading league, games won—
8—Warren E. Spahn, Boston NL, 1949-50; Milwaukee NL, 53-57-58-59-60-61
6—Walter P. Johnson, Washington AL, 1913-14-15-16-18-24.
    Robert W. A. Feller, Cleveland AL, 1939-40-41-46 (tied)-47-51.

G—Most consecutive games won, lifetime—
24—Carl O. Hubbell, New York NL, 1936 (16); 1937 (8).
17—John T. Allen, Cleveland AL, 1936 (2); 1937 (15).

H—Most consecutive games won, season—
See table, page 53.

I—Most games won, from one club, season—
12—Charles Radbourne, Providence NL, from Cleveland, 1884.
  9—Edward M. Reulbach, Chicago NL, from Brooklyn, 1908.
    Edward A. Walsh, Chicago AL, from New York and Boston, 1908.

J—Most consecutive years winning 30 or more games—
7—Timothy J. Keefe, Metropolitan AA, 1883-41, 1884-35; New York NL, 1885-32, 1886-42, 1887-35; 1888-35, 1889-30.
5—John G. Clarkson, Chicago NL, 1885-53, 1886-35, 1887-38; Boston NL, 1888-33, 1889-49.
4—Charles A. Nichols, Boston NL, 1891-33, 1892-35, 1893-32, 1894-31.
3—Christopher Mathewson, New York NL, 1903-30, 1904-33, 1905-31.
    Grover C. Alexander, Philadelphia NL, 1915-31, 1916-33, 1917-30.
    Charles A. Nichols, Boston NL, 1896-30, 1897-32, 1898-33.

K—Most consecutive years, winning 20 or more games—
14—Denton T. Young, Cleve. NL, 1891-98; St. Louis NL, 1899-1900; Bos. AL, 1901-1904.
12—Christopher Mathewson, New York NL, 1903-14.
10—Walter P. Johnson, Washington AL, 1910-19.
    Charles A. Nichols, Boston NL, 1890-99.

L—Most years winning 20 or more games—
16—Denton T. Young, Cleveland, St. L. NL; Boston AL, 1891±1904, 1907-08.
13—Christopher Mathewson, New York NL, 1901; 1903-14.
    Warren E. Spahn, Boston-Milwaukee NL, 1947, 49-51, 53-54, 56-61, 63.
12—Walter P. Johnson, Washington AL, 1910-19; 1924-25.

M—Most years, 20 or more wins, left hander (since 1901)—
13—Warren E. Spahn, Boston-Milw. NL, 1947 (21), 1949 (21), 1950 (21), 1951 (22), 1953 (23), 1954 (21), 1956 (20), 1957 (21), 1958 (22), 1959 (21), 1960 (21), 1961 (21), 1963 (23).
  8—Robert M. Grove, Phila.-Boston AL, 1927 (20), 1928 (24), 1929 (20), 1930 (28), 1931 (31), 1932 (25), 1933 (24), 1935 (20).

N—Winning 20 or more games, pitching in two major leagues, same season—
21—Joseph J. McGinnity, Baltimore AL (13)-New York NL (8), 1902.
    Henry L. Borowy, New York AL (10)-Chicago NL (11), 1945.
20—Patrick J. Flaherty, Chicago AL (1)-Pittsburgh NL (19)-1904.

GAMES LOST

O—Most games lost, lifetime—
315—Denton T. Young, Clev. NL (136) 1890-98; St.L. NL (33) 1899-00; Bos. AL (112) 1901-08; Clev. AL (29) 1909-11; Bos. NL (5) 1911.

P—Most games lost, league—
279—Walter P. Johnson, Washington AL, 21 years, 1907-1927.
251—Eppa Rixey, Phila.-Cinn. NL, 21 years, 1912-33. (In Service 1918.)

Q—Most games lost, season—
48—John Coleman, Philadelphia NL, 1883.   26—John Townsend, Washington AL, 1904.
29—Victor G. Willis, Boston NL, 1905.   Robert Groom, Washington AL, 1909.

SHUTOUTS

A—Most shutout games, lifetime—
113—Walter P. Johnson, Washington AL, 21 years, 1907-27.
90—Grover C. Alexander, Phil. (61), 1911-17; Chi. (24), 1918-26; St. Louis (5), NL, 1926-29.

B—Most shutout games, left-hander, lifetime—
70—Edward S. Plank, Phil. AL (60) 1901-14; St. L. FL (6) 1915; St. L. AL (4) 1916-17.
63—Warren E. Spahn. Bos. NL (27) 1947-52; Mil. NL (36) 1953-64.

C—Most shutout games, season—
16—Grover C. Alexander, Philadelphia NL, 1916.
13—John W. Coombs, Philadelphia AL, 1910.

D—Most shutout games, left-hander, season—
11—Sanford Koufax, Los Angeles NL, 1963.
9—George H. Ruth, Boston AL, 1916.

E—Most consecutive shutout games, season—
5—G. Harris White, Chicago AL, Sept. 12, 16, 19, 25, 30, 1904.
4—Mordecai P. Brown, Chicago NL, June 13, 25, July 2, 4 (A.M.), 1908.
Grover C. Alexander, Philadelphia NL, Sept. 7, 13, 17, 21, 1911.
Edward M. Reulbach, Chicago NL, Sept. 19, 26 (2 games), Oct. 1, 1908.
Wm. C. Lee, Chicago NL, Sept. 5, 11, 17, 22, 1938.
(1 1-3 relief, without being scored upon), Sept. 7.
Salvatore A. Maglie, New York NL, Aug. 26, 30, Sept. 4, 9, 1950.
(Pitched 45 consecutive innings without being scored upon.)

F—Most shutout games from one club, season—
5—Charles B. Baldwin, Detroit NL vs. Philadelphia, 1886.
Anthony J. Mullane, Cincinnati AA vs. New York, 1887.
Thomas J. Hughes, Washington AL, vs. Cleveland, 1905.
Grover C. Alexander, Philadelphia NL, vs. Cincinnati, 1916.

G—Most consecutive shutout innings—
56—Walter P. Johnson, Washington AL, April 10 (2d inn.) to May 14 (4th inn.) 1913.
46 1-3—Carl O. Hubbell, New York NL, July 13 to Aug. 1, 1933.

H—Most consecutive shutout innings, game—
21—Joseph Oeschger, Boston NL, vs Brooklyn 1-1 tie game, 26 innings, May 1, 1920.
(Leon J. Cadore, Brooklyn NL, in this same game had 20 shutout innings.)
20—Joseph Harris, Boston AL, vs Philadelphia (Boston lost, 4-1) 24 innings, Sept. 1, 1906.

I—Double-header shutout—
1—Edward M. Reulbach, Chicago NL, vs Brooklyn (5 to 0, 3 to 0), Sept. 26, 1908.

J—Pitching shutouts in first two games—
2—James Hughes, Baltimore NL, April 18, 22, 1898.
Joseph Doyle, New York AL, August 25, 30, 1906.
John A. Marcum, Philadelphia AL, Sept. 7, 11, 1933.
David M. Ferriss, Boston AL, April 29, May 6, 1945.
Allan Worthington, New York NL, July 6, 11, 1953.
Karl Spooner, Brooklyn NL, Sept. 22, 26, 1954.

BASES ON BALLS

K—Most bases on balls, lifetime—
1775—Early Wynn, Wash. (460) AL, 1939, 41-44, 46-48; Clev. (877) AL, 1949-57, 63; Chi. (438) AL, 1958-62.
1713—Amos W. Rusie, Ind. (114) NL, 1889; N.Y. (1596) NL, 1890-95, 97-98; Cin. (3) NL, 1901.
1434—(NL since 1900): Warren E. Spahn, Bos. (587) NL, 1942-46-52; Mil. (791) NL, 1953-64; N.Y. (35) NL, 1965; S.F. (21) NL, 1965.

L—Most bases on balls, season—
276—Amos W. Rusie, New York NL, 64 games, 1890.
208—Robert Feller, Cleveland AL, 39 games, 1938.
185—Samuel Jones, Chicago NL, 36 games, 1955.

M—Most bases on balls, game—
16—William George, New York NL, AM game, May 30, 1887.
George Van Haltren, Chicago NL, June 27, 1887.
Henry Gruber, Cleveland PL, April 19, 1890.
Bruno P. Haas, Philadelphia AL, 2d game, June 23, 1915.
14—Henry Mathewson, New York NL, Oct. 5, 1906.

N—Most bases on balls, inning—
8—William D. Gray, Wash. AL vs. Chi. (7 in success.), 2d inn., 1st game, Aug. 28, 1909.
7—Anthony J. Mullane, Balto. NL vs. Bos. (3 in success.) 1st inn. AM g., June 18, 1894.
Robert Ewing, Cincinnati NL vs. Chicago, 4th inn., April 19, 1902.

O—Most consecutive innings, no bases on balls—(1900 to Date)—
84 1-3—William C. Fischer, Kansas City AL, Aug. 3 to Sept. 20, 1962.
68—Christy Mathewson, New York NL, June 19 to July 18, 1913.

P—Fewest bases on balls, game over 9 innings—
0—Charles B. Adams, Pittsburgh NL vs. New York, 21 inns., July 17, 1914.
Denton T. Young, Boston AL vs. Philadelphia, 20 inns., July 4, 1905.
Carl O. Hubbell, New York NL vs. St. Louis, 18 inns., July 2, 1933, 1st g.

A—Most strikeouts, lifetime—

3497—Walter P. Johnson, Wash. AL, 1907-27 (right-hander).
2583—Warren E. Spahn, Bos.-Mil.-N.Y.-S.F. NL, 1942, 46-65 (left-hander).

B—Most strikeouts, league—

3497—Walter P. Johnson, Wash. AL, 1907-27 (right-hander)
2583—Warren E. Spahn, Bos.-Mil.-N.Y.-S.F. NL, 1942, 46-65 (left-hander)
2499—Christopher Mathewson, N.Y.-Cin. NL, 1900-16 (right-hander).
2266—Robert M. Grove, Phil.-Bos. AL, 1925-41 (left-hander).

C—Most strikeouts, season—

505—Matthew Kilroy, Balt. AA, 1886 (Distance 50 ft.).
382—Sanford Koufax, L.A. NL, 1965 (left-hander).
348—Robert A. Feller, Clev. AL, 1946 (right-hander).
343—George E. Waddell, Phil. AL, 1904 (left-hander).
270—Robert Gibson, St. L. NL, 1965 (right-hander)

D—Most years leading league, strikeouts—

12—Walter P. Johnson, Wash. AL, 1910, 12-19, 21, 23-24.
7—Arthur C. Vance, Brk. NL, 1922-28.

E—Most consecutive years leading league, strikeouts—

8—Walter P. Johnson, Wash. AL, 1912-19.
7—Arthur C. Vance, Brk. NL, 1922-28.

F—Most years, 300-or-more strikeouts—

2—George E. Waddell, Phil. AL, 1903-04.
Walter P. Johnson, Wash. AL, 1910, 12.
Sanford Koufax, L.A. NL, 1963, 65.

G—Most years, 200-or-more strikeouts—

7—George E. Waddell, Phil. AL, 1902-08.
Walter P. Johnson, Wash. AL, 1910-16.
6—Donald S. Drysdale, L.A. NL, 1959-60, 62-65.

H—Most consecutive years, 200-or-more strikeouts—

7—George E. Waddell, Phil. AL, 1902-08.
Walter P. Johnson, Wash. AL, 1910-16.
5—John G. Clarkson, Chi.-Bos. NL, 1885-89.
Sanford Koufax, L.A. NL, 1961-65.

I—Most years, 100-or-more strikeouts—

18—Walter P. Johnson, Wash. AL, 1908-19, 21-26.
17—Warren E. Spahn, Bos.-Mil. NL, 1947-63.

J—Most consecutive years, 100-or-more strikeouts—

17—Warren E. Spahn, Bos.-Mil. NL, 1947-63.
13—Edward S. Plank, Phil. AL, 1902-14. (also St.L. FL, 1915).

K—Most strikeouts, game (9 inns., since 1900)—

18—Robert A. Feller, Clev. AL vs Det., Oct. 2, 1938 (lost).
Sanford Koufax, L.A. NL vs S.F., Aug. 31, 1959; vs Chi., Apr. 24, 1962.

L—Most strikeouts, night game (9 inns.)—

18—Sanford Koufax, L.A. NL vs S.F., Aug. 31, 1959.
17—William C. Monbouquette, Bos. AL vs Wash., May 12, 1961.

M—Most strikeouts, extra inning game—

21—Thomas E. Cheney, Wash. AL vs Balt. (16 inns.), Sept. 12, 1962 (night).
18—Warren E. Spahn, Bos. NL vs Chi. (15 inns.), June 14, 1952.
James W. Maloney, Cin. NL vs N.Y. (11 inns.), June 14, 1965 (night).
Christopher J. Short, Phil. NL vs N.Y. (15 inns.), Oct. 2, 1965 (night).

N—Most strikeouts, first game (since 1900)—

15—Karl B. Spooner, Brk. NL vs N.Y., Sept. 22, 1954.
12—Elmer G. Myers, Phil. AL vs Wash., Oct. 6, 1915.

O—Most strikeouts, 2 consecutive games—

31—Sanford Koufax, L.A. NL, Aug. 24 (13)-Aug. 31 (18), 1959.
28—Robert A. Feller, Clev. AL, Sept. 27 (10)-Oct. 2 (18), 1938.

P—Most games, 10-or-more strikeouts, lifetime—

82—Sanford Koufax, Brk.-L.A. NL, 1955-65.
54—Robert A. Feller, Clev. AL, 1936-41, 45-56.

Q—Most consecutive strikeouts, game—

9—Michael F. Welch, N.Y. NL, Aug. 28, 1884.
Since 1900:
8—Matthew C. Surkont, Mil. NL, May 25, 1953.
John J. Podres, L.A. NL, July 2, 1962.
James W. Maloney, Cin. NL, May 21, 1963.
7—Rinold G. Duren, L.A. AL, June 9, 1961.
Dennis D. McLain, Det. AL, June 15, 1965.

R—Most strikeouts, inning—

4—By many. Last:
Donald S. Drysdale, L.A. NL vs Phil. (2d inn.), Apr. 17, 1965.

PITCHERS' RECORDS—Continued
HIT BATSMEN

A—Most hit batsmen, lifetime, league—
204—Walter P. Johnson, Washington AL, 1907-27.
152—Joseph J. McGinnity, Balt.-Brk.-N.Y. NL, 1899-1900, 02-08.
B—Most hit batsmen, season—
41—Joseph McGinnity, Brooklyn NL, 1900.
26—John Warhop, New York AL, 1909.
C—Most hit batsmen, one pitcher, game—
6—Edward Knouff, Baltimore AA, April 25, 1887.
5—John J. Healy, Indianapolis NL, April 30, 1887.
Emerson P. Hawley, Pittsburgh NL, May 9, 1896.
Fred C. Bates, Cleveland NL, July 17, 1899.
4—By many AL pitchers. Last:
Kenneth F. McBride, Los Angeles AL, April 23, 1964.
D—Most hit batsmen, inning—
3—Emerson P. Hawley, Pittsburgh NL, 7th inn., May 9, 1896.
Walter Thornton, Chicago NL, 4th inn., May 18, 1898.
Charles L. Phillippe, Pittsburgh NL, 1st inn., Sept. 25, 1905.
Melvin A. Gallia, Washington AL, 1st inn., 2nd game, June 20, 1913.
Harry C. Harper, New York AL, 8th inn., Aug. 25, 1921.
Ray Boggs, Boston NL, 9th inn., Sept. 17, 1928.
Thomas S. Morgan, New York AL, 3rd inn., June 30, 1954.
Steven G. Ridzik, New York NL, 6th inn., July 16, 1956.
Raul R. Sanchez, Cincinnati NL, 8th inn., 1st game, May 15, 1960.

WILD PITCHES

E—Most wild pitches, season (1900 to date)—
30—Leon K. Ames, New York NL, 1905.
21—Walter P. Johnson, Washington AL, 1910.
R. Earl Wilson, Boston AL, 1963.
F—Most wild pitches (1900 to date) game—
5—C. Wheatley, Detroit AL, Sept. 27, 1912.
Lawrence Cheney, Brooklyn NL, July 9, 1918.
G—Most wild pitches, inning (1900 to date)—
4—Walter P. Johnson, Washington AL, 4th inn., Sept. 21, 1914.
3—By many NL pitchers. Last:
Ernest G. Broglio, St. Louis NL, 7th inn., May 19th, 1964

BALKS

H—Most balks, season—
8—Robert J. Shaw, Milwaukee NL, 1963.
6—John J. Boehling, Washington AL, 1915.
Victor J. Raschi, New York AL, 1950.
I—Most balks, game—
5—Robert J. Shaw, Milwaukee NL, May 4, 1963.
4—Victor J. Raschi, New York AL, May 3, 1950.
J—Most balks, inning—
3—Milburn J. Shoffner, Cleveland AL, 3d inn., May 12, 1930
James P. Owens, Cincinnati NL, 2d inn., Apr. 24, 1963.
Robert J. Shaw, Milwaukee NL, 3d inn., May 4, 1963.

LEADING LEAGUE IN WON & LOST PCT. and EARNED RUN AVERAGE, SAME YEAR
(Fifteen or more decisions)
NATIONAL LEAGUE

1915—Grover C. Alexander, Philadelphia NL ....756 W & L   1.22 ER
1923—Adolfo Luque, Cincinnati NL ....771 W & L   1.93 ER
1926—Ray Kremer, Pittsburgh NL............................769 W & L   2.61 ER
1932—Lonnie Warneke, Chicago NL..........................786 W & L   2.37 ER
1936—Carl O. Hubbell, New York NL.......................813 W & L   2.31 ER
1938—William C. Lee, Chicago NL ....710 W & L   2.66 ER
1941—Elmer R. Riddle, Cincinnati NL......................826 W & L   2.24 ER
1952—J. Hoyt Wilhelm, New York NL ....833 W & L   2.43 ER
1954—John A. Antonelli, New York NL ....750 W & L   2.29 ER
1964—Sanford Koufax, Los Angeles NL ....792 W & L   1.74 ER
1965—Sanford Koufax, Los Angeles NL ....765 W & L   2.04 ER

AMERICAN LEAGUE

1913—Walter P. Johnson, Washington AL...................837 W & L   1.09 ER
1924—Walter P. Johnson, Washington AL...................767 W & L   2.72 ER
1925—Stanley Coveleskie, Washington AL ....800 W & L   2.84 ER
1929—Robert M. Grove, Philadelphia AL....................769 W & L   2.82 ER
1930—Robert M. Grove, Philadelphia AL....................848 W & L   2.54 ER
1931—Robert M. Grove, Philadelphia AL....................886 W & L   2.05 ER
1934—Vernon Gomez, New York AL..........................839 W & L   2.33 ER
1938—Robert M. Grove, Boston AL...........................778 W & L   3.07 ER
1943—Spurgeon F. Chandler, New York AL..................833 W & L   1.64 ER
1953—Edmund W. Lopat, New York AL ....800 W & L   2.43 ER
1956—Edward C. Ford, New York AL.........................760 W & L   2.47 ER

Pitchers who in their lifetime have won three hundred or more games

Name and Club	Years	G	W	L	PC.
Alexander, Grover C., Phil.-Chi.-St. L. NL............	20, 1911-1930	696	373	208	.642
Clarkson, John G., Wor.-Chi.-Bos.-Clev. NL	12, 1882-1894	529	328	175	.652
Galvin, James F., 3-NL, 1-AA, 1-PL, 1-NA	15, 1875-1892	684	365	309	.542
Grove, Robert M., Phil.-Bos. AL	17, 1925-1941	616	300	141	.680
Johnson, Walter P., Washington AL.................	21, 1907-1927	802	416	279	.599
Keefe, Timothy J., Troy-N.Y.-Phila. NL; Met. AA, N.Y., PL	14, 1880-1893	587	346	225	.606
Mathewson, Christopher, N.Y.-Cinn. NL...........	17, 1900-1916	634	373	188	.665
Nichols, Chas. A., Bos.-St. L.-Phila. NL...........	15, 1890-1906	586	360	202	.641
Plank, Edward S., Phila.-St. L. AL; St. L. FL.......	17, 1901-1917	620	325	190	.631
Radbourne, Chas., Buff.-Prov.-Bost.-Cin. NL	11, 1881-1891	517	308	191	.617
Spahn, Warren E., Bos.-Mil.-N.Y.-S.F. NL	21, 1942-1965	750	363	245	.597
Welch, Michael, Troy-New York NL.................	13, 1880-1892	540	316	214	.596
Wynn, Early, Wash.-Clev.-Chi. AL	23, 1939-1963	691	300	244	.551
Young, Denton T., 3-NL, 2-AL	22, 1890-1911	906	511	315	.619

Two hundred or more games

Name and Club	Years	G	W	L	PC.
Bender,, Charles A., Phil. AL, Balt. FL, Phil. NL	16, 1903-1925	452	212	128	.624
Brown, Mordecai P.,St. L.-Chi.-Cinn., NL; St. L.-Bk.-Ch. FL	14, 1903-1916	480	239	130	.647
Buffington, C. G., Bos.-Phil.-Balt. NL; Phila. PL; Bos. AA.................................	11, 1882-1892	409	223	150	.598
Caruthers, Robert L., Six Clubs AA, NL.............	10, 1884-1893	333	217	93	.700
Cicotte, Edward V., Det.-Bos.-Chi. AL.............	14, 1905-1920	499	209	148	.585
Cooper, A. Wilbur, Pitts.-Chi. NL; Det. AL........	15, 1912-1926	516	216	178	.548
Coveleskie, Stanley, Phil.-Cleve.-Wash.-N.Y. AL.......	14, 1912-1928	449	216	142	.603
Dauss, George, Detroit AL.....................	15, 1912-1926	537	218	184	.542
Derringer, Paul, St. L.-Cinn.-Chi. NL.............	15, 1931-1945	579	223	212	.513
Faber, Urban C., Chicago AL....................	20, 1914-1933	669	253	211	.545
Feller, Robert W. A., Cleveland AL	18, 1936-1956	570	266	162	.621
Fitzsimmons, Fred L., N.Y., Brooklyn NL...........	19, 1925-1943	513	217	146	.598
Ford, Edward C., New York AL	14, 1950-1965	469	232	97	.705
Griffith, Clark C., Seven Clubs AA-NL-AL..........	19, 1891-1914	428	237	140	.629
Grimes, B. A., Six Clubs NL-One AL..............	19, 1916-1934	615	270	212	.560
Haines, Jesse J., Cinn.-St. L. NL.................	19, 1918-1937	555	210	158	.571
Harder, Melvin L., Cleveland AL.................	20, 1928-1947	582	223	186	.545
Hoyt, Waite C., 4 AL-3 NL......................	21, 1918-1938	675	237	182	.566
Hubbell, Carl O., New York NL..................	16, 1928-1943	535	253	154	.622
Jones, Sam P., Six Clubs AL....................	22, 1914-1935	645	228	216	.514
King, Charles F., Seven Clubs....................	10, 1886-1897	359	206	153	.574
Lemon, Robert G., Cleveland AL.................	13, 1946-1958	460	207	128	.618
Lyons, Theo. A., Chicago AL....................	21, 1923-1946	594	260	230	.531
Marquard, R. W., N. Y.-Bkl.-Cinn.-Bos. NL........	18, 1908-1925	537	201	177	.532
Mays, Carl W., Bos.-N.Y. AL; Cinn.-N.Y. NL.......	15, 1915-1929	490	203	128	.613
McCormick, James, Ind.-Cleve.-Prov.-Chic.-Pitts. NL; Cin. UA..................................	10, 1878-1887	483	264	217	.549
McGinnity, Joseph J., 3-NL, 1-AL	10, 1899-1908	467	247	142	.633
Mullane, Anthony J., Eight Clubs NL—AA...........	14, 1881-1894	564	282	221	.561
Mullin, George, Det.-Wash. AL; Ind. FL	14, 1902-1915	492	228	193	.542
Newhouser, Harold, Detroit, Cleveland AL	16, 1939-1954	486	207	150	.580
Newsom, Louis N., 3 NL—6 AL	20, 1929-1953	600	211	222	.48
Pennock, Herbert J., Phil.-Bos.-N.Y. AL	22, 1912-1934	617	241	163	.597
Pierce, W. William, Det.-Chi. AL; S.F. NL.........	18, 1945-1964	585	211	169	.555
Powell, John, Cleve.-St. L. NL; St. L.-N.Y. AL......	17, 1897-1913	551	248	258	.490
Quinn, John P., 4-AL, 3-NL, 1-FL................	23, 1909-1933	753	247	216	.533
Rixey, Eppa, Phil.-Cinn. NL....................	21, 1912-1933	692	266	251	.515
Roberts, Robin E., Phil.-Hou. NL; Balt. AL........	18, 1948-1965	652	281	237	.542
Root, Charles H., St. L. AL; Chicago NL	17, 1923-1941	632	201	160	.556
Ruffing, Charles H., Bos.-New York-Chic. AL.......	22, 1924-1947	624	273	225	.548
Rusie, Amos, Ind.-N.Y.-Cin. NL	10, 1889-1901	457	251	173	.592
Stivetts, John, St. L.-Bos.-Cleve NL.............	11, 1889-1899	358	209	122	.631
Terry, William J., Bkn. AA, Bkn.-Balt.-Pitts.-Chi. NL	14, 1884-1897	467	204	196	.510
Uhle, George, Cleve.-Det.-N.Y. AL; N.Y. NL.......	17, 1919-1936	513	200	166	.546
Weyhing, August P., Ten Clubs AA, PL, NL, AL........	14, 1887-1901	523	265	236	.529
White, Wm. H., Bos.-Cinn., Det. NL; Cinn. AA......	10, 1877-1886	407	228	166	.579
Whitehill, Earl O., Det.-Wash.-Cleve.-Chi; Chi. NL......	17, 1923-1939	540	218	186	.540
Willis, Victor, Bos.-Pitts.-St. L. NL.................	13, 1898-1910	500	244	207	.541

Leading Pitchers in Major Leagues
WON AND LOST PERCENTAGE, 1876-1899
(20 or more decisions)
NATIONAL LEAGUE

Year	Name and Club	W.	L.	PC.	Year	Name and Club	W.	L.	PC.
1876	Albert G. Spalding, Chi...	47	13	.783	1888	Timothy J. Keefe, N.Y...	35	12	.745
1877	Thomas H. Bond, Boston	40	17	.702	1889	John G. Clarkson, Boston	49	19	.721
1878	Thomas H. Bond, Boston	40	19	.678	1890	Thomas J. Lovett, Bklyn..	31	11	.738
1879	John M. Ward, Prov. ...	46	19	.708	1891	John Ewing, N.Y.........	21	8	.724
1880	Fred. E. Goldsmith, Chi.	21	3	.875	1892	Denton T. Young, Clev...	36	10	.783
1881	Lawrence J. Corcoran, Chi.	31	14	.689	1893	August P. Wehing, Phila.	24	9	.727
1882	Lawrence J. Corcoran, Chi.	27	13	.675	1894	Jouett L. Meekin, N.Y....	36	10	.783
1883	James McCormick, Clev...	27	13	.675	1895	William L. Hoffer, Balt...	29	8	.784
1884	Chas. G. Radbourne, Prov.	60	12	.833	1896	William L. Hoffer, Balt.	26	7	.788
1885	Michael F. Welch, N.Y...	44	11	.800	1897	Jeremiah Nops, Balt......	19	5	.792
1886	John A. Flynn, Chi......	23	6	.793	1898	Edward M. Lewis, Boston	25	8	.758
1887	Charles J. Ferguson, Phila.	24	10	.683	1899	James J. Hughes, Bklyn...	26	6	.813

HIGHEST WON AND LOST PERCENTAGE 1900- to Date
(15 or more decisions)

Year	NATIONAL LEAGUE — Name and Club	W.	L.	PC.	AMERICAN LEAGUE — Name and Club	W.	L.	PC.
1900	Joseph J. McGinnity, Bklyn.	29	9	.763	Not Organized			
1901	Samuel L. Leever, Pitts...	14	5	.737	Clark C. Griffith, Chi.........	24	7	.774
1902	John D. Chesbro, Pitts....	28	6	.824	William Bernhard, Cleve.......	18	5	.783
1903	Samuel L. Leever, Pitts...	25	7	.781	Earl L. Moore, Cleve.........	22	7	.759
1904	Joseph J. McGinnity, N.Y.	35	8	.814	John D. Chesbro, N.Y........	41	12	.774
1905	Samuel L. Leever, Pitts...	20	5	.800	George E. Waddell, Phila....	27	10	.730
1906	Edward M. Reulbach, Chi.	19	4	.826	Edward S. Plank, Phila......	19	6	.760
1907	Edward M. Reulbach, Chi.	17	4	.810	William E. Donovan, Detroit.	25	4	.862
1908	Edward M. Reulbach, Chi.	24	7	.774	Edward A. Walsh, Chicago.....	40	15	.727
1909	S. Howard Camnitz, Pitts.	25	6	.806	George J. Mullin, Detroit......	29	8	.784
	Chris. Mathewson, N.Y...	25	6	.806				
1910	Chas. L. Phillippe, Pitts...	14	2	.875	Charles A. Bender, Phila.....	23	5	.821
1911	Rich. W. Marquard, N.Y...	24	7	.774	Charles A. Bender, Phila.....	17	5	.773
1912	Claude R. Hendrix, Pitts...	24	9	.727	Joseph Wood, Bos...........	34	5	.872
1913	Albert Humphries, Chi....	16	4	.800	Walter P. Johnson, Wash.....	36	7	.837
1914	William L. James, Boston	26	7	.788	Charles A. Bender, Phila.....	17	3	.850
1915	Grover C. Alexander, Phila.	31	10	.756	Joseph Wood, Boston........	14	5	.737
1916	Thomas Hughes, Bos......	16	3	.842	H. Coveleskie, Detroit........	23	10	.697
1917	Ferd. N. Schupp, NY....	21	7	.750	Edward L. Klepfer, Cleve.....	13	4	.765
1918	Claude R. Hendrix, Chi....	20	7	.741	Sam P. Jones, Bos...........	16	5	.762
1919	Walter J. Reuther, Cinn...	19	6	.760	E. V. Cicotte, Chi...........	29	7	.805
1920	Burleigh A. Grimes, Bklyn.	23	11	.676	James C. Bagby, Cleve.......	31	12	.721
1921	Charles B. Adams, Pitts..	14	5	.737	Carl W. Mays, N.Y...........	27	9	.750
	Chas. F. Glazner, Pitts...	14	5	.737				
1922	Philip B. Douglas, NY....	11	4	.733	Leslie J. Bush, N.Y..........	26	7	.788
1923	Adolfo Luque, Cinn.......	27	8	.771	Herbert J. Pennock, N.Y......	19	6	.760
1924	Emil Yde, Pitts.........	16	3	.842	Walter P. Johnson, Wash.....	23	7	.767
1925	Wm. H. Sherdel, St. L....	15	6	.714	S. Coveleskie, Wash..........	20	5	.800
1926	Ray Kremer, Pitts.......	20	6	.769	George E. Uhle, Cleve........	27	11	.711
1927	Lawrence J. Benton, NY...	17	7	.708	Waite C. Hoyt, N.Y..........	22	7	.759
1928	Lawrence J. Benton, NY...	25	9	.735	A. F. Crowder, St. L.........	21	5	.808
1929	Charles H. Root, Chi.....	19	6	.760	Robert M. Grove, Phila.......	20	6	.769
1930	Fred Fitzsimmons, NY....	19	7	.731	Robert M. Grove, Phila.......	28	5	.848
1931	Jesse L. Haines, St. L.....	12	3	.800	Robert M. Grove, Phila.......	31	4	.886
1932	Lonnie Warneke, Chi.....	22	6	.786	John T. Allen, N.Y..........	17	4	.810
1933	Lyle Tinning, Chi........	13	6	.684	Robert M. Grove, Phila.......	24	8	.750
1934	Jerome H. Dean, St. L....	30	7	.811	Vernon Gomez, N.Y..........	26	5	.839
1935	William C. Lee, Chi......	20	6	.769	Eldon L. Auker, Detroit......	18	7	.720
1936	Carl O. Hubbell, NY.....	26	6	.813	Irving D. Hadley, N.Y........	14	4	.778
1937	Carl O. Hubbell, NY.....	22	8	.733	John T. Allen, Cleve.........	15	1	.938
1938	William C. Lee, Chi......	22	9	.710	Robert M. Grove, Bos........	14	4	.778
1939	Paul Derringer, Cinn.....	25	7	.781	R. Atley Donald, N.Y........	13	3	.813
1940	Fred L. Fitzsimmons, Bkn.	16	2	.889	Lynwood T. Rowe, Detroit.	16	3	.842
1941	Elmer R. Riddle, Cinn....	19	4	.826	Vernon Gomez, N.Y..........	15	5	.750
1942	Howard W. Krist, St. L....	13	3	.813	Ernest E. Bonham, N.Y.......	21	5	.808
1943	Clyde M. Shoun, Cinn.....	14	5	.737	Spurgeon F. Chandler, N.Y.....	20	4	.833
	J. Whitlow Wyatt, Bkn...	14	5	.737				
1944	Theodore Wilks, St. L....	17	4	.810	Cecil C. Hughson, Bos........	18	5	.783
1945	Harry D. Brecheen, St. L..	15	4	.789	Robert C. Muncrief, St. L.....	13	4	.765
1946	Lynwood T. Rowe, Phila...	11	4	.733	David M. Ferriss, Bos........	25	6	.806
1947	Lawrence Jansen, NY....	21	5	.808	Frank J. Shea, N.Y..........	14	5	.737
1948	Truett B. Sewell, Pitts....	13	3	.813	John H. Kramer, Bos.........	18	5	.783
1949	Ralph T. Branca, Bkn.....	13	5	.722	Ellis R. Kinder, Bos.........	23	6	.793
1950	Salvatore A. Maglie, N.Y..	18	4	.818	Victor J. Raschi, N.Y.........	21	8	.724
1951	Elwin C. Roe, Bkn.	22	3	.880	Robert W. A. Feller, Cleve....	22	8	.733
					Morris W. Martin, Phil.......	11	4	.733
1952	J. Hoyt Wilhelm, N.Y.....	15	3	.833	Robert C. Shantz, Phil........	24	7	.774
1953	Carl D. Erskine, Bkn.....	20	6	.769	Edmund W. Lopat, N.Y.......	16	4	.800
1954	John A. Antonelli, N.Y. ...	21	7	.750	Sandalio S. Consuegra, Chi. ...	16	3	.842
	J. Hoyt Wilhelm, N.Y. ...	12	4	.750				
1955	Donald Newcombe, Bkn. ...	20	5	.800	Thomas J. Byrne, N. Y.........	16	5	.762

HIGHEST WON AND LOST PERCENTAGE
1900- to Date—(continued)
(15 or more decisions)

NATIONAL LEAGUE Name and Club	W.	L.	PC.	AMERICAN LEAGUE Name and Club	W.	L.	PC.
1956 Donald Newcombe, Bkn...	27	7	.794	Edward C. Ford, N. Y.........	19	6	.760
1957 Robert R. Buhl, Mil......	18	7	.720	{ Richard E. Donovan, Chi......	16	6	.727
				{ Thomas V. Sturdivant, N.Y....	16	6	.727
1958 { Warren E. Spahn, Mil....	22	11	.667	Robert L. Turley, N.Y.	21	7	.750
{ S. Lewis Burdette, Mil....	20	10	.667				
1959 El Roy L. Face, Pitts....	18	1	.947	Robert J. Shaw, Chi..........	18	6	.750
1960 Lyndall D. McDaniel, St.L.	12	4	.750	James A. Coates, N.Y.........	13	3	.813
1961 John J. Podres, L.A.	18	5	.783	Edward C. Ford, N.Y.........	25	4	.862
1962 Robert T. Purkey, Cin. ...	23	5	.821	Raymond E. Herbert, Chi.	20	9	.690
1963 Ronald P. Perranoski, L.A..	16	3	.842	Edward C. Ford, N.Y.........	24	7	.774
1964 Sanford Koufax, L.A.	19	5	.792	Wallace E. Bunker, Balt.	19	5	.792
1965 Sanford Koufax, L.A.	26	8	.765	James T. Grant, Minn.	21	7	.750

LOWEST EARNED RUN AVERAGE (1912 to Date)

	NATIONAL LEAGUE	Inn. Pit.	E.R. Ave.	AMERICAN LEAGUE	Inn. Pit.	E.R Ave.
1912	C. Tesreau, N.Y..........	243	1.96	Not tabulated		
1913	C. Mathewson, N.Y........	306	2.06	W. P. Johnson, Wash........	346	1.09
1914	W. L. Doak, St. L........	256	1.72	H. B. Leonard, Boston.......	222	1.01
1915	G. C. Alexander, Phila....	376	1.22	J. Wood, Boston	157	1.49
1916	G. C. Alexander, Phila.....	389	1.55	G. H. Ruth, Boston	324	1.75
1917	G. C. Alexander, Phila.....	388	1.85	E. V. Cicotte, Chicago	346	1.53
1918	J. L. Vaughn, Chi.........	290	1.74	W. P. Johnson, Wash........	325	1.28
1919	G. C. Alexander, Chi......	235	1.72	W. P. Johnson, Wash........	290	1.49
1920	G. C. Alexander, Chi......	363	1.91	J. R. Shawkey, N.Y.........	267	2.46
1921	W. L. Doak, St. L.........	209	2.58	U. C. Faber, Chicago........	331	2.48
1922	W. D. Ryan, N.Y...........	192	3.00	U. C. Faber, Chicago........	353	2.81
1923	A. Luque, Cinn...........	322	1.93	S. Coveleskie, Cleve.......	228	2.76
1924	A. C. Vance, Bklyn........	309	2.16	W. P. Johnson, Wash........	278	2.72
1925	A. Luque, Cinn...........	291	2.63	S. Coveleskie, Wash........	241	2.84
1926	Ray Kremer, Pitts........	231	2.61	R. M. Grove, Phila.........	258	2.51
1927	Ray Kremer, Pitts........	226	2.47	W. Wilcy Moore, N.Y........	213	2.28
1928	A. C. Vance, Bklyn........	280	2.09	E. G. Braxton, Wash........	218	2.52
1929	Wm. Walker, N.Y..........	178	3.08	R. M. Grove, Phila.........	275	2.82
1930	A. C. Vance, Bklyn........	259	2.61	R. M. Grove, Phila.........	291	2.54
1931	Wm. Walker, N.Y..........	239	2.26	R. M. Grove, Phila.........	289	2.05
1932	L. Warneke, Chicago......	277	2.37	R. M. Grove, Phila.........	292	2.84
1933	C. O. Hubbell, N.Y........	309	1.66	M. M. Pearson, Cleveland	135	2.33
1934	C. O. Hubbell, N.Y........	313	2.30	V. Gomez, N.Y.............	282	2.33
1935	D. E. Blanton, Pitts.......	254	2.59	R. M. Grove, Bos...........	273	2.70
1936	C. O. Hubbell, N.Y........	303	2.31	R. M. Grove, Bos...........	253	2.81
1937	J. R. Turner, Bos.........	257	2.38	V. Gomez, N.Y.............	278	2.33
1938	W. C. Lee, Chicago.......	291	2.66	R. M. Grove, Bos...........	164	3.07
1939	W. H. Walters, Cinn.......	319	2.29	R. M. Grove, Bos...........	191	2.54
1940	W. H. Walters, Cinn.......	305	2.48	R. W. Feller, Cleve.........	320	2.62
1941	E. R. Riddle, Cinn........	217	2.24	T. S. Lee, Chicago.........	300	2.37
1942	M. C. Cooper, St. L.......	279	1.77	T. A. Lyons, Chicago.......	180	2.10
1943	H. J. Pollet, St. L........	118	1.75	S. F. Chandler, N.Y........	253	1.64
1944	E. B. Heusser, Cinn.......	193	2.38	P. H. Trout, Detroit	352	2.12
1945	H. L. Borowy, Chicago....	122	2.14	H. Newhouser, Detroit	313	1.81
1946	H. J. Pollet, St. L........	266	2.10	H. Newhouser, Detroit	293	1.94
1947	W. E. Spahn, Boston......	290	2.33	S. F. Chandler, N.Y........	128	2.46
1948	H. D. Brecheen, St. L......	233	2.24	H. E. Bearden, Cleve.......	230	2.43
1949	G. B. Koslo, N.Y..........	212	2.50	M. L. Parnell, Boston.......	295	2.78
1950	J. T. Hearn, St. L., N.Y....	134	2.49	E. Wynn, Cleveland	214	3.20
1951	C. Nichols, Bos.	156	2.88	S. Rogovin, Det.-Chi........	217	2.78
1952	J. H. Wilhelm, N.Y.	159	2.43	A. P. Reynolds, N.Y........	244	2.07
1953	W. E. Spahn, Milw.	266	2.10	E. W. Lopat, N.Y..........	178	2.43
1954	J. A. Antonelli, N.Y........	259	2.29	E. M. Garcia, Cleve........	259	2.64
1955	R. B. Friend, Pitts........	200	2.84	W. W Pierce, Chicago.......	206	1.97
1956	S. L. Burdette, Milw.......	256	2.71	E. C. Ford, N.Y............	226	2.47
1957	J. J. Podres, Bklyn........	196	2.66	R. C. Shantz, N.Y..........	173	2.45
1958	S. L. Miller, S.F.	182	2.47	E. C. Ford, N.Y............	219	2.01
1959	S. Jones, S.F..............	271	2.82	J. H. Wilhelm, Balt.........	226	2.19
1960	M. F. McCormick, S.F.	253	2.70	F. M. Baumann, Chi.........	185	2.68
1961	W. E. Spahn, Mil..........	263	3.01	R. E. Donovan, Wash........	169	2.40
1962	S. Koufax, L.A............	184	2.54	H. J. Aguirre, Det..........	216	2.21
1963	S. Koufax, L.A............	311	1.88	G. C. Peters, Chi	243	2.33
1964	S. Koufax, L.A............	223	1.74	W. D. Chance, L.A.........	278	1.65
1965	S. Koufax, L.A............	336	2.04	S. E. McDowell, Clev........	273	2.18

NOTE: Qualifiers 1912-1951 required 10 complete games; since 1952 must pitch one inning for each of team's scheduled games.

CONSECUTIVE GAMES WON—SEASON

19—Keefe, T. J., New York NL 1888
   Marquard, R. W., New York NL 1912
18—Radbourne, C., Providence NL 1884
17—Welch, M., New York NL 1883
   Luby, J. P., Chicago NL 1890
   Face, E. L., Pittsburgh NL 1959
16—McCormick, J., Chicago NL 1886
   Wood, Joseph, Boston AL 1912
   Johnson, W., Washington AL 1912
   Grove, R. M., Philadelphia AL 1931
   Rowe, L. T., Detroit.........................1934
   Hubbell, Carl O., New York NL 1936
   Blackwell, Ewell, Cincinnati NL 1947
   Sanford, John S., San Francisco NL 1962
15—Stratton, W. S., Louisville AA 1890
   Vance, A. C., Brooklyn NL 1924
   Crowder, A. F., Washington AL 1932
   Allen, John, Cleveland AL 1937
14—Flynn, John, Chicago NL 1886
   McGinnity, J. J., N. Y. NL (in addition to 2 ties) .1904
   McCormick, J., Cincinnati UA 1884
   Chesbro, J., New York AL 1909
   Reulbach, E., Chicago NL 1909
   Johnson, W., Washington AL 1913
   Bender, C. A., Philadelphia AL 1914
   Grove, R. M., Philadelphia AL 1928
   Ford, Edward C., New York AL 1961
13—Corcoran, Lawrence, Chicago NL 1880
   Buffington, Charles, Boston NL 1884
   Young, Denton T., Cleveland NL 1892
   Dwyer, Frank, Cincinnati NL 1896
   Mathewson, C., New York NL 1909
   Phillippe, C. A., Pittsburgh NL 1910
   Johnson, W., Washington AL 1924
   Coveleskie, S., Washington AL 1925
   Grimes, B. A., New York NL 1927
   Ferrell, Wesley C., Cleveland AL 1930
   Newsom, L. N., Detroit AL 1940
   Kinder, Ellis R., Boston AL 1949
   Lawrence, Brooks, Cincinnati NL 1956
12—White, William, Cincinnati AA 1882
   Clarkson, John, Chicago NL 1885
   Ferguson, Charles, Philadelphia NL 1886
   Young, Denton T., Boston AL 1901
   Chesbro, John D., Pittsburgh NL 1902
   Wiltse, G. L., New York NL 1904
   Reulbach, E. M., Chicago NL 1906

Ford, Russell, New York AL 1910
Rudolph, R. T., Boston NL 1914
Zachary, J. T., New York AL 1929
Earnshaw, George, Philadelphia AL 1931
Allen, John, Cleveland AL 1938
Donald, R. Atley, New York AL 1939
Ferriss, David M., Boston AL 1946
Ford, Edward C., New York AL 1963

CONSECUTIVE GAMES LOST—SEASON

19—Nabors, John, Philadelphia AL 1916
18—Curtis, Clifton C., Boston NL 1910
   Craig, Roger L., New York NL 1963
16—Sheehan, Thos., Philadelphia AL 1916
   Hughey, James, Cleveland NL 1899
   Dean, Henry, Cincinnati NL 1876
   Anderson, N. Craig, New York NL 1962
14—Gilmore, Frank, Washington NL 1887
   Bates, Frank C., Cleveland NL 1899
   Pastorius, J. W., Brooklyn NL 1908
   Brown, Chas. E., Boston NL 1910
   Judson, Howard K., Chicago AL 1949
   Calvert, Paul L. E., Washington AL 1949
13—Moffet, Samuel R., Cleveland NL 1884
   Morton, Guy, Cleveland AL 1914
   Grimes, B. A., Pittsburgh NL 1917
   Oeschger, J., Boston NL 1922
   Henry, F., Chicago AL 1930
   Cantwell, B. C., Boston NL 1935
   Harris, Luman, Philadelphia AL 1943
   McCall, Robert L., Chicago NL 1948
12—Purcell, William, Cincinnati NL 1880
   Nichols, Frederick, Baltimore AA 1882
   Coleman, John, Philadelphia NL 1883
   Crowell, William, Cleveland AA 1888
   Thielman, Henry, Cincinnati NL 1902
   Eason, Malcolm W., Brooklyn NL 1905
   Schneider, P. J., Cincinnati NL 1914
   Marquard, R., New York NL 1914
   Miller, R. L., Philadelphia NL 1928
   Ruffing, Charles H., Boston AL 1929
   Johnson, Silas K., Cincinnati NL 1933
   Butcher, A. Maxwell, Phil.-Pitt. NL 1939
   Mulcahy, H. N., Philadelphia NL 1940
   Masterson, Walter, Washington AL 1940
   Newsom, Louis N., Philadelphia AL 1945
   Gerkin, Stephen P., Philadelphia AL 1945
   Bishop, Charles T., Philadelphia AL 1953
   Miller, Robert L., New York NL 1962

NO HIT GAMES

MOST NO-HIT GAMES LIFETIME

4—Sanford Koufax, Los Angeles NL, 1962-63-64-65.
3—Lawrence J. Corcoran, Chicago NL, 1880-82-84.
   Denton T. Young, Boston NL-AL, 1897; 1904-08.
   Robert W. A. Feller, Cleveland AL, 1940-46-51.

SPECIAL MENTION

1959—Harvey Haddix, Jr., Pittsburgh vs Milwaukee NL, May 26
   (Pitched 12 "perfect" innings. Allowed hit in 13th and lost).

NO-HIT GAMES—10 OR MORE INNINGS

	Score
Edward J. Kimber, Brk. AA vs Toledo, Oct. 4, 1884 (10 inns. Called, darkness)	0—0
Harry M. McIntire, Brk. NL vs Pitt., Aug. 1, 1906 (10 2/3 inns. Lost in 13 inns, allowed 4 hits)	0—1
George L. Wiltse, N.Y. NL vs Phil, July 4, 1908 (10 inns.)	1—0
Frederick A. Toney, Cin. NL vs Chi., May 2, 1917 (10 inns.)	1—0
James W. Maloney, Cin. NL vs N.Y., June 14, 1965 (10 inns. Allowed 2 hits in 11th, lost)	0—1
James W. Maloney, Cin. NL vs Chi., Aug. 19, 1965 (10 inns.)	1—0

PERFECT GAME—9 INNINGS

Year	Name, Club and Date	Score
1880—	John Lee Richmond, Worcester vs Cleve. NL, June 12..	1—0
	John M. Ward, Providence vs Buffalo NL, June 17 AM..	5—0
1904—	Denton T. Young, Boston vs Philadelphia AL, May 5..	3—0
1908—	Adrian C. Joss, Cleveland vs Chicago AL, Oct. 2..	1—0
1917—	Ernest C. Shore, Bos. vs Wash. AL, June 23 (1st g.)..	*4—0
1922—	C. C. Robertson, Chicago vs Detroit AL, April 30..	2—0
†1956—	Donald J. Larsen, N.Y. AL vs Bkn. NL, Oct. 8..	2—0
1964—	James P. Bunning, Phil. NL vs N.Y., June 21 (1st g.)	6—0
1965—	Sanford Koufax, L.A. NL vs Chi., Sept. 9 ..	1—0

*Starting pitcher, "Babe" Ruth, was banished from game by umpire Owens after giving first batter, Morgan, a base on balls. Shore relieved and, while pitching to second batter, Morgan was caught stealing. Shore then retired next 26 batters to complete "perfect" game.
†World Series game.

PITCHER WINNING 2 COMPLETE GAMES IN ONE DAY

Alexander, Grover C., Philadelphia NL, Sept. 23, 1916.
Alexander, Grover C., Philadelphia NL, Sept. 3, 1917.
Baldwin, Mark, Pittsburgh NL, Sept. 12, 1891.
Baldwin, Mark, Pittsburgh NL, May 30, 1892.
Bell, Herman S., St. Louis NL, July 19, 1924.
Clarkson, John G., Boston NL, Sept. 12, 1889.
Collins, Ray W., Boston AL, Sept. 22, 1914.
Crane, Edward, New York PL, Sept. 27, 1890.
Cunningham, Elmore, Buffalo PL, Aug. 20, 1890.
Cummings, W. A., Hartford NL, Sept. 9, 1876.
Davenport, Arthur D., St. Louis AL, July 29, 1916.
Demaree, Albert W., Philadelphia NL, Sept. 20, 1916.
Doak, William L., St. Louis NL, Sept. 18, 1917.
Ferguson, Charles, Philadelphia NL, Oct. 9, 1886.
Galvin, James, Buffalo NL, July 12, 1879.
Galvin, James, Buffalo NL, July 4, 1882.
Gruber, Henry, Cleveland PL, July 26, 1890.
Hecker, Guy J., Louisville AA, July 4, 1884.
Hutchinson, William F., Chicago NL, May 30, 1890.
Keefe, Timothy J., Mets AA (NY), vs Columbus, July 4, 1883.
Levsen, Emil H., Cleveland AL, Aug. 28, 1926.
McGinnity, Joseph J., New York NL, Aug. 1, 1903
McGinnity, Joseph J., New York NL, Aug. 8, 1903.
McGinnity, Joseph J., New York NL, Aug. 31, 1903.
Mays, Carl W., Boston AL, Aug. 30, 1918.
Mullane, Anthony J., Cincinnati AA, Sept. 20, 1888.
Mullin, George J., Detroit AL, Sept. 22, 1906.
Owen, Frank M., Chicago AL, July 1, 1905.
Perritt, William D., New York NL, Sept. 9, 1916.
Radbourne, Charles, Providence NL, May 30, 1884.
Reulbach, Edward M., Chicago NL, Sept. 26, 1908.
Rusie, Amos, New York NL, Sept. 26, 1891.
Seymour, J. Bentley, New York NL, June 3, 1897.
Scanlon, William D., Brooklyn NL, Oct. 3, 1905.
Shocker, Urban J., St. Louis AL, Sept. 6, 1924.
Stuart, John D., St. Louis NL, July 10, 1923.
Summers, Oren E., Detroit AL, Sept. 25, 1908.
Toney, Fred, Cincinnati NL, July 1, 1917.
Walsh, Edward A., Chicago AL, Sept. 29, 1905.
Ward, John, Providence NL, Aug. 8, 1878.
Watson, John R., Boston NL, Aug. 13, 1921.
Whitney, Michael, Troy NL, July 4, 1881.
Whitney, James E., Washington NL, Aug. 20, 1887.
Young, Denton T., Cleveland NL, Oct. 4, 1890.

1875—Joseph E. Borden, Philadelphia vs Chicago NA, July 28.............. 4–0
1876—George Washington Bradley, St. Louis vs Hartford NL, July 15........ 2–0
1880—John Lee Richmond, Worcester vs Cleveland NL, June 12.............. 1–0
John M. Ward, Providence vs Buffalo NL, June 17, AM.............. 5–0
Lawrence J. Corcoran, Chicago vs Boston NL, August·19.............. 6–0
James F. Galvin, Buffalo vs Worcester NL, August 20.............. 1–0
1882—Anthony J. Mullane, Louisville vs Cincinnati AA, Sept. 11............ 2–0
Guy J. Hecker, Louisville vs Pittsburgh AA, Sept. 19.................. 3–1
Lawrence J. Corcoran, Chicago vs Worcester NL, Sept. 20............ 5–0
1883—Charles Radbourne, Providence vs Cleveland NL, July 25............ 8–0
Hugh Dailey, Cleveland vs Philadelphia NL, Sept. 13................. 1–0
1884—Lawrence J. Corcoran, Chicago vs Providence NL, June 27............ 6–0
James F. Galvin, Buffalo vs Detroit NL, August 4.................... 18–0
Albert W. Atkisson, Philadelphia vs Pittsburgh AA, May 24.......... 10–1
Edward Morris, Columbus vs Pittsburgh AA, May 29................. 5–0
Frank T. Mountain, Columbus vs Washington AA, June 5............. 12–0
Richard L. Burns, Cincinnati vs Kansas City UA, August 26.......... 3–1
Edward L. Cushman, Milwaukee vs Washington UA, Sept. 28......... 5–0
1885—John G. Clarkson, Chicago vs Providence NL, July 27.............. 4–0
Charles J. Ferguson, Philadelphia vs Providence NL, August 29...... 1–0
1886—William H. Terry, Brooklyn vs St. Louis AA, July 24.............. 1–0
Albert W. Atkisson, Philadelphia vs New York AA, May 1............ 3–2
Matthew Kilroy, Baltimore vs Pittsburgh AA, October 6............. 6–0
1888—William H. Terry, Brooklyn vs Louisville AA, May 27............. 4–0
Henry Porter, Kansas City vs Baltimore AA, June 6............... 4–0
Edward W. Seward, Philadelphia vs Cincinnati AA, July 26......... 12–2
August P. Weyhing, Philadelphia vs. Kansas City AA, July 31........ 4–0
1890—Ledell H. Titcomb, Rochester vs Syracuse AA, Sept. 15.............. 7–0
1891—Thomas J. Lovett, Brooklyn vs New York NL, June 22.............. 4–0
Amos W. Rusie, New York vs Brooklyn NL, July 31.................. 6–0
•Theodore Breitenstein, St. Louis vs Louisville AA, Oct. 4 (1st game).... 8–0
1892—John E. Stivetts, Boston vs Brooklyn NL, August 6................ 11–0
Alex. B. Sanders, Louisville vs Baltimore NL, August 22............ 6–2
•Chas. L. Jones, Cincinnati vs Pittsburgh NL, Oct. 15 (1st game in NL).. 7–1
1893—William V. Hawke, Baltimore vs Washington NL, August 16......... 5–0
1897—Denton T. Young, Cleveland vs Cincinnati NL, Sept. 18.............. 6–0
1898—Theodore Breitenstein, Cincinnati vs Pittsburgh NL, April 22........ 11–0
James Hughes, Baltimore vs Boston NL, April 22.................... 8–0
Frank L. Donohue, Philadelphia vs Boston NL, July 8............... 5–0
Walter M. Thornton, Chicago vs Brooklyn NL, August 21............ 2–0
1899—Charles F. Phillippe, Louisville vs New York NL, May 25........... 7–0
Victor G. Willis, Boston vs Washington NL, August 7............... 7–1
1900—Frank Hahn, Cincinnati vs Philadelphia NL, July 12............... 4–0
1901—Christopher Mathewson, New York vs St. Louis NL, July 15......... 5–0
Earl L. Moore, Cleveland vs Chicago AL, May 9. Moore pitched nine
innings against Chicago, the latter not making a hit in that time,
but Cleveland lost the game in the tenth inning................... 2–4
1902—James J. Callahan, Chicago vs Detroit AL, Sept. 20 (1st game)........ 3–0
1903—Charles Fraser, Philadelphia vs Chicago NL, Sept. 18.............. 10–0
1904—Denton T. Young, Boston vs Philadelphia AL, May 5.............. 3–0
Jesse N. Tannehill, Boston vs Chicago AL, August 17............... 6–0
Robert K. Wicker. Chicago vs New York NL, June 11, 12 innings; Mertes,
NY, made a single in the tenth inning......................... 1–0
1905—Christopher Mathewson, New York vs Chicago NL, June 13.......... 1–0
Weldon Henley, Philadelphia vs St. Louis AL, July 22 (1st game)..... 6–0
William H. Dinneen, Boston vs Chicago AL, Sept. 27 (1st game)...... 2–0
Frank E. Smith, Chicago vs Detroit AL, Sept. 6 (2d game).......... 15–0
1906—John C. Lush, Philadelphia vs Brooklyn NL, May 1................ 1–0
Malcolm W. Eason, Brooklyn vs St. Louis NL, July 20.............. 2–0
1907—Frank X. Pfeffer, Boston vs Cincinnati NL, May 8................ 6–0
Nicholas Maddox, Pittsburgh vs Brooklyn NL, Sept. 20............. 2–1
1908—Denton T. Young, Boston vs New York AL, June 30................ 8–0
George N. Rucker, Brooklyn vs Boston NL, Sept. 5 (2d game)........ 6–0
Robert S. Rhoades, Cleveland vs Boston AL, Sept. 18............... 2–1
Frank E. Smith, Chicago vs Philadelphia AL, Sept. 20.............. 1–0
Adrian C. Joss, Cleveland vs Chicago AL, October 2............... 1–0

• First major league start.

1909—Leon K. Ames, New York vs Brooklyn NL, April 15. Ames pitched nine innings against Brooklyn, the latter not making a hit in that time, but New York lost the game in the thirteenth inning .... 0—3
1910—Adrian C. Joss, Cleveland vs Chicago AL, April 20 .... 1—0
    Charles A. Bender, Philadelphia vs Cleveland AL, May 12 .... 4—0
    Thomas J. Hughes, New York vs Cleveland AL, August 30. Hughes pitched nine innings. Cleveland not making a hit in that time. Cleveland made its first hit in the tenth inning and won the game in the eleventh .... 0—5
1911—Joseph Wood, Boston vs St. Louis AL, July 29 (1st game) .... 5—0
    Edward A. Walsh, Chicago vs Boston AL, August 27 .... 5—0
1912—George E. Mullin, Detroit vs St. Louis AL, July 4, (P.M.) .... 7—0
    Earl Hamilton, St. Louis vs Detroit AL, August 30 .... 5—1
    Charles M. Tesreau, New York vs Philadelphia NL, Sept. 6 (1st game).. 3—0
1914—James Scott, Chicago vs Washington AL, May 14. Washington scored in the tenth inning .... 0—1
    Joseph D. Benz, Chicago vs Cleveland AL, May 31 .... 6—1
    George A. Davis, Boston vs Philadelphia NL, Sept. 9 (2d game) ...... 7—0
    Edward F. LaFitte, Brooklyn vs Kansas City, FL, Sept. 19 (1st game).. 6—2
1915—Richard W. Marquard, New York vs Brooklyn NL, April 15 .... 2—0
    James S. Lavender, Chicago vs New York NL, August 31 (1st game).... 2—0
    Claude R. Hendrix, Chicago vs Pittsburgh FL, May 15 .... 10—0
    Frank L. Allen, Pittsburgh vs St. Louis FL, April 24 .... 2—0
    Miles G. Main, Kansas City vs Buffalo FL, August 16 .... 5—0
    Arthur D. Davenport, St. Louis vs Chicago FL, Sept. 7 (1st game)..... 3—0
1916—Thomas J. Hughes, Boston vs Pittsburgh NL, June 16 .... 2—0
    George Fostor, Boston vs New York AL, June 21 .... 2—0
    Leslie A. Bush, Philadelphia vs Cleveland AL, August 26 .... 5—0
    Hubert B. Leonard, Boston vs St. Louis AL, August 30 .... 4—0
1917—Edward V. Cicotte, Chicago vs St. Louis AL, April 14 .... 11—0
    George Mogridge, New York vs Boston AL, April 24 .... 2—1
    James L. Vaughn, Chicago vs Cincinnati NL, May 2. (Toney, Cincinnati, pitched ten no-hit innings in the same game) .... 0—1
    Ernest Koob, St. Louis vs Chicago AL, May 5 .... 1—0
    Robert Groom, St. Louis vs Chicago AL, May 6 (2d game) .... 3—0
    Ernest G. Shore, Boston vs Washington AL, June 23 (1st game) .... 4—0
1918—Hubert B. Leonard, Boston vs Detroit AL, June 3 .... 5—0
1919—Horace O. Eller, Cincinnati vs St. Louis NL, May 11 .... 6—0
    Raymond Caldwell, Cleveland vs New York AL, Sept. 10 (1st game).... 3—0
1920—Walter P. Johnson, Washington vs Boston AL, July 1 .... 1—0
1922—Chas. C. Robertson, Chicago vs Detroit AL, April 30 .... 2—0
    Jesse Barnes, New York vs Philadelphia NL, May 7 .... 6—0
1923—Samuel Jones, New York vs Philadelphia AL, Sept. 4 .... 2—0
    Howard Ehmke, Boston vs Philadelphia AL, Sept. 7 .... 4—0
1924—Jesse J. Haines, St. Louis vs Boston NL, July 17 .... 5—0
1925—Arthur C. Vance, Brooklyn vs Philadelphia NL, Sept. 13 (1st game).... 10—1
1926—Theodore A. Lyons, Chicago vs Boston AL, August 21 .... 6—0
1929—Carl O. Hubbell, New York vs Pittsburgh NL, May 8 .... 11—0
1931—Wesley C. Ferrell, Cleveland vs St. Louis AL, April 29 .... 9—0
    Robert J. Burke, Washington vs Boston AL, August 8 .... 5—0
1934—Louis N. Newsom, St. Louis vs Boston AL, Sept. 18 .... 1—2
    (pitched nine hitless innings, allowed one hit in tenth).
    Paul Dean, St. Louis vs Brooklyn NL, Sept. 21 (2d game) .... 3—0
1935—Vernon Kennedy, Chicago vs Cleveland AL, August 31 .... 5—0
1937—William Dietrich, Chicago vs St. Louis AL, June 1 .... 8—0
1938—John Vander Meer, Cincinnati vs Boston NL, June 11 .... 3—0
    John Vander Meer, Cincinnati vs Brooklyn NL, June 15 (night) .... 6—0
    M. Monte Pearson, New York vs Cleveland AL, Aug. 27 (2d game) ...... 13—0

1940—Robert W. Feller, Cleveland vs Chicago AL, April 16 (Opening Day)... 1—0
    James O. Carleton, Brooklyn vs Cincinnati NL, April 30............ 3—0
1941—Lonnie Warneke, St. Louis vs Cincinnati NL, August 30 .... 2—0
1944—James A. Tobin, Boston vs Brooklyn NL, April 27 .... 2—0
    Clyde M. Shoun, Cincinnati vs Boston NL, May 15 .... 1—0
1945—Richard J. Fowler, Philadelphia vs St. Louis AL, Sept. 9 (2d game).... 1—0
1946—Edward M. Head, Brooklyn vs Boston NL, April 23................. 5—0
    Robert W. A. Feller, Cleveland vs New York AL, April 30.......... 1—0
1947—Ewell Blackwell, Cincinnati vs Boston NL, June 18 (night).......... 6—0
    Donald P. Black, Cleveland vs Philadelphia AL, July 10 (1st game)...... 3—0
    William McCahan, Philadelphia vs Washington AL, Sept. 3.......... 3—0
1948—Robert G. Lemon, Cleveland vs Detroit AL, June 30 (night) .... 2—0
    Rex E. Barney, Brooklyn vs New York NL, Sept. 9 (night)............ 2—0
1950—Vernon E. Bickford, Boston vs Brooklyn NL, August 11 (night)........ 7—0
1951—Clifford D. Chambers, Pittsburgh vs Boston NL, May 6 (2d game) ...... 3—0
    Robert W. A. Feller, Cleveland vs Detroit AL, July 1 (1st game) ...... 2—1
    Allie P. Reynolds, New York vs Cleveland AL, July 12 (night) .... 1—0
    Allie P. Reynolds, New York vs Boston AL, September 28 (1st game) ... 8—0
1952—Carl D. Erskine, Brooklyn vs Chicago NL, June 19 .... 5—0
    Virgil O. Trucks, Detroit vs Washington AL, May 15 .... 1—0
    Virgil O. Trucks, Detroit vs New York AL, Aug. 25 .... 1—0
1953—°Alva L. Holloman, St. Louis vs Philadelphia AL, May 6 (night) ...... 6—0
1954—James A. Wilson, Milwaukee vs Philadelphia NL, June 12............. 2—0
1955—Samuel Jones, Chicago vs Pittsburgh NL, May 12................... 4—0
1956—Carl D. Erskine, Brooklyn vs New York NL, May 12 .... 3—0
    Melvin L. Parnell, Boston vs Chicago AL, July 14 .... 4—0
    Salvatore A. Maglie, Brooklyn vs Philadelphia NL, Sept. 25 (night) .... 5—0
1957—Robert C. Keegan, Chicago vs Washington AL, Aug. 20 (night) .... 6—0
1958—James P. Bunning, Detroit vs Boston AL, July 20 .... 3—0
    J. Hoyt Wilhelm, Baltimore vs New York AL, Sept. 20 .... 1—0
1959—See Haddix game page 54.
1960—Donald E. Cardwell, Chicago vs St. Louis NL, May 15 .... 4—0
    Selva Lewis Burdette, Milwaukee vs Philadelphia NL, Aug. 18 (night) .. 1—0
    Warren E. Spahn, Milwaukee vs Philadelphia NL, Sept. 16 (night) ..... 4—0
1961—Warren E. Spahn, Milwaukee vs San Francisco NL, April 28 (night) .... 1—0
1962—Robert Belinsky, Los Angeles vs Baltimore AL, May 5 (night) .... 2—0
    Robert E. Wilson, Boston vs Los Angeles AL, June 26 (night) .... 2—0
    Sanford Koufax, Los Angeles vs New York NL, June 30 (night) .... 5—0
    William C. Monbouquette, Boston vs Chicago AL, Aug. 1 (night) ...... 1—0
    John F. Kralick, Minnesota vs Kansas City AL, Aug. 26 .... 1—0
1963—Sanford Koufax, Los Angeles vs San Francisco NL, May 11 (night) .... 8—0
    Donald E. Nottebart, Houston vs Philadelphia NL, May 17 (night) ..... 4—1
    Juan A. Marichal, San Francisco vs Houston NL, June 15 .... 1—0
1964—Kenneth T. Johnson, Houston vs Cincinnati NL, April 23 (night) (lost) .. 0—1
    Sanford Koufax, Los Angeles vs. Philadelphia NL, June 4 (night) ...... 3—0
    James P. Bunning, Philadelphia vs New York NL, June 21 (1st game) .. 6—0
1965—Sanford Koufax, Los Angeles vs Chicago NL, Sept. 9 (night) .... 1—0
    David M. Morehead, Boston vs Cleveland AL, Sept. 16 .... 2—0
    See Maloney games page 54.

٭ First major league start.

CLUB PITCHING RECORDS

A—Most complete games, season—
148–Boston AL, 1904
146–St. Louis NL, 1904.

B—Fewest complete games, season—
18–Kansas City AL, 1964-65.
27–Chicago NL, 1958.

C—Most runs, season—
1199–Philadelphia NL, 1930.
1064–St. Louis AL, 1936.

D—Fewest runs, season—
379–Chicago NL, 1906.
435–Philadelphia AL, 1910.

E—Most hits, season—
1993–Philadelphia NL, 1930.
1776–St. Louis AL, 1936.

F—Fewest hits, season—
1163–New York AL, 1955.
1174–Pittsburgh NL, 1909.

G—Most bases on balls, season—
812–New York AL, 1949.
671–Brooklyn NL, 1946.

H—Fewest bases on balls, season—
295–New York NL, 1921.
359–Detroit AL, 1909.

I—Most strikeouts, season—(154 game schedule)—
1122–Los Angeles NL, 1960.
896–Detroit AL, 1946.

II—Most strikeouts, season (162 game schedule)—
1162–Cleveland AL, 1964.
1122–Cincinnati NL, 1964.

J—Fewest strikeouts, season—
356–Boston AL, 1930.
357–New York NL, 1921.

K—Most hit batsmen, season—
81–Philadelphia AL, 1911.
68–Brooklyn NL, 1903.

L—Fewest hit batsmen, season—
5–St. Louis AL, 1945.
10–St. Louis NL, 1948.

M—Most wild pitches, season—
83–Cincinnati NL, 1965.
73–Minnesota AL, 1964.

N—Fewest wild pitches, season—
9–Cincinnati NL, 1944.
10–St. Louis AL, 1930.
Cleveland AL, 1943.

O—Most balks, season—
20–New York NL, 1963.
14–New York AL, 1950.

P—Fewest balks, season—
0–By many clubs. Last:
Pittsburgh NL, 1965.
Chicago AL, 1965.

Q—Lowest earned run average, season—
2.16–Chicago AL, 1917.
2.18–Philadelphia NL, 1915.

R—Highest earned run average, season—
6.70–Philadelphia NL, 1936.
6.24–St. Louis AL, 1936.

S—Most pitchers winning 20 or more games, season—
4–Chicago AL, 1920.
3–Pittsburgh NL, 1902.
New York NL, 1904, 05, 13, 20.
Cincinnati NL, 1923.

T—Most pitchers losing 20 or more games, season—
4–Boston NL, 1905.
Boston NL, 1906.
3–Washington AL, 1904.
St. Louis AL, 1905.
Philadelphia AL, 1916.

U—Most home runs allowed season (154 game schedule)–
187–Kansas City AL, 1956.
185–St. Louis NL, 1955.

V—Most home runs allowed season (162 game schedule)–
220–Kansas City AL, 1964.
192–New York NL, 1962.

CLUB BATTING RECORDS

A—Highest percentage, season—
.343—Philadelphia NL, 132 games, 1894.
.319—New York NL, 154 games, 1930.
.316—Detroit AL, 154 games, 1921.

B—Lowest percentage, season—
.207—Washington NL, 136 games, 1888.
.212—Chicago AL, 156 games, 1910.
.213—Brooklyn NL, 154 games, 1908.

C—Highest percentage, pennant winner, season—
.328—Baltimore NL, 129 games, 1894.
.31422—St. Louis NL, 154 games, 1930.
.30746—New York AL, 155 games, 1927.

D—Lowest percentage, pennant winner, season—
.228—Chicago AL, 154 games, 1906 (8th in batting per cent)
.245—Los Angeles NL, 162 games, 1965 (7th in batting per cent).

AT BAT–CLUB

E—Most times at bat, one club, season—
5705—New York AL, 164 games, 1964.
5686—Pittsburgh NL, 163 games, 1965.
5667—Philadelphia NL, 156 games, 1930.
5646—Cleveland AL, 157 games, 1936.

F—Fewest times at bat, one club, season—
4725—Philadelphia NL, 149 games, 1907.
4827—Chicago AL, 153 games, 1913.

G—Most times at bat, both clubs, 9-inning game—
110—Boston NL (66) vs Detroit (44), June 9, 1883.
99—New York NL (56) vs Cincinnati (43), June 9, 1901.
New York NL (58) vs Philadelphia (41), July 11, 1931.
96—Cleveland AL (51) vs Phila. (45), April 29, 1952.

H—Most times at bat, one club, 9-inning game—
66—Boston NL vs Detroit, June 9, 1883.
Chicago NL vs Buffalo, July 3, 1883.
58—New York NL vs Philadelphia, 2d game, Sept. 2, 1925.
New York NL vs Philadelphia, July 11, 1931.
56—New York NL vs Philadelphia, June 28, 1939.

I—Most times facing pitcher, one club, inning—
23—Chicago NL, 7th inning, Sept. 6, 1883.
23—Boston AL, 7th inning, June 18, 1953.
21—Brooklyn NL, 1st inning, May 21, 1952.

I-I—Most men reaching base consecutively in one inning (since 1900)
19—Brooklyn NL, 1st inning, May 21, 1952.
13—Kansas City AL, 2nd inning, Apr. 21, 1956.

JJ—Most batters reaching base in one inning—
20—Boston AL vs. Detroit, 7th inn., June 18, 1953.
19—Boston AL vs. Baltimore, 1st inn., June 18, 1896.
Brooklyn NL vs. Cincinnati, 1st inn., May 21, 1952.

RUNS–CLUB

J—Most players, 100 or more runs, one club, season—
7—Boston NL, Duffy (160), Lowe (158), Long (136), Nash (132), Bannon (130), McCarthy (118), Tucker (112), 1894.
6—New York AL, Gehrig (163), Ruth (149), Combs (130), Chapman (120), Sewell (102), Lazzeri (100), 1931.
6—Brooklyn NL, Snider (132), Gilliam (125), Robinson (109), Reese (108), Campanella (103), Hodges (101), 1953.

K—Most runs, one club, season—
1221—Boston NL, 133 games, 1894.
1067—New York AL, 155 games, 1931.
1004—St. Louis NL, 154 games, 1930.

L—Fewest runs in a season (150 or more games)—
372—St. Louis NL, 154 games, 1908.
380—Washington AL, 156 games, 1909.

M—Most opponents' runs, season—
1199—Philadelphia NL, 156 games, 1930.
1064—St. Louis AL, 155 games, 1936.

N—Most runs, pennant winner, season—
1065—New York AL, 155 games, 1936.
1004—St. Louis NL, 154 games, 1930.
(Baltimore NL had 1170, playing 129 games, 1894.)

O—Most runs, 4 consecutive games, one club—
88—Chicago NL, July 20-27, 1876.
65—Boston AL, June 5-8, 1950.

Most runs, 3 consecutive games, one club—
71—Chicago NL, July 20-25, 1876.
56—Boston AL, June 7-9, 1950.

P—Most runs, one club, game—
36—Chicago NL (36) vs Louisville (7), June 29, 1897.
29—Boston AL (29) vs St. Louis (4), June 8, 1950
Chicago AL (29) vs K.C. (6), April 23, 1955.
28—St. L. NL (28), 2d g. vs Phila. (6), July 6, 1929.

Q—Most runs, both clubs, 9-inning game—
49—Chicago NL (26) vs Phila. (23), Aug. 25, 1922.
36—Boston AL (22) vs Philadelphia (14), June 29, 1950.

R—Most runs, one club, inning—
18—Chicago NL, 7th inning, Sept. 6, 1883.
17—Boston AL, 7th inning, June 18, 1953.
15—Brooklyn NL, 1st inning, May 21, 1952.

S—Most runs, both clubs, inning—
19—Wash. AA (14), Balto. (5), 1st inn., June 17, 1891.
18—Chicago NL, Detroit (0), 7th inn., Sept. 6, 1883.
17—Boston NL (10), New York (7), 9th inn., June 20, 1912.
Boston AL (17), Detroit (0) 7th inn., June 18, 1953.

CLUB BATTING RECORDS—Continued

Most RUNS (10 or more in an inning) ONE CLUB

NATIONAL	AMERICAN

First Inning—
16—Boston, June 18, 1894
15—Brooklyn, May 21, 1952
   14—Cleve., 2d g., June 18, 1950

Second Inning—
13—New York, July 19, 1890
11—Cinn., July 22, 1926
   Brooklyn, April 29, 1930
   Phila., July 14, 1934
   13—Kansas City, April 21, 1956

Third Inning—
14—Cleveland, Aug. 7, 1889
12—St. L., 1st g., Sept. 16, 1926
   N. Y., 2d g., June 1, 1930
   12—New York, Sept. 11, 1949

Fourth Inning—
15—Hartford, May 13, 1876
14—Chicago, Aug. 25, 1922
   13—Chicago, Sept. 26, 1943

Fifth Inning—
13—Chicago, Aug. 16, 1890
12—New York, Sept. 3, 1926
   14—New York, July 6, 1920

Sixth Inning—
14—Phila., PL, June 26, 1890
12—Phila., 1st g., July 21, 1923
   Chi., 2d g., Aug. 21, 1935
   13—Cleve., 1st g., July 7, 1923
   Detroit, June 17, 1925

Seventh Inning—
18—Chicago, Sept. 6, 1883
12—Chicago, May 28, 1925
   Brooklyn, August 30, 1953
   17—Boston, June 18, 1953

Eighth Inning—
13—Brooklyn, Aug. 8, 1954.
   13—Phila., June 15, 1925

Ninth Inning—
14—Baltimore, April 24, 1894
12—San Francisco, Aug. 23, 1961
   11—New York, May 3, 1951

Tenth Inning—
10—Boston, June 17, 1887.

Eleventh Inning—
10—Kansas City, July 21, 1886.
   Twelfth Inning—
   11—N.Y., 1st g., July 26, 1928

Thirteenth Inning—
10—Cinn., May 15, 1919

A—Most runs, two consecutive innings, one club—
21—Pitts. NL, 12 in 3d inn., 9 in 4th inn., June 6, 1894.
19—Boston AL, 9 in 2d inn., 10 in 3d inn., May 2, 1901.
   Boston AL, 2 in 6th inn., 17 in 7th inn., June 18, 1953.

RUNS BATTED IN—CLUB

B—Most players, 100 or more runs batted in, one club, season—
5—New York AL, Dickey (107), DiMaggio (125), Gehrig (152), Lazzeri (109), Selkirk (107), 1936.
4—Pittsburgh NL, Wright (121), Barnhart (114), Traynor (106), Cuyler (102), 1925.
Chicago NL, Wilson (159), Hornsby (149), Stephenson (110), Cuyler (102), 1929.
Philadelphia NL, Klein (145), Hurst (125), O'Doul (122), Whitney (115), 1929.

C—Most runs batted in, one club, season—
995—New York AL, 155 games, 1936.
942—St. Louis AL, 154 games, 1930.

D—Most runs batted in, both clubs, game—
43—Chicago NL (24), vs Philadelphia (19), Aug. 25, 1922.
35—Boston AL (21), Philadelphia (14), June 29, 1950.

E—Most runs batted in, one club, game—
29—Boston AL vs. St. Louis, June 8, 1950.
26—New York NL vs Brooklyn, 1st g., April 30, 1944.

F—Most runs batted in, one club, inning—
17—Boston AL, 7th inn., June 18, 1953.
15—Chicago NL, 7th inn., Sept. 6, 1883.
Brooklyn NL, 1st inn., May 21, 1952.

BASE HITS—CLUB

G—Most hits, one club, season—
1783—Philadelphia NL, 156 games, 1930.
1724—Detroit AL, 154 games, 1921.

H—Fewest hits, one club season (150 or more games)—
1044—Brooklyn NL, 154 games, 1908.
1061—Chicago AL, 156 games, 1910.

I—Most players 200 or more hits, one club, season—
4—Phila. NL, O'Doul 254, Klein 219, Thompson 202, Whitney 200, 1929.
Detroit AL, Walker 213, Gehringer 209, Fox 208, Greenberg 200, 1937.

J—Most hits, both clubs, 9-inning game—
51—Phila. NL (26) vs Chicago (25), Aug. 25, 1922.
45—Phila. AL (27) vs Boston (18), July 8, 1902.
Detroit AL (28) vs New York (17), Sept. 29, 1928.

K—Most hits, one club, 9-inning game—
36—Philadelphia NL, Aug. 17, 1894.
31—New York NL, June 9, 1901.
30—New York AL, Sept. 28, 1923.

CLUB BATTING RECORDS—Continued

A—Most hits, one club, inning—
18—Chicago NL, 7th inning, Sept. 6, 1883.
14—Boston AL, 7th inning, June 18, 1953.
12—St. Louis AL, 1st inning, April 22, 1925.

B—Most players making 2 or more hits, one club, inning—
6—Chicago NL, (Williamson 3, Burns, 3, Pfeffer 3, Goldsmith 2, Billy Sunday 2, Kelly 2), 7th inn., Sept. 6, 1883.
5—Phila AL, (Hartsel, Davis, Lave, Cross, Seybold, Murphy), 6th inn., July 8, 1902.
New York AL, (Mays, Miller, Peckinpaugh, Ruth, Schang), 9th inn., Sept. 10, 1921.

C—Most players making 5 or more hits, one club, game—(9 inn.)—
4—Phila. NL, (Hamilton 5, Thompson 6, Sullivan 5, Grady 5), Aug. 17, 1894.
3—N.Y. NL, (VanHaltren 5, Selbach 6, Hickman 5), June 9, 1901.
Detroit AL, Vitt 5, Cobb 5, Veach 5), July 30, 1917.
New York NL, (Groh 5, Youngs 5, O'Connell 5), June 1, 1923.
Chicago AL, (Kreevich 5, Bonura 5, Appling 5), Sept. 11, 1936.

CC—Most players making 4-or-more hits, one club, game—
7—Chicago NL vs Cleveland, July 24, 1894.
5—San Francisco NL vs Los Angeles, May 13, 1958.
4—By many. Last: Bos. AL vs St. L., June 8, 1950.

D—Most successive hits, one club, inning—
10—Boston AL, 9th inn., June 2, 1901.
St. Louis NL, 4th inn., Sept. 17, 1920.
St. Louis NL, 6th inn., June 12, 1922.
Chicago NL, 1st game, 4th inn., Sept. 7, 1929.
Brooklyn NL, 6th inn., June 23, 1930.

E—Most successive hits, one club, game—
12—St. Louis NL, 4th (10) and 5th (2) inn., Sept. 17, 1920.
Brooklyn NL, 6th (10) and 7th (2) inn., June 23, 1930.
10—Boston AL, 9th inn., June 2, 1901.

F—Fewest hits, both clubs, game—
1—Chicago NL (0) vs L.A. (1), Sept. 9, 1965.
2—Philadelphia AA (1), Baltimore (1), Aug. 20, 1886.
Chicago NL (1), vs Pitts. (1), A. M. game, July 4, 1906.
Chicago NL (0) vs Cin. (2), 10 inn., May 2, 1917.
Cleveland AL (1), vs St. Louis (1), April 23, 1952.
Baltimore AL (1), vs Chicago (1), June 21, 1956.
Baltimore AL (1), vs Kansas City (1), Sept. 12, 1964.

TOTAL BASES—CLUB

G—Most total bases, one club, season—
2703—New York AL, 155 games, 1936.
2684—Chicago NL, 156 games, 1930.

H—Fewest total bases, one club, season—
1310—Chicago AL, 156 games, 1910.
1358—Brooklyn NL, 154 games, 1908.

I—Most total bases, both clubs, 9-inning game—
79—St. L. NL, (12-1b, 5-2b, 1-3b, 4-hr; total 41) vs Philadelphia (10-1b, 2-2b, 6-hr; total 38), May 11, 1923.
77—New York AL, (12-1b, 2-2b, 2-3b, 7-hr; total 50) vs. Phila. (6-1b, 2-2b, 3-3b, 2-hr; total 27), June 3, 1932.

J—Most total bases, one club, 9-inning game (since 1900)—
60—Boston AL, (11-1b, 9-2b, 1-3b, 7-hr) June 8, 1950.
50—S.F. NL, (15-1b, 3-2b, 3-3b, 5-hr), May 13, 1958.

K—Most total bases, one club, inning—
29—Chicago NL, (10-1b, 6-2b, 1-3b, 1-hr, 7th inn., Sept. 6, 1883.
27—San Francisco NL, (5-1b, 1-2b, 5-hr), 9th inn., Aug. 23, 1961.
25—Boston AL, (1-2b, 2-3b, 4-hr) 6th inn., Sept. 24, 1940.

LONG HITS—CLUB

L—Most long hits, one club, season—
580—N. Y. AL, (315-2b, 83-3b, 182-hr), 155 games, 1936.
566—St. Louis NL, (373-2b, 89-3b, 104-hr), 154 games, 1930.

M—Fewest long hits, one club, season—
124—Chicago AL, 156 games, (116-2b, 56-3b, 7-hr), 1910.
182—Boston NL, 155 games, (124-2b, 43-3b, 15-hr), 1909.

N—Most long hits, one club, 9-inning game—
17—Boston AL (9-2b, 1-3b, 7-hr), June 8, 1950.
16—Chicago NL (14-2b, 2-3b), July 3, 1883.
13—St. Louis NL, (7-2b, 1-3b, 5-hr), April 18, 1925.
St. Louis NL, (13-2b), 2d game, July 12, 1931.
St. Louis NL, (4-2b, 2-3b, 7-hr) May 7, 1940.
Milwaukee NL, (6-2b, 7-hr) July 31, 1954.

O—Most long hits, both clubs, 9-inning game—
24—St. L. NL, (13-2b) vs Chi. (10-2b, 1-hr), 2d g., July 12, 1931
18—Bos. AL (3-2b, 5-3b, 2-hr) vs Wash. AL (4-2b, 1-3b, 3-hr), April 26, 1902.
Wash. AL, (8-2b, 1-3b, 1-hr) vs Detroit (7-2b, 1-3b), July 24, 1921.
New York AL, (5-2b, 0-3b, 5-hr) vs Phila. (3-2b, 0-3b 5-hr), 2d game, May 22, 1930.
New York AL, (2-2b, 2-3b, 7-hr) vs Phila. (2-2b, 3-3b, 2-hr), June 3, 1932.
Boston AL (9-2b, 1-3b, 7-hr) vs St. Louis (1-2b), June 8, 1950.

P—Fewest long hits in 18 inning game—
0—New York AL vs Chicago, 11 singles each, Aug. 21, 1933.

Q—Most long hits, one club, inning—
8—Chicago NL, 7th inn. (6-2b, 1-3b, 1-hr), Sept. 6, 1883.
7—St. Louis AL, 6th inn. (7-2b), Aug. 25, 1936, 1st g.
Boston NL, 1st inn. (1-2b, 2-3b, 4-hr) Sept. 24, 1940, 2d game.
Phila. NL, 8th inn. (1-2b, 1-3b, 5-hr), June 2, 1949.
New York AL, 9th inn. (2-2b, 2-3b, 3-hr), May 3, 1951.

EXTRA BASES ON LONG HITS—CLUB

R—Most extra bases on long hits, one club, season—
1027—N.Y. AL, (315 on 2b, 166 on 3b, 546 on hr), 155 games, 1936
1016—Brooklyn NL (274 on 2b, 118 on 3b, 624 on hr), 155 games, 1953.

CLUB BATTING RECORDS—Continued

A—Fewest extra bases on long hits, one club, season—
249—Chi. AL, 156 games (116 on 2-b, 112 on 3-b, 21 on hr.) 1910.
255—Boston NL, 155 games (124 on 2-b, 86 on 3-b, 45 on hr.) 1909.

B—Most extra bases on long hits, one club, 9-inning game—
32—Boston AL (9 on 2b, 2 on 3b, 21 on hr) June 8, 1950.
29—St. L. NL (4 on 2b, 4 on 3b, 21 on hr) May 7, 1940.

C—Most extra bases on long hits, one club, in an inning—
18—Philadelphia NL (1 on 2b, 2 on 3b, 15 on hr) June 2, 1949.
17—Boston NL (1 on 2b, 4 on 3b, 12 on hr) 2d g, Sept. 24, 1940.

ONE-BASE HITS (Singles)—CLUB

D—Most 1-base hits (singles) season—
1338—Philadelphia NL, 132 games, 1894.
1297—Pittsburgh NL, 155 games, 1922.
1298—Detroit AL, 154 games, 1921.

E—Fewest 1-base hits (singles), season—
837—Washington AL, 154 games, 1959.
846—Brooklyn NL, 154 games, 1908.

F—Most 1-base hits (singles) one club, 9-inning game—
28—Philadelphia NL, Aug. 17, 1894.
Boston NL, April 20, 1896.
24—Cleveland AL, July 29, 1928.
Boston AL, June 18, 1953.
23—New York NL, Sept. 21, 1931.

G—Most 1-base hits (singles), both clubs, 9-inning game—
37—Balto. NL (21) vs Wash. (16) Aug. 8, 1896.
36—Chicago AL (21) vs Boston (15) Aug. 15, 1922.
New York NL (22), vs Cinn. (14) June 9, 1901.

H—Most 1-base hits (singles), one club, inning—
11—St. Louis NL, 1st inn., April 22, 1925.
Boston AL, 7th inn, June 18, 1953.

TWO-BASE HITS (doubles)—CLUB

I—Most consecutive years leading in 2-base hits.
8—Cleveland AL, 1916-17-18-19-20-21-22-23.
5—St. Louis NL, 1920-21-22-23-24.

J—Most 2-base hits, one club, season—
373—St. Louis NL, 154 games, 1930.
358—Cleveland AL, 154 games, 1930.

K—Fewest 2-base hits, one club, season—
110—Brooklyn NL, 154 games, 1908.
116—Chicago AL, 156 games, 1910.

L—Most 2-base hits, one club, 9-inning game—
14—Chicago NL vs Buffalo, July 3, 1883.
13—St. Louis NL, 2d game, July 12, 1931.
11—Detroit AL, July 14, 1934.

M—Most 2-base hits, both clubs, 9 inning game—
23—St. L. NL (13) vs Chi. (10) 2d game, July 12, 1931.
16—Cleveland AL (9) vs New York (7) July 21, 1921.

N—Most 2-base hits, one club, inning—
7—Boston NL, 1st inn, 1st g, Aug. 25, 1936.
6—Washington AL, 8th inn., June 9, 1934.

THREE-BASE HITS (Triples)—CLUB

O—Most 3-base hits, one club, season—
153—Baltimore NL, 129 games, 1894.
129—Pittsburgh NL, 152 games, 1912.
112—Baltimore AL, 134 games, 1901.
Boston AL, 141 games, 1903.

P—Fewest 3-base hits, one club, season—
19—Boston NL, 150 games, 1942.
Baltimore AL, 154 games, 1958.

Q—Most 3-base hits, one club, 9-inning game—
9—Baltimore NL, 1st game, Sept. 3, 1894.
8—Pittsburgh NL, 2d game, May 30, 1925.
6—Chicago AL, Sept. 17, 1920.
Detroit AL, June 17, 1922.

R—Most 3-base hits, both clubs, 9-inning game—
11—Baltimore NL (9), Cleveland (2), 1st game, Sept. 3, 1894.
9—Pittsburgh NL (6) vs. Chicago (3), 2d game, July 4, 1904.
Pittsburgh (8) vs. St. Louis (1), 2d game, May 30, 1925.
Detroit AL (6) vs. New York (3), June 17, 1922.

S—Most 3-base hits, one club, inning—
4—Chicago AL, 8th inn., Sept. 15, 1901, 2nd game.
Chicago NL, 4th inn., July 2, 1895.
Brooklyn NL, 1st inn., April 17, 1898.
Cleveland AL, 3d inn. (in succession), Aug. 23, 1902.
Cincinnati NL, 5th inn., May 8, 1922.
Boston AL, 2d inn., July 22, 1926.
New York NL, 4th inn. (in succession) May 6, 1934.
New York NL, 1st inn. July 17, 1936.

T—Most 3-base hits with bases filled, one club, one game—
2—By many clubs.
Last performed by: Milwaukee NL (W. Bruton, 1st, 6th inning, August 2, 1959 (2nd game).

CLUB BATTING RECORDS—Continued
HOME RUNS—CLUB

A—Most years, leading in home runs (1900 to date)—
  34—New York AL (see table page 67).
  24—New York NL (see table page 67).

B—Most years, 100 or more home runs—
  42—New York AL, 1920-21, 23, 25-43, 46-65.
  26—New York NL, 1925; 27-32; 34-35; 37-39; 42; 45-57.

C—Most consecutive years, 100 or more home runs—
  20—New York AL, 1946-65.
  16—Chicago NL, 1950-65.

D—Most home runs, one club season (154 game schedule)—
  221—New York NL, 155 games, 1947.
       Cincinnati NL, 155 games, 1956.

E—Most home runs, one club season (162 game schedule)—
  193—New York AL, 155 games, 1960.

F—Most home runs, season (active clubs)—
  240—New York AL, 163 games, 1961.

AMERICAN LEAGUE	
New York, 1961	240
Minnesota, 1963	225
Detroit, 1962	209
Los Angeles, 1961	189
Boston, 1964	186
Cleveland, 1962	180
Kansas City, 1957; 64	166
Baltimore, 1964	162
Chicago, 1961	138
Washington, 1963	138

NATIONAL LEAGUE	
Cincinnati, 1956	221
San Francisco, 1962	204
Milwaukee, 1957	199
Chicago, 1958	182
Los Angeles, 1958	172
Pittsburgh, 1947	156
Philadelphia, 1929	153
St. Louis, 1953	143
New York, 1962	139
Houston, 1962	105

G—Most home runs, one club, 2 consecutive games—
  13—New York AL, June 28, 28, 1939.
      San Francisco NL, Apr. 29, 30, 1961.

H—Most home runs, one club, 3 consecutive games—
  15—Minnesota AL, Aug. 26, 29, 29, 1963.
  14—Milwaukee NL, Aug. 30, 30, Sept. 2, 1953.
      Milwaukee NL, May 30, 30, 31, 1956.
      San Francisco NL, Apr. 29, 30, May 2, 1961.
      Milwaukee NL, June 8, 9, 10, 1961.

I—Most home runs, one club, 4 consecutive games—
  17—Minnesota AL, Aug. 26, 29, 29, 30, 1963.
  16—Milwaukee NL, Aug. 30, 30, Sept. 2, 3, 1953.
      Milwaukee NL, May 28, 30, 30, 31, 1956.
      Milwaukee NL, June 8, 9, 10, 11 (1st g), 1961.

J—Most home runs, one club, 5 consecutive games—
  19—New York NL, July 7-11, 1954.
      Minnesota AL, Aug. 26-30, 1963.

K—Most home runs, one club, 6 consecutive games—
  22—New York NL, July 6-July 11 (1st g.), 1954.
  21—Cleveland AL, May 15-20, 1962.

L—Most home runs, one club, 7 consecutive games—
  24—New York NL, July 5 (2nd g.)-July 11 (1st g.), 1954.
      Cleveland AL, May 15-21, 1962.

M—Most home runs, one club, 8 consecutive games—
  26—New York NL, July 5-July 11 (1st g.), 1954.
      Cleveland AL, May 13 (2d gm)-21, 1962.

N—Most home runs, one club, 9 consecutive games—
  28—Cleveland AL, May 13-21, 1962.
  27—New York NL, July 4 (2nd g.)-July 11 (1st g.), 1954.

O—Fewest home runs (135 or more games), one club season—
  3—Chicago AL, 156 games, 1908.
  5—St. Louis NL, 137 games, 1903.
     Philadelphia NL, 137 games, 1902.

P—Most home runs, one club, game—
  8—New York AL, vs. Philadelphia, 1st g., June 28, 1939.
     Milwaukee NL, vs. Pittsburgh, 1st g., Aug. 30, 1953.
     Cincinnati NL vs Milwaukee, Aug. 18, 1956.
     San Francisco NL vs Milwaukee, 1st g., Apr. 30, 1961.
     Minnesota AL vs Washington, 1st g., Aug. 29, 1963.

Q—Most home runs, both clubs, game—
  11—New York AL (6) vs. Detroit (5), June 23, 1950.
  10—Phila. NL (6) vs. St. Louis (4), May 11, 1923.
      Pitts. NL (7) vs. St. Louis (3), Aug. 16, 1947.
      Milw. NL (7) vs. Bkn. (3), July 31, 1954.
      Cinn. NL (8) vs Milw. (2), Aug. 18, 1956.
      S.F. NL (8) vs Milw. (2), Apr. 30, 1961.

R—Most players on club hitting 50 or more home runs—
  2—New York AL, 1961.

S—Most players on club hitting 40 or more home runs—
  2—New York AL, 1927, 30, 31, 61.
     Brooklyn NL, 1953, 54.
     Cincinnati NL, 1955.
     Detroit AL, 1961.
     San Francisco NL, 1961.

T—Most players on club, hitting 30 or more home runs—
  3—Phil. NL, 1929; N.Y. AL, 1941; N.Y. NL, 1947; Bklyn. NL,
     1950, 53; Cin. NL, 1956; Wash. AL, 1959; Mil. NL, 1961, 65;
     Minn. AL, 1963, 64, 65; S.F. NL, 1963, 64.

U—Most players on club, hitting 20 or more home runs—
  6—New York AL, 1961.
     Minnesota AL, 1964.
     Milwaukee AL, 1965.

V—Most home runs, 2 players, one club, season—
  115—New York AL, 1961. (Maris 61, Mantle 54).
  93—Chicago NL, 1930. (Wilson 56, Hartnett 37).

W—Most home runs at park, season—
  219—Cincinnati NL (Crosley Field), 1957.
  248—Los Angeles AL (Wrigley Field), 1961.

CLUB BATTING RECORDS—Continued

A—Most players 2 or more home runs, game, club—
3—Pitts. NL (Kiner 3, Greenberg 2, Cox 2), Aug. 16, 1947.
Boston AL (Doerr 3, Dropo 2, Williams 2), June 8, 1950.
N.Y. NL (Mays 2, Spencer 2, Westrum 2), July 8, 1956.
Cinn. NL (Thurman 3, Robinson 2, Kluszewski 2), Aug. 18, 1956.
N.Y. AL (Mantle 2, Maris 2, Skowron 2), May 30, 1961.

B—Most home runs in succession, club, inning—
4—Mil. NL, 7th inn., June 8, 1961 (Mathews, Aaron, Adcock, Thomas).
Clev. AL, 6th inn., July 31, 1963 (Held, Ramos, Francona, Brown).
Minn. AL, 11th inn., May 2, 1964 (Oliva, Allison, Hall, Killebrew).

C—Most home runs, one club, in an inning—
5—New York NL, 4th inn., June 6, 1939 (Danning, Demaree, Whitehead, Salvo, Moore).
Philadelphia NL, 8th inn., June 2, 1949 (Seminick (2), Rowe, Jones, Ennis).
San Francisco NL, 9th inn., Aug. 23, 1961 (Cepeda, F. Alou, Davenport, Orsino, Mays).
4—Boston AL, 6th inn., 1st g., Sept. 24, 1940 (Williams, Foxx, Cronin, Tabor).
Detroit AL, 4th inn., June 23, 1950 (Trout, Priddy, Wertz, Evers).
Boston AL, 6th inn., May 22, 1957 (Mauch, Williams, Gernert, Malzone).
Boston AL, 7th inn., Aug. 26, 1957 (Zauchin, Lepcio, Piersall, Malzone).
Cleveland AL, July 31, 1963 (see Item "B" above).
Minnesota AL, May 2, 1964 (see Item "B" above).

D—Most times 3 or more home runs in an inning, club, lifetime—
27—New York NL, 1932-1957.
26—New York AL, 1919-1962.

E—Most times 3 consecutive HR, inning, one club—
8—New York NL, 1932,39(2),48,49,53,54,56.
5—Cleveland AL, 1902,39,50,51,62.

F—Most home runs (only runs of game)—
5—By 4 NL clubs. Last: Chi., Apr. 21, 1964.
4—By 8 AL clubs. Last: Wash., June 8, 1964.

G—Most home runs, both clubs, one inning—
5—St. L. AL (3) vs. Phila. (2), 9th inn., June 8, 1928.
New York NL (5) vs. Cin. (0), 4th inn., June 6, 1939.
Philadelphia NL (5) vs. Cin. (0), 8th inn., June 2, 1949.
Detroit AL (4) vs. N.Y. (1) 4th inn., June 23, 1950
New York NL (3) vs. Boston (2), 3rd inn., July 6, 1951.
Cincinnati NL (3) vs. Bkn. (2), 7th inn., June 11, 1954.
San Francisco NL (5) vs Cin. (0), 9th inn., Aug. 23, 1961.
Philadelphia NL (3) vs. Chi. (2), 5th inn., April 17, 1964.

H—Most home runs with bases filled, club, season—
10—Det. AL, 1938.
9—Chicago NL, 1929.

I—Most home runs with bases filled, one club, game—
2—By many clubs. Last:
Minnesota AL, July 18, 1962 (1st inn.: Killebrew, Allison).

J—Most consecutive games one or more home runs, one club—
25—New York AL (40 home runs), June 1-29, 1941.
24—Brooklyn NL (39 home runs), June 18-July 10, **1953.**

K—Most home runs hit in consecutive games—
40—New York AL (25 consecutive games), June 1-29, **1941,**
39—Brooklyn NL (24 consecutive games), June 18-July **10, 1953.**

SACRIFICE HITS—CLUB

L—Most sacrifice hits, one club, season—
310—Boston AL, 157 games, 1917.
270—Chicago NL, 158 games, 1908.

M—Fewest sacrifice hits, one club, season (no Sac. Flies)
32—New York NL, 154 games, 1957.
35—Boston AL, 162 games, 1964.

N—Most sacrifice hits, one club, game—
8—Cincinnati NL, May 6, 1926.
New York AL, May 4, **1918.**
Chicago AL, July 11, **1927.**
St. Louis AL, July 23, 1928.

O—Most sacrifice hits, both clubs, game—
11—Wash. AL, 7, vs. Boston 4, Sept. 1, 1926.
9—N.Y. NL, 5, vs. Chi. 4, August 29, 1921.
Cincinnati NL, 8, vs. Phila. 1, May 6, 1926.

P—Most sacrifice hits, one club, inning—
3—Cleveland AL vs St.L. (5th inn.), July 10, 1949.
Chicago NL vs Mil. (6th inn.), Aug. 26, 1962.

Q—Most sacrifice flies, one club, game—
5—Chicago AL vs. Detroit, Sept 27, 1924.
4—By many clubs.

R—Most sacrifice flies, one club, inning—
3—Chicago AL vs Clev., 2d g. (5th inn.), July 1, 1962.

GROUNDED INTO DOUBLE PLAY—CLUB

S—Most times, club—season—
170—Philadelphia AL, 1950.
166—St. Louis NL, 1958.

T—Fewest times, club, season—
75—St. Louis NL, 1945.
91—New York AL, 1963.

HIT BATSMEN—CLUB

U—Most hit batsmen, one club, season—
75—Chicago AL, 154 games, 1956.
53—Philadelphia NL, 161 games, 1962.

V—Fewest hit batsmen, one club, season—
5—Philadelphia AL, 154 games, 1937.
9—Philadelphia NL, 152 games, 1939.

CLUB BATTING RECORDS—Continued

A—Most hit batsmen, one club, game—
6—Brooklyn AA vs. Baltimore, Apr. 25, 1887.
New York AL vs. Washington, June 20, 1913.
5—Detroit NL vs. Indianapolis, Apr. 30, 1887.
Pittsburgh NL vs. Cleveland, Apr. 23, 1890.
Washington NL vs. Pittsburgh, May 9, 1896.

B—Most hit batsmen, both clubs, game—
9—Detroit NL (5), Indianapolis (4), Apr. 30, 1887.
7—N. Y. NL (4), Bos. (3). 2d g., Aug. 1, 1903.
Brk. NL (4), N.Y. (3), July 17, 1900.
Detroit AL (4), Wash. (3), 2d g., Aug. 24, 1914.

C—Most hit batsmen, one club, inning—
4—Boston NL vs Pitt. (2d inn.), Aug. 19, 1893.
3—By 3 AL & 3 NL, since 1900. Last:
Boston AL vs N.Y. (3d inn.), June 30, 1954.
Philadelphia NL vs Cin. (8th inn.), May 15, 1960.

BASES ON BALLS—CLUB

D—Most bases on balls, one club, season—
835—Boston AL, 155 games, 1949.
732—Brooklyn NL, 155 games, 1947.

E—Fewest bases on balls, one club, season—
283—Philadelphia NL, 153 games, 1920.
356—Philadelphia AL, 156 games, 1920.

F—Most bases on balls, one club, game—
18—Detroit AL, May 9, 1916.
Cleveland AL, May 20, 1948.
17—Brooklyn NL, Aug. 27, 1903.
New York, NL, 1st game, Apr. 30, 1944.

G—Most bases on balls, both clubs, game—
30—Detroit AL (18) vs. Philadelphia (12), May 9, 1916.
24—New York NL (15) vs. Brooklyn (9), Aug. 9, 1951.

H—Most bases on balls, one club, inning—
11—New York AL, 3d inn., Sept. 11, 1949.
9—Cincinnati, 5th inn., April 24, 1957.

I—Most bases on balls, by pinch hitters, inning—
3—Pittsburgh NL, 9th inning, June 3, 1911.
Brooklyn NL (consecutive), 7th inn., April 22, 1922.
Boston NL, 9th inning, 1st g., June 2, 1932.
Chicago NL, 7th inning, July 29, 1947.
Baltimore AL, 7th inning, Apr. 22, 1955.
Washington AL, 9th inning, 2d g, May 14, 1961, (cons.).

J—Most consecutive bases on balls, inning—
7—Chicago AL vs Wash. (1st g., 2d inn.), Aug. 28, 1909.
6—New York NL vs. Philadelphia, 6th inn., July 7, 1909.
St. Louis NL vs. Philadelphia, 5th inn., Sept. 14, 1928.
New York NL vs Brooklyn, 2d inn, 1st g, April 30, 1944.

STRIKEOUTS—CLUB

K—Most strikeouts, one club, season (154 game schedule)—
1054—Philadelphia NL, 1960.
883—Washington AL, 1960.

L—Most strikeouts, one club, season (162 game schedule)—
1129—New York NL, 1965.
1125—Washington AL, 1965.

M—Fewest strikeouts, one club, season—
308—Cincinnati NL, 153 games, 1921.
326—Philadelphia AL, 155 games, 1927.

N—Most strikeouts, club, game (9 inn.)—
18—Detroit AL vs Clev. 1st g., Oct. 2, 1938.
San Francisco NL vs L.A., Aug. 31, 1959.
Chicago NL vs L.A., Apr. 24, 1962.
Boston AL vs Det., June 15, 1965.

O—Most strikeouts, both clubs, game (9 inn.)—
26—Phil. NL (16) vs Pitt. (10), July 29, 1965.
25—Bos. AL (13) vs Det. (12), May 24, 1963.
Clev. AL (15) vs N.Y. (10), July 6, 1963.

P—Most strikeouts, club, game (extra inn.)—
22—New York NL vs S.F., May 31, 1964 (23 inn.).
21—Baltimore AL vs Wash., Sept. 12, 1962 (16 inn.).

Q—Most strikeouts, both clubs, game (extra inn.)—
36—N.Y. NL (22) vs S.F. (14), 2 g., May 31, 1964 (23 inn.).
Pitt. NL (19) vs Cin. (17), Sept. 30, 1964 (16 inn.).
33—Wash. AL (19) vs Clev. (14), June 14, 1963 (19 inn.).

R—Most strikeouts, club, double-header (18 inn.)—
25—Los Angeles AL vs Clev., July 31, 1963.
24—Chicago NL vs St. L., July 30, 1933.
Philadelphia NL vs L.A., June 29, 1960.

S—Most strikeouts, both clubs, double-header (18 inn.)—
40—Clev. AL (23) vs L.A. (17), Sept. 29, 1962.
Phil. NL (21) vs Chi. (19), Sept. 23, 1965.

T—Most strikeouts, club, double-header (extra inn.)—
31—Pittsburgh NL vs Phil., Sept. 22, 1958 (23 inn.).
New York NL vs Phil., Oct. 2, 1965 (27 inn.).
27—Cleveland AL vs Bos., Aug. 25, 1963 (24 inn.).

U—Most strikeouts, both clubs, double-header (extra inn.)—
47—N.Y. NL (29) vs S.F. (18), May 31, 1964 (32 inn.).
44—Clev. AL (27) vs Bos. (17), Aug. 25, 1963 (24 inn.).

V—Most strikeouts, club, consecutive games—
28—Philadelphia AL, June 2 (14), 3 (14), 1933.
27—Chicago NL, Apr. 22 (9), 24 (18), 1962.

W—Most strikeouts, pinch-hitters, club, game—
4—By many. Last:
Washington AL vs Clev., May 1, 1957.
Chicago NL vs N.Y., Sept. 21, 1962.

X—Most strikeouts, pinch-hitters, club, inn.—
3—By many. Last:
St. Louis NL vs Cin., May 10, 1961 (9th inn.).
Los Angeles AL vs Bos., June 1, 1964 (9th inn.).

CLUB FIELDING RECORDS

A—Highest percentage, one club, season—
.985—Baltimore AL, 1964.
.9831—Cincinnati NL, 1958.

B—Consecutive years leading in fielding—
6—Boston AL, 1916–972, 17–972, 18–971, 19–975, 20–972, 21–975
4—Chicago NL, 1905-962, 06-969, 07-967, 08-969.

C—Most chances accepted, one club, season—
6655—Chicago AL, 157 games, 1907.
6472—New York NL, 155 games, 1920.

D—Fewest chances accepted one club, season—
5470—Cleveland AL, 147 games, 1945.
5545—Philadelphia NL, 154 games, 1955.

E—Most putouts, one club, season—
4466—Los Angeles NL, 165 games, 1962.
4520—New York AL, 164 games, 1964.

F—Fewest putouts, one club, season—
3887—Philadelphia NL, 149 games, 1907.
3907—Cleveland AL, 147 games, 1945.

G—Most assists, one club, season—
2446—Chicago AL, 157 games, 1907.
2293—St. Louis NL, 154 games, 1917.

H—Fewest assists, one club, season—
1437—Philadelphia NL, 156 games, 1957.
1443—Detroit AL, 161 games, 1962.

I—Most assists, both clubs, 9-inning game—
45—New York AL (23), Chicago (22), Aug. 21, 1905.
44—Brook. NL (23), New York (21), April 21, 1903.
   New York NL (25), Cincinnati (19), May 15, 1909.

J—Fewest assists, both clubs, game—
5—Baltimore AL (3) vs. Cleveland (2), Aug. 31, 1955.
6—Philadelphia NL (1), vs Chicago (5), May 2, 1957.
   Philadelphia NL (3), vs S.F. (3), May 13, 1959.

K—Most assists, one club, 9-inning game—
28—Pittsburgh NL, vs. New York, June 7, 1911.
27—St. Louis AL vs. Philadelphia, Aug. 16, 1919.

L—Fewest assists, one club, 9-inning game—
0—Cleveland AL vs New York, July 4, 1945 (1st game).
1—By many N.L. clubs. Last:
   Philadelphia NL vs Milwaukee, June 16, 1965.

M—Most assists, infield, one club, 9-inning game—
26—Brooklyn NL vs. Pittsburgh, June 14, 1906.
   Pittsburgh NL vs. New York, June 7, 1911.
   Boston NL vs. New York, June 24, 1918.
   Boston NL vs. New York, June 30, 1919.
   St. Louis AL vs. Philadelphia, Aug. 16, 1919.

N—Most assists, infield (without battery), one club, 9-inning game—
21—Detroit AL (0-1b, 5-2b, 4-3b, 12ss.), 2d game, Sept. 2, 1901.
   New York NL (1b-0, 2b-7, 3b-5, ss-9), July 13, 1919.
   Phila. NL (1-1b, 8-2b, 5-3b, 7-ss), 2d game, May 30, 1931.
   Brooklyn NL (3-1b, 11-2b, 2-3b, 5-ss.), 2d g., Aug. 18, 1935.
   Washington AL (1-1b, 9-2b, 3-3b, 8-ss.), 1st g., Sept. 2, 1935.

O—Fewest assists, infield (without battery), one club, game—
0—By 11 clubs. Last:
   Philadelphia NL vs Chi., May 2, 1957.

P—Fewest chances offered outfield, club, game, 10 or more inns.—
0—New York NL, 10 innings, Aug. 8, 1899.
   St. Louis AL, 11 inn., April 23, 1905.

Q—Fewest chances offered outfield, both clubs, game—
2—Pittsburgh NL (1), Brooklyn NL (1), Aug. 26, 1910.
   Cincinnati NL, (1), Brooklyn (1), May 7, 1941.
3—St. Louis AL (2), Chicago (1), April 24, 1908.
   New York AL (2), Boston (1), May 4, 1911.
   New York AL (2), Detroit (1, error), May 9, 1930.
   Cleveland AL (0), New York (3), July 24, 1965.

R—Most putouts by outfield, one club, 9-inning game—
19—Pittsburgh NL vs. Cincinnati, 2nd g., July 5, 1948.
18—Cleveland AL vs. St. Louis, Sept. 28, 1929.
   New York AL vs. Boston, Oct. 1, 1933.

S—Fewest putouts by outfield, club, game, 10 or more inns.—
0—New York NL, 13 inn., April 15, 1909.
   St. Louis AL, 11 inn., April 23, 1905.

T—Most putouts by outfield, both clubs, 9-inning game—
30—Chicago NL, 16, Philadelphia 14, Aug. 7, 1953.
29—Washington AL 17, St. Louis 12, May 3, 1939.

U—Fewest putouts by outfield, both clubs, game—
1—St. Louis AA 1, New York 0, June 30, 1886.
   Pittsburgh NL 1, Brooklyn 0, Aug. 26, 1910.
2—New York AL 2, Detroit 0, May 9, 1930.

V—Most assists by outfield, one club, 9-inning game—
5—Pittsburgh NL vs. Philadelphia, Aug. 23, 1910.
   New York AL vs. Boston, 2d game, Sept. 5, 1921.
   Cleveland AL vs. St. Louis, May 1, 1928.

W—Most errors, outfield, game, since 1900—
5—Baltimore AL, Aug. 19, 1902.
4—By many clubs
   Last club: Milwaukee NL, July 21, 1953.

CLUB FIELDING RECORDS—Continued

A—Most errors, season—
425—Detroit AL, 136 games, 1901.
408—Brooklyn NL, 155 games, 1905.

B—Fewest errors (150 or more games), season—
95—Baltimore AL, 163 games, 1964.
100—Cincinnati NL, 154 games, 1958.

BB—Most errorless games, season (150 or more games)—
91—New York AL, 164 games, 1964.
87—Cincinnati NL, 162 games, 1965.

C—Most errors, one club, game—
12—Detroit AL vs. Chicago, May 1, 1901.
     Chicago AL vs. Detroit, May 6, 1903.
11—St. Louis NL vs Pittsburgh, April 19, 1902.
     Boston NL vs. St. Louis, June 11, 1906.
     St. Louis NL vs. Cincinnati, 2d game, July 3, 1909.

D—Most errors, both clubs, game—
18—Chicago AL (12) vs. Detroit (6), May 6, 1903.
15—St. Louis NL (11) vs. Pitts. (4), April 19, 1902.
     Boston NL (10) vs. Chicago (5), Oct. 3, 1904.

D-D—Most consecutive errorless games, season—
12—Detroit AL, July 27-Aug. 7, 1963.
11—Cincinnati NL, July 6-17, 1953.

E—Fewest passed balls, one club, season—
0—New York AL, 155 games, 1931.
2—Boston NL, 153 games, 1943.

EE—Most passed balls, one club, season—
49—Baltimore AL, 155 games, 1959.
42—Boston NL, 156 games, 1905.

F—Most double plays, club, season—
217—Philadelphia AL, 154 games, 1949.
198—Los Angeles NL, 154 games, 1958.

G—Most double plays, one club, game—
7—New York AL, Aug. 14, 1942.
6—Cincinnati NL, June 20, 1925.
     Pittsburgh NL, Sept. 23, 1925.
     New York NL, May 15, 1928.
     New York NL, Aug. 12, 1932.
     Philadelphia NL (in 8 inn. of 10 inn. game), April 21, 1935.
     Pittsburgh NL, 1st g., Sept. 6, 1948.
     St. Louis NL, Aug. 20, 1954.
     New York NL, May 2, 1957.

H—Most double plays, both clubs, game—
9—Detroit AL (5) vs. Washington (4), May 21, 1925.
     Chicago NL (5) vs. Cincinnati (4), July 3, 1929.
     Cleveland AL (6) vs. Detroit (3), Sept. 27, 1952.
     New York AL (6) vs. Kansas City (3), July 31, 1955.
     Los Angeles NL (5) vs Pittsburgh (4), April 15, 1961.
     Cleveland AL (5) vs Boston (4), May 9, 1965.

I—Most double plays, one club, doubleheader—
10—Washington AL (5 each game) vs. Chicago, Aug. 18, 1943.
9—St. Louis NL (4 in 1st, 5 in 2nd) vs. Cincinnati, June 11, 1944.

I-I—Most consecutive games making double plays—
25—Boston AL (38 double plays), May 7 to June 4, 1951.
     Cleveland AL (38 double plays), Aug. 21 2nd g. to Sept. 12, 1953.
23—Brooklyn NL (36 double plays), Aug. 7 to Aug 27, 1952.

TRIPLE PLAYS

J—Most triple plays, one club, season—
3—Cincinnati AA, 1882.
     Detroit AL, 1911.
     Boston AL, 1924.
     Philadelphia NL, 1964.
     Chicago NL, 1965.

K—Most triple plays unassisted—
1—Neal Ball, Cleve. AL, 2d inn., first game, July 19, 1909.
     George H. Burns, Boston AL, 2d inn., Sept. 14, 1923.
     Ernest K. Padgett, Bos. NL, 4th inn., 2d game, Oct. 6, 1923.
     F. Glenn Wright, Pittsburgh NL, 9th inn., May 7, 1925.
     James E. Cooney, Chicago NL, 4th inn., AM, 1st g, May 30, 1927.
     John H. Neun, Detroit AL, 9th inn., May 31, 1927.

CLUB PINCH HITTING RECORDS

A—Most hits one club, game—
6—Brooklyn NL vs Philadelphia, Sept. 9, 1926.
4—Cleveland AL vs Chicago, April 22, 1930.
Philadelphia AL vs Detroit, Sept. 18, 1940.
Detroit AL vs Chicago, April 22, 1953.
Kansas City AL vs Detroit, Sept. 1, 1958.
New York AL vs Cleveland (1st g), Aug. 26, 1960.

B—Most hits one club, inning—
4—Chicago NL vs. Brk., May 21, 1927 (9th inn., 2d gm.).
Philadelphia AL vs. Det., Sept. 18, 1940 (9th inn., 2d gm.).

C—Most home runs one club, season—
12—Cincinnati NL, 1957.
10—New York AL, 1961.

D—Most home runs one club, game—
2—By many clubs. Last:
New York NL, Sept. 17, 1963.
Cleveland AL, 2d gm., Aug. 15, 1965.

E—Most home runs, one club, inning—
2—New York NL (Robert Hofman, James Rhodes) vs. St. Louis, June 20, 1954, 6th inn.
New York AL (Robert Cerv, Elston Howard) vs Kansas City, July 23, 1955, 1st inn.
San Francisco NL (Henry Sauer, Robert Schmidt) vs Milwaukee, June 4, 1958 (10th inn.).
Los Angeles NL (Frank Howard, William Skowron) vs Chicago, Aug. 8, 1963, 5th inn.

F—Most home runs both clubs, game—
3—Philadelphia NL (2), St. Louis (1), June 2, 1928.
St. Louis NL (2), Brooklyn (1), July 21, 1930.
2—By many clubs.

G—Most pinch hitters used one club, game—
9—Los Angeles NL vs St.L., Sept. 22, 1959.
8—Baltimore AL vs Chicago, May 28, 1954.

H—Most pinch hitters used both clubs, game—
14—New York NL (7) vs Chi. (7), May 2, 1956 (17 inns.).
12—Washington AL (8) vs N.Y. (4), Sept. 20, 1960 (11 inns.).
11—Chicago NL (7) vs Los Angeles (4), Oct. 1, 1961.
10—Baltimore AL (6), New York (4), April 26, 1959.

HH—Most pinch hitters, club, inning—
6—San Francisco NL, 9th inn., May 5, 1958.
5—By many A.L. clubs. Last:
Chicago AL, 7th inn., April 19, 1965.

I—Most pinch hitters, both clubs, inning—
8—Chicago AL (5) vs Baltimore (3), 7th inn., May 18, 1957.
Philadelphia NL (5) vs St. Louis (3), 8th inn., April 30, 1961.

CLUB BASE RUNNING RECORDS

J—Most stolen bases (1900 to date), one club, season—
347—New York NL, 154 games, 1911.
288—Washington AL, 155 games, 1913.

K—Fewest stolen bases, one club, season—
13—Washington AL, 154 games, 1957.
17—St. Louis NL, 157 games, 1949.

L—Most stolen bases, one club, game—
19—Philadelphia AA vs. Syracuse, April 22, 1890.
17—New York NL, vs Pittsburgh, May 23, 1890.
15—New York AL vs St. Louis, Sept. 23, 1911.
11—St. Louis NL vs Pitts. 2d game (5 innings), Aug. 13, 1916.
New York NL vs Boston, June 20, 1912.

M—Most stolen bases, both clubs, game—
21—Philadelphia AA (19) vs. Syracuse (2), April 22, 1890.
20—New York NL (17) vs Pittsburgh (3), May 23, 1890.
16—New York NL (11) vs Boston (5), June 20, 1912.
15—New York AL (15) vs St. Louis (0), Sept. 28, 1911.
St. Louis AL (8) vs Detroit (7), Oct. 1, 1916.

N—Most stolen bases, one club, inning—
8—Washington AL, 1st inning, July 19, 1915.
Philadelphia NL, 9th inning, 1st gm., July 7, 1919.

O—Most caught stealing bases, one club, season—
149—Chicago NL, 154 games, 1924.
119—Chicago AL, 156 games, 1923.

P—Most caught stealing bases, one club, season—
8—Milwaukee NL, 154 games, 1958.
11—Kansas City AL, 154 games, 1960.
Cleveland AL, 161 games, 1961.

LEFT ON BASES—CLUB

Q—Most left on bases, one club, season—
1334—St. Louis AL, 157 games, 1941.
1278—Brooklyn NL, 155 games, 1947.

R—Fewest left on bases, one club, season—
925—Kansas City AL, 154 games, 1957.
964—Chicago NL, 154 games, 1924.

S—Most left on bases, one club, 9 inning game—
20—New York AL vs Boston, Sept. 21, 1956.
18—By 8 NL clubs.

T—Fewest left on bases, one club, game, 10 or more innings—
0—Phila. AL vs N. Y., 14 innings, 2d game, June 22, 1929.

U—Most left on bases, both clubs, game—
30—Brk. NL (16) vs Pitt. (14), June 30, 1893.
N.Y. AL (15) vs Chi. (15), Aug. 27, 1935, (1st g).
N.Y. NL (17) vs Phil. (13), July 18, 1943, (1st g).
L.A. AL (15) vs Wash. (15), July 21, 1961.

V—Most left on bases, both clubs, extra inning game—
44—Chi. NL (23) vs Cin. (21), Aug. 9, 1942 (18 inn.).
43—Det. AL (23 vs N.Y. (20), June 24, 1962 (22 inn.).

CLUB LEADERS IN HOME RUNS
°High for Club, League
1901 to Date

	National	Club	Total League	American	Club	Total League
1901	St. Louis	39	225	Boston	36	226
1902	Brooklyn	19	96	Washington	47	256
1903	Pittsburgh	33	147	Boston	48	182
1904	New York	31	175	Philadelphia	41	163
1905	New York	39	182	Boston	29	153
1906	Brooklyn	25	126	Philadelphia	31	123
1907	New York	23	141	Philadelphia	22	101
1908	Brooklyn	28	151	St. Louis	21	114
1909	New York	26	151	Boston	21	109
1910	Chicago	34	214	Boston	44	144
1911	Philadelphia	60	314	Boston-Philadelphia	35	193
1912	New York	48	284	Boston	28	149
1913	Philadelphia	73	311	Philadelphia	33	158
1914	Philadelphia	62	266	Philadelphia	28	148
1915	Philadelphia	58	225	New York	31	159
1916	Chicago	46	239	New York	34	142
1917	New York	39	202	New York	27	133
1918	St. Louis	27	138	Philadelphia	22	97
1919	Philadelphia	42	206	New York	45	239
1920	Philadelphia	64	261	New York	115	370
1921	Philadelphia	88	460	New York	134	477
1922	Philadelphia	116	530	Philadelphia	111	524
1923	Philadelphia	112	538	New York	105	441
1924	New York	95	498	New York	98	396
1925	New York	114	634	New York-St. Louis	110	533
1926	St. Louis	90	439	New York	121	424
1927	New York	109	483	New York	158	439
1928	New York	118	610	New York	133	483
1929	Philadelphia	153	754	New York	142	596
1930	Chicago	171	892	New York	152	673
1931	New York	101	492	New York	155	576
1932	Philadelphia	122	649	Philadelphia	173	708
1933	New York	82	460	New York	144	608
1934	New York	126	656	Philadelphia	144	688
1935	New York	123	662	Philadelphia	112	663
1936	Philadelphia	103	607	New York	182	758
1937	New York	111	624	New York	174	806
1938	New York	125	611	New York	174	864
1939	New York	116	649	New York	166	796
1940	St. Louis	119	688	New York	155	883
1941	Brooklyn	101	597	New York	151	734
1942	New York	109	538	New York	108	533
1943	New York	81	432	New York	100	473
1944	St. Louis	100	575	New York	96	459
1945	New York	114	577	New York	93	430
1946	New York	121	562	New York	136	653
1947	New York	221°	886	New York	115	679
1948	New York	164	845	Cleveland	155	710
1949	Brooklyn	152	936	Boston	131	769
1950	Brooklyn	194	1100	Cleveland	164	973
1951	Brooklyn	184	1024	Cleveland-New York	140	839
1952	Brooklyn	153	907	Cleveland	148	794
1953	Brooklyn	208	1197	Cleveland	160	879
1954	New York-Brooklyn	186	1114	Cleveland	156	823
1955	Brooklyn	201	1263	New York	175	961
1956	Cincinnati	221°	1219	New York	190	1075
1957	Milwaukee	199	1178	Kansas City	166	1024
1958	Chicago	182	1183	New York	164	1057
1959	Milwaukee	177	1159	Cleveland	167	1091
1960	Milwaukee	170	1042	New York	193	1086
1961	Milwaukee	188	1196	New York	240°	1534
1962	San Francisco	204	1449°	Detroit	209	1552°
1963	San Francisco	197	1215	Minnesota	225	1489
1964	San Francisco	165	1211	Minnesota	221	1551
1965	Milwaukee	196	1318	Boston	165	1370

GENERAL CLUB RECORDS

A—Most games played, season (154 game schedule)
162—Detroit AL, 1904
160—Cincinnati NL, 1915.

B—Most games played, season (162 game schedule)—
165—L.A., S.F. NL, 1962.
164—Clev., N.Y. AL, 1964.

C—Fewest games played, season (154 game schedule)—
147—Cleveland AL (2 ties, 9 unplayed), 1945.
149—Philadelphia NL (2 ties, 7 unplayed), 1907, 1934.

D—Shortest and longest game by time—
51 minutes—N. Y. NL (6), Phila (1), 1st game, Sept. 28, 1919.
55 minutes—St. L. AL (6) vs N. Y. (2), 2d game, Sept. 26, 1926.
7:23—S.F. NL (8) at N.Y. (6), 23 inn., 2 g., May 31, 1964.
7:00—N.Y. AL (9) at Det. (7), 22 inn., June 24, 1962.

Longest nine inning game—
4:18—San Francisco NL (7) at Los Angeles (8), Oct. 2, 1962.
3:54—Detroit AL (17) vs Kansas City (14), 2d game, July 23, 1961.

Longest night game, by time—
5:13—St. Louis NL (7) at Houston (7), Apr. 25, 1962 (17 inns.).
—Los Angeles NL (4) vs. Phil. (3), Sept. 19, 1964 (16 inn.).
4:58—Baltimore AL (8) vs. Bos. (7), June 23, 1954 (17 inn.).

SHUTOUT GAMES—CLUB

E—Fewest shutout games, club, season—
6—Philadelphia NL, won 3, lost 3, 1930.
7—Baltimore AL, won 4, lost 3, 1901.
Philadelphia AL, won 5, lost 2, 1902.
New York AL, won 4, lost 3, 1926.
Philadelphia NL, won 4, lost 2, tied 1, 1929.
Chicago AL, won 2, lost 5, 1930.
New York AL, won 4, lost 3, 1931.

F—Most shutout games (1900 to date) season—
47—Chicago AL, won 22, lost 24, tie 1, 1910.
46—St. Louis NL, won 13, lost 33, 1908.

G—Fewest times shutout, season—
0—New York AL, 155 games, 1932 (1 only in 1927 and 1933).
Boston and Philadelphia NL, 132 game schedule, 1894.
1—Pittsburgh NL, by Phila (1-0, July 1, 1901), 139 games, 1901.
1—Brooklyn NL, by New York (6-0, July 11, 1953), 155 games 1953.

H—Most consecutive games, scoring—
308—New York AL, Aug. 2, 1931-Aug. 3, 1933.
185—Philadelphia NL, Aug. 11, 1893-May 11, 1895.

I—Clubs not making any shutouts, season's play—
(12 club league, playing only 132 games.)
Chi. NL, 1894; Wash. NL, 1894, 95, 98; Brk. NL, 1898; St. L. NL, 1898; Clev. NL, 1899.

J—Most shutout games won, club, season—
32—Chicago NL, 1907, 09.
30—Chicago AL, 1906 (also 2 tied).

K—Fewest shutout games won, club, season (1900 to date)—
1—Philadelphia AL, 1919.
Chicago AL, 1924.
Boston NL, 1928.
Washington AL, 1956.

L—Most shutout games, lost, club, season—
33—St. Louis NL, 1908.
29—Washington AL, 1909.

M—Fewest shutout games, lost, club, season—
0—New York AL, 155 games, 1932.
1—Pittsburgh NL, 139 games, 1901
Brooklyn NL, 155 games, 1953.

N—Largest score, shutout game—
28-0—Providence NL vs Philadelphia, Aug. 21, 1883.
21-0—Detroit AL vs Cleveland, 7 innings, Sept. 15, 1901
New York AL vs Phila., 8 inn., 2d g., Aug. 13, 1939
19-0—Chicago NL vs New York, June 7, 1906.
Pittsburgh NL vs St. Louis, Aug. 3, 1961.

O—Longest game without scoring—
20 innings—Pittsburgh NL vs Boston (won in 21 inn., 2-0)
Aug. 1, 1918.
19 innings—Cincinnati NL vs Brooklyn (0-0), Sept. 11, 1946.
18 innings—Detroit AL vs Washington (0-0), July 16, 1909.

P—Most Consecutive 1-0 Losses—
3—Brooklyn NL, Sept. 7, 7, 8, 1908
St. Louis AL, Apr. 25, 26, 27, 1909
Washington AL, May 7, 8, 10, 1909
Pittsburgh NL, Aug. 31, 31, Sept. 1, 1917
Philadelphia NL, May 11, 12, 13, 1960

Q—Longest 1-0 game—18 innings—
Providence NL (1), Detroit (0) (home run), Aug. 17, 1882.
Washington AL (1), Chicago (0), May 15, 1918.
New York NL (1), St. Louis (0), (1st game), July 2, 1933.
Washington AL (1), Chicago (0) (1st game), June 8, 1947.

GENERAL CLUB RECORDS—Continued

A—Most consecutive shutout games, won, club—
6—Pitt. NL, June 2, 3, 4, 5, 6, 8, 1903.
4—Clev. AL, June 24, 25, 26, 27, 1903.
N.Y. AL, May 11, 14, 15, 16, 1932.
Clev. AL, Aug. 15, 17, 18, 20, 1948.
Balt. AL, June 24, 25, 26, 28, 1957.

B—Most consecutive shutout games, lost, club—
4—Bos. NL, May 19 (0-15), 21 (0-8), 21 (0-1), 23 (0-5), 1906.
Bos. NL, Aug. 2 (0-3), 3 (0-4), 4 (0-1), 6 (0-4), 1906.
St. Louis AL, Aug. 25 (0-3), 26 (0-8), 29 (0-3), 30 (0-4), 1913.
Cinn. NL, July 30 (0-5), 31 (0-3), Aug. 1 (0-6), 3 (0-6), 1908.
Cinn. NL, July 31 (0-5), Aug. 1 (0-1), 2 (0-3), 3 (0-18), 1931.
Wash. AL, Sept. 19(0-2), 20(0-2), 22(0-2), 1958.
Hou. NL, June 20(0-5), 21(0-3), 22(0-3), 23(0-4), 1963.
Wash. AL, Sept. 1(0-3), 2(0-9), 4(0-1), 5(0-4), 1964.

C—Most consecutive innings shutting out opponents—
56—Pittsburgh NL, June 1 (last 2 innings), June 2 (9), June 3 (9), June 4 (9), June 5 (9), June 6 (6), June 8 (9), June 9 (first 3 innings), 1903.
47—Cleveland AL, Aug. 15, 1st g. (last 3 innings), 2d g. (9), Aug. 17 (9), Aug. 18 (9), Aug. 20 (9), Aug. 21 (1st 8 innings), 1948.

D—Most consecutive innings shut out by opponents—
48—Philadelphia AL, Sept. 22 (last 7 innings), Sept. 23, 1st g. (9), Sept. 23, 2nd g. (9), Sept. 24 (9), Sept. 25 (9), Sept. 26 (5), 1906.
45—Cincinnati NL, July 29 (4), July 31 (9), Aug. 1 (9), Aug. 2 (9), Aug. 3 (9), Aug. 4 (5), 1931.

E—Largest score, both clubs, game—
26-23—Chicago NL, Phila., Aug. 25, 1922.
22-14—Boston AL, Philadelphia, June 29, 1950.

F—Scoring in every inning, 9 inning game—
By 2 AA & 6 NL clubs only. Last:
St. Louis (15) NL, vs. Chi. (2), Sept. 13, 1964.

FF—Scoring in 8 innings (No At-Bats in 9th)—
By several NL & 4 AL clubs. Last:
Chicago (12) AL vs. Bos. (8), May 11, 1949.
New York (13) NL, vs. Cin. (3), July 19, 1949.

G—Most consecutive innings, scoring, club—
16—Boston AL (Sept. 15 (2), 16 (8), 17 (6), 1903).
14—New York NL, (July 18 (3), 19 (8), 20 (3), 1949).

PERCENTAGE—CLUB

H—Highest percentage games won, season—
.798—Chicago NL (won 67, lost 17), 1880.
.763—Chicago NL (won 116, lost 36), 1906.
.721—Cleveland AL (won 111, lost 43), 1954.
I—Highest percentage games won for tailender, season—
.454—New York NL, won 69, lost 83, 1915.
.431—Chicago AL, won 66, lost 87, 1924.

J—Lowest percentage games won, winning championship—
.564 Los Angeles NL (W88-L68), 1959.
.575 Detroit AL (W88-L65), 1945,
K—Lowest percentage of games won, season—
.130—Cleveland NL (won 20, lost 134), 1899,
.235—Philadelphia AL (won 36, lost 117), 1916.
.248—Boston NL (won 38, lost 115), 1935.

CONSECUTIVE VICTORIES

NATIONAL LEAGUE

Games	Club	H.	Rd.	Year
26	New York	26	0	1916
21	Chicago	11	10	1880
	Chicago	18	3	1935
	Providence	16	4	1884
20	Chicago	14	4	1885
	Baltimore	13	5	1894
	New York	13	5	1904
17	Boston	16	1	1897
	New York	14	3	1907
	New York	5	11	1916
16	Philadelphia	14	2	1887
	Philadelphia	11	5	1890
	Pittsburgh	12	4	1909
	New York	11	4	1912
	New York	13	3	1951
15	Detroit	12	3	1886
	Pittsburgh	11	4	1903
	Brooklyn	3	12	1924
	Chicago	11	4	1936
	New York	8	7	1936

AMERICAN LEAGUE

Games	Club	H.	Rd.	Year
19	Chicago	11	8	1906
18	New York	6	13	1947
17	New York	3	15	**1953**
	Washington	1	16	1912
16	Philadelphia	5	12	1931
	New York	12	4	1926
15	New York	12	3	1906
	Philadelphia	13	2	1913
	Boston	11	4	1946
	New York	9	6	1960

AMERICAN ASSOCIATION

Games	Club	H.	Rd.	Year
15	St. Louis	15	0	1887

NATIONAL ASSOCIATION

Games	Club	H.	Rd.	Year
26	Boston		..	**1875**

UNION ASSOCIATION

Games	Club	H.	Rd.	Year
20	St. Louis	16	4	1884

CONSECUTIVE DEFEATS

NATIONAL LEAGUE

Games	Club	H.	Rd.	Year
24	Cleveland	5	19	1899
23	Pittsburgh	1	22	1890
	Philadelphia	6	17	1961
20	Louisville	0	20	1894
19	Boston	3	16	1906
	Cincinnati	6	13	1914
18	Cincinnati	9	9	1876
	Louisville	0	18	1894
17	Washington	7	10	1894
	New York	7	10	1962
16	Troy	11	5	1882
	Detroit	11	5	1884
	Cleveland	0	16	1899
	Boston	5	11	**1907**
	Boston	8	8	1911
	Brooklyn	0	16	1944
15	St. Louis	11	4	1909
	Boston	0	15	1927
	Boston	0	15	1935
	New York	8	7	1963

AMERICAN LEAGUE

Games	Club	H.	Rd.	Year
20	Boston	1	19	1906
	Philadelphia	1	19	1916
	Philadelphia	3	17	1943
18	Philadelphia	0	18	1920
	Washington	8	10	1948
	Washington	3	15	**1959**
17	Boston	14	3	1926
16	Boston	9	7	1907
15	Boston	10	5	1927
	Philadelphia	10	5	1937

AMERICAN ASSOCIATION

Games	Club	H.	Rd.	Year
26	Louisville	5	21	1889

GENERAL CLUB RECORDS—Continued

A—Most games won, season (154 game schedule)—
116—Chicago NL, 1906.
111—Cleveland AL, 1954.
Most games won, season (162 game schedule)—
109—New York AL, 1961.
103—San Francisco NL, 1962.

B—Most games lost, season (154 game schedule)—
134—Cleveland NL, 1899.
117—Philadelphia AL, 1916.
115—Boston NL, 1935.
Most games lost, season (162 game schedule)—
120—New York NL, 1962.
106—Washington AL, 1963.

C—Most consecutive games won at start of season—
20—St. Louis UA, April 20 to May 22, 1884.
12—New York NL, May 1 to May 16, 1884.
10—Brooklyn NL, April 13 to April 21, 1955.
  Pittsburgh NL, April 10 to April 22, 1962.
9—St. Louis AL, April 18 to April 28, 1944.

D—Most consecutive games lost at start of season—
13—Washington AL, April 14 to May 4, 1904.
  Detroit AL, April 14 to May 2, 1920.
11—Detroit NL, May 1 to May 15, 1884.
9—Brooklyn NL, April 16 to April 26, 1918.
  Boston NL, April 19 to May 6, 1919.
  New York NL, April 11 to April 22, 1962.

E—Most years winning 100 or more games, 1900 to date, season—
11—New York AL, 110—1927, 101—1928, 107—1932, 102—1936, 102—1937, 106—1939, 101—1941, 103—1942, 103—1954, 109—1961, 104—1963.
5—Chicago NL, 116—1906, 107—1907, 104—1909, 104—1910, 100—1935.

F—Most years losing 100 or more games, season—
14—Philadelphia NL, 100—1904, 103—1921, 104—1923, 103—1927, 109—1928, 102—1930, 106—1936, 105—1938, 106—1939, 103—1940, 111—1941, 109—1942 (5 successive years), 108—1945, 107—1961.
11—Phila. AL, 109—1915, 117—1916, 104—1919, 106—1920, 100—1921, (3 consecutive yrs.), 100—1936, 100—1940, 105—1943, 105—1946, 102—1950, 103—1954.

G—Most consecutive years winning 100 or more games—
3—Phila. AL, 1929—104, 1930—102, 1931—107.
  St. Louis NL, 1942—106, 1943—105, 1944—105

H—Earliest pennant clinching—since 1900—
September 4, 1941—New York AL.
September 8, 1955, Brooklyn NL.

LEAGUE WINNERS—LARGEST MARGIN

NATIONAL LEAGUE

Year	Winner	won	lost	pct.	Runnerup	won	lost	pct.	G.B.
1902	Pittsburgh	103	36	.741	Brooklyn	75	63	.543	27½
1906	Chicago	116	36	.763	New York	96	56	.632	20
1943	St. Louis	105	49	.682	Cincinnati	87	67	.565	18
1907	Chicago	107	45	.704	Pittsburgh	91	63	.591	17
1944	St. Louis	105	49	.682	Pittsburgh	90	63	.588	14½
1955	Brooklyn	98	55	.641	Milwaukee	85	69	.552	13½
1904	New York	106	47	.693	Chicago	93	60	.608	13
1953	Brooklyn	105	49	.682	Milwaukee	92	62	.597	13
1910	Chicago	104	50	.675	New York	91	63	.591	13
1931	St. Louis	101	53	.656	New York	89	65	.572	13
1913	New York	101	51	.664	Phila.	88	63	.583	12½
1940	Cincinnati	100	53	.654	Brooklyn	88	65	.575	12

AMERICAN LEAGUE

Year	Winner	won	lost	pct.	Runnerup	won	lost	pct.	G.B.
1936	New York	102	51	.667	Detroit	83	71	.539	19½
1927	New York	110	44	.714	Phila.	91	63	.591	19
1929	Phila.	104	46	.693	New York	88	66	.571	18
1941	New York	101	53	.656	Boston	84	70	.545	17
1939	New York	106	45	.702	Boston	89	62	.589	17
1923	New York	98	54	.645	Detroit	83	71	.539	16
1903	Boston	91	47	.659	New York	75	60	.556	14½
1910	Phila.	102	48	.680	New York	88	63	.583	14½
1912	Boston	105	47	.691	Wash.	91	61	.599	14
1911	Phila.	101	50	.669	Detroit	89	65	.578	13½
1931	Phila.	107	45	.704	New York	94	59	.614	13½
1943	New York	98	56	.636	Wash.	84	69	.549	13½
1932	New York	107	47	.695	Phila.	94	60	.610	13
1937	New York	102	52	.662	Detroit	89	65	.578	13
1946	Boston	104	50	.675	Detroit	92	62	.597	12
1947	New York	97	57	.630	Detroit	85	69	.552	12

LEAGUE WINNERS—SMALLEST MARGIN

NATIONAL LEAGUE

Year	Winner	Runnerup	GB
1908	Chi.	N.Y., Pitt.	1
1946	St.L.	Brk.	*
1949	Brk.	St.L.	1
1951	N.Y.	Brk.	**
1956	Brk.	Mil.	1
1959	L.A.	Mil.	**
1962	S.F.	L.A.	1
1964	St.L.	Cin., Phil.	1

* Tied. 2 game playoff.
** Tied. 3 game playoff.

AMERICAN LEAGUE

Year	Winner	Runnerup	GB
1904	Bos.	N.Y.	1½
1907	Det.	Phil.	1½
1908	Det.	Clev.	½
1922	N.Y.	St.L.	1
1940	Det.	Clev.	1
1944	St.L.	Det.	1
1945	Det.	Wash.	1½
1948	Clev.	Bos.	*
1949	N.Y.	Bos.	1
1964	N.Y.	Chi.	1

* Tied. 1 game playoff.

A—Most consecutive years losing 100 or more games—
5—Philadelphia NL, 105–1938, 106–1939, 103–1940, 111–1941, 109–1942.
4—Washington, AL, 1961-100, 1962-101, 1963-106, 1964-100.

B—Most games won from one club, season—
21 to 1—New York AL, (21) in succession, St. Louis (1), 1927.
Pittsburgh NL, (21) Cincinnati (1), 1937.
Chicago NL, (21) Boston (1), 1909.
Chicago NL, (21) Cincinnati (1), 1945.

C—Fewest games won from one club, season—
1—National League: Boston (lost 21), from Chicago, 1909.
Boston (lost 20), from Pittsburgh, 1909.
Cincinnati (lost 21), from Pittsburgh, 1937.
Cincinnati (lost 21), from Chicago, 1945.
Houston (lost 17), from Philadelphia, 1962.
1—American League: St. L. (lost 21), from New York, 1927.
Boston (lost 17), from Minnesota, 1965.

D—Most consecutive games won, season—
26—N. Y. NL, Sept. 7 (1st game) to Sept. 30, (1 tie), 1916.
19—Chicago AL, Aug. 2-23, 1906.
New York AL, June 29 (2d game) to July 17 (2d game), 1947.

E—Most consecutive games lost, season—
26—Louisville AA, May 22, 1889.
24—Cleveland NL, Aug. 26-Sept. 16, 1899.
23—Philadelphia NL, July 29-Aug. 20 (1st g), 1961.
20—Boston AL, May 1-29, 1906.
Philadelphia AL, July 21-Aug. 8, 1916; Aug. 7-Aug. 24, (1st game), 1943.

F—Most consecutive games won at home—
26—New York NL, 1916.
22—Philadelphia AL, 1931.

G—Most consecutive games lost at home—
20—St. Louis AL, 1953.
14—Boston NL, 1911.

H—Longest tie games, by innings—
26—Brooklyn NL (1), Boston (1), May 1, 1920.
24—Detroit AL (1), Philadelphia (1), July 21, 1945.

I—Longest scoreless tie game, by innings—
19—Cincinnati NL vs. Brooklyn, Sept. 11, 1946.
18—Detroit AL vs Washington, July 16, 1909.

J—Most consecutive games won on road—
17—New York NL, 1916.
16—Washington AL, 1912.

K—Most consecutive games lost on road—
22—Pittsburgh NL, 1890.
New York NL, 1963.
19—Philadelphia AL, 1916.

L—Most games won at home—
65—New York AL (lost 16), 1961, (162 game schedule).
62—New York AL (lost 15), 1932.
61—Boston NL (lost 15), 1898.
San Francisco NL (lost 21), 1962, (162 game schedule).
60—St. Louis NL (lost 17), 1942.
Brooklyn NL (lost 17), 1953.

M—Most games lost at home—
59—St. Louis AL, 1939.
58—New York NL, 1962 (162 game schedule).

N—Most games won on road—
60—Chicago NL (lost 15), 1906.
54—New York AL (lost 20), 1939.

O—Most games lost on road—
65—Boston NL, 1935.
64—Philadelphia AL, 1916.

P—Most innings, consecutive extra inn. games, same clubs—
46—Cleveland AL vs St. L., May 1-5, 1910 (4 games).
45—Brooklyn NL vs Pitt., Aug. 20-22, 1917 (3 games).

Q—Most innings, 2 consecutive extra inn. games, club—
45—Boston NL, May 1-3, 1920.
36—Boston AL, July 12-13, 1951.
Chicago AL, July 12-13, 1951.

R—Most innings, 3 consecutive extra inn. games, club—
58—Brooklyn NL, May 1-3, 1920.
41—Cleveland AL, Apr. 18-21, 1935.

S—Most innings, 4 consecutive extra inn. games, club—
59—Pittsburgh NL, Aug. 18-22, 1917.
51—Chicago AL, Aug. 23-26, 1915.
Detroit AL, May 11-14, 1943.

T—Most consecutive extra inn. games, club—
5—Detroit AL, Sept. 9-13, 1908 (54 inns.).
4—Pittsburgh NL, Aug. 18-22, 1917 (59 inns.).

U—Most consecutive extra inn. games, same clubs—
4—Chicago AL vs Det., Sept. 9-12, 1908 (43 inns.).
Cleveland AL vs St. L., May 1-5, 1910 (46 inns.).
Boston AL vs St. L., May 31-June 2, 1943 (45 inns.).
3—Brooklyn NL vs Pitt., Aug. 20-22, 1917 (45 inns.).
Chicago AL vs Pitt., Aug. 18-20, 1961 (33 inns.).

V—Most games, one day, club—
3—Brk. NL vs Pitt. (10-9, 3-2, 8-4), Sept. 1, 1890.
Balt. NL vs Lou. (4-3, 9-1, 12-1), Sept. 7, 1896.
Pitt. NL vs Cin. (4-13, 3-7, 6-0), Oct. 2, 1920.

GENERAL CLUB RECORDS—Continued
DOUBLE-HEADERS

A—Most double-headers played in succession—
9—Boston NL vs Brooklyn, Sept. 4, 5.
   Philadelphia, Sept. 7, 8.
   New York, Sept. 10, 11, 13, 14.
   Chicago, Sept. 15, 1928.
8—Washington AL vs Philadelphia, July 27, 28.
   Chicago, July 29, 30, 31.
   Cleveland, Aug. 3, 4, 5, 1909.

B—Most consecutive double-headers won—
5—New York AL vs Washington, Aug. 30, 31, Sept. 1.
   Philadelphia, Sept. 3.
   Boston, Sept. 4, 1906.
4—Brooklyn NL vs Philadelphia, Sept. 1, 2, 3.
   Boston, Sept. 4, 1924.
   New York NL vs Boston, Sept. 10, 11, 13, 14, 1928.

C—Most consecutive double-headers lost—
5—Boston NL vs Philadelphia, Sept. 8.
   New York, Sept. 10, 11, 13, 14, 1928.
4—Boston AL vs New York, June 29, July 2.
   Washington, July 4, 5, 1921.

D—Most times winning two games, one day, one season—
20—Chicago NL, 1945.   Washington AL, 1945.
14—St. Louis AL, 1942.   Boston AL, 1946
   New York AL, 1943.
   Cleveland AL, 1943.
   (Tied series breaks streak.)

E—Most consecutive series won, season—
14—New York NL, 1912.
13—New York AL, 1943.

PLAYERS USED

F—Most players used in a season—
56—Philadelphia AL, 1915.
53—Brooklyn NL, 1944.

G—Most players used in a game, one club—
26—New York AL vs Boston, Sept. 29, 1956, 13 inn.
25—St. Louis NL vs Los Angeles, April 16, 1959, 9 inn.
   Milwaukee NL vs. Philadelphia, Sept. 26, 1964.
24—Washington AL vs Baltimore, Sept. 24, 1960.

H—Most players used in a game, both clubs—
48—New York NL (25) vs Chicago (23), May 2, 1956, 17 inn.
44—New York AL (26) vs Boston (18), Sept. 29, 1956, 13 inn.
   Kansas City AL (22) vs. Minnesota (22), Sept. 29, 1964, 15 inn.
43—Milwaukee NL (25) vs. Philadelphia (18), Sept. 26, 1964.
40—Detroit AL (21) vs. Kansas City (19), May 24, 1955.

I—Most pitchers used in a game, one club—
9—St. Louis AL vs Chicago, Oct. 2, 1949.
8—By many NL clubs. Last:
   San Francisco NL vs Cincinnati, Oct. 1, 1965.

II—Most pitchers, one club, double-header—
13—Milwaukee NL vs. Philadelphia, May 12, 1963, 23 inn.
12—Cleveland AL vs Detroit, Sept. 7, 1959.
11—By 5 clubs. Last: Pitt. NL vs S.F., Sept. 7, 1964.

J—Most pitchers used in a game, both clubs—
14—Chicago NL (7) vs New York (7) July 23, 1944 (2d game).
   Cincinnati NL (8) vs Milwaukee (6) April 26, 1959.
   Cleveland AL (7) vs Kansas City (7) April 23, 1961.

JJ—Most pitchers, both clubs, double-header—
22—Milwaukee NL (11) vs. New York (11), July 26, 1964.
21—Detroit AL (11) vs. Kansas City (10), July 23, 1961.

K—Most pitchers, one club, extra inning game—
9—Cincinnati NL vs Houston, July 8, 1962, 2d g. (13 inns.).
   Los Angeles AL vs Minnesota, Apr. 16, 1963 (13 inn.).
   Minnesota AL vs. Chicago, July 23, 1964 (13 inn.).

L—Most pitchers, both clubs, extra inning game—
17—Los Angeles AL (9) vs Minn. (8), Apr. 16, 1963, 13 inn.
15—St. Louis NL (8) vs Phila. (7) May 4, 1954, 11 inn.

M—Most pitchers used, inning, one club—
5—By many clubs. Last:
   Philadelphia NL vs Pittsburgh (9th inn.), Sept. 18, 1965.

MANAGERIAL RECORDS

N—Most years as manager—
53—Connie Mack, Pittsburgh NL, 1895-96; Milwaukee 1900;
   Philadelphia AL, 1901-1950.
33—John J. McGraw, Baltimore NL, 1899; Baltimore AL, 1901-02 (part); New York NL 1902 (part), 1932 (part).

O—Managers' championship record—
10 yrs—J. J. McGraw, N.Y. NL: 1904-05, 11-13, 17, 21-24.
   C. D. Stengel, N.Y. AL: 1949-53, 55-58, 60.
9 yrs—C. Mack, Phil. AL: 1902, 05, 10-11, 13-14, 29-31.
   J. V. McCarthy, Chi. NL: 1929; N.Y. AL: 1932, 36-39, 41-43.

P—Managers' consecutive championship records—
5 years—Charles D. Stengel, New York AL, 1949-50-51-52-53.
4 years—Harry Wright, Boston NA, 1872-73-74-75.
   Charles A. Comiskey, St. Louis AA, 1885-86-87-88.
   John J. McGraw, New York NL, 1921-22-23-24.
   Jos. V. McCarthy, New York NL, 1936-37-38-39.
   Charles D. Stengel, New York AL, 1955-56-57-58.

GENERAL CLUB RECORDS—Continued

PENNANT WINNERS—1901—to Date

NATIONAL		AMERICAN	
New York	15	New York	29
Chicago	10	Philadelphia	9
St. Louis	10	Detroit	7
Brooklyn	9	Boston	7
Pittsburgh	4	Chicago	5
Cincinnati	4	Washington	3
Los Angeles	3	Cleveland	3
Boston	2	St. Louis	1
Philadelphia	2	Minnesota	1
Milwaukee	2		
San Francisco	1		

TAIL ENDERS—1901—to Date

NATIONAL		AMERICAN	
Brooklyn	1	Detroit	1
New York (since 1962)	4	Baltimore	1
New York (thru 1957)	4	Cleveland	1
Chicago	5	New York	2
Pittsburgh	7	Washington (since 1961)	2
Cincinnati	8	Chicago	4
Boston	9	Kansas City	4
Philadelphia	22	Washington	10
		Boston	11
		St. Louis	11
		Philadelphia	18

A—Most Pennants won—

29—New York AL: 1921-23, 26-28 (M. J. Huggins, mgr., 6); 1932, 36-39, 41-43 (J. V. McCarthy, mgr., 8); 1947 (S. R. Harris, mgr.); 1949-53, 55-58, 60 (C. D. Stengel, mgr., 10); 1961-63 (R. G. Houk, mgr. 3); 1964 (L. P. Berra, mgr.).

17—New York NL: 1888-89 (J. J. Mutrie, mgr., 2); 1904-05, 11-13, 17, 21-24 (J. J. McGraw, mgr., 10); 1933, 36-37 (W. H. Terry, mgr., 3); 1951, 54 (L. R. Durocher, mgr., 2).

B—Winning Pennant in first season, as Manager—

NATIONAL LEAGUE	
Spalding, A. G., Chicago	1876
Wright, Geo., Providence	1879
Chance, F. L., Chicago	1906
Moran, P. J., Philadelphia	1915
Street, Chas. E., St. Louis	1933
Grimm, Chas. J., Chicago	1932
Hartnett, Chas. L., Chi.	1938
Dyer, Edwin H., St. Louis	1946

AMERICAN LEAGUE	
Griffith, Clark C., Chicago	1901
Jennings, Hugh A., Det.	1907
Gleason, William J., Chi.	1919
Harris, Stanley R., Wash.	1924
Cronin, Joseph E., Wash.	1933
Cochrane, Gordon S., Det.	1934
Houk, Ralph G., N.Y.	1961
Berra, Lawrence P. N.Y.	1964

C—Fewest pennants won—
0—Balt., K.C., L.A., Wash. (since 1961) AL. Hou., N.Y. (since 1962) NL.

D—Consecutive Pennants, club—
5—American League—New York, 1949-53; 1960-64.
4—National Association—Boston, 1872-73-74-75.
American Association—St. Louis, 1885-86-87-**88.**
National League—New York, 1921-22-23-24.

E—Most Times Finished in Last Place (Since 1901)—
22—Phil. NL, 1904, 19-21, 23, 26-28, 30, 36, 38-42, 44-45, **47, 58-61.**
18—Phil. AL, 1915-21, 35-36, 38, 40-43, 45-46, 50, 54.

F—Fewest times finished in last place (1901 to date)—
0—Houston, Los Angeles, Milwaukee, San Francisco NL.
Baltimore, Los Angeles, Minnesota, AL.

G—Most consecutive times finished in last place—
7—Philadelphia AL, 1915-16-17-18-19-20-21.
5—Philadelphia NL, 1938-39-40-41-42.

H—Most seasons Umpiring—
34—Robert D. Emslie, 1891-1924 in National League.
33—Thomas H. Connolly, 1898-1900 in National League. 1901-1931 in American League.

GENERAL LEAGUE RECORDS
NATIONAL LEAGUE—AMERICAN LEAGUE

I—Highest batting percentage, season, league—
.303—National League, 1930.
.292—American League, 1921.

J—Lowest batting percentage, season, league—
.2395—National League, 1908.
.23912—American League, 1908.

K—Most times at bat, season—
55,449—National League (10 teams) 1962.
55,239—American League (10 teams) 1962.

RUNS—LEAGUE

L—Most runs, league, season—
7,342—American League (10 teams) 1961.
7,278—National League (10 teams) 1962.

GENERAL LEAGUE RECORDS—Continued

RUNS—LEAGUE

A—Fewest runs, league (150 or more games), season—
4,136—National League, 1908.
4,272—American League, 1909.

B—Most runs league, 4 games, one day—
101—National League—Boston 11, Pittsburgh 9 (20); Washington 14, Chicago 6 (20); New York 26, Indianapolis 6 (32); Detroit 19, Philadelphia 10 (29), May 17, 1887.

C—Most players 100 or more runs, league, season—
24—American League, 1936.
19—National League, 1929.

RUNS BATTED IN—LEAGUE

D—Most runs batted in, league, season—
6,842—American League (10 teams), 1961.
6,760—National League (10 teams), 1962.

E—Most players 100 or more runs batted in, league, season—
18—American League, 1936.
17—National League, 1930.

BASE HITS—LEAGUE

F—Most hits, league, season—
14,453—National League (10 teams), 1962.
14,068—American League (10 teams), 1962.

G—Fewest hits, league (150 or more games), season—
9,566—National League, 1907.
9,719—American League, 1908.

H—Most players, making 200 or more hits, league, season—
12—National League, 1929, 1930.
9—American League, 1936, 1937.

I—Most years, no player making 200 hits, league, season—
23—National League (7 in succession, 1913-1919).
19—American League,
(7 years none made by either league.)

TOTAL BASES—LEAGUE

J—Most total bases, league, season—
21,781—National League (10 teams), 1962.
21,762—American League (10 teams), 1962.

LONG HITS—EXTRA BASES ON LONG HITS—LEAGUE

K—Most long hits, league, season—
4,190—A.L. (2238-2b, 400-3b, 1552-hr) (10 teams), 1962.
3,977—N.L. (2075-2b, 453-3b, 1449-hr) (10 teams), 1962.

L—Most extra bases on long hits, season, league—
7,694—A.L. (2238-2b, 800-3b, 4656-hr) (10 teams), 1962.
7,328—N.L. (2075-2b, 906-3b, 4347-hr) (10 teams), 1962.

SINGLES, DOUBLES, TRIPLES—LEAGUE

M—Most 1-base hits (singles), league, season—
10,476—National League (10 teams), 1962.
9,878—American League (10 teams), 1962.

N—Most 2-base hits (doubles), league, season—
2,400—American League, 1936.
2,386—National League, 1930.

O—Most 3-base hits (triples), league, season—
694—American League, 1921.
685—National League, 1912.

HOME RUNS—LEAGUE

P—Most home runs, league, season—
1,552—American League (10 teams), 1962.
1,449—National League (10 teams), 1962.

Q—Fewest home runs (150 or more games), league, season—
101—American League in 1907.
126—National League in 1906.

R—Most players making three home runs, game, season—
7—National League, 1950.
5—American League, 1930, 1932, 1950.

S—Most players making two or more home runs, game, season—
98—American League (10 teams), 1964.
84—National League, 1955.

T—Most players making 20 or more home runs, season—
25—National League (10 teams), 1962.
American League (10 teams), 1964.

U—Most players making 30 or more home runs, season—
10—National League (10 teams), 1965.
9—American League (10 teams), 1964.

V—Most players making 40 or more home runs, season—
6—National League, 1954, 1955.
American League (10 teams), 1961.

W—Most players making 50 or more home runs, season—
2—American League, 1938, 1961.
National League, 1947.

X—Most clubs making 100 or more home runs, season—
10—National League (10 teams), 1962.
American League (10 teams), 1964.

LEAGUE BATTING RECORDS—Continued

A—Most home runs, one league, one day—
30—American League (10 games), June 10, 1962, June 14, 1964.
28—National League (8 games), July 8, 1962.

B—Most home runs, both leagues, one day—
54—A.L. (30, 10 gs), N.L. (24, 10 gs), June 10, 1962.

C—Most home runs, both leagues, same day, 8 games—
30—AL (18)—NL (12), June 23, 1950; June 2, 1960.

D—Most home runs by pinch-hitters, league, season—
50—American League (10 teams), 1961.
45—National League (10 teams), 1962.

E—Most home runs with bases filled, season, league—
48—American League (10 teams), 1961.
37—National League (10 teams), 1962.

F—Most home runs with bases filled by pinch hitters, season—
7—American League (10 teams), 1961.
4—National League, 1959.

G—Fewest home runs with bases filled, season, league—
0—American League, 1918 (curtailed season).
1—American League, 1906, 07, 09, 15.
National League, 1920.

H—Most home runs with bases filled, season, both leagues—
77—AL (48)—NL (29), 1961 (18 teams).
68—NL (35)—AL (33), 1950 (16 teams).

I—Most home runs with bases filled, one day—
3—By American League 7. Last: Chi., Det., N.Y., Aug, 19, 1962.
By National League 5. Last: Chi.-Cin.-St.L., Aug. 13, 1959.

J—Most .300 batsmen (100 or more games), season—
43—National League (8 teams), 1930.
33—American League (8 teams), 1924, 1930.

K—Fewest .300 batsmen, season—
2—American League, 1905.
4—National League, 1907.

L—Most sacrifice hits, season, league—
1,731—American League, 1917.
1,655—National League, 1908.

LL—Fewest sacrifice hits, season, league—
510—National League, 1957.
531—American League—1958.

M—Most bases on balls, season, league—
5,902—American League (10 teams), 1961.
5,265—National League (10 teams), 1962.

N—Most strikeouts, season, league—
9,956—American League (10 teams), 1964.
9,649—National League (10 teams), 1965.

O—Fewest strikeouts, season, league—
3,245—American League, 1924.
3,359—National League, 1926.

LEAGUE FIELDING

P—Highest fielding percentage, season, league—
.9797—American League, 1964.
.9773—National League, 1956.

Q—Lowest fielding percentage, season, league—
.9374—American League, 1901.
.9494—National League, 1903.

R—Most putouts, season, league—
43,932—National League (10 teams), 1965.
43,847—American League (10 teams), 1964.

S—Most putouts, season, league—
32,235—American League, 1938.
32,296—National League, 1906.

T—Most assists, season, league—
18,008—National League (10 teams), 1965.
17,269—American League (10 teams), 1961.

U—Fewest assists, season, league—
13,219—American League, 1958.
13,345—National League, 1956.

V—Most chances accepted, season, league—
61,940—National League (10 teams), 1965.
60,997—American League (10 teams), 1964.

W—Most errors, season, league—
2,889—American League, 1901.
2,590—National League, 1904.

X—Fewest errors, season, league—
1,002—American League, 1958.
1,082—National League, 1956.

Y—Fewest passed balls, season, league—
53—American League, 1949.
65—National League, 1936.

Z—Most double plays, season, league—
1,596—National League (10 teams), 1962.
1,585—American League (10 teams), 1961.

O—Total number of no-hit games—165
  80—National League.
  62—American League.
  1—National Association, 1875.
  15—American Association, 1882-1891.
  2—Union Association, 1884.
  5—Federal League, 1914-1915.
P—Most no-hit games, league, season—
  5—American League, 1917.
  4—National League, 1880, 1898.
    American Association, 1884, 1888.
    Federal Association, 1915.
Q—Years no-hit games pitched, both leagues—
  20-1901, 04-05, 08, 12, 14, 16-17, 19, 34, 38, 40, 46-48, 51-52, 56, 62, 65.
R—Most years, without no-hit games, by either league—
  13—1913, 1921, 1927, 1928, 1930, 1932, 1933, 1936, 1939, 1942, 1943, 1949, 1959.
S—Most years, without no-hit games, one league—
  31—AL, 1903, 06-07, 09, 13, 15, 21-22, 24-25, 27-30, 32-33, 36, 39, 41-44, 49-50, 54-55, 59-61, 63-64.
  27—NL, 1902, 10-11, 13, 18, 20-21, 23, 26-28, 30-33, 35-37, 39, 42-43, 45, 49, 53, 57-59.
T—Most no-hit games in a day, league—
  2—National League, April 22, 1898.
U—Most 1-hit games, season—
  15—National League, 1965 (10 teams).
  13—American League, 1910.
  12—National League, 1906, 11.
V—Most 2-hit games, season—
  34—National League, 1963.
  33—American League, 1963.
W—Most 3-hit games, season—
  67—National League, 1963.
  56—American League, 1909.
X—Most tie games, season—
  19—American League, 1910.
  16—National League, 1913.
Y—Most tie games in a day, league—
  3—National League, April 26, 1897.
Z—Fewest tie games, season (1900 to date)—
  0—National League, 1925, 1954, 1958.
    American League, 1930, 1963, 1965.
AA—Most extra inning games, season—
  91—American League, 1943, 65.
  89—National League, 1965.
BB—Longest membership in league—
  90 yrs.—Chicago NL, 1876-1965.
  65 yrs.—Bos., Chi., Clev., Det. AL, 1901-65.

LEAGUE FIELDING RECORDS—Continued

A—Most triple plays, season, league—
  7—National—1905, 1910, 1929.
    American—1922, 1936.
B—Fewest triple plays, season, league—
  0—National League—1928, 1938, 1941, 1943, 1945, 1946, 1959, 1961.
    American League 1904, 1933, 1942, 1956, 1961, 1962.
C—Triple plays in a day—
  2—National—Brooklyn (1), New York (1), May 29, 1897.
    National—Boston (1), Chicago (1), Aug. 30, 1921.

LEAGUE BASE RUNNING

D—Most stolen bases, league, season—
  1,810—American League, 1912.
  1,691—National League, 1911.
E—Fewest stolen bases, league, season—
  337—National League, 1954.
  278—American League, 1950.
F—Most left on bases, league, season—
  11,680—American League (10 teams), 1961.
  11,416—National League (10 teams), 1962.

LEAGUE GAMES RECORDS

G—Most games played, season, (8 teams, 154 game schedule)—
  631—American League, 1914, 1917.
GG—Most games played, season, (10 teams, 162 game schedule)—
  625—National League, 1964.
  814—American League, 1965.
H—Fewest games played one season (154 game schedule)—
  813—National League, 1965.
  608—American League, 1933.
  608—National League, 1934.
I—Most unplayed games one season (except 1918)—
  19—American League, 1901.
  14—National League, 1938.
J—Fewest unplayed games one season—
  0—NL: 1908, 30, 32, 36, 47, 49, 51, 53-54, 56-61, 63-65.
    AL: 1922, 30, 40-41, 44, 46-47, 49-52, 54-56, 59-60, 64-65.
K—Most shutout games played, one season—
  164—National League, 1908.
  146—American League, 1909.
L—Fewest shutout games played, one season—
  41—American League, 1925.
  48—National League, 1930.
M—Most shutout games, league, one day—
  5—National—July 13, 1888; June 24, 1892; July 21, 1896; July 8, 1907; Sept. 9, 1916.
    American—Sept. 7, 1903; Aug. 5, 1909.
N—Most 1-0 games, (1900 to date)—season—
  43—National League, 1907.
  41—American League, 1908.

Longest Games in the Major Leagues

NATIONAL LEAGUE

26 inn.—Brk. 1, Bos. 1 (tie) ....May 1, 1920		
23 inn.—Brk. 2, Bos. 2 (tie) ...June 27, 1939		
S.F. 8, N.Y. 6 (2d g) ..May 31, 1964		
22 inn.—Brk. 6, Pitt. 5 ....Aug. 22, 1917		
. Chi. 4, Bos. 3 ....May 17, 1927		
21 inn.—N. Y. 3 Pitts. 1 ......July 17, 1914		
Chi. 2, Phila. 1 ......July 17, 1918		
Pitts. 2, Bos. 0 ....Aug. 1, 1918		
20 inn.—Chi. 7, Cinn. 7 (tie)...June 30, 1892		
Chi. 2, Phila. 1 ......Aug. 24, 1905		
Bklyn. 9, Phila. 9 (tie)..Apr. 30, 1919		
St. L. 8, Chi. 7 ......Aug. 28, 1930		
Bklyn. 6, Bos. 2.......July 5, 1940		
19 inn.—Chi. 3, Pitts. 2 ......June 22, 1902		
Pitts. 7, Bos. 6 ......July 31, 1912		
Chi. 4, Bklyn. 3 ......June 17, 1915		
St. L. 8, Phila. 8 (tie)..June 13, 1918		
Bos. 2, Bklyn. 1 ......May 3, 1920		

Chi. 3, Bos. 2 ....Aug. 17, 1932
Bklyn. 9, Chi. 9 (tie)....May 17, 1939
Cinn. 0, Bklyn 0 (tie)..Sept. 11, 1946
Phil. 8, Cin. 7 (N, 2 g) Sept. 15, 1950
Pitt. 4, Mil. 3 (N) ....July 19, 1955
18 inn.—Prov. 1, Det. 0 ......Aug. 17, 1882
Bklyn. 7, St. L. 7 (tie) .Aug. 17, 1902
Chi. 2, St. L. 1 ......June 24, 1905
Bklyn. 4, St. L. 3 ....July 29, 1914
Pitts. 3, Chi. 2, (2d g) .June 28, 1916
Phila. 10, Bklyn. 9 ....June 1, 1919
N. Y. 9, Pitts. 8 ......July 7, 1922
Chi. 7, Bos. 2 ......May 14, 1927
N. Y. 1, St. L. 0, 1st g..July 2, 1933
St. L. 8, Cinn. 6 (1st g.)..July 1, 1934
Chi. 10, Cinn. 8 (1st g.).Aug. 9, 1942
Phila. 4, Pitts. 3......June 9, 1949
Cinn. 7, Chi. 6 (2nd g.)..Sept. 7, 1951
N.Y. 0, Phil. 0 (N, 2 g) Oct. 2, 1965

AMERICAN LEAGUE

24 inn.—Phila. 4, Bos. 1 ......Sept. 1, 1906	
Det. 1, Phila. 1 (tie) ..July 21, 1945	
22 inn.—N.Y. 9, Det. 7 ......June 24, 1962	
21 inn.—Det. 6, Chi. 5 ......May 24, 1929	
20 inn.—Phila. 4, Bos. 2, ..July 4 (p.m.) 1905	
19 inn.—Wash. 5, Phila. 4 ....Sept. 27, 1912	
Chi. 5, Cleve. 4 ......June 24, 1915	
Cleve. 3, N. Y. 2 ......May 24, 1918	
St. L. 8, Wash. 6 ......Aug. 9, 1921	
Chi. 5, Bos. 4 (N) ......July 13, 1951	
Clev. 4, St. L. 3 (N) ..July 1, 1952	
Clev. 3, Wash. 2 (N) ..June 14, 1963	

18 inn.—Chi. 6, N. Y. 6 (tie) ...June 25, 1903
Det. 0, Wash. 0 (tie)....July 16, 1909
Wash. 1, Chi. 0 ......May 15, 1918
Det. 7, Wash. 6 ......Aug. 4, 1918
Bos. 12, N.Y. 11 (1st g)..Sept. 5, 1927
Phila. 18, Cleve. 17 ....July 10,1932
N. Y. 3, Chi. 3 (tie)....Aug. 21, 1933
Wash. 1, Chi. 0 (1st g.)..June 8, 1947
Wash. 5. St. L. 5 (tie) ..June 20, 1952
Chi. 1, Balt. 1 (N) ....Aug. 6, 1959

WORLD SERIES ROSTERS

1965-LOS ANGELES N.L. vs. MINNESOTA A.L.

Los Angeles N.L. 4 victories; Minnesota A.L. 3 victories

Date	Winning Team and Pitcher		Losing Team and Pitcher		Where Played
Oct. 6—Minnesota (Grant)	....	8	Los Angeles (Drysdale) ...		2 Minnesota
Oct. 7—Minnesota (Kaat)	....	5	Los Angeles (Koufax)		1 Minnesota
Oct. 9—Los Angeles (Osteen)	....	4	Minnesota (Pascual)		0 Los Angeles
Oct. 10—Los Angeles (Drysdale)	....	7	Minnesota (Grant)		2 Los Angeles
Oct. 11—Los Angeles (Koufax)	....	7	Minnesota (Kaat)		0 Los Angeles
Oct. 13—Minnesota (Grant)	....	5	Los Angeles (Osteen)		1 Minnesota
Oct. 14—Los Angeles (Koufax)	....	2	Minnesota (Kaat)		0 Minnesota

Managers—Walter E. Alston, Los Angeles; Sabath A. Mele, Minnesota.

Los Angeles—John Roseboro, Jeffrey A. Torborg, catchers; James T. Brewer, Donald S. Drysdale, Michael D. Kekich, Sanford Koufax, Robert L. Miller, Claude W. Osteen, Ronald Perranoski, John J. Podres, John N. Purdin, Howard D. Reed, J. Nicholas Willhite, pitchers; Ronald R. Fairly, James Gilliam, John E. Kennedy, James K. Lefebvre, Donald E. LeJohn, M. Wesley Parker, Richard J. Tracewski, Maurice M. Wills, infielders; Willie M. Crawford, William H. Davis, Louis B. Johnson, Wallace W. Moon, outfielders.

Minnesota—Earl J. Battey, John J. Sevcik, Gerald R. Zimmerman, catchers; David W. Boswell, James T. Grant, James L. Kaat, John C. Klippstein, James J. Merritt, Melvin F. Nelson, Camilo Pascual, James E. Perry, William Pleis, Richard L. Stigman, Allan F. Worthington, pitchers; Harmon C. Killebrew, Gerald D. Kindall, Donald R. Mincher, Frank R. Quilici, Richard J. Rollins, Zoilo Versalles, infielders; W. Robert Allison, Jimmie R. Hall, Joseph R. Nossek, Pedro Oliva, Hilario Valdespino, outfielders.

WORLD SERIES ROSTERS

1964-ST. LOUIS N.L. vs NEW YORK A.L.

St. Louis N.L., 4 victories; New York A.L. 3 victories

Date	Winning Team and Pitcher	Losing Team and Pitcher	Where Played
Oct. 7—St. Louis (Sadecki) 9		New York (Ford) 5	St. Louis
Oct. 8—New York (Stottlemyre) 8		St. Louis (Gibson) 3	St. Louis
Oct. 10—New York (Bouton) 2		St. Louis (Schultz) 1	New York
Oct. 11—St. Louis (Craig) 4		New York (Downing) 3	New York
Oct. 12—St. Louis (Gibson) ....°5		New York (Mikkelsen) 2	New York
Oct. 14—New York (Bouton) 8		St. Louis (Simmons) 3	St. Louis
Oct. 15—St. Louis (Gibson) 7		New York (Stottlemyre) 5	St. Louis

°10 innings.

Managers—John J. Keane, St. Louis; Lawrence P. Berra, New York.

St. Louis—J. Timothy McCarver, Robert G. Uecker, catchers; Roger L. Craig, Miguel S. Cuellar, Robert Gibson, Robert W. Humphreys, Gordon C. Richardson, Raymond M. Sadecki, George W. Schultz, Curtis T. Simmons, Ronald W. Taylor, Ray C. Washburn, pitchers; Kenton L. Boyer, Gerald P. Buchek, Richard M. Groat, M. Julian Javier, C. Dallan Maxvill, Edward W. Spiezio, William D. White, infielders; Louis C. Brock, Curtis C. Flood, Charles W. James, T. Michael Shannon, Robert R. Skinner, Carl W. Warwick, outfielders.

New York—John E. Blanchard, Elston G. Howard, catchers; James A. Bouton, Alphonso E. Downing, Edward C. Ford, Steve A. Hamilton, Peter J. Mikkelsen, Harold E. Reniff, Roland F. Sheldon, William C. Stafford, Melvin L. Stottlemyre, Ralph W. Terry, Stanley W. Williams, pitchers; Cletis L. Boyer, Pedro Gonzalez, J. Michael Hegan, Anthony C. Kubek, Philip F. Linz, Joseph A. Pepitone, Robert C. Richardson, infielders; Hector H. Lopez, Mickey C. Mantle, Roger E. Maris, Archie F. Moore, Jr., Thomas M. Tresh, outfielders.

1963—LOS ANGELES N.L. vs NEW YORK A.L.

Los Angeles N.L. 4 victories; New York A.L. 0 victories

Date	Winning Team and Pitcher	Losing Team and Pitcher	Where Played
Oct. 2—Los Angeles (Koufax) 5		New York (Ford) 2	New York
Oct. 3—Los Angeles (Podres) 4		New York (Downing) 1	New York
Oct. 5—Los Angeles (Drysdale) 1		New York (Bouton) 0	Los Angeles
Oct. 6—Los Angeles (Koufax) 2		New York (Ford) 1	Los Angeles

Managers—Walter E. Alston, Los Angeles; Ralph G. Houk, New York.

Los Angeles—Douglas J. Camilli, John Roseboro, catchers; Richard C. Calmus, Donald S. Drysdale, Sanford Koufax, Robert L. Miller, Ronald P. Perranoski, John J. Podres, Peter G. Richert, Kenneth D. Rowe, Lawrence Sherry, pitchers; Marvin Breeding, Ronald R. Fairly, James Gilliam, Kenneth McMullen, William J. Skowron, Richard J. Tracewski, Maurice M. Wills, infielders; Herman T. Davis, William H. Davis, Alfred Ferrara, Frank O. Howard, Wallace W. Moon, Ray Lee Walls, outfielders.

New York—Lawrence P. Berra, Elston G. Howard, catchers; James A. Bouton, Marshall Bridges, Alphonso E. Downing, Edward C. Ford, Steve A. Hamilton, William G. Kunkel, Thomas J. Metcalf, Harold E. Reniff, William C. Stafford, Ralph W. Terry, Stanley W. Williams, pitchers; Cletis L. Boyer, Harry J. Bright, Anthony C. Kubek, Philip F. Linz, Joseph A. Pepitone, Robert C. Richardson, infielders; John E. Blanchard, Hector H. Lopez, Mickey C. Mantle, Roger R. Maris, John B. Reed, Thomas M. Tresh, outfielders.

1962—NEW YORK A.L. vs SAN FRANCISCO N.L.

New York A.L. 4 victories; San Francisco N.L. 3 victories

Date	Winning Team and Pitcher	Losing Team and Pitcher	Where Played
Oct. 4—New York (Ford) 6		San Francisco (O'Dell) ... 2	San Francisco
Oct. 5—San Francisco (Sanford) 2		New York (Terry) 0	San Francisco
Oct. 7—New York (Stafford) 3		San Francisco (Pierce) ... 2	New York
Oct. 8—San Francisco (Larsen) 7		New York (Coates) 3	New York
Oct. 10—New York (Terry) 5		San Francisco (Sanford) .. 3	New York
Oct. 15—San Francisco (Pierce) 5		New York (Ford) 2	San Francisco
Oct. 16—New York (Terry) 1		San Francisco (Sanford) .. 0	San Francisco

Managers—Ralph G. Houk, New York; Alvin R. Dark, San Francisco.

New York—John E. Blanchard, Elston G. Howard, catchers; Luis E. Arroyo, James A. Bouton, Marshall Bridges, Truman E. Clevenger, James A. Coates, Buddy L. Daley, Edward C. Ford, Roland F. Sheldon, William C. Stafford, Ralph W. Terry, Robert L. Turley, pitchers; Cletis L. Boyer, Anthony Kubek, Philip F. Linz, Richard D. Long, Robert C. Richardson, William J. Skowron, infielders; Lawrence P. Berra, Hector H. Lopez, Mickey C. Mantle, Roger E. Maris, John B. Reed, Thomas M. Tresh, outfielders.

San Francisco—L. Edgar Bailey, Jr., Thomas F. Haller, John Orsino, catchers; Bobby D. Bolin, James F. Duffalo, Bob Roy Garibaldi, Donald J. Larsen, Juan A. Marichal, Michael F. McCormick, Stuart L. Miller, William O. O'Dell, W. William Pierce, John S. Sanford, pitchers; Ernest F. Bowman, Orlando Cepeda, James H. Davenport, Charles J. Hiller, Willie L. McCovey, Jose A. Pagan, infielders; Felipe R. Alou, Mateo R. Alou, Carl Boles, Harvey E. Kuenn, Jr., Willie H. Mays, Jr., Robert C. Nieman, outfielders.

1961—NEW YORK A.L. vs CINCINNATI N.L.

New York A.L. 4 victories; Cincinnati N.L. 1 victory

Date	Winning Team and Pitcher		Losing Team and Pitcher		Where Played
Oct. 4—New York (Ford)	2	Cincinnati (O'Toole)	0	New York
Oct. 5—Cincinnati (Jay)	6	New York (Terry)	2	New York
Oct. 7—New York (Arroyo)	3	Cincinnati (Purkey)	2	Cincinnati
Oct. 8—New York (Ford)	7	Cincinnati (O'Toole)	0	Cincinnati
Oct. 9—New York (Daley)	13	Cincinnati (Jay)	5	Cincinnati

Managers—Ralph G. Houk, New York; Frederick C. Hutchinson, Cincinnati.

New York—John E. Blanchard, Elston G. Howard, catchers; Luis E. Arroyo, Truman E. Clevenger, James A. Coates, Buddy L. Daley, Alphonso Downing, Edward C. Ford, Harold Reniff, Roland F. Sheldon, William C. Stafford, Ralph W. Terry, Robert L. Turley, pitchers; Cletis L. Boyer, Joseph P. DeMaestri, William F. Gardner, Robert H. Hale, Anthony C. Kubek, Robert C. Richardson, William J. Skowron, infielders; Lawrence P. Berra, Hector H. Lopez, Mickey C. Mantle, Roger E. Maris, John B. Reed, outfielders.

Cincinnati—John Edwards, Darrell D. Johnson, Gerald R. Zimmerman, catchers; James P. Brosnan, William R. Henry, James W. Hook, Kenneth R. Hunt, Joseph R. Jay, Kenneth Johnson, James W. Maloney, Howard R. Nunn, James J. O'Toole, Robert T. Purkey, pitchers; Donald L. Blasingame, Leonardo L. Cardenas, Elio R. Chacon, Gordon C. Coleman, Gene L. Freese, Richard E. Gernert, Edward M. Kasko, infielders; David R. Bell, Gerald T. Lynch, Vada E. Pinson, Walter C. Post, Frank Robinson, outfielders.

1960—PITTSBURGH N.L. vs NEW YORK A.L.

Pittsburgh N.L. 4 victories; New York A.L. 3 victories

Date	Winning Team and Pitcher		Losing Team and Pitcher		Where Played
Oct. 5—Pittsburgh (Law)	6	New York (Ditmar)	4	Pittsburgh
Oct. 6—New York (Turley)	16	Pittsburgh (Friend)	3	Pittsburgh
Oct. 8—New York (Ford)	10	Pittsburgh (Mizell)	0	New York
Oct. 9—Pittsburgh (Law)	3	New York (Terry)	2	New York
Oct. 10—Pittsburgh (Haddix)	5	New York (Ditmar)	2	New York
Oct. 12—New York (Ford)	12	Pittsburgh (Friend)	0	Pittsburgh
Oct. 13—Pittsburgh (Haddix)	10	New York (Terry)	9	Pittsburgh

Managers—Daniel E. Murtaugh, Pittsburgh; Charles D. Stengel, New York.

Pittsburgh—Forrest H. Burgess, Robert C. Oldis, Harold W. Smith, catchers; Thomas E. Cheney, Jr., Elroy L. Face, Robert B. Friend, Joseph C. Gibbon, Fred A. Green, Harvey Haddix, Jr., Clement W. Labine, Vernon S. Law, Wilmer D. Mizell, George A. Witt, pitchers; Eugene Baker, Richard M. Groat, Donald A. Hoak, William S. Mazeroski, Glenn R. Nelson, J. Richard Schofield, Richard L. Stuart, infielders; Joseph O. Christopher, Gino N. Cimoli, Roberto W. Clemente, Robert R. Skinner, William C. Virdon, outfielders.

New York—Lawrence P. Berra, John E. Blanchard, Elston G. Howard, catchers; Luis Arroyo, James A. Coates, Arthur J. Ditmar, Rinold G. Duren, Jr., Edward C. Ford, Eli Grba, Duane F. Maas, Robert C. Shantz, William Stafford, Ralph W. Terry, Robert L. Turley, pitchers; Cletis L. Boyer, Joseph P. DeMaestri, Anthony C. Kubek, Jr., R. Dale Long, Gilbert J. McDougald, Robert C. Richardson, William J. Skowron, Jr., infielders; Robert H. Cerv, Hector H. Lopez, Mickey C. Mantle, Roger E. Maris, outfielders.

1959—LOS ANGELES N.L. vs CHICAGO A.L.

Los Angeles N.L. 4 victories; Chicago A.L. 2 victories

Date	Winning Team and Pitcher		Losing Team and Pitcher		Where Played
Oct. 1—Chicago (Wynn)	11	Los Angeles (Craig)	0	Chicago
Oct. 2—Los Angeles (Podres)	4	Chicago (Shaw)	3	Chicago
Oct. 4—Los Angeles (Drysdale)	3	Chicago (Donovan)	1	Los Angeles
Oct. 5—Los Angeles (Sherry)	5	Chicago (Staley)	4	Los Angeles
Oct. 6—Chicago (Shaw)	1	Los Angeles (Koufax)	0	Los Angeles
Oct. 8—Los Angeles (Sherry)	9	Chicago (Wynn)	3	Chicago

Managers—Walter E. Alston, Los Angeles; Alfonso R. Lopez, Chicago.

Los Angeles—Joseph B. Pignatano, John Roseboro, catchers; Clarence N. Churn, Roger L. Craig, Donald S. Drysdale, John C. Klippstein, Sanford Koufax, Clement W. Labine, Daniel E. McDevitt, John J. Podres, Lawrence Sherry, Stanley W. Williams, pitchers; James Gilliam, Gilbert R. Hodges, Charles L. Neal, Maurice M. Wills, Donald W. Zimmer, infielders; Donald L. Demeter, Charles A. Essegian, Jr., Ronald R. Fairly, Carl A. Furillo, Norman H. Larker, Wallace W. Moon, Eldon J. Repulski, Edwin D. Snider, outfielders.

Chicago—Earl J. Battey, Jr., J. Sherman Lollar, John A. Romano, catchers; Rodolfo Arias, Richard E. Donovan, A. Barry Latman, Omar J. Lown, Kenneth F. McBride, Raymond L. Moore, W. William Pierce, Robert J. Shaw, Gerald L. Staley, Early Wynn, pitchers; Luis E. Aparicio, Norman D. Cash, Samuel Esposito, J. Nelson Fox, William D. Goodman, Theodore B. Kluszewski, John M. Phillips, C. Earl Torgeson, infielders; James H. Landis, Jr., James McAnany, Manuel J. Rivera, Alphonse E. Smith, outfielders.

1958—NEW YORK A.L. vs. MILWAUKEE N.L.

New York A.L. 4 victories; Milwaukee N.L. 3

Date	Winning Team and Pitcher		Losing Team and Pitcher		Where Played
Oct. 1—Milwaukee (Spahn)	°4	New York (Duren)	3	Milwaukee
Oct. 2—Milwaukee (Burdette)	13	New York (Turley)	5	Milwaukee
Oct. 4—New York (Larsen)	4	Milwaukee (Rush)	0	New York
Oct. 5—Milwaukee (Spahn)	3	New York (Ford)	0	New York
Oct. 6—New York (Turley)	7	Milwaukee (Burdette)	0	New York
Oct. 8—New York (Duren)	°4	Milwaukee (Spahn)	3	Milwaukee
Oct. 9—New York (Turley)	6	Milwaukee (Burdette)	2	Milwaukee

°10 innings.

Managers—Charles D. Stengel, New York; Fred G. Haney, Milwaukee.
New York—Lawrence P. Berra, Elston G. Howard, Darrell D. Johnson, catchers; Murry M. Dickson, Arthur J. Ditmar, Rinold G. Duren, Jr., Edward C. Ford, John C. Kucks, Donald J. Larsen, Duane F. Maas, Zachary C. Munroe, Robert C. Shantz, Thomas V. Sturdivant, Virgil O. Trucks, Robert L. Turley, pitchers; Andrew A. Carey, Anthony C. Kubek, Jerry D. Lumpe, Gilbert J. McDougald, Robert C. Richardson, William J. Skowron, Marvin E. Throneberry, infielders; Henry A. Bauer, Mickey C. Mantle, Norman L. Siebern, Enos B. Slaughter, outfielders.
Milwaukee—Delmar W. Crandall, Delbert W. Rice, catchers; Robert R. Buhl, Selva L. Burdette, Donald E. Conley, Ernest T. Johnson, Donald J. McMahon, Juan Pizarro, Humberto V. Robinson, Robert R. Rush, Warren E. Spahn, Robert Trowbridge, Carleton F. Willey, pitchers; Joseph W. Adcock, Harry A. Hanebrink, John Logan, Felix L. Mantilla, Edwin L. Mathews, Albert F. Schoendienst, Frank J. Torre, Kendell C. Wise, infielders; Henry L. Aaron, William H. Bruton, John W. Covington, Andrew Pafko, outfielders.

1957—MILWAUKEE N.L. vs. NEW YORK A.L.

Milwaukee N.L. 4 victories; New York A.L. 3

Date	Winning Team and Pitcher		Losing Team and Pitcher		Where Played
Oct. 2—New York (Ford)	3	Milwaukee (Spahn)	1	New York
Oct. 3—Milwaukee (Burdette)	4	New York (Shantz)	2	New York
Oct. 5—New York (Larsen)	12	Milwaukee (Buhl)	3	Milwaukee
Oct. 6—Milwaukee (Spahn)	°7	New York (Grim)	5	Milwaukee
Oct. 7—Milwaukee (Burdette)	1	New York (Ford)	0	Milwaukee
Oct. 9—New York (Turley)	3	Milwaukee (Johnson)	2	New York
Oct. 10—Milwaukee (Burdette)	5	New York (Larsen)	0	New York

°10 innings.

Managers—Fred G. Haney, Milwaukee; Charles D. Stengel, New York.
Milwaukee—Delmar W. Crandall, Delbert W. Rice, Carl E. Sawatski, catchers; Robert R. Buhl, Selva L. Burdette, Donald E. Conley, Ernest T. Johnson, David Jolly, Donald J. McMahon, William T. Phillips, Juan Pizarro, Warren E. Spahn, Robert Trowbridge, pitchers; Joseph W. Adcock, Vernal L. Jones, John Logan, Felix L. Mantilla, Edwin L. Mathews, Melvin E. Roach, Albert F. Schoendienst, Frank J. Torre, infielders; Henry A. Aaron, John W. Covington, John DeMerit, Robert S. Hazle, Andrew Pafko, outfielders.

New York—Lawrence P. Berra, Darrell Johnson, catchers; Thomas J. Byrne, Alva W. Cicotte, Arthur J. Ditmar, Edward C. Ford, Robert A. Grim, John C. Kucks, Donald J. Larsen, Robert C. Shantz, Thomas V. Sturdivant, Robert L. Turley, pitchers; Andrew A. Carey, Gerald F. Coleman, Joseph E. Collins, Anthony C. Kubek, Jerry D. Lumpe, Gilbert J. McDougald, Robert C. Richardson, William J. Skowron, infielders; Henry A. Bauer, Elston G. Howard, Mickey C. Mantle, Harry L. Simpson, Enos B. Slaughter, outfielders.

1956—NEW YORK A.L. vs. BROOKLYN N.L.

New York A.L. 4 victories; Brooklyn N.L. 3

Date	Winning Team and Pitcher		Losing Team and Pitcher		Where Played
Oct. 3—Brooklyn (Maglie)	6	New York (Ford)	3	Brooklyn
Oct. 5—Brooklyn (Bessent)	13	New York (Morgan)	8	Brooklyn
Oct. 6—New York (Ford)	5	Brooklyn (Craig)	3	New York
Oct. 7—New York (Sturdivant)	6	Brooklyn (Erskine)	2	New York
Oct. 8—New York (Larsen)	2	Brooklyn (Maglie)	0	New York
Oct. 9—Brooklyn (Labine)	°1	New York (Turley)	0	Brooklyn
Oct. 10—New York (Kucks)	9	Brooklyn (Newcombe)	0	Brooklyn

°10 innings.

Managers—Charles D. Stengel, New York; Walter E. Alston, Brooklyn.
New York—Lawrence P. Berra, Charles R. Silvera, catchers; Thomas J. Byrne, Walter G. Coleman, Edward C. Ford, Robert A. Grim, John C. Kucks, Donald J. Larsen, Maurice J. McDermott, Thomas S. Morgan, Thomas V. Sturdivant, Robert L. Turley, pitchers; Andrew A. Carey, Thomas E. Carroll, Gerald F. Coleman, Joseph E. Collins, Gordon W. Hunter, Alfred M. Martin, Gilbert J. McDougald, William J. Skowron, infielders; Henry A. Bauer, Robert H. Cerv, Elston G. Howard, Mickey C. Mantle, Norman L. Siebern, Enos B. Slaughter, George W. Wilson, outfielders.
Brooklyn—Roy Campanella, Homer Howell, Albert B. Walker, catchers; Fred D. Bessent, Roger L. Craig, Donald S. Drysdale, Carl D. Erskine, Sanford Koufax, Clement W. Labine, Kenneth K. Lehman, Salvatore A. Maglie, Donald Newcombe, Edward J. Roebuck, pitchers; Humberto Fernandez, James Gilliam, Gilbert R. Hodges, Ransom J. Jackson, Charles L. Neal, Harold H. Reese, Jack R. Robinson, infielders; Edmundo Amoros, Gino W. Cimoli, Carl ? Furillo, Loren D. Mitchell, Edwin D. Snider, outfielders.

1955—BROOKLYN N.L. vs. NEW YORK A.L.

Brooklyn N.L. 4 victories; New York A.L. 3

Date	Winning Team and Pitcher		Losing Team and Pitcher		Where Played
Sept. 28—New York (Ford)	6	Brooklyn (Newcombe)	5	New York
Sept. 29—New York (Byrne)	4	Brooklyn (Loes)	2	New York
Sept. 30—Brooklyn (Podres)	8	New York (Turley)	3	Brooklyn
Oct. 1—Brooklyn (Labine)	8	New York (Larsen)	5	Brooklyn
Oct. 2—Brooklyn (Craig)	5	New York (Grim)	3	Brooklyn
Oct. 3—New York (Ford)	5	Brooklyn (Spooner)	1	New York
Oct. 4—Brooklyn (Podres)	2	New York (Byrne)	0	New York

Managers—Walter E. Alston, Brooklyn; Charles D. Stengel, New York.

Brooklyn—Roy Campanella, Homer E. Howell, Albert B. Walker, catchers; Fred D. Bessent, Roger L. Craig, Carl D. Erskine, Sanford Koufax, Clement W. Labine, William Loes, Russell C. Meyer, Donald Newcombe, John J. Podres, Edward J. Roebuck, Karl B. Spooner, pitchers; James Gilliam Donald A. Hoak, Gilbert R. Hodges, Frank W. Kellert, Jack R. Robinson, Harold H. Reese, Donald W. Zimmer, infielders; Edmundo Amoros, Carl A. Furillo, George T. Shuba, Edwin D. Snider, outfielders.

New York—Lawrence P. Berra, Charles A. Silvera, catchers; Thomas J. Byrne, Walter G. Coleman, Edward C. Ford, Robert A. Grim, John C. Kucks, Donald J. Larsen, Thomas S. Morgan, Thomas V. Sturdivant, Robert L. Turley, Robert G. Wiesler, pitchers; Andrew A. Carey, Thomas E. Carroll, Gerald F. Coleman, Joseph E. Collins, Frank J. Leja, Gilbert J. McDougald, Alfred M. Martin, Philip F. Rizzuto, William Edward Robinson, William J. Skowron, infielders; Henry A. Bauer, Robert H. Cerv, Elston G. Howard, Mickey C. Mantle, Irving A. Noren, outfielders.

1954—NEW YORK N.L. vs. CLEVELAND A.L.

New York N.L. 4 victories; Cleveland A.L. 0

Date	Winning Team and Pitcher		Losing Team and Pitcher		Where Played
Sept. 29—New York (Grissom)	*5	Cleveland (Lemon)	2	New York
Sept. 30—New York (Antonelli)	3	Cleveland (Wynn)	1	New York
Oct. 1—New York (Gomez)	6	Cleveland (Garcia)	2	Cleveland
Oct. 2—New York (Liddle)	7	Cleveland (Lemon)	4	Cleveland

* 10 innings.

Managers—Leo E. Durocher, New York; Alfonso R. Lopez, Cleveland.

New York—Raymond F. Katt, Wesley N. Westrum, catchers; John A. Antonelli, Elmer N. Corwin, Paul Giel, Ruben Gomez, Marvin Grissom, James T. Hearn, Alex Konikowski, Donald E. Liddle, Salvatore Maglie, John W. McCall, Hovt J. Wilhelm, Allan Worthington, pitchers; Joseph Amalfitano, Foster Castleman, Alvin R. Dark, William F. Gardner, Robert G. Hofman, Carroll W. Lockman, Henry Thompson, David C. Williams, infielders; Monte M. Irvin, Willie E. Mays, Donald F. Mueller, James L. Rhodes, William M. Taylor, outfielders.

Cleveland—Newton M. Grasso, James E. Hegan, Harold R. Naragon, catchers; Robert W. Feller, Edward M. Garcia, Robert N. Hooper, Arthur J. Houtteman, Robert G. Lemon, Donald L. Mossi, Raymond E. Narleski, Harold Newhouser, Early Wynn, pitchers; Roberto Avila, Samuel J. Dente, William V. Glynn, Henry Majeski, Rudolph V. Regalado, Albert L. Rosen, George B. Strickland, Victor W. Wertz, infielders; Lawrence E. Doby, Loren D. Mitchell, David E. Philley, David Pope, Alphonse E. Smith, Waldon T. Westlake, outfielders.

1953—NEW YORK A.L. vs. BROOKLYN N.L.

New York A.L. 4 victories; Brooklyn N.L. 2

Date	Winning Team and Pitcher		Losing Team and Pitcher		Where Played
Sept. 30—New York (Sain)	9	Brooklyn (Labine)	5	New York
Oct. 1—New York (Lopat)	4	Brooklyn (Roe)	2	New York
Oct. 2—Brooklyn (Erskine)	3	New York (Raschi)	2	Brooklyn
Oct. 3—Brooklyn (Loes)	7	New York (Ford)	3	Brooklyn
Oct. 4—New York (McDonald)	11	Brooklyn (Podres)	7	Brooklyn
Oct. 5—New York (Reynolds)	4	Brooklyn (Labine)	3	New York

Manager—Charles D. Stengel, New York; Charles W. Dressen, Brooklyn.

New York—Lawrence P. Berra, Charles A. Silvera, Gus Triandos, catchers; Edward C. Ford, Thomas A. Gorman, Stephen C. Kraly, Robert L. Kuzava, Edmund W. Lopat, James L. McDonald, William P. Miller, Victor J. Raschi, Allie P. Reynolds, John F. Sain, Arthur L. Schallock, pitchers; Donald R. Bollweg, Andrew A. Carey, Gerald F. Coleman, Joseph E. Collins, Alfred M. Martin, Gilbert J. McDougald, Guillermo P. Miranda, John R. Mize, Philip F. Rizzuto, infielders; Henry A. Bauer, Mickey C. Mantle, Irving A. Noren, William B. Renna, Eugene R. Woodling, outfielders.

Brooklyn—Roy Campanella, Albert H. Walker, catchers; Joseph Black, Carl D. Erskine, James R. Hughes, Clement W. Labine, William Loes, Russell C. Meyer, Robert Milliken, Ervin Palica, John Podres, Elwin C. Roe, Benjamin S. Wade, pitchers; Wayne C. Belardi, William R. Cox, James Gilliam, Gilbert R. Hodges, Robert M. Morgan, Harold H. Reese, infielders; William J. Antonello, Carl A. Furillo, Jack R. Robinson, George T. Shuba, Edwin D. Snider, Donald N. Thompson, Richard H. Williams, outfielders.

1952—NEW YORK A. L. vs. BROOKLYN N. L.

New York A.L. 4 victories; Brooklyn N.L. 3

Date	Winning Team and Pitcher	Losing Team and Pitcher	Where Played
Oct. 1—Brooklyn (Black) 4	New York (Reynolds) 2	Brooklyn
Oct. 2—New York (Raschi) 7	Brooklyn (Erskine) 1	Brooklyn
Oct. 3—Brooklyn (Roe) 5	New York (Lopat) 3	New York
Oct. 4—New York (Reynolds) ... 2	Brooklyn (Black) 0	New York
Oct. 5—Brooklyn (Erskine) *6	New York (Sain) 5	New York
Oct. 6—New York (Raschi) 3	Brooklyn (Loes) 2	Brooklyn
Oct. 7—New York (Reynolds) 4	Brooklyn (Black) 2	Brooklyn

* 11 innings.

Managers—Charles D. Stengel, New York; Charles W. Dressen, Brooklyn.

New York—Lawrence P. Berra, Ralph G. Houk, Charles A. Silvera, catchers; Ewell Blackwell, Thomas A. Gorman, Robert L. Kuzava, Edmund W. Lopat, James L. McDonald, William P. Miller, Joseph P. Ostrowski, Victor J. Raschi, Allie P. Reynolds, John F. Sain, Ray W. Scarborough, pitchers; Loren R. Babe, James E. Brideweser, Joseph E. Collins, Alfred M. Martin, Gilbert J. McDougald, John R. Mize, Philip F. Rizzuto, infielders; Henry A. Bauer, Mickey C. Mantle, Irving A. Noren, Eugene R. Woodling, outfielders.

Brooklyn—Roy Campanella, Albert H. Walker, catchers; Joseph Black, Ralph T. Branca, Carl D. Erskine, Clyde E. King, Clement W. Labine, Joseph B. Landrum, Kenneth Lehman, William Loes, Raymond L. Moore, Elwin C. Roe, John W. Rutherford, Benjamin S. Wade, pitchers; Everett L. Bridges, William R. Cox, Gilbert R. Hodges, Robert Morgan, Glenn R. Nelson, Harold H. Reese, Jack R. Robinson, infielders; Edmundo Amoros, Carl A. Furillo, Thomas F. Holmes, Andrew Pafko, George Shuba, Edwin D. Snider, Richard Williams, outfielders.

1951—NEW YORK A. L. vs. NEW YORK N. L.

New York A. L. 4 victories; New York N.L. 2

Date	Winning Team and Pitcher	Losing Team and Pitcher	Where Played
Oct. 4—Giants (Koslo) 5	Yankees (Reynolds) 1	Yankee Stadium
Oct. 5—Yankees (Lopat) 3	Giants (Jansen) 1	Yankee Stadium
Oct. 6—Giants (Hearn) 6	Yankees (Raschi) 2	Polo Grounds
Oct. 7—Postponed rain.		
Oct. 8—Yankees (Reynolds) 6	Giants (Maglie) 2	Polo Grounds
Oct. 9—Yankees (Lopat) 13	Giants (Jansen) 1	Polo Grounds
Oct. 10—Yankees (Raschi) 4	Giants (Koslo) 3	Yankee Stadium

Managers—Charles D. Stengel, Yankees; Leo E. Durocher, Giants.

Yankees—Lawrence P. Berra, Ralph G. Houk, Charles A. Silvera, catchers; Robert C. Hogue, Robert L. Kuzava, Edmund Lopat, Thomas S. Morgan, Joseph P. Ostrowski, Frank Overmire, Victor J. Raschi, Allie P. Reynolds, John F. Sain, Arthur Shallock, Frank J. Shea, pitchers; Robert W. Brown, Gerald F. Coleman, Joseph E. Collins, John L. Hopp, Alfred M. Martin, Gilbert J. McDougald, John R. Mize, Philip F. Rizzuto, infielders; Henry A. Bauer, Joseph P. DiMaggio, Mickey C. Mantle, Eugene R. Woodling, outfielders.

Giants—Rafael Noble, Wesley W. Westrum. Salvatore A. Yvars, catchers; Elmer N. Corwin, James T. Hearn, Lawrence J. Jansen, Sheldon L. Jones, Montia C. Kennedy, Alexander J. Konikowski, George B. Koslo, Salvatore A. Maglie, George F. Spencer, pitchers; Alvin R. Dark, Carroll W. Lockman, Jack W. Lohrke, William J. Rigney, Henry L. Schenz, Edward R. Stanky, Henry T. Thompson, Robert B. Thomson, David Williams, infielders; Clinton C Hartung, Monford Irvin, Willie Mays, Donald F. Mueller, outfielders.

1950—NEW YORK A. L. vs. PHILADELPHIA N. L.

New York A.L. 4 victories; Philadelphia N.L. 0

Date	Winning Team and Pitcher	Losing Team and Pitcher	Where Played
Oct. 4—New York (Raschi)...... 1	Philadelphia (Konstanty) . 0	Philadelphia
Oct. 5—New York (Reynolds) ... *2	Philadelphia (Roberts) ..., 1	Philadelphia
Oct. 6—New York (Ferrick) ... 3	Philadelphia (Meyer) 2	New York
Oct. 7—New York (Ford) 5	Philadelphia (Miller) 2	New York

*10 innings.

Managers—Charles D. Stengel, New York; Edwin M. Sawyer, Philadelphia.

New York—Lawrence P. Berra, Ralph G. Houk, Charles A. Silvera, catchers; Thomas J. Byrne, Thomas J. Ferrick, Edward C. Ford, Edmund Lopat, Joseph P. Ostrowski, Joseph F. Page, Victor J. Raschi, Allie P. Reynolds. Fred J. Sanford, pitchers; Robert W. Brown, Gerald F. Coleman, Joseph E. Collins, John L. Hopp, William R. Johnson, Alfred M. Martin, John R. Mize, Philip F. Rizzuto, infielders; Henry A. Bauer, Joseph P. DiMaggio, Jack E. Jensen, Clifford F. Mapes, Eugene R. Woodling, outfielders.

Philadelphia—Stanley E. Lopata. Andrew W. Seminick, Kenneth J. Silvestri, catchers; Milo Candini, Emory N. Church. Sylvester U. Donnelly, Kenneth A. Heintzelman, Kenneth W. Johnson, C. James Konstanty, Russell C. Meyer, Robert J. Miller, Robin E. Roberts, John S. Thompson, pitchers; James H. Bloodworth, Ralph J. Caballero, Michael M. Goliat, Granville W. Hamner, Willie E. Jones, Edward S. Waitkus, infielders; Richie Ashburn, Delmer Ennis, Stanley Hollmig, John L. Mayo, Richard A. Sisler, Richard C. Whitman, outfielders.

1949—NEW YORK A. L. vs. BROOKLYN N. L.

New York A.L. 4 victories; Brooklyn N.L. 1

Date	Winning Team and Pitcher		Losing Team and Pitcher		Where Played
Oct. 5—New York (Reynolds)...	1	Brooklyn (Newcombe) ...	0	New York
Oct. 6—Brooklyn (Roe)	1	New York (Raschi)	0	New York
Oct. 7—New York (Page)	4	Brooklyn (Branca)	3	Brooklyn
Oct. 8—New York (Lopat)	6	Brooklyn (Newcombe) ...	4	Brooklyn
Oct. 9—New York (Raschi)	10	Brooklyn (Barney)	6	Brooklyn

Managers—Charles D. Stengel, New York; Burton E. Shotton, Brooklyn.
New York—Lawrence P. Berra, Constantine G. Niarhos, Charles A. Silvera, catchers; Ralph X. Buxton, Thomas J. Byrne, Edmund Lopat, Clarence W. Marshall, Joseph F. Page, Duane X. Pillette, Victor J. Raschi, Allie P. Reynolds, Fred J. Sanford, pitchers; Robert W. Brown, Gerald F. Coleman, Thomas D. Henrich, William R. Johnson, John R. Mize, Philip F. Rizzuto, George H. Stirnweiss, infielders; Henry A. Bauer, Joseph P. DiMaggio, Charles E. Keller, John H. Lindell, Clifford F. Mapes, Eugene R. Woodling, outfielders.
Brooklyn—Roy Campanella, C. Bruce Edwards, catchers; John K. Banta, Rex E. Barney, Ralp T. Branca, Carl D. Erskine, Joseph H. Hatten, Paul E. Minner, Donald Newcombe, Ervin Palica, Elwin C. Roe, pitchers; William R. Cox, Gilbert R. Hodges, John D. Jorgensen, Edward T. Miksis, Harold H. Reese, Jack R. Robinson, infielders; Thomas N. Brown, Carl A. Furillo, Eugene V. Hermanski, Myron W. McCormick, Luis Olmo, Marvin D. Rackley, Edwin D. Snider, Richard C. Whitman, outfielders.

1948—CLEVELAND A. L. vs. BOSTON N. L.

Cleveland A.L. 4 victories; Boston N.L. 2

Oct. 6—Boston (Sain)	1	Cleveland (Feller)	0	Boston
Oct. 7—Cleveland (Lemon)	4	Boston (Spahn)	1	Boston
Oct. 8—Cleveland (Bearden) ...	2	Boston (Bickford)	0	Cleveland
Oct. 9—Cleveland (Gromek) ...	2	Boston (Sain)	1	Cleveland
Oct. 10—Boston (Spahn)	11	Cleveland (Feller)	5	Cleveland
Oct. 11—Cleveland (Lemon)	4	Boston (Voiselle)	3	Boston

Managers—Louis Boudreau, Cleveland; William H. Southworth, Boston.
Cleveland—James E. Hegan, Joseph J. Tipton, catchers; H. Eugene Bearden, Donald P. Black, Russell O. Christopher, Robert W. A. Feller, Stephen J. Gromek, Edward F. Klieman, Robert G. Lemon, Robert C. Muncrief, Leroy Paige, Samuel W. Zoldak, pitchers; John Berardino, Raymond O. Boone, Louis Boudreau, Joseph L. Gordon, Kenneth F. Keltner, W. Edward Robinson, Albert F. Rosen, infielders; Alfred H. Clark, Lawrence E. Doby, Henry A. Edwards, Walter F. Judnich, Robert D. Kennedy, L. Dale Mitchell, Harold A. Peck, Thurman L. Tucker, outfielders.
Boston—Philip S. Masi, William F. Salkeld, catchers; Charles H. Barrett, Vernon D. Bickford, Robert C. Hogue, Albert H. Lyons, Nelson T. Potter, John F. Sain, Clyde M. Shoun, Warren E. Spahn, William S. Voiselle, Ernest D. White, pitchers; Alvin R. Dark, Robert I. Elliott, Frank A. McCormick, Cornelius J. Ryan, Raymond F. Sanders, Sebastian D. Sisti, Edward R. Stanky, Robert H. Sturgeon, C. Earl Torgeson, infielders; Clinton A. Conaster, J. Geoffrey Heath, Thomas F. Holmes, Myron W. McCormick, Marvin A. Rickert, James W. Russell, outfielders.

1947—NEW YORK A. L. vs. BROOKLYN N. L.

New York A.L. 4 victories; Brooklyn N.L. 3

Sept. 30—New York (Shea)	5	Brooklyn (Branca)	3	New York
Oct. 1—New York (Reynolds) ..	10	Brooklyn (Lombardi) ...	3	New York
Oct. 2—Brooklyn (Casey)	9	New York (Newsom) ...	8	Brooklyn
Oct. 3—Brooklyn (Casey)	3	New York (Bevens)	2	Brooklyn
Oct. 4—New York (Shea)	2	Brooklyn (Barney)	1	Brooklyn
Oct. 5—Brooklyn (Branca)	8	New York (Page)	6	New York
Oct. 6—New York (Page)	5	Brooklyn (Gregg)	2	New York

Managers—Stanley R. Harris, New York; Burton E. Shotton, Brooklyn.
New York—Lawrence P. Berra, Ralph G. Houk, J. Sherman Lollar, Aaron A. Robinson, catchers; Floyd C. Bevens, Spurgeon F. Chandler, Karl A. Drews, Randall P. Gumpert, Donald R. Johnson, Louis N. Newsom, Joseph F. Page, Victor J. Raschi, Allie P. Reynolds, Frank J. Shea, Charles W. Wensloff, pitchers; Robert W. Brown, Linus R. Frey, William R. Johnson, George H. McQuinn, John D. Phillips, Philip F. Rizzuto, George H. Stirnweiss, infielders; Alfred A. Clark, Joseph P. DiMaggio, Thomas D. Henrich, Charles E. Keller, John H. Lindell, outfielders.
Brooklyn—Robert R. Bragan, C. Bruce Edwards, Gilbert R. Hodges, catchers; Daniel R. Bankhead, Rex E. Barney, Henry B. Behrman, Ralph T. Branca, Hugh T. Casey, Harold D. Gregg, Joseph H. Hatten, Clyde E. King, Victor A. Lombardi, J. Harry Taylor, pitchers; Thomas M. Brown, John D. Jorgensen, Harry A. Lavagetto, Edward T. Miksis, Harold H. Reese, Jack R. Robinson, Stanley A. Rojek, Edward R. Stanky, Floyd E. Vaughan, infielders; Carl A. Furillo, Albert F. Gionfriddo, Eugene V. Hermanski, Harold P. Reiser, Frederick R. Walker, outfielders.

1946—ST. LOUIS N. L. vs. BOSTON A. L

St. Louis N.L. 4 victories; Boston A.L. 3

Date	Winning Team and Pitcher		Losing Team and Pitcher		Where Played
Oct. 6—Boston (Johnson)	......	°3	St. Louis (Pollet)	 2	St. Louis
Oct. 7—St. Louis (Brecheen)	..	3	Boston (Harris)	 0	St. Louis
Oct. 9—Boston (Ferriss)	......	4	St. Louis (Dickson)	 0	Boston
Oct. 10—St. Louis (Munger)	...	12	Boston (Hughson)	 3	Boston
Oct. 11—Boston (Dobson)	......	6	St. Louis (Brazle)	 3	Boston
Oct. 13—St. Louis (Brecheen)	...	4	Boston (Harris)	 1	St. Louis
Oct. 15—St. Louis (Brecheen)	...	4	Boston (Klinger)	 3	St. Louis

°10 innings.

Managers—Edwin H. Dyer, St. Louis; Joseph E. Cronin, Boston.

St. Louis—Joseph H. Garagiola, Clyde F. Kluttz, Delbert W. Rice, catchers; Charles H. Barrett, John A. Beazley, Alpha E. Brazle, Harry D. Brecheen, Kenneth W. Burkhart, Murry M. Dickson, John Grodzicki, Howard W. Krist, George D. Munger, Howard J. Pollet, Frederick A. Schmidt, Theodore Wilks, pitchers; Joffre J. Cross, Vernal L. Jones, George J. Kurowski, Martin W. Marion, Stanley F. Musial, Albert F. Schoendienst, infielders; Elvin C. Adams, Ervin F. Dusak, William F. Endicott, Terry B. Moore, Walter A. Sessi, Richard A. Sisler, Enos B. Slaughter, Harry W. Walker, outfielders.

Boston—Edward J. McGah, Roy R. Partee, Harold E. Wagner, catchers; James C. Bagby, Mace S. Brown, Joseph G. Dobson, Clement J. Dreisewerd, David M. Ferriss, Maurice C. Harris, Cecil C. Hughson, Earl D. Johnson, Robert H. Klinger, Dominic J. Ryba, Charles T. Wagner, William H. Zuber, pitchers; Paul M. Campbell, Robert P. Doerr, Donald J. Gutteridge, Michael F. Higgins, Edward C. Pellagrini, John M. Pesky, Glen D. Russell, Rudolph P. York, infielders; D. Leon Culberson, Dominic P. DiMaggio, John P. Lazor, Thomas R. McBride, George M. Metkovich, Wallace Moses, Theodore S. Williams, outfielders.

1945—DETROIT A. L. vs. CHICAGO N. L.

Detroit A.L. 4 victories; Chicago N.L. 3

Oct. 3—Chicago (Borowy)	....	9	Detroit (Newhouser)	 0	Detroit
Oct. 4—Detroit (Trucks)	......	4	Chicago (Wyse)	 1	Detroit
Oct. 5—Chicago (Passeau)	...	3	Detroit (Overmire)	 0	Detroit
Oct. 6—Detroit (Trout)	....	4	Chicago (Prim)	 1	Chicago
Oct. 7—Detroit (Newhouser)	...	8	Chicago (Borowy)	 4	Chicago
Oct. 8—Chicago (Borowy)	....	°8	Detroit (Trout)	 7	Chicago
Oct. 10—Detroit (Newhouser)	...	9	Chicago (Borowy)	 3	Chicago

°12 innings.

Managers—Stephen F. O'Neill, Detroit; Charles J. Grimm, Chicago.

Detroit—James E. Miller, Paul R. Richards, Robert V. Swift, catchers; Alton B. Benton, Thomas D. Bridges, George J. Caster, Zebelon V. Eaton, Arthur J. Houtteman, Leslie C. Mueller, Harold Newhouser, Frank Overmire, Walter W. Pierce, James A. Tobin, Paul H. Trout, Virgil O. Trucks, Walter W. Wilson, pitchers; Edward J. Borom, R. Joseph Hoover, Robert P. Maier, Edward J. Mayo, John J. McHale, James P. Outlaw, James L. Webb, Rudolph P. York, infielders; Roger M. Cramer, Roy J. Cullenbine, Henry B. Greenberg, Charles C. Hostetler, Edward F. Mierkowicz, Harvey W. Walker, outfielders.

Chicago—Paul A. Gillespie, Thompson O. Livingston, Clyde E. McCullough, Leonard O. Rice, Dewey E. Williams, catchers; Hiram G. Bithorn, Henry L. Borowy, Robert H. Chipman, Paul M. Derringer, Paul W. Erickson, Edward M. Hanyzewski, Claude W. Passeau, Raymond L. Prim, Walter D. Signer, Raymond F. Starr, Harold H. Vandenberg, Lonnie Warneke, Henry W. Wyse, pitchers; Heinz Becker, Seymour Block, Philip J. Cavarretta, Stanley C. Hack, Roy J. Hughes, Donald S. Johnson, Leonard R. Merullo, William C. Schuster, infielders; Harry L. Lowrey, William B. Nicholson, Andrew Pafko, Edward Sauer, Frank E. Secory, outfielders.

1944—ST. LOUIS N. L. vs. ST. LOUIS A. L.

St. Louis N.L. 4 victories; St. Louis A.L. 2

Oct. 4—Browns (Galehouse)	...	2	Cardinals (M. Cooper)	... 1	Sportsman's Park
Oct. 5—Cardinals (Donnelly)	...	°3	Browns (Muncrief)	 2	Sportsman's Park
Oct. 6—Browns (Kramer)	......	6	Cardinals (Wilks)	 2	Sportsman's Park
Oct. 7—Cardinals (Brecheen)	...	5	Browns (Jakucki)	 1	Sportsman's Park
Oct. 8—Cardinals (M. Cooper)	..	2	Browns (Galehouse)	 0	Sportsman's Park
Oct. 9—Cardinals (Lanier)	...	3	Browns (Potter,	 1	Sportsman's Park

°11 innings.

Managers—William H. Southworth. Cardinals; J. Luther Sewell, Browns.

Cardinals—W. Walker Cooper, Robert W. Keely, J. Kenneth O'Dea, catchers; Harry D. Brecheen, Eldred W. Byerly, Morton C. Cooper, Sylvester U. Donnelly, Alvin J. Jurisich, H. Max Lanier, Frederick A. Schmidt, Theodore Wilks, pitchers; George D. Fallon, George J. Kurowski, Martin W. Marion, Raymond F. Sanders, Emil M. Verban, infielders; August S. Bergamo, Debs C. Garms, John L. Hopp, Daniel W. Litwhiler, John L. Martin, Stanley F. Musial, outfielders.

Browns—Myron C. Hayworth, Frank Mancuso, Thomas R. Turner, catchers; George J. Caster, Dennis W. Galehouse, Albert W. Hollingsworth, G. Willis Hudlin, Sigmund J. Jakucki, John H. Kramer, Robert C. Muncrief, Nelson T. Potter, A. Newman Shirley, Samuel W. Zoldak, pitchers; Floyd W. Baker, Mark J. Christman, Ellis Clary, Donald J. Gutteridge, George H. McQuinn, Vernon D. Stephens, infielders; Milton J. Byrnes, Michael G. Chartak, Michael A. Kreevich, Chester P. Laabs, Eugene Moore, Allen L. Zarilla, outfielders.

1943—NEW YORK A. L. vs. ST. LOUIS N. L.

New York A.L. 4 victories; St. Louis N.L. 1

Date	Winning Team and Pitcher		Losing Team and Pitcher		Where Played
Oct. 5—New York (Chandler) ..	4	St. Louis (Lanier)	2	New York
Oct. 6—St. Louis (M. Cooper)..	4	New York (Bonham)	3	New York
Oct. 7—New York (Borowy) ...	6	St. Louis (Brazle)	2	New York
Oct. 10—New York (Russo)	2	St. Louis (Brecheen)	1	St. Louis
Oct. 11—New York (Chandler) ..	2	St. Louis (M. Cooper) ...	0	St. Louis

Managers—Joseph V. McCarthy, New York; William H. Southworth, St. Louis.

New York—William M. Dickey, Ralston B. Hemsley, Kenneth E. Sears, catchers; Ernest E. Bonham, Henry L. Borowy, Marvin H. Breuer, Thomas J. Byrne, Spurgeon F. Chandler, R. Atley Donald, John J. Murphy, Marius U. Russo, James R. Turner, Charles W. Wensloff, William H. Zuber, pitchers; Frank P. Crosetti, Nicholas R. Etten, Joseph L. Gordon, Oscar R. Grimes, William R. Johnson, George Stirnweiss, infielders; Charles E. Keller, John H. Lindell, Arthur B. Metheny, George T. Stainback, C. Roy Weatherly, outfielders. St. Louis—W. Walker Cooper, J. Kenneth O'Dea, Samuel Narron, catchers; Alpha Brazle, Harry D. Brecheen, Morton C. Cooper, Murry M. Dickson, Harry E. Gumbert, Howard W. Krist, H. Max Lanier, George Munger, Ernest D. White, pitchers; George Fallon, Debs Garms, Louis F. Klein, George J. Kurowski, Martin W. Marion, Raymond F. Sanders, infielders; J. Franklin Demaree, John L. Hopp, Daniel W. Litwhiler, Stanley F. Musial, Harry W. Walker, outfielders.

1942—ST. LOUIS N. L. vs. NEW YORK A. L.

St. Louis N.L. 4 victories; New York A.L. 1

Sept. 30—New York (Ruffing) ...	7	St. Louis (M. Cooper) ...	4	St. Louis
Oct. 1—St. Louis (Beazley)	4	New York (Bonham)	3	St. Louis
Oct. 3—St. Louis (White)	2	New York (Chandler) ...	0	New York
Oct. 4—St. Louis (Lanier)	9	New York (Donald)	6	New York
Oct. 5—St. Louis (Beazley)	4	New York (Ruffing)	2	New York

Managers—William H. Southworth, St. Louis; Joseph V. McCarthy, New York.

St. Louis—W. Walker Cooper, J. Kenneth O'Dea, Samuel Narron, catchers; John Beazley, Morton C. Cooper, Murry M. Dickson, Harry E. Gumbert, Howard W. Krist, H. Max Lanier, Lloyd A. Moore, Howard J. Pollet, Ernest D. White, pitchers; James R. Brown, Frank A. J. Crespi, John L. Hopp, George J. Kurowski, Martin W. Marion, Raymond F. Sanders, infielders; Terry B. Moore, Stanley F. Musial, Enos B. Slaughter, H. Coaker Triplett, Harry W. Walker, outfielders. New York—William M. Dickey, Ralston B. Hemsley, Warren V. Rosar, catchers; Ernest E. Bonham, Henry L. Borowy, Marvin H. Breuer, Spurgeon F. Chandler, R. Atley Donald, Vernon Gomez, John H. Lindell, John J. Murphy, Charles H. Ruffing, Marius U. Russo, James R. Turner, pitchers; Frank P. J. Crosetti, Joseph L. Gordon, John A. Hassett, Gerald E. Priddy, Philip F. Rizzuto, Robert A. Rolfe, infielders; Roy J. Cullenbine, Joseph P. DiMaggio, Charles E. Keller, George A. Selkirk, George T. Stainback, outfielders.

1941—NEW YORK A. L. vs. BROOKLYN N. L.

New York A.L. 4 victories; Brooklyn N.L. 1

Oct. 1—New York (Ruffing) ...	3	Brooklyn (Davis)	2	New York
Oct. 2—Brooklyn (Wyatt)	3	New York (Chandler) ...	2	New York
Oct. 4—New York (Russo)	2	Brooklyn (Casey)	1	Brooklyn
Oct. 5—New York (Murphy) ...	7	Brooklyn (Casey)	4	Brooklyn
Oct. 6—New York (Bonham) ...	3	Brooklyn (Wyatt)	1	Brooklyn

Managers—Joseph V. McCarthy, New York; Leo E. Durocher, Brooklyn.

New York—William Dickey, Warren Rosar, Kenneth J. Silvestri, catchers; Ernest E. Bonham, Norman Branch, Marvin H. Breuer, Spurgeon Chandler, Atley Donald, Vernon Gomez, John J. Murphy, Stephen Peek, Charles H. Ruffing, Marius U. Russo, Charles Stanceu, pitchers; Frank P. Crosetti, Joseph Gordon, Gerald Priddy, Philip F. Rizzuto, Robert A. Rolfe, John P. Sturm, infielders; Stanley D. Bordagaray, Joseph P. DiMaggio, Thomas D. Henrich, Charles E. Keller, George A. Selkirk, outfielders. Brooklyn—Herman L. Franks, Arnold M. Owen, catchers; Edward J. Albosta, John T. Allen, Hugh T. Casey, Curtis B. Davis, Thomas K. Drake, Fred Fitzsimmons, Lawrence H. French, Luke D. Hamlin, W. Kirby Higbe, Newel W. Kimball, J. Whitlow Wyatt, pitchers; Adolph Camilli, Peter Coscarart, Leo E. Durocher, William J. Herman, Harry A. Lavagetto, Harold H. Reese, Lewis S. Riggs, infielders; August J. Galan, Joseph M. Medwick, Harold P. Reiser, Fred Walker, James C. Wasdell, outfielders.

1940—CINCINNATI N. L. vs. DETROIT A. L.

Cincinnati N.L. 4 victories; Detroit A.L. 3

Date	Winning Team and Pitcher		Losing Team and Pitcher		Where Played
Oct. 2—Detroit (Newsom)	....	7	Cincinnati (Derringer)	... 2	Cincinnati
Oct. 3—Cincinnati (Walters)	...	5	Detroit (Rowe)	 3	Cincinnati
Oct. 4—Detroit (Bridges)	......	7	Cincinnati (Turner)	 4	Detroit
Oct. 5—Cincinnati (Derringer)	..	5	Detroit (Trout)	 2	Detroit
Oct. 6—Detroit (Newsom)	.....	8	Cincinnati (Thompson)	.. 0	Detroit
Oct. 7—Cincinnati (Walters)	...	4	Detroit (Rowe)	 0	Cincinnati
Oct. 8—Cincinnati (Derringer)	..	2	Detroit (Newsom)	 1	Cincinnati

Managers—William B. McKechnie, Cincinnati; Delmar D. Baker, Detroit.

Cincinnati—William Baker, Ernest N. Lombardi, James Wilson, catchers; Joseph N. Beggs, Paul Derringer, Witt Guise, John R. Hutchings, Lloyd A. Moore, Elmer R. Riddle, Milburn J. Shoffner, Eugene E. Thompson, James R. Turner, John S. VanderMeer, William H. Walters, pitchers; Linus R. Frey, Edwin Joost, Frank A. McCormick, William H. Myers, Lewis S. Riggs, William M. Werber, infielders; Morris Arnovich, Harry Craft, Ival R. Goodman, Myron W. McCormick, James A. Ripple, outfielders.
Detroit—William J. Sullivan, George R. Tebbets, catchers; Alton Benton, Thomas D. Bridges, John Gorsica, Fred Hutchinson, Archie R. McKain, Harold Newhouser, Louis N. Newsom, Lynwood T. Rowe, Thomas Seats, Clay Smith, Paul H. Trout, pitchers; Richard Bartell, Frank D. Croucher, Charles L. Gehringer, M. Frank Higgins, L. D. Meyers, P. Rudolph York, infielders; H. Earl Averill, Bruce D. Campbell, Ervin Fox, Henry Greenberg, W. Barney McCosky, George T. Stainback, outfielders.

1939—NEW YORK A. L. vs. CINCINNATI N. L.

New York A.L. 4 victories; Cincinnati N.L. 0

Oct. 4—New York (Ruffing)	....	2	Cincinnati (Derringer)	... 1	New York
Oct. 5—New York (Pearson)	...	4	Cincinnati (Walters)	 0	New York
Oct. 7—New York (Hadley)	....	7	Cincinnati (Thompson)	.. 3	Cincinnati
Oct. 8—New York (Murphy)	...	°7	Cincinnati (Walters)	 4	Cincinnati
°10 innings.					

Managers—Joseph V. McCarthy, New York; William B. McKechnie, Cincinnati.

New York—William Dickey, Arndt Jorgens, Warren Rosar, catchers; Spurgeon Chandler, Atley Donald, Vernon Gomez, Irving D. Hadley, Oral C. Hildebrand, John J. Murphy, Monte M. Pearson, Charles H. Ruffing, Marius U. Russo, Steve Sundra, pitchers; Frank P. Crosetti, Ellsworth T. Dahlgren, H. Louis Gehrig, Joseph Gordon, Wm. H. Knickerbocker, Robert A. Rolfe, infielders; Joseph P. DiMaggio, Thomas D. Henrich, Charles E. Keller, Alvin L. Powell, George A. Selkirk, outfielders.
Cincinnati—Willard Hershberger, Ernest N. Lombardi, catchers; Paul Derringer, Lee T. Grissom, Henry W. Johnson, Lloyd A. Moore, John Niggeling, Milburn G. Shoffner, Eugene E. Thompson, John S. VanderMeer, William H. Walters, pitchers; Linus R. Frey, Edwin Joost, Frank A. McCormick, William H. Myers, Lewis S. Riggs, Leslie G. Scarsella, William M. Werber, infielders; Walter A. Berger, Antonio Bongiovanni, Stanley Bordagaray, Harry Craft, Lee Gamble, Ival R. Goodman, Al H. Simmons, outfielders.

1938—NEW YORK A. L. vs. CHICAGO N. L.

New York A.L. 4 victories; Chicago N.L. 0

Oct. 5—New York (Ruffing)	....	3	Chicago (Lee)	 1	Chicago
Oct. 6—New York (Gomez)	...	6	Chicago (Dean)	 3	Chicago
Oct. 8—New York (Pearson)	...	5	Chicago (Bryant)	 2	New York
Oct. 9—New York (Ruffing)	....	8	Chicago (Lee)	 3	New York

Managers—Joseph V. McCarthy, New York; Charles L. Hartnett, Chicago.

New York—William Dickey, Joseph C. Glenn, Arndt Jorgens, catchers; Ivy P. Andrews, Spurgeon F. Chandler, Wesley C. Ferrell, Vernon Gomez, Irving D. Hadley, John J. Murphy, Monte M. Pearson, Charles H. Ruffing, Steve Sundra, pitchers; Frank P. Crosetti, H. Louis Gehrig, Joseph Gordon, Wm. H. Knickerbocker, Robert A. Rolfe, Ellsworth T. Dahlgren, infielders; Joseph P. DiMaggio, Thomas D. Henrich, Myril O. Hoag, Alvin J. Powell, George A. Selkirk, outfielders.
Chicago—Robert Garbark, Charles L. Hartnett, J. Kenneth O'Dea, catchers; Claiborne H. Bryant, James O. Carleton, Jerome H. Dean, Lawrence H. French, William C. Lee, Vance L. Page, Charles H. Root, Jack Russell, pitchers; Philip Cavarretta, James A. Collins, Stanley C. Hack, William Herman, William F. Jurges, Anthony M. Lazzeri, infielders; James Asbell, J. Frank Demaree, August J. Galan, Joseph A. Marty, Carl N. Reynolds, outfielders.

1937—NEW YORK A. L. vs. NEW YORK N. L.

New York A.L. 4 victories; New York N.L. 1

Date	Winning Team and Pitcher		Losing Team and Pitcher		Where Played
Oct. 6—Yankees (Gomez)	8	Giants (Hubbell)	1	Yankee Stadium
Oct. 7—Yankees (Ruffing)	8	Giants (Melton)	1	Yankee Stadium
Oct. 8—Yankees (Pearson)	5	Giants (Schumacher)	1	Polo Grounds
Oct. 9—Giants (Hubbell)	7	Yankees (Hadley)	3	Polo Grounds
Oct. 10—Yankees (Gomez)	4	Giants (Melton)	2	Polo Grounds

Managers—Joseph V. McCarthy, Yankees; William H. Terry, Giants.

Yankees—William Dickey, Joseph C. Glenn, Arndt Jorgens, catchers; Ivy P. Andrews, Spurgeon F. Chandler, Vernon Gomez, Irving D. Hadley, Frank Makosky, Perce L. Malone, John J. Murphy, Monte M. Pearson, Charles H. Ruffing, Kemp C. Wicker, pitchers; Frank P. Crosetti, H. Louis Gehrig, Donald Heffner, Anthony M. Lazzeri, Robert A. Rolfe, Jack Saltzgaver, infielders; Joseph P. DiMaggio, Thomas D. Henrich, Myril O. Hoag, Alvin J. Powell, George A. Selkirk, outfielders.

Giants—Harry Danning, Edward Madjeski, August R. Mancuso, catchers; Thomas C. Baker, J. Donald Brennan, Clydell Castleman, S. Richard Coffman, Harry E. Gumbert, Carl O. Hubbell, Clifford G. Melton, Harold H. Schumacher, Alfred J. Smith, pitchers; Richard Bartell, Louis P. Chiozza, Michael J. Haslin, Samuel A. Leslie, John J. McCarthy, Melvin T. Ott, John C. Ryan, Burgess U. Whitehead, infielders; Walter A. Berger, Henry C. Leiber, Joseph G. Moore, James Ripple, outfielders.

1936—NEW YORK A. L. vs. NEW YORK N. L.

New York A.L. 4 victories; New York N.L. 2

Sept. 30—Giants (Hubbell)	6	Yankees (Ruffing)	1	Polo Grounds
Oct. 2—Yankees (Gomez)	18	Giants (Schumacher)	4	Polo Grounds
Oct. 3—Yankees (Hadley)	2	Giants (Fitzsimmons)	1	Yankee Stadium
Oct. 4—Yankees (Pearson)	5	Giants (Hubbell)	2	Yankee Stadium
Oct. 5—Giants (Schumacher)	°5	Yankees (Malone)	4	Yankee Stadium
Oct. 6—Yankees (Gomez)	13	Giants (Fitzsimmons)	5	Polo Grounds

°10 innings.

Managers—Joseph V. McCarthy, Yankees; William H. Terry, Giants.

Yankees—William Dickey, Joseph C. Glenn, Arndt Jorgens, catchers; John J. Broaca, Walter G. Brown, Vernon Gomez, Irving D. Hadley, Perce L. Malone, John J. Murphy, Monte M. Pearson, Charles H. Ruffing, Kemp C. Wicker, pitchers; Frank P. Crosetti, H. Louis Gehrig, Donald Heffner (ill), Anthony M. Lazzeri, Robert A. Rolfe, Jack Saltzgaver, infielders; Joseph P. DiMaggio, Roy C. Johnson, Alvin J. Powell, Robert I. Seeds, George A. Selkirk, outfielders.

Giants—Harry Danning, August R. Mancuso, Roy Spencer, catchers; Clydell Castleman, S. Richard Coffman, Fred Fitzsimmons, Frank Gabler, Harry E. Gumbert, Carl O. Hubbell, Harold H. Schumacher, Alfred J. Smith, pitchers; Richard Bartell, Travis C. Jackson, Mark A. Koenig, Samuel A. Leslie, Edward Mayo, William H. Terry, Burgess U. Whitehead, infielders; George W. Davis, Henry C. Leiber, Joseph G. Moore, Melvin T. Ott, James Ripple, outfielders.

1935—DETROIT A. L. vs. CHICAGO N. L.

Detroit A.L. 4 victories; Chicago N.L. 2

Oct. 2—Chicago (Warneke)	3	Detroit (Rowe)	0	Detroit
Oct. 3—Detroit (Bridges)	8	Chicago (Root)	3	Detroit
Oct. 4—Detroit (Rowe)	°6	Chicago (French)	5	Chicago
Oct. 5—Detroit (Crowder)	2	Chicago (Carleton)	1	Chicago
Oct. 6—Chicago (Warneke)	3	Detroit (Rowe)	1	Chicago
Oct. 7—Detroit (Bridges)	4	Chicago (French)	3	Detroit

°11 innings.

Managers—Gordon S. Cochrane, Detroit; Charles J. Grimm, Chicago.

Detroit—Gordon S. Cochrane, c.; Eldon L. Auker, p.; Thomas D. Bridges, p.; Herman E. Clifton, inf.; Alvin F. Crowder, p.; Ervin Fox, of.; Charles L. Gehringer, 2b.; Leon A. Goslin, of.; Henry Greenberg, 1b.; Raymond H. Hayworth, c.; Elon G. Hogsett, p.; Roxie Lawson, p.; Marvin J. Owen, inf.; Frank Reiber, c.; William G. Rogell, ss.; Lynwood T. Rowe, p.; Henry G. Schuble, inf.; Hubert Shelly, of.; Victor Sorrell, p.; Joseph Sullivan, p.; Gerald H. Walker, of.; Joyner C. White, of.

Chicago—Charles J. Grimm, 1b.; James O. Carleton, p.; Hugh Casey, p.; Philip Cavarretta, 1b.; J. Frank Demaree, of.; Elwood G. English, inf.; Lawrence H. French, p.; August J. Galan, of.; Stanley C. Hack, 3b.; Chas. L. Hartnett, c.; Roy Henshaw, p.; William Herman, 2b.; William F. Jurges, ss.; Charles H. Klein, of.; Fabian Kowalik, p.; William C. Lee, p.; Fred C. Linstrom, of.; James K. O'Dea, c.; Charles H. Root, p.; George T. Stainback, of.; Walter Stephenson, c.; Lonnie Warneke, p.; Clyde Shoun, p.

1934—ST. LOUIS N. L. vs. DETROIT A. L.

St. Louis N.L. 4 victories; Detroit A.L. 3

Date	Winning Team and Pitcher		Losing Team and Pitcher		Where Played
Oct. 3—St. Louis (J. Dean)	...	8	Detroit (Crowder)	 3	Detroit
Oct. 4—Detroit (Rowe)	....	°3	St. Louis (W. Walker)	... 2	Detroit
Oct. 5—St. Louis (P. Dean)	...	4	Detroit (Bridges)	 1	St. Louis
Oct. 6—Detroit (Auker)	....	10	St. Louis (W. Walker)	... 4	St. Louis
Oct. 7—Detroit (Bridges)	......	3	St. Louis (J. Dean)	... 1	St. Louis
Oct. 8—St. Louis (P. Dean)	...	4	Detroit (Rowe)	 3	Detroit
Oct. 9—St. Louis (J. Dean)	....	11	Detroit (Auker)	 0	Detroit

°12 innings.

Managers—Frank F. Frisch, St. Louis; Gordon S. Cochrane, Detroit.

St. Louis—Frank F. Frisch, 2b.; James O. Carleton, p.; Jerome H. Dean, p.; Paul Dean, p.; Jesse J. Haines, p.; William Hallahan, p.; James Mooney, p.; Arthur C. Vance, p.; William H. Walker, p.; James A. Collins, 1b.; John L. Martin, 3b.; Leo A. Durocher, ss.; Joseph M. Medwick, of.; Ernest Orsatti, of.; John H. Rothrock, of.; Charles P. Fullis, of.; C. R. Crawford, util.; William DeLancey, c.; Virgil L. Davis, c.; B. U. Whitehead, inf.; Francis Healy, c.
Detroit—Gordon S. Cochrane, c.; Eldon L. Auker, p.; Thomas D. Bridges, p.; Alvin F. Crowder, p.; Charles W. Fischer, p.; Luke D. Hamlin, p.; Elon C. Hogsett, p.; Fred Marberry, p.; Lynwood T. Rowe, p.; Victor G. Sorrell, p.; Henry Greenberg, 1b.; Charles L. Gehringer, 2b.; Marvin J. Owen, 3b.; William G. Rogell, ss.; Herman E. Clifton, inf.; Henry G. Schuble, inf.; Frank J. Doljack, of.; Ervin Fox, of.; Leon A. Goslin, of.; Gerald H. Walker, of.; Joyner C. White, of.; Raymond H. Hayworth, c.

1933—NEW YORK N. L. vs. WASHINGTON A. L.

New York N.L. 4 victories; Washington A.L. 1

Oct. 3—New York (Hubbell)	...	4	Washington (Stewart)	... 2	At New York
Oct. 4—New York (Schumacher)		6	Washington (Crowder)	.. 1	At New York
Oct. 5—Washington (Whitehill)		4	New York (Fitzsimmons)	. 0	At Washington
Oct. 6—New York (Hubbell)	...	°2	Washington (Weaver)	... 1	At Washington
Oct. 7—New York (Luque)	.....	†4	Washington (Russell)	... 3	At Washington

°11 innings.
†10 innings.

Managers—William H. Terry, New York; Joseph E. Cronin, Washington.

New York—William H. Terry, 1b.; Herman C. Bell, p.; William W. Clark, p.; Hugh M. Critz, 2b.; George W. Davis, of.; Harry Danning, c.; Charles Dressen, 3b.; Fred Fitzsimmons, p.; Carl O. Hubbell, p.; Travis C. Jackson, 3b.; R. Byrne James, of.; Adolfo Luque, p.; August R. Mancuso, c.; Joseph G. Moore, of.; Frank J. O'Doul, of.; Melvin T. Ott, of.; Leroy Parmelee, p.; Homer H. Peel, of.; Paul R. Richards, c.; John C. Ryan, ss.; John T. Salveson, p.; Harold H. Schumacher, p.; Glenn E. Spencer, p.; John L. Vergez, 3b.
Washington—Joseph E. Cronin, ss.; Morris Berg, c.; Oswald L. Bluege, 3b.; Robert Boken, util.; W. Cliff Bolton, c.; Alvin F. Crowder, p.; Leon A. Goslin, of.; David S. Harris, of.; John L. Kerr, 2b.; Joseph Kuhel, 1b.; Henry E. Manush, of.; Charles S. Myer, 2b.; Edgar C. Rice, of.; Jack Russell, p.; Fred W. Schulte, of.; J. Luke Sewell, c.; Walter C. Stewart, p.; Alphonse T. Thomas, p.; Monte M. Weaver, p.; Earl O. Whitehill, p.; Alexander B. McColl, p.; Robert J. Burke, p.; Edwin V. Chapman, p.

1932—NEW YORK A. L. vs. CHICAGO N. L.

New York A.L. 4 victories; Chicago 0

Sept. 28—New York (Ruffing)	...	12	Chicago (Bush)	 6	At New York
Sept. 29—New York (Gomez)	....	5	Chicago (Warneke)	 2	At New York
Oct. 1—New York (Pipgras)	...	7	Chicago (Root)	 5	At Chicago
Oct. 2—New York (Moore)	...	13	Chicago (May)	 6	At Chicago

Managers—Joseph V. McCarthy, New York; Charles J. Grimm, Chicago.

New York—William Dickey, Arndt Jorgens, catchers; John T. Allen, Walter G. Brown, Charles Devens, Vernon Gomez, Daniel K. MacFayden, Wilcey W. Moore, Herbert J. Pennock, George W. Pipgras, Charles H. Ruffing, Edwin L. Wells, pitchers; Frank P. Crosetti, Edward S. Farrell, H. Louis Gehrig, Lynford H. Lary, Anthony M. Lazzeri, Joseph M. Sewell, infielders; Samuel D. Byrd, W. Benjamin Chapman, Earle B. Combs, Myril O. Hoag, George H. Ruth, outfielders.
Chicago—Charles L. Hartnett, Ralston B. Hemsley, James W. Taylor, catchers; Guy T. Bush, Burleigh A. Grimes, Leroy G. Herrmann, Perce L. Malone, Frank S. May, Charles H. Root, Robert E. Smith, Lyle Tinning, Lonnie Warneke, pitchers; Elwood G. English, Charles J. Grimm, Stanley C. Hack, William Herman, William F. Jurges, Mark A. Koenig, infielders; Hazen S. Cuyler J. Frank Demaree, Marvin J. Gudat, John F. Moore, J. Riggs Stephenson, outfielders.

84

1931—ST. LOUIS N. L. vs. PHILADELPHIA A. L.

St. Louis N.L. 4 victories, Philadelphia A.L. 3

Date	Winning Team and Pitcher	Losing Team and Pitcher	Where Played
Oct. 1—Philadelphia (Grove) ... 6	St. Louis (Derringer) 2	At St. Louis
Oct. 2—St. Louis (Hallahan) ... 2	Philadelphia (Earnshaw) .. 0	At St. Louis
Oct. 5—St. Louis (Grimes) 5	Philadelphia (Grove) 2	At Philadelphia
Oct. 6—Philadelphia (Earnshaw). 3	St. Louis (Johnson) 0	At Philadelphia
Oct. 7—St. Louis (Hallahan)... 5	Philadelphia (Hoyt) 1	At Philadelphia
Oct. 9—Philadelphia (Grove) ... 8	St. Louis (Derringer) 1	At St. Louis
Oct. 10—St. Louis (Grimes) 4	Philadelphia (Earnshaw).. 2	At St. Louis

Managers—Charles E. Street, St. Louis; Connie Mack, Philadelphia.

St. Louis—Earl J. Adams, 3b.; F. Raymond Blades, of.; James L. Bottomley, 1b.; Frank F. Frisch, 2b.; Charles M. Gelbert, ss.; Charles J. Hafey, of.; August R. Mancuso, c.; George R. Watkins, of.; James Wilson, c.; Burleigh A. Grimes, p.; Jesse J. Haines, p.; William Hallahan, p.; Sylvester W. Johnson, p.; James K. Lindsey, p.; Charles F. Rhem, p.; Andrew A. High, util.; Ernest R. Orsatti, of.; D'Arcy R. Flowers, 3b.; Paul Derringer, p.; Anthony Kaufmann, p.;Walter Roettger, of.; James A. Collins, 1b.; Miguel Gonzales, c.; John L. Martin, of.; Allyn M. Stout, p.

Philadelphia—Max F. Bishop, 2b.; John P. Boley, ss.; Gordon S. Cochrane, c.; James J. Dykes, 3b.; James E. Foxx, 1b.; George W. Haas, of.; Edmund J. Miller, of.; Al H. Simmons, of.; George L. Earnshaw, p.; Robert M. Grove, p.; George Walberg, p.; LeRoy Mahaffey, p.; Edwin A. Rommel, p.; Dibrell Williams, ss.; Roger M. Cramer, of.; Waite C. Hoyt, p.; John Heving, c.; Lewis Krausse, p.; James N. Peterson, p.; James W. Moore, of.; Henry McDonald, p.; Eric McNair, 2b.; Joseph Palmisano, c.; Philip J. Todt, 1b.

1930—PHILADELPHIA A. L. vs. ST. LOUIS N. L.

Philadelphia A.L. 4 victories; St. Louis N.L. 2

Oct. 1—Philadelphia (Grove) ... 5	St. Louis (Grimes) 2	At Philadelphia
Oct. 2—Philadelphia (Earnshaw). 6	St. Louis (Rhem) 1	At Philadelphia
Oct. 4—St. Louis (Hallahan) ... 5	Philadelphia (Walberg) .. 0	At St. Louis
Oct. 5—St. Louis (Haines) 3	Philadelphia (Grove) 1	At St. Louis
Oct. 6—Philadelphia (Grove) ... 2	St. Louis (Grimes) 0	At St. Louis
Oct. 8—Philadelphia (Earnshaw). 7	St. Louis (Hallahan) 1	At Philadelphia

Managers—Connie Mack, Philadelphia; Charles E. Street, St. Louis.

Philadelphia—Max F. Bishop, 2b.; John P. Boley, ss.; Gordon S. Cochrane, c.; James J. Dykes, 3b.; James E. Foxx, 1b.; George W. Haas, of.; Edmund J. Miller, of.; Al H. Simmons, of.; D. Eric McNair, 3b.; James W. Moore, of.; William Shores, p.; George L. Earnshaw, p.; Robert M. Grove, p.; John P. Quinn, p.; George Walberg, p.; Edward T. Collins, 2b.; Frank Higgins, 3b.; LeRoy Mahaffey, p.; Charles S. Perkins, p.; Ralph F. Perkins, c.; Edwin A. Rommel, p.; Walter H. Schang, c.; Homer W. Summa, of.; Dibrell Williams, 2b.

St. Louis—Earl J. Adams, 3b.; Ray Blades, of.; James L. Bottomley, 1b.; Taylor L. Douthit, of.; Frank F. Frisch, 2b.; Charles Gelbert, ss.; Charles J. Hafey, of.; Gus R. Mancuso, c.; George A. Watkins, of.; James Wilson, c.; Burleigh A. Grimes, p.; Herman Bell, p.; Jesse J. Haines, p.; William Hallahan, p.; Sylvester Johnson, p.; James K. Lindsey, p.; Charles F. Rhem, p.; George A. Fisher. of.; Albert F. Grabowski, p.; Andrew High, 3b.; Ernest Orsatti, of.; George L. Puccinelli, of.

1929—PHILADELPHIA A. L. vs. CHICAGO N. L.

Philadelphia A.L. 4 victories; Chicago 1

Oct. 8—Philadelphia (Ehmke) .. 3	Chicago (Root) 1	At Chicago
Oct. 9—Philadelphia (Earnshaw). 9	Chicago (Malone) 3	At Chicago
Oct. 11—Chicago (Bush) 3	Philadelphia (Earnshaw). 1	At Philadelphia
Oct. 12—Philadelphia (Rommel) . 10	Chicago (Blake) 8	At Philadelphia
Oct. 14—Philadelphia (Walberg) . 3	Chicago (Malone) 2	At Philadelphia

Managers—Connie Mack, Philadelphia; Joseph V. McCarthy, Chicago.

Philadelphia—Max F. Bishop, of.; John P. Boley, ss.; William R. Breckinridge, p.; George Burns, 1b.; Gordon S. Cochrane, c.; Edward T. Collins, 2b.; James Cronin, c.; James J. Dykes, 3b.; George L. Earnshaw, p.; Howard E. Ehmke, p.; James E. Foxx, 1b.; Walter E. French, of.; Robert M. Grove, p.; George W. Haas, of.; Samuel D. Hale, 3b.; DeWitt LeBourveau, of.; Edmund J. Miller, of.; Ralph F. Perkins, c.; John P. Quinn, p.; Edwin A. Rommel, p.; William Shores, p.; Al H. Simmons, of.; Homer W. Summa, of.; George Walberg, p.; C. Carroll Yerkes, 3b.

Chicago—Clyde Beck, 3b.; Clarence V. Blair, ss.; J. Fred Blake, p.; Guy T. Bush, p.; Harold Carlson, p.; Hazen S. Cuyler, of.; Mike Cvengros, p.; Elwood English, ss.; Miguel A. Gonzales, p.; Henry M. Grampp, p.; Charles J. Grimm, 1b.; Charles L. Hartnett, c.; Clifton Heathcote, of.; Rogers Hornsby, 2b.; N. A. McMillan, 3b.; Perce Malone, p.; John F. Moore, of.; Arthur N. Nehf, p.; Kenneth Penner, p.; Charles H. Root, p.; John Schulte, c.; J. Riggs Stephenson, of.; James W. Taylor, c.; Charles J. Tolson, 1b.; Lewis R. Wilson, of.

1928—NEW YORK A. L. vs. ST. LOUIS N. L.

New York A.L. 4 victories, St. Louis N.L. 0

Date	Winning Team and Pitcher		Losing Team and Pitcher		Where Played
Oct. 4—New York (Hoyt)	.....	4	St. Louis (Sherdel)	 1	At New York
Oct. 5—New York (Pipgras)	....	9	St. Louis (Alexander)	... 3	At New York
Oct. 7—New York (Zachary)	...	7	St. Louis (Haines)	 3	At St. Louis
Oct. 9—New York (Hoyt)	......	7	St. Louis (Sherdel)	 3	At St. Louis

Managers—Miller J. Huggins, New York; William B. McKechnie, St. Louis.

New York—Benjamin O. Bengough, c.;T. Patrick Collins, c.; Earle B. Combs, cf.; William Dickey, c.; Joseph A. Dugan, 3b.; Leo E. Durocher, 2b.; Cedric M. Durst, of.; Michael Gazella, 3b.; H. Louis Gehrig, 1b.; John Grabowski, c.; Fred Heimach, p.; Waite C. Hoyt, p.; Mark A. Koenig, ss.; Anthony M. Lazzeri, 2b.; Robert W. Meusel, of.; Benjamin Paschal, of.; Jezebel T. Zachary, p.; Herbert J. Pennock, p.; George W. Pipgras, p.; Eugene Robertson, 3b.; George H. Ruth, cf.; Wilfred D. Ryan, p.; Myles L. Thomas, p. St. Louis—Grover C. Alexander, p.; Ray Blades, of.; James L. Bottomley, 1b.; Taylor L. Douthit, of.; Fred Frankhouse, p.; Frank F. Frisch, 2b.; Charles J. Hafey, of.; Harold Haid, p.; Jesse J. Haines, p.; George W. Harper, of.; Andrew A. High, 3b.; Roscoe A. Holm, of.; Sylvester W. Johnson, p.; Walter J. Maranville, ss.; John L. Martin, of.; Clarence E. Mitchell, p.; Ernest Orsatti, of.; Arthur C. Reinhart, p.; Charles F. Rhem, p.; Walter Roettger, of.; William L. Sherdel, p.; Thomas J. Thevenow, ss.; N. Howard Williamson, of.; James Wilson, c.; Earl Smith, c.

1927—NEW YORK A. L. vs. PITTSBURGH N. L.

New York A.L. 4 victories; Pittsburgh 0

Oct. 5—New York (Hoyt)	......	5	Pittsburgh (Kremer)	 4	At Pittsburgh
Oct. 6—New York (Pipgras)	....	6	Pittsburgh (Aldridge)	... 2	At Pittsburgh
Oct. 7—New York (Pennock)	....	8	Pittsburgh (Meadows)	... 1	At New York
Oct. 8—New York (Moore)	....	4	Pittsburgh (Miljus)	 3	At New York

Managers—Miller J. Huggins, New York; Owen J. Bush, Pittsburgh.

New York—H. Louis Gehrig, 1b.; Anthony M. Lazzeri, 2b.; Joseph A. Dugan, 3b.; Mark A. Koenig, ss.; George H. Ruth, rf.; Earle B. Combs, cf.; Robert W. Meusel, lf.; T. Patrick Collins, c.; Benjamin O. Bengough, c.; John Grabowski, c.; Waite C. Hoyt, p.; Wilcey Moore, p.; Herbert J. Pennock, p.; G. W. Pipgras, p.; Cedric Durst, of.; Michael Gazella, 3b.; Joseph Giard, p.; Ray Morehart, 2b.; Benjamin Paschal, of.; W. H. Ruether, p.; J. R. Shawkey, p.; Urban J. Shocker, p.; Myles L. Thomas, p.; Julian Wera, 3b. Pittsburgh—Joseph Harris, 1b.; George F. Grantham, 2b.; Harold Rhyne, 2b.; Harold J. Traynor, 3b.; F. Glenn Wright, ss.; Paul G. Waner, rf.; Lloyd J. Waner, cf.; Clyde L. Barnhart, lf.; John B. Gooch, c.; Earl Smith, c.; Roy H. Spencer, c.; Victor E. Aldridge, p.; Michael Cvengros, p.; Ralph F. Dawson, p.; Ray Kremer, p.; John Miljus, p.; H. Lee Meadows, p.; Carmen Hill, p.; Henry Groh, 3b.; Emil O. Yde, p.; Frederick Brickell, of.; Joseph Cronin, ss.; Hazen S. Cuyler, of.

1926—ST. LOUIS N. L. vs. NEW YORK A. L.

St. Louis N.L. 4 victories; New York 3

Oct. 2—New York (Pennock)	..	2	St. Louis (Sherdel)	 1	At New York
Oct. 3—St. Louis (Alexander)	.	6	New York (Shocker)	 2	At New York
Oct. 5—St. Louis (Haines)	.....	4	New York (Ruether)	... 0	At St. Louis
Oct. 6—New York (Hoyt)	.....	10	St. Louis (Reinhart)	... 5	At St. Louis
Oct. 7—New York (Pennock)	...	°3	St. Louis (Sherdel)	... 2	At St. Louis
Oct. 9—St. Louis (Alexander)	.	10	New York (Shawkey)	... 2	At New York
Oct. 10—St. Louis (Haines)	.....	3	New York (Hoyt)	 2	At New York

°10 innings.

Managers—Rogers Hornsby, St. Louis; Miller J. Huggins, New York.

St. Louis—James L. Bottomley, 1b.; Rogers Hornsby, 2b.; Lester R. Bell, 3b.; Thomas J. Thevenow, ss.; William H. Southworth, rf.; Tayor L. Douthit, cf.; Roscoe A. Holm, cf.; Charles J. Hafey, lf.; Robert A. O'Farrell, c.; Grover C. Alexander, p.; Herman S. Bell, p.; Jesse J. Haines, p.; William A. Hallahan, p.; H. Victor Keen, p.; Arthur C. Reinhart, p.; Charles F. Rhem, p.; William L. Sherdel, p.; D'Arcy R. Flowers, util.; George Toporcer, util.; Raymond Blades, of.; Edgar Clough, p.; S. Johnson, p.; Allan Sothoron, p.; Henry Vick, c. New York—H. Louis Gehrig, 1b.; Anthony M. Lazzeri, 2b.; Joseph A. Dugan, 3b.; Michael Gazella, 3b.; Mark A. Koenig, ss.; George H. Ruth, rf.-lf.; Earle B. Combs, cf.; Robert Meusel, lf.; T. Patrick Collins, c.; Henry Severeid, c.; Waite C. Hoyt, p.; Samuel P. Jones, p.; Herbert J. Pennock, p.; Walter H. Ruether, p.; J. Robert Shawkey, p.; Urban J. Shocker, p.; Myles Thomas, p.; Benjamin Paschal, util.; Spencer Adams, util.; W. E. Beall, p.; B. O. Bengough, c.; E. G. Braxton, p.; R. E. Carlyle, of.; Herb McQuaid, p.; Aaron L. Ward, 2b.

1925—PITTSBURGH N. L. vs. WASHINGTON A. L.

Pittsburgh N.L. 4 victories; Washington A.L. 3

Date	Winning Team and Pitcher		Losing Team and Pitcher		Where Played
Oct. 7—	Washington (Johnson) ..	4	Pittsburgh (Meadows) ...	1	At Pittsburgh
Oct. 8—	Pittsburgh (Aldridge) ..	3	Washington (Coveleskie) .	2	At Pittsburgh
Oct. 10—	Washington (Ferguson)..	4	Pittsburgh (Kremer)	3	At Washington
Oct. 11—	Washington (Johnson) ..	4	Pittsburgh (Yde)	0	At Washington
Oct. 12—	Pittsburgh (Aldridge) ..	6	Washington (Coveleskie) .	3	At Washington
Oct. 13—	Pittsburgh (Kremer) ...	3	Washington (Ferguson) ..	2	At Pittsburgh
Oct. 15—	Pittsburgh (Kremer) ...	9	Washington (Johnson) ...	7	At Pittsburgh

Managers—William B. McKechnie, Pittsburgh; Stanley R. Harris, Washington.

Pittsburgh—George F. Grantham, 1b.; John J. McInnis, 1b.; George E. Moore, 2b.; Harold J. Traynor, 3b.; F. Glenn Wright, ss.; Clyde L. Barnhart, lf.; Max G. Carey, cf.; Hazen S. Cuyler, rf.; Carson L. Bigbee, of.; Earl Smith, c.; John B. Gooch, c.; H. Lee Meadows, p.; John D. Morrison, p.; Victor E. Aldridge, p.; Ray Kremer, p.; Emil O. Yde, p.; Charles B. Adams, p.; John Oldham, p.; B. A. Culloton, p.; Jewel Ens, 3b.; George Haas, of.; John Rawlings, 2b.; Thomas Sheehan, p.; Roy H. Spencer, c.; L. F. Thompson, 2b.

Washington—Joseph Judge, 1b.; Stanley R. Harris, 2b.; Spencer D. Adams, 2b.; Oswald L. Bluege, 3b.; Charles S. Myer, 3b.; Roger T. Peckinpaugh, ss.; Leon A. Goslin, lf.; Edgar C. Rice, cf.; Joseph Harris, rf.; G. Earl McNeely, of.; Herold Ruel, c.; Henry Severeid, c.; Walter Johnson, p.; Stanley Coveleskie, p.; Alexander Ferguson, p.; Fred Marberry, p.; Nobel W. Ballou, p.; Jezebel T. Zachary, p.; Robert H. Veach, of.; Walter H. Ruether, p.; Harry Leibold, of.; Ernest L. Jeanes, of.; Allan Russell, p.; Everett Scott, ss.; Bennet Tate, c.

1924—WASHINGTON A. L. vs. NEW YORK N. L.

Washington A.L. 4 victories; New York N.L. 3

Oct. 4—	New York (Nehf)	4	Washington (Johnson) ...	3	At Wash. (12 inn.)
Oct. 5—	Washington (Zachary) ..	4	New York (Bentley)	3	At Washington
Oct. 6—	New York (McQuillan) ..	6	Washington (Marberry) ..	4	At New York
Oct. 7—	Washington (Mogridge) .	7	New York (Barnes)	4	At New York
Oct. 8—	New York (Bentley) ...	6	Washington (Johnson) ...	2	At New York
Oct. 9—	Washington (Zachary) ..	2	New York (Nehf)	1	At Washington
Oct. 10—	Washington (Johnson) ..	4	New York (Bentley)	3	At Wash. (12 inn.)

Managers—Stanley R. Harris, Washington; John J. McGraw, New York.

Washington—Joseph Judge, 1b.; E. R. Shirley, 1b.; Stanley R. Harris, 2b.; Oswald L. Bluege, 3b.; T. C. Taylor, 3b.; Roger T. Peckinpaugh, ss.; Harry Leibold, lf.; G. Earl McNeely, cf.; Edgar C. Rice, rf.; Leon A. Goslin, lf.; George Fisher, of.; Herold Ruel, c.; Bennett Tate, c.; Walter Johnson, p.; Fred Marberry, p.; Joseph Martina, p.; George Mogridge, p.; Warren H. Ogden, p.; Allan Russell, p.; Byron F. Speece, p.; Jezebel T. Zachary, p.; W. M. Hargrave, c.; R. J. Miller, 3b.; Paul Zahniser, p.;

New York—George L. Kelly, 1b.; William H. Terry, 1b.; Frank F. Frisch, 2b.; Henry K. Groh, 3b.; Fred C. Lindstrom, 3b.; Travis Jackson, ss.; Emil F. Meusel, lf.; Lewis R. Wilson, lf.; Ross Youngs, rf.; W. H. Southworth, cf.; Howard E. Baldwin, p.; Virgil P. Barnes, p.; John M. Bentley, p.; Wayland O. Dean, p.; Claude Jonnard, p.; Hugh A. McQuillan, p.; Arthur N. Nehf, p.; Wilfred D. Ryan, p.; John R. Watson, p.; Henry M. Gowdy, c.; Frank Snyder, c.; W. H. Huntzinger, p.; Ernest Maun, p.; James O'Connell, of.

1923—NEW YORK A. L. vs. NEW YORK N. L.

New York A.L. (Yankees) 4 victories; New York N.L. (Giants), 2

Oct. 10—	New York N (Ryan)....	5	New York A (Bush)	4	At Yankee Stad.
Oct. 11—	New York A (Pennock).	4	New York N (McQuillan).	2	At Polo Grounds
Oct. 12—	New York N (Nehf)....	1	New York A (Jones)	0	At Yankee Stad.
Oct. 13—	New York A (Shawkey).	8	New York N (Scott)	4	At Polo Grounds
Oct. 14—	New York A (Bush) ...	8	New York N (Bentley) ..	1	At Yankee Stad.
Oct. 15—	New York A (Pennock)	6	New York N (Nehf)	4	At Polo Grounds

Managers—John J. McGraw, New York N.L.; Miller J. Huggins, New York A.L.

New York A.L. (Yankees)—Walter Pipp, 1b.; Aaron Ward, 2b.; Joseph Dugan, 3b.; L. Everett Scott, ss.; Ernest R. Johnson, ss.; Robert Meusel, lf.; Lawton W. Witt, cf.; George H. Ruth, rf.; Henry L. Haines, of.; Harvey Hendrick, of.; Elmer J. Smith, of.; Walter H. Schang, c.; Fred C. Hoffman, c.; Leslie J. Bush, p.; Waite C. Hoyt, p.; Samuel P. Jones, p.; Herbert J. Pennock, p.; J. Robert Shawkey, p.; Carl W. Mays, p.; Michael J. McNally, of.; Ben O. Bengough, c.; Michael Gazella, 3b.; George W. Pipgras, p.; Oscar Roettger, p.

New York N.L. (Giants)—George L. Kelly, 1b.; Frank F. Frisch, 2b.; Fred Maguire, 2b.; Henry K. Groh, 3b.; Travis Jackson, 3b.-ss.; David J. Bancroft, ss.; Emil F. Meusel, lf.; W. A. Cunningham, cf.; Charles D. Stengel, cf.; Ross Youngs, rf.; James J. O'Connell, of.; Frank Snyder, c.; Henry M. Gowdy, c.; Alexander Gaston, c.; Virgil E. Barnes, p.; John N. Bentley, p.; Claude Jonnard, p.; Hugh A. McQuillan, p.; Arthur N. Nehf, p.; Wilfred D. Ryan, p.; John W. Scott, p.; John R. Watson, p.; Dennis Gearin, p.; Ralph Shinners, of.

1922—NEW YORK N. L. vs. NEW YORK A. L.

New York N.L. (Giants) 4 victories; New York A.L. (Yankees) none; 1 tie game

Date	Winning Team and Pitcher		Losing Team and Pitcher		Where Played
Oct. 4—New York N (Ryan)	....	3	New York A (Bush)	 2	At Polo Grounds
Oct. 5—New York N (Tie)	....	3	New York A (Tie)	 3	At P. G (10 inn.)
Oct. 6—New York N (Scott)	...	3	New York A (Hoyt)	 0	At Polo Grounds
Oct. 7—New York N (McQuillan)		4	New York A (Mays)	 3	At Polo Grounds
Oct. 8—New York N (Nehf)	....	5	New York A (Bush)	 3	At Polo Grounds

Managers—John J. McGraw, New York N.L.; Miller J. Huggins, New York A.L.

New York N.L. (Giants)—George L. Kelly, 1b.; Frank F. Frisch, 2b.; Henry K. Groh, 3b.; David J. Bancroft, ss.; Emil F. Meusel, lf.; Charles D. Stengel, cf.; Lee King, cf.; William A. Cunningham, cf.; Ross Youngs, rf.; Frank Snyder, c.; Earl Smith, c.; Jesse Barnes, p.; Hugh A. McQuillan, p.; Arthur N. Nehf, p.; Wilfred D. Ryan, p.; John W. Scott, p.; Virgil J. Barnes, p.; Clinton Blume, p.; Alex. Gaston, c.; Carmen Hill, p.; Claude Jonnard, p.; John Rawlings, 2b.; Davis Robertson, of.

New York A.L. (Yankees)—Walter C. Pipp, 1b.; Aaron Ward, 2b.; Michael J. McNally, 2b.; Joseph Dugan, 3b.; J. Frank Baker, 3b.; L. Everett Scott, ss.; Robert Meusel, lf.; Lawton W. Witt, cf.; Norman McMillan, cf.; George H. Ruth, rf.; Elmer Smith, rf.; Walter H. Schang, c.; Waite C. Hoyt, p.; Leslie J. Bush, p.; Carl W. Mays, p.; J. Robert Shawkey, p.; Samuel P. Jones, p.; Albert DeVormer, c.; Frank O'Doul, p.; Fred Hoffman, c.; George Murray, p.; Camp Skinner, of.

1921—NEW YORK N. L. vs. NEW YORK A. L.

New York N.L. (Giants) 5 victories; New York A.L. (Yankees) 3

Oct. 5—New York A (Mays)	...	3	New York N (Douglas)	.. 0	At Polo Grounds
Oct. 6—New York A (Hoyt)	....	3	New York N (Nehf)	 0	At Polo Grounds
Oct. 7—New York N (Barnes)	..	13	New York A (Quinn)	 5	At Polo Grounds
Oct. 9—New York N (Douglas)	..	4	New York A (Mays)	 2	At Polo Grounds
Oct. 10—New York A (Hoyt)	....	3	New York N (Nehf)	 1	At Polo Grounds
Oct. 11—New York N (Barnes)	..	8	New York A (Shawkey)	.. 5	At Polo Grounds
Oct. 12—New York N (Douglas)		2	New York A (Mays)	 1	At Polo Grounds
Oct. 13—New York N (Nehf)	...	1	New York A (Hoyt)	 0	At Polo Grounds

Managers—John J. McGraw, New York N.L.; Miller J. Huggins, New York A.L.

New York N.L. (Giants)—George L. Kelly, 1b.; John W. Rawlings, 2b.; Frank F. Frisch, 3b.-2b.; David J. Bancroft, ss.; Emil F. Meusel, lf.; George J. Burns, cf.; Ross Youngs, rf.; Frank Snyder, c.; Earl Smith, c.; Jesse L. Barnes, p.; Philip B. Douglas, p.; Fred A. Toney, p.; Arthur N. Nehf, p.; Edward Brown, of.; W. A. Cunningham, of.; Cecil A. Causey, p.; Alex Gaston, c.; Miguel Gonzales, c.; Walter H. Kopf, ss.; Wilfred D. Ryan, p.; Harry F. Sallee, p.; Patrick J. Shea, p.; Charles D. Stengel, of.

New York A.L. (Yankees)—Walter C. Pipp, 1b; Aaron L. Ward, 2b.; Michael J. McNally, 3b.; J. Frank Baker, 3b.; Roger T. Peckinpaugh, ss.; George H. Ruth, lf.; Wilson Fewster, cf.; Elmer Miller, cf.; Robert Meusel, rf.; W. H. Shang, c.; Al Devormer, c.; Waite C. Hoyt, p.; Carl Mays, p.; J. J. Quinn, p.; J. Robert Shawkey, p.; W. H. Collins, p.; William Piercy, p.; H. C. Harper, p.; Thomas Rogers, p.; Alex Ferguson, p.; N. L. Hawks, of.; John Mitchell, ss.; R. F. Roth, of.

1920—CLEVELAND A. L. vs. BROOKLYN N. L.

Cleveland A.L. 5 victories; Brooklyn N.L. 2

Oct. 5—Cleveland (Coveleskie)	.	3	Brooklyn (Marquard)	 1	At Brooklyn
Oct. 6—Brooklyn (Grimes)	....	3	Cleveland (Bagby)	 0	At Brooklyn
Oct. 7—Brooklyn (Smith)	......	2	Cleveland (Caldwell)	... 1	At Brooklyn
Oct. 9—Cleveland (Coveleskie)	.	5	Brooklyn (Cadore)	 1	At Cleveland
Oct. 10—Cleveland (Bagby)	.....	8	Brooklyn (Grimes)	 1	At Cleveland
Oct. 11—Cleveland (Mails)	.....	1	Brooklyn (Smith)	 0	At Cleveland
Oct. 12—Cleveland (Coveleskie)	.	3	Brooklyn (Grimes)	 0	At Cleveland

Managers—Tris Speaker, Cleveland; Wilbert J. Robinson, Brooklyn.

Cleveland—George H. Burns, 1b.; William R. Johnston, 1b.; William Wambsganss, 2b.; W. Lawrence Gardner, 3b.; Joseph W. Sewell, ss.; Harry Lunte, ss.; Joseph P. Evans, lf.; Charles D. Jamieson, lf.; John G. Graney, lf.; Tris E. Speaker, cf.; Elmer Smith, rf.; Joseph Wood, rf.; Steve F. O'Neill, c.; Chester D. Thomas, c.; Leslie G. Nunamaker, c.; James C. Bagby, p.; Ray B. Caldwell, p.; Stanley Coveleskie, p.; Walter Mails, p.; George E. Uhle, p.; W. R. Clark, p.; G. R. Ellison, p.; Guy Morton, p.

Brooklyn—Edward J. Konetchy, 1b.; Raymond H. Schmandt, 1b.; Peter J. Kilduff, 2b.; James H. Johnston, 3b.; John T. Sheehan, 3b.; Ivan M. Olson, ss.-2b.; Zack D. Wheat, lf.; Henry H. Myers, cf.; Thomas H. Griffith, rf.; Bernie M. Nels, rf.; Otto Miller, c.; Ernest G. Krueger, c.; L. J. Cadore, p.; Burleigh A. Grimes, p.; Albert L. Mamaux, p.; Richard W. Marquard, p.; Clarence E. Mitchell, p.; Ed J. Pfeffer, p.; Sherrod M. Smith, p.; William G. Lamar, of.; William F. McCabe, inf.; Harold H. Elliott, c.; John K. Miljus, p.; George B. Mohart, p.; James W. Taylor, c.; Charles W. Ward, ss.

1919—CINCINNATI N. L. vs. CHICAGO A L.

Cincinnati N.L. 5 victories; Chicago A.L. 3

Date	Winning Team and Pitcher		Losing Team and Pitcher		Where Played
Oct. 1—Cincinnati (Ruether)	...	9	Chicago (Cicotte	....	1	At Cincinnati
Oct. 2—Cincinnati (Sallee)	.....	4	Chicago (Williams)	.....	2	At Cincinnati
Oct. 3—Chicago (Kerr)	....	3	Cincinnati (Fisher)	.....	0	At Chicago
Oct. 4—Cincinnati (Ring)	......	2	Chicago (Cicotte)	.....	0	At Chicago
Oct. 6—Cincinnati (Eller)	......	5	Chicago (Williams)	.....	0	At Chicago
Oct. 7—Chicago (Kerr)	....	5	Cincinnati (Ring)	......	4	At Cinn. (10 inns.)
Oct. 8—Chicago (Cicotte)	......	4	Cincinnati (Sallee)	....	1	At Cincinnati
Oct. 9—Cincinnati (Eller)	......	10	Chicago (Williams)	....	5	At Chicago

Managers—Patrick J. Moran, Cincinnati; William Gleason, Chicago.

Cincinnati—J. E. Daubert, 1b.; M. C. Rath, 2b.; H. K. Groh, 3b.; W. L. Kopf, ss.; L. Duncan, lf.; A. Earl Neale, rf.; Edd J. Roush, cf.; W. A. Rariden, c.; I. B. Wingo, c.; W. H. Ruether, p.; H. O. Eller, p.; H. F. Sallee, p.; J. J. Ring, p.; Adolfo Luque, p.; R. L. Fisher, p.; S. R. Magee, of.; J. L. Smith, inf.; A. W. Allen, c.; A. Roy Mitchell, p.; R. B. Bressler, of.; Charles H. See, of.; E. F. Gerner, p.; H. W. Schreiber, inf.

Chicago—C. A. Gandil, 1b.; E. T. Collins, 2b.; G. D. Weaver, 3b.; C. A. Risberg, ss.; Joseph Jackson, lf.; Harry Leibold, rf.-cf.; J. F. Collins, rf-cf.; Oscar Felsch, cf.-rf.; R. W. Schalk, c.; Byrd Lynn, c.; Richard Kerr, p.; E. V. Cicotte, p.; Claude Williams, p.; R. H. Wilkinson, p.; G. C. Lowdermilk, p.; William James, p.; J. E. Mayer, p.; Edward Murphy, of.; Fred McMullin, 3b.; Urban C. Faber, p.; Joseph Jenkins, c.; H. McD. McCellan, inf.; John J. Sullivan, p.

1918—BOSTON A. L. vs. CHICAGO N. L.

Boston A.L. 4 victories; Chicago N.L. 2

Sept. 5—Boston (Ruth)	....	1	Chicago (Vaughn)	......	0	At Chicago
Sept. 6—Chicago (Tyler)	......	3	Boston (Bush)	....	1	At Chicago
Sept. 7—Boston (Mays)	....	2	Chicago (Vaughn)	......	1	At Chicago
Sept. 9—Boston (Ruth)	....	3	Chicago (Douglas)	.....	2	At Boston
Sept. 10—Chicago (Vaughn)	....	3	Boston (Jones)	....	0	At Boston
Sept. 11—Boston (Mays)	....	2	Chicago (Tyler)	....	1	At Boston

Managers—E. G. Barrow, Boston; Fred P. Mitchell, Chicago.

Boston—John McInnis, 1b.; D. W. Shean, 2b.; Fred Thomas, 3b.; Everett Scott, ss.; George Whiteman, lf.; George H. Ruth, lf.-p.; Amos Strunk, cf.; H. B. Hooper, rf.; S. L. Agnew, c.; W. H. Schang, c.; L. J. Bush, p.; C. W. Mays, p.; S. P. Jones, p.; L. Miller, of.; Jean Dubuc. p.; George Cochrane, inf.; John F. Coffey, inf.; W. W. Kinney, p.; Walter Mayer, c.; William Pertica, p.; Charles Wagner, inf.

Chicago—F. C. Merkle, 1b.; Charles Pick, 2b.; William Wortman, 2b.; Charles Deal, 3b.; Rollie Zeider, 3b.; Charles Hollocher, ss.; Leslie Mann, lf.; G. H. Paskert, cf.; Max Flack, rf.; William Killefer, c.; Robert O'Farrell, c.; J. L. Vaughn, p.; G. H. Tyler, p.; P. B. Douglas, p.; C. R. Hendrix, p.; W. F. McCabe, inf.; Turner Barber, of.; Paul Carter, p.; T. A. Clarke, c.; F. Otto Knabe, inf.; E. G. Martin, p.; James R. Walker, p.

1917—CHICAGO A. L. vs. NEW YORK N. L.

Chicago A.L. 4 victories, New York N.L. 2

Oct. 6—Chicago (Cicotte)	......	2	New York (Sallee)	......	1	At Chicago
Oct. 7—Chicago (Faber)	......	7	New York (Anderson)	...	2	At Chicago
Oct. 10—New York (Benton)	....	2	Chicago (Cicotte)	......	0	At New York
Oct. 11—New York (Schupp)	....	5	Chicago (Faber)	....	0	At New York
Oct. 13—Chicago (Faber)	......	8	New York (Sallee)	......	5	At Chicago
Oct. 15—Chicago (Faber)	......	4	New York (Benton)	.....	2	At New York

Managers—Clarence H. Rowland, Chicago; John J. McGraw, New York.

Chicago—C. A. Gandil, 1b.; E. T. Collins, 2b.; F. McMullin, 3b.; G. D. Weaver, ss.; J. Jackson, lf.; O. Felsch, cf.; J F. Collins, rf.; H. Leibold, rf.; R. W. Schalk, c.; E. V. Cicotte, p.; U. C. Faber, p.; E. A. Russell, p.; C. Williams, p.; D. C. Danforth, p.; C. A. Risberg, ss.; B. Lynn, c.; Joseph D. Benz, p.; Robert M. Byrne, 3b.; R. L. Hasbrook, inf.; Joseph Jenkins, c.; T. C. Jourdan, 1b.; J. Edward Murphy, of.; James Scott, p.; M. G. Wolfgang, p.

New York—W. Holke, 1b.; C. L. Herzog, 2b.; H. Zimmerman, 3b.; A. Fletcher, ss.; G. J. Burns, lf.; B. Kauff, cf.; D. Robertson, rf.; J. Thorpe, rf.; L. McCarty, c.; W. A. Rariden, c.; H. F. Sallee, p.; C. J. Benton, p.; F. M. Schupp, p.; W. D. Perritt, p.; F. Anderson, p.; C. M. Tesreau, p.; J. W. Wilhout, of.; A. W. Baird, inf.; Albert W. Demaree, p.; George Gibson, c.; John Lobert, 3b.; John J. Murray, of.; John Onslow, c.; James L. Smith, inf.

1916—BOSTON A. L. vs. BROOKLYN N. L.

Boston A.L. 4 victories; Brooklyn N.L. 1

Date	Winning Team and Pitcher		Losing Team and Pitcher		Where Played
Oct. 7—Boston (Shore)	6		Brooklyn (Marquard)	5	At Boston
Oct. 9—Boston (Ruth)	2		Brooklyn (Smith)	1	At Bos. (14 inn.)
Oct. 10—Brooklyn (Coombs)	4		Boston (Mays)	3	At Brooklyn
Oct. 11—Boston (Leonard)	6		Brooklyn (Marquard)	2	At Brooklyn
Oct. 12—Boston (Shore)	4		Brooklyn (Pfeffer)	1	At Boston

Managers—William Carrigan, Boston; Wilbert J. Robinson, Brooklyn.

Boston—Richard Hoblitzel, 1b.; H. C. Janvrin, 2b.; W. L. Gardner, 3b.; Everett Scott, ss.; George Lewis, lf.; James Walsh, cf.; C. Walker, cf.; C. H. Shorten, cf.; Harry B. Hooper, rf.; F. L. Cady, c.; C. D. Thomas, c.; William Carrigan, c.; George H. Ruth, p.; George Foster, p.; H. B. Leonard, p.; C. W. Mays, p.; Ernest Shore, p.; M. J. McNally, inf.; D. C. Gainor, inf.; Olaf Henriksen, of.; Samuel Agnew, c.; John J. Barry, ss.; S. L. Gregg, p.; Samuel P. Jones, p.; Charles Wagner, inf.; J. W. Wyckoff, p.
Brooklyn—J. E. Daubert, 1b.; Fred Merkle, 1b.; George Cutshaw, 2b.; H. Mowrey, 3b.; Ivan Olson, ss.; Zack Wheat, lf.; H. H. Myers, cf.; J. H. Johnston, rf.; Charles Stengel, rf.; O. Miller, c.; J Meyers, c.; J. Coombs, p.; E. Pfeffer, p.; R. Marquard, p.; S. Smith, p.; L. Cheney, p.; N. Rucker, p.; W. G. Dell, p.; O. O'Mara, inf.; G. Getz, inf.; E. S. Appleton, p.; J. Walter Mails, p.

1915—BOSTON A. L. vs. PHILADELPHIA N. L.

Boston A.L. 4 victories; Philadelphia N.L. 1

Oct. 8—Philadelphia (Alexander)	3		Boston (Shore)	1	At Philadelphia
Oct. 9—Boston (Foster)	2		Philadelphia (Mayer)	1	At Philadelphia
Oct. 11—Boston (Leonard)	2		Philadelphia (Alexander)	1	At Boston
Oct. 12—Boston (Shore)	2		Philadelphia (Chalmers)	1	At Boston
Oct. 13—Boston (Foster)	5		Philadelphia (Rixey)	4	At Philadelphia

Managers—William Carrigan, Boston; Patrick J. Moran, Philadelphia.

Boston—D. C. Gainor, 1b.; Richard Hoblitzel, 1b.; J. J. Barry, 2b.; W. L. Gardner, 3b.; Everett Scott, ss.; H. C. Janvrin, ss.; George Lewis, lf.; Tris Speaker, cf.; H. B. Hooper, rf.; F. L. Cady, c.; C. D. Thomas, c.; William Carrigan, c.; George Foster, p.; H. B. Leonard, p.; Ernest Shore, p.; George H. Ruth, p.; O. Henriksen, of.; Ray W. Collins, p.; S. A. Gregg, p.; Carl W. Mays, p.; Michael J. McNally, inf.; Charles Wagner, inf.; Joseph Wood, p.
Philadelphia—Fred W. Luderus, 1b.; George Whitted, 1b.-lf.; J. A. Niehoff, 2b.; M. J. Stock, 3b.; D. J. Bancroft, ss.; Beals Becker, rf.-lf.; George H. Paskert, cf.; C. C. Cravath, rf.; R. M. Burns, c.; G. C. Alexander, p.; George Chalmers, p.; J. E. Mayer, p.; E. J. Rixey, p.; O. J. Dugey, of.; William Killefer, c.; R. M. Byrne, 3b.; John B. Adams, c.; S. F. Baumgartner, p.; Albert W. Demaree, p.; George W. McQuillan, p.; Ben Tincup, p.; Harry Weiser, of.

1914—BOSTON N. L. vs. PHILADELPHIA A. L.

Boston N.L. 4 victories; Philadelphia A.L. 0

Oct. 9—Boston (Rudolph)	7		Philadelphia (Bender)	1	At Philadelphia
Oct. 10—Boston (James)	1		Philadelphia (Plank)	0	At Philadelphia
Oct. 12—Boston (James)	5		Philadelphia (Bush)	4	At Bos. (12 inn.)
Oct. 13—Boston (Rudolph)	3		Philadelphia (Shawkey)	2	At Boston

Managers—George T. Stallings, Boston; Connie Mack, Philadelphia.

Boston—C. J. Schmidt, 1b.; J. J. Evers. 2b.; Chas. Deal. 3b.; W. J. Maranville, ss.; L. Mann, lf.-rf.; G. B. Whitted, cf.; T. Cather, lf.; J. Connolly, lf.; J. H. Moran, rf.; H. Gowdy, c.; W. L. James, p.; R. Rudolph, p.; G. Tyler, p.; J. Devore, p.; L. W. Gilbert, Eugene Cocrehan, p.; E. S. Cottrell. p.; Richard Crutcher, p.; G. A. Davis, p.; Oscar J. Dugey, of.; Otto Hess, p.; W. G. Martin, inf.; J. Carlisle Smith, 3b.; Paul Strand, p.; Albert Whaling, c.
Philadelphia—John McInnis, 1b.; E. T. Collins, 2b.; J. F. Baker. 3b.; J. J. Barry, ss.; R. Oldring. lf.; A. Strunk, cf.; J. Walsh. cf.; T. P. Murphy, rf.; W. H. Schang, c.; J. Lapp. c.; C. A. Bender, p.; L. J. Bush, p.; H. J. Pennock, p.; E. S. Plank. p.; R. J. Shawkey. p.; H. J. Wyckoff, p.; R. B. Bressler, p.; John W. Coombs, p.; L. G. Davies, p.; Harry H. Davis, 1b.; William L. Kopf, ss.; James McAvoy, c.; J. Ira Thomas, c.; C. Thompson, of.

1913—PHILADELPHIA A. L. vs. NEW YORK N. L.

Philadelphia A.L. 4 victories; New York N.L. 1

Date	Winning Team and Pitcher		Losing Team and Pitcher		Where Played
Oct. 7—Philadelphia (Bender) ..	6	New York (Marquard) ...	4	At New York
Oct. 8—New York (Mathewson).	3	Philadelphia (Plank)	0	At Phila. (10 inn.)
Oct. 9—Philadelphia (Bush) ...	8	New York (Tesreau)	2	At New York
Oct. 10—Philadelphia (Bender) ..	6	New York (Demaree)	5	At Philadelphia
Oct. 11—Philadelphia (Plank) ...	3	New York (Mathewson) ..	1	At New York

Managers, Connie Mack, Philadelphia; John J. McGraw, New York.

Philadelphia—John McInnis, 1b.; E. T. Collins, 2b.; J. F. Baker, 3b., J. J. Bary, ss.; R. Oldring, lf.; Amos Strunk, cf.; E. Murphy, rf.; W. H. Schang, c.; J. Lapp, c.; C. A. Bender, p.; E. S. Plank, p.; L. J. Bush, p.; C. W. Brown, p.; John W. Coombs, p.; Harry H. Davis, 1b.; Thomas F. Daly, c.; Byron W. Houck, p.; John L. Lavan, ss.; Daniel F. Murphy, inf.; William Orr, inf.; Herbert J. Pennock, p.; J. Robert Shawkey, p.; J. Ira Thomas, c.; James Walsh, of.; J. W. Wyckoff, p.
New York—Fred Merkle, 1b.; George Wiltse, 1b.; Fred Snodgrass, cf.-1b.; Larry Doyle, 2b.; Charles Herzog, 3b.; Arthur Shafer, cf.-3b.; Arthur Fletcher, ss.; Jack Murray, lf.-rf.; George Burns, lf.; J. B. McLean, c.; Arthur Wilson, c.; J. T. Meyers, c.; Christy Mathewson, p.; R. W. Marquard, p.; Al Demaree, p.; Charles Tesreau, p.; Claude Cooper, c.; Otis Crandall, p.; Harold McCormick, lf.; Eddie Grant, inf.; Arthur Fromme, p.; Grover C. Hartley, c.; James Thorpe, of.

1912—BOSTON A. L. vs. NEW YORK N. L.

Boston A.L. 4 victories; New York N.L. 3, 1 tie game

Oct. 8—Boston (Wood)	4	New York (Tesreau)	3	At New York	
Oct. 9—Boston (Tie)	6	New York (Tie)	6	At Bos. (11 inn.)	
Oct. 10—New York (Marquard) ..	2	Boston (O'Brien)	1	At Boston	
Oct. 11—Boston (Wood)	3	New York (Tesreau)	1	At New York	
Oct. 12—Boston (Bedient)	2	New York (Mathewson) ..	1	At Boston	
Oct. 14—New York (Marquard) ..	5	Boston (O'Brien)	2	At New York	
Oct. 15—New York (Tesreau) ...	11	Boston (Wood)	4	At Boston	
Oct. 16—Boston (Wood)	3	New York (Mathewson) ..	2	At Bos. (10 inn.)	

Managers—J. Garland Stahl, Boston; John J. McGraw, New York.

Boston—J. G. Stahl, 1b.; S. Yerkes, 2b.; W. L. Gardner, 3b.; C. Wagner, ss.; J. Lewis, lf.; T. E. Speaker, cf.; H. Hooper, rf.; F. E. Cady, c.; W. Carrigan, c.; J. Wood, p.; H. Bedient, p.; C. Hall, p.; Ray Collins, p.; T. O'Brien, p.; O. Henriksen, of.; N. Ball, inf.; C. Engle, util.; Hugh Bradley, inf.; M. Krugg, inf.; L. G. Nunamaker, c.; Larry A. Pape, p.; Chester D. Thomas, c.
New York—Fred Merkle, 1b.; Larry Doyle, 2b.; Charles L. Herzog, 3b.; Arthur Fletcher, ss.; Arthur Shafer, ss.; Jack Murray, lf.-rf.; Fred Snodgras, cf.; Josh Devore, lf.-rf.; Beals Becker, cf.; J. T. Meyers, c.; Arthur Wilson, c.; Christy Mathewson, p.; R. W. Marquard, p.; Charles Tesreau, p.; Leon Ames, p.; Otis Crandall, p.; Harold McCormick, cf.; George J. Burns, of.; Henry K. Groh, 3b.; Grover C. Hartley, c.; George L. Wiltse, p.

1911—PHILADELPHIA A. L. vs. NEW YORK N. L.

Philadelphia A.L. 4 victories; New York N.L. 2

Oct. 14—New York (Mathewson).	2	Philadelphia (Bender) ...	1	At New York	
Oct. 16—Philadelphia (Plank)...	3	New York (Marquard) ..	1	At Philadelphia	
Oct. 17—Philadelphia (Coombs) .	3	New York (Mathewson) ..	2	At N. Y. (11 inn.)	
Oct. 24—Philadelphia (Bender) ..	4	New York (Mathewson) ..	2	At Philadelphia	
Oct. 25—New York (Crandall) ..	4	Philadelphia (Plank)	3	At N. Y. (10 inn.)	
Oct. 26—Philadelphia (Bender) ..	13	New York (Ames)	2	At Philadelphia	

Managers—Connie Mack, Philadelphia; John J. McGraw, New York.

Philadelphia—H. Davis, 1b.; E. T. Collins, 2b.; J. F. Baker, 3b.; J. J. Barry, ss.; B. Lord, lf.; R. Olding, cf.; D. Murphy, rf.; I. Thomas, c.; J. Lapp, c.; C. Bender, p.; J. Coombs, p.; E. S. Plank, p.; J. McInnis, 1b.; Amos Strunk, cf.; David C. Danforth, p.; Claude Derrick, inf.; T. F. Hartsel, of.; Harry W. Krause, p.; P. J. Livingston, c.; David Martin, p.; Harry R. Morgan, p.
New York—Fred Merkle, 1b.; Larry Doyle, 2b.; Charles Herzog, 3b.; Arthur Fletcher, ss.; Josh Devore, lf.; Fred Snodgrass, cf.; Jack Murray, rf.; Beals Becker, cf.; J. T. Meyers, c.; Arthur Wilson, c.; Christy Mathewson, p.; R. W. Marquard, p.; Otis Crandall, p.; George Wiltse, p.; Leon Ames, p.; Arthur Devlin, 3b.; Louis Drucke, p.; Grover C. Hartley, c.; J. Eugene Paulette, 1b.

1910—PHILADELPHIA A. L. vs. CHICAGO N. L.

Philadelphia A.L. 4 victories; Chicago N.L. 1

Date	Winning Team and Pitcher		Losing Team and Pitcher		Where Played
Oct. 17—Philadelphia (Bender)	..	4	Chicago (Overall)	1	At Philadelphia
Oct. 18—Philadelphia (Coombs)	.	9	Chicago (Brown)	3	At Philadelphia
Oct. 20—Philadelphia (Coombs)	.	12	Chicago (McIntire)	5	At Chicago
Oct. 22—Chicago (Brown)		4	Philadelphia (Bender)	3	At Chgo. (10 inn.)
Oct. 23—Philadelphia (Coombs)	.	7	Chicago (Brown)	2	At Chicago

Managers—Connie Mack, Philadelphia, Frank L. Chance, Chicago.

Philadelphia—H. Davis, 1b.; E. T. Collins, 2b.; J. F. Baker, 3b.; J. J. Barry, ss.; B. Lord, cf.-lf.; F. Hartsel, lf.; A. Strunk, cf.; D. Murphy, rf.; I. Thomas, c.; J. Lapp, c.; J. Coombs, p.; C. Bender, p.; Frank M. Atkins, p.; Patrick Donohue, c.; James H. Dygert, p.; Claude Derrick, inf.; B. F. Houser, 1b.; Harry W. Krause, p.; P. J. Livingston, c.; Harry R. Morgan, p.; John J. McInnis, 1b.; R. H. Oldring, of.; Edward S. Plank, p. Chicago—F. Chance, 1b.; H. Zimmerman, 2b.; H. Steinfeldt, 3b.; Joe Tinker, ss.; J. Sheckard, lf.; A. Hofman, cf.; F. Schulte, rf.; J. G. Kling, c.; J. Archer, c.-1b.; O. Overall, p.; H. McIntire, p.; M. Brown, p.; L. Ritchie, p.; E. Reulbach, p.; J. Pfeister, p.; L. Cole, p.; C. Beaumont, of.; T. Needham, c.; John J. Evers, 2b.; William A. Foxen, p.; John F. Kane, inf.; Frank X. Pfeffer, p.; Orlie F. Weaver, p.

1909—PITTSBURGH N. L. vs. DETROIT A. L.

Pittsburgh N.L. 4 victories, Detroit A.L. 3

Oct. 8—Pittsburgh (Adams)	...	4	Detroit (Mullin)	1	At Pittsburgh
Oct. 9—Detroit (Donovan)	.....	7	Pittsburgh (Camnitz)	2	At Pittsburgh
Oct. 11—Pittsburgh (Maddox)	...	8	Detroit (Summers)	6	At Detroit
Oct. 12—Detroit (Mullin)		5	Pittsburgh (Leifield)	0	At Detroit
Oct. 13—Pittsburgh (Adams)	....	8	Detroit (Summers)	4	At Pittsburgh
Oct. 14—Detroit (Mullin)		5	Pittsburgh (Willis)	4	At Detroit
Oct. 16—Pittsburgh (Adams)	...	8	Detroit (Donovan)	0	At Detroit

Managers—Fred C. Clarke, Pittsburgh; Hugh Jennings, Detroit.

Pittsburgh—W. Abstein, 1b.; J. Miller, 2b.; R. Byrne, 3b.; T. Leach, 3b.-cf.; J. Wagner, ss.; F. Clarke, lf.; H. Hyatt, rf.; O. Wilson, rf.; G. Gibson, c.; C. Adams, p.; H. Camnitz, p.; V. Willis, p.; N. Maddox, p.; F. Leifield, p.; C. Phillippe, p.; P. F. O'Connor, c.; E. Abbaticchio, 1b.; Chester M. Brandon, p.; Samuel W. Frock, p.; Samuel A. Leever, p.; Eugene, Moore, p.; William B. Powell, p.; Michael E. Simon, c. Detroit—T. Jones, 1b.; J. Delahanty, 2b.; G. Moriarty, 3b.; C. O'Leary, 3b.; D. Bush, ss.; M. McIntyre, lf.; D. Jones, cf.; S. Crawford, rf.-1b.; T. Cobb, rf.; C. Schmidt, c.; O. Stanage, c.; G. Mullin, p.; W. Donovan, p.; E. Summers, p.; R. Works, p.; E. Willett, p.; H. W. Beckindorf, c.; Edward H. Killian, p.; George H. Speer, p.

1908—CHICAGO N. L. vs. DETROIT A. L.

Chicago N.L. 4 victories; Detroit A.L. 1

Oct. 10—Chicago (Brown)		10	Detroit (Summers)	6	At Detroit
Oct. 11—Chicago (Overall)	....	6	Detroit (Donovan)	1	At Chicago
Oct. 12—Detroit (Mullin)		8	Chicago (Pfiester)	3	At Chicago
Oct. 13—Chicago (Brown)		3	Detroit (Summers)	0	At Detroit
Oct. 14—Chicago (Overall)	.....	2	Detroit (Donovan)	0	At Detroit

Managers—Frank L. Chance, Chicago; Hugh Jennings, Detroit.

Chicago—F. Chance, 1b.; G. E. Howard, 1b.; J. J. Evers, 2b.; H. Steinfeldt, 3b.; Joe Tinker, ss.; J. Sheckard, lf.; A. Hofman, cf.; F. Schulte, rf.; J. G. Kling, c.; M. Brown, p.; E. Reulbach, p.; J. Pfiester, p.; O. Overall, p.; Blaine Durbin, p.; Charles C. Fraser, p.; Floyd M. Kroh, p.; Carl L. Lundgren, p.; William R. Marshall, c.; Patrick J. Moran, c.; James F. Slagle, of.; Henry Zimmerman, inf. Detroit—C. Rossman, 1b.; J. Downs, 2b.; H. Schaefer, 2b.-3b.; W. Coughlin, 3b.; C. O'Leary, ss.; M. McIntyre, lf.; S. Crawford, rf.; T. Cobb, cf.; D. Jones, f.; C. Schmidt, c.; I. Thomas, c.; E. Killian, p.; E. Summers, p.; W. Donovan, p.; G. Mullin, p.; G. Winters, p.; Wade H. Killefer, inf.; George F. Suggs, p.; Robert E. Willett, p.

1907—CHICAGO N. L. vs. DETROIT A. L.

Chicago N.L. 4 victories; Detroit none, 1 tie game

Date	Winning Team and Pitcher		Losing Team and Pitcher		Where Played
Oct. 8—Chicago (Tie)	3	Detroit (Tie)	3	At Chgo. (12 inn.)
Oct. 9—Chicago (Pfiester)	3	Detroit (Mullin)	1	At Chicago
Oct. 10—Chicago (Reulbach)	5	Detroit (Siever)	1	At Chicago
Oct. 11—Chicago (Overall)	6	Detroit (Donovan)	1	At Detroit
Oct. 12—Chicago (Brown)	2	Detroit (Mullin)	0	At Detroit

Managers—Frank L. Chance, Chicago; Hugh Jennings, Detroit.

Chicago—F. Chance, 1b.; G. E. Howard, 1b.; J. J. Evers, 2b.; H. Steinfeldt, 3b.; Joe Tinker, ss.; J. Sheckard, lf.; J. Slagle, cf.; Frank Schulte, rf.; J. G. Kling, c.; M. Brown, p.; E. Reulbach, p.; J. Pfiester, p.; O. Overall, p.; Blaine Durbin, p.; Charles C. Fraser, p.; Carl L. Lundgren, p.; Patrick J. Moran, c.; Arthur F. Hofman, util.; Thomas J. Walsh, c.; Henry Zimmerman, inf.

Detroit—C. Rossman, 1b.; H. Schaefer, 2b.; W. Coughlin, 3b.; C. O'Leary, ss.; D. Jones, lf.; S. Crawford, rf.; T. Cobb, cf.; S. Schmidt, c.; Fred Payne, c.; J. Archer, c.; E. Killian, p.; G. Mullin, p.; W. Donovan, p.; E. Siever, p.; Jerry Downs, util.; Robert L. Lowe, 2b.; Matthew McIntyre, of.; Robert E. Willett, p.

1906—CHICAGO A. L. vs. CHICAGO N. L.

Chicago A.L. 4 victories; Chicago N.L. 2

Oct. 9—Chicago A (Altrock)	2	Chicago N (Brown)	1	At Chgo. Nat. Pk.
Oct. 10—Chicago N (Reulbach)	7	Chicago A (White)	1	At Chgo. Am. Pk.
Oct. 11—Chicago A (Walsh)	3	Chicago N (Pfiester)	0	At Chgo. Nat. Pk.
Oct. 12—Chicago N (Brown)	1	Chicago A (Altrock)	0	At Chgo. Am. Pk.
Oct. 13—Chicago A (Walsh)	8	Chicago N (Pfiester)	6	At Chgo. Nat. Pk.
Oct. 14—Chicago A (White)	8	Chicago N (Brown)	3	At Chgo. Am. Pk.

Managers—Fielder Jones, Chicago A.L.; Frank L. Chance, Chicago N.L.

Chicago (White Sox)—J. Donohue, 1b.; F. Isbell, 2b.; Geo. Rohe, 3b.; Lee Tannehill, ss.; G. Davis, ss.; P. Dougherty, f.; F. Jones, f.; E. Hahn, f.; W. Sullivan, c.; G. H. White, p.; Frank Owen, p.; E. Walsh, p.; N. Altrock, p.; Edward W. McFarland, c.; Roy Patterson, p.; Frank E. Smith, p.; W. J. O'Neil, inf.; J. H. Hart, c.; Louis Fiene, p.; August Dundon, inf.; Jay K. Towne, c.

Chicago (Cubs)—F. Chance, 1b.; J. J. Evers, 2b.; H. Steinfeldt, 3b.; Joe Tinker, ss.; J. Sheckard, f.; A. Hofman, f.; F. Schulte, f.; J. G. Kling, c.; M. Brown, p.; E. Reulbach, p.; J. Pfiester, p.; O. Overall, p.; H. H. Gessler, of.; Charles W. Harper, p.; Carl L. Lundgren, p; Patrick J. Moran, c; James F. Slagle, of; John W. Taylor, p; Thomas J. Walsh, c.

1905—NEW YORK N. L. vs. PHILADELPHIA A. L.

New York N.L. 4 victories; Philadelphia A.L. 1

Oct. 9—New York (Mathewson)	3	Philadelphia (Plank)	0	At Philadelphia
Oct. 10—Philadelphia (Bender)	3	New York (McGinnity)	0	At New York
Oct. 12—New York (Mathewson)	9	Philadelphia (Coakley)	0	At Philadelphia
Oct. 13—New York (McGinnity)	1	Philadelphia (Plank)	0	At New York
Oct. 14—New York (Mathewson)	2	Philadelphia (Bender)	0	At New York

Managers—John J. McGraw, New York; Connie Mack, Philadelphia.

New York—Dan McGann, 1b.; W. O. Gilbert, 2b.; A. Devlin, 3b.; W. Dahlen, ss.; S. Mertes, of.; M. Donlin, of.; G. Browne, of.; R. Bresnahan, c.; F. Bowerman, c.; Christy Mathewson, p.; J. McGinnity, p.; L. Ames, p.; William J. Clarke, c.; Claude Elliott, p.; Sam Strang, inf.; Luther Taylor, p.; George L. Wiltse, p.

Philadelphia—H. Davis, 1b.; D. Murphy, 2b.; Lave Cross, 3b.; Monte Cross, ss.; F. T. Hartsel, f.; B. Lord, f.; R. Seybold, f.; O. Shreckengost, c.; M. R. Powers, c.; E. S. Plank, p.; C. Bender, p.; A. Coakley, p.; D. Hoffman, of.; H. L. Barton, of.; James H. Dygert, p.; W. Henley, p.; J. W. Knight, inf.; George E. Waddell, p.

NO GAMES IN 1904

1903—BOSTON A. L. vs. PITTSBURGH N. L.

Boston A.L. 5 victories; Pittsburgh N.L. 3
(Not under Brush rules)

Oct. 1—Pittsburgh (Phillippe)	7	Boston (Young)	3	At Boston
Oct. 2—Boston (Dinneen)	3	Pittsburgh (Leever)	0	At Boston
Oct. 3—Pittsburgh (Phillippe)	4	Boston (Hughes)	2	At Boston
Oct. 6—Pittsburgh (Phillippe)	5	Boston (Dinneen)	4	At Pittsburgh
Oct. 7—Boston (Young)	11	Pittsburgh (Kennedy)	2	At Pittsburgh
Oct. 8—Boston (Dinneen)	6	Pittsburgh (Leever)	3	At Pittsburgh
Oct. 10—Boston (Young)	7	Pittsburgh (Phillipe)	3	At Pittsburgh
Oct. 13—Boston (Dinneen)	3	Pittsburgh (Phillippe)	0	At Boston

Managers—J. J. Collins, Boston; F. C. Clarke, Pittsburgh.

Boston—G. LaChance, 1b.; H. Ferris, 2b.; J. Collins, 3b.; F. Parent, ss.; P. Dougherty, of.; C. Stahl, of.; J. Freeman, of.; J. J. O'Brien, of.; L. Criger, c.; C. Farrell, c.; D. T. Young, p.; W. Dinneen, p.; T. Hughes, p.

Pittsburgh—W. Bransfield, 1b.; C. C. Ritchey, 2b.; T. Leach, 3b.; J. Wagner, ss.; Fred Clarke, lf.; C. H. Beaumont, cf.; J. D. Sebring. rf.; E. Phelps, c.; H. Smith, c.; Charles Phillippe, p.; Sam Leever, p.; W. Kennedy, p.; F. W. Veil, p.; John Thompson, p.

ROSTERS OF CHAMPIONSHIP TEAMS AND RESULTS OF LEAGUE COMPETITION, 1871-1904

1904 New York NL Champions
John J. McGraw, Manager

Ames, L.	p	McGann, D	1b
Bowerman, F.	c	McGinnity, J	p
Bresnahan, R.	of	Mathewson, C	p
Browne, G	of	Mertes, S.	lf
Dahlen, W.	ss	Taylor, L.	p
Devin, A.	3b	Warner, J. J.	c
Dunn, John	2b	Wiltse, G.	p
Gilbert, W. O.	2b		

1904 Boston AL Champions
James J. Collins, Manager

Collins, J. J.	3b	LaChance, G.	1b
Criger, L	c	Parent, F	ss
Dinneen, W. H.	p	Selbach, A.	of
Farrell, C.	c	Stahl, C.	of
Ferris, Hobe	2b	Tannehill, J.	p
Freeman, J.	of	Winters, G.	p
Gibson, N. R.	p	Young, D. T.	p

1902 Pittsburgh NL Champions
Fred C. Clarke, Manager

Beaumont, C. H.	of	Leever, S.	p
Bransfield, W.	1b	O'Connor, J.	c
Burke, Jas.	2b-of	Phillippe, C.	p
Chesbro, J.	p	Ritchey, C. C.	2b
Clarke, F. C.	of	Sebring, J. D.	of
Conroy, W.	ss	Smith, H.	c
Davis, H.	of	Tannehill, J.	p
Doheny, E.	p	Wagner, J.	lf-of
Leach, T.	3b	Zimmer, C.	c

1902 Philadelphia AL Champions
Connie Mack, Manager

Castro, L.	2b	Mitchell, F.	p
Cross, L.	3b	Murphy, D.	2b
Cross, M.	ss	Plank, E. S.	p
Davis, H.	1b	Powers, M. B.	c
Fultz, D.	2b-of	Seybold, R. A.	of
Hartsel, F. F.	of	Schreckengost, O.	c
Hustings, B. J.	p.	Waddell, G. E.	p

1901 Pittsburgh NL Champions
Fred C. Clarke, Manager

Beaumont, C. H.	of	O'Connor, J.	c
Bransfield, W.	1b	Phillippe, C	p
Chesbro, J.	p	Poole, Ed.	ut
Clarke, F. C.	of	Ritchey, C. C.	2b
Davis, A. L.	of	Tannehill, J.	p
Ely, Fred	ss	Wagner, J.	ss-of
Leach, T.	3b	Yeager, G.	c
Leever, S.	p	Zimmer, C.	c

1901 Chicago AL Champions
Clark C. Griffith, Manager

Burke, J.	3b	Katoll, J.	p
Callahan, J. J.	p	McFarland, H.	of
Foster, C.	ut	Mertes, S.	2b
Griffith, C. C.	p	Patterson, R	p
Hartman, F.	3b	Platt, W.	p
Hoy, W. E.	of	Shugart, F.	ss
Isbell, F.	1b	Sugden, J.	c
Jones, F.	of	Sullivan, W.	c

1900 Brooklyn NL Champions
Edward H. Hanlon, Manager

Cross, L.	3b	Keeler, W.	of
Dahlen, W. H.	ss	Kelley, J. J.	1b-of
Daly, T. P.	2b	Kennedy, W.	p
DeMont'lle, E.	2b	Kitson, F.	p
Farrell, C.	c	McGinnity, J.	p
Jennings, H.	1b	McGuire, J.	c
Jones, F. A.	of	Sheckard, J.	of

1899 Brooklyn NL Champions
Edward H. Hanlon, Manager

Anderson, J.	of	Jones, F. A.	of
Casey, James	3b	Keeler, W.	of
Dahlen, W.	ss	Kelley, J. J.	of
Daly, T. P.	2b	Kennedy, W.	p
Dunn, John	p	McGann, D.	1b
Farrell, C.	c	McGuire, J.	c
Hughes, J.	p	McJames, J.	p
Jennings, H.	1b		

1898 Boston NL Champions
Frank G. Selee, Manager

Bergen, M.	c	Lowe, R. L.	of
Collins, J. J.	3b	Nichols, C. A.	p
Duffy, H.	of	Stahl, C.	of
Hamilton, W.	of	Stivetts, J. E.	p
Hickman, C	ut	Tenney, F.	1b
Klobedanz, F. A.	p	Willis, V.	p
Lewis, E. M.	p	Yeager, G.	c
Long, H. C.	ss		

1897 Temple Cup Series
Edward H. Hanlon, Manager
Baltimore 4 Boston 1

Bowerman, F.	c	Kelley, J. J.	of
Corbett, Jos.	p	McGraw, J. J.	3b
Doyle, J.	1b	Nops, J.	p
Hoffer, W.	p	Reitz, H.	2b
Jennings, H.	ss	Robinson, W.	c
Keeler, W.	of	Stenzel, J.	of

1897 Boston
Frank G. Selee, Manager

Bergen, M.	c	Long, H. C.	ss
Collins, J. J.	3b	Lowe, R. L.	2b
Duffy, H.	of	Nichols, C. A.	p
Ganzel, C.	c	Stahl, C.	of
Hamilton, W.	of	Stivetts, J. E.	p
Hickman, C.	p	Tenney, F.	1b
Klobedanz, F. A.	p		

1896 Temple Cup Series
Baltimore 4 Cleveland 0

Edward Hanlon, Manager		Oliver Tebeau, Manager	
Brodie, W.	of	Blake, H.	of
Clarke, W	c	Burkett, J.	of
Corbett, Jos.	p	Chamberlain, E.	p
Doyle, J.	1b	Childs, C.	2b
Hoffer, W.	p	Cuppy, G.	p
Jennings, H	ss	McAleer, J.	of
Keeler, W.	of	McGarr, J.	3b
Kelley, J. J.	of	McKean, E.	ss
McGraw, J. J.	3b	Tebeau, O.	1b
Reitz, H.	2b	Wallace, R.	p
Robinson, W.	c	Young, D. T.	p
		Zimmer, C.	c

1895 Temple Cup Series
Cleveland 4 Baltimore 1

Oliver Tebeau, Manager		Edward Hanlon, Manager	
Blake, H.	of	Brodie, W.	of
Burkett, J.	of	Carey, G.	1b
Childs, C.	2b	Clarke, W.	c
Cuppy, G.	p	Esper, C.	p
McAleer, J.	of	Gleason, W	2b
McGarr, J.	3b	Hoffer, W.	p
McKean, E.	ss	Jennings, H.	ss
Tebeau, O.	1b	Keeler, W.	of
Young, D. T.	p	Kelley, J. J.	of
Zimmer, C.	c	McGraw, J. J.	3b
		McMahon, W.	p
		Robinson, W.	c

1894 Temple Cup Series
New York 4 Baltimore 0

John M. Ward, Manager		Edward Hanlon, Manager	
Burke, E.	of	Bonner, W.	of
Davis, G.	3b	Brodie, W.	of
Doyle, J.	1b	Brouthers, D.	1b
Farrell, C.	c	Esper, C.	p
Fuller, W.	ss	Gleason, W.	p
Meekin, J.	p	Hawke, W.	p
Rusie, A.	p	Hemming, G.	p
Tiernan, M.	of	Jennings, H.	ss
VanHaltren, G.	of	Keeler, W.	of
Ward, J. M.	2b	Kelley, J. J.	of
		McGraw, J. J.	3b
		Reitz, H.	2b
		Robinson, W.	ss

1893 Boston NL Champions

Bennett, C. W.	c	McCarthy, T. F.	of
Carroll, C.	of	Merritt, W.	c
Duffy, H.	of	Nash, W. H.	3b
Ganzel, C.	c	Nichols, C. A.	p
Gastright, H.	p	Staley, H. E.	p
Long, H. C.	ss	Stivetts, J.	p
Lowe, R. L.	2b	Tucker, T. J.	1b

1892 Play-Off—Split Season
Boston 5 Cleveland 0 (1-tie)

Frank G. Selee, Manager		Oliver Tebeau, Manager	
Bennett, C.	c	Burkett, J.	of
Duffy, H.	of	Childs, C.	2b
Ganzel, C.	c	Clarkson, J.	p
Kelly, M. J.	c	Cuppy, G.	p
Long, H. C.	ss	McAleer, J.	of
Lowe, R. L.	of	McKean, E.	ss
McCarthy, T. F.	of	O'Connor, J.	of
Nash, W. H.	3b	Tebeau, O.	3b
Nichols, C. A.	p	Virtue, J.	1b
Quinn, J.	2b	Young, D. T.	p
Staley, H. E.	p	Zimmer, C.	c
Stivetts, J. F.	p		
Tucker, T. J.	1b		

1891—No Series
1891 Boston NL Champions
Frank G. Selee, Manager

Bennett, C.	c	Nash, W. H.	3b
Brodie, W.	of	Nichols, C. A.	p
Clarkson, J.	p	Quinn, J.	2b
Ganzel, C.	c	Staley, H. E.	p
Kelly, M. J.	of	Stovey, H.	of
Long, H. C.	ss	Sullivan, M.	of
Lowe, R. L.	of-2b	Tucker, T. J.	1b

1891 Boston AA Champions
Arthur Irwin, Manager

Brouthers. D.	1b	Joyce, Wm.	3b
Brown, T.	cf	Kelly, M.	c
Buffington, C.	p	Murphy, L.	c
Daley, Wm.	p	O'Brien, J.	p
Duffy, H.	rf	Radford, P.	ss
Farrell, C.	c	Richardson, H.	lf
Griffith, C.	p	Stricker, J.	2b
Haddock, G.	p		

1890
National vs American Asso. Series
Brooklyn 3 Louisville 3 (1-tie)

W. McGunnigle, Manager		John C. Chapman, Manager	
Burns, T.	of	Dailey, Edw. M.	p
Bushong, A.	c	Ehret, P.	p
Carruthers, R.	p	Hamburg, E.	of
Clark, R.	c	Meekin, J.	p
Collins, H.	2b	Raymond, P.	3b
Corkhill, J.	of	Ryan, J.	c
Daly, T.	c	Shinnock, T.	2b
Donovan, P. J.	of	Stratton, S.	p
Foutz, D.	1b	Taylor, H.	1b
Hughes, J.	p	Tomney, P.	ss
Lovett, T.	p	Weaver, W.	of
O'Brien, W.	of	Weckbecker, P.	c
Pickney, G.	3b	Wolf, W.	of
Smith, G.	ss		
Terry, W. H.	p		

1889 New York NL Brooklyn AA
New York 6 Brooklyn 3

James Mutrie, Manager		W. McGunnigle, Manager	
Brown, W.	c	Burns, T.	of
Connor, R.	1b	Bushong, A.	c
Crane, E.	p	Carruthers, R.	p
Ewing, W. B.	c	Clark, R.	c
Gore, Geo.	of	Collins, H.	2b
Keefe, T.	p	Corkhill, J.	of
O'Day, H.	p	Foutz, D.	1b
O'Rourke, J.	of	Hughes, J.	p
Richardson, D.	2b	Lovett, T.	p
Tiernan, M.	of	O'Brien, W.	of
Ward, John M.	ss	Pinckney, G.	3b
Welch, M.	p	Smith, G.	ss
Whitney, A.	3b	Terry, W. H.	p
		Visner, J.	c

1888 New York NL St. Louis AA
New York 6 St. Louis 4

James Mutrie, Manager		Chas. Comiskey, Manager	
Brown, W.	c	Chamberlain, E.	p
Connor, R.	1b	Comiskey, C.	1b
Crane, E.	p	King, C.	p
Ewing, W. B.	c	Latham, W. A.	3b
George, W.	p	Lyons, H.	of
Keefe, T.	p	McCarthy, T.	of
Murphy, P.	c	Milligan, J.	c
O'Day, H.	p	O'Neill, J. F.	of
O'Rourke, J.	of	Robinson, W.	2b
Richardson, D.	2b	White, W.	ss
Slattery, M.	of		
Tiernan, M.	of		
Ward, John M.	ss		
Welch, M.	p		
Whitney, A.	3b		

NATIONAL LEAGUE   AMERICAN ASSOCIATION

1887 Detroit NL St. Louis AA
Detroit 10 St. Louis 5

W. H. Watkins, Manager		Chas. Comiskey, Manager	
Baldwin, C. B.	p	Boyle, L.	c
Bennett, C.	c	Bushong, A.	c
Brouthers, D.	1b	Carruthers, R.	p
Conway, O. J.	p	Comiskey, C.	1b
Dunlap, F.	2b	Foutz, D.	p-of
Ganzel, C.	1b-c	Gleason, W.	ss
Getzein, C.	p	King, C.	p
Hanlon, E.	of	Latham, W. A.	3b
Richardson, H	of	O'Neill, J. F.	of
Rowe, J.	ss	Robinson, W.	2b
Thompson, S.	of	Welch, G.	of
Twitchell, L.	p		
White, J.	3b		

1886 St. Louis AA Chicago NL
St. Louis 4 Chicago 2

Chas. Comiskey, Manager		Adrian. C. Anson, Manager	
Bushong, A.	c	Anson, A. C.	1b
Carruthers, R.	p	Burns, T.	3b
Comiskey, C.	1b	Clarkson, J.	p
Foutz, D.	of-p	Dalrymple, A.	of
Gleason, W.	ss	Flint, F.	c
Hudson, N.	p	Gore, Geo.	of
Latham, W. A.	3b	Kelly, M. J.	c
O'Neill, J. F.	of	McCormick, J.	p
Robinson, W.	2b	Pfeffer, F.	2b
Welch, C.	of	Ryan, J.	of
		Williamson, E.	ss

1885 Chicago NL St. Louis AA
Chicago 3 St. Louis 3 (1-tie)

Adrian. C. Anson, Manager		Chas. Comiskey, Manager	
Anson, A. C.	1b	Bushong, A.	c
Burns, T.	3b	Carruthers, R.	p
Clarkson, J.	p	Comiskey, C.	1b
Dalrymple, A.	of	Foutz, D.	of-p
Flint, F.	c	Gleason, W.	ss
Gore, Geo.	of	Latham, W. A.	3b
Holliday, F.	of	Nicol, H.	of
Kelly, M. J.	c	O'Neill, J. F.	of
McCormick, J.	p	Robinson, W.	2b
Pfeffer, F.	2b	Welch, C.	of
Sunday, W.	of		
Williamson, E.	ss		

1884 Providence NL Mets. AA
Providence 3 Mets. O

F. C. Bancroft, Manager		James Mutrie, Manager	
Carroll, C.	of	Brady, S.	of
Denny, J.	3b	Esterbrook, T.	3b
Farrell, J.	2b	Holbert, W.	c
Gilligan, B.	c	Keefe, T.	p
Hines, P.	of	Kennedy, E.	of
Irwin, A.	ss	Lynch, J.	p
Nava, V.	c	Nelson, J.	ss
Radbourne, C.	p	Orr, D.	1b
Radford, P.	of	Reipschlager, C.	c
Start, J.	1b	Roseman, J.	of
		Troy, J.	2b

1883—No Series
1883 Boston NL Champions
John F. Morrill, Manager

Buffington, C.	p	Radford, P.	of
Burdock, J.	2b	Smith, C.	ss
Hackett, M.	c	Sutton, E.	3b
Hines, M.	c	Whitney, J.	p
Hornung, J.	of	Wise, Sam	ss
Morrill, J. F.	1b		

1883 Philadelphia AA Champions
Lew. Simmons, Manager

Birdsall, A.	lf	Mathews, R.	p
Blakiston, R.	cf	Moynahan, M.	ss
Bradley, G. W.	p	O'Brien, J.	c
Corey, F.	3b	Rowan, E.	c
Jones, C. W.	p	Stovey, H.	1b
Knight, A.	cf	Stricker, J.	2b

1882—No Series
1882 Chicago NL Champions
Adrian C. Anson, Manager

Anson, A. C.	1b	Gore, Geo.	of
Burns, T. E.	ss-2b	Kelly, M. J.	of
Corcoran, L.	p	Nicol, H.	of
Dalrymple, A.	of	Quest, J.	2b
Flint, F. S.	c	Williamson, E.	3b
Goldsmith, F.	p		

1882 Cincinnati AA Champions
Charles Fulmer, Manager

Carpenter, W. W.	3b	Powers, P.	c
Fulmer, C.	ss	Snyder, C. N.	c
Luff, H. T.	1b	Sommer, J.	lf
Macullar, J.	cf	Stearns, D.	1b
McCormick, H.	p	Wheeler, H.	rf
McPhee, J. A.	2b	White, W. H.	p

1881 Chicago NL Champions
Adrian C. Anson, Manager

Anson, A. C.	1b	Gore, Geo.	of
Burns, T. E.	ss	Kelly, M. J.	of
Corcoran, L.	p	Nicol, H.	of
Dalrymple, A.	of	Quest, J.	2b
Flint, F. S.	c	Williamson, E.	3b
Goldsmith, F.	p		

1880 Chicago NL Champions
Adrian C. Anson, Manager

Anson, A. C.	1b	Goldsmith, F.	p
Burns, T. E.	ss	Gore, Geo.	of
Corcoran, L.	p	Kelly, M. J.	of
Dalrymple, A.	of	Quest, J.	2b
Flint, F. S.	c	Williamson, E.	3b

1879 Providence NL Champions
George Wright, Manager

Brown, J.	c	O'Rourke, J.	1b-of
Gross, E.	c	Start, Joe	1b
Hague, W.	3b	Ward, John M.	p
Hines, Paul	of	Wright, G.	ss
McGeary, M.	2b	York, Tom	of
Mathews, R.	p		

1878 Boston NL Champions
Harry Wright, Manager

Bond, T. H.	p	O'Rourke, J.	of
Burdock, J. J.	2b	Schaefer, H. C.	sub
Leonard, A. J.	of	Snyder, C. N.	c
Manning, J. E.	of	Sutton, E. B.	3b
Morrill, J. F.	1b	Wright, G.	ss

1877 Boston NL Champions
Harry Wright, Manager

Bond, Tom	p	O'Rourke, J.	of
Brown, L.	c	Schafer, H.	ss
Leonard, A.	ss	Sutton, E.	3b
Morrill, J.	2b	White, James	1b
Murnane, T.	p	Wright, Geo.	2b

1876 First Year, National League
Chicago Champions
Albert G. Spalding, Manager

Addy, R.	of	Hines, Paul	of
Anson, A. C.	3b-1b	McVey, C. A.	1b
Barnes, R.	2b	Peters, J.	ss
Bielaskie, O.	of	Spalding, A. G.	p
Glenn, J.	of	White, James	c

WORLD SERIES

	WINNERS NAT. LEAGUE		LOSERS BOTH LEAGUES		WINNERS AM. LEAGUE	
Year	Club	Manager	Club	Manager	Club	Manager
			FOUR (4) GAME SERIES			
1914	Boston	George T. Stallings	Philadelphia AL	Connie Mack		
1927			Pittsburgh NL	Owen J. Bush	New York	Miller J. Huggins
1928			St. Louis NL	William B. McKechnie	New York	Miller J. Huggins
1932			Chicago NL	Charles J. Grimm	New York	Joseph V. McCarthy
1938			Chicago NL	C. L. Hartnett	New York	Joseph V. McCarthy
1939			Cincinnati NL	William B. McKechnie	New York	Joseph V. McCarthy
1950			Philadelphia NL	Edwin M. Sawyer	New York	Charles D. Stengel
1954	New York	Leo E. Durocher	Cleveland AL	Alfonso R. Lopez		
1963	Los Angeles	Walter E. Alston	New York AL	Ralph G. Houk		
			FIVE (5) GAME SERIES			
1905	New York	John J. McGraw	Philadelphia AL	Connie Mack		
1907	Chicago	Frank L. Chance	Detroit AL	Hugh Jennings		(1 tie game)
1908	Chicago	Frank L. Chance	Detroit AL	Hugh Jennings		
1910			Chicago NL	Frank L. Chance	Philadelphia	Connie Mack
1913			New York NL	John J. McGraw	Philadelphia	Connie Mack
1915			Philadelphia NL	Patrick J. Moran	Boston	William Carrigan
1916			Brooklyn NL	Wilbert Robinson	Boston	William Carrigan
1922	New York	John J. McGraw	New York AL	Miller J. Huggins		(1 tie game)
1929			Chicago NL	Joseph V. McCarthy	Philadelphia	Connie Mack
1933	New York	William H. Terry	Washington AL	Joseph E. Cronin		
1937			New York NL	Wm. H. Terry	New York	Joseph V. McCarthy
1941			Brooklyn NL	Leo E. Durocher	New York	Joseph V. McCarthy
1942	St. Louis	William H. Southworth	New York AL	Joseph V. McCarthy		
1943			St. Louis NL	William H. Southworth	New York	Joseph V. McCarthy
1949			Brooklyn NL	Burton E. Shotton	New York	Charles D. Stengel
1961			Cincinnati NL	Frederick C. Hutchinson	New York	Ralph G. Houk
			SIX (6) GAME SERIES			
1906			Chicago NL	Frank L. Chance	Chicago	Fielder Jones
1911			New York NL	John J. McGraw	Philadelphia	Connie Mack

WORLD SERIES

	WINNERS NAT. LEAGUE		LOSERS BOTH LEAGUES		WINNERS AM. LEAGUE	
Year	Club	Manager	Club	Manager	Club	Manager
			SIX (6) GAME SERIES—Continued			
1917			New York NL	John J. McGraw	Chicago	Clarence H. Rowland
1918			Chicago NL	Fred L. Mitchell	Boston	Edward G. Barrow
1923			New York NL	John J. McGraw	New York	Miller J. Huggins
1930			St. Louis NL	Charles E. Street	Philadelphia	Connie Mack
1935			Chicago NL	Charles J. Grimm	Detroit	Gordon S. Cochrane
1936			New York NL	William H. Terry	New York	Joseph V. McCarthy
1944	St. Louis	William H. Southworth	St. Louis AL	J. Luther Sewell		
1948			Boston NL	William H. Southworth	Cleveland	Louis Boudreau
1951			New York NL	Leo F. Durocher	New York	Charles D. Stengel
1953			Brooklyn NL	Charles W. Dressen	New York	Charles D. Stengel
1959	Los Angeles	Walter E. Alston	Chicago AL	Alfonso R. Lopez		
			SEVEN (7) GAME SERIES			
1909	Pittsburgh	Fred C. Clarke	Detroit AL	Hugh Jennings		
1920			Brooklyn NL	Wilbert Robinson	Cleveland	Tris Speaker
1924			New York NL	John J. McGraw	Washington	Stanley R. Harris
1925	Pittsburgh	William B. McKechnie	Washington AL	Stanley R. Harris		
1926	St. Louis	Rogers Hornsby	New York AL	Miller J. Huggins		
1931	St. Louis	Charles E. Street	Philadelphia AL	Connie Mack		
1934	St. Louis	Frank F. Frisch	Detroit AL	Gordon S. Cochrane		
1940	Cincinnati	William B. McKechnie	Detroit AL	Delmar D. Baker		
1945			Chicago NL	Charles J. Grimm	Detroit	Stephen F. O'Neill
1946	St. Louis	Edwin H. Dyer	Boston AL	Joseph E. Cronin		
1947			Brooklyn NL	Burton E. Shotton	New York	Stanley R. Harris
1952			Brooklyn NL	Charles W. Dressen	New York	Charles D. Stengel
1955	Brooklyn	Walter E. Alston	New York AL	Charles D. Stengel		
1956			Brooklyn NL	Walter E. Alston	New York	Charles D. Stengel
1957	Milwaukee	Fred G. Haney	New York AL	Charles D. Stengel		
1958			Milwaukee NL	Fred G. Haney	New York	Charles D. Stengel
1960	Pittsburgh	Daniel E. Murtaugh	New York AL	Charles D. Stengel		
1962			San Francisco NL	Alvin R. Dark	New York	Ralph G. Houk
1964	St. Louis	John J. Keane	New York AL	Lawrence P. Berra		
1965	Los Angeles	Walter E. Alston	Minnesota AL	Sabath A. Mele		
			EIGHT (8) GAME SERIES			
1903			Pittsburgh NL	Fred C. Clarke	Boston	James J. Collins
1912		(1 tie game)	New York NL	John J. McGraw	Boston	J. Garland Stahl
1919	Cincinnati	Patrick J. Moran	Chicago AL	William Gleason		
1921	New York	John J. McGraw	New York AL	Miller J. Huggins		

98

WORLD SERIES RECORDS
INDIVIDUAL BATTING RECORDS

A—Most series played—
14—Lawrence P. Berra, N.Y. AL, 1947, 49-53, 55-58, 60-63.
12—Mickey C. Mantle, N.Y. AL, 1951-53, 55-58, 60-64.
10—George H. Ruth, Bos. AL, 1915-16, 18; N.Y. AL, 1921-23, 26-28, 32.
Joseph P. DiMaggio, N.Y. AL, 1936-39, 41-42, 47, 49-51.
8—Frank F. Frisch, N.Y. NL, 1921-24; St.L. NL, 1928, 30-31, 34.

B—Most times on winning club—
10—Lawrence P. Berra, New York AL.

BB—Most times on losing club—
6—Harold H. Reese, Brooklyn NL

C—Most series batting .300 or better—
6—G. H. Ruth, N.Y. AL, 1921—.313, 1923—.368, 1926—.300, 1927—.400, 1928—.625, 1932—.333.

D—Highest batting percentage, total series—
.363—J. Franklin Baker, Phila.-N.Y. AL, (6 series, 25 games, 91 ab. 33 hits) 1910, '11, '13, '14, '21, '22.

E—Highest batting percentage, 4 or more games, one series—
.625—4 game series, George H. Ruth, New York, AL, 1928.
.500—5 game series, John B. McLean, New York, NL, 1913.
Joseph Gordon, New York AL, 1941.
Robert W. Brown, New York AL, 1949.
.500—6 game series, Davis A. Robertson, New York NL, 1917.
Alfred M. Martin, New York AL, 1953.
.500—7 game series, John L. Martin, St. Louis NL, 1931.
John H. Lindell, New York AL, 1947.
.400—8 game series, Charles L. Herzog, New York NL, 1912.

F—Most games played, total series—
75—Lawrence P. Berra, New York AL.
50—Frank F. Frisch, New York (26)—St. Louis (24) NL.

G—Most games played with one club—
75—Lawrence P. Berra, New York AL.

RUNS

H—Most runs, total series—
42—Mickey C. Mantle, N.Y. AL, 1951-53, 55-58, 60-64.

I—Most runs, one series—
9—4 game series, George H. Ruth, New York AL, 1928.
Henry L. Gehrig, New York AL, 1932.
6—5 game series, J. Frank Baker and D. F. Murphy, Philadelphia AL, 1910.
Harry B. Hooper, Boston AL, 1916.
Al H. Simmons, Philadelphia AL, 1929.
8—6 game series, George H. Ruth, New York AL, 1923.
Alvin J. Powell, New York AL, 1936.
8—7 game series, Thomas W. Leach, Pittsburgh NL, 1909.
John L. Martin, St. Louis NL, 1934.
William R. Johnson, New York AL, 1947.
Mickey C. Mantle, New York AL, 1960, 64.
Robert C. Richardson, New York AL, 1960.
8—8 game series, Fred N. Parent, Boston AL, 1903.

J—Most runs, game—
4—George H. Ruth, New York AL, Oct. 6, 1926.
Earle B. Combs, New York AL, Oct. 2, 1932.
Frank P. Crosetti, New York AL, Oct. 2, 1936.
Enos B. Slaughter, St. Louis NL, Oct. 10, 1946.

K—Most consecutive games, one or more runs, one or more series—
9—George H. Ruth, New York AL, 2, 1927; 4, 1928; 3, 1932.

L—Most runs, inning—
2—Frank F. Frisch, New York NL vs. New York AL, 7th inning, Oct. 7, 1921.
James E. Foxx, Al. H. Simmons, Philadelphia AL vs. Chicago NL, 7th inning, Oct. 12, 1929.

TIMES AT BAT

M—Most times at bat, total series—
259—Lawrence P. Berra, N.Y. AL.
197—Frank F. Frisch, N.Y.-St.L. NL.

WORLD SERIES INDIVIDUAL BATTING—Continued

A—Most times at bat, one series—
  19—4 game series, Mark A. Koenig, New York AL, 1928.
  23—5 game series, Harold C. Janvrin, Boston AL, 1916.
      Joseph G. Moore, New York NL, 1937.
      Robert C. Richardson, New York AL, 1961.
  28—6 game series, Joseph G. Moore, New York NL, 1936.
  33—7 game series, Stanley R. Harris, Washington AL, 1924.
      Edgar C. Rice, Washington AL, 1925.
  36—8 game series, James J. Collins, Boston AL, 1903.

B—Most times at bat, 9-inning game—
  6—By many players. Last:
      Robert C. Richardson, New York AL, Oct. 9, 1961.
      Anthony C. Kubek, New York AL, Oct. 9, 1961.

C—Most times at bat, inning—
  2—By many players.

RUNS BATTED IN (officially adopted in 1920)

D—Most runs batted in, total series—
  40—Mickey C. Mantle, N.Y. AL, 1951-53, 55-58, 60-64.

E—Most runs batted in, one series—
  9—4 game series, Henry L. Gehrig, New York AL, 1928.
  8—5 game series, Daniel F. Murphy, Philadelphia AL, 1910.
  10—6 game series, Theodore B. Kluszewski, Chicago AL, 1959.
  12—7 game series, Robert C. Richardson, New York AL, 1960.
  8—8 game series, Thomas W. Leach, Pittsburgh NL, 1903.
      Louis B. Duncan, Cincinnati NL, 1919.

F—Most runs batted in, game—
  6—Robert C. Richardson, New York AL, (4) 1st inn., (2) 4th inn., Oct. 8, 1960.

G—Most runs batted in, inning—
  4—Elmer J. Smith, Cleveland AL, 1st inning, Oct. 10, 1920.
      Anthony M. Lazzeri, New York AL, 3d inning, Oct. 2, 1936.
      Gilbert J. McDougald, New York AL, 3d inning, Oct. 9, 1951.
      Mickey C. Mantle, New York AL, 3d inning, Oct. 4, 1953.
      Lawrence P. Berra, New York AL, 2nd inning, Oct. 5, 1956.
      William J. Skowron, New York AL, 7th inning, Oct. 10, 1956.
      Robert C. Richardson, New York AL, 1st inning, Oct. 8, 1960.
      Charles J. Hiller, San Francisco NL, 7th inning, Oct. 8, 1962.
      Kenton L. Boyer, St. Louis NL, 6th inning, Oct. 11, 1964.
      Joseph A. Pepitone, New York AL, 8th inning, Oct. 14, 1964.

H—Most runs batted in, consecutive times at bat—
  7—James L. Rhodes, New York NL on first 4 times bat, 1954.

BASE HITS

I—Most base hits, total series—
  71—Lawrence P. Berra, New York AL, 1947, 49-53, 55-58, 60-61.
  58—Frank F. Frisch, N.Y. NL, 1921-24; St. L. NL, 1928, 30-31, 34.

J—Most base hits, one club, total series—
  71—Lawrence P. Berra, New York AL.

K—Most consecutive games, one or more base hits, total series—
  17—Henry A. Bauer, New York AL, 1956-7, 1957-7, 1958-3.

L—Most base hits, one series—
  10—4 game series, George H. Ruth, New York AL, 1928.
  9—5 game series, Edward T. Collins, J. Frank Baker, Philadelphia AL, 1910.
      J. Frank Baker, Philadelphia AL, 1913.
      Henry K. Groh, New York NL, 1922.
      Joseph G. Moore, New York NL, 1937.
      Robert C. Richardson, New York AL, 1961.
  12—6 game series, Alfred M. Martin, New York AL, 1953.
  13—7 game series, Robert C. Richardson, New York AL, 1964.
  12—8 game series, Charles L. Herzog, New York NL, 1912;
      Joseph J. Jackson, Chicago AL, 1919.

M—Most base hits, inning—
  2—By 13 players. Last:
      Frank R. Quilici, Minn. AL, Oct. 6, 1965 (3rd inn.).

N—Most hitless times at bat, series—
  21—James T. Scheckard, Chicago NL (6 games) 1906.
      William D. Sullivan, Chicago AL (6 games) 1906.
      John J. Murray, New York NL (6 games) 1911.
      Gilbert R. Hodges, Brooklyn NL (7 games) 1952.

O—Most consecutive hitless times at bat, total series—
  31—Marvin J. Owen, Detroit AL, last 12 times at bat in 1934 series and first 19 times at bat in 1935 series.

MAKING ONE OR MORE BASE HITS IN EACH GAME, ONE SERIES

Year	Name and Club	G.	H.	2B.	3B.	HR.
1907	Frank Schulte, Chicago NL	5	5	..	..	..
1908	Frank Schulte, Chicago NL	5	7	..	..	..
1910	Edward T. Collins, Philadelphia AL	5	9	4	1	..
	Daniel F. Murphy, Philadelphia AL	5	7	2	1	1
1914	John J. Evers, Boston NL	4	7	..	..	..
	Charles J. Schmidt, Boston NL	4	5	..	..	..
1915	Harry B. Hooper, Boston AL	5	7	..	..	2
	George E. Lewis, Boston AL	5	8	..	..	1
1916	Harry B. Hooper, Boston AL	5	7	1	1	..
1917	Davis A. Robertson, New York NL	6	11	1	1	..
1922	Walter C. Pipp, New York AL	5	6	1	..	..
	Robert W. Meusel, New York AL	5	6	1	..	..
	Henry K. Groh, New York NL	5	9	..	1	..
	Emil F. Meusel, New York NL	5	5	..	..	1
1923	George H. Ruth, New York AL	6	7	1	1	2
	Aaron L. Ward, New York AL	6	10	..	..	1
	Walter H. Schang, New York AL	6	7	1	..	..
1924	Stanley R. Harris, Washington AL	7	11	1	..	2
	George L. Kelly, New York NL	7	9	1	..	1
1925	Joseph Harris, Washington AL	7	11	..	..	2
1926	James L. Bottomley, St. Louis NL	7	10	3	..	..
	Earle B. Combs, New York AL	7	10	2	..	..
1927	Lloyd J. Waner, Pittsburgh NL	4	6	1	1	..
	Clyde L. Barnhart, Pittsburgh NL	4	5	1	..	..
	Mark A. Koenig, New York AL	4	9	2	..	..
1928	George H. Ruth, New York AL	4	10	3	..	3
	Henry L. Gehrig, New York AL	4	6	1	..	4
1929	Edmund J. Miller, Philadelphia AL	5	7	1	..	..
	J. Riggs Stephenson, Chicago NL	5	6	1	..	..
1930	James E. Foxx, Philadelphia AL	6	7	2	1	1
1932	Henry L. Gehrig, New York AL	4	9	1	..	3
	William Dickey, New York AL	4	7	..	..	..
	George H. Ruth, New York AL	4	5	..	..	2
	J. Riggs Stephenson, Chicago NL	4	8	1	..	..
	Charles L. Hartnett, Chicago NL	4	5	2	..	1
1933	George W. Davis, New York NL	5	7	1	..	..
1934	John L. Martin, St. Louis NL	7	11	3	1	..
	Charles L. Gehringer, Detroit AL	7	11	1	..	1
1935	Ervin Fox, Detroit AL	6	10	2	1	..
1936	George Selkirk, New York AL	6	8	..	1	2
	Richard Bartell, New York NL	6	8	3	..	1
1937	Joseph G. Moore, New York NL	5	8	3	..	1
	A. M. Lazzeri, New York AL	5	6	..	1	1
1938	Jos. Gordon, New York AL	4	6	2	..	1
	H. L. Gehrig, New York AL	4	4	..	..	..
	S. C. Hack, Chicago NL	4	8	1	..	..
	P. Cavarretta, Chicago NL	4	6	1	..	..
1939	C. E. Keller, New York AL	4	7	1	1	3
	J. P. DiMaggio, New York AL	4	5	..	..	1
	Wm. Dickey, New York AL	4	4	..	..	2
1941	J. P. Sturm, New York AL	5	6	..	..	..
	Jos. Gordon, New York AL	5	7	1	1	1
1943	W. Walker Cooper, St. Louis NL	5	5	..	..	..
1944	Raymond F. Sanders, St. Louis NL	6	6	..	..	1
1947	Thomas D. Henrich, New York AL	7	10	2	..	1
1950	Eugene R. Woodling, New York AL	4	6	..	..	..
1951	Alvin R. Dark, New York NL	6	10	3	..	1
	Philip F. Rizzuto, New York AL	6	8	..	..	1
1953	Alfred M. Martin, New York AL	6	12	1	2	2
1954	Victor W. Wertz, Cleveland AL	4	8	2	1	1
	Alvin R. Dark, New York NL	4	7	1	..	..
	Henry Thompson, New York NL	4	4	1	..	..
1955	Lawrence P. Berra, New York AL	7	10	1	..	1
1956	Henry A. Bauer, New York AL	7	9	..	..	1
	Alfred M. Martin, New York AL	7	8	..	..	2
1957	Henry A. Bauer, New York AL	7	8	2	1	2
	Henry Aaron, Milwaukee NL	7	11	..	1	3
1960	Roberto W. Clemente, Pittsburgh NL	7	9	..	..	..
1961	Robert C. Richardson, New York AL	5	9	1	..	..
1964	Robert C. Richardson, New York AL	7	13	2	..	..
	J. Timothy McCarver, St. Louis NL	7	11	1	1	1
1965	Ronald R. Fairly, Los Angeles NL	7	11	3	..	2

Beaumont, C. H., Pitt. NL, Oct. 8, 1903
Burns, G. J., N. Y., NL, Oct. 7, 1921
Carey, M. G., Pitt. NL, Oct. 15, 1925
Cobb, T. R., Det. AL, Oct. 12, 1908
Collins, J. A., St. L. NL, Oct. 9, 1934
Dickey, W. M., N. Y. AL, Oct. 5, 1938
Doyle, L. J., N. Y. NL, Oct. 25, 1911
Dugan, J. A., N. Y. AL, Oct. 14, 1923
Frisch, F. F., N. Y. NL, Oct. 5, 1921
Garagiola, J. H., St. L. NL, Oct. 10, 1946
Gilliam, J. W., L. A. NL, Oct. 6, 1959
Goslin, L. A., Wash. AL, Oct. 7, 1924
Greenberg, H. B., Det. AL, Oct. 6, 1934
Hack, S. C., Chi. NL, Oct. 8, 1945
Hahn, E. W., Chi. AL, Oct. 14, 1906
Irvin, M. M., N. Y. NL, Oct. 4, 1951

Isbell, W. F., Chi. AL, Oct. 13, 1906
Keller, C. E., N. Y. AL, Oct. 5, 1941
Kurowski, G. J., St. L. NL, Oct. 10, 1946
Leach, T. W., Pitt. NL, Oct. 1, 1903
Lindstrom, F. C., N. Y. NL, Oct. 8, 1924
Mantle, M. C., N. Y. AL, Oct. 8, 1960
Medwick, J. M., St. L. NL, Oct. 3, 1934
Moses, W., Bos. AL, Oct. 10, 1946
Murphy, D. F., Phil. AL, Oct. 26, 1911
Ott, M. T., N. Y. NL, Oct. 3, 1933
Slaughter, E. B., St. L. NL, Oct. 10, 1946
Snyder, F. J., N. Y. NL, Oct. 7, 1921
Wertz, V. W., Clev. AL, Sept. 29, 1954
Wills, M. M., L. A. NL, Oct. 11, 1965
Youngs, R. M., N. Y. NL, Oct. 13, 1923

ONE-BASE HITS (Singles)

A—Most one-base hits (singles), total series—
    49—Lawrence P. Berra, New York AL, 1947, 49-53, 55-58, 60-61.
    45—Frank F. Frisch, N.Y. NL, 1921-24; St. L. NL, 1928, 30-31, 34.
B—Most one-base hits (singles), one series—
    7—4 game series, John J. Evers, Boston NL, 1914;
        J. Riggs Stephenson, Chicago NL, 1932;
        Mark A. Koenig, New York AL, 1927;
        William Dickey, New York AL, 1932;
        Stanley C. Hack, Chicago NL, 1938.
        Alvin R. Dark, New York NL, 1954.
        Donald F. Mueller, New York NL, 1954.
    8—5 game series, Frank L. Chance, Chicago NL, 1908.
        J. Franklin Baker, Philadelphia AL, 1913.
        Henry K. Groh, New York NL, 1922.
        Joseph G. Moore, New York NL, 1937.
        Robert C. Richardson, New York NL, 1961.
    10—6 game series, Robert A. Rolfe, New York AL, 1936.
        Monford Irvin, New York NL, 1951.
    12—7 game series, Edgar C. Rice, Washington AL, 1925.
    9—8 game series, John T. Myers, New York NL, 1912.
        James D. Sebring, Pittsburgh NL, 1903.
C—Most one-base hits (singles), game—
    4—By 8 players. Last performed:
        James Gilliam, Los Angeles NL vs Chicago AL, Oct. 6, 1959
D—Most one-base hits, inning—
    2—James E. Foxx, Phil. AL (7th inn.), Oct. 12, 1929.
        Joseph G. Moore, N.Y. NL (6th inn.), Oct. 4, 1933.
        Joseph P. DiMaggio, N.Y. AL (9th inn.), Oct. 6, 1936.
        Henry E. Leiber, N.Y. NL (2d inn.), Oct. 9, 1937.
        Robert H. Cerv, N.Y. AL (1st inn.), Oct. 8, 1960.

TWO-BASE HITS (Doubles)

E—Most two-base hits, total series—
    10—Frank F. Frisch, N.Y. NL, 1922, 24; St. L. NL, 1930-31, 34.
        Lawrence P. Berra, N.Y. AL, 1951-53, 55-58.
F—Most two-base hits, one series—
    3—4 game series, Henry M. Gowdy, Boston NL, 1914;
        George H. Ruth, New York AL, 1928.
    4—5 game series, Edward T. Collins, Philadelphia AL, 1910.
    5—6 game series, Charles J. Hafey, St. Louis NL, 1930.
    6—7 game series, Ervin Fox, Detroit AL, 1934.
    4—8 game series, John J. Murray, New York NL, 1912;
        Charles L. Herzog, New York NL, 1912;
        George D. Weaver, Chicago AL, 1919;
        George J. Burns, New York NL, 1921.
G—Most two-base hits, game—
    4—Frank Isbell, White Sox vs Cubs, Oct. 13, 1906.
H—Players scoring three (3) on a two bagger—
    1—Frank F. Frisch, St. Louis NL, 3d inning, Oct. 10, 1934.
    Paul R. Richards, Detroit AL, 1st inning, Oct. 10, 1945.
THREE-BASE HITS (Triples)
I—Most three-base hits, total series—
    4—Thomas W. Leach, Pitt. NL, 1903, 09.
        Tristam E. Speaker, Bos. AL, 1912, 15; Clev. AL, 1920.
        William R. Johnson, New York AL, 1943, 47.
J—Most three-base hits, one series—
    2—4 game series, Henry L. Gehrig, New York AL, 1927.
        H. Thomas Davis, Los Angeles NL, 1963.
    5 game series, Edward T. Collins, Philadelphia AL, 1913.
        Robert W. Brown, New York AL, 1949.
    6 game series, George Rohe, Chicago AL, 1906;
        Robert W. Meusel, New York AL, 1923.
        Alfred M. Martin, New York AL, 1953.
    3—7 game series, William R. Johnson, New York AL, 1947.
    4—8 game series, Thomas W. Leach, Pittsburgh NL, 1903.

WORLD SERIES INDIVIDUAL BATTING—Continued

A—Most three-base hits, game—
2—Walter H. Ruether, Cincinnati NL, Oct. 1, 1919.
Thomas W. Leach, Pittsburgh NL, Oct. 1, 1903.
Patrick H. Dougherty, Boston AL, Oct. 7, 1903.
Robert C. Richardson, New York AL, Oct. 12, 1960.
H. Thomas Davis, Los Angeles NL, Oct. 3, 1963.

HOME RUNS

B—Most home runs, total series—
18—Mickey C. Mantle, N.Y. AL, 1952(2), 53(2), 55, 56(3), 57, 58(2), 60(3), 63, 64(3), 1964.
C—Most home runs, one series—
4—4 game series, Henry L. Gehrig, New York AL, 1928.
2—5 game series, Harry B. Hooper, Boston AL, 1915.
W. Lawrence Gardner, Boston AL, 1916.
Aaron L. Ward, New York AL, 1922.
J. E. Foxx, G. W. Haas, Al H. Simmons, Phila. AL, 1929.
Melvin T. Ott, New York NL, 1933.
Charles E. Keller, New York AL, 1942.
John E. Blanchard, New York AL, 1961.
3—6 game series, Geo. H. Ruth, N.Y. AL, 1923; Theo. B. Kluszewski, Chi. AL, 1959.
4—7 game series, George H. Ruth, New York AL, 1926.
Edwin D. Snider, Brooklyn NL, 1952, 1955.
Henry A. Bauer, New York AL, 1958.
2—8 game series, Patrick H. Dougherty, Boston AL, 1903.
D—Most home runs, game—
3—George H. Ruth, New York AL, Oct. 6, 1926; Oct. 9, 1928.
E—Making two (2) home runs in a game—
By 19 players. Last:
Mickey C. Mantle, New York AL, Oct. 6, 1960.
F—Most home runs, 3 consecutive games—
4—Henry L. Gehrig, New York AL, Oct. 5 (1), Oct. 7 (2), Oct. 9 (1), 1928.
G—Home runs with bases filled, game—
1—Elmer J. Smith, Cleveland AL, 1st inning, Oct. 10, 1920.
Anthony M. Lazzeri, New York AL, 3d inning, Oct. 2, 1936.
Gilbert J. McDougald, New York AL, 3d inning. Oct. 9, 1951.
Mickey C. Mantle, New York AL, 3d inning, Oct. 4, 1953.
Lawrence P. Berra, New York AL, 2nd inning, Oct. 5, 1956.
William J. Skowron, Jr., New York AL, 7th inning, Oct. 10, 1956.
Robert C. Richardson, New York AL, 1st inning, Oct. 8, 1960.
Charles J. Hiller, San Francisco NL, 7th inning, Oct. 8, 1962.
Kenton L. Boyer, St. Louis NL, 6th inning, Oct. 11, 1964.
Joseph A. Pepitone, New York AL, 8th inning. Oct, 14. 1964,
H—Most home runs winning games, one series—
2—Charles D. Stengel, New York NL, Oct. 10, 12, 1923.
Rudolph P. York, Boston AL, Oct. 6, 9, 1946.
I—Most home runs winning games, total series—
3—Henry B. Greenberg, Detroit AL, Oct. 3, 1935; Oct. 6, 1940; and Oct. 4, 1945.
J—Leadoff batter hitting home run, game—
Patrick H. Dougherty, Bos. AL, Oct. 2, 1903.
David J. Jones, Det. AL, Oct. 13, 1909.
Philip F. Rizzuto, N.Y. AL, Oct. 5, 1942.
L. Dale Mitchell, Clev. AL, Oct. 10, 1948.
Eugene R. Woodling, N.Y. AL, Oct. 4, 1953.
Alphonse E. Smith, Clev. AL, Sept. 30, 1954.
William H. Bruton, Mil. NL, Oct. 2, 1958.

TOTAL BASES

K—Most total bases, total series—
123—Mickey C. Mantle, N.Y. AL, 1951-53; 55-58; 60-64.
L—Most total bases, one series—
22—4 game series, George H. Ruth, New York AL, 1928.
14—5 game series, James E. Foxx, Philadelphia AL, 1929.
23—6 game series, Alfred M. Martin, New York AL, 1953.
24—7 game series, Edwin D. Snider, Brooklyn NL, 1952.
18—8 game series, Charles L. Herzog, New York NL, 1912.
Joseph J. Jackson, Chicago AL, 1919.
M—Most total bases, game—
12—George H. Ruth, New York AL (3-hr), Oct. 6, 1926 and Oct. 9, 1928.
N—Most total bases, inning—
5—Ross Youngs, New York NL (1-2b, 1-3b), 7th inning, Oct. 7, 1921;
Al H. Simmons, Philadelphia AL (1-1b, 1-hr), 7th inning, Oct. 12, 1929.

LONG HITS (Doubles, Triples, Homers)

O—Most long hits, one series—
6—4 game series, George H. Ruth, New York AL, 1928.
4—5 game series, Daniel F. Murphy, Phil. AL, 1910.
Edward T. Collins, Phil. AL, 1910.
Elston G. Howard, New York AL, 1961.
5—6 game series, George H. Ruth, New York AL, 1923.
Charles J. Hafey, St. Louis NL, 1930.
Alfred M. Martin, New York AL, 1953.
James Gilliam, Brooklyn NL, 1953.
6—7 game series, Ervin Fox, Detroit AL (6-2b), 1934.
Edwin D. Snider, Brooklyn NL, 1952.
5—8 game series, John J. Murray, Charles L. Herzog, New York NL, 1912.
George D. Weaver, Chicago AL, 1919.
George J. Burns, N. Y. NL, 1921.

WORLD SERIES INDIVIDUAL BATTING—Continued

A—Most long hits, total series—
    26—Mickey C. Mantle, N.Y. AL, (6-2b, 2-3b, 18-hr), 1951-53; 55-58; 60-64.
B—Most long hits in a game—
    4—Frank Isbell, Chicago AL vs Chicago NL, four (4) doubles, Oct. 13, 1906.
C—Most long hits, inning—
    2—Ross Youngs, New York NL (1-2b, 1-3b), 7th inning, Oct. 7, 1921.

EXTRA BASES ON LONG HITS

D—Most extra bases on long hits, total series—
    64—Mickey C. Mantle, N.Y. AL, 1951-53; 55-58; 60-64.
E—Most extra bases on long hits, one series—
    13—4 game series, Henry L. Gehrig, New York AL, 1928 (1-2b, 4-hr).
    7—5 game series, James E. Foxx, Philadelphia AL, 1929 (1-2b, 2-hr).
        John E. Blanchard, New York AL, 1961 (1-2b, 2-hr).
    12—6 game series, George H. Ruth, New York AL, 1923 (1-2b, 1-3b, 3-hr).
    14—7 game series, Edwin D. Snider, Brooklyn NL, 1952 (2-2b, 4-hr).
    10-8 game series, Patrick H. Dougherty, Boston AL, 1903 (2-3b, 2-hr).
F—Most extra bases on long hits, game—
    9—George H. Ruth, New York AL (3-hr), Oct. 6, 1926, and (3-hr), Oct. 9, 1928.
G—Most extra bases on long hits, inning—
    3—By many.
H—Hitting into unassisted triple play—
    1—Clarence E. Mitchell, Brooklyn NL, Oct. 10, 1920.

SACRIFICE HITS

I—Most sacrifice hits, total series—
    8—Edward T. Collins, Phila. Chi. AL, 1910 (1), 11 (2), 13 (2), 14 (1), 19 (2).
J—Most sacrifice hits, one series—
    5—Fred C. Clarke, Pittsburgh NL, 1909.
        Jacob E. Daubert, Cincinnati NL, 1919.
K—Most sacrifice hits, game—
    3—Joseph B. Tinker, Chicago NL, Oct. 12, 1906.
        Wesley N. Westrum, New York NL, Oct. 2, 1954 (2-sh, 1-sf).

BASES ON BALLS

L—Most bases on balls, total series—
    43—Mickey C. Mantle, N.Y. AL, 1951-53; 55-58; 60-64.
M—Most bases on balls, one series—
    7—4 game series, Henry Thompson, New York NL, 1954.
    7—5 game series, James T. Sheckard, Chicago NL, 1910.
        Gordon S. Cochrane, Philadelphia AL, 1929.
        Joseph Gordon, New York AL, 1941.
    8—6 game series, George H. Ruth, New York AL, 1923.
    11—7 game series, George H. Ruth, New York AL, 1926.
    8—8 game series, Henry K. Groh, Cincinnati NL, 1919.
N—Most bases on balls, game—
    4—Fred C. Clarke, Pittsburgh NL, Oct. 14, 1909.
        Richard C. Hoblitzel, Boston AL, Oct. 9, 1916.
        Ross M. Youngs, New York NL, Oct. 10, 1924.
        George H. Ruth, New York AL, Oct. 10, 1926.
        Jack R. Robinson, Brooklyn NL, Oct. 5, 1952.
O—Most consecutive bases on balls—
    5—Henry L. Gehrig, N.Y. AL, Oct. 7 (6-7 inns.), Oct. 9 (2, 4-5 inns.), 1928.

STRIKE OUTS

P—Most strikeouts, total series—
    54—Mickey C. Mantle, N.Y. AL, 1951-53; 55-58; 60-64.
Q—Most strikeouts, one series—
    7—4 game series, Robert W. Meusel, New York AL, 1927.
    8—5 game series, Rogers Hornsby, Chicago NL, 1929.
        Edwin D. Snider, Brooklyn NL, 1949.
    9—6 game series, James L. Bottomley, St. Louis NL, 1930.
    11—7 game series, Edwin L. Mathews, Jr., Milwaukee NL, 1958.
    10—8 game series, George L. Kelly, New York NL, 1921.
R—Most strikeouts, game—
    5—George W. Pipgras, New York AL, 3d game, Oct. 1, 1932.
S—Most consecutive strikeouts, one or more games—
    5—Josh Devore, New York NL, Oct. 16, 1911 (4); Oct. 17, 1911 (1).
        George Mogridge, Washington AL, Oct. 7, 1924 (4); Oct. 10, 1924 (1).
        George W. Pipgras, New York AL, Oct. 1, 1932.
        Mickey C. Mantle, New York AL, Oct. 2(4)-Oct. 3, 1953.
        T. Michael Shannon, St. Louis NL, Oct.. 12(2)-Oct. 14(3), 1964.
T—Fewest strikeouts (most at-bats), one series—
    0—Edd J. Roush, Cincinnati NL, 1919 (28 at bats).
        Charles L. Gehringer, Detroit AL, 1940 (28 at bats).
        James W. Gilliam, Los Angeles NL, 1965 (28 at bats).

WORLD SERIES .300 BATSMEN

SIX SERIES

Ruth, G. H., N.Y. AL..1921 .313 1923 .368 1926 .300 1927 .400 1928 .625 1932 .333

FIVE SERIES

Berra, L.P., N.Y. AL .1953 .429 1955 .417 1956 .360 1957 .320 1960 .318

FOUR SERIES

Brown, R. W., N.Y. AL 1947	1.000	1949	.500	1950	.333	1951	.357
DiMaggio, J. P., N.Y. AL....1936	.346	1939	.313	1942	.333	1950	.308
Frisch, F. F., N.Y. NL....1921	.300	1922	.471	1923	.400	1924	.333
Gehrig, H. L., N.Y. AL....1926	.348	1927	.308	1928	.545	1932	.529
Rizzuto, P. F., N.Y. AL....1942	.381	1947	.308	1951	.320	1953	.316
Rolfe, R. A., N.Y. AL......1936	.400	1937	.300	1941	.300	1942	.353
Skowron, W. J. N.Y. AL-L.A. NL 1955	.333	1960	.375	1961	.353	1963	.375
Snider, E. D., Brooklyn NL.1952	.345	1953	.320	1955	.320	1956	.304
Woodling, E. R., N.Y. AL..1949	.400	1950	.429	1952	.348	1953	.300

THREE SERIES

Baker, J. Frank, Phila. AL..............1910	.409	1911	.375	1913	.450
Collins, E. T., Phila. and Chi. AL 1910	.429	1913	.421	1917	.409
Combs, Earl B., New York AL 1926	.357	1927	.313	1932	.375
Evers, J. J., Chi. and Bos. NL............1907	.350	1908	.350	1914	.438
Foxx, Jas. E., Philadelphia AL............1929	.350	1930	.333	1931	.348
Greenberg, Henry B., Detroit AL 1934	.321	1940	.357	1945	.304
Hodges, Gilbert R., Brooklyn-Los Angeles NL 1953	.364	1956	.304	1959	.391
Mantle, Mickey C., New York AL .. 1952	.345	1960	.400	1964	.333
Reese, Harold H., Brooklyn NL 1947	.304	1949	.316	1952	.345
Richardson, Robert C., New York AL 1960	.367	1961	.391	1964	.406
Schang, W. H., Phila.-Bos.-N.Y. AL 1913	.357	1918	.444	1923	.318
Simmons, Al H., Philadelphia AL 1929	.300	1930	.364	1931	.333

TWO SERIES

Aaron, Henry, Milwaukee NL 1957	.393	1958	.333
Barry, John J., Philadelphia AL 1911	.368	1913	.300
Bauer, Henry A., New York AL 1955	.429	1958	.323
Blanchard, John E., New York AL 1960	.455	1961	.400
Cavarretta, Philip J., Chicago NL 1938	.462	1945	.423
Chance, Frank L., Chicago NL 1908	.421	1910	.353
Dark, Alvin R., New York NL 1951	.417	1954	.412
Dickey, William M., New York AL 1932	.438	1938	.400
Furillo, Carl A. Brooklyn NL 1947	.353	1953	.333
Gehringer, Charles L., Detroit AL......................1934	.379	1935	.375
Gordon, Joseph L., New York AL 1938	.400	1941	.500
Goslin, Leon A., Washington AL 1924	.344	1925	.308
Grimm, Charles J., Chicago NL......................1929	.389	1932	.333
Hack, Stanley C., Chicago NL......................1938	.471	1945	.367
Hofman, Arthur F., Chicago NL......................1906	.304	1908	.316
Hooper, Harry B., Boston AL......................1915	.350	1916	.333
Howard, Elston G., New York AL 1960	.462	1963	.333
Jackson, Joseph, Chicago AL 1917	.304	1919	.375
Keller, Charles E., New York AL 1939	.438	1941	.389
Lewis, George E., Boston AL......................1915	.444	1916	.353
Maranville, Walter J., Bos.-St. L. NL......................1914	.308	1928	.308
Martin, Alfred M., New York AL......................1953	.500	1955	.320
Martin, John L., St. Louis NL......................1931	.500	1934	.355
Meyers, John T., New York NL......................1911	.300	1912	.357
Murphy, Daniel F., Philadelphia AL......................1910	.350	1911	.304
Ott, Melvin T., New York NL......................1933	.389	1936	.304
Ripple, James A., N.Y.-Cinn. NL......................1936	.333	1940	.333
Schulte, Frank, Chicago NL......................1908	.389	1910	.353
Slaughter, Enos B., St. Louis NL-New York AL......................1946	.320	1956	.350
Snyder, Frank J., New York NL......................1921	.364	1922	.333
Speaker, Tris E., Bos.-Cleve. AL......................1912	.300	1920	.320
Stengel, Charles D., Bklyn.-N.Y. NL......................1916	.364	1923	.417
Stephenson, J. Riggs, Chicago NL......................1929	.316	1932	.444
Weaver, George D., Chicago AL......................1917	.333	1919	.324
Youngs, Ross, New York NL......................1922	.375	1923	.348

INDIVIDUAL .400 HITTERS, OR BETTER
PLAYING IN ALL GAMES, EACH SERIES

	Year	G.	AB.	R.	H.	2B.	3B.	HR.	TB.	PC.
Ruth, George H., New York AL	1928	4	16	9	10	3	..	3	22	.625
Gowdy, Henry M., Boston NL	1914	4	11	3	6	3	1	1	14	.545
Gehrig, H. L., New York AL	1928	4	11	5	6	1	..	4	19	.545
Gehrig, Henry L., New York AL	1932	4	17	9	9	1	..	3	19	.529
McLean, John B., New York NL	1913	5	12	1	6	..	..	..	6	.500
Robertson, Davis A., New York NL	1917	6	22	3	11	1	1	..	14	.500
Koenig, Mark A., New York AL	1927	4	18	5	9	2	..	..	11	.500
Martin, John L., St. Louis NL	1931	7	24	5	12	4	..	1	19	.500
Martin, Alfred J., New York AL	1953	6	24	5	12	1	2	2	23	.500
Wertz, Victor W., Cleveland AL	1954	4	16	2	8	2	1	1	15	.500
Gordon, Joseph, New York AL	1941	5	14	2	7	1	1	1	13	.500
McCarver, J. Timothy. St. Louis NL	1964	7	23	4	11	1	1	1	17	.478
Groh, Henry K., New York NL	1922	5	19	4	9	..	1	..	11	.474
Steinfeldt, Harry M., Chicago NL	1907	5	17	2	8	1	1	..	11	.471
Frisch, Frank F., New York NL	1922	5	17	3	8	1	..	..	9	.471
Wilson, Lewis L., Chicago NL	1929	5	17	2	8	..	1	..	10	.471
Hack, Stanley C., Chicago NL	1938	4	17	3	8	1	..	..	9	.471
Cavarretta, Philip, Chicago NL	1938	4	13	1	6	1	..	..	7	.462
Carey, Max G., Pittsburgh NL	1925	7	24	6	11	4	..	..	15	.458
Irvin, Monford, New York NL	1951	6	24	3	11	..	1	..	13	.458
Powell, Alvin J., New York AL	1936	6	22	8	10	1	..	1	14	.455
Baker, J. Frank, Philadelphia AL	1913	5	20	2	9	..	..	1	12	.450
Lewis, George E., Boston AL	1915	5	18	1	8	1	..	1	12	.444
Stephenson, J. Riggs, Chicago NL	1932	4	18	2	8	1	..	..	9	.444
Harris, Joseph, Washington AL	1925	7	25	5	11	2	..	3	22	.440
Keller, Charles E., New York AL	1939	4	16	8	7	1	1	3	19	.438
Evers, John J., Boston NL	1914	4	16	2	7	..	..	..	7	.438
Luderus, Fred W., Philadelphia NL	1915	5	16	1	7	2	..	1	12	.438
Dickey, William, New York AL	1932	4	16	2	7	..	..	..	7	.438
McQuinn, George H., St. Louis AL	1944	6	16	2	7	2	..	1	12	.438
Collins, Edward T., Philadelphia AL	1910	5	21	5	9	4	..	..	13	.429
Berra, Lawrence P., New York AL	1953	6	21	3	9	1	..	1	13	.429
Hamner, Granville W., Philadelphia NL	1950	4	14	1	6	2	1	..	10	.429
Woodling, Eugene R., New York AL	1950	4	14	2	6	..	..	..	6	.429
Cavarretta, Philip J., Chicago NL	1945	7	26	7	11	2	..	1	16	.423
Chance, Frank L., Chicago NL	1908	5	19	4	8	..	..	..	8	.421
Collins, Edward T., Philadelphia AL	1913	5	19	5	8	..	2	..	12	.421
Dykes, James J., Philadelphia AL	1929	5	19	2	8	1	..	..	9	.421
Ward, Aaron, New York AL	1923	6	24	4	10	..	..	1	13	.417
Stengel, Charles D., New York NL	1923	6	12	3	5	..	..	2	11	.417
Thevenow, Thomas J., St. Louis NL	1926	7	24	5	10	1	..	1	14	.417
Dark, Alvin R., New York NL	1951	6	24	5	10	3	..	1	16	.417
Berra, Lawrence P., New York AL	1955	7	24	5	10	1	..	1	14	.417
Verban, Emil M., St. Louis NL	1944	6	17	1	7	..	..	..	7	.412
Walker, Harry W., St. Louis NL	1946	7	17	3	7	2	..	..	9	.412
Dark, Alvin R., New York NL	1954	4	17	2	7	..	..	..	7	.412
Bruton, William H., Milwaukee NL	1958	7	17	2	7	..	..	1	10	.412
Baker, J. Frank, Philadelphia AL	1910	5	22	6	9	3	..	..	12	.409
Collins, Edward T., Chicago AL	1917	6	22	4	9	1	..	..	10	.409
Richardson, Robert C., New York AL	1964	7	32	3	13	2	..	..	15	.406
Rossman, Claude, Detroit AL	1907	5	20	1	8	..	1	..	10	.400
Herzog, Charles L., New York NL	1912	8	30	6	12	4	1	..	18	.400
Frisch, Frank F., New York NL	1923	6	25	2	10	..	1	..	12	.400
Ruth, George H., New York AL	1927	4	15	4	6	..	..	2	12	.400
Waner, Lloyd J., Pittsburgh NL	1927	4	15	5	6	1	..	..	9	.400
Cochrane, Gordon S., Philadelphia AL	1929	5	15	5	6	1	..	..	7	.400
Rolfe, Robert A., New York AL	1936	6	25	5	10	..	..	..	10	.400
Lazzeri, Anthony M., New York AL	1937	5	15	3	6	..	1	1	11	.400
Gordon, Joseph, New York AL	1938	4	15	3	6	2	..	1	11	.400
Dickey, William, New York AL	1938	4	15	2	6	..	..	1	9	.400
McCormick, Frank A., Cincinnati NL	1939	4	15	1	6	1	..	..	7	.400
Mantle, Mickey C., New York AL	1960	7	25	8	10	1	..	3	20	.400
Davis, H. Thomas, Los Angeles NL	1963	4	15	..	6	..	2	..	10	.400

106

LEADING BATSMEN WORLD SERIES,
1903 to Date

PLAYING IN ALL GAMES, EACH SERIES

Year	National League	G.	A.B.	H.	T.B.	PC.	American League	G.	A.B.	H.	T.B.	PC.
1903	J. D. Sebring, Pitts	8	30	11	16	.367	C. S. Stahl, Bos	8	33	10	17	.303
1904	No series						No series					
1905	M. J. Donlin, N. Y.	5	19	6	7	.316	T. F. Hartsel, Phila	5	17	5	6	.294
1906	A. Hofman, Chicago	6	23	7	8	.304	George Rohe, Chi.	6	21	7	12	.333
							J. A. Donohue, Chi.	6	18	6	10	.333
1907	H. Steinfeldt, Chicago	5	17	8	11	.471	C. Rossman, Detroit	5	20	8	10	.400
1908	F. L. Chance, Chicago	5	19	8	8	.421	T. R. Cobb, Detroit	5	19	7	8	.368
1909	J. P. Wagner, Pitts	7	24	8	12	.333	J. C. Delahanty, Det	7	26	9	13	.346
1910	F. Schulte, Chicago	5	17	6	9	.353	E. T. Collins, Phila	5	21	9	13	.429
	F. L. Chance, Chicago	5	17	6	9	.353						
1911	L. Doyle, New York	6	23	7	12	.304	J. F. Baker, Phila	6	24	9	17	.375
1912	C. Herzog, New York	8	30	12	18	.400	Tris Speaker, Boston	8	30	9	14	.300
1913	J. B. McLean, N. Y.	5	12	6	6	.500	J. F. Baker, Phila	5	20	9	12	.450
1914	H. Gowdy, Boston	4	11	6	14	.545	J. F. Baker, Phila	4	16	4	6	.250
1915	F. W. Luderus, Phila	5	16	7	12	.438	G. E. Lewis, Boston	5	18	8	12	.444
1916	Ivan M. Olson, Bklyn	5	16	4	6	.250	G. E. Lewis, Boston	5	17	6	10	.353
1917	D. Robertson, N. Y.	6	22	11	14	.500	E. T. Collins, Chi	6	22	9	10	.409
1918	C. Pick, Chicago	6	18	7	8	.389	J. P. McInnis, Bos	6	20	5	5	.250
							G. Whiteman, Bos	6	20	5	7	.250
1919	A. E. Neale, Cinn	8	28	10	13	.357	J. J. Jackson, Chi	8	32	12	18	.375
1920	Z. Wheat, Bklyn	7	27	9	11	.333	S. F. O'Neill, Cleve	7	21	7	10	.333
1921	E. Meusel, N. Y.	8	29	10	17	.345	W. H. Schang, N. Y.	8	21	6	9	.286
1922	H. K. Groh, N. Y.	5	19	9	11	.474	R. Meusel, N. Y.	5	20	6	7	.300
1923	C. D. Stengel, N. Y.	6	12	5	11	.417	A. L. Ward, N. Y.	6	24	10	13	.417
1924	F. C. Lindstrom, N.Y.	7	30	10	12	.333	J. I. Judge, Wash.	7	26	10	11	.385
	F. F. Frisch, N. Y.	7	30	10	16	.333						
1925	M. G. Carey, Pitts	7	24	11	15	.458	J. Harris, Wash.	7	25	11	22	.440
1926	T. J. Thevenow, St. L.	7	24	10	14	.417	E. B. Combs, N. Y.	7	28	10	12	.357
1927	L. J. Waner, Pitts	4	15	6	9	.400	M. A. Koenig, N. Y.	4	18	9	11	.500
1928	W. J. Maranville, St.L.	4	13	4	5	.308	G. H. Ruth, N. Y.	4	16	10	22	.625
1929	L. R. Wilson, Chi	5	17	8	10	.471	J. J. Dykes, Phila	5	19	8	9	.421
1930	C. M. Gelbert, St. L.	6	17	6	8	.353	A. H. Simmons, Phila	6	22	8	16	.364
1931	J. L. Martin, St. L.	7	24	12	19	.500	J. E. Foxx, Phila	7	23	8	11	.348
1932	J. R. Stephenson, Chi.	4	18	8	9	.444	H. L. Gehrig, N. Y.	4	17	9	19	.529
1933	M. T. Ott, N. Y.	5	18	7	13	.389	F. W. Schulte, Wash.	5	21	7	11	.333
1934	J. M. Medwick, St. L.	7	29	11	16	.379	C. L. Gehringer, Det	7	29	11	15	.379
1935	W. Herman, Chi	6	24	8	15	.333	E. Fox, Detroit	6	26	10	15	.385
1936	R. Bartell, N. Y.	6	21	8	14	.381	A. J. Powell, N. Y.	6	22	10	14	.455
1937	Jos. G. Moore, N. Y.	5	23	9	10	.391	A. M. Lazzeri, N. Y.	5	15	6	11	.400
1938	S. C. Hack, Chi.	4	17	8	9	.471	J. Gordon, N. Y.	4	15	6	11	.400
							W. Dickey, N. Y.	4	15	6	9	.400
1939	F. A. McCormick, Cinn.	4	15	6	7	.400	C. E. Keller, N.Y.	4	16	7	19	.438
1940	W. M. Werber, Cinn	7	27	10	14	.370	B. D. Campbell, Det.	7	25	9	13	.360
1941	J. M. Medwick, Bklyn	5	17	4	5	.235	J. Gordon, N. Y.	5	14	7	13	.500
1942	J. R. Brown, St. L.	5	20	6	6	.300	P. F. Rizzuto, N. Y.	5	21	8	11	.381
1943	M. W. Marion, St. L.	5	14	5	10	.357	W. R. Johnson, N. Y.	5	20	6	9	.300
1944	E. M. Verban, St. L.	6	17	7	7	.412	G. H. McQuinn, St.L.	6	16	7	12	.438
1945	P. J. Cavarretta, Chi.	7	26	11	16	.423	R. M. Cramer, Det.	7	29	11	11	.379
1946	H. W. Walker, St. L.	7	17	7	9	.412	R. P. York, Boston	7	23	6	15	.261

(R. P. Doerr hit .409 in 6 games.)

Year	National League	G.	AB.	H.	TB.	PC.	American League	G.	AB.	H.	TB.	PC.
1947	H. H. Reese, Bklyn	7	23	7	8	.304	T. D. Henrich, N. Y.	7	31	10	15	.323
	(C. A. Furillo hit .353 in 6 games.)						(J. H. Lindell hit .500 in 6 games.)					
1948	R. I. Elliott, Boston	6	21	7	13	.333	L. E. Doby, Cleve.	6	22	7	11	.318
	(C. E. Torgeson hit .389 in 5 games.)											
1949	H. H. Reese, Bklyn,	5	19	6	10	.316	T. D. Henrich, N. Y.	5	19	5	8	.263
							(R. W. Brown hit .500 in 4 games.)					
1950	G. W. Hamner, Phila.	4	14	6	10	.429	E. R. Woodling, N.Y.	4	14	6	6	.429
1951	M. Irvin, New York	6	24	11	13	.458	P. F. Rizzuto, N.Y.	6	25	8	11	.320
							(R. W. Brown hit .357 in 5 games)					
1952	E. D. Snider, Bklyn	7	29	10	24	.345	E. R. Woodling, N.Y.	7	23	8	14	.348
	H. H. Reese, Bklyn	7	29	10	13	.345	(John R. Mize hit .400 in 5 games)					
1953	G. R. Hodges, Bklyn	6	22	8	11	.364	A. M. Martin, N.Y.	6	24	12	23	.500
1954	A. R. Dark, N.Y.	4	17	7	7	.412	V. W. Wertz, Cleve.	4	16	8	15	.500
1955	E. D. Snider, Bklyn.	7	25	8	21	.320	L. P. Berra, N.Y.	7	24	10	14	.417
1956	G. R Hodges, Bklyn.	7	23	7	12	.304	L. P. Berra, N.Y.	7	25	9	20	.360
	E. D. Snider, Bklyn.	7	23	7	11	.304						
1957	H. Aaron, Milw.	7	28	11	22	.393	G. F. Coleman, N.Y.	7	22	8	10	.364
1958	W. Bruton, Milw.	7	17	7	10	.412	H. A. Bauer, N.Y.	7	31	10	22	.323
1959	G. R. Hodges, L.A.	6	23	9	14	.391	T. B. Kluszewski, Chi.	6	23	9	19	.391
1960	W. S. Mazeroski, Pitt.	7	25	8	16	.320	M. C. Mantle, N.Y.	7	25	10	20	.400
1961	W. C. Post, Cin.	5	18	6	10	.333	R. C. Richardson, N.Y.	5	23	9	10	.319
1962	J. A. Pagan, S.F.	7	19	7	10	.368	T. M. Tresh, N.Y.	7	28	9	13	.321
1963	H. T. Davis, L.A.	4	15	6	10	.400	E. G. Howard, N.Y.	4	15	5	5	.333
1964	J. T. McCarver, St. L.	7	23	11	17	.478	R. C. Richardson, N.Y.	7	32	13	15	.406
1965	R. R. Fairly, L.A.	7	29	11	20	.379	Z. Versalles, Minn.	7	28	8	14	.286
							H. C. Killebrew, Minn.	7	21	6	9	.286

HOME RUNS, WORLD SERIES, 1903 to Date

Year	NATIONAL LEAGUE	No.	AMERICAN LEAGUE	No.
1903	James B. Sebring (Pittsburgh)	1	P. J. Dougherty (2) (Boston)	2
1904	No Series		No Series	
1905	None (New York)	0	None (Philadelphia)	0
1906	None (Chicago)	0	None (Chicago)	0
1907	None (Chicago)	0	None (Detroit)	0
1908	Joseph B. Tinker (Chicago)	1	None (Detroit)	0
1909	Fred C. Clarke (2) (Pittsburgh)	2	D. J. Jones, S. Crawford (Detroit)	2
1910	None (Chicago)	0	Daniel F. Murphy (Philadelphia)	1
1911	None (New York)	0	J. F. Baker (2), R. N. Oldring (Phila).	3
1912	Lawrence J. Doyle (New York)	1	W. L. Gardner (Boston)	1
1913	Fred C. Merkle (New York)	1	J. F. Baker, W. H. Schang (Phila.)	2
1914	Henry W. Gowdy (Boston)	1	None (Philadelphia)	0
1915	Fred W. Luderus (Phila.)	1	H. B. Hooper (2), G. E. Lewis (Boston)	3
1916	Henry H. Myers (Brooklyn)	1	W. L. Gardner (2) (Boston)	2
1917	Benjamin M. Kauff (2) (N. Y.)	2	Oscar C. Felsch (Chicago)	1
1918	None (Chicago)	0	None (Boston)	0
1919	None (Cincinnati)	0	Joseph J. Jackson (Chicago)	1
1920	None (Brooklyn)	0	J. C. Bagby, E. J. Smith (Cleve.)	2
1921	F. Snyder, E. F. Meusel (N. Y.)	2	G. H. Ruth, W. Fewster (N. Y.)	2
1922	Emil F. Meusel (New York)	1	Aaron L. Ward (2) (New York)	2
1923	C. D. Stengel (2), R. Youngs, F. Snyder, E. F. Meusel (New York)	5	G. H. Ruth (3), A. L. Ward, J. A. Dugan (New York)	5
1924	G. L. Kelly, W. H. Terry, J. N. Bentley, W. D. Ryan (New York)	4	L. A. Goslin (3), S. R. Harris (2) (Washington)	5
1925	H. S. Cuyler, F. G. Wright, G. E. Moore, H. Traynor (Pittsburgh)	4	J. I. Judge, R. T. Peckinpaugh, J. Harris (3), L. A. Goslin (3) (Wash.)	8
1926	W. H. Southworth, L. R. Bell, T. J. Thevenow, J. J. Haines (St. L.)	4	George H. Ruth (4) (New York)	4
1927	None (Pittsburgh)	0	George H. Ruth (2) (New York)	2
1928	James L. Bottomley (St. L.)	1	H. L. Gehrig (4), G. H. Ruth (3), R. W. Meusel, C. Durst (New York)	9
1929	Charles J. Grimm (Chicago)	1	J. E. Foxx (2), G. W. Haas (2), Al H. Simmons (2) (Phila.)	6
1930	T. L. Douthit, G. Watkins (St. L.)	2	G. S. Cochrane (2), Al H. Simmons (2), J. J. Dykes, J. E. Foxx (Phila)	6
1931	J. L. Martin, G. Watkins (St. L.)	2	Al H. Simmons (2), J. E. Foxx, (Phila)	3
1932	H. S. Cuyler, F. Demaree, C. L. Hartnett (Chicago)	3	H. L. Gehrig (3), G. H. Ruth (2), A. Lazzeri (2), E. B. Combs (N. Y.)	8
1933	M. T. Ott (2) W. H. Terry, (N. Y.)	3	L. A. Goslin, F. W. Schulte (Wash.)	2
1934	J. M. Medwick, W. DeLancey (St. L.)	2	C. L. Gehringer, H. Greenberg (Det.)	2
1935	F. Demaree (2) C. L. Hartnett, W. Herman, C. H. Klein (Chicago)	5	Henry Greenberg (Detroit)	1
1936	J. G. Moore, R. Bartell, M. T. Ott, J. Ripple (New York)	4	H. L. Gehrig (2), G. Selkirk (2), W. Dickey, A. Lazzeri, A. J. Powell (New York)	7
1937	M. T. Ott (New York)	1	J. P. DiMaggio, H. L. Gehrig, M. O. Hoag, A. M. Lazzeri (New York)	4
1938	J. Marty, J. K. O'Dea (Chicago)	2	F. P. Crosetti, T. D. Henrich, J. P. DiMaggio, W. Dickey, J. Gordon (New York)	5
1939	None (Cincinnati)	0	C. E. Keller (3), J. P. DiMaggio, W. Dickey (2), E. T. Dahlgren (N.Y.)	7
1940	J. A. Ripple, Wm. H. Walters (Cinn.)	2	B. D. Campbell, H. Greenberg, P. R. York, M. F. Higgins (Detroit)	4
1941	H. P. Reiser (Brooklyn)	1	T. D. Henrich, J. Gordon (N. Y.)	2
1942	E. B. Slaughter, G. J. Kurowski, (St. Louis)	2	C. E. Keller (2), P. F. Rizzuto (N. Y.)	3
1943	M. W. Marion, R. F. Sanders, St. L.	2	J. L. Gordon, W. M. Dickey (N. Y.)	2
1944	S. F. Musial, R. F. Sanders, D. W. Litwhiler (St. L.)	3	G. H. McQuinn (St. Louis)	1
1945	Philip J. Cavarretta (Chicago)	1	Henry B. Greenberg (2) (Detroit)	2
1946	Enos B. Slaughter (St. Louis)	1	R. P. York (2), R. P. Doerr, D. L. Culberson (Boston)	4

HOME RUNS, WORLD SERIES, 1903 to Date—Continued

Year	NATIONAL LEAGUE	No.	AMERICAN LEAGUE
1947	Fred R. Walker (Brooklyn)	1	J. P. DiMaggio (2), T. D. Henrich, L. P. Berra (New York)........... 4
1948	R. I. Elliott (2), M. A. Rickert, W. F. Salkeld (Boston)	4	L. E. Doby, L. D. Mitchell, J. E. Hegan, J. L. Gordon (Cleve.)..... 4
1949	H. H. Reese, L. Olmo, G. R. Hodges, R. Campanella (Brooklyn)	4	T. D. Henrich, J. P. DiMaggio (N. Y.). 2
1950	None (Philadelphia)	0	J. P. DiMaggio, L. P. Berra (N. Y.)... 2
1951	A. R. Dark, C. W. Lockman (New York)	2	J. Collins, E. R. Woodling, J. P. DiMaggio, G. J. McDougald, P. F. Rizzuto (N.Y.) 5
1952	E. D. Snider (4), H. H. Reese, J. R. Robinson (Brooklyn)	6	J. R. Mize (3), L. P. Berra (2), M. C. Mantle (2), A. M. Martin, G. J. McDougald, E. R. Woodling (N.Y.) 10
1953	J. Gilliam (2), E. D. Snider, R. Campanella, G. R. Hodges, C. A. Furillo, W. R. Cox, G. Shuba (Brooklyn)	8	G. J. McDougald (2), M. C. Mantle (2), A. M. Martin (2), J. E. Collins, L. P. Berra, E. R. Woodling (N.Y.) 9
1954	J. L. Rhodes (2) (New York)	2	A. E. Smith, V. W. Wertz, H. Majeski (Cleve.) 3
1955	E. Amoros, R. Campanella (2), C. A. Furillo, G. R. Hodges, E. D. Snider (4) Brooklyn	9	L. P. Berra, R. H. Cerv, J. E. Collins (2), E. G. Howard, M. C. Mantle, G. J. McDougald, W. J. Skowron (New York) 8
1956	G. R. Hodges, J. R. Robinson, E. D. Snider, Brooklyn	3	H. A. Bauer, L. P. Berra (3), E. G. Howard, M. C. Mantle (3), A. M. Martin (2), W. J. Skowron, E. B. Slaughter, New York 12
1957	H. Aaron (3), D. W. Crandall, J. Logan, E. L. Mathews, F. J. Torre (2), Milwaukee	8	H. A. Bauer (2), L. P. Berra, E. G. Howard, A. Kubek (2), M. C. Mantle, New York 7
1958	W. H. Bruton, S. L. Burdette, D. W. Crandall, Milwaukee	3	H. A. Bauer (4), M. C. Mantle (2), G. J. McDougald (2), W. J. Skowron (2), New York 10
1959	C. A. Essegian (2), C. L. Neal (2), G. R. Hodges, W. W. Moon, E. D. Snider (Los Angeles)	7	T. B. Kluszewski (3), J. S. Lollar (Chicago) 4
1960	W. S. Mazeroski (2), G. R. Nelson, H. W. Smith (Pittsburgh)	4	M. C. Mantle (3), R. E. Maris (2), W. J. Skowron (2), L. P. Berra, E. G. Howard, R. C. Richardson (New York) 10
1961	G. C. Coleman, W. C. Post, F. Robinson (Cincinnati)	3	J. E. Blanchard (2), L. P. Berra, H. Lopez E. G. Howard, R. E. Maris, W. J. Skowron (New York) 7
1962	E. L. Bailey, T. F. Haller, C. J. Hiller, W. L. McCovey, J. A. Pagan (San Francisco)	5	C. L. Boyer, R. E. Maris, T. M. Tresh, New York 3
1963	F. O. Howard, J. Roseboro, W. J. Skowron (Los Angeles)	3	M. C. Mantle, T. M. Tresh (New York) 2
1964	K. L. Boyer(2), L. C. Brock, J. T. McCarver, T. M. Shannon (St. Louis)	5	M. C. Mantle(3), P. F. Linz(2), T. M. Tresh(2), C. L. Boyer, R. E. Maris, J. A. Pepitone (New York)..10
1965	R. R. Fairly (2), L. B. Johnson (2), M. W. Parker (Los Angeles)	5	W. R. Allison, J. T. Grant, H. C. Killebrew, D. R. Mincher, P. Oliva, Z. Versalles (Minnesota) 6

INDIVIDUAL FIELDING RECORDS

SPECIAL FIELDING RECORDS

Triple play unassisted—
Wm. Wambsganss, Cleve. AL (at 2-b), Oct. 10, 1920.

Double play, unassisted, outfielder—
Tris E. Speaker, Boston AL, Oct. 15, 1912.

FIRST BASEMEN'S FIELDING RECORDS

CHANCES ACCEPTED

A—Most chances accepted, one series—
55–4 game, Charles J. Schmidt, Boston NL, 1914.
73–5 game, Richard C. Hoblitzel, Boston AL, 1916.
87–6 game, John A. Donahue, Chicago AL, 1906.
80–7 game, James L. Bottomley, St. Louis NL, 1926.
93–8 game, George L. Kelly, New York NL, 1921.
    Walter C. Pipp, New York AL, 1921.

B—Most chances accepted, game—
19–Edward J. Konetchy, Bklyn. NL (17-po, 2-a), Oct. 7, 1920.
    Geo. L. Kelly, New York NL (19-po), Oct. 15, 1923.

C—Fewest chances offered, game—
2—Walter C. Pipp, N.Y. AL, Oct. 11, 1921 (2-po).

PUTOUTS

D—Most putouts, one series—
52–4 game, Charles J. Schmidt, Boston NL, 1914.
69–5 game, Richard C. Hoblitzel, Boston AL, 1916.
79–6 game, John A. Donahue, Chicago AL, 1906.
79–7 game, James L. Bottomley St. Louis NL, 1926.
92–8 game, Walter C. Pipp, New York AL, 1921.

E—Most putouts, game—
19—George L. Kelly, New York NL, Oct. 15, 1923.

ASSISTS

F—Most assists, one series—
6–4 game, Victor W. Wertz, Cleveland AL, 1954
    Joseph A. Pepitone, New York AL, 1963.
5–5 game, Claude Rossman, Detroit AL, 1908.
    Adolph Camilli, Brooklyn NL, 1941.
    Raymond F. Sanders, St. Louis NL, 1943.
    William J. Skowron, New York AL, 1961.
9–6 game, Fred C. Merkle, Chicago NL, 1918.
8–7 game, Rudolph P. York, Detroit AL, 1945.
7–8 game, George L. Kelly, New York NL, 1921.

G—Most assists, game—
4—Marvin J. Owen, Detroit AL, Oct. 6, 1935.
    Donald R. Mincher, Minnesota AL, Oct. 7, 1965.

ERRORS

H—Most errors, one series—
1–4 game, John P. McInnis, Boston AL, 1914;

    Henry L. Gehrig, New York AL, 1932;
    Victor W. Wertz, Cleveland AL, 1954.
    Joseph A. Pepitone, New York AL, 1963.
3–5 game, Frank L. Chance, Chicago NL, 1908;
    Harry H. Davis, Philadelphia AL, 1910.
3–6 game, Henry Greenberg, Detroit AL, 1935.
5–7 game, William H. Abstein, Pittsburgh NL, 1909.
3–8 game, Fred C. Merkle, New York NL, 1912.

I—Most errors, game—
2—By 8 players.

II—Most double plays, one series—
11—Gilbert R. Hodges, Brooklyn NL, 1955.

SECOND BASEMEN'S FIELDING RECORDS

CHANCES ACCEPTED

J—Most chances accepted, one series—
28–4 game, Anthony M. Lazzeri, New York AL, 1927.
43–5 game, Joseph L. Gordon, New York AL, 1943.
39–6 game, Charles L. Gehringer, Detroit AL, 1935.
54–7 game, Stanley R. Harris, Washington AL, 1924.
52–8 game, Edward T. Collins, Chicago AL, 1919.
    Aaron L. Ward, New York AL, 1921.

K—Most chances accepted, game—
13—Claude C. Ritchey, Pitt. NL, Oct. 10, 1903 (5-po, 8-a).
    Stanley R. Harris, Wash. AL, Oct. 11, 1925 (6-po, 7-a).

L—Fewest chances offered, game—
0—Charles T. Pick, Chicago NL, Sept. 7, 1918.
    Max F. Bishop, Philadelphia AL, Oct. 6, 1931.
    Gerald F. Coleman, New York AL, Oct. 8, 1949.

PUTOUTS

M—Most putouts, one series—
13–4 game, Michael M. Goliat, Philadelphia NL, 1950.
20–5 game, Joseph L. Gordon, New York AL, 1943.
18–6 game, Charles L. Neal, Los Angeles NL, 1959.
26–7 game, Stanley R. Harris, Washington AL, 1924.
22–8 game, Maurice C. Rath, Cincinnati NL, 1919.

N—Most putouts, game—
8—Stanley R. Harris, Washington AL, Oct. 8, 1924.

ASSISTS

O—Most assists, one series—
18–4 game, Anthony M. Lazzeri, New York AL, 1927.
23–5 game, Joseph L. Gordon, New York AL, 1943.
27–6 game, Aaron L. Ward, New York AL, 1923.
31–7 game, Robert P. Doerr, Boston AL, 1946.
34–8 game, Aaron L. Ward, New York AL, 1921.

SECOND BASEMEN'S FIELDING RECORDS—Continued

A—Most assists, game—
8—Claude C. Ritchey, Pittsburgh NL, Oct. 10, 1903.
  Herman Schaefer, Detroit AL, Oct. 12, 1907.
  Harold C. Janvrin, Boston AL, Oct. 7, 1916;
  Edward T. Collins, Chicago AL, Oct. 15, 1917;
  Stanley R. Harris, Washington AL, Oct. 7, 1924.
  Joseph L. Gordon, New York AL, Oct. 5, 1943.
  Robert P. Doerr, Boston AL, Oct. 9, 1946.

ERRORS

B—Most errors, one series—
2—4 game, Anthony M. Lazzeri, New York AL, 1928.
  Joseph Gordon, New York AL, 1938.
  William Herman, Chicago NL, 1938.
4—5 game, Daniel F. Murphy, Philadelphia AL, 1905.
5—6 game, Frank Isbell, Chicago AL, 1906.
3—7 game, John B. Miller, Pittsburgh NL, 1909.
  Charles Gehringer, Detroit AL, 1934.
4—8 game, Lawrence J. Doyle, New York NL, 1912.

C—Most errors, game—
3—Daniel F. Murphy, Philadelphia AL, Oct. 12, 1905.
  Charles S. Myer, Washington AL, Oct. 3, 1933.

THIRD BASEMEN'S FIELDING RECORDS

CHANCES ACCEPTED

D—Most chances accepted, one series—
25—4 game, J. Frank Baker, Philadelphia AL, 1914.
25—5 game, W. Lawrence Gardner, Boston AL, 1916.
27—6 game, Robert B. Thomson, New York NL, 1951.
34—7 game, M. Frank Higgins, Detroit AL, 1940.
37—8 game, Frank F. Frisch, New York NL, 1921.

E—Most chances accepted, game—
10—M. Frank Higgins, Detroit AL (1-po, 9-a), October 5, 1940.

PUTOUTS

F—Most putouts, one series—
10—4 game, J. Frank Baker, Philadelphia AL, 1914.
10—5 game, Henry M. Steinfeldt, Chicago NL, 1907.
14—6 game, Robert A. Rolfe, New York AL, 1936.
13—7 game, George J. Kurowski, St. Louis NL, 1946.
13—8 game, Frank F. Frisch, New York NL, 1921.

G—Most putouts, game—
4—By 9 players.

ASSISTS

H—Most assists, one series—
15—4 game, J. Frank Baker, Philadelphia AL, 1914.
18—5 game, W. Lawrence Gardner, Boston AL, 1916.
16—6 game, George Rohe, Chicago AL, 1906.
30—7 game, M. Frank Higgins, Detroit AL, 1940.
24—8 game, Frank Frisch, New York NL, 1921.

I—Most assists, game—
9—M. Frank Higgins, Detroit AL, October 5, 1940.

ERRORS

J—Most errors, one series—
2—4 game, Robert A. Rolfe, New York AL, 1938.
4—5 game, Harry M. Steinfeldt, Chicago NL, 1910.
3—6 game, George Rohe, Chicago AL, 1906.
  Charles L. Herzog, New York NL, 1911.
  Travis C. Jackson, New York NL, 1936.
  Robert I. Elliott, Boston NL, 1948.
4—7 game, John L. Martin, St. Louis NL, 1934.
  Gilbert J. McDougald, New York AL, 1952.
4—8 game, W. Lawrence Gardner, Boston AL, 1912.
  Thomas W. Leach, Pittsburgh NL, 1903.

K—Most errors, game—
3—John L. Martin, St. Louis NL, Oct. 6, 1934.

SHORTSTOP'S FIELDING RECORDS

CHANCES ACCEPTED

L—Most chances accepted, one series—
26—4 game, John J. Barry, Philadelphia AL, 1914.
  Frank P. Crosetti, New York AL, 1938.
38—5 game, Joseph B. Tinker, Chicago NL, 1907.
37—6 game, Philip F. Rizzuto, New York AL, 1951.
42—7 game, Charles M. Gelbert, St. Louis NL, 1931.
51—8 game, Charles A. Risberg, Chicago AL, 1919.

M—Most chances accepted, game—
13—George D. Weaver, Chicago AL (7-po, 6-a), Oct. 7, 1917.

N—Fewest chances offered, game—
0—John P. Boley, Philadelphia AL, Oct. 8, 1929.
  David J. Bancroft, Philadelphia NL, Oct. 12, 1915.
  Harold H. Reese, Brooklyn NL, Oct. 1, 1947.
  Philip F. Rizzuto, New York AL, Oct. 7, 1949.

PUTOUTS

O—Most putouts, one series—
16—4 game, Frank P. Crosetti, New York AL, 1938.
15—5 game, Joseph B. Tinker, Chicago NL, 1907.
  Philip F. Rizzuto, New York AL, 1942.
16—6 game, William F. Jurges, Chicago NL, 1935.
18—7 game, Philip F. Rizzuto, New York AL, 1947.
24—8 game, Charles Wagner, Boston AL, 1912.

P—Most putouts, game—
7—George D. Weaver, Chicago AL, Oct. 7, 1917.
  Philip F. Rizzuto, New York AL, Oct. 5, 1942.

ASSISTS

A—Most assists, game—
10—John Logan, Milwaukee NL, Oct. 9, 1957 (10 inn.).
9—Roger Peckinpaugh, New York AL, Oct. 5, 1921.
B—Most assists, one series—
21—4 game, John J. Barry, Philadelphia AL, 1914.
25—5 game, L. Everett Scott, Boston AL, 1916.
25—6 game, L. Everett Scott, Boston AL, 1918.
29—7 game, Charles M. Gelbert, St. Louis NL, 1931.
30—8 game, Frederick A. Parent, Boston AL, 1903.

ERRORS

C—Most errors, one series—
4—4 game, Frank P. Crosetti, New York AL, 1932.
4—5 game, Ivan N. Olson, Brooklyn NL, 1916.
     Elwood G. English, Chicago NL, 1929.
4—6 game, Arthur Fletcher, New York AL, 1911.
     George D. Weaver, Chicago AL, 1917.
8—7 game, Roger Peckinpaugh, Washington AL, 1925.
6—8 game, John P. Wagner, Pittsburgh NL, 1903.
D—Most errors, game—
3—John J. Barry, Phila. AL, Oct. 26, 1911.
     Arthur Fletcher, N.Y. NL, Oct. 9, 1912.
     George D. Weaver, Chicago AL, Oct. 13, 1917.
E—Most unassisted double plays, one series—
2—Joseph B. Tinker, Chicago NL, 1907.

OUTFIELDERS' FIELDING RECORDS
CHANCES ACCEPTED

F—Most chances accepted, one series—
16—4 game, Earl B. Combs, New York AL, 1927.
20—5 games, Joseph P. DiMaggio, New York AL, 1942.
22—6 game, Michael A. Kreevich, St. Louis AL, 1944.
26—7 game, Andrew Pafko, Chicago NL, 1945.
33—8 game, Edd J. Roush, Cincinnati NL, 1919.
G—Most chances accepted, game—
8—Edd J. Roush, Cincinnati NL, Oct. 1, 1919.
     Henry E. Leiber, New York NL, Oct. 2, 1936.

PUTOUTS

H—Most putouts, one series—
16—4 game, Earle B. Combs, New York AL, 1927.
20—5 game, Joseph P. DiMaggio, New York AL, 1942.
20—6 game, Michael A. Kreevich, St. Louis AL, 1944.
     Marvin A. Rickert, Boston NL, 1948.
24—7 game, Myron W. McCormick, Cincinnati NL, 1940.
     Andrew Pafko, Chicago NL, 1945.
30—8 game, Edd J. Roush, Cincinnati NL, 1919.

I—Most putouts, game—
8—Center Fielders—Edd J. Roush, Cin. NL, Oct. 1, 1919.
7—Right Fielders—John J. Murray, N. Y. NL, Oct. 14, 1912.
     Raymond Blades, St. Louis NL, Oct. 5, 1930.
     Edmund Miller, Philadelphia AL, Oct. 5, 1930.
6—Left Fielders—George E. Lewis, Boston AL, Oct. 12, 1915; Oct. 11, 1916.
     Emil F. Meusel, New York NL, Oct. 10, 1923.
     Charles J. Hafey, St. Louis NL, Oct. 7, 1926.
     Harry L. Lowrey, Chicago NL, Oct. 8, 1945.
     Myron W. McCormick, Boston NL, Oct. 8, 1948.
     Harvey E. Kuenn, San Francisco NL, Oct. 4, 1962.
     Thomas M. Tresh, New York AL, Oct. 16, 1962.
     H. Thomas Davis, Los Angeles NL, Oct. 3, 1963.

J—Most putouts, one inning—
3—By many. Last:
     Roger E. Maris, New York AL, 3rd inn., Oct. 11, 1964.

ASSISTS

K—Most assists, one series—
2—4 game, By many players.
2—5 game, By many players.
2—6 game, By many players.
4—7 game, Edgar C. Rice, Washington AL, 1924.
3—8 game, Harry Hooper, Boston AL, 1912.
     Edd J. Roush, Cincinnati NL, 1919.
     Patrick H. Dougherty, Boston AL, 1903.
L—Most assists, game—
2—By 8 players.

ERRORS

M—Most errors, game—
2—John F. Collins, Chicago AL, Oct. 10, 1917.
     Ross Youngs, New York NL, Oct. 11, 1923.
     Ernest R. Orsatti, St. Louis NL, Oct. 3, 1934.
     Donald F. Mueller, New York NL, Sept. 29, 1954.
     Edwin D. Snider, Los Angeles NL, Oct. 1, 1959.
N—Most errors, inning—
2—Edwin D. Snider, Los Angeles NL, 3d inn., Oct. 1, 1959.
O—Most errors, one series—
2—4 games, Lloyd J. Waner, Pittsburgh NL, 1927.
     Donald F. Mueller, New York NL, 1954.

William A. Rariden, New York NL, Oct. 10, 1917.
William P. Delancey, St. Louis NL, Oct. 8, 1934.

ERRORS

G—Most errors, one series—
2–4 game, James Wilson, St. Louis NL, 1928.
2–5 game, Charles Schmidt, Detroit AL, 1907.
 W. Walker Cooper, St. Louis NL, 1943.
2–6 game, Ray W. Schalk, Chicago AL, 1917.
5–7 game, Charles Schmidt, Detroit AL, 1909.
3–8 game, Louis Criger, Boston AL, 1903.

H—Most errors, game—
2–Louis Criger, Boston AL, Oct. 1, 1903.
 James Wilson, St. Louis NL, Oct. 7, 1928.

DOUBLE PLAYS

I—Most double plays started, one series—
3–Walter H. Schang, New York AL, 1921.
J—Most double plays started, game—
2–Charles Schmidt, Detroit AL, Oct. 14, 1909.
 Walter H. Schang, New York AL, Oct. 11, 1921.
JJ—Most runners thrown out stealing, game—
6–John W. Lapp, Philadelphia AL, Oct. 17, 1911 (11 inns.).

PITCHERS' FIELDING RECORDS

CHANCES ACCEPTED

K—Most chances accepted, one series—
6–4 game, George A. Tyler, Boston NL, 1914.
 Chas. H. Ruffing, New York AL, 1938.
10–5 game, Christy Mathewson, New York NL, 1905.
 Mordecai P. Brown, Chicago NL, 1910.
17–6 game, Nick Altrock, Chicago AL, 1906.
 James L. Vaughn, Chicago NL, 1918.
12–7 game, George Mullin, Detroit AL, 1909.
13–8 game, Christopher Mathewson, New York NL, 1912.
L—Most chances accepted, game—
11–Nick Altrock, Chicago AL (3-po, 8-a), Oct. 12, 1906.

PUTOUTS

M—Most putouts, one series—
3–4 game, Edward C. Ford, New York AL, 1963.
4–5 game, George Foster, Boston AL, 1915.
 Robert T. Purkey, Cincinnati NL, 1961.
6–6 game, Nick Altrock, Chicago AL, 1906.
 James L. Vaughn, Chicago NL, 1918.
5–7 game, James L. Kaat, Minnesota AL, 1965.
2–8 game, Philip Douglas, New York NL, 1921.
 Charles L. Phillippe, Pittsburgh NL, 1903.

OUTFIELDERS' FIELDING RECORDS—Continued

Most errors, one series (continued)—
2–5 game, Five (5) players, 1905, 1907, 1908, 1922, 1943.
3–6 game, John J. Murray, New York NL, 1911.
 John F. Collins, Chicago AL, 1917.
2–7 game, Zachary D. Wheat, Brooklyn NL, 1920.
 Ernest R. Orsatti, St. Louis NL, 1934.
 Leon A. Goslin, Detroit AL, 1934.
 Mickey C. Mantle, New York AL, 1964.
2–8 game, Joshua D. Devore, New York NL, 1912.
 Tristan E. Speaker, Boston AL, 1912.
 Oscar Felsch, Chicago AL, 1919.
 Edd J. Roush, Cincinnati NL, 1919.

CATCHERS' FIELDING RECORDS

CHANCES ACCEPTED

A—Most chances accepted, one series—
43–4 game, John Roseboro, Los Angeles NL, 1963.
61–5 game, Gordon S. Cochrane, Philadelphia AL, 1929.
56–6 game, Roy Campanella, Brooklyn NL, 1953.
66–7 game, Lawrence P. Berra, New York AL, 1952.
62–8 game, Louis Criger, Boston AL, 1903.
B—Most chances accepted, game—
18–John Roseboro, Los Angeles NL, Oct. 2, 1963.

PUTOUTS

C—Most putouts, one series—
43–4 game, John Roseboro, Los Angeles NL, 1963.
59–5 game, Gordon S. Cochrane, Philadelphia AL, 1929.
55–6 game, W. Cooper, St. Louis NL, 1944.
60–7 game, Lawrence P. Berra, New York AL, 1958.
54–8 game, Louis Criger, Boston AL, 1903.
D—Most putouts, game—
18–John Roseboro, Los Angeles NL, Oct. 2, 1963.

ASSISTS

E—Most assists, one series—
5–4 game, Charles L. Hartnett, Chicago NL, 1932.
 Wm. Dickey, New York AL, 1938.
9–5 game, Charles Schmidt, Detroit AL, 1907.
 Edward Burns, Philadelphia NL, 1915.
12–6 game, John T. Meyers, New York NL, 1911.
11–7 game, Charles Schmidt, Detroit AL, 1909.
15–8 game, Ray W. Schalk, Chicago AL, 1919.
F—Most assists, game—
6–John W. Lapp, Philadelphia AL, Oct. 17, 1911 (11 inns.).
4–John G. Kling, Chicago NL, Oct. 9, 1907; Oct. 11, 1907; Oct. 14, 1908.
 Charles Schmidt, Det. AL, Oct. 11, 1907; Oct. 14, 1908.
 George Gibson, Pittsburgh NL, Oct. 12, 1909.

A—Most putouts, game—
5—James L. Kaat, Minnesota AL, Oct. 7, 1965.
AA—Most putouts, inning—
2—By 4 pitchers. Last:
Robert T. Purkey, Cincinati NL, 9th inn., Oct. 7, 1961.

ASSISTS

B—Most assists, one series—
5-4 game, Leslie J. Bush, Philadelphia AL, 1914.
George Tyler, Boston NL, 1914.
William L. James, Boston NL, 1914.
W. Wiley Moore, New York AL, 1927.
Monte M. Pearson, New York AL, 1939.
10-5 game, Mordecai P. Brown, Chicago NL, 1910.
12-6 game, Mordecai P. Brown, Chicago NL, 1906.
12-7 game, George Mullin, Detroit AL, 1909.
12-8 game, Christy Mathewson, New York NL, 1912.

C—Most assists, game—
8—Nick Altrock, Chicago AL, Oct. 12, 1906.
Lonnie Warneke, Chicago NL, Oct. 2, 1935.

ERRORS

D—Most errors, one series—
1-4 game, seven (7) players, 1914, 27, 28, 32, 39, 54 (2).
2-5 game, John W. Coombs, Philadelphia AL, 1910.
H. Max Lanier, St. Louis NL, 1942.
2-6 game, Nelson T. Potter, St. Louis AL, 1944.
2-7 game, Charles Phillippe, Pittsburgh NL, 1909.
Allie P. Reynolds, New York AL, 1952.
2-8 game, Edward V. Cicotte, Chicago AL, 1919.

E—Most errors, game—
2—By 5 pitchers.
Last: Nelson T. Potter, St. Louis AL, Oct. 5, 1944.

PITCHERS' RECORDS

F—Pitching in most series—
11—Edward C. Ford, New York AL, 1950, 53, 55-58, 60-64.
FF—Pitching in most games, total series—
22—Edward C. Ford, New York AL, 1950,53(2),55(2),56(2),57(2),58(3),60(2),61(2),62(3),63(2),64.

G—Pitching in most games, one series—
6—Hugh T. Casey, Brooklyn NL, 1947.
GG—Most games started, total series—
22—Edward C. Ford, New York AL (see Item FF above).

VICTORIES AND DEFEATS

H—Most victories, total series—
10—Edward C. Ford, New York AL, 1950(1),55(2),56(1),57(1),60(2),61(2),62(1).

I—Most defeats, total series—
8—Edward C. Ford, New York AL, 1953,56,57,58,62,63(2),64.

J—All victories, no defeats—
6—Vernon L. Gomez, New York AL, 1932 (1), 36 (2), 37 (2), 38 (1).

K—Most games won, one series—
2-4 game, R. Rudolph, Boston NL, 1914.
W. L. James, Boston NL, 1914.
W. C. Hoyt, New York AL, 1928.
C. H. Ruffing, New York AL, 1938.
Sanford Koufax, Los Angeles NL, 1963.
3-5 game, C. Mathewson, New York, 1905.
J. W. Coombs, Phila. AL, 1910.
3-6 game, U. C. Faber, Chicago AL, 1917.
3-7 game, C. B. Adams, Pitts. NL, 1909.
S. Coveleskie, Cleve. AL, 1920.
Harry D. Brechen, St. Louis NL, 1946 (only left-hander to win 3 games).
S. Lewis Burdette, Milwaukee NL, 1957.
3-8 game, Joseph Wood, Boston AL, 1912.
C. Phillippe, Pitts. NL, 1903.
W. H. Dinneen, Bos. AL, 1903.

L—Most games lost, one series—
2-4 game, W. H. Sherdel, St. Louis NL, 1928.
W. C. Lee, Chicago NL, 1938.
W. H. Walters, Cinn. NL, 1939.
E. C. Ford, New York AL, 1963.
2-5 game, by many.
2-6 game, by many.
2-7 game, by many.
3-8 game, C. P. Williams, Chicago AL, 1919.

M—Pitchers winning three games, losing none, series—
Christy Mathewson, New York NL, 1905.
Charles B. Adams, Pittsburgh NL, 1909.
John W. Coombs, Philadelphia AL, 1910.
Stanley Coveleskie, Cleveland AL, 1920.
Harry D. Brecheen, St. Louis NL, 1946.
S. Lewis Burdette, Milwaukee NL, 1957.

N—Pitchers winning and losing longest game—
14 innings—winner—George H. Ruth, Boston AL, 2-1, Oct. 9, 1916.
Loser—Sherrod M. Smith, Brooklyn NL (pitched 13 1/3 inns.—complete game).

EARNED RUNS

O—Most earned runs, pitcher winning two (2) or more games, series—
3-4 game, W. C. Hoyt, New York AL, 1928.
C. H. Ruffing, New York AL, 1938.
8-5 game, J. W. Coombs, Phila. AL, 1910.
8-6 game, Vernon Gomez, New York AL, 1936.
14-7 game, Harold Newhouser, Detroit AL, 1945.
10-8 game, Joseph Wood, Boston AL, 1912.

PITCHERS' RECORDS—Continued

A—Fewest earned runs, pitchers winning two (2) or more games series—
0-4 game, W. L. James, Boston NL, 1914.
0-5 game, C. Mathewson, New York NL, 1905.
  C. O. Hubbell, New York NL, 1933.
  E. C. Ford, New York AL, 1961.
1-6 game, L. Warneke, Chicago NL, 1935.
  Edmund W. Lopat, New York AL, 1951.
  Lawrence Sherry, Los Angeles NL, 1959.
0-7 game, J. J. Haines, St. Louis NL, 1926.
  E. C. Ford, New York AL, 1960.
0-8 game, W. C. Hoyt, New York AL, 1921.

SHUTOUT GAMES

B—Most shutout games, total series—
4—Christy Mathewson, New York NL, 1905 (3), 1913.
C—Most shutout games, one series—
3—Christy Mathewson, New York NL, 1905.
D—Most hits allowed, no runs—
10—Spurgeon F. Chandler, N. Y. AL, Oct. 11, 1943.
8—Christy Mathewson, N. Y. NL, Oct. 8, 1913.
  John J. Podres, Brooklyn NL, Oct. 4, 1955.

COMPLETE GAMES

E—Pitching most complete games, one series—
2-4 game, R. Rudolph, Boston NL, 1914.
  W. C. Hoyt, New York AL, 1928.
  C. H. Ruffing, New York AL, 1938.
  S. Koufax, Los Angeles NL, 1963.
3-5 game, C. H. Mathewson, New York NL, 1905.
  J. W. Coombs, Phila. AL, 1910.
3-6 game, C. A. Bender, Phila. AL, 1911.
  J. L. Vaughn, Chicago NL, 1918.
3-7 game, C. B. Adams, Pitts. NL, 1909.
  Geo. Mullin, Detroit AL, 1909.
  S. Coveleskie, Cleveland AL, 1920.
  W. P. Johnson, Washington AL, 1925.
  Louis N. Newsom, Detroit AL, 1940.
  S. Lewis Burdette, Milwaukee NL, 1957.
5-8 game, C. Phillippe, Pittsburgh NL, 1903.

INNINGS PITCHED

F—Most innings pitched, total series—
146—Edward C. Ford, New York AL, 1950, 53, 55-58, 60-64.
G—Most innings pitched, one series—
18-4 game, R. Rudolph, Boston NL, 1914.
  W. C. Hoyt, New York AL, 1928.
  C. H. Ruffing, New York AL, 1938.
  S. Koufax, Los Angeles NL, 1963.

27-5 game, C. Mathewson, New York NL, 1905.
  J. W. Coombs, Phila. AL, 1910.
27-6 game, C. Mathewson, New York NL, 1911.
  Urban C. Faber, Chicago AL, 1917.
  James L. Vaughn, Chicago NL, 1918.
32-7 game, Geo. Mullin, Detroit AL, 1909.
44-8 game, C. Phillippe, Pittsburgh NL, 1903.

H—Most consecutive innings pitched, no runs, one series—
27—Christy Mathewson, New York NL, 1905.
I—Most consecutive innings pitched, no runs, total series—
33 2/3—Edward C. Ford, New York AL (1960—18, 61—14, 62—1 2/3).
J—Perfect no hit game—
  Donald J. Larsen, New York AL, Oct. 8, 1956.
K—Most consecutive innings, no hits, game—
9—Donald J. Larsen, New York AL, Oct. 8, 1956.
KK—Most consecutive innings no hits, total series—
11-1/3—Donald J. Larsen, New York AL, 1956-57.

STRIKE OUTS

L—Most strikeouts, one pitcher, total series—
94—Edward C. Ford, New York AL, 1950, 53, 55-58, 60-64.
M—Most strikeouts, one series—
23-4 game, S. Koufax, Los Angeles NL, 1963.
18-5 game, C. Mathewson, New York NL, 1905.
20-6 game, C. A. Bender, Phila. AL, 1911.
31-7 game, Robert Gibson, St. Louis NL, 1964.
28-8 game, W. H. Dinneen, Boston AL, 1903.
N—Most strikeouts, one pitcher, game—
15—Sanford Koufax, Los Angeles NL, Oct. 2, 1963.
O—Most strikeouts in succession, game—
6—Horace O. Eller, Cincinnati NL (3 in 2d, 3 in 3d), Oct. 6, 1919.
P—Striking out first five batters—
  Morton C. Cooper, St. Louis NL, Oct. 11, 1943.
  Sanford Koufax, Los Angeles NL, Oct. 2, 1963.
Q—Retiring side on three pitched balls—
3—Christy Mathewson, N. Y. NL, 11th inn., Oct. 9, 1912; also
  5th inning, Oct. 16, 1912.
  George Walberg, Phila. AL, 7th inn., Oct. 12, 1929.
  Ernest E. Bonham, N. Y. AL, 7th inn., Oct. 6, 1941.

BASES ON BALLS

R—Most bases on balls, one pitcher, total series—
34—Edward C. Ford, New York AL, 1950, 53, 55-58, 60-64.

PITCHERS' RECORDS—Continued

A—Most bases on balls, one series—
8—4 game, Robert G. Lemon, Cleveland AL, 1954.
14—5 game, J. W. Coombs, Phila. AL, 1910.
11—6 game, G. A. Tyler, Chicago NL, 1918.
  Vernon Gomez, New York AL, 1936.
  Allie P. Reynolds, New York AL, 1951.
11—7 game, W. P. Johnson, Wash. AL, 1924.
  Flyod C. Bevens, New York AL, 1947.
13—8 games, A. N. Nehf, New York NL, 1921.

B—Most bases on balls, game—
10—Floyd C. Bevens, N.Y. AL, Oct. 3, 1947.

C—Most bases on balls, inning—
4—William E. Donovan, Det. AL, Oct. 16, 1909 (2nd inn.).
  Arthur C. Reinhart, St. L. NL, Oct. 6, 1926 (5th inn.).
  Guy T. Bush, Chi. NL, Sept. 28, 1932 (6th inn.).

D—Most games, no bases on balls, one series—
4—Charles L. Phillippe, Pitt. NL, 1903.

E—Most consecutive inns., no bases on balls, one series—
27—Charles L. Phillippe, Pitt. NL, 1903.

WILD PITCHES—HIT BATSMEN

F—Most wild pitches, total series—
5—Harold H. Schumacher, N.Y. NL, 1933 (2), 36 (2), 37.

G—Most wild pitches, one series—
3—Charles M. Tesreau, N.Y. NL, 1912.
Most wild pitches, game—
2—By 7 pitchers. Last:
  James A. Bouton, N.Y. AL, Oct. 5, 1963. .
Most wild pitches, inning—
2—By 4 pitchers. Last:
  James O. Carleton, Chi. NL, Oct. 9, 1932 (8th inn.).

H—Most hit batsmen, total series—
4—Edward S. Plank, Phila. AL, 1905, 1911, 1913, 1914.
  Wm. E. Donovan, Det. AL, 1907 (3), 1909 (1).

I—Most hit batsmen, one series—
3—William E. Donovan, Detroit AL, 1907.
Most hit batsmen, game—
2—By 10 pitchers. Last:
  Robert B. Friend, Pitt. NL, Oct. 12, 1960.

HOME RUNS—OFF PITCHER

J—Most home runs off pitcher, total series—
8—Burleigh A. Grimes, Brk. NL, 1920(2); St. L. NL, 1930(3);
  31; Chi. NL, 1932(2).
  Charles H. Root, Chi. NL, 1929(2), 32(4), 35, 38.
  Allie P. Reynolds, N.Y. AL, 1947, 51, 52(2), 53(4).
  Donald Newcombe, Brk. NL, 1949, 55(3), 56(4).
  Edward C. Ford, N.Y. AL, 1955(2), 56(2), 62, 63(2), 64.

K—Most home runs allowed, game—
4—Charles H. Root, Chi. NL, Oct. 1, 1932.
  Eugene E. Thompson, Cin. NL, Oct. 7, 1939.

L—Most home runs allowed, inning—
2—By many pitchers. Last:
  Robert Gibson, St. L. NL, Oct. 15, 1964 (9th inn.).

PITCHERS USED

M—Most pitchers used in a game, both clubs—
10—New York AL (6), Brooklyn NL (4), 6th game, Oct. 5, 1947
  New York AL (7), Brooklyn (3), 2nd game, Oct. 5, 1956.
  Cincinnati NL (8), New York AL (2), 5th game, Oct. 9, 1961.

N—Most pitchers used in a game, one club—
8—Cincinnati NL, 5th game, Oct. 9, 1961.

NN—Most pitchers used in one series, both clubs—
20—Pittsburgh NL (10); vs. New York AL (10), 1960, 7 games.

World Series Club Batting Records

BATTING PERCENTAGE

O—Highest batting percentage, one series—
.313—4 game, New York AL, 1932.
.316—5 game, Philadelphia AL, 1910.
.302—6 game, New York AL, 1936.
.338—7 game, New York AL, 1960.
.270—8 game, New York NL, 1912.

P—Lowest batting percentage, one series—
.171—4 game, New York AL, 1963.
.161—5 game, Philadelphia AL, 1905.
.175—6 game, New York NL, 1911.
.195—7 game, Brooklyn NL, 1956.
  Minnesota AL, 1965.
.207—8 game, New York AL, 1921.

Q—Lowest batting percentage of club winning series—
.206—4 game, New York AL, 1939.
.209—5 game, New York NL, 1905.
.186—6 game, Boston AL, 1918.
.199—7 game, New York AL, 1962.
.220—8 game, Boston AL, 1912.

R—Highest batting percentage of club losing series—
.253—4 game, Chicago NL, 1932.
.249—5 game, Chicago NL, 1929.
.300—6 game, Brooklyn NL, 1953.
.338—7 game, New York AL, 1960.
.270—8 game, New York NL, 1912.

S—Highest percentage, game—
.513—N. Y. NL (39 ab, 20 hits), Oct. 7, 1921.

TIMES AT BAT

T—Most times at bat, one club, total series—
5,500—New York AL, 29 series.
2,631—New York NL, 14 series.

WORLD SERIES CLUB BATTING RECORDS—Continued

A—Most times at bat, one club, one series—
146—4 game, Chicago NL, 1932.
178—5 game, New York AL, 1942.
215—6 game, New York AL, 1936.
269—7 game, Boston AL, 1903.

B—Most times at bat, one club, game—
48—Detroit AL, 6th game, Oct. 8, 1945 (12 inns.).
45—New York AL, 4th game, Oct. 2, 1932 (9 inns.),
New York AL, 6th game, Oct. 6, 1936 (9 inns.).

C—Most times at bat, both clubs, game—
94—Detroit AL (48) vs Chicago NL (46), Oct. 8, 1945 (12 inns.).
84—N. Y. AL (45) vs Chi. NL (39), Oct. 2, 1932 (9 inns.),
New York AL (45) vs Pitt. NL (39), Oct. 6, 1960.

D—Most players facing pitcher one club, inning—
15—Philadelphia AL, 7th inning, Oct. 12, 1929.

E—Players facing pitcher twice, one club, inning—
6—Philadelphia AL, 7th inning, Oct. 12, 1929.

RUNS—CLUB

F—Most runs, both clubs, one series—
56—4 game, New York AL (37) vs Chicago NL (19), 1932.
50—5 game, Chicago NL (15) vs Philadelphia AL (35), 1910.
66—6 game, New York AL (43) vs New York NL (23), 1936.
82—7 game, New York AL (55) vs Pitt. NL (27), 1960.
63—8 game, Boston AL (39) vs Pittsburgh NL (24), 1903.

G—Most runs, one club, one series—
37—4 game, New York AL, 1932.
35—5 game, Philadelphia AL, 1910.
43—6 game, New York AL, 1936.
55—7 game, New York AL, 1960.
39—8 game, Boston AL, 1903.

H—Most runs, losing club, one series—
19—4 game, Chicago NL, 1932.
18—5 game, New York AL, 1942.
27—6 game, Brooklyn NL, 1953.
57—7 game, New York AL, 1960.
31—8 game, New York NL, 1912.

I—Fewest runs, both clubs, one series—
16—4 game, New York AL (11) vs Philadelphia NL (5), 1950.
Los Angeles NL (12) vs New York AL (4), 1963.
18—5 game, New York NL (15) vs Philadelphia AL (3), 1905.
29—6 game, Chicago NL (10) vs Boston AL (9), 1918.
29—7 game, Brooklyn NL (8) vs Cleveland AL (21), 1920.
51—8 game, New York NL (29) vs New York AL (22), 1921.

J—Fewest runs, one club, one series—
4—4 game, New York AL, 1963.
3—5 game, Philadelphia AL, 1905.
9—6 game, Boston AL, 1918.
8—7 game, Brooklyn NL, 1920.
20—8 game, Chicago AL, 1919.

K—Most runs, both clubs, game—
22—New York AL (18) vs New York NL (4), Oct. 2, 1936.

L—Most runs, one club, game—
18—New York AL vs New York NL, Oct. 2, 1936.

M—Most runs in first inning, one club—
7—Milwaukee NL, Oct. 2, 1958.

N—Most runs in ninth inning, one club—
7—New York AL, Oct. 6, 1936.

O—Most runs in an inning, one club—
10—Philadelphia AL, 7th inning, Oct. 12, 1929.

OO—Most runs, both clubs, one inning—
11—Philadelphia AL (10), Chicago NL (1), 7th inn., Oct. 12, 1929.
Brooklyn NL (6), New York AL (5), 2nd inn., Oct. 5, 1956.

P—Largest winning margin, single game—
14—New York AL (18) vs New York NL (4), Oct. 2, 1936.

Q—Most runs in extra inning, one club—
3—New York AL, 10th inning, Oct. 8, 1913.
New York AL, 10th inning, Oct. 8, 1939.
Milwaukee NL, 10th inning, Sept. 29, 1954.
St. Louis NL, 10th inning, Oct. 12, 1964.

RUNS BATTED IN

R—Most runs batted in, one club, one series—
36—4 game, New York AL, 1932.
29—5 game, Philadelphia AL, 1910.
41—6 game, New York AL, 1936.
54—7 game, New York AL, 1960.
35—8 game, Boston AL, 1903.

S—Most runs batted in, both clubs, one series—
52—4 game, New York AL (36) vs Chicago NL (16), 1932.
42—5 game, Philadelphia AL (29) vs Chicago NL (13), 1910.
61—6 game, New York AL (41) vs New York NL (20), 1936.
80—7 game, New York AL (54) vs Pittsburgh NL (26), 1960.
58—8 game, Boston AL (35) vs Pittsburgh NL (23), 1903.

T—Most runs batted in, one club, one game—
18—New York AL, 2d game, Oct. 2, 1936.

TT—Most runs batted in, both clubs, game—
21—New York AL (18), New York NL (3), Oct. 2, 1936.
Brooklyn NL (13), New York AL (8), Oct. 5, 1956.

BASE HITS—CLUB

U—Most base hits, both clubs, one series—
82—4 game, New York AL (45) vs Chicago NL (37), 1932.
91—5 game, Philadelphia AL (56) vs Chicago NL (35), 1910.
151—6 game, New York AL (91) vs Pittsburgh NL (60), 1960.
134—8 game, New York AL (74) vs. Boston AL (60), 1912.
135—8 game, Boston AL (71) vs Pittsburgh NL (64), 1903.

V—Most base hits, one club, one series—
45—4 game, New York AL, 1932.
56—5 game, Philadelphia AL, 1910.

WORLD SERIES CLUB BATTING RECORDS—Continued

Most base hits, one club, one series (continued)—
65—6 game, New York AL, 1936.
91—7 game, New York NL, 1960.
74—8 game, New York NL, 1912.
A—Most base hits, one club, game—
20—New York NL, Oct. 7, 1921.
   St. Louis NL, Oct. 10, 1946.
B—Most base hits, one club, inning—
10—Philadelphia AL, 7th inning, Oct. 12, 1929.
C—Fewest base hits, both clubs, one series—
47—4 game, Los Angeles NL (25) vs New York AL (22), 1963.
57—5 game, New York NL (32) vs Philadelphia AL (25), 1905.
69—6 game, Chicago NL (37) vs Boston AL (32), 1918.
95—7 game, San Francisco NL (51) vs New York AL (44), 1962.
121—8 game, New York NL (71) vs New York AL (50), 1921.
D—Fewest base hits, one club, one series—
22—4 game, Philadelphia AL, 1914.
   New York AL, 1963.
25—5 game, Philadelphia AL, 1905.
32—6 game, Boston AL, 1918.
42—7 game, Brooklyn NL, 1956.
   Minnesota AL, 1965.
50—8 game, New York AL, 1921.
E—Most base hits, both clubs, game—
32—New York AL (19) vs Pittsburgh NL (13), Oct. 6, 1960.
   New York AL, Oct. 6, 1921.
F—Fewest base hits, both clubs, game—
5—Giants (3), Yankees (2), Oct. 6, 1921.
  New York AL (5), Brooklyn NL (0), Oct. 8, 1956.
G—Fewest base hits, one club, game—
0—Brooklyn NL, Oct. 8, 1956.
H—Most consecutive hits, one club, inning—
8—New York NL, 7th inning, Oct. 7, 1921.
I—Scoring one or more runs, making one or more hits in a game, by each player (9) one club—
New York AL (18 runs, 17 hits), 2d game, Oct. 2, 1936.

ONE BASE HITS (Singles)—CLUB

J—Most 1-base hits, one club, one series—
31—4 game, New York AL, 1932.
46—5 game, New York NL, 1922.
49—6 game, New York NL, 1936.
64—7 game, New York NL, 1960.
55—8 game, New York NL, 1912.
K—Fewest 1-base hits, one club, one series—
13—4 game, Philadelphia AL, 1914.
19—5 game, Brooklyn NL, 1941.
17—6 game, Philadelphia AL, 1930.
27—7 game, Minnesota AL, 1965.
39—8 game, Boston AL, 1912.

L—Most 1-base hits, both clubs, one series—
55—4 game, New York AL (31) vs Chicago NL (24), 1932.
70—5 game, New York NL (39) vs Washington AL (31), 1933.
87—6 game, Chicago AL (47) vs New York NL (40), 1917.
109—7 game, New York AL (64) vs Pittsburgh NL (45), 1960.
96—8 game, Boston AL (49) vs Pittsburgh NL (47), 1903.
M—Most 1-base hits (singles), one club, game—
15—New York NL, Oct. 7, 1921.
   New York AL, Oct. 6, 1936.
MM—Most 1-base hits (singles), both clubs, game—
23—New York AL (13) vs Pittsburgh NL (10), Oct. 6, 1960.
N—Fewest 1-base hits (singles), one club, game—
0—Philadelphia AL, Oct. 1, 8, 1930.
  Brooklyn NL, Oct. 3, 1947; Oct. 8, 1956.
  New York AL, Oct. 4, 1952.

TWO BASE HITS (Doubles)—CLUB

O—Most 2-base hits, one club, one series—
9—4 game, Philadelphia AL, 1914.
19—5 game, Philadelphia AL, 1910.
15—6 game, Philadelphia AL, 1911.
19—7 game, St. Louis NL, 1946.
14—8 game, New York NL, 1912; Boston AL, 1912.
P—Most 2-base hits, both clubs, one series—
15—4 game, Philadelphia AL (9) vs Boston NL (6), 1914.
30—5 game, Philadelphia AL (19) vs Chicago NL (11), 1910.
26—6 game, Philadelphia AL (15) vs New York NL (11), 1911.
29—7 game, Detroit AL (16) vs Pittsburgh NL (13), 1909.
28—8 game, New York NL (14) vs Boston AL (14), 1912.
Q—Fewest 2-base hits, one club, one series—
3—4 game, Cin. NL 1939; N.Y. AL 1950; N.Y. NL 1954; L.A. NL & N.Y. AL 1963.
1—5 game, Detroit AL, 1907.
2—6 game, Boston AL, 1918; New York NL, 1923.
4—7 game, New York NL, 1955.
4—8 game, Boston AL, 1903.
R—Fewest 2-base hits, both clubs, one series—
6—4 game, Los Angeles NL (3) vs New York AL (3), 1963.
6—5 game, Philadelphia NL (4) vs Boston AL (2), 1915.
7—6 game, Chicago NL (5) vs. Brooklyn NL (2), 1918.
12—7 game, New York AL (5) vs Brooklyn NL (8), 1955.
11—8 game, Boston AL (4) vs Pittsburgh NL (7), 1903.
S—Most 2-base hits, one club, game—
8—Chicago AL, Oct. 13, 1906.
  Pittsburgh NL, Oct. 15, 1925.
T—Most 2-base hits, both clubs, game—
11—Chicago AL, (8) vs Chicago NL (3), 5th g., Oct. 13, 1906.
U—Most 2-base hits, one club, inning—
3—By 9 clubs. Last:
  Chicago AL, Oct. 1, 1959 (3rd inn.).

THREE BASE HITS (Triples)—CLUB

A—Most 3-base hits, one club, one series—
2–4 game, Bos. NL, 1914; N.Y. AL 1927; Chi. NL, 1932; L.A. NL, 1963.

6–5 game, Boston AL, 1916.
4–6 game, N.Y. NL, 1917; N.Y. AL, 1923, 1953.
5–7 game, St. Louis NL, 1934; New York AL, 1947.
16–8 game, Boston AL, 1903.

B—Most 3-base hits, both clubs, one series—
3–4 game, New York AL (2) vs Pittsburgh NL (1), 1927.
11–5 game, Boston AL (6) vs Brooklyn NL (5), 1916.
7–6 game, New York AL (4) vs New York NL (3), 1923.
6–7 game, St. Louis NL (5) vs Detroit AL (1), 1934.
    New York AL (5) vs Brooklyn NL (1), 1947.
25–8 game, Boston AL (16) vs Pittsburgh NL (9), 1903.

C—Most 3-base hits, one club, game—
5–Boston AL, Oct. 7, 10, 1903.

CC—Most 3-base hits, one club, inning—
2–By 8 clubs. Last: New York AL, Sept. 30, 1953 (1st inn.).

D—Most 3-base hits, both clubs, game—
7–Boston AL (5) vs. Pittsburgh NL (2), Oct. 10, 1903.

E—Fewest 3-base hits, one club, one series—
0–4 game, By 5 clubs.
    5 game, By 10 clubs.
    6 game, By 7 clubs.
    7 game, By 11 clubs.
1–8 game, New York AL, 1921.

F—Fewest 3-base hits, both clubs, one series—
1–4 game, St. Louis NL (1) vs New York AL (0), 1928.
    Cleveland AL (1) vs New York NL (0), 1954.
0–5 game, N. Y. NL (0) vs Phila. AL (0), 1905;
    New York NL (0) vs Wash. AL (0), 1933.
0–6 game, Cleveland AL (0) vs Boston NL (0), 1948.
0–7 game, St. Louis NL (0) vs Phila. AL (0), 1931.
5–8 game, New York NL (4) vs New York AL (1), 1921.

HOME RUNS—CLUB

G—Total home runs, 1903 to date—
395–American League, 244.
    National League, 151.

H—Most home runs, total Series—
163–New York AL.
33–Brooklyn NL.

I—Most home runs, one club, one series—
9–4 game, New York AL, 1928.
7–5 game, New York AL, 1961.
9–6 game, New York AL, 1953.
12–7 game, New York AL, 1956.
2–8 game, N. Y. NL, 1921; N. Y. AL, 1921; Bos. AL, 1903.

J—Most home runs, both clubs, one series—
11–4 game, New York AL (8) vs. Chicago NL (3), 1932.
10–5 game, New York AL (7) vs Cincinnati NL (3), 1961.
17–6 game, New York AL (9) vs. Brooklyn NL (8), 1953.
17–7 game, New York AL (9) vs. Brooklyn NL (8), 1955.
4–8 game, New York NL (2) vs. New York AL (2), 1921.

K—Fewest home runs, both clubs, one series—
1–4 game, Philadelphia AL (0) vs. Boston NL (1), 1914.
0–5 game, New York NL vs. Phila. AL, 1905.
    Chicago NL vs. Detroit AL, 1907
    Chicago NL vs. Chicago AL, 1906.
0–6 game, Chicago NL vs. Boston AL, 1918.
2–7 game, Cleveland AL (2) vs. Brooklyn NL (0), 1920.
1–8 game, Chicago AL (1) vs. Cincinnati NL (0), 1919.

L—Fewest home runs, one club, one series—
0–4 game, Philadelphia AL, 1914;
    Pittsburgh NL, 1927.
    Cincinnati NL, 1939.
0–5 game, New York NL, Philadelphia AL, 1905;
    Chicago NL, Detroit AL, 1907;
    Chicago NL, 1910; Detroit AL, 1908.
0–6 game, Chicago NL, Chicago AL, 1906;
    New York NL, 1911;
    Chicago NL, Boston AL, 1918.
0–7 game, Brooklyn NL, 1920.
0–8 game, Cincinnati NL, 1919.

M—Most home runs, one club, game—
5–New York AL, Oct. 9, 1928.

N—Most home runs, both clubs, game—
6–New York AL (4), Chicago NL (2), Oct. 1, 1932.
    New York AL (4), Brooklyn NL (2), Oct. 4, 1953.

O—Most home runs, 2 consecutive innings, one club—
4–New York AL, George H. Ruth and Henry L. Gehrig (in succession), 7th inning;
    Cedric Durst and George H. Ruth, 8th inning, Oct. 9, 1928.

P—Most home runs, one club, inning—
2–By 19 clubs. Last: New York AL, 9th inn., Oct. 15, 1964.

Q—Most home runs, both clubs, inning—
3–New York NL (2) vs New York AL (1), Oct. 11, 1921 (2d inn.).

A—Most consecutive games, home runs, one series—
7—Washington AL, 1925.

B—Most consecutive games, home runs, total series—
9—New York AL, 1952.

TOTAL BASES—CLUB

C—Most total bases one club, one series—
75—4 game, New York AL (31-1b, 6-2b, 8-hr), 1932.
80—5 game, Phila. AL (35-1b, 19-2b, 1-3b, 1-hr), 1910.
103—6 game, Brooklyn NL, (42-1b, 13-2b, 1-3b, 8-hr), 1953.
142—7 game, New York AL, 1960.
113—8 game, Boston AL (49-1b, 4-2b, 16-3b, 2-hr), 1903.

D—Most total bases, both clubs, one series—
133—4 game, New York AL (75); Chicago NL (58), 1932.
128—5 game, Phila. AL (80); Chicago NL (48), 1910.
200—6 game, Brooklyn NL(103); New York AL (97), 1953.
225—7 game, New York AL (142) vs Pittsburgh NL (83), 1960.
205—8 game, Boston AL (113); Pittsburgh NL (92), 1903.

E—Fewest total bases, one club, one series—
31—4 game, Philadelphia AL (13-1b, 9-2b), 1914.
New York AL (17—1b, 3—2b, 2—hr), 1963.
30—5 game, Philadelphia AL (20-1b, 5-2b), 1905.
40—6 game, Boston AL (27-1b, 2-2b, 3-3b), 1918.
51—7 game, Brooklyn NL (38-1b, 5-2b, 1-3b), 1920.
65—8 game, New York AL (40-1b, 7-2b, 1-3b, 2-hr), 1921.

EE—Fewest total bases, one club, game—
0—Brooklyn NL, Oct. 8, 1956.

F—Fewest total bases, both clubs, one series—
72—4 game, New York AL (31); Los Angeles NL (41), 1963.
69—5 game, Phila. AL (30); New York NL, (39), 1905.
84—6 game, Boston AL, 40); Brooklyn NL, (44) 1918.
123—7 game, Brooklyn NL, (51); Cleve. AL (72), 1920.
163—8 game, New York NL, (65); New York NL, (98), 1921.

G—Most total bases, one club, game—
32—New York AL, 15 hits (8-1b, 2-2b, 5-hr), Oct. 9, 1928.
New York AL, 19 hits (12-1b, 4-2b, 3-hr), Oct. 2, 1932.

H—Most total bases, both clubs, game—
47—N.Y. AL, 27 (4-1b, 2-2b, 1-3b, 4-hr) vs. Brooklyn NL
20 (12-1b, 2-hr), Oct. 4, 1953.

I—Most total bases, one club, inning—
17—Phil AL (7-1b, 1-2b, 2-hr), Oct. 12, 1929 (7th inn.).

LONG HITS—CLUB

J—Most long hits, one club, one series—
16—4 game, New York AL (7-2b, 9-hr), 1928.
21—5 game, Phila. AL (19-2b, 1-3b, 1-hr), 1910.
22—6 game, Brooklyn NL (13-2b, 1-3b, 8-hr), 1953.
27—7 game, New York AL (13-2b, 4-3b, 10-hr), 1960.
22—8 game, Boston AL (4-2b, 16-3b, 2-hr), 1903.

K—Most long hits, both clubs, one series—
27—4 game, N. Y. AL (14) vs. Chi. NL (13), 1932.
33—5 game, Phila. AL (21) vs. Chicago NL (12), 1910.
41—6 game, Bkn. NL (22), vs. New York AL (19), 1953.
42—7 game, New York AL (27) vs Pittsburgh NL (15), 1960.
40—8 game, Boston AL (21) vs. New York NL (19), 1912.

L—Fewest long hits, one club, one series—
4—4 game, Cincinnati NL (3-2b, 1-3b), 1939.
3—5 game, Detroit AL (1-2b, 2-3b), 1907.
5—6 game, Boston AL (2-2b, 3-3b), 1918.
6—7 game, Brooklyn NL (5-2b, 1-3b), 1920.
10—8 game, New York AL (7-2b, 1-3b, 2-hr), 1921.

M—Fewest long hits, both clubs, one series—
13—4 game, Phila. NL (7) vs. N.Y. AL (6), 1950.
L.A. NL (8) vs N.Y. AL (5) 1963.
10—5 game, Chi. NL (7) vs. Det. AL (3), 1907.
11—6 game, Chi. NL (6) vs. Bos. AL (5), 1918.
19—7 game, Cleve. AL (13) vs. Bklyn NL (6), 1920.
29—8 game, N. Y. NL (19) vs. N. Y. AL (10), 1921.

N—Most long hits, one club, game—
9—Pittsburgh (8-2b, 1-3b), Oct. 15, 1925.

O—Most long hits, both clubs, game—
11—By 3 clubs. Last: N.Y. AL (7) vs Cin. NL (4), Oct. 9, 1961.

EXTRA BASES ON LONG HITS

P—Most extra bases on long hits, one club, one series—
34—4 game, New York AL (7 on 2b, 27 on hr), 1928.
31—5 game, New York AL (21 on 2b, 2 on 3b, 8 on hr), 1953.
41—6 game, New York AL (13 on 2b, 8 on 3b, 27 on hr), 1953.
51—7 game, New York AL (13 on 2b, 8 on 3b, 30 on hr), 1960.
42—8 game, Boston AL (4 on 2b, 32 on 3b, 6 on hr), 1903.

Q—Most extra bases on long hits, both clubs, one series—
51—4 game, Chicago NL (8 on 2b, 4 on 3b, 9 on hr);
New York AL (6 on 2b, 24 on hr), 1932.
48—5 game, New York AL (21 on 2b, 2 on 3b, 8 on hr); Cincinnati NL (8 on 2b, 9 on hr) 1961.
80—6 game, N.Y. AL (6 on 2b, 8 on 3b, 27 on hr); Bkn NL
(13 on 2b, 2 on 3b, 24 on hr) 1953.
74—7 game, N.Y. AL (13 on 2b, 8 on 3b, 30 on hr);
Pittsburgh NL (11 on 2b, 12 on hr) 1960.
70—8 game, Bos. AL (4 on 2b, 32 on 3b, 6 on hr);
Pittsburgh NL (7 on 2b, 18 on 3b, 3 on hr), 1903.

WORLD SERIES CLUB BATTING RECORDS—Continued
BASES ON BALLS – CLUB

A—Most bases on balls, one club, one series—
24–4 game, New York AL, 1932.
24–5 game, New York AL, 1961.
26–6 game, New York AL, 1936.

B—Most bases on balls, both clubs, one series—
38–7 game, New York AL, 1951.
27–8 game, New York AL, 1921.

B—Most bases on balls, both clubs, one series—
38–4 game, New York AL (24) vs Chicago NL (14), 1932.
37–5 game, N. Y. AL (23) vs. Bklyn. NL (14), 1941.
51–6 game, New York NL (26) vs. New York NL (25), 1951.
68–7 game, New York AL (38) vs. Brooklyn NL (30). 1947.
49–8 game, New York NL (27) vs New York NL (22), 1921.

C—Fewest bases on balls, one club, one series—
4–4 game, Pittsburgh NL, 1927.
5–5 game, Philadelphia AL, 1905.
4–6 game, Philadelphia AL, 1911.
9–7 game, St. Louis NL, 1931.
13–8 game, Boston AL, 1903.

D—Fewest bases on balls, both clubs, one series—
15–4 game, Cinn. NL (6) vs. N. Y. AL (9), 1939.
17–5 game, Phila. AL (7) vs. N. Y. NL (8), 1913.
15–6 game, N.Y. NL (6) vs. Chi. NL (11), 1917.
30–7 game, Pitt. NL (12) vs. N.Y. AL (18), 1960.
27–8 game, Bos. AL (13) vs. Pitt. NL (14), 1903.

E—Most bases on balls, both clubs, game—
19—New York AL (11) vs. Milwaukee NL (8), Oct. 5, 1957.

F—Fewest bases on balls, both clubs, game—
11—Brooklyn NL, Oct. 5, 1956.
New York AL, Oct. 5, 1957.

STRIKEOUTS

G—Most strikeouts, one club, one series—
37–4 game, New York AL, 1963.
50–5 game, Chicago NL, 1929.
49–6 game, St. Louis AL, 1944.
56–7 game, Milwaukee NL, 1958.
45–8 game, Pittsburgh NL, 1903.

H—Most strikeouts, both clubs, one series—
62–4 game, New York AL (37) vs Los Angeles NL (25), 1963.
77–5 game, Chicago NL (50) vs. Phila. AL (27), 1929.
92–6 game, St. Louis AL (49) vs. St. Louis NL (43), 1944.
98–7 game, Milwaukee NL (56) vs N.Y. AL (42), 1958.
82–8 game, N. Y. NL (38) vs. N. Y. AL (44), 1921.

I—Fewest strikeouts, one club, one series—
7–4 game, Pittsburgh NL, 1927.

15–5 game, New York NL, 1922.
14–6 game, Chicago NL, 1918.
20–7 game, Brooklyn NL, 1920.
22–8 game, Cincinnati NL, 1919.

J—Fewest strikeouts, both clubs, one series—
32–4 game, Pittsburgh NL (7); New York AL (25), 1927.
35–5 game, Philadelphia AL (16) vs New York NL (19), 1913.
New York NL (15) vs New York AL (20), 1922.
35–6 game, Chicago NL (14); Boston AL (21), 1918.
41–7 game, Brooklyn NL (20); Cleveland AL (21), 1920.
50–8 game, Cincinnati NL (22) vs Chicago AL (28), 1919.

K—Most strikeouts, one club, 9 inning, game—
15—New York AL, 1st game, Oct. 2, 1963.
14—New York AL, 3d game, Oct. 2, 1953.
13—Chicago NL, 1st game, Oct. 8; also 2nd game, Oct. 9, 1929.

L—Most strikeouts, both clubs, game—
25—New York AL (15) vs Los Angeles NL (10), Oct. 2, 1963.

M—Fewest strikeouts, both clubs, game—
0—Pittsburgh NL vs New York AL, Oct. 13, 1960.

SACRIFICE HITS

N—Most sacrifice hits, one club, one series—
8–4 game, New York NL, 1954.
12–5 game, Boston AL, 1916.
14–6 game, Chicago NL 1906.
12–7 game, St. Louis NL, 1926.
Pittsburgh NL, 1909.
13–8 game, Cincinnati NL, 1913.

O—Fewest sacrifice hits, one club, one series—
1–4 game, Chi. NL, 1932, 38; N.Y. AL 1932, 38, 63.
0–5 game, N.Y. NL, 1937; N.Y. AL, 1941; Brk. NL, 1941; Cin. NL, 1961
0–6 game, N.Y. AL, 1923; N.Y. AL. 1951.
1–7 game, N.Y. AL, 1955.
2–8 game, Pitt. NL, 1903; Bos. AL 1903.

P—Most sacrifice hits, both clubs, one series—
12–4 game, Pitts. NL (6) vs. N.Y. AL (6), 1927.
18–5 game, Bos. AL (12) vs. Bklyn NL (6), 1916.
20–6 game, Chi. NL (14) vs. Chi. AL (6), 1906.
22–7 game, St. L. NL (12) vs. N. Y. AL (10), 1926.
20–8 game, Cinn. NL (13) vs. Chi. AL (7), 1919.

Q—Fewest sacrifice hits, both clubs, one series—
2–4 game, Chi. NL (1) vs. N. Y. AL (1), 1932, 1938.
0–5 game, New York AL (0), Brooklyn NL (0), 1941.
2–6 game, New York AL (0) vs. New York NL (2), 1951.
6–7 game, New York AL (3) vs Brooklyn NL (3), 1947.
Pittsburgh NL (3) vs New York NL (3), 1960.
New York AL (2) vs San Francisco NL (4), 1962.
6–8 game, Pittsburgh AL (4) vs Boston AL (4), 1903.

World Series Pinch Hitting Data

A—Most players used as pinch hitters, both clubs, one series—
19-4 game, Cleveland AL (16), New York NL (3), 1954.
19-5 game, Cincinnati NL (15), New York AL (4), 1961.
22-6 game, Los Angeles NL (13), Chicago NL (9), 1959.
30-7 game, Brooklyn NL (19), New York AL (11), 1947.
10-8 game, New York NL (5), Boston AL (5), 1912.

B—Most players used as pinch hitters, one club, one series—
16-4 game, Cleveland AL, 1954.
15-5 game, Cincinnati NL, 1961.
13-6 game, St. Louis AL, 1944; Los Angeles NL, 1959.
19-7 game, Brooklyn NL, 1947.
6-8 game, Chicago AL, 1919.

C—Most players used as pinch hitters, club, game—
6—Los Angeles NL, Oct. 6, 1959.

D—Fewest players, used as pinch hitters, both clubs, one series—
3-4 game, Boston NL (2), Phila. AL (1), 1914.
Cinn. NL (3), N.Y. AL (0), 1939.
2-5 game, New York NL (2), Phila. AL (0), 1905.
4-6 game, Philadelphia AL (0) vs New York NL (4), 1911.
8-7 game, Pittsburgh NL (3), Detroit AL (5), 1909.
5-8 game, Boston AL (4), Pittsburgh NL (1), 1903.
New York NL (2), New York AL (3), 1921.

E—Fewest players, used as pinch hitters, one club, one series—
0-4 game, N. Y. AL (0), 1939.
0-5 game, Philadelphia AL (0), 1910, 13.
0-6 game, Philadelphia AL, 1911.
3-7 game, Pittsburgh NL, 1909.
1-8 game, Pittsburgh NL, 1903.

F—Participating in four or more games, total series—

Blanchard, J.E., N.Y. AL	10	
Leibold, H. L., Chi.-Wash AL	8	
Lopez, Hector H., N.Y. AL	8	
Mize, John R., N.Y. AL	8	
O'Dea, J. K., Chi., St. L. NL	7	
Furillo, Carl, Brk.-L.A. NL	7	
McCormick, H. E., N.Y., NL	7	
Mitchell, Dale, ClevAL-BrkNL	7	
Howard, E. G., N.Y., AL	6	
Henriksen, Olaf, Bos. AL	6	
Bentley, John N. N.Y., NL	5	
Blades, Ray, St. Louis NL	5	
Lavagetto, H. A., Bklyn. NL	5	
Nelson, G. R., Brk.-Pitt. NL	5	
Orsatti, Ernest R., St. L., NL	5	
Paschal, Benj. N. Y., AL	5	
Secory, Frank E., Chicago NL	5	
Smith, Earl, N.Y., Pitts. NL	5	
Warwick, Carl W., St.L. NL	5	
Berra, Lawrence P., N.Y. AL	4	
Brown, Robert W., N.Y. AL	4	
Collins, Joseph P., N.Y. AL	4	
Rigney, William J., N.Y. NL	4	
Shuba, George T., Bklyn NL	4	
Skinner, Robt. R., St.L. NL	4	

G—Most times used as pinch hitters, one series—
5—Harry E. McCormick, New York NL, 1912.
Benj. Paschal, New York AL, 1926.
Frank E. Secory, Chicago NL, 1945.
Harry A. Lavagetto, Brooklyn NL, 1947.
Carl W Warwick, St.Louis NL, 1964.

H—Most strike outs, by pinch hitters, in one or more games—
3—Charles L. Hartnett, Chicago NL, Oct. 8, 9, 12, 1929.
Ralston B. Hemsley, Chicago NL, Sept. 29, Oct. 1, 2, 1932.

I—Most base hits—total series—
3—Robert W. Brown, New York AL (3), 1947.
John R. Mize, New York AL (2), 1949, (1) 1952.
J. Kenneth O'Dea, Chicago NL (1) 1935, St. Louis NL (1) 1942, (1) 1944.
James L. Rhodes, New York NL (3), 1954.
Carl A. Furillo, Bklyn. NL (2) 1947, L.A. NL (1) 1959.
Robert H. Cerv, N.Y. AL, 1955, 56, 60.
John E. Blanchard, N.Y. AL, 1960, 61, 64.
Carl W. Warwick, St.L. NL, 1964 (3).

J—Home run by pinch hitter—
2—Charles A. Essegian, Jr., Los Angeles, NL, 7th inn. Oct. 2 and 9th inn. Oct. 8, 1959.
1—Lawrence P. Berra, New York AL, 7th inn., Oct. 2, 1947.
John R. Mize, New York AL, 9th inn., Oct. 3, 1952.
George Shuba, Brooklyn NL, 6th inn., Sept. 30, 1953.
James L. Rhodes, New York NL, 10th inn., Sept. 29, 1954.
Henry Majeski, Cleveland AL, 5th inn., Oct. 2, 1954.
Robert H. Cerv, New York AL, 7th inn., Oct. 2, 1955.
Elston G. Howard, New York AL, 9th inn., Oct. 5, 1960.
John E. Blanchard, New York AL, 8th inn., Oct. 7, 1961.

K—Pinch hitter winning game with home run—
James L. Rhodes, New York NL, 10th inn., Sept. 29, 1954.

L—Most runs batted in by pinch hitter, one game—
3—James L. Rhodes, New York NL, Sept. 29, 1954.
Henry Majeski, Cleveland AL, Oct. 2, 1954.

M—Most runs batted in by pinch hitter, series—
6—James L. Rhodes, New York NL, 4-game series, 1954.

N—Most runs batted in by pinch hitter, consecutive times at bat—
6—James L. Rhodes, New York NL, (3), Sept. 29; (1), Sept. 30; (2), Oct. 1, 1954.

O—Most total bases by pinch hitter, series—
6—James L. Rhodes, New York NL, 2 on 1b, 4 on hr, 1954.

P—Player winning game on first time at bat—
James L. Rhodes, New York NL, 3-run home run in 10th inn., Sept. 29, 1954.

World Series Pitchers—1903 to Date

(Won and Lost Record)

Pitcher, Club, Year	W	L
Ford, N.Y.AL, 1950, 53, 55-58, 60-64..	10	8
Ruffing, N.Y. AL, 1932, 36-39, 41-42 ..	7	2
Reynolds, N.Y. AL, 1947, 49-53	7	2
Gomez, N.Y. AL, 1932, 36-38	6	0
Bender, Phil. AL, 1905, 10-11, 13-14 ..	6	4
Hoyt, N.Y.-Phil. AL, 1921-22, 26-28; 31	6	4
Coombs, Phil.AL-Brk.NL, 1910-11; 16	5	0
Pennock, N.Y. AL, 1923, 26-27	5	0
Raschi, N.Y. AL, 1949-53	5	3
Brown, Chi. NL, 1906-08, 10	5	4
Mathewson, N.Y. NL, 1905, 11-13 ...	5	5
Pearson, N.Y. AL, 1936-39	4	0
Bridges, Det. AL, 1934-35, 40	4	1
Brecheen, St.L. NL, 1943-44, 46	4	1
Lopat, N.Y. AL, 1949, 51-53	4	1
Podres, Brk.-L.A. NL, 1953,55; 59, 63	4	1
Grove, Phil. AL, 1930-31	4	2
Hubbell, N.Y. NL, 1933, 36-37	4	2
Burdette, Mil. NL, 1957-58	4	2
Larsen, N.Y. AL-S.F. NL, 1955-58; 62	4	2
Koufax, L.A. NL, 1959, 63, 65	4	3
Earnshaw, Phil. AL, 1929-31	4	3
Spahn, Bos.-Mil. NL, 1948; 57-58 ...	4	3
Turley, N.Y. AL, 1955-58, 60	4	3
Nehf, N.Y. NL, 1921-24	4	4
Adams, Pitt. NL, 1909	3	0
Ruth, Bos. AL, 1916, 18	3	0
Zachary, Wash.-N.Y. AL, 1924;·28 ..	3	0
Pipgras, N.Y. AL, 1927-28, 32	3	0
Dinneen, Bos. AL, 1903	3	1
Overall, Chi. NL, 1907-08, 10	3	1
Wood, Bos. AL, 1912	3	1
Shore, Bos. AL, 1915-16	3	1
Faber, Chi. AL, 1917	3	1
Haines, St.L. NL, 1926, 28, 30	3	1
Hallahan, St.L. NL, 1930-31	3	1
Drysdale, L.A. NL, 1959, 63, 65	3	1
Phillippe, Pitt. NL, 1903	3	2
Alexander, Phil.-St.L. NL, 1915; 26, 28	3	2
Coveleskie, Clev-Wash.AL, 1920; 25 .	3	2
Borowy, N.Y. AL-Chi. NL, 1943; 45..	3	2
Mullin, Det. AL, 1907-09	3	3
Johnson, Wash. AL, 1924-25	3	3
Mays, Bos.-N.Y. AL, 1916, 18; 21-22..	3	4
Grimes, Brk.-St.L. NL, 1920; 30-31 ..	3	4
Walsh, Chi. AL, 1906	2	0
Reulbach, Chi. NL, 1906-07	2	0
Rudolph, Bos. NL, 1914	2	0
James, Bos. NL, 1914	2	0
Foster, Bos. AL, 1915	2	0
Leonard, Bos. AL, 1915-16	2	0
Kerr, Chi. AL, 1919	2	0
Eller, Cin. NL, 1919	2	0
Barnes, N.Y. NL, 1921	2	0
Ryan, N.Y. NL, 1922-23	2	0
Moore, N.Y. AL, 1927, 32	2	0
P. Dean, St.L. NL, 1934	2	0
Murphy, N.Y. AL, 1939, 41	2	0
Beazley, St.L. NL, 1942	2	0
Russo, N.Y. AL, 1941, 43	2	0
Shea, N.Y. AL, 1947	2	0
Sherry, L.A. NL, 1959	2	0
Law, Pitt. NL, 1960	2	0
Haddix, Pitt. NL, 1960	2	0
Roe, Brk. NL, 1949, 52-53	2	1
Young, Bos. AL, 1903	2	1
McQuillan, N.Y. NL, 1922-24	2	1
Aldridge, Pitt. NL, 1925, 27	2	1
Warneke, Chi. NL, 1932, 35	2	1
Hadley, N.Y. AL, 1936-37, 39	2	1
Lanier, St.L. NL, 1942-44	2	1
Newhouser, Det. AL, 1945	2	1
Page, N.Y. AL, 1947, 49	2	1
Bouton, N.Y. AL, 1963-64	2	1
Gibson, St.L. NL, 1964	2	1
Grant, Minn. AL 1965	2	1
Douglas, Chi.-N.Y. NL, 1918; 21 ,..	2	2

Pitcher, Club, Year	W	L
Kremer, Pitt. NL, 1925, 27	2	2
Schumacher, N.Y. NL, 1933, 36-37 ..	2	2
J. Dean, St.L.-Chi. NL, 1934; 38 ...	2	2
Walters, Cin. NL, 1939-40	2	2
Newsom, Det.-N.Y. AL, 1940; 47 ...	2	2
Chandler, N.Y. AL, 1941-43	2	2
Casey, Brk. NL, 1941, 47	2	2
Sain, Bos. NL-N.Y. AL, 1948; 52-53..	2	2
Lemon, Clev. AL, 1948, 54	2	2
Erskine, Brk. NL, 1952-53, 56	2	2
Labine, Brk. NL, 1953, 55-56	2	2
Craig, Brk-LA-StL.NL, 1955-56; 59; 64	2	2
Cicotte, Chi. AL, 1917, 19	2	3
M. Cooper, St.L. NL, 1942-44	2	3
Derringer, StL-Cin.NL, 1931; 39-40 .	2	4
Terry, N.Y. AL, 1960-62	2	4
Plank, Phil. AL, 1905, 11, 13-14	2	5
Marquard, N.Y.-Brk. NL, 1911-13; 16, 20	2	5
Bush, Phil.-Bos.-N.Y. AL, 1913-14; 18; 22-23	2	5
Rowe, Det. AL, 1934-35, 40	2	5
Maddox, Pitt. NL, 1909	1	0
Crandall, N.Y. NL, 1911	1	0
Bedient, Bos. AL, 1912	1	0
Schupp, N.Y. NL, 1917	1	0
Mails, Clev. AL, 1920	1	0
Mogridge, Wash. AL, 1924	1	0
Ehmke, Phil. AL, 1929	1	0
Rommel, Phil. AL, 1929	1	0
Luque, N.Y. NL, 1933	1	0
Whitehill, Wash. AL, 1933	1	0
White, St.L. NL, 1942	1	0
Donnelly, St.L. NL, 1944	1	0
Kramer, St.L. AL, 1944	1	0
Trucks, Det. AL, 1945	1	0
Passeau, Chi. NL, 1945	1	0
Johnson, Bos. AL, 1946	1	0
Ferriss, Bos. AL, 1946	1	0
Munger, St.L. NL, 1946	1	0
Dobson, Bos. AL, 1946	1	0
Bearden, Clev. AL, 1948	1	0
Gromek, Clev. AL, 1948	1	0
Ferrick, N.Y. AL, 1950	1	0
Hearn, N.Y. NL, 1951	1	0
McDonald, N.Y. AL, 1953	1	0
Grissom, N.Y. NL, 1954	1	0
Antonelli, N.Y. NL, 1954	1	0
Gomez, N.Y. NL, 1954	1	0
Liddle, N.Y. NL, 1954	1	0
Bessent, Brk. NL, 1956	1	0
Kucks, N.Y. AL, 1956	1	0
Sturdivant, N.Y. AL, 1956	1	0
Arroyo, N.Y. AL, 1961	1	0
Daley, N.Y. AL, 1961	1	0
Stafford, N.Y. AL, 1962	1	0
Sadecki, St.L, N.L., 1964	1	0
McGinnity, N.Y. NL, 1905	1	1
Altrock, Chi. AL, 1906	1	1
White, Chi. AL, 1906	1	1
Benton, N.Y. NL, 1917	1	1
Tyler, Chi. NL, 1918	1	1
Ring, Cin. NL, 1919	1	1
Ruether, Cin. NL-N.Y. AL, 1916; 26..	1	1
Bagby, Clev. AL, 1920	1	1
Scott, N.Y. AL, 1922-23	1	1
Ferguson, Wash. AL, 1925	1	1
Bush, Chi. NL, 1929, 32	1	1
Walberg, Phil. AL, 1929-30	1	1
Auker, Det. AL, 1934	1	1
Wyatt, Brk. NL, 1941	1	1
Galehouse, St.L. AL, 1944	1	1
Koslo, N.Y. NL, 1951	1	1
Byrne, N.Y. AL, 1955	1	1
Duren, N.Y. AL, 1958	1	1
Shaw, Chi. AL, 1959	1	1
Jay, Cin. NL, 1961	1	1

(Won and Lost Record)—Continued

Pitcher, Club, Year	W	L
Pierce, S.F. NL, 1962	1	1
Stottlemyre, N.Y. AL, 1964	1	1
Osteen, L.A. NL, 1965	1	1
Smith, Brk NL, 1916, 20	1	2
Vaughn, Chi. NL, 1918	1	2
Crowder, Wash.-Det. AL, 1933; 34-35	1	2
Bonham, N.Y. AL, 1941-43	1	2
Trout, Det. AL, 1940, 45	1	2
Branca, Brk. NL, 1947, 49	1	2
Black, Brk. NL, 1952	1	2
Loes, Brk. NL, 1952-53, 55	1	2
Maglie, N.Y.-Brk. NL, 1951; 56	1	2
Wynn, Clev.-Chi. AL, 1954; 59	1	2
Sanford, S.F. NL, 1962	1	2
Kaat, Minn. AL, 1965	1	2
Pfeister, Chi. NL, 1906-08	1	3
Tesreau, N.Y. NL, 1912-13	1	3
Sallee, N.Y.-Cin. NL, 1917; 19	1	3
Bentley, N.Y. NL, 1923-24	1	3
Shawkey, Phil-NY AL, 1914; 21, 23, 26	1	3
Donovan, Det. AL, 1907-09	1	4
Hughes, Bos. AL, 1903	0	1
Kennedy, Pitt. NL, 1903	0	1
Coakley, Phil. AL, 1905	0	1
Siever, Det. AL, 1907	0	1
Camnitz, Pitt. NL, 1909	0	1
Leifield, Pitt. NL, 1909	0	1
Willis, Pitt. NL, 1909	0	1
McIntire, Chi. NL, 1910	0	1
Ames, N.Y. NL, 1911	0	1
Demaree, N.Y. NL, 1913	0	1
Mayer, Phil. NL, 1915	0	1
Chalmers, Phil. NL, 1915	0	1
Rixey, Phil. NL, 1915	0	1
Pfeffer, Brk. NL, 1916	0	1
Anderson, N.Y. NL, 1917	0	1
Fisher, Cin. NL, 1919	0	1
Caldwell, Clev. AL, 1920	0	1
Cadore, Brk. NL, 1920	0	1
Quinn, N.Y. AL, 1921	0	1
Marberry, Wash. AL, 1924	0	1
Barnes, N.Y. NL, 1924	0	1
Yde, Pitt. NL, 1925	0	1
Shocker, N.Y. AL, 1926	0	1
Reinhart, St.L. NL, 1926	0	1
Miljus, Pitt. NL, 1928	0	1
Blake, Chi. NL, 1929	0	1
Rhem, St.L. NL, 1930	0	1
Johnson, St.L. NL, 1931	0	1
May, Chi. NL, 1932	0	1
Stewart, Wash. AL, 1933	0	1
Weaver, Wash. AL, 1933	0	1
Russell, Wash. AL, 1933	0	1
Carleton, Chi. NL, 1935	0	1
Bryant, Chi. NL, 1935	0	1
Turner, Cin. NL, 1940	0	1
Davis, Brk. NL, 1941	0	1
Donald, N.Y. AL, 1942	0	1
Wilks, St.L. NL, 1944	0	1
Potter, St.L. AL, 1944	0	1
Muncrief, St.L. AL, 1944	0	1
Jakucki, St.L. AL, 1944	0	1
Overmire, Det. AL, 1945	0	1
Wyse, Chi. NL, 1945	0	1
Prim, Chi. NL, 1945	0	1
Pollet, St.L. NL, 1946	0	1
Dickson, St.L. NL, 1946	0	1
Hughson, Bos. AL, 1946	0	1
Klinger, Bos. AL, 1946	0	1
Lombardi, Brk. NL, 1947	0	1
Bevens, N.Y. AL, 1947	0	1
Gregg, Brk. NL, 1947	0	1
Bickford, Bos. NL, 1948	0	1
Voiselle, Bos. NL, 1948	0	1
Konstanty, Phil. NL, 1950	0	1
Roberts, Phil. NL, 1950	0	1
Meyer, Phil. NL, 1950	0	1
Miller, Phil. NL, 1950	0	1
Garcia, Clev. AL, 1954	0	1
Spooner, Brk. NL, 1955	0	1
Morgan, N.Y. AL, 1956	0	1
Johnson, Mil. NL, 1957	0	1
Buhl, Mil. NL, 1957	0	1
Shantz, N.Y. AL, 1957	0	1
Rush, Mil. NL, 1958	0	1
Donovan, Chi. AL, 1959	0	1
Staley, Chi. AL, 1959	0	1
Mizell, Pitt. NL, 1960	0	1
Purkey, Cin. NL, 1961	0	1
Coates, N.Y. AL, 1962	0	1
O'Dell, S.F. NL, 1962	0	1
Schultz, St.L. NL, 1964	0	1
Mikkelsen, N.Y. AL, 1964	0	1
Simmons, St.L. NL, 1964	0	1
Pascual, Minn. AL, 1965	0	1
Leever, Pitt. NL, 1903	0	2
O'Brien, Bos. AL, 1912	0	2
Jones, Bos.-N,Y, AL, 1918; 23	0	2
Meadows, Pitt. NL, 1925, 27	0	2
Walker, St.L. NL, 1934	0	2
French, Chi. NL, 1935	0	2
Melton, N.Y. NL, 1937	0	2
Lee, Chi. NL, 1938	0	2
Thompson, Cin. NL, 1939-40	0	2
Brazle, St.L. NL, 1943, 46	0	2
Harris, Bos. AL, 1946	0	2
Feller, Clev. AL, 1948	0	2
Barney, Brk. NL, 1947, 49	0	2
Jansen, N.Y. NL, 1951	0	2
Grim, N.Y. AL, 1955, 57	0	2
Ditmar, N.Y. AL, 1960	0	2
Friend, Pitt. NL, 1960	0	2
O'Toole, Cin. NL, 1961	0	2
Downing, N.Y. AL, 1963-64	0	2
Williams, Chi. AL, 1919	0	3
Malone, Chi. NL-N.Y. AL, 1929; 36	0	3
Root, Chi. NL, 1929, 32, 35	0	3
Fitzsimmons, N.Y. NL, 1933, 36	0	3
Summers, Det. AL, 1908-09	0	4
Sherdel, St.L. NL, 1926, 28	0	4
Newcombe, Brk. NL, 1949, 55-56	0	4

CLUB FIELDING RECORDS

A—Highest percentage, fielding, one series—
.993—4 game, New York AL, 1963.
1.000—5 game, New York AL, 1937.
.996—6 game, Phil. AL, 1931; St. Louis NL, 1944.
.992—7 game, Phil. AL, 1931; N.Y. AL, 1955; Brk. NL, 1956.
.984—8 game, New York NL, 1921.

B—Lowest percentage, fielding, one series—
.949—4 game, New York AL, 1932.
.942—5 game, Brooklyn NL, 1916.
.938—6 game, New York NL, 1911.
.934—7 game, Detroit AL, 1909.
.944—8 game, Pittsburgh NL, 1903.

C—Most putouts, one club, one series—
117—4 game, Boston NL, 1914.
147—5 game, Boston AL, 1916.
167—6 game, Philadelphia AL, 1911.
201—7 game, Washington AL, 1924.
222—8 game, Boston AL, 1912.

D—Most putouts for outfielders, game—
15—New York NL, rf. 7; cf. 6; lf. 2; Oct. 14, 1912.
Boston AL, rf. 5; cf. 5; lf. 5; Oct. 6, 1948.

E—Most putouts, outfielders, both clubs, game—
23—Pitt. N.L. (13) vs New York A.L. (10), Oct. 6, 1927.

F—Fewest chances offered, outfielders, game—
0—New York N.L., Sept. 30, 1936.

G—Fewest putouts for outfielders, game, 1 club—
0—New York NL vs New York AL, Oct. 5, 1921.
New York NL vs New York AL, Sept. 30, 1936.

H—Most assists, one club, one series—
67—4 game, Philadelphia AL, 1914.
90—5 game, Boston AL, 1916.
99—6 game, Chicago AL, 1906.
99—7 game, Washington AL, 1924.
115—8 game, Chicago AL, 1919.

I—Fewest assists, one club, one series—
28—4 game, New York AL, 1928.
40—5 game, Philadelphia AL, 1929.
Brooklyn NL, 1949.
41—6 game, Philadelphia AL, 1930.
57—7 game, Minnesota AL, 1965.
96—8 game, Pittsburgh NL, 1903.
Cincinnati NL, 1919.

J—Most assists, one club, game—
21—Boston AL, Sept. 9, 1918.
Chicago AL, Oct. 7, 1917.

K—Fewest assists, one club, game—
3—St. Louis NL, Oct. 5, 1934.   New York AL, Oct. 16, 1962.
Boston NL, Oct. 6, 1948.   Minnesota AL, Oct. 6, 1965.

L—Fewest assists, both club, game—
8—Philadelphia AL (5), St. Louis NL (3), Oct. 2, 1930.

M—Most errors, one club, one series—
8—4 game, New York AL, 1932.   19—7 game, Detroit AL, 1909.
13—5 game, Brooklyn NL, 1916.   18—8 game, Pittsburgh NL, 1903.
16—6 game, New York NL, 1911.

N—Fewest errors, one club, one series—
1—4 game, New York NL, 1963.
0—5 game, New York AL, 1937.
1—6 game, Bos. AL, 1918; St.L. NL, 1944; N.Y. AL, 1953.
2—7 game, Phila. AL, 1931; N.Y. AL, 1955-56, Bklyn. NL, 1956.
5—8 game, New York NL, 1921.

O—Most errors, one club, game—
6—Chicago AL, Oct. 13, 1906; Oct. 13, 1917.
Pittsburgh NL, Oct. 12, 1909.

P—Most errorless games, one club, one series—
5—New York NL, 8 games, 1921.
Philadelphia AL, 7 games, 1931.
New York AL, 5 games, 1937, 6 games, 1953, 7 games, 1955.
Boston AL, 6 games, 1918.
St. Louis NL, 6 games, 1944.
Brooklyn NL, 7 games, 1956.

Q—Most errorless games, both clubs, one series—
9—Philadelphia AL (5), vs. St. Louis NL (4), 7 games, 1931.

R—Most successive errorless games, one club, one series—
5—Philadelphia AL, Oct. 1, 2, 5, 6, 7, 1931, 7 games.
New York AL, Oct. 6, 7, 8, 9, 10, 1937, 5 games.
New York AL, Sept. 29, 30, Oct. 1, 2, 3, 1955, 7 games.

S—Most double plays, both clubs, one series—
19—Brooklyn NL 12, New York AL 7, 7 games, 1955.

T—Fewest double plays, both clubs, one series—
4—Philadelphia AL (2), New York NL (2), 5 games, 1905.
Philadelphia AL (2), New York NL (2), 6 games, 1911.
New York NL (2), Cleveland AL (2), 4 games, 1954.

U—Most double plays, one club, one series—
12—Brooklyn NL, 7 games, 1955.

V—Fewest double plays, one club, one series—
1—New York NL, 1913.   Brooklyn NL, 1949.
New York AL, 1932, 1961.   Philadelphia NL, 1950.
Cincinnati NL, 1939.   Los Angeles NL, 1963.

W—Most double plays, one club, game—
4—Philadelphia AL, Oct. 9, 1914.   Cleveland AL, Oct. 11, 1948.
Boston AL, Sept. 7, 1916.   New York AL, Oct. 8, 1951.
Chicago NL, Sept. 29, 1932.

X—Most double plays, both clubs, game—
6—Brooklyn NL (3) vs New York AL (3), Sept. 29, 1955

INDIVIDUAL BASE RUNNING

C—Most stolen bases, individual, total series—
14—Edward T. Collins, Phila.-Chic. AL, 1910 (4), 1911 (2), 1913 (3), 1914 (1), 1917 (3), 1919 (1).

D—Most stolen bases, individual, one series—
2–4 game, Charles Deal, Walter J. Maranville, Bos. NL, 1914.
6–5 game, James F. Slagle, Chicago NL, 1907.
3–6 game, Edward T. Collins, Chicago AL, 1917.
6–7 game, John P. Wagner, Pittsburgh, 1909.
4–8 game, Joshua Devore, New York NL, 1912.

E—Most times stealing home base, player, game—
1—William F. Dahlen, New York NL, 5th inning, Oct. 12, 1905.
George S. Davis, Chicago NL, 3rd inning, Oct. 13, 1906.
James F. Slagle, Chicago NL, 7th inning, Oct. 11, 1907.
Tyrus R. Cobb, Detroit AL, 3d inning, Oct. 9, 1909.
Charles L. Herzog, New York NL, 1st inning, Oct. 14, 1912.
Charles J. Schmidt, Boston NL, 8th inning, Oct. 9, 1914.
Michael J. McNally, N. Y. AL, 5th inning, Oct. 5, 1921.
Robert W. Meusel, New York NL, 8th inning, Oct. 6, 1921.
Robert W. Meusel, New York AL, 6th inning, Oct. 7, 1928.
Monford Irvin, New York NL, 1st inning, Oct. 4, 1951.
Jack R. Robinson, Brooklyn NL, 8th inning, Sept. 28, 1955.
J. Timothy McCarver, St.Louis NL, 4th inning, Oct. 15, 1964.

CLUB BASE RUNNING

F—Most stolen bases, one club, one series—
9–4 game, Boston NL, 1914.
18–5 game, Chicago NL, 1907.
8–6 game, Chicago NL, 1906.
18–7 game, Pittsburgh NL, 1909.
12–8 game, New York NL, 1912.

G—Most stolen bases, both clubs, one series—
11–4 game, Boston NL (9), Phila. AL (2), 1914.
25–5 game, Chicago NL (18), Detroit AL (7), 1907.
14–6 game, Chicago NL (8), Chicago AL (6), 1906.
24–7 game, Pittsburgh NL (18), Detroit AL (6), 1909.
18–8 game, New York NL (12), Boston AL (6), 1912.

H—Fewest stolen bases, both clubs, one series—
1–4 game, N. Y. AL (0), Cinn. (1), 1939.
Cleveland AL (0), New York NL (1), 1954.
1–5 game, Chic. NL, (1), Phila. AL (0), 1929; N. Y. NL (0), Wash. AL (1), 1933; N. Y. NL (1), N. Y. AL (0), 1937.
Cin. NL(0), N. Y. AL (1), 1961.
0–6 game, St. Louis NL, St. Louis AL, 1944.
1–7 game, Cinn. NL (1), Det. AL (0), 1940.
12–8 game, Cincinnati NL (7), Chicago AL (5). 1919.

I—Fewest stolen bases, one club, one series—
0–4 game, Pitt. NL, 1927; N.Y. AL, 1932, 39, 63; Chi. NL, 1938; Clev. AL, 1954.
5 game, Phil. AL, 1929; N.Y. NL, 1933; N.Y. AL, 1937; Brk. NL, 1941; St. L. NL, 1942; Cin. NL, 1961.
6 game, Phil. AL, 1930; N.Y. NL, 1936; St. L. NL, 1944; St. L. AL, 1944; N.Y. AL, 1951.
7 game, Phil. AL, 1931; Det. AL, 1940; N.Y. AL, 1960.
5–8 game, Bos. AL, 1903; Chi. AL, 1919.

J—Most stolen bases, club, game—
7—Chicago NL, Oct. 8, 1907 (10 inns.).
5—New York NL, Oct. 12, 1905.
Chicago NL, Oct. 10, 1906; Oct. 9, 1907.

CLUB LEFT ON BASE

K—Most left on bases, one club, one series—
37–4 game, Cleveland AL, 1954.
42–5 game, New York AL, 1941.
51–6 game, Detroit AL, 1935; St. Louis NL, 1944.
64–7 game, Detroit AL, 1934.
55–8 game, Boston AL, 1912.

L—Most left on bases, both clubs, one series—
65–4 game, Cleveland AL (37), New York NL (28), 1954.
76–5 game, New York NL (39), Washington AL (37), 1933.
96–6 game, Brooklyn NL (49), New York AL (47), 1953.
116–7 game, New York NL (59), Washington AL (57), 1924.
108–8 game, Boston AL (58), Pittsburgh NL (50), 1903.
Boston AL (55), New York NL (53), 1912.

M—Fewest left on bases, one club, one series—
16–4 game, New York AL, 1939.
24–5 game, New York NL, 1913.
29–6 game, Philadelphia AL, 1911.
36–7 game, Minnesota AL, 1965.
43–8 game, New York AL, 1921.

N—Fewest left on bases, both clubs, one series—
39–4 game, Cincinnati NL (23), New York AL (16), 1939.
54–5 game, Philadelphia AL (30), New York NL (24), 1913.
60–6 game, Philadelphia AL (29), New York NL (31), 1911.
82–7 game, Brooklyn NL (39), Cleveland AL (43), 1920.
Brooklyn NL (42), New York AL (40), 1956.
San Francisco NL (39), New York AL (43), 1962.
97–8 game, New York AL (54), New York NL (43), 1921.

O—Most left on bases, one club, game—
14—Chicago NL, Oct. 18, 1910. Milwaukee NL, Oct. 5, 1957.

P—Most left on bases, both clubs, game—
23—Chicago NL (14), Philadelphia AL (9), Oct. 18, 1910.

Q—Fewest left on bases, one club, game—
0–Brooklyn NL, Oct. 8, 1956. Los Angeles NL, Oct. 6, 1963.

R—Fewest left on bases, both clubs, game—
3–New York AL (3), Brooklyn (0), Oct. 8, 1956.

GENERAL CLUB RECORDS
SERIES AND SEASON PLAYED

A—Highest percentage games won, one series—
1.000—Chicago NL, 1907, 5 game (1 tie).
Boston NL, 1914, 4 game.
New York NL, 1922, 5 game (1 tie) 1954.
New York AL, 1927-28, 1932, 1938, 1939, 1950, 4 game.
Los Angeles NL, 1963, 4 game.

B—Lowest percentage games won, one series—
.000—Detroit AL, 1907, 5 game (1 tie).
Philadelphia AL, 1914, 4 game.
New York AL, 1922, 5 game (1 tie); 1963, 4 game.
Pittsburgh NL, 1927, 4 game.
St. Louis NL, 1928, 4 game.
Chicago NL, 1932, 1938, 4 game.
Cincinnati NL, 1939, 4 game.
Philadelphia NL, 1950, 4 game.
Cleveland AL, 1954, 4 game.

C—Club playing most series—
29—New York AL.
14—New York NL.

D—Club winning most games—
99—New York AL (29 series).
39—New York NL (14 series).

E—Club losing most games—
65—New York AL (29 series).
41—New York NL (14 series).

F—Most consecutive games won, one series—
4—Boston AL, 1903, 15.
Chicago NL, 1907.
Boston NL, 1914.
Cleveland AL, 1920.
New York NL, 1922, 54.
New York AL, 1927-28, 32, 38-39, 50.
St. Louis NL, 1942.
Los Angeles NL, 1963.

G—Most consecutive games lost, one series—
4—Pittsburgh NL, 1903, 27.
Detroit AL, 1907.
Philadelphia AL, 1914.
Philadelphia NL, 1915, 50.
Brooklyn NL, 1920.
New York AL, 1922, 42, 63.
St. Louis NL, 1928.
Chicago NL, 1932, 38.
Cincinnati NL, 1939.
Cleveland AL, 1954.

H—Most consecutive games won, total series—
12—New York (Yankees) AL, 1927, 1928, 1932.
8—New York NL, 1921, 1922 (1 tie), 1923.

I—Most consecutive games lost, total series—
8—Philadelphia NL, 1915, 1950.
New York AL, 1921, 1922 (1 tie), 1923.

J—Series winners—
4 game series, Boston NL, 1914, New York NL, 1954.
New York AL, 1927-28, 32, 38-39, 50, 58, 61, 62.
Los Angeles NL, 1963.

5 game series, New York NL, 1905, 1922 (1 tie), 1933.
Chicago NL, 1907 (1 tie), 1908.
Philadelphia AL, 1910, 1913, 1929.
Boston AL, 1915, 1916.
New York AL, 1937, 1941, 1943, 1949, 1961.
St. Louis NL, 1942.

6 game series, Chicago AL, 1906, 1917.
Philadelphia AL, 1911, 1930.
Boston AL, 1918.
New York AL, 1923, 1936, 1951, 1953.
Detroit AL, 1935.
St. Louis NL, 1944.
Cleveland AL, 1948.
Los Angeles NL, 1959.

7 game series, Cleveland AL, 1920.
Pittsburgh NL, 1909, 1925, 1960.
Washington AL, 1924.
St.Louis NL, 1926, 1931, 1934, 1946, 1964.
Cincinnati, 1940.
Detroit AL, 1945.
New York AL, 1947, 1952, 1956, 1958, 1962.
Brooklyn NL, 1955.
Milwaukee NL, 1957.
Los Angeles NL, 1965.

8 game series, Cincinnati, NL, 1919.
Boston AL, 1912 (1 tie).
Boston AL, 1903.
New York NL, 1921.

K—Most times winners—total series—
20—New York AL.
7—St.Louis NL.

L—Most times losers—total series—
9—New York NL.
New York AL.

GENERAL CLUB RECORDS—Continued

A—Series losers—
4 game series, Philadelphia AL, 1914.
  Pittsburgh NL, 1927.
  St. Louis NL, 1928.
  Chicago NL, 1932, 1938.
  Cincinnati NL, 1939.
  Philadelphia NL, 1950.
  Cleveland AL, 1954.
  New York AL, 1963.
5 game series, Philadelphia AL, 1905.
  Detroit AL, 1907 (1 tie), 1908.
  Chicago NL, 1910, 1929.
  New York NL, 1913, 1937.
  Philadelphia NL, 1915.
  Brooklyn NL, 1916, 1941, 1949.
  New York AL, 1922 (1 tie), 1942.
  Washington AL, 1933.
  St. Louis NL, 1943.
  Cincinnati NL, 1961.
6 game series, Chicago NL, 1906, 1918, 1935.
  New York NL, 1911, 1917, 1923, 1936, 1951.
  St. Louis NL, 1930.
  St. Louis AL, 1944.
  Boston NL, 1948.
  Brooklyn NL, 1953.
  Chicago AL, 1959.
7 game series, Brooklyn NL, 1920, 1947, 1952, 1956.
  Detroit AL, 1909, 1934, 1940.
  New York NL, 1924.
  Washington AL, 1925.
  New York AL, 1926, 1955, 1957, 1960, 1964.
  Philadelphia AL, 1931.
  Chicago NL, 1945.
  Boston AL, 1946.
  Milwaukee NL, 1958.
  San Francisco NL, 1962.
  Minnesota AL, 1965.
8 game series, Chicago AL, 1919.
  New York NL, 1912 (1 tie).
  New York AL, 1921.
  Pittsburgh NL, 1903.

B—Largest score in a game—
(22)—N. Y. AL (18) vs. N. Y. NL (4) 2d g, Oct. 2, 1936.

C—Longest game by innings, game—
14—Bost AL vs. Brooklyn NL (2-1), Oct. 9, 1916.

D—Longest game, by time—
3:28—Detroit AL vs. Chicago NL, Oct. 8, 1945 (12 inns.)
3:26—Brooklyn NL vs. New York AL, Oct. 5, 1956 (9 inns.).

E—Shortest game, by time—
1:25—Chicago NL vs. Detroit AL, Oct. 14, 1908.

F—Most no-hit games, one series—
1—New York AL (D. J. Larsen) vs Brooklyn NL, Oct. 8, 1956.

G—Most 1-hit games, one series—
1—Chicago NL (E. M. Reulbach) vs. Chicago AL, Oct. 10, 1906.
  Chicago NL (C. W. Passeau) vs. Detroit AL, Oct. 5, 1945.
  New York AL (F. C. Bevens) lost vs. Brooklyn NL, Oct. 3, 1947.

H—Most 2-hit games, one series—
2—Chicago AL, Oct. 11 and Chicago NL, Oct. 12, 1906.
  St. Louis NL, Oct. 5 and Phila. AL, Oct. 6, 1931.

I—Most 3-hit games, one series—
3—Cincinnati NL, October 3, 1919.
  Chicago AL, Oct. 5 and 6, 1919.

J—Most games, extra base hits only, one series—
2—Philadelphia AL vs. St. Louis NL, 1st game (1-2b, 2-3b, 2-hr) Oct. 1, and 6th game (5-2b, 2-hr), Oct. 8, 1930.

K—Most shutout games won, 1903 to date—
77—National League 43, American League 34.

L—Most shutout games, one series, both clubs—
5—New York NL (4), Philadelphia AL (1), 1905.

M—Largest score, shutout game—
12-0—New York AL vs Pittsburgh NL, Oct. 12, 1960.

N—Lowest score shutout game—
1-0—See table page 131.

O—Most consecutive innings, shutting out opponents, one series—
28—N. Y. NL, Oct. 10 (1), Oct. 12 (9), Oct. 13 (9), Oct. 14 (9), 1905.

P—Series, without any shutout games—
18—4 game series, 1927, 1928, 1932, 1938, 1954.
  5 game series, 1910, 1915, 1916, 1929, 1937, 1941.
  6 game series, 1911, 1936, 1951, 1953.
  7 game series, 1924, 1947, 1964.
  8 game series, 1912.

Q—Most tie games, one series—
1—Chicago NL, vs. Detroit AL (12 innings), 1907.
  New York NL vs. Boston AL (11 innings), 1912.
  New York NL vs. New York AL (10 innings), 1922.

R—Longest tie game-12 innings—
  Chicago NL vs. Detroit AL (3-3), Oct. 8, 1907.

GENERAL SERIES RECORDS

S—Won & Lost—

American League	W	L
Boston	5	1
Chicago	2	2
Cleveland	2	1
Detroit	2	5
Minnesota	0	1
New York	20	9
Philadelphia	5	3
St. Louis	0	1
Washington	1	2

National League	W	L
Boston		1-1
Brooklyn		1-8
Chicago		2-8
Cincinnati		2-2
Los Angeles		3-0
Milwaukee		1-1
New York		5-9
Philadelphia		0-2
Pittsburgh		3-2
St. Louis		7-3
San Francisco		0-1

GENERAL SERIES RECORDS—Continued

Manager and number of times contending—

NATIONAL

Manager	Times
Alston, Walter E., Brk.-L.A.	5
Bush, Owen J., Pittsburgh	4
Chance, Frank L., Chicago	4
Clarke, Fred C., Pittsburgh	2
Dark, Alvin R., S.F.	1
Dressen, Charles W., Bklyn.	2
Durocher, Leo E., Bkn-N.Y.	3
Dyer, Edwin H., St. Louis	1
Frisch, Frank F., St. Louis	1
Grimm, Charles J., Chicago	3
Haney, Fred G., Milwaukee	2
Hartnett, Charles L., Chicago	1
Hornsby, Rogers, St. Louis	1
Hutchinson, Frederick, Cin.	1
Keane, John J., St.L.	1
McCarthy, Jos. V., Chicago	1
McGraw, John J., New York	9
McKechnie, Wm. B., Pitts., St. L., Cincinnati	4
Mitchell, Fred F., Chicago	1
Moran, Pat. J., Phila., Cinn.	2
Murtaugh, Daniel E., Pitt.	1
Robinson, Wilbert, Brooklyn	2
Sawyer, Edwin M., Phila.	1
Shotton, Burton E., Bklyn.	2
Southworth, William H., St.L.-Bos.	4
Stallings, George T., Boston	1
Street, Charles E., St. Louis	2
Terry, William H., N. Y.	3

AMERICAN

Manager	Times
Baker, Delmar D., Detroit	1
Barrow, Edward G., Boston	1
Berra, Lawrence P., N.Y.	1
Boudreau, Louis, Cleveland	1
Carrigan, William F., Boston	2
Cochrane, Gordon S., Detroit	2
Collins, James J., Boston	1
Cronin, Jos. E., Wash.-Bos.	2
Gleason, William, Chicago	1
Harris, Stanley R., W.-N.Y.	3
Houk, Ralph G., N.Y.	3
Huggins, Miller J., N. Y.	6
Jennings, Hugh, Detroit	3
Jones, Fielder, Chicago	1
Lopez, Alfonso R., Clev.-Chi.	2
Mack, Connie, Phila.	8
McCarthy, Jos. V., N. Y.	8
Mele, Sabath A., Minnesota	1
O'Neill, Stephen F., Detroit	1
Rowland, Clarence H., Chi.	1
Sewell, J. Luther, St. Louis	1
Speaker, Tris E., Cleveland	1
Stahl, J. Garland, Boston	1
Stengel, Charles D., N.Y.	10

Manager winning most World Series—
7—J. V. McCarthy, N.Y. AL, 1932-36-37-38-39-41-43.
C. D. Stengel, N.Y. AL, 1949-50-51-52-53-56-58.

UMPIRES WHO HAVE OFFICIATED IN WORLD SERIES

Umpire	Lg.	Years
Ballanfant, Lee	NL	1940 46 51 55
Barlick, Albert J.	NL	1946 50 51 54 58 62
Barr, George	NL	1937 42 48 49
Basil, Stephen	AL	1937
Berry, Charles F.	AL	1946 50 54 58 62
Boggess, Lynton R.	NL	1952 56 60
Boyer, James M.	AL	1947
Brennan, Wm.	NL	1911
Byron, Wm. J.	NL	1914
Burkhart, W. Kenneth	NL	1962 64
Chill, Ollie P.	AL	1921
Chylak, Nester	AL	1957 60
Conlan, John B.	NL	1945 50 54 57 61
Connolly, T. H.	AL	1903 08 10 11 13 16 20 24
Crawford, Henry C.	NL	1961 63
Dascoli, Frank	NL	1953 59
Dinneen, W. H.	AL	1911 14 16 20 24 26 29 32
Dixon, Hal H.	NL	1959
Donatelli, August J.	NL	1955 57 61
Dunn, T. P.	AL	1944
Egan, John	NL	1913
Evans, W. G.	AL	1909 12 15 17 19 23
Flaherty, John F.	AL	1955 58 65
Geisel, Harry	AL	1930 34 36
Gore, Arthur	NL	1941 47 52
Gorman, Thomas	NL	1951 53
Grieve, Wm.	AL	1956 58 63
Hart, E. (Bob)	AL	1923
Hildebrand, G.	AL	1914 18 22 26
Honochick, G. J.	AL	1952 55 60 62
Hubbard Cal.	AL	1938 42 46 49
Hurley, Edwin H.	AL	1949 53 59 65
Jackowski, Wm.	NL	1958 60
Johnstone, J. E.	NL	1906 09
Jorda, Louis D.	NL	1945 49
Klem, W. J.	NL	1908 11 12 13 14 15 17 1918 20 22 24 26 29 31 32 34 40
Kolls, Louis	AL	1938
Landes, Stanley A.	NL	1960 62
McCormick, W. J.	NL	1922 25
McGowan, W. A.	AL	1928 31 35 39 41 44 47 50
McKinley, William F.	AL	1950 57 64
Magerkurth, G. L.	NL	1932 36 42 47
Moran, Charles B.	NL	1927 29 33 38
Moriarty, G.	AL	1921 25 30 33 35
Nallin, R. F.	AL	1919 23 27 31
Napp, L.A.	AL	1954 56 63
O'Day, H.	NL	1903 05 07 08 10 16 18 20 23 26
O'Loughlin, F.	AL	1906 09 12 15 17
Ormsby, E. T.	AL	1927 33 37 40
Owens, C. B.	AL	1918 22 25 28 34
Paparella, A. J.	AL	1948 51 57 63
Passarella, A. M.	AL	1945 49 52
Pipgras, G.	AL	1944
Pinelli, R. A. C.	NL	1939 41 47 48 52 56
Pfirman, C.	NL	1928 33 36
Quigley, E. C.	NL	1916 19 21 24 27 35
Reardon, J. E.	NL	1930 34 39 43 49
Rice, John L.	AL	1959 63
Rigler, Jos. W.	NL	1910 12 13 15 17 19 21 25 28 30
Rommel, Edwin A.	AL	1943 47
Rue, Jos. W.	AL	
Runge, Edward P.	AL	1956 61
Sears, John	NL	1938 44
Secory, Frank E.	NL	1957 59 64
Sheridan, John	AL	1905 07 08 10
Smith, Vincent A.	AL	1955
Smith, W. Alaric	NL	1964
Soar, A. Henry	AL	1953 56 62 64
Stark, Albert D.	NL	1931 35
Stevens, John W.	AL	1951 54 60
Stewart, Robert W.	AL	1961 65
Stewart, Wm.	NL	1937 48 53
Sudol, Edward L.	NL	1965
Summers, William R.	AL	1936 39 42 45 48 51 55 59
Umont, Frank	AL	1958 61
Vangrafflan, Roy P.	AL	1929 32
Vargo, Edward P.	NL	1965
Venzon, Anthony	NL	1963 65
Warneke, L.	NL	1954

GENERAL SERIES RECORDS—Continued

A—Most players participating, one series, club—
24-4 game, Cleveland AL, 1954.
25-5 game, Brooklyn NL, 1949.
24-6 game, New York NL, 1951; Los Angeles NL, 1959.
26-7 game, Detroit AL, 1945; Boston AL, 1946.
19-8 game, Chicago AL, 1919; New York AL, 1921.

B—Most players, both clubs, one series—
39-4 games, Cleveland AL (24), New York NL (15), 1954.
45-5 game, Brooklyn (25) vs. New York AL (20), 1949.
45-6 game, New York NL (24) vs New York AL (21), 1951.
    Los Angeles NL (24) vs Chicago AL (21), 1959.
51-7 game, Detroit AL (26), Chicago NL (25), 1945.
36-8 game, Chicago AL (19) vs. Cinn. NL (17), 1919.

C—Fewest players, club, one series—
13-4 game, Los Angeles NL, 1963.
12-5 game, N.Y. NL, 1905; Phil. AL, 1910, 13.
14-6 game, Chicago NL, 1906; Phila. AL, 1911.
16-7 game, Detroit AL, 1909.
13-8 game, New York NL, 1921; Boston AL, 1903.

D—Fewest players, both clubs, one series—
31-4 game, Boston NL (15), Phila. AL (16), 1914.
25-5 game, New York NL (12), Phila. AL (13), 1905.
29-6 game, New York NL (15), Phila. AL (14), 1911.
33-7 game, Detroit AL (16), Pitt. NL (17), 1909.
27-8 game, Pittsburgh NL (14), Boston AL (13), 1903.

E—Most players, club, game—
21—New York AL, 6th game, Oct. 5, 1947 (9 inns.).
    Cincinnati NL, 5th game, Oct. 9, 1961 (9 inns.).

F—Most players, both clubs, game—
38—New York AL (21), Brooklyn NL (17), 6th g., Oct. 5, 1947
    Det. AL (19), Chic. NL (19), 6th g., Oct. 8, 1945 (12 inns.).

G—Largest attendance, one series—
251,507—4 game series, Cleveland AL—New York NL, 1954.
277,312—5 game series, Cardinals—Yankees, 1943.
420,784—6 game series, Chicago AL—Los Angeles NL, 1959.
394,712—7 game series, Milwaukee NL—New York AL, 1957.
269,976—8 game series, Giants—Yankees, 1921.

H—Smallest attendance, one series—
111,009—4 game series, Boston NL—Philadelphia AL, 1914.
62,232—5 game series, Chicago NL—Detroit AL, 1908.
99,845—6 game series, Chicago AL—Chicago NL, 1906.
145,295—7 game series, Pittsburgh NL—Detroit AL, 1909.
100,429—8 game series, Pittsburgh NL—Boston AL, 1903.

I—Largest attendance, game—
92,706—Chicago AL at Los Angeles NL, Coliseum, Oct. 6, 1959.

J—Smallest attendance, game—
6,210—Det. AL vs. Chi. NL, at Det. 5th game, Oct. 14, 1908.

K—Total attendance, 1903-to date
15,054,990 (366 games).

L—Largest gate receipts, one series—
$1,995,189.09—4 game series, L.A. NL-N.Y. AL, 1963.
1,480,059.95—5 game series, N.Y. AL-Cin. NL, 1961.
2,628,809.44—6 game series, N.Y. NL-Phil. AL, 1959.
2,975,041.60—7 game series, L.A. NL-Minn. AL, 1965.
900,233.00—8 game series, N.Y. NL-N.Y. AL, 1921.

M—Smallest receipts, one series—
$225,739.00—4 game series, Bos. NL-Phil. AL, 1914.
68,436.81—5 game series, N.Y. NL-Phil. AL, 1905.
106,550.00—6 game series, Chi. AL-Chi. NL, 1906.
188,302.50—7 game series, Pitt. NL-Det. AL, 1909.
50,000.00—8 game series, Pitt. NL-Bos. AL, 1903.

N—Largest receipts, game—
$552,774.77—Chi. AL at L.A. NL, Oct. 6, 1959.

O—Smallest receipts, game—
$8,348.00—N.Y. NL at Phil. AL, Oct 12, 1905.

P—Largest receipts, players' pool—
$1,017,546.43—L.A. NL vs N.Y. AL, 1963 (4 games).

Q—Smallest receipts, players' pool—
$27,394.20—N.Y. NL vs Phil. AL, 1905 (5 games).

R—Largest receipts, winning player—
$12,794.00—L.A. NL, 1963 (4 games).

S—Smallest receipts, winning player—
$1,102.51—Bos. AL, 1918 (6 games).

T—Largest receipts, losing player—
$7,874.32—N.Y. AL, 1963 (4 games).

U—Smallest receipts, losing player—
$382.00—Phil. AL, 1905 (5 games).

GENERAL SERIES RECORDS—Continued
LOW HIT GAMES

Perfect no hit game—
1956—Oct. 8: Donald J. Larsen, New York AL.

Games of one hit—
1906—Oct. 10: E. M. Reulbach, Chicago NL.
1945—Oct. 5: C. W. Passeau, Chicago NL.
1947—Oct. 3: F. C. Bevens, New York AL (lost).

Games of two hits—
1906—Oct. 11: Walsh, Chicago AL; Oct. 12: Brown, Chicago NL.
1913—Oct. 11: Plank, Philadelphia AL.
1914—Oct. 10: James, Boston NL.
1921—Oct. 6: Hoyt, New York AL.
1931—Oct. 5: Grimes, St. L. NL; Oct. 6: Earnshaw, Phila. AL.
1939—Oct. 5: Pearson, New York AL.
1944—Oct. 4: M. Cooper, St. Louis NL (lost).
1948—Oct. 6: Feller, Cleveland AL (lost).
1949—Oct. 5: Reynolds, New York AL.
1950—Oct. 4: Raschi, New York AL.
1958—Oct. 5: Spahn, Milwaukee NL.
1961—Oct. 4: Ford, New York AL.
1963—Oct. 6: Ford and Reniff, New York AL (lost).

Games of three hits—
1908—Oct. 14: Overall, Chicago NL.
1910—Oct. 17: Bender, Philadelphia AL.
1911—Oct. 17: Coombs, Philadelphia AL (11 innings).
1912—Oct. 12: Bedient, Boston AL.
1915—Oct. 9: Foster, Boston AL; Oct. 11: Leonard, Boston AL.
1916—Oct. 12: Shore, Boston AL.
1918—Sept. 12: Mays, Boston AL.
1919—Oct. 3: Kerr, Chi. AL; Oct. 4: Ring, Cinn. NL, Oct. 6: Eller, Cinn. NL.
1920—Oct. 7: S. Smith, Bklyn. NL; Oct. 12: Mails, Cleve. AL.
1921—Oct. 9: Nehf, New York NL.
1923—Oct. 14: Bush, New York AL.
1926—Oct. 2: Pennock, New York AL.
1927—Oct. 7: Pennock, New York AL.
1928—Oct. 4: Hoyt, New York AL.
1930—Oct. 6: Earnshaw and Grove, Philadelphia AL.

1931—Oct. 2: Hallahan, St. Louis NL.
1940—Oct. 3: Walters, Cinn. NL.; Oct. 6: Newsom, Det. AL.
1944—Oct. 9: Lanier and Wilks, St. Louis NL.
1952—Oct. 2: Raschi, New York AL.
1956—Oct. 10: Kucks, New York AL.
1962—Oct. 5: Sanford, San Francisco NL.
Oct. 15: Pierce, San Francisco NL.
1963—Oct. 5: Drysdale, Los Angeles NL.
1965—Oct. 14: Koufax, Los Angeles NL.

Games of four hits—
1903—Oct. 2: Dinneen, Bos. AL; Oct. 3: Phillippe, Pitts. NL;
Oct. 13: Dinneen, Boston AL.
1905—Oct. 9: Mathewson, N. Y. NL; Oct. 10: Bender, Phila. AL; Oct. 12: Mathewson, N. Y. NL; Oct. 13: Plank, Phila. AL.
1906—Oct. 9: Brown, Chicago NL; Oct. 9: Altrock, Chicago AL; Oct. 11: Pfiester, Chicago NL.
1908—Oct. 11: Overall, Chi. NL; Oct. 13: Brown, Chi. NL.
1911—Oct. 16: Marquard and Crandall, N. Y. NL; Oct. 26: Bender, Phila. AL.
1918—Sept. 9 Tyler and Douglas, Chicago NL.
1919—Oct. 2: Williams, Chi. AL; Oct. 6: Williams and Mayer, Chi. AL.
1921—Oct. 13: Nehf, New York NL.
1922—Oct. 6: J. Scott, New York NL.
1923—Oct. 12: Jones, New York AL.
1924—Oct. 9: Nehf and Ryan, New York NL.
1926—Oct. 3: Alexander, St. Louis NL.
1928—Oct. 5: Pipgras, New York AL.
1930—Oct. 5: Haines, St. Louis NL.
1936—Oct. 5: Fitzsimmons, New York NL.
1941—Oct. 4: Russo, N. Y. AL; Oct. 6: Bonham, N. Y. AL.
1946—Oct. 7: Brecheen, St. L. NL; Oct. 11: Dobson, Bos. AL.
1947—Sept. 30: Branca, Behrman, Casey, Brooklyn NL (lost);
Oct. 4: Shea, New York AL.
1948—Oct. 6: Sain, Boston NL.
1952—Oct. 4: Reynolds, New York AL;
Oct. 4: Black and Rutherford, Brooklyn NL.
1954—Sept. 30: Wynn and Mossi, Cleveland AL.
Oct. 1; Gomez and Wilhelm, New York NL.
1956—Oct. 9: Turley, New York AL (10 inn., lost).
1957—Oct. 9: Turley, New York AL.
1958—Oct. 4: Rush and McMahon, Milwaukee NL (lost).
1960—Oct. 8: Ford, New York AL.
1961—Oct. 5: Jay, Cincinnati NL.
1962—Oct. 16: Terry, New York AL.
Oct. 5: Stafford, New York AL.
1963—Oct. 5: Bonton and Reniff, New York AL (lost).
1965—Oct. 11: Koufax, Los Angeles NL.

HEAVY BATTING GAMES

Thirteen hits—
1911—Oct. 26: Philadelphia AL 13, New York NL **4.**
1920—Oct. 10: Brooklyn NL 13, Cleveland AL 12.
1921—Oct. 11: New York NL 13, New York AL **7.**
1923—Oct. 13: New York AL 13, New York NL 13.
1924—Oct. 7: Washington AL 13, New York NL **6.**
  —Oct. 8: New York NL 13, Washington AL **9.**
1925—Oct. 12: Pittsburgh NL 13, Washington AL **8.**
1926—Oct. 9: St. Louis NL 13, New York AL **8.**
1934—Oct. 3: St. Louis NL 13, Detroit AL 8
1940—Oct. 4: Detroit AL 13, St. Louis NL 10.
  —Oct. 6: Detroit AL 13, Cincinnati NL 10.
1945—Oct. 3: Chicago NL 13, Detroit NL 3.
1947—Oct. 5: Brooklyn NL 13, New York AL 13.
1953—Oct. 5: New York AL 13, Brooklyn NL **8.**
1959—Oct. 8: Los Angeles NL (13), Chicago AL **(6).**
1960—Oct. 5: New York AL 13, Pittsburgh NL 19.
  Oct. 6: Pittsburgh NL 13, New York AL 19.
  Oct. 13: New York AL 13, Pittsburgh NL 11.

Fourteen hits—
1903—Oct. 7: Boston AL 14, Pittsburgh NL **6.**
1906—Oct. 14: Chicago AL 14, Chicago NL **7.**
1908—Oct. 10: Chicago NL 14, Detroit AL 10.
1910—Oct. 18: Philadelphia AL 14, Chicago NL **8.**
1917—Oct. 13: Chicago AL 14, New York NL 12.
1919—Oct. 1: Cincinnati NL 14, Chicago AL 14.
1923—Oct. 14: New York NL 14, New York AL **3.**
1926—Oct. 6: New York AL 14, St. Louis NL 14.
1953—Oct. 4: Brooklyn NL 14, New York AL **11.**
1965—Oct. 11: Los Angeles NL 14, Minnesota AL 4.

Fifteen hits—
1910—Oct. 20: Philadelphia AL 15, Chicago NL **6.**
1925—Oct. 15: Pittsburgh NL 15, Washington NL **11.**
1928—Oct. 9: New York AL 15, St. Louis NL 11.
1929—Oct. 12: Philadelphia AL 15, Chicago NL 10.
1947—Oct. 1: New York AL 15, Brooklyn NL **9.**
1947—Oct. 5: New York AL 15, Brooklyn NL 12.
1958—Oct. 2: Milwaukee NL 15, New York AL **7.**
1961—Oct. 9: New York AL 15, Cincinnati NL 11.

Sixteen hits—
1912—Oct. 15: New York NL 16, Boston AL **8.**
1919—Oct. 9: Cincinnati NL 16, Chicago AL 10.
1960—Oct. 8: New York AL 16, Pittsburgh NL 4.

Seventeen hits—
1934—Oct. 7: St. Louis NL 17; Detroit AL **6.**
1936—Oct. 4: New York NL 17, New York NL **6.**
  —Oct. 6: New York AL 17, New York NL **9.**
1960—Oct. 12: New York AL 17, Pittsburgh NL **7.**

Nineteen hits—
1932—Oct. 2: New York AL 19, Chicago NL 9.
1960—Oct. 6: New York AL 19, Pittsburgh NL 13.

Twenty hits—
1921—Oct. 7: New York NL 20, New York AL 8.
1946—Oct. 10: St. Louis NL 20, Boston AL 9.

SHUTOUT GAMES

1 to 0 games—
1905—Oct. 13: McGinnity, N. Y. NL vs Plank, Phila., AL.
1906—Oct. 12: Brown, Chi. NL vs Altrock, Chi. AL.
1914—Oct. 10: James, Boston AL vs Plank, Phila. AL.
1918—Sept. 9: Ruth, Boston AL vs Vaughn, Chicago NL.
1920—Oct. 11: Mails, Cleveland AL vs Smith, Brooklyn NL.
1921—Oct. 13: Nehf, New York NL vs Hoyt, New York AL.
1923—Oct. 12: Nehf, New York NL vs Jones, Bush, N. Y. AL.
1948—Oct. 6: Sain, Boston NL vs Feller, Cleveland AL.
1949—Oct. 5: Reynolds, N. Y. AL vs Newcombe, Bklyn NL.
1950—Oct. 6: Roe, Bklyn NL vs Raschi, N. Y. AL.
1956—Oct. 9: Raschi, N.Y. AL vs Konstanty, Phila. NL.
1957—Oct. 7: Labine, Bklyn. vs Turley, N. Y. AL (10 inn.).
1959—Oct. 6: Burdette, Milw. NL vs Ford, Turley N.Y. AL.
  Oct. 6: Shaw, Pierce, Donovan, Chi. AL vs Koufax, Williams, L.A. NL.
1962—Oct. 16: Terry, N.Y. AL vs Sanford, O'Dell, S.F. NL.
1963—Oct. 5: Drysdale, L.A. NL vs Bouton, Reniff, N.Y. AL.

2 to 0 games—
1905—Oct. 14: Mathewson, N. Y. NL vs Bender, Phila. AL.
1907—Oct. 12: Brown, Chicago NL vs Mullin, Detroit AL.
1908—Oct. 14: Overall, Chicago NL vs Donovan, Detroit AL.
1917—Oct. 6: Benton, New York NL vs Cicotte, Chicago AL.
1919—Oct. 4: Ring, Cincinnati NL vs Cicotte, Chicago AL.
1930—Oct. 6: Earnshaw, Grove, Phila. AL vs Grimes, St.L. NL.
1931—Oct. 2: Hallahan, St. L. NL vs Earnshaw, Phila. AL.
1942—Oct. 3: White, St. Louis NL vs Chandler, Breuer, Turner, New York AL.
1943—Oct. 11: Chandler, New York AL vs M. Cooper, Lanier, Dickson, St. Louis NL.
1944—Oct. 8: M. Cooper, St. L. NL vs Galehouse, St. L. AL.
1948—Oct. 8: Bearden, Cleveland AL vs Bickford, Voiselle, Barrett, Boston NL.
1952—Oct. 4: Reynolds, New York AL vs Black, Rutherford, Brooklyn NL.
1955—Oct. 4: Podres, Brooklyn NL vs. Byrne, Grim, Turley, New York AL.
1956—Oct. 8: Larsen, N. Y. AL vs Maglie, Bklyn.
1961—Oct. 4: Ford, N.Y. AL vs O'Toole, Brosnan, Cin. NL.
1962—Oct. 5: Sanford, S.F. NL vs Terry, Daley, N.Y. AL.
1965—Oct. 14: Koufax, L.A. NL vs 5 p. Minn. AL.

WORLD SERIES RECORDS—Continued

3 to 0 games—

1903—Oct. 3: Dinneen, Boston AL vs Leever, Pittsburgh NL.
1903—Oct. 12: Dinneen, Boston AL vs Phillippe, Pitts. NL.
1905—Oct. 9: Mathewson, N. Y. NL vs Plank, Phila. AL.
1905—Oct. 10: Bender, Phila AL vs McGinnity, Ames, N. Y. NL.
1906—Oct. 11: Walsh, Chicago AL vs Pfiester, Chicago NL.
1908—Oct. 13: Brown, Chi. NL vs Summers, Winter, Det. AL.
1913—Oct. 8: Mathewson N.Y. NL vs Plank, Phila. AL. (10 inn.)
1918—Sept. 10: Vaughn, Chi. NL vs Jones, Bos. AL.
1919—Oct. 3: Kerr, Chi. AL vs Fisher, Luque, Cinn. NL.
1920—Oct. 6: Grimes, Bklyn NL vs Bagby, Uhle, Cleve. AL.
1920—Oct. 12: Coveleskie, Clev. AL vs Grimes, Mamaux, Bk. NL.
1921—Oct. 5: Mays, N. Y. AL vs Douglas, J. Barnes, N. Y. NL.
1922—Oct. 6: Hoyt, New York AL vs Nehf, New York NL.
1931—Oct. 6: Earnshaw, Phila. AL, vs Johnson, St. Louis NL.
1935—Oct. 2: Warneke, Chicago NL vs Rowe, Detroit AL.
1945—Oct. 5: Passeau, Chi. NL vs Overmire, Benton, Det. AL.
1946—Oct. 7: Brecheen, St. L. NL vs Harris, Dobson, Bos. AL.
1958—Oct. 5: Spahn, Milw. NL vs Ford, Kucks, Dickson, N.Y. AL.

4 to 0 games—

1925—Oct. 11: Johnson, Wash. AL vs Yde, Morrison, Adams, Pittsburgh NL.
1926—Oct. 5: Haines, St.L. NL vs Ruether, Shawkey, Thomas, New York AL.
1933—Oct. 5: Whitehill, Wash. AL vs Fitzsimmons, Bell, N. Y. NL.
1939—Oct. 5: Pearson, N. Y. AL vs Walters, Cinn. NL.
1940—Oct. 7: Walters, Cinn. NL vs 3 p. Detroit AL.
1946—Oct. 9: Ferris, Boston AL vs Dickson, Wilks, St. L. NL.
1958—Oct. 4: Larsen and Duren, N.Y. AL vs Rush, McMahon, Milw. NL.
1965—Oct. 9: Osteen, L.A. NL vs 3 p. Minn. AL.

5 to 0 games—

1909—Oct. 12: Mullin, Det. AL vs Leifield. Phillippe, Pitts. NL.
1917—Oct. 11: Schupp, N. Y. NL vs Faber, Danforth, Chi. AL.
1919—Oct. 6: Eller, Cinn. NL vs Williams, Mayer, Chi. AL.
1930—Oct. 4: Hallahan, St.L.NL vs Walberg, Shores, Phil. AL.
1957—Oct. 10: Burdette, Milwaukee NL vs 5 p. N.Y. AL.

7 to 0 games—

1958—Oct. 6: Turley, New York AL vs 3 p. Mil. NL.
1961—Oct. 8: Ford and Coates, New York AL vs 3 p. Cin. NL.
1965—Oct. 11: Koufax, L.A. NL vs 3 p. Minn. AL.

8 to 0 games—

1909—Oct. 16: Adams, Pitts. NL vs Donovan, Mullin, Det. AL.
1940—Oct. 6: Newsom, Det. AL vs 4 p. Cincinnati NL.

9 to 0 games—

1905—Oct. 12: Mathewson, N. Y. NL vs Coakley, Phila. AL.
1945—Oct. 3: Borowy, Chicago NL vs 4 p. Detroit AL.
1956—Oct. 10: Kucks, N. Y. AL vs 5 p. Brooklyn NL.

10 to 0 games—

1960—Oct. 8: Ford, N.Y. AL vs Pittsburgh NL.

11 to 0 games—

1934—Oct. 9: J. Dean, St. Louis NL vs 6 p. Detroit AL.
1959—Oct. 1: Wynn, Staley, Chi. AL vs 5 p. L.A. NL.

12 to 0 games—

1960—Oct. 12: Ford, N.Y. AL vs Pittsburgh NL.

DRAWN AND HIGH SCORE GAMES

Drawn games—

1907—Oct. 8: Chicago NL 3, Detroit AL 3, 12 innings.
1912—Oct. 8: Boston AL 6, New York NL 6, 11 innings.
1922—Oct. 5: Giants 3, Yankees 3, 10 innings.

High score games (9 innings), 10 or more runs—

1903—Oct. 7: Boston AL 11, Pittsburgh NL 2
1908—Oct. 10: Chicago NL 10: Detroit AL 6.
1910—Oct. 20: Philadelphia AL 12, Chicago NL 5,
1911—Oct. 26: Philadelphia AL 13, New York NL 2.
1912—Oct. 15: New York NL 11, Boston AL 4,
1919—Oct. 3: Cincinnati NL 10, Chicago AL 5.
1921—Oct. 5: Giants NL 13, Yankees AL 5,
1926—Oct. 6: New York NL 10, St. Louis NL 5.
Oct. 9: St. Louis NL 10, New York AL 2.
1929—Oct. 12: Philadelphia AL 10, Chicago NL 8.
1932—Sept. 28: New York AL 12, Chicago NL 6.
Oct. 2: New York AL 13, Chicago NL 6.
1934—Oct. 6: Detroit AL 10, St. Louis NL 4.
Oct. 9: St. Louis NL 11, Detroit AL 0.
1936—Oct. 2: New York AL 18, New York NL 4.
Oct. 9: New York AL 13, New York NL 5.
1946—Oct. 10: St. Louis NL 12, Boston AL 3.
1947—Oct. 1: New York AL 10, Brooklyn NL 3.
1948—Oct. 9: Boston NL 11, Cleveland AL 5.
1949—Oct. 9: New York AL 10, Brooklyn NL 6.
1951—Oct. 6: New York AL 13, New York NL 1.
1956—Oct. 5: Brooklyn NL 13, New York AL 8.
1957—Oct. 2: Milwaukee NL 13, New York AL 5.
1958—Oct. 1: Milwaukee NL 13, New York AL 5.
1959—Oct. 1: Chicago AL 11, Los Angeles NL 0.
1960—Oct. 6: New York AL 16, Pittsburgh NL 3.
Oct. 8: New York AL 10, Pittsburgh NL 0.
Oct. 12: New York AL 12, Pittsburgh NL 0.
1961—Oct. 13: Pittsburgh NL 10, New York AL 9.
Oct. 9: New York AL 13, Cincinnati NL 5.

WORLD SERIES RECORDS—Continued

EXTRA INNING GAMES

Fourteen innings—
1916—Oct. 9: Boston AL 2, Brooklyn NL 1.

Twelve innings—
1907—Oct. 8: Chicago NL 3, Detroit AL 3 (tie).
1914—Oct. 12: Boston NL 5, Philadelphia AL 4.
1924—Oct. 4: New York NL 4, Washington AL 3.
  Oct. 10: Washington AL 4, New York NL 3.
1934—Oct. 4: Detroit AL 3, St. Louis NL 2.
1945—Oct. 8: Chicago NL 8, Detroit AL 7.

Eleven innings—
1911—Oct. 17: Philadelphia AL 3, New York NL 2.
1912—Oct. 9: New York NL 6, Boston AL 6 (tie).
1933—Oct. 6: New York NL 2, Washington AL 1.
1935—Oct. 4: Detroit AL 6, Chicago NL 5.
1944—Oct. 5: St. Louis NL 3, St. Louis AL 2.
1952—Oct. 5: Brooklyn NL 6, New York AL 5.

Ten innings—
1910—Oct. 22: Chicago NL 4, Philadelphia AL 3.
1911—Oct. 25: New York NL 4, Philadelphia AL 3.
1912—Oct. 16: Boston AL 3, New York NL 2.
1913—Oct. 8: New York NL 3, Philadelphia AL 0.
1919—Oct. 7: Chicago AL 5, Cincinnati NL 4.
1922—Oct. 5: New York NL 3, New York AL 3 (tie).
1926—Oct. 7: New York AL 3, St. Louis NL 2.
1933—Oct. 7: New York NL 4, Washington AL 3.
1936—Oct. 4: New York NL 5, New York AL 4.
1939—Oct. 8: New York NL 7, Cincinnati NL 4.
1946—Oct. 6: Boston AL 3, St. Louis NL 2.
1950—Oct. 5: New York AL 2, Philadelphia NL 1.
1954—Sept. 29: New York NL 5, Cleveland AL 2.
1956—Oct. 9: Brooklyn NL 1, New York AL 0
1957—Oct. 6: Milwaukee NL 7, New York AL 5.
1958—Oct. 1: New York AL 4, Milwaukee NL 5.
  Oct. 8: New York AL 4, Milwaukee NL 3.
1964—Oct. 12: St.Louis NL 5, New York AL 2.

Most consecutive extra inning games, one series—
2—New York NL (2) vs Washington AL (1) 11 innings, Oct. 6, 1933.
  New York NL (4) vs Washington AL (3) 10 innings, Oct. 7, 1933.

WORLD SERIES WINNERS

American League—
20—New York, 1923, 1927, 1928, 1932, 1936, 1937, 1938, 1939, 1941, 1943, 1947, 1949, 1950, 1951, 1952, 1953, 1956, 1958, 1961, 1962.
5—Boston, 1903, 1912, 1915, 1916, 1918.
  Philadelphia, 1910, 1911, 1913, 1929, 1930.
2—Chicago, 1906, 1917.
  Detroit, 1935, 1945.
  Cleveland, 1920, 1948.
1—Washington, 1924.

National League—
7—St.Louis, 1926, 1931, 1934, 1942, 1944, 1946, 1964.
5—New York, 1905, 1921, 1922, 1933, 1954.
3—Pittsburgh, 1909, 1925, 1960.
  Los Angeles, 1959, 1963, 1965.
2—Chicago, 1907, 1908
  Cincinnati, 1919, 1940.
1—Boston, 1914.
  Brooklyn, 1955.
  Milwaukee, 1957.

WORLD SERIES LOSERS

American League—
9—New York 1921, 1922, 1926, 1942, 1955, 1957, 1960, 1963, 1964.
5—Detroit, 1907, 1908, 1909, 1934, 1940.
3—Philadelphia, 1905, 1914, 1931.
2—Washington, 1925, 1933.
  Chicago, 1919, 1959.
1—St. Louis, 1944.
  Boston, 1946.
  Cleveland, 1954.
  Minnesota, 1965.

National League—
9—New York, 1911, 1912, 1913, 1917, 1923, 1924, 1936, 1937, 1951.
8—Chicago, 1906, 1910, 1918, 1929, 1932, 1935, 1938, 1945.
  Brooklyn, 1916, 1920, 1941, 1947, 1949, 1952, 1953, 1956.
3—St. Louis, 1928, 1930, 1943.
2—Pittsburgh, 1903, 1927.
  Philadelphia, 1915, 1950.
  Cincinnati, 1939, 1961.
1—Boston, 1948.
  Milwaukee, 1958.
  San Francisco, 1962.

WORLD SERIES WINNERS AND RECEIPTS

Year	National League	No Series in 1904	American League	Games Won	Attend-ance	Receipts	Players' Total	1 Winning Share	1 Losing Share
1903	Pittsburgh		*Boston	3–5	100,429	$ 50,000.00	$ 32,612.00	$1,182.00	$1,316.25
1905	*New York		Philadelphia	4–1	91,723	68,436.81	27,394.20	1,142.00	382.22
1906	Chicago		*Chicago	2–4	99,845	106,550.00	33,401.70	1,874.63	439.50
1907	*Chicago		Detroit	4–0†	78,068	101,728.50	54,933.39	2,142.85	1,945.96
1908	*Chicago		Detroit	4–1	62,232	94,975.50	46,114.92	1,317.58	870.00
1909	*Pittsburgh		Detroit	4–3	145,295	188,302.50	66,924.90	1,825.22	1,274.76
1910	Chicago		*Philadelphia	1–4	124,222	173,980.00	79,071.93	2,062.79	1,375.16
1911	New York		*Philadelphia	2–4	179,851	342,364.50	127,910.61	3,654.58	2,436.39
1912	New York		*Boston	3–4†	252,037	490,833.00	147,572.28	4,024.68	2,566.47
1913	New York		*Philadelphia	1–4	151,000	325,980.00	135,164.16	3,246.36	2,164.22
1914	*Boston		Philadelphia	4–0	111,009	225,739.00	121,898.94	2,812.28	2,031.65
1915	Philadelphia		*Boston	1–4	143,351	320,361.50	144,899.55	3,780.25	2,520.17
1916	Brooklyn		*Boston	1–4	162,859	385,590.50	162,927.45	3,910.26	2,834.82
1917	New York		*Chicago	2–4	186,654	425,878.00	152,888.58	3,669.32	2,442.21
1918	Chicago		*Boston	2–4	128,483	179,619.00	69,527.70	1,102.51	671.09
1919	*Cincinnati		Chicago	5–3	236,928	722,414.00	260,349.66	5,207.07	3,254.36
1920	Brooklyn		*Cleveland	2–5	178,737	564,800.00	214,882.74	4,168.00	2,419.60
1921	*Giants		Yankees	5–3	269,976	900,233.00	292,522.23	5,265.00	3,510.00
1922	*New York		New York	4–0†	185,947	605,475.00	247,309.71	4,545.71	2,842.86
1923	New York		*New York	2–4	301,430	1,063,815.00	368,783.04	6,143.49	4,112.88
1924	New York		*Washington	3–4	283,665	1,093,104.00	331,092.51	5,959.64	3,820.29
1925	*Pittsburgh		Washington	4–3	282,848	1,182,854.00	339,644.19	5,332.72	3,734.60
1926	*St. Louis		New York	4–3	328,051	1,207,864.00	372,300.51	5,584.51	3,417.75
1927	Pittsburgh		*New York	0–4	201,705	783,217.00	399,440.67	5,782.24	3,985.47
1928	St. Louis		*New York	0–4	199,072	777,290.00	419,736.60	5,813.20	4,181.30
1929	Chicago		*Philadelphia	1–4	190,490	859,494.00	388,086.66	5,620.57	3,782.01
1930	St. Louis		*Philadelphia	2–4	212,619	953,772.00	323,865.00	5,038.07	3,536.68
1931	*St. Louis		Philadelphia	4–3	231,567	1,030,723.00	320,303.46	4,467.59	3,023.09
1932	*New York		Chicago	0–4	191,998	713,377.00	363,822.27	5,231.77	4,244.60
1933	*New York		Washington	4–1	163,076	679,365.00	284,665.68	4,256.72	3,019.86
1934	*St. Louis		Detroit	4–3	281,510	1,128,995.27‡	327,950.46	5,389.57	3,354.68
1935	Chicago		*Detroit	2–4	286,672	1,173,794.00‡	397,360.24	6,544.76	4,198.53

WORLD SERIES WINNERS AND RECEIPTS (Continued)

Year	National League	American League	Games Won	Attendance	Receipts	Players' Total	1 Winning Share	1 Losing Share
1936	New York	*New York	2–4	302,924	$1,304,399.00‡	$460,002.66‡	$6,430.55‡	$4,655.58‡
1937	New York	*New York	1–4	238,142	1,085,994.00‡	459,629.35	6,471.11	4,489.96
1938	Chicago	*New York	0–4	200,833	851,166.00	434,094.66	5,782.76	4,674.87
1939	Cincinnati	*New York	0–4	183,849	845,329.09‡	431,117.84	5,541.89	4,193.39
1940	*Cincinnati	Detroit	4–3	281,927	1,322,328.21‡	404,414.04‡	5,803.62‡	3,531.81‡
1941	Brooklyn	*New York	1–4	235,773	1,107,762.00‡	474,184.54‡	5,943.31‡	4,829.40‡
1942	*St. Louis	New York	4–1	277,101	1,205,249.00‡	427,579.41	6,192.53	3,351.77
1943	St. Louis	*New York	1–4	277,312	1,205,784.00‡	488,005.74	6,139.46	4,321.96
1944	*St. Louis	St. Louis	4–2	206,708	1,006,122.00‡	309,590.91	4,626.01	2,743.79
1945	Chicago	*Detroit	3–4	333,457	1,592,454.00‡	475,579.04‡	6,443.34‡	3,930.22‡
1946	*St. Louis	Boston	4–3	250,071	1,227,900.00v	304,141.05	3,742.34	2,140.89
1947	Brooklyn	*New York	3–4	389,763	2,021,348.92x	493,674.82	5,830.03	4,081.19
1948	Boston	*Cleveland	2–4	358,362	1,923,685.56y	548,214.99	6,772.07	4,570.73
1949	Brooklyn	*New York	1–4	236,716	1,479,627.88z	490,855.84	5,626.74	4,272.74
1950	Philadelphia	*New York	0–4	196,009	1,928,669.03z	486,371.21	5,737.95	4,081.34
1951	New York	*New York	2–4	341,977	2,708,457.47z	560,562.37	6,446.09	4,951.03
1952	Brooklyn	*New York	3–4	340,706	2,747,753.01z	500,003.28	5,982.65	4,200.64
1953	Brooklyn	*New York	2–4	307,350	2,979,269.41z	691,341.61	8,280.68	6,178.42
1954	*New York	Cleveland	4–0	251,507	2,741,203.38z	881,763.72	11,147.90	6,712.50
1955	*Brooklyn	New York	4–3	362,310	3,512,515.34z	737,853.59	9,768.21	5,598.58
1956	Brooklyn	*New York	3–4	345,903	3,333,254.59z	758,561.63	8,714.76	6,934.34
1957	*Milwaukee	New York	4–3	394,712	5,475,978.94**	709,027.55	8,924.36	5,606.06
1958	Milwaukee	*New York	3–4	393,909	5,397,223.03**	726,044.55	8,759.10	5,896.08
1959	*Los Angeles	Chicago	4–2	420,784	5,628,809.44**	893,301.40	11,231.18	7,275.17
1960	*Pittsburgh	New York	4–3	349,813	5,480,627.88**	682,144.82	8,417.94	5,214.64
1961	Cincinnati	*New York	1–4	223,247	4,730,059.95**	645,928.28	7,389.13	5,356.37
1962	San Francisco	*New York	3–4	376,864	6,128,891.11**	863,281.71	9,882.74	7,291.49
1963	*Los Angeles	New York	4–0	247,279	5,495,189.09**	1,017,546.43	12,794.00	7,874.32
1964	*St. Louis	New York	4–3	321,807	5,743,187.96**	696,520.15	8,622.19	5,309.29
1965	*Los Angeles	Minnesota	4–3	364,326	6,475,041.60**	885,612.21	10,297.43	6,634.36

* Indicates World Champions.
† 1 drawn game.
B Not under Brush rules.
‡ Including $100,000 radio receipts.

v including $175,000 radio receipts.
x Including $175,000 radio and $65,000 television receipts.
y Including $200,000 radio and $90,000 television receipts.
z Including all receipts from Radio and Television.
**Including share of Radio and Television receipts.

No Series in 1904

	G	AB	R	H	2B	3B	HR	TB	PC	SH	BB	HP	SO	SB	RBI
1903—Pittsburgh NL	8	271	24	65	7	9	1	93	.240	2	14	1	45	9	..
Boston AL	8	283	39	71	4	16	2	113	.251	2	13	2	27	5	..
1905—New York NL	5	153	15	32	7	..	..	39	.209	5	19	2	26	11	..
Philadelphia AL	5	155	3	25	5	..	..	30	.161	3	5	1	25	2	..
1906—Chicago NL	6	185	18	36	9	..	..	45	.195	14	18	2	28	8	..
Chicago AL	6	187	22	37	10	3	..	53	.198	6	18	3	38	6	..
1907—Chicago NL	6	167	19	43	6	1	..	51	.257	9	12	4	25	18	..
Detroit AL	5	173	6	36	1	2	..	41	.208	3	9	1	22	7	..
1908—Chicago NL	5	164	24	48	4	2	1	59	.293	9	13	..	26	14	..
Detroit AL	5	158	15	32	5	..	..	37	.203	5	12	2	26	5	..
1909—Pittsburgh NL	7	223	34	49	13	1	2	70	.220	12	20	6	34	18	..
Detroit AL	7	234	28	55	16	..	2	77	.235	4	20	4	22	6	..
1910—Chicago NL	5	158	15	35	11	1	..	48	.222	7	18	..	31	3	..
Philadelphia AL	5	177	35	56	19	1	1	80	.316	7	17	2	24	7	..
1911—New York NL	6	189	13	33	11	1	..	46	.175	6	14	3	44	4	..
Philadelphia AL	6	205	27	50	15	..	3	74	.244	9	4	..	31	4	..
1912—New York NL	8	274	31	74	14	4	1	99	.270	7	22	3	39	12	..
Boston AL	8	273	25	60	14	6	1	89	.220	8	19	1	36	6	..
1913—New York NL	5	164	15	33	3	1	1	41	.201	2	8	3	19	5	..
Philadelphia AL	5	174	23	46	4	4	2	64	.264	7	7	..	16	5	..
1914—Boston NL	4	135	16	33	6	2	1	46	.244	3	15	1	18	9	..
Philadelphia AL	4	128	6	22	9	..	..	31	.172	3	13	..	28	2	..
1915—Philadelphia NL	5	148	10	27	4	1	1	36	.182	5	10	2	25	2	..
Boston AL	5	159	12	42	2	2	3	57	.264	7	11	1	25	1	..
1916—Brooklyn NL	5	170	13	34	2	5	1	49	.200	6	14	2	19	1	..
Boston AL	5	164	21	39	7	6	2	64	.238	12	18	..	25	1	..
1917—New York NL	6	199	17	51	5	4	2	70	.256	3	6	2	27	3	..
Chicago AL	6	197	21	54	6	..	1	63	.274	3	11	..	28	6	..
1918—Chicago NL	6	176	10	37	5	1	..	44	.210	4	18	2	14	3	..
Boston AL	6	172	9	32	2	3	..	40	.186	8	16	1	21	3	..
1919—Cincinnati NL	8	251	35	64	10	7	..	88	.255	13	25	5	22	7	..
Chicago AL	8	263	20	59	10	3	1	78	.224	7	15	3	30	5	..
1920—Brooklyn NL	7	215	8	44	5	..	..	51	.205	5	10	..	20	1	7
Cleveland AL	7	217	21	53	9	2	2	72	.244	3	21	..	21	2	18
1921—New York NL	8	264	29	71	13	4	2	98	.269	6	22	1	38	7	26
New York AL	8	241	22	50	7	1	2	65	.207	9	27	1	44	6	20
1922—New York NL	5	162	18	50	2	1	1	57	.309	5	12	..	15	1	18
New York AL	5	158	11	32	6	1	2	46	.203	6	8	2	20	2	11
1923—New York NL	6	201	17	47	2	3	5	70	.243	..	12	1	18	1	17
New York AL	6	205	30	60	8	4	5	91	.293	6	20	1	22	1	29
1924—New York NL	7	253	27	66	9	2	4	85	.261	7	25	2	40	3	23
Washington AL	7	248	26	61	9	..	5	85	.246	6	29	..	34	5	25
1925—Pittsburgh NL	7	230	25	61	12	2	4	89	.265	6	17	4	32	7	22
Washington AL	7	225	26	59	8	..	8	91	.262	11	17	2	33	2	23
1926—St. Louis NL	7	239	31	65	12	1	4	91	.272	12	11	1	30	2	30
New York AL	7	223	21	54	10	1	4	78	.242	10	31	1	31	1	17
1927—Pittsburgh NL	4	130	10	29	6	1	..	37	.223	6	4	1	7	..	10
New York AL	4	136	23	38	6	2	2	54	.279	6	13	1	25	2	19
1928—St. Louis NL	4	131	10	27	5	1	1	37	.206	2	11	1	29	3	9
New York AL	4	134	27	37	7	..	9	71	.276	5	13	1	12	4	24
1929—Chicago NL	5	173	17	43	6	2	1	56	.249	2	13	..	50	1	15
Philadelphia AL	5	171	26	48	5	..	6	71	.281	7	13	1	27	..	26
1930—St. Louis NL	6	190	12	38	10	1	2	56	.200	4	11	..	33	1	11
Philadelphia AL	6	178	21	35	10	2	6	67	.197	7	24	1	32	..	20
1931—St. Louis NL	7	229	19	54	11	..	2	71	.236	4	9	..	41	8	17
Philadelphia AL	7	227	22	50	5	..	3	64	.220	4	28	1	46	..	20
1932—Chicago NL	4	146	19	37	8	2	3	58	.253	1	11	..	24	2	16
New York AL	4	144	37	45	6	..	8	75	.313	1	23	4	26	..	36
1933—New York NL	5	176	16	47	5	..	3	61	.267	6	11	..	21	..	16
Washington AL	5	173	11	37	4	..	2	47	.214	3	13	..	24	1	11
1934—St. Louis NL	7	262	34	73	14	5	2	103	.279	4	11	1	31	2	32
Detroit AL	7	250	23	56	12	1	2	76	.224	6	25	2	43	4	20
1935—Chicago NL	6	202	18	48	6	2	5	73	.238	7	11	1	29	1	17
Detroit AL	6	206	21	51	11	1	1	67	.248	3	25	2	27	1	18
1936—New York NL	6	203	23	50	9	..	4	71	.246	7	21	..	33	..	20
New York AL	6	215	43	65	8	1	7	96	.302	3	26	1	35	1	41
1937—New York NL	5	169	12	40	6	..	1	49	.237	..	11	..	21	1	12
New York AL	5	169	28	42	6	4	4	68	.249	2	21	1	21	..	25
1938—Chicago NL	4	136	9	33	4	1	2	45	.243	1	6	..	26	..	8
New York AL	4	135	22	37	6	1	5	60	.274	1	11	1	16	3	21
1939—Cincinnati NL	4	133	8	27	3	1	..	32	.203	2	6	1	22	1	8
New York AL	4	131	20	27	4	1	7	54	.206	2	9	..	20	..	18
1940—Cincinnati NL	7	232	22	58	14	..	2	78	.250	4	15	..	30	1	24
Detroit AL	7	228	28	56	9	3	4	83	.246	3	30	..	30	..	24
1941—Brooklyn NL	5	159	11	29	7	2	1	43	.182	..	14	..	21	..	11
New York AL	5	166	17	41	5	1	2	54	.247	..	23	2	18	2	16

(Continued on following page)

	G	AB	R	H	2B	3B	HR	TB	PC	SH	BB	HP	SO	SB	RBI
1942—St. Louis NL	5	163	23	39	4	2	2	53	.239	7	17	..	19	..	23
New York AL	5	178	18	44	6	..	3	59	.247	1	8	..	22	3	14
1943—St. Louis NL	5	165	9	37	5	..	2	48	.224	5	11	..	26	1	8
New York AL	5	159	17	35	5	2	2	50	.220	4	12	..	30	3	14
1944—St. Louis NL	6	204	16	49	9	1	3	69	.240	7	19	..	43	..	15
St. Louis AL	6	197	12	36	9	1	1	50	.183	1	23	..	49	..	9
1945—Chicago NL	7	247	29	65	16	3	1	90	.263	10	19	..	48	2	27
Detroit AL	7	242	32	54	10	..	2	70	.223	3	33	2	22	3	32
1946—St. Louis NL	7	232	28	60	19	2	1	86	.259	8	19	2	30	3	27
Boston AL	7	233	20	56	7	1	4	77	.240	3	22	1	28	2	18
1947—Brooklyn NL	7	226	29	52	13	1	1	70	.230	3	30	1	32	7	26
New York AL	7	238	38	67	11	5	4	100	.282	3	38	2	37	2	35
1948—Boston NL	6	187	17	43	6	..	4	61	.230	7	16	..	19	1	16
Cleveland AL	6	191	17	38	7	..	4	57	.199	3	12	1	26	2	16
1949—New York AL	5	164	21	37	10	2	2	57	.226	3	18	..	27	2	20
Brooklyn NL	5	162	14	34	7	1	4	55	.210	2	15	1	38	1	14
1950—New York AL	4	135	11	30	3	1	2	41	.222	2	13	1	12	1	10
Philadelphia NL	4	128	5	26	6	1	..	34	.203	6	7	1	24	1	3
1951—New York AL	6	199	29	49	7	2	5	75	.246	0	26	1	23	0	25
New York NL	6	194	18	46	7	1	2	61	.237	2	25	1	22	2	15
1952—New York AL	7	232	26	50	5	2	10	89	.216	2	31	1	32	1	24
Brooklyn NL	7	233	20	50	7	0	6	75	.215	6	24	5	48	1	18
1953—New York AL	6	201	33	56	6	4	9	97	.279	4	25	4	43	2	32
Brooklyn NL	6	213	27	64	13	1	8	103	.300	2	15	2	30	2	26
1954—New York NL	4	130	21	33	3	..	2	42	.254	8	17	..	24	1	20
Cleveland AL	4	137	9	26	5	1	3	42	.190	3	16	1	23	..	9
1955—Brooklyn NL	7	223	31	58	8	1	9	95	.260	8	33	2	38	2	30
New York AL	7	222	26	55	4	2	8	87	.248	1	22	1	39	3	15
1956—New York AL	7	229	33	58	6	..	12	100	.253	4	21	..	43	2	33
Brooklyn NL	7	215	25	42	8	1	3	61	.195	2	32	..	47	1	24
1957—Milwaukee NL	7	225	23	47	6	1	8	79	.209	6	22	3	40	1	22
New York AL	7	230	25	57	7	1	7	87	.248	3	22	..	34	1	25
1958—New York AL	7	233	29	49	5	1	10	86	.210	2	21	..	42	1	29
Milwaukee NL	7	240	25	60	10	1	3	81	.250	4	27	..	56	1	24
1959—Los Angeles NL	6	203	21	53	3	1	7	79	.261	3	12	..	27	5	19
Chicago AL	6	199	23	52	10	..	4	74	.262	3	20	2	33	2	19
1960—Pittsburgh NL	7	234	27	60	11	..	4	83	.256	3	12	3	26	2	26
New York AL	7	269	55	91	13	4	10	142	.338	2	18	2	40	..	54
1961—New York AL	5	165	27	42	8	1	7	73	.255	3	24	0	25	1	26
Cincinnati NL	5	170	13	35	8	0	3	52	.206	0	8	3	27	0	11
1962—New York AL	7	221	20	44	6	1	3	61	.199	1	21	2	39	4	17
San Francisco NL	7	226	21	51	10	2	5	80	.226	4	12	1	39	1	19
1963—Los Angeles NL	4	117	12	25	3	2	3	41	.214	3	11	0	25	2	12
New York AL	4	129	4	22	2	0	2	30	.170	1	5	1	37	0	4
1964—St. Louis NL	7	240	32	61	8	3	5	90	.254	6	18	..	39	3	29
New York AL	7	239	33	60	11	..	10	101	.251	3	25	2	54	2	33
1965—Los Angeles NL	7	234	24	64	10	1	5	91	.274	6	13	3	31	9	21
Minnesota AL	7	215	20	42	7	2	6	71	.195	2	19	0	54	2	19

ALL-STAR GAME PERFORMANCE RECORDS

SERVICE

MOST GAMES, LIFETIME
24   S. F. Musial, St.L. NL
18   T. S. Williams, Bos. AL

MOST CONSECUTIVE GAMES, LIFETIME
24   S. F. Musial, St.L. NL
14   M. C. Mantle, N.Y. AL

BATTING—GAME

MOST OFFICIAL AT BATS, GAME
7   W. E. Jones, Phil. NL 1950 (14 inn)
6   By 5 AL & 3 NL players (ex inn gm)
5   By 15 AL & 18 NL players (9 inn)

MOST RUNS SCORED, GAME
4   T. S. Williams, Bos. AL 1946
3   By 3 AL & 2 NL players

MOST HITS, GAME
4   J. M. Medwick, St. L. NL 1937
    T. S. Williams, Bos. AL 1946

MOST TOTAL BASES, GAME
10   T. S. Williams, Bos. AL 1946
9   J. F. Vaughan, Pitt. NL 1941
    A. L. Rosen, Clev. AL 1954

MOST ONE BASE HITS, GAME
3   By 3 AL & 3 NL players
    Last: H. C. Killebrew, Minn. AL 1964

MOST TWO BASE HITS, GAME
2   By 1 AL & 3 NL players
    Last: E. Banks, Chi. NL 1959

MOST THREE BASE HITS, GAME
1   By many players, Last:
    B. C. Robinson, Balt. AL 1964

MOST HOME RUNS, GAME
2   J. F. Vaughan, Pitt. NL 1941 (cons)
    T. S. Williams, Bos. AL 1946
    A. L. Rosen, Clev. AL 1954 (cons)

MOST RUNS BATTED IN, GAME
5   T. S. Williams, Bos..AL 1946
    A. L. Rosen, Clev. AL 1954
4   By 3 AL & 1 NL players

MOST BASES ON BALLS, GAME
3   C. L. Gehringer, Det. AL 1934
    P. J. Cavarretta, Chi. NL 1944

MOST STRIKEOUTS, GAME
3   By many players, Last:
    J. Roseboro, L. A. NL 1961 (cons)

MOST STOLEN BASES, GAME
2   W. H. Mays, S.F. NL 1963

MOST CAUGHT STEALING, GAME
1   By 5 AL & 7 NL players. Last:
    R. W. Clemente, Pitt. NL 1962

MOST HIT BY PITCHER, GAME
1   By many players. Last:
    E. G. Howard, N.Y. AL 1964

BATTING—LIFETIME

HIGHEST BATTING AVERAGE (20 ABs)
.500 C. L. Gehringer, Det. AL (20-10)
.433 W. J. Herman, Chi.-Brk. NL (30-13)

MOST OFFICIAL AT BATS, LIFETIME
63   S. F. Musial, St.L. NL
46   T. S. Williams, Bos. AL

MOST RUNS SCORED, LIFETIME
18   W. H. Mays, N.Y.-S. F. NL
10   T. S. Williams, Bos. AL

BATTING—LIFETIME, Cont.

MOST HITS, LIFETIME
21   W. H. Mays, N.Y.-S. F. NL
14   T. S. Williams, Bos. AL

MOST TOTAL BASES, LIFETIME
40   S. F. Musial, St.L. NL
29   T. S. Williams, Bos. AL

MOST HOME RUNS, LIFETIME
6   S. F. Musial, St. L. NL
4   T. S. Williams, Bos. AL

MOST RUNS BATTED IN, LIFETIME
12   T. S. Williams, Bos. AL
10   S. F. Musial, St. L. NL

MOST STOLEN BASES, LIFETIME
6   W. H. Mays, N.Y.-S.F. NL

PITCHING—GAME

MOST INNINGS, GAME
6   V. L. Gomez, N. Y. AL 1934
5   L. J. Jansen, N. Y. NL 1950

MOST RUNS, GAME
5   C. W. Passeau, Chi. NL 1941 (5 E. R.)
    S. S. Consuegra, Chi. AL 1954 (5 E. R.)
    E. C. Ford, N. Y. AL 1955 (3 E. R.)
    J. W. Maloney, Cin. NL 1965 (5 E. R.)

MOST HITS, GAME
7   T. J. Bridges, Det. AL 1937
6   L. Warnecke, Chi. NL 1933
    C. W. Passeau, Chi. NL 1941

MOST HITS, INNING
5   S. S. Consuegra, Chi. AL 1954
4   By 4 NL pitchers

MOST BASES ON BALLS, GAME
5   W. A. Hallahan, St. L. NL 1933

MOST BASES ON BALLS, INNING
3   E. Wynn, Chi. AL 1959
2   By many pitchers.

MOST STRIKEOUTS, GAME
6   C. O. Hubbell, N. Y. AL 1934
    J. S. VanderMeer, Cin. NL 1943
    L. J. Jansen, N. Y. NL 1950

MOST CONSECUTIVE STRIKEOUTS, GAME
5   C. O. Hubbell, N. Y. NL 1934

MOST STRIKEOUTS, INNING
(Only men faced)
3   J. F. Sain, Bos. NL 1948 (5 inn)
    R. C. Shantz, Phil. AL 1952 (5 inn)

MOST STRIKEOUTS, CONSECUTIVE INNINGS
6   C. O. Hubbell, N. Y. NL 1934 (1-2 inn)

PITCHING—LIFETIME

MOST GAMES, LIFETIME
7   E. Wynn, Clev.-Chi. AL (6 cons.)
    W. E. Spahn, Bos.-Mil. NL
    J. P. Bunning, Det. AL-Phil. NL

MOST GAMES WON, LIFETIME
3   V. L. Gomez, N. Y. AL 1933, 35, 37
2   R. B. Friend, Pitt. NL 1956, 60
    J. A. Marichal, S.F. NL 1962, 64

MOST GAMES LOST, LIFETIME
2   M. M. Cooper, St. L. NL 1942, 43
    C. W. Passeau, Chi. NL 1941, 46
    E. C. Ford, N. Y. AL 1959, 60

LOWEST ERA, LIFETIME
0.00 M. L. Harder, Clev. AL (13 inns)
1.13   J. P. Bunning, Det. AL-Phil. NL (16 inns)
1.32 E. Blackwell, Cin. NL (13⅔ inns)

MOST INNINGS PITCHED, LIFETIME
18   V. L. Gomez, N. Y. AL (5 gs)
14⅓ D. S. Drysdale, L. A. NL (6gs)

RECORD OF ALL-STAR GAMES

FIRST GAME

At Chicago (AL), July 6, 1933 R.H.E.
Nationals ......0 0 0 0 0 2 0 0 0—2 8 0
Americans ......0 1 2 0 0 1 0 0 .—4 9 1
Batteries—HALLAHAN, Warneke, Hubbell, P.; J. Wilson, Hartnett, C.; GOMEZ, Crowder, Grove, P.; R. Ferrell, C.
Paid attendance—47,595.

THIRD GAME

At Cleveland (AL), July 8, 1935 R.H.E.
Nationals ......0 0 0 1 0 0 0 0 0—1 4 1
Americans ......2 1 0 0 1 0 0 0 .—4 8 0
Batteries—WALKER, Schumacher, Derringer, J. Dean, P.; J. Wilson, Hartnett, C.; GOMEZ, Harder, P.; Hemsley, C.
Paid attendance—69,831.

FIFTH GAME

At Washington (AL), July 7, 1937 R.H.E.
Nationals ......0 0 0 1 1 1 0 0 0—3 13 0
Americans .....0 0 2 3 1 2 0 0 .—8 13 2
Batteries—J. DEAN, Hubbell, Blanton, Grissom, Mungo, Walters, P.; Hartnett, Mancuso, C.; GOMEZ, Bridges, Harder, P.; Dickey, C.
Paid attendance—31,391.

SEVENTH GAME

At New York (AL), July 11, 1939 R.H.E.
Nationals ......0 0 1 0 0 0 0 0 0—1 7 1
Americans .....0 0 0 2 1 0 0 0 .—3 6 1
Batteries—Derringer, LEE, Fette, P.; Lombardi, C.; Ruffing, BRIDGES, Feller, P.; Dickey, C.
Paid attendance—62,892.

NINTH GAME

At Detroit (AL), July 8, 1941 R.H.E.
Nationals ......0 0 0 0 0 1 2 2 0—5 10 2
Americans ......0 0 0 1 0 1 0 1 4—7 11 3
Batteries — Wyatt, Derringer, Walters, PASSEAU, P.; Owen, Lopez, Danning, C.; Feller, Lee, Hudson, SMITH, P.; Dickey, Hayes, C.
Paid attendance—54,674.

ELEVENTH GAME

At Philadelphia (AL), July 13, 1943 R.H.E.
Nationals ....1 0 0 0 0 1 0 1—3 10 1
Americans ....0 3 1 0 1 0 0 0 x—5 8 2
Batteries—M. COOPER, Vander Meer, Sewell, Javery, C.; W. Cooper, Lombardi, C.; LEONARD, Newhouser, Hughson, P.; Early, C.
Paid attendance—31,938.

NO GAME IN 1945

THIRTEENTH GAME

At Boston (AL), July 9, 1946 R.H.E.
Nationals ....0 0 0 0 0 0 0 0 0— 0 3 0
Americans .....2 0 0 1 3 0 2 4 x—12 14 1
Batteries—PASSEAU, Higbe, Blackwell, Sewell, P.; W. Cooper, Masi, C.; FELLER, Newhouser, Kramer, P.; Hayes, Rosar, H. Wagner, C.
Paid attendance—34,906.

FIFTEENTH GAME

At St. Louis (AL), July 12, 1948 R.H.E.
Nationals .....2 0 0 0 0 0 0 0 0—2 8 0
Americans .....0 1 1 3 0 0 0 0 x—5 6 0
Batteries—Branca, SCHMITZ, Sain, Blackwell, P.; Cooper, Masi, C.; Masterson, RASCHI, J. Coleman, P.; Rosar, Tebbetts, C.
Paid attendance—34,009.

SECOND GAME

At New York (NL), July 10, 1934 R.H.E.
Americans .....0 0 0 2 6 1 0 0 0—9 14 1
Nationals .....1 0 3 0 3 0 0 0 0—7 8 1
Batteries—Gomez, Ruffing, HARDER, P.; Dickey, Cochrane, C.; Hubbell, Warneke, MUNGO, J. Dean, Frankhouse, P.; Hartnett, Lopez, C.
Paid attendance—48,363.

FOURTH GAME

At Boston (NL), July 7, 1936 R.H.E.
Americans .....0 0 0 0 0 3 0 0—3 7 1
Nationals .....0 2 0 0 2 0 0 0 .—4 9 0
Batteries—GROVE, Harder, Rowe, P.; R. Ferrell, Dickey, C.; J. DEAN, Davis, Hubbell, Warneke, P.; Hartnett, C.
Paid attendance—25,556.

SIXTH GAME

At Cincinnati (NL), July 6, 1938 R.H.E.
Americans .....0 0 0 0 0 0 0 0 1—1 7 4
Nationals .....1 0 0 1 0 0 2 0 .—4 8 0
Batteries—GOMEZ, Allen, Grove, P.; Dickey, C.; VANDER MEER, Lee, Brown, P.; Lombardi, C.
Paid attendance—27,067.

EIGHTH GAME

At St. Louis (NL), July 9, 1940 R.H.E.
Americans .....0 0 0 0 0 0 0 0 0—0 3 1
Nationals .....3 0 0 0 0 0 1 .—4 7 0
Batteries—RUFFING, Newsom, Feller, P.; Dickey, Hayes, Hemsley, C.; DERRINGER, Walters, Wyatt, French, Hubbell, P.; Lombardi, Phelps, Danning, C.
Paid attendance—32,373.

TENTH GAME

At New York (NL), July 6, 1942 R.H.E.
Americans .....3 0 0 0 0 0 0 0—3 7 0
Nationals .....0 0 0 0 0 0 1 0—1 6 1
Batteries—CHANDLER, Benton, P.; Tebbetts, C.; M. COOPER, Vander Meer, Passeau, Walters, P.; W. Cooper, Lombardi, C.
Paid attendance—34,178.

TWELFTH GAME

At Pittsburgh (NL), July 11, 1944 R.H.E.
Americans .....0 1 0 0 0 0 0 0 0—1 6 3
Nationals .....0 0 4 0 0 2 1 x—7 12 1
Batteries—Borowy, HUGHSON, Muncrief, Newhouser, Newsom, P.; Hemsley, Hayes, C.; Walters, RAFFENSBERGER, Sewell, Tobin, P.; W. Cooper, Mueller, C.
Paid attendance—29,589.

FOURTEENTH GAME

At Chicago (NL), July 8, 1947 R.H.E.
Americans .....0 0 0 0 1 1 0 0—2 8 0
Nationals .....0 0 0 1 0 0 0 0 0—1 5 1
Batteries—Newhouser, SHEA, Masterson, Page, P.; Rosar, C.; Blackwell, Brecheen, SAIN, Spahn, P.; W. Cooper, Edwards, Masi, C.
Paid attendance—41,123.

SIXTEENTH GAME

At Brooklyn (NL), July 12, 1949 R.H.E.
Americans .....4 0 0 2 0 2 3 0 0—11 13 1
Nationals ......2 1 2 0 0 2 0 0 0— 7 12 5
Batteries—Parnell, TRUCKS, Brissie, Raschi, P.; Tebbetts, Berra, C.; Spahn, NEWCOMBE; Munger, Bickford, Pollett, Blackwell, P.; Seminick, Campanella, C.
Paid attendance—32,577.

137B

RECORD OF ALL STAR GAMES (continued)

SEVENTEENTH GAME
At Chicago (AL), July 11, 1950   R.H.E.

Nationals ...02000000100001–4 10 0
Americans ..00102000000000–3 8 1

Batteries—Roberts, Newcombe, Konstanty, Jansen, BLACKWELL, P.; Campanella, C.; Raschi, Lemon, Houtteman, Reynolds, GRAY, Feller, P.; Berra, Hegan, C.

Paid attendance–46,127.

NINETEENTH GAME
At Philadelphia (NL), July 8, 1952   R.H.E.

Americans 00020–2 5 0
Nationals 10020–3 3 0

Game called at end of fifth—rain.
Batteries—Raschi, LEMON, Shantz, P; Berra, C; Simmons, RUSH, P; Campanella, C.

Paid attendance–32,785.

TWENTY-FIRST GAME
At Cleveland (AL), July 13, 1954   R.H.E.

Nationals 00052000 2– 9 14 0
Americans 00412103 x–11 17 1

Batteries—Roberts, Antonelli, Spahn, Grissom, CONLEY, Erskine, P; Campanella, Burgess, C; Ford, Consuegra, Lemon, Porterfield, Keegan, STONE, Trucks, P; Berra, C.

Paid attendance–68,751.

TWENTY.THIRD.GAME
At Washington (AL), July 10, 1956   R.H.E.

Nationals 0012112 00–7 11 0
Americans 0000030 00–3 11 0

Batteries—FRIEND, Spahn, Antonelli, P; Bailey, Campanella, C; PIERCE, Ford, Wilson Brewer, Score, Wynn, P; Berra, Lollar, C.

Paid attendance–28,843.

TWENTY-FIFTH GAME
At Baltimore (AL), July 8, 1958   R.H.E.

Nationals 210000000–3 4 2
Americans 110011 00x–4 9 2

Batteries—Turley, Narleski, WYNN, O'-Dell, P; Triandos, Berra, C; Spahn, FRIEND, Jackson, Farrell, P; Crandall, C.

Paid attendance–48,829.

TWENTY-SEVENTH GAME
At Los Angeles (NL), Aug. 3, 1959 R.H.E.

Americans 012000110–5 6 0
Nationals 100010100–3 6 3

Batteries—WALKER, Wynn, Wilhelm, O'Dell, McLish, P; Berra, Lollar, C; DRYSDALE, Conley, S. Jones, Face, P; Crandall, Smith, C.

Paid Attendance–55,105.

TWENTY-NINTH GAME
At New York (AL), July 13, 1960 R.H.E.

Nationals 021000102–6 10 0
Americans 000000000–0 8 0

Batteries—LAW, Podres, Williams, Jackson, Henry, McDaniel, P; Crandall, Burgess, Bailey, C; FORD, Wynn, Staley, Lary, Bell, P; Berra, Lollar, C.

Paid Attendance–38,362.

EIGHTEENTH GAME
At Detroit (AL), July 10, 1951   R.H.E.

Nationals 10030211 0–8 12 1
Americans 010110000–3 10 2

Batteries—Roberts, MAGLIE, Newcombe, Blackwell, P.; Campanella, C.; Garver, LOPAT, Hutchinson, Parnell, Lemon, P.; Berra, C.

Paid attendance–52,075.

TWENTIETH GAME
At Cincinnati (NL), July 14, 1953   R.H.E.

Americans 000000001–1 5 0
Nationals 000201 2 x–5 10 0

Batteries—Pierce, REYNOLDS, Garcia, Paige, P; Berra, C; Roberts, SPAHN, Simmons, Dickson, P; Campanella, C.

Paid attendance–30,846.

TWENTY-SECOND GAME
At Milwaukee (NL), July 12, 1955   R.H.E.

Americans ..400001000000–5 10 2
Nationals 00000230001–6 13 1

Batteries—Pierce, Wynn, Ford, SULLIVAN, P; Berra, C; Roberts, Haddix, Newcombe, Jones, Nuxhall, CONLEY, P; Crandall, Burgess, Lopata, C.

Paid attendance–45,643.

TWENTY-FOURTH GAME
At St. Louis (NL), July 9, 1957   R.H.E.

Americans 020001003–6 10 0
Nationals 000000203–5 9 1

Batteries—BUNNING, Loes, Wynn, Pierce, Mossi, Grim, P; Berra, C; SIMMONS, Burdette, Sanford, Jackson, Labine, P; Bailey, C.

Paid attendance–30,693.

TWENTY-SIXTH GAME
At Pittsburgh (NL), July 7, 1959   R.H.E.

Americans 000100030–4 8 0
Nationals 10000022 x–5 9 1

Batteries—Wynn, Duren, Bunnning, FORD, Daley, P; Triandos, Lollar, C.; Drysdale, Burdette, Face, ANTONELLI, Elston, P; Crandall, C.

Paid Attendance–35,277.

TWENTY-EIGHTH GAME
At Kansas City (AL), July 11, 1960 R.H.E.

Nationals 311000 0 0–5 12 4
Americans 000001020–3 6 1

Batteries—FRIEND, McCormick, Face, Buhl, Law, P; Crandall, Burgess, C; MONBOUQUETTE, Estrada, Coates, Bell, Lary, Daley, P; Berra, Howard, C.

Paid Attendance–30,619.

THIRTIETH GAME
At San Francisco (NL), July 11, 1961 R.H.E.

Americans ...000001 00 2 0–4 4 2
Nationals ...010110010 2–5 11 5

Batteries—Ford, Lary, Donovan, Bunning, Fornieles, WILHELM, P; Romano, Berra, Howard, C; Spahn, Purkey, McCormick, Face, Koufax, MILLER, P; Burgess, C.

Paid Attendance–44,115.

137C

RECORD OF ALL-STAR GAMES—Continued

THIRTY-FIRST GAME

At Boston (AL), July 31, 1961   R.H.E.
Nationals .....0 0 0 0 0 1 0 0 0—1 5 1
Americans ....1 0 0 0 0 0 0 0 0—1 4 0
  Batteries—Bunning, Schwall, Pascual, P;
Romano, Howard, C; Purkey, Mahaffey,
Koufax, Miller, P; Burgess, Roseboro, C.
  Paid Attendance—31,851.

THIRTY-THIRD GAME

At Chicago (NL), July 30, 1962   R.H.E.
Americans .....0 0 1 2 0 1 3 0 2—9 10 0
Nationals .....0 1 0 0 0 0 1 1 1—4 8 0
  Batteries—Stenhouse, HERBERT, Aguirre,
Pappas, P; Battey, Howard, C; Podres,
MAHAFFEY, Gibson, Farrell, Marichal, P;
Crandall, Roseboro, C.
  Paid Attendance—38,359.

THIRTY-FIFTH GAME

At New York (NL), July 7, 1964   R.H.E.
American ....1 0 0 0 0 2 1 0 0—4 9 1
National ....0 0 0 2 1 0 0 0 4—7 8 0
  Batteries—Chance, Wyatt, Pascual, RAD-
ATZ, P; Howard, C; Drysdale, Bunning,
Short, Farrell, MARICHAL, P; Torre, Ed-
wards, C.
  Paid Attendance—50,850.

THIRTY-SECOND GAME

At Washington (AL), July 10, 1962 R.H.E.
Nationals .....0 0 0 0 0 2 0 1 0—3 8 0
Americans ....0 0 0 0 0 1 0 0 0—1 4 0
  Batteries—Drysdale, MARICHAL, Purkey,
Shaw, P; Crandall, C; Bunning, PASCUAL,
Donovan, Pappas, P; Battey, Romano, C.
  Paid Attendance—45,480.

THIRTY-FOURTH GAME

At Cleveland (AL), July 9, 1963   R.H.E.
National ....0 1 2 0 1 0 0 1 0—5 6 0
American ....0 1 2 0 0 0 0 0 0—3 11 1
  Batteries—O'Toole, JACKSON, Culp, Woode-
shick, Drysdale, P; Bailey, Edwards, C; Mc-
Bride, BUNNING, Bouton, Pizarro, Radatz,
P; Battey, Howard, C.
  Paid Attendance—44,160.

THIRTY-SIXTH GAME

At Minnesota (AL), July 13, 1965   R.H.E.
National ....3 2 0 0 0 0 1 0 0—6 11 0
American ....0 0 0 1 4 0 0 0 0—5 8 0
  Batteries—Marichal, Maloney, Drysdale,
KOUFAX, Farrell, Gibson, P; Torre, C;
Pappas, Grant, Richert, McDOWELL, Fish-
er, P; Battey, Freehan, C.
  Paid Attendance—46,706.

PLAYERS SELECTED FOR ALL-STAR GAMES

1965—NATIONAL LEAGUE—Eugene W. Mauch, Philadelphia, Manager. CHICAGO—Banks, 1b; Santo, 3b; Williams, of. CINCINNATI—Cardenas, ss; Edwards, c; Ellis, p; Maloney, p; Robinson, of; Rose 2b. HOUSTON—Farrell, p. LOS ANGELES—Drysdale, p; Koufax, p; Wills, ss. MILWAUKEE—H. Aaron, of; Torre, c. NEW YORK—Kranepool, 1b. PHILADEL-PHIA—Allen, 3b; Callison, of; Rojas, 2b. PITTSBURGH—Clemente, of; Stargell, of; Veale, p. ST. LOUIS—Gibson, p. SAN FRANCISCO—Marichal, p; Mays, of. AMERICAN LEAGUE —Alfonso R. Lopez, Chicago, Manager. BALTIMORE—Pappas, p; Robinson, 3b. BOSTON—Mantilla, 2b. CHICAGO—Fisher, p; Skowron, 1b. CLEVELAND—Alvis, 3b; Colavito, of; Davalillo, of; McDowell, p. DETROIT—Freehan, c; Horton, of; Kaline, of; McAuliffe, ss. KANSAS CITY—O'Donoghue, p. LOS ANGELES—R. Lee, p. MINNESOTA—Battey, c; Grant, p; Hall, of; Killebrew, 1b; Oliva, of; Versalles, ss. NEW YORK—Howard, c; Mantle, of; Pepitone, 1b; Richardson, 2b; Stottlemyre, p. WASHINGTON—Richert, p.

1964—AMERICAN LEAGUE—Alfonso R. Lopez, Chicago, Manager. BALTIMORE—B. Robin-son, 3b; Siebern, 1b. BOSTON—Bressoud, ss; Malzone, 3b; Radatz, p. CHICAGO—Peters, p; Pizarro, p. CLEVELAND—Kralick, p: DETROIT—Freehan, c; Lumpe, 2b. KANSAS CITY—Colavito, of; Wyatt, p. LOS ANGELES—Chance, p; Fregosi, ss. MINNESOTA—Allison, 1b; Hall, of; Killebrew, of; Oliva, of; Pascual, p. NEW YORK—Ford, p; Howard, c; Mantle, of; Pepitone, 1b; Richardson, 2b. WASHINGTON—Hinton, of. NATIONAL LEAGUE—Walter E. Alston, Los Angeles, Manager. CHICAGO—Ellsworth, p; Santo, 3b; Williams, of. CINCIN-NATI—Cardenas, ss; Edwards, c. HOUSTON—Farrell, p. LOS ANGELES—Drysdale, p; Kou-fax, p. MILWAUKEE—Aaron, of; Torre, c. NEW YORK—Hunt, 2b. PHILADELPHIA—Bun-ning, p; Callison, of; Short, p. PITTSBURGH—Burgess, c; Clemente, of; Mazeroski, 2b; Star-gell, of. ST. LOUIS—Boyer, 3b; Flood, of; Groat ss; White, 1b. SAN FRANCISCO—Cepeda, 1b; Marichal, p; Mays, of.

1963—NATIONAL LEAGUE—Alvin R. Dark, San Francisco, Manager. CHICAGO—Jackson, p; Santo, 3b. CINCINNATI—O'Toole, p; Edwards, c. HOUSTON—Woodeshick, p. LOS AN-GELES—Drysdale, p; Koufax, p; Wills, ss; T. Davis, of. MILWAUKEE—Spahn, p; Torre, c; H. Aaron, of. NEW YORK—Snider, of. PHILADELPHIA—Culp, p. PITTSBURGH—Clemente, of. ST. LOUIS—Boyer, 3b; Groat, ss; Javier, 2b; White, 1b; Musial, of. SAN FRANCISCO—Marichal, p; Bailey, c; Cepeda, 1b; Mays, of; McCovey, of. AMERICAN LEAGUE—Ralph G. Houk, New York, Manager. BALTIMORE—Aparicio, ss; Robinson, 3b. BOSTON—Monbou-quette, p; Radatz, p; Malzone, 3b; Yastrzemski, of. CHICAGO—Pizarro, p; Fox, 2b. CLEVE-LAND—Grant, p. DETROIT—Bunning, p; Kaline, of. KANSAS CITY—Siebern, 1b. LOS ANGELES—McBride, p; Pearson, of; Wagner, of. MINNESOTA—Battey, c; Versalles, ss; Allison, of; Killebrew, of. NEW YORK—Bouton, p; Howard, c; Pepitone, 1b; Richardson, 2b; Tresh, of. WASHINGTON—Leppert, c.

1962 (Both)—NATIONAL LEAGUE—Fred Hutchinson, Cincinnati, Mgr. CHICAGO—Banks, 1b; Altman, of; Williams, of. CINCINNATI—Purkey, p; Robinson, of. HOUSTON—Farrell, p; LOS ANGELES—Drysdale, p; Koufax, p; Podres, p; Roseboro, c; Wills, ss; T. Davis, of. MILWAUKEE—Shaw, p; Spahn, p; Crandall, c; Bolling, 2b; Mathews, 3b; H. Aaron, of. NEW YORK—Ashburn, of. PHILADELPHIA—Mahaffey, p; Callison, of. PITTSBURGH—Groat, ss; Mazeroski, 2b; Clemente, of. ST. LOUIS—Gibson, p; Boyer, 3b; Musial, of. SAN FRANCISCO—Marichal, p; Cepeda, 1b; Davenport, 3b; F. Alou, of; Mays, of. AMERICAN LEAGUE—Ralph G. Houk, New York, Mgr. BALTIMORE—Pappas, p. Wilhelm, p; Gentile, 1b; B. Robinson, 3b. BOSTON—Monbouquette, p; Runnels, 1b. CHICAGO—Herbert, p; Aparicio, ss; Landis, of. CLEVELAND—Donovan, p; Romano, c. DETROIT—Aguirre, p; Bunning, p; Colavito, of; Kaline, of. KANSAS CITY—Siebern, 1b. LOS ANGELES—McBride, p; Moran, 2b; L. Thomas, of; Wagner, of. MINNESOTA—Kaat, p; Pascual, p; Battey, c; Rollins, 3b. NEW YORK—Terry, p; Howard, c; Richardson, 2b; Tresh, ss; Berra, of; Mantle, of; Maris, of. WASHINGTON—Stenhouse, p.

PLAYERS SELECTED FOR ALL STAR GAMES—Cont'd.

1961 (Both Games)—NATIONAL LEAGUE—Daniel E. Murtaugh, Pittsburgh, Mgr. CHICAGO —Banks, ss; Zimmer, 2b; Altman, of. CINCINNATI—Jay, p; Purkey, p; Kasko, ss; F. Robinson, of. LOS ANGELES—Drysdale, p; Koufax, p; Roseboro, c; Wills, ss. MILWAUKEE—Spahn, p; Bolling, 2b; Mathews, 3b; Aaron, of. PHILADELPHIA—Mahaffey, p. PITTSBURGH—Face, p; Burgess, c; Stuart, 1b; Clemente, of. ST. LOUIS—Boyer, 3b; White, 1b; Musial, of. SAN FRANCISCO—McCormick, p; Miller, p; Bailey, c; Cepeda, of; Mays, of. AMERICAN LEAGUE—Paul R. Richards, Baltimore, Mgr. BALTIMORE—Wilhelm, p; Gentile, 1b; B. Robinson, 3b; Brandt, of. BOSTON—Fornieles, p; Schwall, p. CHICAGO—Pierce, p; Aparicio, ss; Fox, 2b; Sievers, 1b. CLEVELAND—Latman, p; Perry, p; Romano, c; Temple, 2b; Francona, of. DETROIT—Bunning, p; Lary, p; Cash, 1b; Colavito, of; Kaline, of. KANSAS CITY—Howser, 3b. LOS ANGELES—Duren, p; McBride, p. MINNESOTA—Pascual, p; Killebrew, 3b. NEW YORK—Arroyo, p; Ford, p; Berra, c; Howard, c; Kubek, ss; Skowron, 1b; Mantle, of; Maris, of. WASHINGTON—Donovan, p.

1960 (Both Games)—NATIONAL LEAGUE—Walter Alston, Los Angeles, Mgr. CHICAGO— Banks, ss. CINCINNATI—Bailey, c; Pinson, of. LOS ANGELES—Podres, p; Williams, p; Larker, 1b; Neal, 2b. MILWAUKEE—Buhl, p; Crandall, c; Adcock, 1b; Mathews, 3b; Aaron, of. PHILADELPHIA—Taylor, 2b. PITTSBURGH—Face, p; Friend, p; Law, p; Burgess, c; Mazerowski, 2b; Groat, ss; Clemente, of; Skinner, of. ST. LOUIS—Jackson, p; McDaniel, p; White, 1b; Boyer, 3b; Musial, of. SAN FRANCISCO—McCormick, p; Cepeda, of; Mays, of. AMERICAN LEAGUE—Alfonso R. Lopez, Chicago, Mgr. BALTIMORE— Estrada, p; Gentile, 1b; Hansen, ss; Robinson, 3b. BOSTON—Monbouquette, p; Runnels, 2b; Malzone, 3b; Williams, of. CHICAGO—Staley, p; Wynn, p; Lollar, c; Fox, 2b; Aparicio, ss; Minoso, of; Smith, of. CLEVELAND—Bell, p; Stigman, p; Power, 1b; Kuenn, of. DETROIT —Lary, p; Kaline, of. KANSAS CITY—B. Daley, p. NEW YORK—Coates, p; Ford, p; Berra, c; Howard, c; Skowron, 1b; Mantle, of; Maris, of. WASHINGTON—Lemon, of.

1959—(1st Game)—NATIONAL LEAGUE—Fred G. Haney, Milwaukee, Mgr. CHICAGO— Banks, ss. CINCINNATI—Robinson, 1b; Temple, 2b; Pinson, of; LOS ANGELES—Drysdale, p; Moon, of. MILWAUKEE—Burdette, p; Spahn, p; Crandall, c; Mathews, 3b; Aaron, of. PHILADELPHIA—Conley, p. PITTSBURGH—Face, p; Burgess, c; Groat, ss; Mazeroski, 2b. ST. LOUIS—Mizell, p; H. Smith, c; K. Boyer, 3b; Musial, 1b; Cunningham, of; White, of. SAN FRANCISCO—Antonelli, p; Cepeda, 1b; Mays, of. AMERICAN LEAGUE—Charles D. Stengel, New York, Mgr. BALTIMORE—Wilhelm, p; Triandos, c. BOSTON—Malzone, 3b; Runnels, 2b; Williams, of. CHICAGO—Pierce, p; Wynn, p; Lollar, c; Aparicio, ss; Fox, 2b. CLEVELAND—Power, 1b; Colavito, of; Minoso, of. DETROIT—Bunning, p; Kaline, of; Kuenn, of. KANSAS CITY—Daley, p. NEW YORK—Duren, p; Ford, p; Berra, c; McDougald, ss; Skowron, 1b; Mantle, of. WASHINGTON—Killebrew, 3b; Sievers, 1b.

1959—(2nd Game)—NATIONAL LEAGUE—Fred G. Haney, Milwaukee, Mgr. CHICAGO— Elston, p; Banks, ss. CINCINNATI—Robinson, 1b; Temple, 2b; Pinson, of. LOS ANGELES —Drysdale, p; Gilliam, 3b; Neal, 2b; Moon, of. MILWAUKEE—Burdette, p; Spahn, p; Crandall, c; Logan, ss; Mathews, 3b; Aaron, of. PHILADELPHIA—Conley, p. PITTSBURGH— Face, p; Burgess, c; Groat, ss; Mazeroski, 2b. ST. LOUIS—H. Smith, c; K. Boyer, 3b; Musial, 1b; Cunningham, of. SAN FRANCISCO—Antonelli, p; S. Jones, p; Cepeda, 1b; Mays, of. AMERICAN LEAGUE—Charles D. Stengel, New York, Mgr. BALTIMORE—O'Dell, p; Walker, p; Wilhelm, p; Woodling, of. BOSTON—Malzone, 3b; Runnels, 2b; Williams, of. CHICAGO—Wynn, p; Lollar, c; Aparicio, ss; Fox, 2b. CLEVELAND—McLish, p; Power, 1b; Colavito, of; Minoso, of. DETROIT—Kaline, of; Kuenn, of. KANSAS CITY—Daley, p; Maris, of. NEW YORK—Duren, p; Berra, c; Howard, 1b; Richardson, 2b; Mantle, of. WASHINGTON—Ramos, p; Killebrew, 3b; Sievers, 1b; Allison, of.

1958—NATIONAL LEAGUE—Fred G. Haney, Milwaukee, Manager. CHICAGO—Banks, ss; Moryn, of; Walls, of. CINCINNATI—Crowe, 1b; Purkey, p; LOS ANGELES—Podres, p; Roseboro, c. MILWAUKEE—Aaron, of; Crandall, c; Logan, ss; Mathews, 3b; McMahon, p; Spahn, p. PHILADELPHIA—Ashburn, of; Farrell, p. PITTSBURGH—Friend, p; Mazeroski, 2b; Skinner, of; Thomas, 3b. ST. LOUIS—Blasingame, 2b; Jackson, p; Musial, 1b. SAN FRANCISCO—Antonelli, p; Mays, of; Schmidt, c. AMERICAN LEAGUE—Charles D. Stengel, New York, Manager. BALTIMORE—O'Dell, p; Triandos, c. BOSTON—Jensen, of; Malzone, 3b; Williams, of. CHICAGO—Aparicio, ss; Fox, 2b; Lollar, c; Pierce, p; Wynn, p. CLEVELAND—Narleski, p; Vernon, 1b. DETROIT—Kaline, of; Kuenn, of. KANSAS CITY— Cerv, of. NEW YORK—Berra, c; Duren, p; Ford, p; Howard, of; Kubek, ss; Mantle, of; McDougald, ss; Skowron, 1b; Turley, p. WASHINGTON—Bridges, ss.

1957—NATIONAL LEAGUE—Walter E. Alston, Brooklyn, Manager. BROOKLYN—Cimoli, of.; Hodges, 1b.; Labine, p. CHICAGO—Banks, ss. CINCINNATI—Bailey, c.; Bell, of.; Hoak, 3b.; McMillan, ss.; Robinson, of.; Temple, 2b. MILWAUKEE—Aaron, of.; Burdette, p.; Logan, ss.; Mathews, 3b.; Schoendienst, 2b.; Spahn, p. NEW YORK—Antonelli, p.; Mays, of. PHILADELPHIA—Sanford, p.; Simmons, p. PITTSBURGH—Foiles, c. ST. LOUIS— Jackson, p.; Moon, of.; Musial, 1b.; Smith, c. AMERICAN LEAGUE—Charles D. Stengel, New York, Manager. BALTIMORE—Kell, 3b.; Loes, p.; Triandos, c. BOSTON—Malzone, 3b.; Williams, of. CHICAGO—Fox, 2b.; Minoso, of.; Pierce, p. CLEVELAND—Mossi, p.; Wertz, 1b.; Wynn, p. DETROIT—Bunning, p.; Kaline, of.; Kuenn, ss.; Maxwell, of. KANSAS CITY —DeMaestri, ss. NEW YORK—Berra, c.; Grim, p.; Howard, c.; Mantle, of.; McDougald, ss.; Richardson, 2b.; Shantz, p.; Skowron, 1b. WASHINGTON—Sievers, of.

PLAYERS SELECTED FOR ALL STAR GAMES—Cont'd.

1956—NATIONAL LEAGUE—Walter E. Alston, Brooklyn, Manager. BROOKLYN—Campanella, c; Gilliam, 2b; Labine, p; Snider, of. CHICAGO—Banks, ss. CINCINNATI—Bailey, c; Bell, of; Kluszewski, 1b; Lawrence, p; McMillan, ss; Nuxhall, p; Robinson, of; Temple, 2b. MILWAUKEE—Aaron, of; Crandall, c; Mathews, 3b; Spahn, p. NEW YORK—Antonelli, p; Mays, of. PHILADELPHIA—Lopata, c; Roberts, p. PITTS-BURGH—Friend, p; Long, 1b. ST. LOUIS—Boyer, 3b; Musial, of; Repulski, of.

AMERICAN LEAGUE—Charles D. Stengel, New York, Manager. BALTIMORE—Kell, 3b. BOSTON—Brewer, p; Piersall, of; Sullivan, p; Vernon, 1b; Williams, of. CHICAGO—Fox, 2b; Lollar, c; Pierce, p; Wilson, p. CLEVELAND—Score, p; Wynn, p. DE-TROIT—Boone, 3b; Kaline, of; Kuenn, ss; Maxwell, of. KANSAS CITY—Power, 1b; Simpson, of. NEW YORK—Berra, c; Ford, p; Kucks, p; Mantle, of; Martin, 2b; McDougald, ss. WASHINGTON—Sievers, 1b.

1955—NATIONAL LEAGUE—Leo E. Durocher, New York, Manager. BROOKLYN—Hodges, 1b; Newcombe, p; Snider, of. CHICAGO—Baker, 2b; Banks, ss; Jackson, 3b; Jones, p; CINCINNATI—Burgess, c; Kluszewski, 1b; Nuxhall, p; MILWAUKEE—Aaron, of; Conley, p; Crandall, c; Logan, ss; Mathews, 3b; NEW YORK—Mays, of; Mueller, of. PHILADELPHIA—Ennis, of; Lopata, c; Roberts, p. PITTSBURGH—Thomas, of. ST. LOUIS—Arroyo, p; Haddix, p; Musial, of; Schoendienst, 2b.

AMERICAN LEAGUE—Alfonso R. Lopez, Cleveland, Manager. BALTIMORE—Wilson, p. BOSTON—Jensen, of; Sullivan, p; Williams, of. CHICAGO—Carrasquel, ss; Donovan, p; Fox, 2b; Lollar, c; Pierce, p. CLEVELAND—Avila, 2b; Doby, of; Rosen, 3b; Score, p; Smith, of; Wynn, p. DETROIT—Hoeft, p; Kaline, of; Kuenn, ss. KANSAS CITY—Finigan, 3b; Power, 1b. NEW YORK—Berra, c; Ford, p; Mantle, of; Turley, p. WASHINGTON—Vernon, 1b.

1954—NATIONAL LEAGUE—Walter E. Alston, Brooklyn, Manager. BROOKLYN—Campanella, c.; Erskine, p.; Hodges, 1b.; Reese, ss.; Robinson, of.; Snider, of. CHICAGO—Jackson, 3b. CINCINNATI—Bell, of.; Kluszewski, 1b. MILWAUKEE—Conley, p.; Crandall, c.; Spahn, p.; Wilson, p. NEW YORK—Antonelli, p.; Dark, ss.; Grissom, p.; Mays, of.; Mueller, of. PHILADELPHIA—Burgess, c.; Hamner, 2b.; Roberts, p. PITTSBURGH—Thomas, of. ST. LOUIS—Jablonski, 3b.; Musial, of.; Schoendienst, 2b.

AMERICAN LEAGUE—Charles D. Stengel, New York, Manager. BALTIMORE—Turley, p. BOSTON—Piersall, of.; Williams, of. CHICAGO—Carrasquel, ss.; Fox, 2b.; Keegan, p.; Lollar, c.; Minoso, of.; Consuegra, p.; Trucks, p. CLEVELAND—Avila, 2b.; Doby, of.; Garcia, p.; Lemon, p.; Rosen, 1b. DETROIT—Boone, 3b.; Kuenn, ss. NEW YORK—Bauer, of.; Berra, c.; Ford, p.; Mantle, of.; Noren, of. PHILADELPHIA—Finigan, 3b. WASHINGTON—Porterfield, p.; Stone, p.; Vernon, 1b.

1953—NATIONAL LEAGUE—Charles W. Dressen, Brooklyn, Manager. BROOKLYN—Campanella, c; Furillo, of.; Hodges, 1b.; Reese, ss.; Robinson, 3b.; Snider, of. CHICAGO—Kiner, of.; McCullough, c. CINCINNATI—Bell, of.; Kluszewski, 1b. MILWAUKEE—Mathews, 3b.; Spahn, p.. NEW YORK—Westrum, c.; Wilhelm, p.; Williams, 2b. PHILADELPHIA—Ashburn, of.; Hamner, ss.; Roberts, p.; Simmons, p. PITTSBURGH—Dickson, p. ST. LOUIS—Haddix, p.; Musial, of.; Schoendienst, 2b.; Slaughter, of.; Staley, p.

AMERICAN LEAGUE—Charles D. Stengel, New York, Manager. BOSTON—Goodman, 2b.; Kell, 3b.; White, c. CHICAGO—Carrasquel, ss.; Fain, 1b.; Fox, 2b.; Minoso, of.; Pierce, p. CLEVELAND—Doby, of.; Garcia, p.; Lemon, p.; Rosen, 3b. DETROIT—Kuenn, ss. NEW YORK—Bauer, of.; Berra, c.; Mantle, of.; Mize, 1b.; Reynolds, p.; Rizzuto, ss.; Sain, p. PHILADELPHIA—Robinson, 1b.; Zernial, of. ST. LOUIS—Hunter, ss.; Paige, p. WASHINGTON—Vernon, 1b.

1952—NATIONAL LEAGUE—Leo E. Durocher, New York, Manager. BOSTON—Spahn, p. BROOKLYN—Campanella, c.; Furillo, of.; Hodges, 1b.; Reese, ss.; Robinson, 2b.; Roe, p.; Snider, of. CHICAGO—Atwell, c.; Rush, p.; Sauer, of. CINCINNATI—Hatton, 3b. NEW YORK— Dark, ss.; Hearn, p.; Lockman, 1b.; Maglie, p.; Thomson, 3b.; Westrum, c. PHILADELPHIA—Hamner, ss.; Roberts, p.; Simmons, p. PITTSBURGH—Kiner, of. ST. LOUIS—Musial, of.; Schoendienst, 2b.; Slaughter, of.; Staley, p.

AMERICAN LEAGUE—Charles D. Stengel, New York, Manager. BOSTON—DiMaggio, of.; Kell, 3b. CHICAGO—Fox, 2b.; Minoso, of.; Robinson, 1b. CLEVELAND—Avilla, 2b.; Doby, of.; Garcia, p.; Hegan, c.; Lemon, p.; Mitchell, of.; Rosen, 3b. DETROIT—Wertz, of. NEW YORK—Berra, c.; Bauer, of.; Mantle, of.; McDougald, 2b.; Raschi, p.; Reynolds, p.; Rizzuto, ss. PHILADELPHIA—Fain, 1b.; Joost, ss.; Shantz, p. ST. LOUIS—Paige, p. WASHINGTON—Jensen, of.; Yost, 3b.

1951—NATIONAL LEAGUE—Edwin M. Sawyer, Philadelphia, Manager. BOSTON—Elliott, 3b; Spahn, p. BROOKLYN—Campanella, c.; Hodges, 1b.; Newcombe, p.; Reese, ss.; Robinson, 2b.; Roe, p.; Snider, of. CHICAGO—Edwards, c.; Leonard, p. CINCIN-NATI—Blackwell, p.; Wyrostek, of. NEW YORK—Dark, ss.; Jansen, p.; Maglie, P. PHILADELPHIA—Ashburn, of.; Ennis, of.; Jones, 3b.; Roberts, p. PITTSBURGH—Kiner, of. ST. LOUIS—Musial, of.; Schoendienst, 2b.; Slaughter, of.; Westlake, of.

AMERICAN LEAGUE—Charles D. Stengel, New York, Manager. BOSTON—DiMaggio, of.; Doerr, 2b.; Parnell, p.; Stephens, 3b.; Williams, of. CHICAGO—Busby, of.; Carrasquel, ss.; Fox, 2b.; Gumpert, p.; Minoso, of.; Robinson, 1b. CLEVELAND—Doby, of.; Hegan, c.; Lemon, p. DETROIT—Hutchinson, p.; Kell, 3b.; Wertz, of. NEW YORK—Berra, c.; DiMaggio, of.; Lopat, p.; Rizzuto, ss. PHILADELPHIA—Fain, 1b.; Shantz, p. ST. LOUIS—Garver, p. WASHINGTON—Marrero, p.

PLAYERS SELECTED FOR ALL STAR GAMES (Continued)

1950—NATIONAL LEAGUE—Burton E. Shotton, Brooklyn, Manager. BOSTON—Cooper, c., Spahn, p.; BROOKLYN—Campanella, c.; Hodges, 1b.; Newcombe, p.; Reese, ss.; Robinson, 2b.; Roe, p.; Snider, of. CHICAGO—Pafko, of.; Rush, p.; Sauer, of. CINCINNATI —Blackwell, p.; Wyrostek, of. NEW YORK—Jansen, p.; Stanky, 2b. PHILADELPHIA—Jones, 3b.; Konstanty, p.; Roberts, p.; Sisler, of. PITTSBURGH—Kiner, of. ST. LOUIS—Marion, ss.; Musial, of.; Schoendienst, 2b.; Slaughter, of.

AMERICAN LEAGUE—Charles D. Stengel, New York, Manager. BOSTON—DiMaggio, of.; Doerr, 2b.; Dropo, 1b.; Stephens, ss.; Williams, of. CHICAGO—Scarborough, p. CLEVELAND—Doby, of.; Feller, p.; Hegan, c.; Lemon, p. DETROIT—Evers, of.; Gray, p.; Houtteman, p.; Kell, 3b. NEW YORK—Berra, c.; Byrne, p.; Coleman, 2b.; DiMaggio, of.; Henrich, 1b.; Raschi, p.; Reynolds, p.; Rizzuto, ss. PHILADELPHIA—Fain, 1b. ST. LOUIS—Lollar, c. WASHINGTON—Michaels, 2b.

1949—AMERICAN LEAGUE—Louis Boudreau, Cleveland, Manager. BOSTON—DiMaggio, of.; Goodman, 1b.; Parnell, p.; Stephens, ss.; Tebbetts, c.; Williams, of. CHICAGO—Michaels, 2b.; CLEVELAND—Doby, of.; Gordon, 2b.; Hegan, c.; Lemon, p.; Mitchell, of. DETROIT—Kell, 3b.; Trucks, p.; Wertz, of. NEW YORK—Berra, c.; DiMaggio, of.; Henrich, of.; Raschi, p.; Reynolds, p. PHILADELPHIA—Brissie, p.; Joost, ss.; Kellner, p. St. LOUIS—Dillinger, 3b. WASHINGTON—Robinson, 1b.

NATIONAL LEAGUE—William H. Southworth, Boston, Manager. BOSTON—Bickford, p.; Spahn, p. BROOKLYN—Branca, p.; Campanella, c.; Hodges, 1b.; Newcombe, p.; Reese, ss.; Robinson, 2b.; Roe, p. CHICAGO—Pafko, of. CINCINNATI—Blackwell, p.; Cooper, c. NEW YORK—Gordon, 3b.; Marshall, of.; Mize, 1b.; Thomson, of. PHILADELPHIA—Seminick, c.; Waitkus, 1b. PITTSBURGH—Kiner, of. ST. LOUIS—Kazak, 3b.; Marion, ss.; Munger, p.; Musial, of.; Pollet, p.; Schoendienst, 2b.; Slaughter, of.

1948—AMERICAN LEAGUE—Stanley R. Harris, New York, Manager. BOSTON—Doerr, 2b.; Stephen, ss.; Tebbetts, c.; Williams, of. CHICAGO—Haynes, p. CLEVELAND—Boudreau, ss.; Feller, p.; Gordon, 2b.; Keltner, 3b.; Lemon, p. DETROIT—Evers, of.; Kell, 3b.; Mullin, of.; Newhouser, p. NEW YORK—Berra, c.; J. DiMaggio, of.; Henrich, of.; McQuinn, 1b.; Page, p.; Raschi, p. PHILADELPHIA—J. Coleman, p.; Rosar, c. ST LOUIS—Zarilla, of. WASHINGTON—Masterson, p.; Vernon, 1b.

NATIONAL LEAGUE—Leo E. Durocher, Bklyn. Manager. BOSTON—Elliott, 3b.; Holmes, of.; Masi, c.; Sain, p.; Stanky, 2b. BROOKLYN—Branca, p.; Reese, ss. CHICAGO—McCullough, c.; Pafko, 3b.; Schmitz, p.; Waitkus, 1b. CINCINNATI—Blackwell, p. NEW YORK—Cooper, c.; Gordon, 3b.; Kerr, ss.; Mize, 1b.; Rigney, 2b.; Thomson, of. PHILADELPHIA—Ashburn, of. PITTSBURGH—Gustine, 3b.; Kiner, of.; E. Riddle, p. ST. LOUIS—Brecheen, p.; Musial, of.; Marion, ss.; Schoendienst, 2b.; Slaughter, of.

1947—AMERICAN LEAGUE—Joseph E. Cronin, Boston, Manager. BOSTON—Doerr, 2b.; Williams, of. CHICAGO—Appling, ss.; York 1b. CLEVELAND—Boudreau, ss.; Gordon, 2b.; Hegan, c. DETROIT—Kell, 3b.; Mullin, cf.; Newhouser, p.; Trout, p. NEW YORK—Chandler, p.; J. DiMaggio, of.; Henrich, of. (replaced Keller, N. Y.); W. Johnson, 3b.; McQuinn, 1b.; Page, p.; A. Robinson, c.; Shea, p. PHILADELPHIA—Rosar, c. ST. LOUIS—Kramer, p. WASHINGTON—Lewis, of.; Masterson, p.; Spence, of.; Wynn, p. (replaced Feller, Cleveland).

NATIONAL LEAGUE—Edwin H. Dyer, St. L., Manager. BOSTON—Masi, c.; Sain, p.; Spahn, p. BROOKLYN—Branca, p.; Edwards, c.; Reese, ss. (replaced Miller, Cinn.); Stanky, 2b.; F. Walker, of. CHICAGO—Cavarretta, 1b.; Pafko, of. CINCINNATI—Blackwell, p.; Haas, of. NEW YORK—W. Cooper, c.; Marshall, of.; Mize, 1b. PHILADELPHIA—Rowe, p.; Verban, 2b.; H. Walker, of. PITTSBURGH—Gustine, 3b. ST LOUIS—Brecheen, p.; Kurowski, 3b. (replaced R. Elliott. Boston); Marion, ss.; Munger, p.; Musial, 1b.; Slaughter, of.

1946—AMERICAN LEAGUE—Stephen F. O'Neill, Detroit, Manager. BOSTON—D. DiMaggio, of.; Doerr, 2b.; Ferriss, p.; Harris, p.; Pesky, ss.; H. Wagner, c.; Williams, of.; York, 1b. CHICAGO—Appling, ss. CLEVELAND—Feller, p.; Hayes, c.; Keltner, 3b. DETROIT—Newhouser, p. NEW YORK—Chandler, p.; Dickey, c.; J. DiMaggio, of.; Gordon, 2b.; Keller, of.; Stirnweiss, 3b. PHILADELPHIA—Chapman, of.; Rosar, c. ST. LOUIS—Kramer, p.; Stephens, ss. WASHINGTON—Spence, of.; Vernon, 1b.

NATIONAL LEAGUE—Chas. J. Grimm, Chicago, Manager. BOSTON—M. Cooper, p.; Hopp, of.; Masi, c. BROOKLYN—Higbe, p.; Reiser, of.; Walker, of. CHICAGO—Cavarretta, of.-1b; Lowrey, of.; Passeau, p.; Schmitz, p. CINCINNATI—Blackwell, p.; Lamanno, c. NEW YORK—W. Cooper, c.; Mize, 1b. PHILADELPHIA—Ennis, of.; McCormick, 1b. (replaced Reese, Bklyn) ; Verban, 2b. (replaced Miller, Cinn.). PITTSBURGH—Gustine, 2b.; Sewell, p. ST. LOUIS—Kurowski, 3b.; Marion, ss.; Musial, of.; Pollet, p.; Schoendienst, 2b.; Slaughter, of.

No Game in 1945.

1944—NATIONAL LEAGUE—Wm. H. Southworth, St. L., Manager. BOSTON—Andrews, p.; Javery, p.; Ryan, 2b.; Tobin, p. BROOKLYN—Galan, of.; Owen, c.; F. Walker, of. CHICAGO—Cavarretta, 1b.; Johnson, 2b.; Nicholson, rf. CINCINNATI—McCormick, 1b.; Miller, ss.; Mueller, c.; Walters, p. NEW YORK—Medwick, lf.; Ott, of.; Voiselle, p. PHILADELPHIA—Raffensberger, p. PITTSBURGH—DiMaggio, cf.; Elliott, 3b.; Sewell, p. ST. LOUIS—W. Cooper, c.; Kurowski, 3b.; Lanier, p.; Marion, ss.; Munger, p.; Musial, of.

AMERICAN LEAGUE—Jos. V. McCarthy, N. Y., Manager. BOSTON—Doerr, 2b.; Foxx, of.; Hughson, p.; Johnson, of. CHICAGO—Grove, p.; Tucker, cf. CLEVELAND—Boudreau, ss.; Cullenbine, of.; Hockett, of.; Keltner, 3b. DETROIT—Higgins, 3b.; Newhouser, p.; Trout, p.; York, 1b. NEW YORK—Borowy, p.; Hemsley, c.; Page, p. PHILADELPHIA—Hayes, c.: Newsom, p. ST. LOUIS—McQuinn, 1b.; Muncrief, p.; Stephens, ss. WASHINGTON—Case, of.; Ferrell, c.; Leonard, p.; Spence, of.

1943—NATIONAL LEAGUE—William H. Southworth, St. L., Manager—BOSTON—Javery, p. BROOKLYN—Galan, of.; Herman, 2b.; Owen, c.; F. Walker, of. CHICAGO—Hack, 3b.; Nicholson, rf.; Passeau, p. CINCINNATI—Frey, 2b.; McCormick, 1b.; Miller, ss.; VanderMeer, p. NEW YORK—Lombardi, c.; Ott, of. PHILADELPHIA—Dahlgren, 1b. PITTSBURGH—DiMaggio, cf.; Fletcher, 1b.; Sewell, p. ST. LOUIS—M. Cooper, p.; W. Cooper, c.; Kurowski, 3b.; Lanier, p.; Marion, ss.; Musial, cf.; Pollett, p.; H. Walker, of.

AMERICAN LEAGUE—Joseph V. McCarthy, N. Y., Manager. BOSTON—Doerr, 2b.; Hughson, p.; Judd, p. CHICAGO—Appling, ss. CLEVELAND—Bagby, p.; Boudreau, ss.; Heath, of.; Keltner, 3b.; Rosar, s.; A. Smith, p. DETROIT—Newhouser, p.; Wakefield, lf.; York, 1b. NEW YORK—Bonham, p.; Chandler, p.; Dickey, c.; Gordon, 2b.; Keller, of.; Lindell, of. PHILADELPHIA—Siebert, 1b. ST. LOUIS—Laabs, cf.; Stephens, ss. WASHINGTON—Case, rf.; Early, c.; R. Johnson, of.; Leonard, p.

1942—NATIONAL LEAGUE—Leo E. Durocher, Bklyn., Manager—BOSTON—Lombardi, c.; Miller, ss. BROOKLYN—Herman, 2b; Medwick, lf.; Owen, c.; Reese, ss.; Reiser, cf.; Vaughan, 3b.; Wyatt, p. CHICAGO—Passeau, p. CINCINNATI—Derringer, p.; F. McCormick, 1b.; Starr, p.; Vander Meer, p.; Walters, p. NEW YORK—Hubbell, p.; Marshall, of.; Melton, p.; Mize, 1b.; Ott, rf. PHILADELPHIA—Litwhiler, of. PITTSBURGH—Elliott, 3b. ST. LOUIS—Brown, 2b.; M. Cooper, p.; W. Cooper, c.; T. Moore, cf.; Slaughter, rf.

AMERICAN LEAGUE—Joseph V. McCarthy, New York, Manager—BOSTON—D. DiMaggio, of.; Doerr, 2b.; Hughson, p.; Williams, lf. CHICAGO—E. Smith, p. CLEVELAND—Bagby, p.; Boudreau, ss.; Keltner, 3b. DETROIT—Benton, p.; Newhouser, p.; Tebbetts, c.; York, 1b. NEW YORK—Bonham, p.; Chandler, p.; W. Dickey, c.; J. DiMaggio, cf.; Gordon, 2b.; Henrich, of.; Rizzuto, ss.; Rosar, c.; Ruffing, p. PHILADELPHIA—Johnson, of.; H. Wagner, c. ST. LOUIS—McQuinn, 1b. WASHINGTON—Hudson, p.; Spence, of.

1941—AMERICAN LEAGUE—Delmar D. Baker, Detroit, Manager. BOSTON—Cronin, ss.; DiMaggio, rf.; Doerr, 2b.; Foxx, 1b.; Williams, lf. CHICAGO—Appling, ss.; Lee, p.; Smith, p. CLEVELAND—Boudreau, ss.; Feller, p.; Heath, rf.; Keltner, 3b. DETROIT—Benton, p.; Tebbetts, c.; York, 1b. NEW YORK—Dickey, c.; DiMaggio, cf.; Gordon, 2b.; Keller, lf.; Ruffing, p.; Russo, p. PHILADELPHIA—Hayes, c. ST. LOUIS—Cullenbine, rf. WASHINGTON—Hudson, p.; Travis, 3b.

NATIONAL LEAGUE—Wm. B. McKechnie, Cinn., Manager. BOSTON—Miller, ss. BROOKLYN—Herman, 2b.; Lavagetto, 3b.; Medwick, lf.; Owen, c.; Reiser, cf.; Wyatt, p. CHICAGO—Hack, 3b.; Nicholson, rf.; Passeau, p. CINCINNATI—Derringer, p.; Frey, 2b.; F. McCormick, 1b.; Walters, p. NEW YORK—Danning, c.; Hubbell, p.; Ott, rf. PHILADELPHIA—Blanton, p. PITTSBURGH—Elliott, rf.; Lopez, c.; Vaughan, ss. ST. LOUIS—Mize, 1b.; Moore, lf.; Slaughter, rf.; Warneke, p.

1940—NATIONAL LEAGUE—Wm. B. McKechnie, Cinn., Manager. BOSTON—Miller, ss.; West, rf. BROOKLYN—Coscarart, 2b.; Durocher, ss.; Lavagetto, 3b.; Medwick, lf.; Phelps, c.; Wyatt, p. CHICAGO—French, p.; Herman, 2b.; Leiber, cf.; Nicholson, rf. CINCINNATI—Derringer, p.; Lombardi, c.; F. McCormick, 1b.; Walters, p. NEW YORK—Danning, c.; Hubbell, p.; Jurges, ss.; J. Moore, lf.; Ott, rf. PHILADELPHIA—Higbe, p.; May, 3b.; Mulcahy, p. PITTSBURGH—Vaughan, ss. ST. LOUIS—Mize, 1b.; T. Moore, cf.

AMERICAN LEAGUE—Jos. E. Cronin, Boston, Manager—BOSTON—Cramer, cf.; Finney, rf.; Foxx, 1b.; Williams, lf. CHICAGO—Appling, ss. CLEVELAND— Boudreau, ss.; Feller, p.; Hemsley, c.; Keltner, 3b.; Mack, 2b.; Milnar, p. DETROIT—Bridges, p.; Greenberg, lf.; Newsom, p. NEW YORK—Dickey, c.; DiMaggio, cf.; Gordon, 2b.; Keller, rf.; Pearson, p.; Ruffing, p.; Rolfe, 3b. PHILADELPHIA—Hayes, c.; Johnson, lf. ST. LOUIS—McQuinn, 1b. WASHINGTON—Leonard, p.; Travis, 3b.

1939—AMERICAN LEAGUE—J. V. McCarthy, N. Y. Manager. BOSTON—Cramer, of.; Cronin, ss.; Foxx, 1b.; Grove, p. CHICAGO—Appling, ss.; Lyons, p. CLEVELAND—Feller, p.; Hemsley, c. DETROIT—Bridges, p.; Greenberg, 1b.; Newsom, p. NEW YORK—Crosetti, ss.; Dickey, c.; DiMaggio, of.; Gomez, p.; Gordon, 2b.; Murphy, p.; Rolfe, 3b.; Ruffing, p.; Selkirk, of. PHILADELPHIA—Hayes, c.; Johnson, of. ST. LOUIS—Hoag, of.; McQuinn, 1b. WASHINGTON—Case, of.

NATIONAL LEAGUE—C. L. Hartnett, Chicago, Manager. BOSTON—Fette, p. BROOKLYN—Camilli, 1b.; Lavagetto, 3b.; Phelps, C.; Wyatt, p. CHICAGO—Hack, 3b.; Herman, 2b.; Lee, p. CINCINNATI—Derringer, p.; Frey, 2b.; Goodman, of.; Lombardi, c.; McCormick, 1b.; VanderMeer, p.; Walters, p. NEW YORK—Danning, c.; Jurges, ss.; Ott, of. PHILADELPHIA—Arnovich, of. PITTSBURGH—Vaughan, ss. ST. LOUIS—Davis, p.; Medwick, of.; Mize, 1b.; Moore, of.; Warneke, p.

PLAYERS SELECTED FOR ALL STAR GAMES (Continued)

1938—NATIONAL LEAGUE—Wm. H. Terry, N. Y., Manager. BOSTON—Cuccinello, 2b.; Turner, p. BROOKLYN—Durocher, ss.; Lavagetto, 3b.; Phelps, c. CHICAGO—Hack, 3b.; Hartnett, c.; Herman, 2b.; Lee, p. CINCINNATI—Derringer, p.; Goodman, of.; Lombardi, c.; McCormick, 1b.; VanderMeer, p. NEW YORK—Hubbell, p.; Leiber, of.; J. Moore, of.; Ott, of. PHILADELPHIA—H. Martin. of. PITTSBURGH—M. Brown, p.; Vaughan, ss.; L. Waner, of. ST. LOUIS—Medwick, of.

AMERICAN LEAGUE—Jos. V. McCarthy, N. Y., Manager. BOSTON—Cramer, of.; Cronin, ss.; Foxx, 1b.-3b.; Grove, p. CHICAGO—Kreevich, of. CLEVELAND—Allen, p.; Feller, p.; Averill, of. DETROIT—Gehringer, 2b.; Greenberg, 1b.; Kennedy, p.; York, c. NEW YORK—Dickey, c.; DiMaggio, of.; Gehrig, 1b.; Gomez, p.; Rolfe, 3b.; Ruffing, p. PHILADELPHIA—R. Johnson, of. ST. LOUIS—Newsom, p. WASHINGTON—R. Ferrell, c.; Lewis, 3b.; Travis, ss.

1937—AMERICAN LEAGUE—Joseph V. McCarthy, N. Y., Manager. BOSTON—Cramer, of.; Cronin, ss.; Foxx, 1b.; Grove, p. CHICAGO—Sewell, c.; Stratton, p. CLEVELAND—Averill, of.; Harder, p. DETROIT—Bridges, p.; Gehringer, 2b.; Greenberg, 1b.; G. Walker, of. NEW YORK—Dickey, c.; DiMaggio, of.; Gehrig, 1b.; Gomez, p.; Murphy (for Stratton, Chicago), p.; Rolfe, 2b. PHILADELPHIA—Moses, of. ST. LOUIS—Bell, of.; Clift, 3b.; West (for Walker, Detroit), of. WASHINGTON—R. Ferrell, c.; W. Ferrell, p.; Myer, 2b.

NATIONAL LEAGUE—Wm. H. Terry, N. Y., Manager—BOSTON—G. Moore, of. BROOKLYN—Mungo, p. CHICAGO—Collins, 1b.; Demaree, of.; Hartnett, c.; Herman, 2b.; Jurges, ss. CINCINNATI—Grissom, p.; Lombardi, c. NEW YORK—Bartell, ss.; Hubbell, p.; Mancuso, s.; J. Moore, of.; Ott, of.; Whitehead, 2b. PHILADELPHIA—Walters, p. PITTSBURGH—Blanton, p.; Vaughan, 3b.; P. Waner, of. ST. LOUIS—J. Dean, p.; J. Martin, of.; Medwick, of.; Mize, 1b.

1936—NATIONAL LEAGUE—Chas. J. Grimm, Chicago, Manager. BOSTON—Berger, of. BROOKLYN—Mungo, p. CHICAGO—C. Davis, p.; Demaree, of.; Galan, of.; Hartnett, c.; Herman, 2b.; Warneke, p. CINCINNATI—Lombardi, c.; Riggs, 2b. NEW YORK—Hubbell, p.; J. Moore, of.; Ott, of. PHILADELPHIA—Whitney, 3b. PITTSBURGH—Suhr, 1b.; Vaughan, ss. ST. LOUIS—Collins, 1b.; J. Dean, p.; Durocher, ss.; Medwick, of.; S. Martin, 2b.

AMERICAN LEAGUE—Jos. V. McCarthy, N. Y., Manager. BOSTON—R. Ferrell, c.; Foxx, 3b.; Grove, p. CHICAGO—Appling, ss.; Radcliff, of. CLEVELAND—Averill, of.; Harder, p. DETROIT—Bridges (place taken by Kennedy, Chicago), p.; Gehringer, 2b.; Goslin, of.; Rowe, p. NEW YORK—Crosetti, ss.; Dickey, c.; DiMaggio, of.; Gehrig, 1b.; Gomez, p.; Pearson, p.; Selkirk, of. PHILADELPHIA—Higgins, 3b. ST. LOUIS—Hemsley, c. WASHINGTON, Chapman, of.

1935—AMERICAN LEAGUE—G. S. Cochrane, Det., Manager. BOSTON—Cronin, ss.; R. Ferrell, c.; Grove, p. CHICAGO—Simmons, of. CLEVELAND—Harder, p.; Vosmik, of. DETROIT—Bridges, p.; Cochrane, c.; Gehringer, 2b.; Rowe, p. NEW YORK—Chapman, of.; Gehrig, 1b.; Gomez, p. PHILADELPHIA—Cramer (replaced Averill of Cleveland), of.; Foxx, 3b.; R. Johnson, of. ST. LOUIS—Hemsley, c.; West, of. WASHINGTON—Bluege, 3b.; Myer, 2b.

NATIONAL LEAGUE—F. F. Frisch, St. L., Manager. BOSTON—Berger, of. BROOKLYN—None. CHICAGO—Hartnett, c.; Herman, 2b. CINCINNATI—Derringer, p. NEW YORK—Hubbell, p.; Mancuso, c.; J. Moore, of.; Ott, of.; Schumacher, p.; Terry, 1b. PHILADELPHIA—Wilson, c. PITTSBURGH—Vaughan, ss.; P. Waner, of. ST. LOUIS—Collins, 1b.; J. Dean, p.; Frisch, 2b.; J. Martin, 3b.; Medwick, of.; Walker, p.; Whitehead, 2b.

1934—AMERICAN LEAGUE—Jos. E. Cronin, Wash., Manager. BOSTON—R. Ferrell, c. CHICAGO—Dykes, 3b.; Simmons, of. CLEVELAND—Averill, of.; Harder, p. DETROIT—Bridges, p.; Cochrane, c.; Gehringer, 2b. NEW YORK—Chapman, of.; Dickey, c.; Gehrig, 1b.; Gomez, p.; Ruffing, p.; Ruth, of. PHILADELPHIA—Foxx, 3b.; Higgins, 3b. ST. LOUIS—West, of. WASHINGTON—Cronin, ss.; Manush, of.; Russell, p.

NATIONAL LEAGUE—Wm. H. Terry, N. Y., Manager. BOSTON—Berger, of.; Frankhouse, p. BROOKLYN—Lopez, c.; Mungo, p. CHICAGO—Cuvler. rf.; Hartnett, c.; Herman, 2b.; Klein, of.; Warneke, p. CINCINNATI—none. NEW YORK—Hubbell, p.; Jackson, ss.; J. Moore, of.; Ott, of.; Terry, 1b. PHILADELPHIA—None. PITTSBURGH—Traynor, 3b.; Vaughan, ss.; P. Waner, of. ST. LOUIS—J. Dean, p.; Frisch, 2b.; J. Martin,3 b.; Medwick, of.

1933—AMERICAN LEAGUE—Connie Mack, Phila., Manager. BOSTON—R. Ferrell, c. CHICAGO—Dykes. 3b.; Simmons, of. CLEVELAND—Averill, of.; W. Ferrell, p.; Hildebrand, p. DETROIT—Gehringer, 2b. NEW YORK—Chapman, of.; Dickey, c.; Gehrig, 1b.; Gomez, p.; Lazzeri. 2b.; Ruth. of. PHILADELPHIA—Foxx, 1b.; Grove, p. ST. LOUIS—West, of. WASHINGTON—Cronin, ss.; Crowder, p.

NATIONAL LEAGUE—J. J. McGraw. N. Y., Manager. BOSTON—Berger, of. BROOKLYN—Cuccinello, 2b. CHICAGO—English, ss.; Hartnett, c.; Warneke, p. CINCINNATI—Hafev. of. NEW YORK—Hubbell, p.; O'Doul. of.; Schumacher, p.; Terry, 1b. PHILADELPHIA—Bartell, ss.; Klein, of. PITTSBURGH—Traynor, 3b.; P. Waner, of. ST. LOUIS—Frisch, 2b.; Hallahan, p.; J. Martin, 3b.; Wilson, c.

MAJOR LEAGUE ALL-STARS
(Selected by Baseball Writers Association)

1931
P—Grove, Phila. AL
P—Earnshaw, Phila. AL
C—Cochrane, Phila. AL
1B—Gehrig, New York AL
2B—Frisch, St. Louis NL
3B—Traynor, Pitts. NL
SS—Cronin, Wash. AL
LF—Simmons, Phila. AL
CF—Averill, Cleve. AL
RF—Ruth, New York AL

1932
P—Warneke, Chicago NL
P—Grove, Phila. AL
C—Dickey, New York AL
1B—Foxx, Phila. AL
2B—Lazzeri, N. Y. AL
3B—Traynor, Pitts. NL
SS—Cronin, Wash. AL
LF—O'Doul, Bklyn. NL
CF—Averill, Cleve. AL
RF—Klein, Phila. NL

1933
P—Hubbell, New York NL
P—Crowder, Wash. AL
C—Dickey, New York AL
1B—Foxx, Phila. AL
2B—Gehringer, Det. AL
3B—Traynor, Pitts. NL
SS—Cronin, Wash. AL
LF—Simmons, Chicago AL
CF—Berger, Boston NL
RF—Klein, Phila. NL

1934
P—Gomez, New York AL
P—J. Dean, St. L. NL
P—Rowe, Detroit AL
C—Cochrane, Det. AL
1B—Gehrig, New York AL
2B—Gehringer, Det. AL
3B—Higgins, Phila. AL
SS—Cronin, Wash. AL
LF—Simmons, Chicago AL
CF—Averill, Cleve. AL
RF—Ott, New York NL

1935
P—J. Dean, St. L. NL
P—Hubbell, New York NL
C—Cochrane, Detroit AL
1B—Greenberg, Detroit AL
2B—Gehringer, Detroit AL
3B—J. Martin, St. Louis NL
SS—Vaughan, Pitts. NL
LF—Medwick, St. Louis NL
CF—Cramer, Phila. AL
RF—Ott, New York NL

1936
P—Hubbell, New York NL
P—J. Dean, St. L. NL
C—Dickey, New York AL
1B—Gehrig, New York AL
2B—Gehringer, Detroit AL
3B—Higgins, Phila. AL
SS—Appling, Chicago AL
LF—Medwick, St. Louis NL
CF—Averill, Cleve. AL
RF—Ott, New York NL

1937
P—Hubbell, New York NL
P—Ruffing, New York AL
C—Hartnett, Chicago NL
1B—Gehrig, New York AL
2B—Gehringer, Detroit AL
3B—Rolfe, New York AL
SS—Bartell, New York NL
LF—Medwick, St. Louis NL
CF—J. DiMaggio, N. Y. AL
RF—P. Waner, Pitts. NL

1938
P—Ruffing, New York AL
P—Gomez, New York AL
P—Vander Meer, Cinn. NL
C—Dickey, New York AL
1B—Foxx, Boston AL
2B—Gehringer, Detroit AL
3B—Rolfe, New York AL
SS—Cronin, Boston AL
LF—Medwick, St. Louis NL
CF—J. DiMaggio, N. Y. AL
RF—Ott, New York NL

1939
P—Ruffing, New York AL
P—Walters, Cinn. NL
P—Feller, Cleveland AL
C—Dickey, New York AL
1B—Foxx, Boston AL
2B—Gordon, New York AL
3B—Rolfe, New York AL
SS—Cronin, Boston AL
LF—Medwick, St. L. NL
CF—J. DiMaggio, N. Y. AL
RF—Williams, Boston AL

1940
P—Feller, Cleveland AL
P—Walters, Cinn. NL
P—Derringer, Cinn. NL
C—Danning, New York NL
1B—F. McCormick, Cinn. NL
2B—Gordon, New York AL
3B—Hack, Chicago NL
SS—Appling, Chicago AL
LF—Greenberg, Det. AL
CF—J. DiMaggio, N. Y. AL
RF—Williams, Boston AL

1941
P—Feller, Cleveland AL
P—Wyatt, Brooklyn NL
P—T. Lee, Chicago AL
C—Dickey, New York AL
1B—Camilli, Bklyn. NL
2B—Gordon, New York AL
3B—Hack, Chicago NL
SS—Travis, Wash. AL
LF—Williams, Boston AL
CF—J. DiMaggio, N. Y. AL
RF—Reiser, Brooklyn NL

1942
P—M. Cooper, St. L. NL
P—Bonham, New York AL
P—Hughson, Boston AL
C—Owen, Brooklyn NL
1B—Mize, New York NL
2B—Gordon, New York AL
3B—Hack, Chicago NL
SS—Pesky, Boston AL
LF—Williams, Boston AL
CF—DiMaggio, N. Y. AL
RF—Slaughter, St. L. NL

1943
P—Chandler, N. Y. AL
P—M. Cooper, St. L. NL
P—Sewell, Pitts. NL
C—W. Cooper, St. L. NL
1B—York, Detroit AL
2B—Herman, Brooklyn NL
3B—W. Johnson, N. Y. AL
SS—Appling, Chicago AL
LF—Wakefield, Det. AL
CF—Musial, St. L. NL
RF—Nicholson, Chic. NL

1944
P—Newhouser, Det. AL
P—M. Cooper, St. L. NL
P—Trout, Detroit AL
C—W. Cooper, St. L. NL
1B—Sanders, St. L. NL
2B—Doerr, Boston AL
3B—Elliott, Pitts. NL
SS—Marion, St. Louis NL
LF—Wakefield, Det. AL
CF—Musial, St. Louis NL
RF—F. Walker, Bklyn. NL

1945
P—Newhouser, Det. AL
P—Ferriss, Boston AL
P—Borowy, N.Y.AL-Chi.NL
C—Richards, Detroit AL
1B—Cavarretta, Chi. NL
2B—Stirnweiss, N. Y. AL
3B—Kurowski, St. L. NL
SS—Marion, St. Louis NL
LF—Rosen, Brooklyn NL
CF—Pafko, Chicago NL
RF—Holmes, Boston NL

1946
P—Newhouser, Detroit AL
P—Feller, Cleveland AL
P—Ferriss, Boston AL
C—Robinson, New York AL
1B—Musial, St. Louis NL
2B—Doerr, Boston AL
3B—Kell, Detroit AL
SS—Pesky, Boston AL
LF—Williams, Boston AL
CF—D. DiMaggio, Boston AL
RF—Slaughter, St. Louis NL

1947
P—Blackwell, Cinn. NL
P—Feller, Cleveland AL
P—Branca, Brooklyn NL
C—W. Cooper, N. Y. NL
1B—Mize, New York NL
2B—Gordon, Cleveland AL
3B—Kell, Detroit AL
SS—Boudreau, Cleveland AL
LF—Williams, Boston AL
CF—J. DiMaggio, N. Y. AL
RF—Kiner, Pittsburgh NL

1948
P—Sain, Boston NL
P—Lemon, Cleveland AL
P—Brecheen, St. L. NL
C—Tebbetts, Boston AL
1B—Mize, New York NL
2B—Gordon, Cleveland AL
3B—R. Elliott, Boston NL
SS—Boudreau, Cleve. AL
LF—Williams, Boston AL
CF—J. DiMaggio, N. Y. AL
RF—Musial, St. Louis NL

142

MAJOR LEAGUE ALL-STARS—Continued

1949
P—Parnell, Boston AL
P—Kinder, Boston AL
P—Page, New York AL
C—Campanella, Bklyn NL
1B—Henrich, New York AL
2B—Robinson, Bklyn. NL
3B—Kell, Detroit AL
SS—Rizzuto, New York AL
LF—Williams, Boston AL
CF—Musial, St. Louis NL
RF—Kiner, Pitts. NL

1950
P—Konstanty, Phila. NL
P—Lemon, Cleveland AL
P—Raschi, New York AL
C—Berra, New York AL
1B—Dropo, Boston AL
2B—Robinson, Brooklyn NL
3B—Kell, Detroit AL
SS—Rizzuto, New York AL
LF—Kiner, Pittsburgh NL
CF—Doby, Cleveland AL
RF—Musial, St. Louis NL

1951
P—Maglie, New York NL
P—Reynolds, New York AL
P—Roe, Brooklyn NL
C—Campanella, Bkn. NL
1B—Fain, Phila. AL
2B—Robinson, Bkn. NL
3B—Kell, Detroit AL
SS—Rizzuto, New York AL
OF—Kiner, Pittsburgh NL
OF—Musial, St. Louis NL
OF—Williams, Boston AL

1952
P—Reynolds, New York AL
P—Roberts, Philadelphia NL
P—Shantz, Philadelphia AL
C—Berra, New York AL
1B—Fain, Philadelphia AL
2B—Robinson, Brooklyn NL
3B—Kell, Boston AL
SS—Rizzuto, New York AL
OF—Mantle, New York AL
OF—Musial, St. Louis NL
OF—Sauer, Chicago NL

1953
P—Porterfield, Wash'ton AL
P—Roberts, Philadelphia NL
P—Spahn, Milwaukee NL
C—Campanella, Brooklyn NL
1B—Vernon, Washington AL
2B—Schoendienst, St. L. NL
3B—Rosen, Cleveland AL
SS—Reese, Brooklyn NL
OF—Furillo, Brooklyn NL
OF—Musial, St. Louis NL
OF—Snider, Brooklyn NL
°OF—Williams, Boston AL
°Honorary Member.

1954
P—Antonelli, New York NL
P—Roberts, Philadelphia NL
P—Lemon, Cleveland AL
C—Berra, New York AL
1B—Kluszewski, Cincinnati NL
2B—Avila, Cleveland AL
3B—Rosen, Cleveland AL
SS—Dark, New York NL
OF—Mays, New York NL
OF—Musial, St. Louis NL
OF—Snider, Brooklyn NL

1955
P—Ford, New York AL
P—Newcombe, Brooklyn, NL
P—Roberts, Philadelphia AL
C—Campanella, Bklyn NL
1B—Kluszewski,Cincinnati NL
2B—Fox, Chicago AL
SS—Banks, Chicago NL
3B—Mathews, Milwaukee NL
OF—Kaline, Detroit AL
OF—Snider, Brooklyn NL
OF—Williams, Boston AL

1956
P—Ford, New York AL
P—Newcombe, Brooklyn NL
P—Pierce, Chicago AL
C—Berra, New York AL
1B—Kluszewski, Cincinnati NL
2B—Fox, Chicago AL
SS—Kuenn, Detroit AL
3B—Boyer, St. Louis NL
OF—Aaron, Milwaukee NL
OF—Mantle, New York AL
OF—Williams, Boston AL

1957
P—Bunning, Detroit AL
P—Pierce, Chicago AL
P—Spahn, Milwaukee NL
C—Berra, New York AL
1B—Musial, St. Louis NL
2B—Schoendienst, Milw. NL
SS—McDougald, N.Y. AL
3B—Mathews, Milw. NL
OF—Williams, Boston AL
OF—Mantle, New York AL
OF—Mays, New York NL

1958
P—Friend, Pittsburgh, NL
P—Spahn, Milwaukee, NL
P—Turley, New York, AL
C—Crandall, Milwaukee, NL
1B—Musial, St. Louis, NL
2B—Fox, Chicago, AL
SS—Banks, Chicago, NL
3B—Thomas, Pittsburgh, NL
OF—Aaron, Milwaukee, NL
OF—Mays, San Francisco, NL
OF—Williams, Boston, AL

1959
P—Antonelli, San Francisco, NL
P—S. Jones, San Francisco, NL
P—Wynn, Chicago, AL
C—Lollar, Chicago, AL
1B—Cepeda, San Francisco, NL
2B—Fox, Chicago, AL
SS—Banks, Chicago, NL
3B—Mathews, Milwaukee, NL
OF—Aaron, Milwaukee, NL
OF—Mays, San Francisco, NL
OF—Minoso, Cleveland, AL

1960
P—Broglio, St. Louis, NL
P—Law, Pittsburgh NL
P—Spahn, Milwaukee NL
C—Crandall, Milwaukee NL
1B—Skowron, New York AL
2B—Mazeroski, Pittsburgh NL
SS—Banks, Chicago NL
3B—Mathews, Milwaukee NL
OF—Minoso, Chicago AL
OF—Mays, San Francisco NL
OF—Maris, New York AL

1961-AL
P—Ford, N.Y.
P—Lary, Det.
C—Howard, N.Y.
1B—Cash, Det.
2B—Richardson, N.Y.
SS—Kubek, N.Y.
3B—Robinson, Balt.
OF—Colavito, Det.
OF—Mantle, N.Y.
OF—Maris, N.Y.

1961—NL
P—Jay, Cin.
P—Spahn, Mil.
C—Burgess, Pitt.
1B—Cepeda, S.F.
2B—Bolling, Mil.
SS—Wills, L.A.
3B—Boyer, St.L.
OF—Robinson, Cin.
OF—Mays, S.F.
OF—Clemente, Pitt.

1962-AL
P—Donovan, Clev.
P—Terry, N.Y.
C—Battey, Minn.
1B—Siebern, K.C.
2B—Richardson, N.Y.
SS—Tresh, N.Y.
3B—Robinson, Balt.
OF—Wagner, L.A.
OF—Mantle, N.Y.
OF—Kaline, Det.

1962—NL
P—Drysdale, L.A.
P—Purkey, Cin.
C—Crandall, Mil.
1B—Cepeda, S.F.
2B—Mazeroski, Pitt.
SS—Wills, L.A.
3B—Boyer, St.L.
OF—T. Davis, L.A.
OF—Mays, S.F.
OF—Robinson, Cin.

1963—AL
P—Ford, N.Y.
P—Peters, Chi.
C—Howard, N.Y.
1B—Pepitone, N.Y.
2B—Richardson, N.Y.
3B—Malzone, Bos.
SS—Aparicio, Balt.
OF—Yastrzemski, Bos.
OF—Pearson, L.A.
OF—Kaline, Det.

1963—NL
P—Koufax, L.A.
P—Marichal, S.F.
C—Edwards, Cin.
1B—White, St. L.
2B—Gilliam, L.A.
3B—Boyer, St.L.
SS—Groat, St.L.
OF—T. Davis, L.A.
OF—Mays, S.F.
OF—H. Aaron, Mil.

1964—AL
P—Chance, L.A.
P—Peters, Chi.
C—Howard, N.Y.
1B—Stuart, Bos.
2B—Richardson, N.Y.
3B—Robinson, Balt.
SS—Fregosi, L.A.
OF—Killebrew, Minn.
OF—Mantle, N.Y.
OF—Oliva, Minn.

1964—NL
P—Bunning, Phil.
P—Koufax, L.A.
C—Torre, Mil.
1B—White, St.L.
2B—Hunt, N.Y.
3B—Boyer, St.L.
SS—Groat, St.L.
OF—Williams, Chi.
OF—Mays, S.F.
OF—Clemente, Pitt.

MAJOR LEAGUE ALL STARS—Continued

1965—AL	1965—NL
P—Grant, Minn.	P—Koufax, L.A.
P—Stottlemyre, N.Y.	P—Marichal, S.F.
C—Battey, Minn.	C—Torre, Mil.
1B—Whitfield, Clev.	1B—McCovey, S.F.
2B—Richardson, N.Y.	2B—Rose, Cin.
3B—Robinson, Balt.	3B—Johnson, Cin.
SS—Versalles, Minn.	SS—Wills, L.A.
OF—Yastrzemski, Bos.	OF—Stargell, Pitt.
OF—Hall, Minn.	OF—Mays, S.F.
OF—Oliva, Minn.	OF—H. Aaron, Mil.

MAJOR LEAGUE MOST VALUABLE PLAYERS

At various times there have been trophies presented to ball players because of their skill and because of the records they have made. Beginning with the Chalmers Award, Base Ball for the first time had a regularly organized vote by writers on the game for the player deemed most valuable to a club in his league, and of course that embraced the league. This continued for four years and was abated when conditions made it seem best to withdraw the selection. After an interval a new competition was organized by which the most valuable player in the American League was named and in 1924 the National League adopted a similar selection, newspaper writers making up that committee. In the American League a winner one year could not be selected again in the following year. In 1929, however, both leagues decided to discontinue the practice. The American League did not make a selection for 1929, but the National League had arranged already for that year.

Under the system in vogue in the Chalmers competition and in the American League competition a vote was cast for one player on each team. Under the National League system ten players were voted for regardless of teams.

CHALMERS AWARD

(Highest possible total, 64 points)

	NATIONAL	Pts.	AMERICAN	Pts.
	(Chalmers Award 64 points)		(Chalmers Award 64 points)	
1911	Schulte, Frank ....Chicago	29	Cobb, Tyrus R. ....Detroit	64
1912	Doyle, Lawrence J. ..New York	48	Speaker, Tris E. ....Boston	59
1913	Daubert, Jacob E. ....Brooklyn	50	Johnson, Walter P. ......Washington	54
1914	Evers, John J. ....Boston	50	Collins, Edward T. ......Philadelphia	63
			(Discontinued after 1914)	

LEAGUE AWARDS

(From 1922 to 1929 inclusive)

	NATIONAL		AMERICAN	
	(Highest possible total, 80 points)		(Highest possible total, 64 points)	
1922	No selection		Sisler, George H. (1B) ......St. Louis	59
1923	No selection		Ruth, George H. (OF) .....New York	64
1924	Vance, Arthur C. (P.)..Brooklyn	74	Johnson, Walter P. (P) ...Washington	55
1925	Hornsby, Rogers (2B)..St. Louis	73	Peckinpaugh, Roger T. (SS) Washington	45
1926	O'Farrell, Robert A. (C.) St. Louis	79	Burns, George H. (1B) ....Cleveland	63
1927	Waner, Paul G. (OF.) Pittsburgh	72	Gehrig, Henry L. (1B).....New York	56
1928	Bottomley, J. L. (1B)..St. Louis	76	Cochrane, Gordon S. (C.) Philadelphia	53
1929	Hornsby, Rogers (2B) ..Chicago	60	No selection.	

SPORTING NEWS AWARDS

1929	No selection		Simmons, Al H., Phila.	40
1930	Terry, Wm. H., N. Y.	47	Cronin, Jos. E., Wash.	52
1931	Klein, Charles H., Phila.	40	Gehrig, H. Louis, N. Y.	40
1932	Klein, Charles H., Phila.	46	Foxx, James E., Phila.	56
1933	Hubbell, Carl O., N. Y.	64	Foxx, James E., Phila.	49
1934	Dean, Jerome H., St. L.	57	Gehrig, H. Louis, N. Y.	51
1935	Vaughan, Floyd E., Pitts. ...	42	Greenberg, Henry, Det.	64
1936	Hubbell, Carl O., N. Y.	61	Gehrig, H. Louis, N. Y.	55
1937	Medwick, Jos. M., St. L.	70	Gehringer, Chas. L., Det.	78
1938	Lombardi, Ernest N., Cinn.	229°	Foxx, James E., Bos.	305°
1939	Walters, Wm. H., Cinn.	303°	DiMaggio, Jos. P., N. Y.	280°
1940	McCormick, Frank A., Cinn. ..	274°	Greenberg, Henry, Det.	292°
1941	Camilli, Adolph, Bklyn.	300°	DiMaggio, Jos. P., N. Y.	291°
1942	Cooper, Morton C., St. L.	263°	Gordon, Joseph L., N. Y.	270°
1943	Musial, Stanley F., St. L.	267°	Chandler, Spurgeon F., N. Y.	246°
1944	Marion, Martin W., St. L. ...	†	Doerr, Robert P., Bos.	
1945	Holmes, Thomas F., Boston ..	†	Mayo, Edward J., Detroit	†

Discontinued after 1945.
°New rating system. †Total points not tabulated.

BASEBALL WRITERS ASSOCIATION AWARDS

(Starting with 1931 season)
°New rating system.

	NATIONAL		AMERICAN	
1931	Frisch, Frank F., St. L.	65	Grove, Robert M., Phila.	78
1932	Klein, Chas. H., Phila.	78	Foxx, James E., Phila.	75
1933	Hubbell, Carl O., N. Y.	77	Foxx, James E., Phila.	74
1934	Dean, Jerome H., St. L.	78	Cochrane, Gordon S., Det.	67
1935	Hartnett, Chas. L., Chi.	75	Greenberg, Henry, Det.	80
1936	Hubbell, Carl O., N. Y.	60	Gehrig, H. Louis, N. Y.	73
1937	Medwick, Jos. M., St. L.	70	Gehringer, Chas. L., Det.	78
1938	Lombardi, Ernest N., Cinn.	229°	Foxx, James E., Bos.	305°
1939	Walters, Wm. H., Cinn.	303°	DiMaggio, Jos. P., N. Y.	280°
1940	McCormick, Frank A., Cinn.	274°	Greenberg, Henry, Det.	292°
1941	Camilli, Adolph, Bklyn.	300°	DiMaggio, Jos. P. N. Y.	291°
1942	Cooper, Morton C., St. L.	263°	Gordon, Joseph L., N. Y.	270°
1943	Musial, Stanley F., St. L.	267°	Chandler, Spurgeon F., N. Y.	246°
1944	Marion, Martin W., St. L.	190°	Newhouser, Harold, Det.	236°
1945	Cavarretta, Philip J., Chicago	279°	Newhouser, Harold, Det.	236°
1946	Musial, Stanley F., St. Louis	319°	Williams, Theodore S., Boston	224°
1947	Elliott, Robert I., Boston	205°	DiMaggio, Joseph P., N. Y.	202°
1948	Musial, Stanley F., St. L.	303°	Boudreau, Louis, Cleveland	324°
1949	Robinson, Jack R., Brooklyn	264°	Williams, Theodore S., Boston	272°
1950	Konstanty, C. James, Phila.	286°	Rizzuto, Philip F., N. Y.	284°
1951	Campanella, Roy, Brooklyn	243°	Berra, Lawrence P., N. Y.	184°
1952	Sauer, Henry, Chicago	226°	Shantz, Robert, Phila.	280°
1953	Campanella, Roy, Brooklyn	297°	Rosen, Al, Cleveland	336°
1954	Mays, Willie, New York	283°	Berra, Lawrence P., New York	230°
1955	Campanella, Roy, Brooklyn	226°	Berra, Lawrence P., New York	218°
1956	Newcombe, Donald, Brooklyn	223°	Mantle, Mickey C., New York	336°
1957	Aaron, Henry, Milwaukee	239°	Mantle, Mickey C., New York	233°
1958	Banks, Ernest, Chicago	283°	Jensen, Jack E., Boston	233°
1959	Banks, Ernest, Chicago	232½°	Fox, J. Nelson, Chicago	295°
1960	Groat, Richard M., Pittsburgh	276°	Maris, Roger E., New York	225°
1961	Robinson, Frank, Cincinnati	219°	Maris, Roger E., New York	202°
1962	Wills, Maurice M., Los Angeles	209°	Mantle, Mickey C., New York	234°
1963	Koufax, Sanford, Los Angeles	237°	Howard, Elston G., New York	248°
1964	Boyer, Kenton L., St. Louis	243°	Robinson, Brooks C., Baltimore	269°
1965	Mays, Willie, San Francisco	224°	Versalles, Zoilo, Minnesota	275°

ROOKIE AWARDS

NATIONAL	AMERICAN
1949 Newcombe, Donald, Brooklyn	Sievers, Roy E., St. Louis
1950 Jethroe, Samuel, Boston	Dropo, Walter O., Boston
1951 Mays, Willie, New York	McDougald, Gilbert, J., New York
1952 Black, Joseph, Brooklyn	Byrd, Harry G., Philadelphia
1953 Gilliam, James, Brooklyn	Kuenn, Harvey E., Detroit
1954 Moon, Wallace W., St. Louis	Grim, Robert A., New York
1955 Virdon, William C., St. Louis	Score, Herbert J., Cleveland
1956 Robinson, Frank, Cincinnati	Aparicio, Luis E., Chicago
1957 Sanford, Jack, Philadelphia	Kubek, Anthony, New York
1958 Cepeda, Orlando, San Francisco	Pearson, Albert, Washington
1959 McCovey, Willie, San Francisco	Allison, William R., Washington
1960 Howard, Frank O., Los Angeles	Hansen, Ronald L., Baltimore
1961 Williams, Billy L., Chicago	Schwall, Donald B., Boston
1962 Hubbs, Kenneth D., Chicago	Tresh, Thomas M., New York
1963 Rose, Peter E., Cincinnati	Peters, Gary C., Chicago
1964 Allen, Richard A., Philadelphia	Oliva, Pedro, Minnesota
1965 Lefebvre, James K., Los Angeles	Blefary, Curtis L., Baltimore

CY YOUNG AWARD

(Best pitcher in major leagues)

1956 Donald Newcombe, Brooklyn NL
1957 Warren Spahn, Milwaukee NL
1958 Robert Turley, New York AL
1959 Early Wynn, Chicago AL
1960 Vernon Law, Pittsburgh NL
1961 Edward C. Ford, New York AL
1962 Donald S. Drysdale, Los Angeles NL
1963 Sanford Koufax, Los Angeles, NL
1964 W. Dean Chance, Los Angeles, AL
1965 Sanford Koufax, Los Angeles, NL

INDEX

144

INDIVIDUAL FIELDING

First Basemen—

Most games played, lifetime 31A
Most games played, season 31B
Highest percentage, season 31C
Consecutive years leading, percentage ..31D
Most years leading 100 games or more..31E
Most chances accepted, lifetime 31EE
Most chances accepted, season 31F
    game, 9 inn. 31G
Fewest chances offered, game 31H
Most consecutive chances accepted 31I
Most putouts, season 31J
    lifetime 31JJ
    game, 9 inn. 31K
Fewest putouts, game 31L
Most assists, season 32A
    years leading in assists 32B
Most assists, game 32C
    errors, season 32D
Fewest errors, season 32E
Most consecutive games, no errors.....32F
    errors, game 32G
    inning 32H
    double plays, season 32I
    unassisted, season 32J
    game 32K
    unassisted, game 32L
    years leading in double plays 32M

Second Basemen—

Most games played, lifetime 32N
    years leading league 32O
    games played, season 32P
    consecutive games played 32Q
Highest percentage, season 33A
Most years leading in percentage 33B
    chances accepted, season 33C
    years leading, chances accepted 33CC
    consecutive chances accepted 33D
    chances, accepted, game 33E
Fewest chances offered, game 33F
Most putouts, season 33G
    years leading 33GG
    game 33H
    assists, season 33I
    game 33J
    errors, season 33K
    game 33L
    consecutive games, no errors 33M
Fewest errors, season 33N
Most double plays, season 33O
    game 34A
    years leading league 34AA

Third Basemen—

Most games played, lifetime 34B
Most games played, season 34C
Highest percentage, season 34D
Most years leading in percentage 34E
Most chances accepted, season 34G
    consecutive errorless chances 34GG
    game 34H
Fewest chances accepted, game 34I
Most putouts, season 34J
    game 34K
    years leading, league 34KK
Most assists, season 34L
    game 34M
    errors, season 34N
    consecutive games, no errors 34O
Fewest errors, season 34P
Most errors, game 35A
    inning 35B
    double plays, season 35C
    game 35D
    unassisted double plays, season 35E
Most Years Leading League, Double
    Plays 35F

Shortstops—

Most games played, lifetime 35G
Most games played, season 35H
Highest percentage, season 35I
Most years leading in percentage 35J
Left handed shortstops 35K
Most chances accepted, season 35L
    game 35M
    consecutive chances accepted 35N
Fewest chances offered, game 35O
Most putouts, season 36A
    game 36B
Most assists, season 36C
    game 36D
Most errors, season 36E
Fewest errors, season 36EE
Most errors, game 36F
    inning 36G
    consecutive games, no errors 36H
    double plays, season 36I
    game 36J
    years leading in double plays 36JJ

Outfielders—

Most games played, lifetime 36K
Most games played, season 36L
Highest percentage, season 36M
Most years leading in percentage 36N
Most chances accepted, season 36O
    game 36P
Fewest chances accepted, game 36Q
Most putouts, season 37A
Most years, 400 putouts or more 37B
    years, leading in putouts 37C
    game 37D
    assists, season 37E
    game 37F
    inning 37FF
    errors, season 37G
Fewest errors, season 37H
Most errors, game 37I
    consecutive games, no errors 37II
    double plays, season 37J
    unassisted double plays, season.....37K

Catchers—

Most games caught, lifetime 37L
Most games caught, season 37M
Highest percentage, season 37N
Most years leading in percentage 37O
    consecutive games caught, league ...37P
Most years, 100 or more games 38A
    consecutive games caught, season ..38AA
    consecutive years, 100 or more games.38B
    years catching, league 38C
    consecutive chances, league 38D
    season 38E
    chances accepted, season 38F
    years leading league, chances 38FF
    game 38G
Fewest chances offered, extra innings..38H
Most putouts, season 38I
    game 38J
    consecutive putouts 38K
Most years leading putouts 38KK
    assists, season 38L
    game 38M
    inning 38N
    errors, season 39A
    game 39B
    inning 39C
Fewest errors, season 39D
Consecutive errorless games 39E
Most passed balls, season 39F
Most passed balls, game 39G
Most passed balls, inning 39H
Fewest passed balls, season 39I
Most thrown out stealing, game 39J
    inning 39K
    double plays, season 39L
    unassisted double plays 39M

INDIVIDUAL FIELDING

INDIVIDUAL PITCHING

INDIVIDUAL PITCHING

CLUB BATTING

LEAGUE BATTING

152

JOSEPH P. DIMAGGIO, NEW YORK AL, 56 GAMES

RECORD BATTING STREAK, 1941

Date	Opp. Club and Pitcher	AB	R	H	2B	3B	HR	RBI
May 15	Chicago—Smith	4	..	1	..	..	..	1
16	Chicago—Lee	4	2	2	..	1	1	1
17	Chicago—Rigney	3	1	1	..	..	..	..
18	St. Louis—Harris (2), Niggeling (1)	3	3	3	1	..	..	1
19	St. Louis—Galehouse	3	..	1	1	..	..	..
20	St. Louis—Auker	5	1	1	..	..	..	1
21	Detroit—Rowe (1), Benton (1)	5	..	2	..	..	..	1
22	Detroit—McKain	4	..	1	..	..	..	1
23	Boston—Newsome	5	..	1	..	..	..	2
24	Boston—Johnson	4	2	1	..	..	..	2
25	Boston—Grove	4	..	1	..	..	..	..
27	Washington—Chase (1), Anderson (2), Carrasquel (1)	5	3	4	..	..	1	3
(Night) 28	Washington—Hudson	4	1	1	..	1	..	..
29	Washington—Sundra	3	1	1	..	..	..	..
30	Boston—Johnson	2	1	1	..	..	..	..
30	Boston—Harris	3	..	1	1	..	..	..
June 1	Cleveland—Milnar	4	1	1	..	..	..	..
1	Cleveland—Harder	4	..	1	..	..	..	..
2	Cleveland—Feller	4	2	2	1	..	..	..
3	Detroit—Trout	4	1	1	..	..	1	1
5	Detroit—Newhouser	5	1	1	..	1	..	1
7	St. Louis—Muncrief (1), Allen (1), Caster (1)	5	2	3	..	..	..	1
8	St. Louis—Auker	4	3	2	..	..	2	4
8	St. Louis—Caster (1), Kramer (1)	4	1	2	1	..	1	3
10	Chicago—Rigney	5	1	1	..	..	..	..
(Night) 12	Chicago—Lee	4	1	2	..	..	1	1
14	Cleveland—Feller	2	..	1	1	..	..	1
15	Cleveland—Bagby	3	1	1	..	..	1	1
16	Cleveland—Milnar	5	..	1	1	..	..	..
17	Chicago—Rigney	4	1	1	..	..	..	..
18	Chicago—Lee	3	..	1	..	..	..	..
19	Chicago—Smith (1), Ross (2)	3	2	3	..	..	1	2
20	Detroit—Newsom (2), McKain (2)	5	3	4	1	..	..	1
21	Detroit—Trout	4	..	1	..	..	..	1
22	Detroit—Newhouser (1), Newsom (1)	5	1	2	1	..	1	2
24	St. Louis—Muncrief	4	1	1	..	..	..	..
25	St. Louis—Galehouse	4	1	1	..	..	1	3
26	St. Louis—Auker	4	..	1	1	..	..	..
27	Philadelphia—Dean	3	1	2	..	..	1	2
28	Philadelphia—Babich (1), Harris (1)	5	1	2	1	..	..	..
29	Washington—Leonard	4	1	1	1	..	..	..
29	Washington—Anderson	5	1	1	..	..	..	1
July 1	Boston—Harris (1), Ryba (1)	4	..	2	..	..	..	1
1	Boston—Wilson	3	1	1	..	..	..	1
2	Boston—Newsome	5	1	1	..	..	1	3
5	Philadelphia—Marchildon	4	2	1	..	..	1	2
6	Philadelphia—Babich (1), Hadley (3)	5	2	4	1	..	..	2
6	Philadelphia—Knott	4	..	2	..	1	..	2
(Night) 10	St. Louis—Niggeling	2	..	1	..	..	..	..
11	St. Louis—Harris (3), Kramer (1)	5	1	4	..	..	1	2
12	St. Louis—Auker (1), Muncrief (1)	5	1	2	1	..	..	1
13	Chicago—Lyons (2), Hallett (1)	4	2	3	..	..	..	..
13	Chicago—Lee	4	..	1	..	..	..	..
14	Chicago—Rigney	3	..	1	..	..	..	..
15	Chicago—Smith	4	1	2	1	..	..	2
16	Cleveland—Milnar (2), Krakauskas (1)	4	3	3	1	..	..	..
	Totals for 56 games	223	56	91	16	4	15	55
							.408 Pct.	

Stopped Night Game, July 17 by Cleveland (Smith and Bagby)

ROGER MARIS HOME RUNS—1961

HR No.	Club's Game	Maris' Game	Date	Inn.	Opponent	Pitcher
1	11	11	Apr. 26	5	at Detroit	Foytack
2	17	17	May 3	7	at Minnesota	Ramos
3	20	20	May 6 (N)	5	at Los Angeles	Grba
4	29	29	May 17	8	Washington	Burnside (L)
5	30	30	May 19 (N)	1	at Cleveland	Perry
6	31	31	May 20	3	at Cleveland	Bell
7	32	32	May 21	1	Baltimore	Estrada
8	35	35	May 24	4	Boston	Conley
9	38	38	May 28	2	Chicago	McLish
10	40	40	May 30	6	at Boston	Conley
11	40	40	May 30	8	at Boston	Fornieles
12	41	41	May 31 (N)	3	at Boston	Muffett
13	43	43	June 2 (N)	3	at Chicago	McLish
14	44	44	June 3	8	at Chicago	Shaw
15	45	45	June 4	3	at Chicago	Kemmerer
16	48	48	June 6 (N)	6	Minnesota	Palmquist
17	49	49	June 7	3	Minnesota	Ramos
18	52	52	June 9 (N)	7	Kansas City	Herbert
19	55	55	June 11	3	Los Angeles	Grba
20	55	55	June 11	7	Los Angeles	James
21	57	57	June 13 (N)	6	at Cleveland	Perry
22	58	58	June 14 (N)	4	at Cleveland	Bell
23	61	61	June 17 (N)	4	at Detroit	Mossi (L)
24	62	62	June 18	8	at Detroit	Casale
25	63	63	June 19 (N)	9	at Kansas City	Archer (L)
26	64	64	June 20 (N)	1	at Kansas City	Nuxhall (L)
27	66	66	June 22 (N)	2	at Kansas City	Bass
28	74	74	July 1	9	Washington	Sisler
29	75	75	July 2	3	Washington	Burnside (L)
30	75	75	July 2	7	Washington	Klippstein
31	77	77	July 4	8	Detroit	Lary
32	78	78	July 5	7	Cleveland	Funk
33	82	82	July 9	7	Boston	Monbouquette
34	84	84	July 13 (N)	1	at Chicago	Wynn
35	86	86	July 15	3	at Chicago	Herbert
36	92	92	July 21 (N)	1	at Boston	Monbouquette
37	95	95	July 25 (N)	4	Chicago	Baumann (L)
38	95	95	July 25 (N)	8	Chicago	Larsen
39	96	96	July 25 (N)	4	Chicago	Kemmerer
40	96	96	July 25 (N)	6	Chicago	Hacker
41	106	105	Aug. 4 (N)	1	Minnesota	Pascual
42	114	113	Aug. 11 (N)	5	at Washington	Burnside (L)
43	115	114	Aug. 12	4	at Washington	Donovan
44	116	115	Aug. 13	4	at Washington	Daniels
45	117	116	Aug. 13	1	at Washington	Kutyna
46	118	117	Aug. 15 (N)	4	Chicago	Pizarro (L)
47	119	118	Aug. 16	1	Chicago	Pierce (L)
48	119	118	Aug. 16	3	Chicago	Pierce (L)
49	123	122	Aug. 20	3	at Cleveland	Perry
50	125	124	Aug. 22 (N)	6	at Los Angeles	McBride
51	129	128	Aug. 26	6	at Kansas City	Walker
52	135	134	Sept. 2	6	Detroit	Lary
53	135	134	Sept. 2	8	Detroit	Aguirre (L)
54	140	139	Sept. 6	4	Washington	Cheney
55	141	140	Sept. 7 (N)	3	Cleveland	Stigman (L)
56	143	142	Sept. 9	7	Cleveland	Grant
57	151	150	Sept. 16	3	at Detroit	Lary
58	152	151	Sept. 17	12	at Detroit	Fox
59	155	154	Sept. 20 (N)	3	at Baltimore	Pappas
60	159	158	Sept. 26 (N)	3	Baltimore	Fisher
61	163	161	Oct. 1	4	Boston	Stallard

At Home—30   On Road—31   Off RHP—49   Off LHP—12   Day—36   Night—25

156

BABE RUTH HOME RUNS—1927

HR No.	Club's Game	Ruth's Game	Date	Inn.	Opponent	Pitcher
1	4	4	Apr. 15	1	Philadelphia	Ehmke
2	11	11	Apr. 23	1	at Philadelphia	Walberg (L)
3	12	12	Apr. 24	6	at Washington	Thurston
4	14	14	Apr. 29	5	at Boston	Harriss
5	16	16	May 1	1	Philadelphia	Quinn
6	16	16	May 1	8	Philadelphia	Walberg (L)
7	24	24	May 10	1	at St. Louis	Gaston
8	25	25	May 11	1	at St. Louis	Nevers
9	29	29	May 17	8	at Detroit	Collins
10	33	33	May 22	6	at Cleveland	Karr
11	34	34	May 23	1	at Washington	Thurston
12	37	37	May 28	7	Washington	Thurston
13	39	39	May 29	8	Boston	MacFayden
14	41	41	May 30	11	at Philadelphia	Walberg (L)
15	42	42	May 31	1	at Philadelphia	Quinn
16	43	43	May 31	5	at Philadelphia	Ehmke
17	47	47	June 5	6	Detroit	Whitehill (L)
18	48	48	June 7	4	Chicago	Thomas
19	52	52	June 11	3	Cleveland	Buckeye (L)
20	52	52	June 11	5	Cleveland	Buckeye (L)
21	53	53	June 12	7	Cleveland	Uhle
22	55	55	June 16	1	St. Louis	Zachary (L)
23	60	60	June 22	5	at Boston	Wiltse (L)
24	60	60	June 22	7	at Boston	Wiltse (L)
25	70	66	June 30	4	Boston	Harriss
26	73	69	July 3	1	at Washington	Lisenbee
27	78	74	July 8	2	at Detroit	Hankins
28	79	75	July 9	1	at Detroit	Holloway
29	79	75	July 9	4	at Detroit	Holloway
30	83	79	July 12	9	at Cleveland	Shaute (L)
31	94	90	July 24	3	at Chicago	Thomas
32	95	91	July 26	1	St. Louis	Gaston
33	95	91	July 26	6	St. Louis	Gaston
34	98	94	July 28	8	St. Louis	Stewart (L)
35	106	102	Aug. 5	8	Detroit	Smith
36	110	106	Aug. 10	3	at Washington	Zachary (L)
37	114	110	Aug. 16	5	at Chicago	Thomas
38	115	111	Aug. 17	11	at Chicago	Connally
39	118	114	Aug. 20	1	at Cleveland	Miller (L)
40	120	116	Aug. 22	6	at Cleveland	Shaute (L)
41	124	120	Aug. 27	8	at St. Louis	Nevers
42	125	121	Aug. 28	1	at St. Louis	Wingard (L)
43	127	123	Aug. 31	8	Boston	Welzer
44	128	124	Sept. 2	1	at Philadelphia	Walberg (L)
45	132	128	Sept. 6	6	at Boston	Welzer
46	132	128	Sept. 6	7	at Boston	Welzer
47	133	129	Sept. 6	9	at Boston	Russell
48	134	130	Sept. 7	1	at Boston	MacFayden
49	134	130	Sept. 7	8	at Boston	Harriss
50	138	134	Sept. 11	4	St. Louis	Gaston
51	139	135	Sept. 13	7	Cleveland	Hudlin
52	140	136	Sept. 13	4	Cleveland	Shaute (L)
53	143	139	Sept. 16	3	Chicago	Blankenship
54	147	143	Sept. 18	5	Chicago	Lyons
55	148	144	Sept. 21	9	Detroit	Gibson
56	149	145	Sept. 22	9	Detroit	Holloway
57	152	148	Sept. 27	6	Philadelphia	Grove (L)
58	153	149	Sept. 29	1	Washington	Lisenbee
59	153	149	Sept. 29	5	Washington	Hopkins
60	154	150	Sept. 30	8	Washington	Zachary (L)

At Home—28   On Road—32   Off RHP—41   Off LHP—19

MOST STOLEN BASES–SEASON
104–Maury Wills–1962
Los Angeles Dodgers NL

No.	Game	Date	Opp.
1	4	Apr. 13	Mil.
2	6	15	Mil.
3	7	16	at S.F.
4	14	24	at Chi.
5	17	27	Pitt.
6	17	27	Pitt.
7	19	29	Pitt.
8	19	29	Pitt.
9	22	May 1	Chi.
10	22	1	Chi.
11	29	10	at Hou.
12	29	10	at Hou.
13	30	11	at St.L.
14	30	11	at St.L.
15	31	12	at St.L.
16	31	12	at St.L.
17	34	16	Hou.
18	34	16	Hou.
19	39	21	S.F.
20	43	25	N.Y.
21	43	25	N.Y.
22	43	25	N.Y.
23	45	27	Phil.
24	47	30	at N.Y.
25	49	31	at N.Y.
26	49	31	at N.Y.
27	49	31	at N.Y.
28	54	June 4	at Phil.
29	56	5	at Pitt.
30	58	7	at Pitt.
31	59	8	at Hou.
32	59	8	at Hou.
33	60	9	at Hou.
34	61	10	at Hou.
35	68	17	Hou.
36	69	18	St.L.
37	70	19	St.L.
38	70	19	St.L.
39	71	20	St.L.
40	78	28	N.Y.
41	78	28	N.Y.
42	80	30	N.Y.
43	84	July 4	Phil.
44	85	4	Phil.
45	86	5	at S.F.
46	86	5	at S.F.
47	94	15	at Phil.
48	97	19	at Cin.
49	100	22	at Chi.
50	104	27	S.F.
51	106	29	S.F.
52	107	Aug. 1	Pitt.
53	109	3	Chi.
54	109	3	Chi.
55	110	4	Chi.
56	110	4	Chi.
57	111	5	Chi.
58	113	6	N.Y.
59	115	8	Phil.
60	115	8	Phil.
61	122	16	at Pitt.
62	122	16	at Pitt.
63	123	17	at Cin.
64	123	17	at Cin.
65	125	19	at Cin.
66	126	20	at Cin.
67	126	20	at Cin.
68	128	23	at Phil.
69	129	24	at N.Y.
70	131	26	at N.Y.
71	131	26	at N.Y.
72	131	26	at N.Y.
73	132	28	Cin.
74	136	Sept. 1	Mil.
75	137	2	Mil.
76	137	2	Mil.
77	141	6	S.F.
78	141	6	S.F.
79	142	7	Pitt.
80	142	7	Pitt.
81	142	7	Pitt.
82	142	7	Pitt.
83	143	8	Pitt.
84	144	9	Pitt.
85	144	9	Pitt.
86	144	9	Pitt.
87	145	10	Chi.
88	145	10	Chi.
89	145	10	Chi.
90	146	11	Chi.
91	148	14	Chi.
92	149	15	Chi.
93	152	18	at Mil.
94	153	19	at Mil.
95	154	21	at St.L.
96	156	23	at St.L.
97	156	23	at St.L.
98	157	25	Hou.
99	157	25	Hou.
100	158	26	Hou.
101	164	Oct. 2	S.F.
102	165	3	S.F.
103	165	3	S.F.
104	165	3	S.F.

Caught Stealing—13

96–Ty Cobb–1915
Detroit Tigers AL

No.	Game	Date	Opp.
1	2	Apr. 15	Clev.
2	3	16	Clev.
3	3	16	Clev.
4	4	17	Clev.
5	9	22	at Clev.
6	10	23	at Clev.
7	12	25	at Clev.
8	13	26	St.L.
9	15	28	St.L.
10	22	May 7	at St.L.
11	22	7	at St.L.
12	24	9	Wash.
13	27	13	Bos.
14	27	13	Bos.
15	30	19	N.Y.
16	30	19	N.Y.
17	30	19	N.Y.
18	30	19	Phil.
19	32	22	Phil.
20	36	26	Wash.
21	39	29	at St.L.
22	39	29	at St.L.
23	42	31	at Chi.
24	44	June 1	at Chi.
25	45	2	at Chi.
26	45	2	at Chi.
27	46	4	at N.Y.
28	46	4	at N.Y.
29	47	5	at N.Y.
30	51	9	at Bos.
31	51	9	at Bos.
32	51	9	at Bos.
33	52	10	at Bos.
34	52	10	at Bos.
35	54	12	at Phil.
36	54	12	at Phil.
37	54	12	at Phil.
38	54	12	at Phil.
39	57	17	at Wash.
40	58	18	at Wash.
41	58	18	at Wash.
42	58	18	at Wash.
43	60	20	St.L.
44	62	23	St.L.
45	63	24	St.L.
46	63	24	St.L.
47	63	24	St.L.
48	64	26	St.L.
49	65	27	Clev.
50	65	27	Clev.
51	66	28	Clev.
52	75	July 9	Bos.
53	75	9	Bos.
54	77	11	Bos.
55	80	13	N.Y.
56	81	14	N.Y.
57	83	18	Phil.
58	84	19	Phil.
59	84	19	Phil.
60	86	21	Phil.
61	87	23	Wash.
62	88	24	Wash.
63	101	Aug. 7	at Phil.
64	102	7	at Phil.
65	102	7	at Phil.
66	108	16	at Clev.
67	108	16	at Clev.
68	108	16	at Clev.
69	110	17	at Clev.
70	110	17	at Clev.
71	110	17	at Clev.
72	113	19	Phil.
73	114	20	Phil.
74	125	31	Chi.
75	125	31	Chi.
76	125	31	Chi.
77	128	Sept. 3	at St.L.
78	130	4	at St.L.
79	131	5	at St.L.
80	132	5	at St.L.
81	134	8	at Chi.
82	135	9	at Clev.
83	136	10	at Clev.
84	139	14	at N.Y.
85	141	16	at Bos.
86	145	21	at Phil.
87	145	21	at Phil.
88	146	22	at Phil.
89	147	23	at Phil.
90	148	24	at Wash.
91	149	25	at Wash.
92	153	29	St.L.
93	154	30	St.L.
94	154	30	St.L.
95	155	Oct. 2	Clev.
96	156	3	Clev.

Caught Stealing—38

ADIRONDACK BATS

Many big-league players actually depend on ADIRONDACK BATS to help keep their batting average ABOVE average

they're livelier!

BATS

"GET A BASKET!"
(WHY NOT?)

The XPG3 gives you a big-as-a-basket catching area topped by the new Basket Web. Flexes in any direction, and it's strong as solid leather. The XPG3 is a "Heart-of-the-Hide" glove by Rawlings. That's the Big League glove line.

"The Finest In The Field!"